PREPARING YOUTH FOR THE 21ST CENTURY: THE TRANSITION FROM EDUCATION TO THE LABOUR MARKET

PROCEEDINGS OF THE
WASHINGTON D.C. CONFERENCE,
23-24 FEBRUARY 1999

ORGANISATION FOR ECONOMIC CO-OPERATION AND DEVELOPMENT

ORGANISATION FOR ECONOMIC CO-OPERATION AND DEVELOPMENT

Pursuant to Article 1 of the Convention signed in Paris on 14th December 1960, and which came into force on 30th September 1961, the Organisation for Economic Co-operation and Development (OECD) shall promote policies designed:

- to achieve the highest sustainable economic growth and employment and a rising standard of living in Member countries, while maintaining financial stability, and thus to contribute to the development of the world economy;
- to contribute to sound economic expansion in Member as well as non-member countries in the process of economic development; and
- to contribute to the expansion of world trade on a multilateral, non-discriminatory basis in accordance with international obligations.

The original Member countries of the OECD are Austria, Belgium, Canada, Denmark, France, Germany, Greece, Iceland, Ireland, Italy, Luxembourg, the Netherlands, Norway, Portugal, Spain, Sweden, Switzerland, Turkey, the United Kingdom and the United States. The following countries became Members subsequently through accession at the dates indicated hereafter: Japan (28th April 1964), Finland (28th January 1969), Australia (7th June 1971), New Zealand (29th May 1973), Mexico (18th May 1994), the Czech Republic (21st December 1995), Hungary (7th May 1996), Poland (22nd November 1996) and Korea (12th December 1996). The Commission of the European Communities takes part in the work of the OECD (Article 13 of the OECD Convention).

FOREWORD

This publication brings together the papers presented at the Conference "Preparing Youth for the 21st Century: The Policy Lessons from the Past two Decades". The Conference, organised jointly by the US Departments of Labor and Education and the OECD, took place in Washington D.C. on 23-24 February 1999. It was opened by Secretary of Labor Alexis Herman, Secretary of Education Richard Riley and myself. The Chair was Ray Marshall, former US Secretary of Labor, who had also chaired the previous OECD high-level conference on youth unemployment held in 1977.

At the time of the 1977 meeting, experts had predicted that the combination of continued economic growth, demographic trends and targeted labour market policies would gradually alleviate the problems of youth unemployment. The intervening two decades have shown that such expectations were over-optimistic. Today, many young people still face serious difficulties in integrating successfully from initial education into the labour market and youth unemployment remains a major political concern in almost all OECD countries. It is for these reasons that I actively pursued the initiative of organising a new Youth Conference in 1999.

This high-level Conference updated the diagnosis of the problems facing young people. In particular, it focussed on assessing the effectiveness of current policies – what has and has not worked and why – that countries have put in place to deal with the range of educational, labour market and social problems. The conference drew a number of lessons for future policy development, especially concerning the key importance of early and persistent intervention to help the most disadvantaged and the central tenets for making labour market policies more effective such as involving employers in the design and implementation of programmes, knowing well the local labour market conditions and making sure that data are constantly gathered in order to evaluate them rigorously.

I want to express my gratitude to the United States for having agreed to co-host this important event, and to Secretary Herman and Secretary Riley for their participation and support. A special thanks goes to Professor Ray Marshall for sharing with us his wisdom and the superb manner in which he chaired the conference.

The lessons drawn from the conference are, of course, not the last word. Ensuring that all our young people have the opportunity to get a good start in the labour market is a continuous process of analytical work and policy development which is a high priority for the OECD. Indeed, we are currently working closely with the government of the United Kingdom on a Ministerial-level follow-up conference that we hope to hold in February 2000.

Donald J. Johnston
Secretary-General of the OECD

The financial contribution of Microsoft Corporation for the publication of the Washington proceedings is warmly acknowledged.

TABLE OF CONTENTS

Workshop 5: Policies to Improve the Employability of Disadvantaged Youth
What Works and for Whom?

Workshop 6: Promoting Job Creation for Disadvantaged Youth
What Works and for Whom?

Rapporteur's Report:

BACKGROUND REPORT

GIVING YOUNG PEOPLE A GOOD START: THE EXPERIENCE OF OECD COUNTRIES

by
Norman Bowers, Anne Sonnet and Laura Bardone
OECD Secretariat, Paris

Introduction

If, some twenty odd years ago, one had asked economists about the future of youth labour market problems most would have been rather optimistic. Demographic developments, sustained economic growth, employment shifts towards youth-intensive sectors and, for those left behind, targeted labour market programmes would contribute greatly to solving the problems identified in youth labour markets. Indeed, these were the conclusions of a major conference held by the OECD in 1977 (see OECD, 1978 in the bibliography).

Unfortunately, developments since then have not borne out this optimism. Despite sharp falls in the size of the youth population and the proliferation of programmes aimed at young people, many still face serious difficulties in integrating successfully into the labour market and youth unemployment remains a major political concern in most OECD countries. It also remains true, however, that countries vary greatly in the degree to which youth have difficulties in getting into jobs and constructing good "careers", and in the relative sizes and composition of at-risk groups.

This paper presents an updated diagnostic of the youth labour market in OECD countries with a particular focus on trends and policy developments since the end of the 1970s. Section I provides a background analysis of the situation of young people in initial education and explores how young people are prepared to enter the labour market. An overview of the youth labour market is then developed in Section II in terms of labour supply, demand and earnings. Section III focuses on the transition from initial education to the labour market, both in the short-term and over a longer period. Finally, Section IV discusses the different strategies for improving youth labour market prospects.

The key issues addressed are: How to ensure more coherent educational, labour market and social policies to assist more young people to get a better start in life? How to develop more effective policies to deal with the specific problems facing disadvantaged young people? How to help more young people settle into good labour market careers?

I. YOUNG PEOPLE IN INITIAL EDUCATION

Introduction

While young people are staying longer in initial education, decreasing the proportion of school drop outs remains a concern in OECD countries.[1] The problem is more acute today because finishing not only compulsory schooling, but also upper secondary education has become a necessary, although not a sufficient, condition for finding a decent job. The minority of youths whose family background, schooling and communities do not equip them with the skills, qualifications, attitudes or motivation required by the labour market are particularly at risk of persistent or intermittent joblessness and a key issue is how to motivate them and make the educational system more relevant to them. The attitudes and living conditions of young people today are key elements to take into consideration (see Box 1).

This section takes stock of the current situation in OECD countries concerning school attendance rates. The following issues are examined: What has happened to school enrolment? To what extent are young people combining school and work? What is the impact of working while still in education in easing the initial transition from school to work? To what extent do youths leave school early without qualifications? What is the proportion of youths not attending school and not employed?

Box 1. **Stylised facts on the attitudes and living conditions of young people today**

1. Young people are relatively happy, unless they are unemployed

Despite deterioration in the youth labour market, young people in general seem optimistic about their future and expect to find an interesting job. They believe that employers attach great importance to qualifications. The attitudes and expectations of young people themselves are conventional: they want the transition to the labour market to lead to full-time jobs that are secure, interesting and well-paid (Bynner *et al.*, 1997). However, expectations have changed concerning gender roles. Young women's educational and career aspirations have become increasingly similar to those of young men.

Youths' positive attitudes towards life can be illustrated by the answers they give in opinion surveys to questions such as: "On the whole, are you very satisfied, fairly satisfied, not very satisfied, or not at all satisfied with the life you lead?". In the Spring 1998 Eurobarometer survey, 84% of all Europeans aged 15-24 years answered that they were very or fairly satisfied compared with 79% of Europeans aged 25 years and over. A critical distinction, however, depends on whether they are unemployed or not. Between 1975 and 1996, in the European countries, 87% of employed young adults were very or fairly satisfied compared with only 67% of the unemployed. This result is statistically highly significant controlling for the age, gender and country.

While the percentage of employed Europeans who are very or fairly satisfied remains roughly constant across age groups, the percentage among the unemployed decreases with age (Table 1).

Importantly, young unemployed people are more likely than other young people to express how important work is in a person's life (Table 2). This stresses the fact that the unemployed clearly would like jobs and do not view work as simply a casual or marginal activity (Oswald, 1997).

2. Youth tend to live longer with their parents now, particularly in southern Europe

In the mid-1990s, almost all teenagers lived with their parents (Table 3). Finland is one exception: only about one-half of those aged 15 to 19 years still live with their parents.[2] In their early twenties, on average two-thirds of young men and one-half of young women stay on in the parental home. After the age of 25, up to 40% of young men still live with their parents compared with only 25% of young women. Over the past decade, the situation has not changed much for teenagers. Concerning 20-24-year olds, however, in most countries young people are staying on longer in the parental home, particularly in southern Europe.

According to the Spring 1997 Eurobarometer survey, when asked why they thought young people were living at home with their parents longer than they used to, almost three-quarters of those aged 15-24 said the main reason was that they could not afford to move out[3] (Table 4).

3. Youths get most of their income from their parents

Almost one-half of young people get most of their income from their parents (Table 5). For 40% of them, the main source of income is from regular work. Casual work is another way of earning money, particularly in Luxembourg and the Netherlands. The social security system is relatively unimportant as an income source, except in Ireland, Finland and the United Kingdom.

4. There may be specific difficulties facing young people living in "jobless households"

Financial dependency on parents is not necessarily an ideal arrangement when nobody has a job in the family. This is not solely a concern for the financial welfare of young people, but there are also issues of family tensions and the nature of day-to-day contacts of people in jobless households with the labour market which may affect their future job prospects. For example, in the United Kingdom, young people with unemployed parents face a substantially higher risk of unemployment themselves (Payne, 1987; Raffe, 1988; Gregg and Machin, 1998). Factors such as poor school attendance and growing up in a family in financial distress matter a lot as empirical research suggests that poverty begets poverty.

Table 6 shows the proportion of unemployed and inactive youths in households where no other person is employed. In all countries, unemployed teenagers are more likely to live in households where nobody is in employment compared with teenagers not in the labour force and who are very likely in education (in fact, for many, participation in education may be contingent upon others in the household having paid work). Unemployed and not in the labour force young adults aged 20-24 years are both confronted with very similar probabilities of being in jobless households (around 30%).

The proportion of young unemployed in households with no other person employed increased slightly between 1985 and 1996 in most countries. However, the risk is quite dissimilar among OECD countries: the share of unemployed youths aged 20-24 in households where nobody is employed was, at over 40%, highest in Finland, Ireland and the United Kingdom. The lowest proportions, in the order of 16 to 25%, were recorded in the southern European countries, Austria, Mexico and Switzerland.

A. School attendance among teenagers and young adults

In many OECD countries, education to at least the upper secondary level is fairly standard and increasing numbers of students are continuing education into their early 20s. In 1997, the proportion of teenagers attending school was, on average, 79%, ranging from a high of 90% in France and Germany to a low of 54% in the United Kingdom (Figure 1). For young adults, the proportion attending school was, on average, 37%. The proportion of youth attending school has risen for both genders over the past decade. (The only exception is male teenagers in the United Kingdom.)

Combining school and work

The biggest change for teenagers over the decade was a growth in the proportion remaining in full-time education and a quasi-stabilisation of those combining education with employment. Figure 1 shows that in 1997, on average 17% of 16-19-year olds were studying and working (16% in 1987), while 61% of them were only studying (52% in 1987). This evolution is almost identical for young adults.

However, the situation varies greatly across countries. In general, combining education and work is relatively common in countries which have either a dual-system apprenticeship programme (Austria, Denmark and Germany) and/or a relatively high incidence of part-time employment (Australia, Canada, Denmark, the Netherlands, the United Kingdom and the United States). Combining school and work was the most common situation for teenagers attending school in the late 1990s compared with full-time studying in only two countries: a high-attendance country such as Denmark where about one-half of 16-19-year olds were working while studying, and a low-attendance country such as the United Kingdom where nearly 30% of teenagers combine both. In these two countries, but also in Australia and the Netherlands, young adults still attending school more often combine work and study. In contrast, the phenomenon of teenage working students is almost non-existent in Belgium, France, Greece, Italy, Portugal and Spain.

One concern about the part-time working of students is the possible impact on their academic performance and final educational attainment (OECD, 1998e). However, the evidence suggests that *overall* there is no tendency for students in part-time jobs to do less well academically than those who do not work. The impact depends partly on the number of hours worked. Several studies indicate a link between poorer attainment and part-time work among students who work for more than 10 hours per week (McKechnie *et al.*, 1998; Robinson, 1998).

There is considerable debate, but little actual research, on the impact of school-work combinations on long-term success rates in integrating into employment and constructing good careers.[4] Ruhm (1997) suggests for the United States that the positive effects of in-school work experience are larger for those who leave the education system after high school than for those who go on to higher education. He also finds that working while in school is more prevalent the more advantaged one's family background, a finding not replicated in British research (Dustmann *et al.*, 1996). In France, full-time university students – the case of 60% of university students less than 28 years old – fare better than part-time attendees in obtaining a good job after leaving university (Béduwe and Cahuzac, 1997).

Early school leavers

Early school leaving without any qualifications increases the risk of exclusion and of poor labour market prospects. The difficulties experienced by early leavers today seem more acute compared with the past several decades. In the United States, high-school drop outs in the cohort entering the labour market in the early 1980s and followed through the early 1990s were more likely to be intermittently unemployed and to rely on part-time jobs for a greater number of years than the ones in the cohort entering the labour market in the late 1960s (Bernhardt *et al.*, 1998). In France, early school leavers without the general *Baccalauréat* fared worse in the late 1990s compared with the late 1980s, mainly because of the rise in unemployment and despite permanent public intervention on the youth labour market (Werquin, 1997).

Early school leavers can be *roughly* approximated by the proportion of teenagers not attending school[5] (Figure 2). Their numbers are substantial in many countries, although there is wide variation. Teenagers not attending school account for, on average, one in five of the age group. They are strongly over-represented in the United Kingdom and Australia where the proportions are 44 and 35%, respectively. Nonetheless, the proportion of teenagers not attending school has decreased everywhere (except for males in the United Kingdom) over the past decade. There is no strong differentiation by gender within countries.

The issue is linked to the emergence of a hard core of young people who are disaffected with the institutions of education and the labour market, and who face a high risk of unemployment and social exclusion. A report on the 1970 British Cohort Study among those aged at 26 years identified three broad groups, who were, respectively, "getting on, getting by, and getting nowhere" (Bynner *et al.*, 1997). Many current concerns focus on the latter group of young people, who face prolonged unemployment or at best employment that is low-paid, insecure and intermittent. They are disadvantaged by their lack of qualifications and basic skills, often compounded by other disadvantages such as poverty, family breakdown, single parenthood, homelessness, poor physical and mental health or a criminal record, or by external problems such as racial or gender discrimination or a lack of local job opportunities. In several countries, such as Canada, concern has been expressed about high and rising proportions of young boys among the population of at-risk youths (Morissette, 1998).

Young people neither in education nor in a job

Figure 3 shows data on a group of young people of policy relevance: those who are not attending school *and* are not employed.[6] However, those young people neither in education nor in the labour market are quite heterogeneous, and it should not be assumed that all of them are experiencing difficulties in the transition from school to work. Some young people may "drop out" of both education and the labour market in order to travel or to undertake community service. However, in most cases, this indicator can be regarded with some confidence as one measure of transition difficulties.

This group includes both the unemployed as well as those who may have become discouraged from actively seeking work. Teenagers neither in education nor in a job accounted for, on average, 9% of the age group in 1997 compared with 12% in 1987. The proportion of teenagers not attending school and not employed is much higher than the OECD average in the United Kingdom, Italy, Spain, Australia and Greece. In general, teenage girls outside of the education system have a higher rate of non-employment than teenage boys, but this gap has narrowed substantially over time, particularly in the southern European countries. Whereas there has been a decline in these rates for teenage girls in all but one country (the United Kingdom) over the past 10 years – reflecting a broader pattern of rising education rates – there have been either small declines for teenage boys or even increases, most notably in the United Kingdom, despite a proliferation of programmes designed to help youths get into jobs. In most countries, the decline has been the result of increases in youths staying on in school (see Figure 1) rather than because more have found jobs.

For young adults, the contrast by gender is starker. Many more women are not in the labour force than men although there is little difference by gender in the proportions of the age group who are unemployed. In general, the same trends apply for teenagers, with declines in the proportion of women neither in education or a job in almost all countries.

Young people with low educational qualifications

As completion of upper secondary education – at almost 75% in the OECD as a whole – has become more the norm in many OECD countries, young persons who fail to complete this level can find themselves particularly penalised in the labour market (OECD, 1997*b*). For example, the unemployment rates of young adults aged 25-29 with low educational attainment are much higher compared with those with attainment at the tertiary/university level. On average in 1996, young adult men with low educational attainment had an unemployment rate of 16% while those with tertiary/university schooling had a rate of about 8% (the respective rates for young adult women are 20 and 9%; see Table 7). Young adults with a university/tertiary education have, however, the highest unemployment rate compared with lower educational attainment in Greece (men only), Italy, Korea and Portugal (men only).

The proportion of 25-29-year-olds who have not completed upper secondary education is still substantial in many countries, although there is wide variation (Figure 4). On average in 1996 almost one in four lacked qualifications beyond the end of compulsory schooling, ranging from over three in four among Turkish women to less than one in ten in Norway, Switzerland (men only), the Czech Republic and Korea.

The reduction in the numbers of young adults with low skills (see Figure 3.2 in OECD, 1998c) has improved neither their relative nor their absolute chances of success in the labour market. Instead, their position has deteriorated as they constitute a smaller and more stigmatised minority who cannot provide evidence of knowledge, competencies and prior work experience; this often leads to a cycle of joblessness interspersed with unstable jobs (OECD, 1998b). For example, in the United Kingdom, as fewer people enter the labour market at the age of 16, those who do so are increasingly seen as the least able.[7]

B. Education and employment activities at key transition ages

A useful initial way to characterise the transition is as the change in the activities of young people from school-going to working/seeking work as they age. It is the time interval during which a cohort of young people moves from near-full enrolment in education to negligible enrolment and from negligible labour market activity to a high level of activity (Galland, 1997; INSEE, 1995, 1997). It can also involve frequent movements between education, the labour market and other activities.[8] In many OECD countries, young people's transition is now beginning at a later age and it is taking longer than a decade ago (OECD, 1996b; OECD, 1998d).[9] As Freeman (see p. 89 in this volume) has expressed it, the "young" today are older than they were several decades ago.

The reasons for a delayed age of entry to full-time work are complex. First, poor job prospects, as exemplified by high youth unemployment rates and falling youth employment rates, have had an influence on the propensity of young people to continue their studies beyond compulsory education. Second, young people are staying on longer in education because it can represent a sound investment in their future. Third, many countries have made substantial efforts to reform curricula and teaching methods so that schools are more attractive to a wider span of young people. Finally, systems of public financial support are increasingly designed to make education a more attractive option than unemployment and inactivity.

An overview of young people's education and employment activities at the ages of 18 and 22 provides a starting point to understanding the different nature of the problems. These ages are key in the transition: the age of 18 roughly represents the end of upper secondary education and the age of 22 the end of the first stage of tertiary education.

Table 8 shows how many 18- and 22-year-olds were in education/training, in employment only, in both or in neither in 1984 and 1997. In 1997, on average, 56% of the cohort of 18-year-olds were in full-time education while among 22-year-olds 46% were in employment only. Thus, education and employment are quite separate activities at ages 18 and 22 for many young people. In terms of the OECD average, the trends over the period are the same for both: a strong increase of youths in full-time education and a much smaller increase in the proportion of those combining education with employment; conversely there has been a strong decrease of those in employment without studying and a smaller decrease of those neither in education nor in employment.

Education and employment activities are partly shaped by national characteristics and policies. In several countries, many young people combine education and work, while in others this is rarely the case. Belgium and the United Kingdom exemplify this contrast. In Belgium, youths rarely work while in school: in 1997, 85% of teenagers aged 18 were in full-time education, only 1% combined education with employment and 3% were in employment only. In the United Kingdom, quite a large proportion of teenagers are working: 18% of those aged 18 were in full-time education, 30% combined education with employment and 38% were only in employment. But interestingly, in both countries, there exists a sizeable group at risk of social marginalisation which is composed of teenagers not in education nor in employment; this group accounted for over 20% of the teenage population in the United Kingdom in 1997 compared with about 12% in Belgium.

Table 9 provides a complementary picture of the schooling and labour market statuses of young persons aged 18 and 22 by gender in 1984 and 1997. The data show large variations across countries in transition patterns, *e.g.* the different proportions in school and the high proportion of young persons in vocational training/apprenticeships in Austria, Denmark and Germany. They also show a general pattern of increases over the period in school attendance and of declines in employment/population ratios.

II. OVERVIEW OF YOUTH IN THE LABOUR MARKET

Introduction

Despite declines in the relative size of the youth cohort (see Box 2) and increases in the level of educational attainment in the past two decades in most OECD countries, the employment and earnings of young people have not improved. Youth labour force participation and employment rates fell across a large number of OECD countries over the period, and the earnings of young workers declined relative to those of older workers in most countries. In several countries, the deterioration of the position of youths on the labour market shows up mainly in relatively high unemployment rates and low employment/population rates. In others, it shows up mainly in falling relative wages for young workers. But in most countries, there is a group of disadvantaged youths facing both kinds of deterioration. Only part of this is due to rising education enrolments as the largest negative trend in employment is among young men not in education (OECD, 1996a). Box 4 at the end of the section (see pp. 17-18) puts together key stylised facts about school-leaving and labour market outcomes for young people today compared with the late 1970s/early 1980s.

Box 2. **The "baby-boom" has turned into a "baby-bust"**

Over the past two decades, the size of the youth cohort relative to that of the working-age population has fallen significantly in most OECD countries (Figure 5). In 1997, youths accounted for 22% of the OECD working-age population, ranging from a low of 17% in Switzerland and Germany to highs of nearly 35% in Turkey and Mexico. In all but two cases, the Czech Republic and Hungary, the youths' share fell over the two decades from 1977. From 1977 to 1997 the average relative decline in the youths' share of the working-age population was about 5 percentage points.

A. Youth participation, employment and unemployment rates

Tables 10 to 12 assess the youth labour market over the past two decades in terms of the classic indicators of labour supply and demand. These data highlight falling participation (Table 10) and employment rates (Table 11), and rising unemployment rates (Table 12). They also reveal wide differences across countries in the levels for persons under the age of 25 years. For example, in 1997, the participation and employment rates of French, Belgian and Korean male teenagers were under 10% compared with almost 70% in Denmark. The differences are somewhat smaller among those aged 20-24 years: the participation/employment rates range from lows of 54/41% for young men in France to highs of 86/81% for young men in Mexico. Participation/employment rates also differ between young men and women: on average in 1997, the gender gap was about 5 percentage points for teenagers and 11 percentage points for the 20-24 age group.

With few exceptions, teenage and young adult unemployment rates are in double-digit figures, and were higher in 1997 than in 1979. Once again, there are large cross-country differences in levels: in 1997, only Austria (men), Denmark, Germany, Japan (women), Korea (women) and Mexico had teenage rates under 10%, while unemployment rates of 35% and over for women were recorded in Belgium, France, Greece, Italy, Poland and Spain (men also).

The trend in unemployment partly reflects the economic cycle, with a boom in the late 1970s and late 1980s followed by a recession in the early 1990s (see Box 3). Over the peak-to-peak period of 1979 and 1989, only in Australia, Canada, Finland, France (women only), Portugal, Sweden and the united States (women only) were declines recorded in teenage unemployment rates; in almost all cases, the declines were modest. In 1997, youth unemployment rates were higher almost everywhere than in 1989.

The need to look beyond unemployment rates in order to gauge youth labour market problems properly is widely recognised (OECD, 1996a, b; EUROSTAT, 1998). When teenagers have low rates of labour force participation and high enrolment rates in education, unemployment rates for this age group refer only to early school leavers. Moreover, they may show a rise even if the proportion of the teenage population that is unemployed has declined.

Box 3. **Youth employment and unemployment rates are very sensitive to cyclical fluctuations**

OECD (1996a) showed that the youth labour market is very sensitive to the overall state of the economy. Estimates of the effect of aggregate labour market conditions on youths in three states – the per cent in education; the per cent employed; and the per cent in the labour force unemployed – were computed by regressing the proportion of each age-gender group from 16 to 29 in each state on the rate of unemployment; a gender dummy; age dummies; and a time trend (see Table 4.18 in OECD, 1996a). Pooling all the countries together, schooling is positively related to unemployment, implying that increases in unemployment lead to increased enrolments, but the very diverse country results belay any easy generalisation. By contrast, there is little ambiguity as to the effect of aggregate unemployment on the proportion of a cohort working or unemployed. The proportion employed falls with unemployment in most countries, with the absolute value of the coefficient often greater than one. The proportion of the cohort unemployed is similarly positively related to aggregate unemployment with a coefficient greater than one almost everywhere. OECD (1996a) also showed that as young people get older, the proportion employed or unemployed becomes less sensitive to aggregate economic conditions.

Hence, some analysts argue that it is important to complement the conventional unemployment rate with the youth unemployment/population ratio. Figure 6 shows both indicators. For the majority of OECD countries, less than one in ten youths were unemployed in 1997. On average, in 1997, 6% of teenagers and 9% of young adults were unemployed by this measure. The two indicators differ mainly in countries where few young persons are in the labour force. Switching from one measure to the other results not only in a substantial change in levels, but also in the ranking of countries.[10] France is a good example because of its relatively low youth participation rate (see also Marchand and Minni, 1997). France has one of the highest youth (15-24) unemployment rates among OECD countries after Spain, Italy and Greece, but comes out better than Finland, Australia, Canada, Poland, Sweden, the United Kingdom and New Zealand when the unemployment/population ratio is considered.

Figure 6 shows another dimension to unemployment, its *duration*. It should be borne in mind that duration refers here to a continuous spell of unemployment rather than repeated spells. Multiple-spell unemployment is, however, very frequent among young people who alternate joblessness with periods of insecure employment or discouragement. The incidence of long-term unemployment (a spell of 12 consecutive months or more) is shown for each country by the lighter colour.[11] The incidence rises as youths grow older: on average, one unemployed teenager in six is in long-term unemployment compared with one unemployed young adult in three. There are, however, huge cross-country differences. In most countries, the majority of unemployed youth (aged 15-24) have been in a spell of unemployment for less than 12 months, except in Italy and Greece (women only).

B. Youth earnings

This section highlights the relative position of youths by examining their earnings relative to those of adults, to those paid in low-wage jobs and to statutory minimum wages.[12] Evidence on earnings mobility is also considered. Low-wage jobs can be a step to a better-paying job but they may also recur and alternate with no pay.

Age-earnings profiles

As youths grow older, they gain experience and earn more. The progression may be slow or fast according to the country and/or the year of entering the labour market. Figure 7 shows the age-earnings profiles for full-time workers by gender for three cohorts in eight countries for which data are available. Three features are worth noting. First, the profiles of young women start at a lower level than young men and have a much flatter slope, except in Australia and the Netherlands. Second, young men in Japan and in France have the steepest profiles. Third, in the seven countries for which recent data are available, the most recent (1995) cohort fares somewhat better than the older ones concerning the level of earnings between 20 and 24 years of age, except in the United States and Australia (young men only).

There is a clear story about youth earnings being persistently low relative to older workers' earnings – between 40 to 80% lower depending on the period and the country (Figure 8). Mean earnings for youths aged 20-24 years in full-time jobs in the late 1970s ranged between a high of 80% of mean earnings of workers aged 35-44 years in Australia to a low of 40% in Korea. The change over the following two decades was in opposite directions in these two countries, a decrease to 68% in Australia and an increase to 50% in Korea. From the late 1970s to the late 1990s, the earnings of youths relative to adults fell in a number of countries for which data are available (the United Kingdom, the United States, Sweden, Canada, New Zealand) or remained stagnant in others (France, Germany, Japan, Finland, the Netherlands). These changes occurred despite national differences in wage formation, a common pattern of decline rather than increase in the size of the youth cohort and an increase in the educational levels of young people relative to adults. As Freeman (see p. 89) has stressed, the decline or stagnation in the relative earnings of young people over the past two decades is quite an unexpected result given that basic economic forces that affect youth wages, including shifts in demand or supply of youth labour and skills, actually went in the opposite direction.

Low-paid jobs

Table 13 shows the likelihood of young workers being in low-paid employment.[13] On average across the 14 countries, nearly 40% of young workers are low paid, but the variation across countries is striking: 63% of all full-time employed youths in the United States are in low-paid jobs compared with under 20% in Austria and Sweden. Given that the overall incidence of low-paid employment varies considerably across countries, it is difficult to discern whether it is much more concentrated amongst youths. An indicator of concentration that abstracts from country differences in the overall incidence of low pay can be constructed by dividing the incidence for youths by the overall incidence of low-paid jobs (column 3 in Table 13). A value greater than one indicates that the risk of low pay for young people is greater than the average risk for all workers. As would be expected, young workers face a much higher-than-average incidence of low-paid employment in all countries.

However, this finding relates to "point-in-time" comparisons and does not allow one to infer anything about mobility in the earnings distribution and how this differs for different age groups. OECD (1997a), drawing on longitudinal data covering six countries (Denmark, France, Germany, Italy, the United Kingdom, and the United States) over the period 1986 to 1991, showed that low-paying jobs are often a stepping stone to better paying jobs, though many also move from low-pay to no pay.[14]

Youths are particularly likely to have been low paid at least once during 1986-1991 and at the beginning of the period when they were youngest (Table 14). However, they move up the earnings distribution more rapidly than older workers, causing their "always low-paid rate" to fall relative to older workers. This pattern holds in all of the countries examined, but is particularly strong in Germany: workers less than 25 in 1986 were four times as likely as all workers to be low paid in that year, but only nearly as likely as all workers to be always low paid during 1986-1991. The United States stands out as having the highest incidence of low-paid employment for youths among the six countries under review: nearly one-half of youths were low paid in 1986, 61% of youths had been in a low-paid job at least once during the five-year period and 14% were always low paid during the whole period. The average cumulative years in low-paid employment is also particularly high in this country. Young workers in the United States who were low paid in 1986 on average accumulated roughly four additional years of low pay during the next five years compared with less than two additional years in Denmark. Persistence in low pay is also high in the United Kingdom. In recent years, both the United Kingdom and the United States have experienced much greater increases in earnings inequality than other OECD countries and persistence in low pay is greater where inequality is greater.

Statutory minimum wages

Youths are much more likely than adults to be in minimum-wage jobs because they generally have less labour market experience than other workers. On the one hand, minimum wages narrow earnings differentials across demographic groups, particularly between the young and the old, and countries with relatively high minimum wages have less earnings inequality and a lower incidence of low pay. On the other hand, if the minimum wage is set at too high a level, young workers may be most vulnerable to job losses.

Indeed, one of the strongest criticisms of minimum wages is that, to the extent they are set at above market-clearing levels, they will price some people with low productivity – and particularly young workers – out of jobs. The econometric evidence reported in OECD (1998b) for nine countries (Belgium, Canada, France, Greece, Japan, the Netherlands, Portugal, Spain and the United States) over the period 1975 to 1996 showed that a 10% increase in the minimum is associated with a 1.5 to 3% decline in *teenage* employment, with no impact on young adults. However, the evidence also shows that hikes in the minimum, on their own, can explain only a very small fraction of the large observed falls in teenage employment rates over the past two decades in almost all countries.[15]

One solution to minimise the potential disemployment effects of a minimum wage on young people is to allow for sub-minimum rates differentiated by age. Over one-half of the seventeen countries[16] which currently have a statutory or national minimum wage apply a reduced rate for young workers.[17] Two features in the setting of these lower rates for young workers are worth noting. With few exceptions, the differential (*i.e.* the gap between the adult minimum and the special youth rate) is quite small – usually about 10-15%. It also applies typically to those aged 18 years and less.

Box 4. **Stylised facts about school-leaving and labour market outcomes for young people today compared with the late 1970s/early 1980s**

They are more educated...

• More youths remain in education beyond compulsory schooling: on average across OECD countries 34% of youths aged 22 were attending school in 1997, compared to 19% in 1984.

• Consequently, there are fewer early school leavers. For instance, the proportion of 18-year-olds not attending school was 33% in 1997, compared with 50% in 1984.

• There are also slightly fewer youths neither in initial education nor in a job: 14% of 16-24-year-olds were not at school and not employed in 1997, compared with 22% in 1984.

• Young people facing the largest barriers to a stable entry into the labour market are more and more those who complete school with qualifications ill-suited to employment or drop outs with no qualifications.

... but their labour market prospects have not tended to improve

• Youth employment rates are lower: in 1997, 44% of the 15-24-year-olds were in employment, compared with 52% in 1979.

• Out-of-school young men have fared particularly badly, as evidenced by a strong trend decline in their employment prospects.

• The employment gap between the youth cohort and the adult cohort has widened.

• Youths in the labour force are more likely to be unemployed: the OECD average unemployment rate for 15-24-year-olds was 16% in 1997, 4 percentage points higher than in 1979.

• While the experience of unemployment is widespread, it is highly concentrated among a disadvantaged group of young people.

• Youths are confronted with stagnant or declining earnings relative to adults, a rather unexpected twist that could have major longer-term consequence in terms of lifelong earnings.

Persistencies across the past two decades

• Transition processes and outcomes differ greatly by country, gender and, often, educational level.

• In many countries, being in full-time education is more common than combining education and work.

• Combining work with schooling is a feature either of apprenticeship countries or of countries with a relatively high incidence of part-time employment.

• Teenage and young adult women perform better at school and have seen a long-term trend increase in their employment prospects compared with their young male counterparts.

• Apprenticeship/dual-system countries clearly do better at getting young people a firm foothold in the labour market.

• Those who fail to get a firm foothold in the labour market form a "hard core" of disaffected young people, a stigmatised minority with cumulative disadvantages, often related to intergenerational factors such as poverty, unstable family backgrounds and life in communities with high overall unemployment.

III. GETTING STARTED, SETTLING IN: A VIEW OF THE TRANSITION FROM INITIAL EDUCATION TO THE LABOUR MARKET

School-to-work transition processes differ sharply across countries, mainly in terms of the time it takes to get into the first job and the amount of labour turnover involved in settling into steady employment. This section will consider the integration of young people only after they have left the education system and will focus on the short-term and longer-term effects of getting started and settling into the labour market.

A. Job prospects one year after leaving initial education

A central issue is how do youths fare once they do leave the education system? OECD (1998b) shed some light on this question by focusing on the labour market outcomes of young people one year after leaving initial education, so-called "new school leavers". "Starting off" in the labour market as unemployed is the case, on average, for one new school leaver in four in OECD countries. The study highlighted that new school leavers on the right track one year after leaving school are those fortunate enough to have a higher level of education and to enter the labour market in a good year. While the job prospects of new school leavers are highly sensitive to the overall state of the labour market, institutional factors matter as well. A range of factors apart from the education system appears to be associated with country differences in the employment rates of new school leavers. Higher employment rates are associated with lower adult unemployment rates, more centralised/co-ordinated systems of wage bargaining and with a strong dual system of vocational education and training.[18]

Cross-country differences are very large. In Germany, Luxembourg, Austria and Denmark, countries with long-standing and highly-developed apprenticeship systems, over three-quarters of young people aged 16-24 years in 1996 were in employment one year after leaving education, whereas less than one-third had a job in Finland and Italy (Figure 9). Over the period 1987 to 1996, only Germany and Ireland posted a significant increase in the proportion of new school leavers finding employment, with the other countries reporting at best a stabilisation, at worse a decline. The deterioration over the decade was particularly marked in France and Greece.

Difficulty in the transition process can be observed not simply in the form of joblessness, but in extended periods after leaving full-time education being spent in temporary, casual or part-time work. Insecure employment is often interspersed with spells of unemployment and with participation in remedial and short-term labour market measures. There have been substantial changes in the types of entry-level jobs available to youths. A common trend, the strength of which varies across countries, is the decline over the past decade in the proportion of new school leavers going directly into permanent, full-time jobs. For those with a job one year after leaving school, it is more often than before a temporary job – in one-third of the cases because the contract covers a period of training – and a part-time job, very often voluntary, in order to combine education and work (Figure 9).

B. A longer-term view of the transition from initial education

The previous sub-section took a short-run perspective to youth insertion into the labour market. The purpose here is to extend that analysis by following youths over time after they leave the educational system permanently using longitudinal data for Australia, France, Germany, Ireland and the United States (see OECD, 1998b for information on data sources and methods).[19]

The main questions addressed are: What are individuals' employment and unemployment experiences over a three to six-year period after permanently leaving initial education? How does that experience vary across countries and levels of educational attainment? How much time do youths spend employed and is there any evidence of "persistence" in labour force status? Is unemployment widely spread or concentrated among a minority who spend a lot of time out of work?

Incidence of employment and unemployment – the first three to five years after permanently leaving education

Tables 15 and 16 record the evolution of employment and unemployment rates for this select group of *permanent* school leavers. Concerning employment, three tendencies are apparent. First, with the exception of Germany, there are large differences in *first-year* employment rates by educational attainment, with rates increasing in line with qualifications. American youths with less than an upper secondary education (*i.e.* high-school dropouts) have quite low employment rates.[20] Second, there are gender differences. Women's employment rates are lower than men's, with the absolute differences generally greater at lower levels of educational attainment (the exception is Irish women with some university/tertiary education). This gap is particularly pronounced in Australia and the United States. Finally, the rates tend to rise over time and the absolute gap between those with less and more education does narrow, especially for young men. However, differences do persist: five years after entering the labour market, between 13 and 25% of young men at the lower end of the education scale are not employed compared with only 1 to 13% of those with some university/tertiary education.

Box 5. **Recourse to youth labour market measures in France**

France is an interesting case because it is the one country for which the data set contains information on participation in subsidised jobs and, as will be emphasised below (see Section IV), such measures add an important dimension to understanding youth labour markets. The first year after leaving school one-third or more of French youth without even the general *Baccalauréat* were employed in subsidised jobs. Other research shows that fully one-half of this cohort went through at least one programme (Werquin, 1997). Although employment rates for this group of new school leavers change little over time, recourse to programmes declines dramatically, while integration into jobs with a permanent contract tends to increase, though fully one-third never obtained such a contract. Not surprisingly, French research has shown that programmes close to regular employment, *e.g. contrats de qualification*, have a higher probability of leading to regular jobs (DARES, 1997).

Some of the tendencies observed with employment are also mirrored in unemployment rates (Table 16). The latter, as in cross-section data, decline as educational qualifications increase. But, there are again large differences across countries, which are more pronounced at lower levels of education. There is, however, no uniform tendency for unemployment rates to decline over time among less-educated youths, except in Australia and the United States.

Time spent in work

The evolution of employment and unemployment rates over time is only one part of the picture of how well or poorly youths become integrated into the labour market. The total amount of time spent in jobs or job-seeking, and whether or not there is persistence in status are also important elements in any judgement about getting a firm foothold in the world of work.

Table 17 shows the average time spent in employment. The figures are calculated conditional upon whether these youths were employed, unemployed or not in the labour force in their first year in the labour market. The closer the values are to one, the closer are these youths to having been continuously in work at the moment of each of the three to six annual interviews [the Irish data, however, refer to the total time spent employed over a 36- (university/tertiary) and a 60-month period].

The overall results are clear. Irrespective of education or gender, getting a job in the first year after permanently leaving school is associated with a greatly increased likelihood of being employed at the moment of each annual interview compared with youths starting off without a job. To some degree, this "persistence" is also higher among the more educated, though the difference is small.[21]

In terms of these youth cohorts overall, the figures in columns one and six of Table 17 should be combined with the very large cross-country differences in employment rates in Table 15. Thus, while youths who do start the transition in a job spend a similar cumulated amount of time in employment in all countries, this covers a significantly larger proportion of youths, especially those with fewer educational qualifications, in Germany, France, and to some extent Ireland, compared with Australia and the United States.

Starting off unemployed or not in the labour force leads to significantly less cumulated time spent in employment over the three to five-year period. There are, however, some cross-country and cross-education differences. Whether the experience of unemployment itself causes further unemployment – the so-called "scarring" hypothesis – has been the subject of considerable debate and some empirical research. Although the evidence is not conclusive, the balance seems to lean towards some evidence of a scarring effect (Franz *et al.*, 1997; Gardecki and Neumark, 1997; Werquin *et al.*, 1997). Though the data in Table 18 cannot be used to prove rigorously that early problems in finding a job *cause* later problems, they do point in this direction.

Another dimension of persistence is shown in Table 18. It records the *distribution* of employment and unemployment. Very few young men, regardless of educational background, were never employed. However, the distribution shows large cross-country differences. At the lower end of educational attainment, over 85% of German men and over 75% of German women were in work during at least four of the annual surveys (these figures are obtained by adding the proportion employed for four and five periods). This compares with 70% for Irish men and 50% for Irish women, and 69% for French men and 63% for French women. The equivalent proportions are much lower for young men and women in Australia and the United States with less than upper secondary education. As educational attainment increases, these cross-country differences diminish among both genders. Results are, not surprisingly, similar for time spent unemployed. Multiple "periods" of unemployment are far more prevalent among American, Australian and French youths. In all countries, the likelihood of being unemployed at any of the survey dates declines with educational attainment.

A useful summary measure which highlights these large differences is to compute how much of this three to five-year period is spent in employment on average. For men with less than upper secondary education in both Australia and the United States, only about two-thirds of the period was spent in work compared with almost 90% in Germany. Moreover, in the first two countries the distribution is highly unequal, with roughly one-half of the total time spent in employment being accounted for by just one-third of these youths. In France, where a six-year period is considered, men with less than upper secondary education spent only half of the total period in employment. The distribution is also highly unequal, with one-half of the total time in employment being accounted for by a little more than one-quarter of these French youth. Box 6 takes a somewhat different look at the experience of unemployment, in particular its concentration over time.

Box 6. **How concentrated is unemployment over time – a longitudinal perspective of the French, German and American experience?**

Many analysts, when focusing on youth unemployment, see it as a very dynamic process. Part of the reason for this stems from the fact that at any point-in-time youth are, in almost all countries, less likely compared with adults, to be long-term unemployed. Job-search models and models of "normal turnover" also often give the impression that much youth unemployment is of a short-term, and hence not very costly, nature.

However, this subsection, following the seminal work of Clark and Summers (1979) and OECD (1984), argues that these theses are a misleading characterisation of much youth unemployment. Instead, much of the observed high rate of youth unemployment is the result of some youths experiencing prolonged spells without work.

In order to shed some light on these issues, this subsection again makes use of longitudinal data.[22] However, unlike the preceding analysis, this subsection has reconstructed the entire unemployment history of youths from retrospective questions to the annual surveys. Thus, for Germany and the United States, the full five-year-period since permanently leaving initial education has been used to calculate the entire time unemployed. For France, unemployment histories have been calculated for a 78-month-period, although these data refer only to the cohort who left the education system at less than the upper secondary level.

Table 19 shows how widespread the experience of unemployment was over the time period. There are three important messages. First, regardless of level of education or gender, it is much more common among American and French youths compared with their German counterparts. Among all American youths in the sample, over one-half had experienced some time unemployed compared with only 28% in Germany. Second, there is no significant difference within countries between young men and women. Third, the experience of any unemployment declines substantially by level of educational qualification, with the drop in unemployment experience being much greater in the United States than in Germany.

Unemployment could be widespread among young people because many of them experience short bouts out of work. However, Table 20 suggests that this would be to misread the actual situation. The apparent concentration of unemployment is shown in detail by looking at the distribution, in months of unemployment.

Among all Germans, the 1.6% of the population who experienced at least two years of unemployment, accounted for 25% of all weeks of unemployment over the five-year period. Similar results are clear for the United States. This degree of concentration is difficult to reconcile with an often expressed view that the main problem of youth unemployment arises from many brief spells of being out of work interspersed by short-term jobs. A key problem, instead, seems to be a semi-permanent mismatch between the capabilities of some young workers and available job opportunities.

There are some differences by level of educational attainment. France is interesting because one-third of the population with less than secondary education experienced two or more years of unemployment (the corresponding figures are 2.8 and 7.2% in Germany and the United States, respectively) accounting for over 60% of all weeks of unemployment (this compares to around 30% in both Germany and the United States). Bearing in mind that unemployment is more widespread among less educated youth, comparing its concentration across levels of education reveals only small differences. In Germany, concentration is little different between those with less than upper secondary and those with completed upper secondary education, while concentration tends to decline a bit among Americans. That said, overall higher levels of education are no guarantee of quickly finding stable employment for all.

IV. STRATEGIES FOR IMPROVING YOUTH LABOUR MARKET PROSPECTS

Introduction

A diagnosis of problems does not immediately lead to coherent policy strategies to solve them. Thus, this section looks at the overall approaches of governments towards youth labour markets, and describes some of the main policy initiatives taken in recent years which are oriented towards improving the school-to-work transition and the access of youths to the regular labour market. Policy in this domain typically straddles the responsibilities of the education, labour market and social welfare authorities, and combines interventions on both the supply and demand sides. On the supply side, policy focuses on the development of young people's employability through school curricula development, the strengthening of the links between education and work, study incentives, remedial training and career counselling. On the demand side, wage-setting and other labour market arrangements may be altered with a view to pricing young people into private-sector jobs, or jobs may be specially created for them in the public/non-profit sectors. In practice, the distinction between these types of policies is not clear-cut. For example, employment subsidies are usually combined with various mixtures of education, training, work experience and support services. Policies also differ in the extent to which they focus on sub-groups of the youth population. Some address school-to-work transition issues for all youths at secondary level, others focus on the disadvantages faced by at-risk youths.

The aims of these policies are multi-fold: a smoother transition to stable, career-oriented and well-paid employment; an effective matching of young workers and jobs; low rates of youth unemployment, particularly long-term unemployment; and the acquisition by youths of the capacity to adapt to a changing work environment throughout their working lives.

The ambition of these goals must be tempered by the recognition of the key role played by socio-economic backgrounds in shaping individuals' educational and employment opportunities throughout their lives. It is quite naive, in fact, to believe that education and active labour market policies aimed at disadvantaged youths can overcome handicaps that have their origin in the economic and social disadvantages faced since early childhood. Only a broader and more long-term policy of poverty reduction and equalisation of socio-economic conditions, that targets support on disadvantaged families and communities, can hope to achieve this. Furthermore, it is important to acknowledge that the aggregate volume of economic activity is the major determinant factor of youth unemployment, and that a sound combination of macroeconomic and structural policies are needed to lay the ground for solving youth labour market problems. A discussion of such a comprehensive strategy is beyond the scope of the present paper.[23] Therefore, the paper takes a restricted view of the strategies for improving youth labour market prospects.

Critically, the ambition of youth policy objectives has seldom been accompanied by systematic programme monitoring and evaluation. When evaluations are available, they usually take a restricted view of the possible impacts of the programmes. Some monitoring activities are limited to measuring participation in the programmes, with little attention being paid to the quality of the programme itself; others look only at the impact on participants employment and/or earnings immediately after they have left the programme; others attempt to measure the net effects of the programmes on aggregate performance indicators like employment and unemployment. There is very little evidence on the long-term effects of these programmes, or as to why the programmes do or do not work. Furthermore, few of the available evaluations, especially for countries other than the United States, are based on experimental methods that allow a rigorous answer to the question: "What would have happened, other things being equal, had the programme not been implemented?".[24]

Rigorous assessment of the effectiveness of the policies discussed here is particularly difficult. Experimental methods are not easily adopted in evaluating policies in the domain of education, as entitlement norms and schooling requirements often rule out the withholding of services from randomly-selected control groups (Ryan and Büchtemann, 1996). Furthermore, policies in this domain may need quite a long time before their impact on youth's employability can be assessed. As for youth labour market programmes that combine different measures, such as training, wage subsidies, job-search assistance, etc. the different elements in each programme and the type of combination between them can contribute to their outcomes, but the evaluator is normally unable to disentangle the importance of these effects. Finally, many of the measures that are discussed here have been so recently implemented that evaluations are scarce.

The section is organised as follows. First, it looks at how initial education and training systems are structured as regards their approach to the school-to-work transition and the provision of the skills required on the labour market. Recent policy developments aimed at strengthening the vocational stream within the education system, ensuring that curricula and qualifications respond to changing work tasks and employment structures, and providing young people with experience in work settings are reviewed. Second, there is a focus on those youths with particular disadvantages in the labour market, and policies of remedial education and training specifically aimed at them are discussed. Third, policies aimed at altering labour market institutions and arrangements with a view toward pricing young people into private-sector jobs, such as youth wages, employer subsidies, special youth contracts and out-of-work income support, are examined. Finally, direct job creation schemes and policies to support self-employment are analysed.

A. Developing young people's employability

Developing young people's employability is a key policy issue for ensuring their successful transition to the labour market and access to career-oriented employment. This involves helping to ensure that they acquire the skills, knowledge and attitudes that will allow them to find work and to cope with unpredictable labour market changes throughout their working lives. Educational systems play a crucial role in preparing youth for the labour market. This section concentrates on examining the main routes through initial education and training into work, and on policies aimed at improving the employability of out-of-school youth. Interest is centred on non-university-bound youth.

Pathways through initial education and into work

Young people move from initial education to employment through a variety of routes or "pathways" that are of particular relevance to policy makers. Education systems in different countries vary greatly in the degree to which general and vocational studies complement each other and in the ways in which they are sequenced. Countries differ, for example, in terms of whether general and vocational streams run in parallel or in integrated programmes, in terms of the timing and nature of the choices that young people have to make between distinct options and labour market destinations, and in terms of the extent to which the vocational stream combines time spent in an education/training institution with time spent at the workplace (OECD, 1998c).

Apprenticeship countries

Austria, Germany, Switzerland and Denmark provide young people with the option of following a vocational pathway at an early age that combines school-based education with training at the workplace. This is the so-called apprenticeship or "dual" system. In Germany, the dual system constitutes the core of vocational education and training: in 1996, over 40% of young *employees* aged between 15 and 24 years had an apprenticeship contract (Table 21). In the same year, apprentices represented around 30% of young employees in Switzerland. In Austria, the dual system attracts a smaller number of pupils – about 24% of employees – due to a highly differentiated provision of school-based vocational education and, in particular, to the so-called five-year technical colleges, giving access to tertiary education.[25] The same share is also lower for Denmark – 25% of young employees.

The main features of the dual system are: trainees are trained in State-recognised occupations requiring formal training, defined in close co-operation with official bodies, management and labour; the apprentice has a formal contract with the firm; the training element is a mix of regular education and on-the-job training supervised by the educational authorities and the social partners; the apprentice's wage is set relatively low compared with the skilled worker rate in the same occupation, but normally rises in accordance with growing productivity as he/she is learning; subsidies to employers may be paid towards the cost of training; and successful completion is certified by a diploma stating that the apprentice fulfils the requirements of the occupation.

As emphasised above, apprenticeship systems in these countries have a good track record in keeping youth unemployment at low levels and at quickly integrating a high proportion of new school leavers into jobs. They do so by raising the incentives and motivation of high-school students to learn; by providing for clear pathways and transitions from school to careers; by expanding the use of contextualised learning that goes beyond firm-specific training; by increasing the relevance of training; and by encouraging employers to upgrade the quality of jobs and to give a chance to young workers (Lerman, 1996).

A widespread consensus on the core elements of the system among all the actors involved, and their high involvement in the design and implementation phases, are key factors for the success of apprenticeship systems. However, this success does not mean that these countries do not face some problems. Concern grew in the 1990s over some global and structural imbalances with which the system is faced. Surpluses or shortages of training places relative to the demand for them have been alternating during the past decade, and the probability is high that a shortage will emerge soon. More importantly, structural mismatches have been identified between the supply of, and demand for, training places, differentiated by occupations, sectors and regions (Bock and Timmermann, 1998). The reasons for these imbalances originate from a change in attitudes on the part of both employers and pupils. On the one hand, the dual system attracts relatively declining numbers of young people, as more and more they tend to choose general rather than vocational education, and full-time vocational/technical schools rather than apprenticeship. On the other hand, employers raise questions as to the cost and appropriateness of training for "rigidly" defined occupations in an era of rapid technological change, and also worry that the quality of applicants is declining as the attractiveness of other pathways rises. For these reasons, they are less willing to invest in high-quality training for apprentices. The continued success of apprenticeship systems shows, however, that these preoccupations are probably exaggerated. It should not be forgotten that the system has been able to adapt to changing job requirements in the past, even if it has done so fairly slowly.

One lesson that can be drawn is that apprenticeships will remain a promising pathway to qualification, employment and further learning if sufficient numbers of attractive training places are offered by employers and if the structure of the supply of apprenticeship places responds to changes in the structure of employment.

Other countries

In other European countries, the most frequent pattern is programmes that take place to a large extent in an education institution rather than at the workplace. This is particularly the case in Greece, Spain and Portugal, where more than 90% of those following a vocational path in 1993-1994 were enrolled in school-based programmes. In France, the Netherlands and Sweden, the vocational programmes that attract most students are those where the training takes place mainly in an education/training institution, but with some time spent at the workplace.

Outside Europe, Australia, Canada, New Zealand and the United States currently have little in the way of vocational training at the level of initial education. In Canada and the United States, the number and range of secondary schools offering vocational programmes have decreased in the past 30 years, due to declining enrolments, changes in the skill and technological requirements of the trades, limited job opportunities and rising aspirations for post-secondary studies. In Australia, vocational education and training has traditionally been offered in the Technical and Further Education colleges (TAFE), involving different types of qualifications and certificates to those issued through the school system. However, the provision of vocational education and training courses as part of the school curriculum in conjunction with TAFE institutes and/or other providers is growing.

In these countries, linkages between education and employment are more informal and decentralised and training decisions by firms and workers are determined by market forces. The assumption is that additional training or skills will be readily acquired after getting a job. High turnover and the risk of poaching, however, can lead to a reluctance to train on the part of employers. In the United States, evidence shows that about 60% of all 25-year-olds obtained no training after high school, and the figures are even higher for non-college youth (Lynch, 1993). Education is also positively correlated with training: those with university qualifications in the United States are roughly five times as likely to receive further training compared with workers with no formal qualification (OECD, 1994). This suggests that the labour market disadvantage of the less educated could persist throughout their careers and the current evidence is that inequalities within the youth cohort have been rising (see Freeman, p. 89 in this volume; Haveman and Knight, 1998).

Finally, Japan relies almost exclusively on formal training provided by the firms. However, there is close co-ordination in the recruitment process between schools and employers. Japanese schools rank graduating students by their academic performance, and associated employers usually hire according to the school's rankings. This screening process increases the incentive for high-school students to perform well in school and gives employers confidence in their potential workers, thus encouraging them to engage in extensive on-the-job training. It has its flaws, though, in that it places an overwhelming emphasis on grades, school performance and recommendations by teachers, thus providing few re-entry opportunities to school drop outs (Lerman, 1996).

Policies aimed at strengthening pathways through initial education and into work

As was noted in the previous sections, completion of upper secondary education has become the norm in almost all OECD countries, having risen over time to at least 75% of school leavers. Those who fail to complete this level find themselves particularly penalised in the labour market, in terms of both employment and earnings. Preventing failure at school is, therefore, one key strategy to ensure a successful transition to work and adult life. However, completing upper secondary education is not a sufficient condition for a stable entry into the labour market. In a number of countries, young people who have completed upper secondary education can be subject to considerable unemployment. Policy in the domain of education, therefore, needs to focus on how to ensure that young people are employable, both at the moment they first enter the labour market and over time.

Integrating vocational and general or academic education

A policy response to meet these challenges has been to attempt to make schooling diverse, flexible and attractive enough to meet the interests and aspirations of the widest possible range of young people in the post-compulsory age group. The development and re-appraisal of the vocational stream within the education system is an important element in such a strategy. At the same time, policy makers are seeking ways to broaden and reinforce advanced general studies even within the vocational stream, thus enhancing integration between vocational and general or "academic" education.

Since the early 1980s, Finland has engaged in an intense and continuous process of educational reforms, both at upper secondary and tertiary levels, designed to meet these objectives. Comprehensive reforms of the education system that go in this same direction have recently taken place in Ireland, Norway, Sweden and Spain (Table 22). Even in the absence of comprehensive reforms, Australia, Canada and the United States have started to develop or revive the provision of vocational courses at the upper secondary level. In the United States, a number of initiatives have been taken over the past decade with the goal to stimulate state and local governments to create a new national system linking school-based and work-based training and ultimately upgrade the careers of young people not pursuing a four-year college degree. In Japan, the authorities have initiated a number of reforms to further develop vocational education in secondary schools, and to generally strengthen the links between the education system and the labour market.

One obstacle to the promotion of secondary-level vocational education has been, in many countries, its low and declining attractiveness, due to the greater value attached to general education by pupils, parents and the society as a whole. Measures to lift the attractiveness of vocational education include the development of double-qualifying pathways, providing qualifications for both work and tertiary education; enhanced permeability between different programmes, that allow young people to keep their options open for as long as possible; and, the promotion of more integrated learning opportunities. Austria and Norway have developed double-qualifying pathways,[26] and, in both countries, overall participation rates in technical and vocational education have been rising (see Box 7). Permeability between different programmes has been promoted by broadening the entry points to vocational education and training and providing opportunities to cross from one pathway to another with minimal loss of time, with an associated broadening of curricula so as to cover a wider range of related occupational tasks (OECD, 1998e). This approach is most typically found in the Nordic countries and in apprenticeship countries, especially in Germany.

Canada, Japan and the United States have developed integrated pathways providing academic courses of study that satisfy entrance requirements for four-year colleges and prepare students for employment through new forms of work-based learning linked to the school curriculum. In the United States, these innovations have been initiated locally, although they have also received support from federal and state legislation, and from non-governmental agencies financed by private foundations. One major example are career academies, which are self-contained groupings of students and teachers within a larger high school, combining academic and vocational curriculum and involving partnerships with employers who provide internships and other services for students. Career academies normally focus on health occupations, business and finance, manufacturing, engineering or computers. Box 7 summarises the results of evaluation studies of such integrated pathways.

The opening up of new pathways is also evident in tertiary education. Shorter and more work-oriented tertiary studies have resulted from the development of the Fachhochschulen (specialist colleges) in German-speaking countries, the higher professional schools in the Czech Republic, the polytechnic institutions in Portugal and Finland, the short-degree courses in Italy, and similar short-cycle tertiary institutions in some other countries. Other institutions that have the potential to produce similar results include the Community colleges in North America that offer school leavers the opportunity to obtain occupational qualifications and/or to prepare them for entry into higher education.

Providing experience in work settings while in education

The belief that young people learn more effectively and are more motivated to learn when learning takes place in context and according to inductive approaches has been one driving force for the introduction of work-based learning within schools (OECD, 1998e). Stern (see p. 155 in this volume) identifies the following potential benefits of work-based learning: the acquisition of knowledge or skills related to employment in particular occupations or industries; the opportunity for career exploration and planning; the possibility to learn more about an industry; and, increased personal and social competence related to work in general.

Linking part-time employment with classroom studies may also enhance students' motivation and educational achievement, while still allowing them to gain valuable work experience. As was noted in Section I, although school-work combinations may have a positive impact on the success of young people in integrating into employment and constructing good careers, there can be a negative link between school attainment and part-time work among students if the number of hours worked is too high. School supervision of students' work appears to mitigate somewhat these negative effects. Therefore, formal structures combining work and schooling have been erected in many countries. These range from full-fledged apprenticeships to short ad-hoc stays in enterprises while attending education.

The workplace component within secondary vocational education has been reinforced in some countries, notably in Sweden, Norway (see Table 22) and the Netherlands. In Australia, school-industry programmes have been introduced to provide students in the senior year of secondary school the opportunity for structured learning in a workplace which is assessed and accredited as part of their schoolwork. In 1996, some 60% of schools provided one of these programmes, but only 12% of senior secondary students participated in them. OECD (1998e) reviewed two studies of the effects of one school-industry programme – the Training in Retail and Commerce (TRAC) project. The results of these studies identified enhanced student outcomes in terms of such things as: motivation and confidence; satisfaction; personal and practical skills; and time-management skills. Furthermore, TRAC graduates appeared to have an unemployment rate approximately half that of non-university-bound school leavers as a whole, and to be 50% more likely to be involved in further education and training through apprenticeships, traineeships or other forms of study.

In Canada and the United States, there is a growing interest in a range of work-study and co-operative education programmes. However, participation in them remains low. In Canada, for example, less than 10% of secondary education students opt for them (Marquardt, 1998). The main obstacles seem to be the reluctance of employers to offer decent workplace opportunities, the low esteem that students and parents have for them, and the reluctance of schools or educational authorities to allocate adequate resources to them and to modify timetables to make workplace attendance a normal part of the educational experience. These obstacles partly relate to the fact that there is usually little connection with what students are doing in their classes and the programmes fail to give formal credit in school and/or vocational qualifications.

Ensuring the relevance of vocational training and education to labour market needs

Against the background of technological innovation, economic restructuring and keener competition, the responsiveness of initial education and training towards changing qualification requirements in the labour market has been a major concern in many countries.

In countries with strong traditions of vocational education and training, there is real concern about how to adjust the content of education. In response to these concerns, there has been an increased emphasis upon the (re-)design of new skill profiles and curricula, and a search for ways to update curricula and qualifications in faster and more flexible ways. In Switzerland, for example, the authorities hope that the responsiveness of vocational training to economic change will be encouraged through the creation of enterprise networks. In such networks, apprentices acquire a broad range of qualifications by moving through several enterprises according to a carefully planned and co-ordinated training programme.

In countries with a less developed vocational education sector, an approach in the hope of creating better linkages between education and employment has been to develop unified qualification frameworks with which to judge attainments, in an attempt to provide the informational and incentive structures needed to spur pupil achievement, encouraging higher educational aspirations and further learning. A system of national standards also helps employers in informing training providers and prospective employees of their skill needs and in evaluating the skill levels of applicants.

In the United Kingdom, vocational education and training after compulsory schooling is organised within a framework of nationally-recognised qualifications: the General National Vocational Qualifications (GNVQs) and the National Vocational Qualifications (NVQs), plus a number of other vocational qualifications. The GNVQ covers a wide range of courses providing full-time vocational education, entirely school-based; the NVQ covers part-time, mainly employment-based, vocational training. While the general architecture of the qualifications and their different levels allow for a high degree of suppleness, critics argue that NVQs have merely superimposed another layer of qualifications without much effect on the quantity and quality of training. A risk associated with this framework and the modularization of post-compulsory education and training is the temptation for young people to abandon an education or training programme before obtaining a qualification.

Whatever the type of links between work skills and the content of education, the involvement of employers and employer organisations in the design of occupational qualifications is very important in tailoring curricula and programmes to labour market needs. This is done either through advisory committees that assist educational authorities, as in the United States and Canada, or through tripartite decision-making bodies with strong employer as well as trade union engagement.

Finally, a common feature across countries is the gradual devolution of certain planning and monitoring tasks from national to sectoral, regional and local levels in order to render education and training provision more immediately responsive to identifiable needs for skilled labour market entrants.

Box 7. **The outcomes of policy developments strengthening pathways through initial education and into work**

The goals of these policies are both *quantitative, i.e.* to increase enrolment rates of students at secondary and tertiary levels and reduce the number of drop outs, and *qualitative, i.e.* to provide young people with the basic skills and competencies relevant to the world of work. As many of these reforms are quite recent, little data are available on the former aspect, but the available evidence for Austria and Norway shows that countries that ensured broad pathways with multiple exit points and that increased opportunities for young people to cross from one pathway to another actually managed to raise the attractiveness of vocational pathways and increase participation rates.

However, as already noted, there remain obstacles to the promotion of these new pathways. In the United States, scepticism on the part of both parents and teachers that the integrated pathways can offer valuable college-preparatory options remains a major barrier to implementing them (see Stern, p. 155 in this volume). In Finland, the "Upper Secondary Experiment" is a pilot project for a reform of upper secondary education, in which the possibilities of individualised pathways based on modularization, networking between schools and the related development of student information and counselling are being explored. However, the outcomes to date from this pilot project have been disappointing, *e.g.* so far the majority of students involved have not taken advantage of the possibility of choosing individualised pathways.

Stern brings together the results of evaluation studies of integrated pathways in the United States. Most of these evaluation studies concern career academies, as they have been in existence for a number of years, and also because, by their design, they allow carrying out experimental evaluations: since they usually serve only a fraction of the students within a high school, other students in the same school can comprise a comparison group for evaluation purposes. Career academy students have been found to be more likely to graduate from high school compared with non-academy students. Furthermore, graduates from career academies have been found in some studies to be more likely to enrol in tertiary education, including four-year colleges and universities. Importantly, however, little is known about what, if any, is the labour market impact of these reforms. Evaluations have not found much difference in the labour market performance of career academy and non-career academy graduates in the first few years after high school, except that some studies have found academy students working more hours per week.

Developing apprenticeship and alternating-training contracts

The success of the German dual system has led many countries to develop apprenticeship systems imitating some of its features, although, as noted above, a whole range of social, economic and political conditions need to be fulfilled for apprenticeship systems to function successfully. Furthermore, apprenticeship-based systems are viewed in some countries as a less preferable option compared with more academic pathways that allow the acquisition of the general competencies and communication skills that are believed to be crucial in a changing working environment. Box 8 below brings together some results of evaluations of apprenticeship in terms of employment and earnings outcomes.

Box 8. The results of evaluations of apprenticeship

The few evaluations of apprenticeships in terms of employment and earnings outcomes have been generally favourable. Ryan (1998) reviews statistical evidence on the economic effects of apprenticeship in advanced economies, both compared with full-time vocational schooling, mostly at upper secondary level, and to youth labour market activity, including employment, unemployment, job training and labour market programmes. The evidence suggests that apprenticeship often generates gains in subsequent employment for participants, particularly relative to job training and labour market programmes, but also relative to full-time vocational education. Benefits in terms of pay are also reasonably well established for males, although in relation more to youth labour market activity than to full-time vocational education. Females appear to do badly, in terms of both access and benefits, in the United Kingdom and the United States. Sollogoub and Ulrich (1997) analysed French evidence on the employment outcomes of apprenticeships compared with the outcomes of vocational education that is solely offered in school. They find that apprenticeship improves the likelihood of employment during the first years on the labour market, but vocational school raises later earnings more than apprenticeship does.

Table 21 sums up the key features of apprenticeship systems in those countries where they account for a relatively important share of youth employment or where concrete measures are being taken to develop them. Norway, France and Ireland provide examples of reforms that have resulted in a genuine increase of apprenticeship opportunities for young people. In Norway, beginning in 1994, apprenticeship has been integrated in a new pathway through upper secondary education. The content of general and vocational education has been broadened and new places have been created in white-collar and service occupations. The reduction in apprentice wages, the creation of co-operative mechanisms to assist smaller firms to train, and the involvement of the social partners in the design of the reform and in its promotion are key elements. In France, legal measures introduced in 1987 aimed not only at encouraging apprenticeship, but also extending it to diplomas beyond the traditional certificate of vocational competence (CAP). Although starting from a very low base, the number of new apprentices has increased by over 50% in four years, to reach 13% of employees of less than 26 years of age in 1997. The proportion of those preparing for a diploma beyond the CAP has shown a steady increase, and now concerns one apprentice in four (Pérot and Simon-Zarca, 1998). In Ireland, the apprenticeship system has recently been designed to provide broad-based training during the initial stages with opportunities to develop specialist skills later, and is based on the achievement of standards rather than on time spent in the programme. Its modular approach is intended to allow for flexibility and cross-skilling and to provide for on-going up-dating of skills. Although the coverage of apprenticeship remains very limited in Ireland, at 5% of employees aged 15-24 years in 1996, the new system seems to be attracting an increasing number of pupils.

In the United Kingdom, the new Modern Apprenticeship scheme (MA) introduced in 1993 has not yet halted the fall in apprentice numbers that started as far back as the early 1960s, but the scheme's design is potentially promising. MA is less restricted by trade demarcations, it covers a broader spread of occupations, and takes a more dynamic view of movement into apprenticeship and progression out to continuing training and further education than did the old system (Gospel, 1998). It aims for a higher standard of attainment than had typically been achieved through the government-sponsored training scheme – Youth Training[27] – which was introduced in 1983 to cater to the rising number of unemployed young people. However, it remains to be seen whether enough firms and young people will be attracted to the programme so as to make a real difference to the number of apprentices.

In Australia, an interesting feature of the apprenticeship system is the existence of "group-training schemes". Under these schemes, the apprentice is recruited by a Group Training Company that receives fees based on wage costs from the participating employers and various forms of financial support from State and Federal governments. These schemes appear to have played a major role in employing apprentices who were discarded by their original employer and in encouraging structured training in areas such as tourism and retailing. However, after growing strongly towards the end of the 1980s, the annual number of new apprenticeship starts has fallen sharply during the 1990s. In an attempt to strengthen and increase the flexibility of the system, a "New Apprenticeships" scheme has been proposed and partly implemented by the new government. The new scheme is supposed to deliver: new places in emerging industries and more multiple workplace apprenticeships through Group Training Companies; more flexible mixes of training and work; integration with the Jobs Pathway Guarantee Program; a user choice of the off-the-job training programme and provider; and, nationally-portable qualifications. It is too early to judge whether this reform will achieve its aims.

B. Education and training for at-risk and unemployed youths

In spite of the efforts made in countries to improve the employability of youth through the education system, a minority still leave school with very limited skills. Exclusion from education, training and employment is often systemic: early school leavers and other at-risk young people are often drawn disproportionately from particular ethnic, social and regional groups. Whatever the causes of their disadvantage, these young people are among the major preoccupations of policy makers as they are particularly vulnerable to repeated spells of unemployment, to long-term unemployment and to intermittent and low-paid work.

Preventing failure at school of at-risk youth

A key policy priority is to discourage young people from dropping out of school or to encourage early school-leavers to return to regular education and training. Some countries have established targeted measures for young people deemed "at risk" of failing at school. In Germany, support measures help disadvantaged young people, in particular migrant children, during compulsory education and during training in the dual system. Such measures include language lessons, compensation of educational deficits, labour market counselling and general help to overcome learning difficulties.

These policies, together with the rapidly rising educational aspirations of migrant families, appear to have led to significant improvements for young second-generation migrants in terms of educational qualifications and participation in the dual system.[28] In the United States, some drop-out prevention programmes, combining academic assistance (tutoring, help with homework, etc.) with adult mentoring, vocational counselling and small payments for school attendance, have proved successful and highly cost-effective. Others, however, have not, indicating that such programmes are difficult to implement (Stanley et al., 1998).

Evaluations of specific programmes to bring out-of-school youths without academic or vocational qualifications back into the system have yielded mixed results. In the United States, such programmes have not proved very successful (op. cit.). The Nordic countries show more promising results. Under the "youth guarantee" concept, every young person up to 20 years of age is entitled to an education at upper-secondary level. For example, in Sweden, any person in this age group not having completed upper-secondary school has the right to be admitted to a programme and to follow an adult education course organised by the municipality. In Norway, a "follow-up service", set up as part of the 1994 education reforms, is designed to reintegrate early leavers back into school and enable them to gain an upper secondary qualification. The service works in close contact with school counsellors and the school psychological service, with the public employment service, and with health, welfare and other community services. Initial monitoring of the follow-up service has yielded positive results, with school drop-out rates falling and very high proportions of those contacted by the service engaged in education and employment.[29] The combination of a trainee place within a firm, which offers subsidised employment and on-the-job training, with some school attendance, has been found to be the most successful approach in re-motivating and re-inserting drop outs. The Nordic countries' experience suggests that satisfactory results can be achieved with a combination of preventive and curative measures which are flexible, tailored to the individual needs and conditions of young people at risk, and integrated across the education, employment and community and social services sectors (OECD, 1998e).

Integrated packages for out-of-school youth

Multi-faceted programmes that combine services ranging from remedial education and training to work experience, job-search assistance, support for returning to formal education and various forms of wage subsidies are becoming the preferred approach for disadvantaged youths in some countries (Table 23). A formal engagement in this direction has been taken by the European Council with the adoption of a guideline for employment policy stating that "governments must offer every young unemployed person either training, retraining, work experience or another employability measure before they have been unemployed for six months".[30] Denmark, Finland, France, the Netherlands and the United Kingdom have already taken legislative steps to implement this guideline.

Since 1996, in Denmark, a special package targets young people under the age of 25 years in receipt of unemployment benefit who have not completed a formal vocational education or training programme. After six months of unemployment, they have the right and the duty to take part in normal education or special courses for at least 18 months, being paid allowances considerably below the level of the unemployment benefit. Survey analysis results indicate positive short-term effects of this initiative on the youth unemployment rate (see Table 23). In fact, one result was that most of the young job seekers had left unemployment before the time they would actually have to start the programme. This was interpreted as a "motivation effect" of the programme, in the sense that the prospect of having to follow mandatory education and the corresponding reduction of the economic benefit meant a strong incentive to leave unemployment and start education or get an ordinary job. It must be stressed, however, that, in the absence of rigorous evaluations, any analysis of the impact of the programme, and of the factors influencing that impact, are only speculative. The Danish labour market has improved considerably since 1994 and that has clearly helped make it easier for youths to shift into ordinary employment (European Commission, 1998).

The Youth Work Guarantee plan (YWG)[31] in the Netherlands and the United Kingdom's New Deal apply the same principles as the Danish package, whereby young people receive benefits only if they attend a training scheme or sign up for a work-experience programme. In exchange the government will try to guarantee a sufficient supply of training and work-experience places. Under the New Deal, all young people aged 18-24 years, who have been claiming Jobseeker's Allowance for 6 months, must first enter an initial Gateway programme which lasts for up to 4 months and consists of intensive counselling and guidance. Then they are offered a choice between 4 options: subsidised work with an employer in the regular labour market; six months' job creation programmes in the environment or voluntary sectors; full-time education and training for up to 12 months without loss of benefit; and entry to self-employment for at least 6 months. Those who refuse to participate in any of these options may have benefit sanctions applied to them. Early indications of the impact of this programme point to increased outflow rates from 6-10 months unemployment for the target group, with positive immediate job prospects for some young people. However, the outflows into the non-job options listed above are higher than those into jobs. These results, based on administrative monitoring data, only offer a partial picture. The programme is being carefully monitored and evaluated and more reliable results are expected soon.

Also outside Europe, programmes offering a different combination of sticks and carrots are becoming more common. In Australia, the Mutual Obligation arrangements offer unemployed youth similar options as the New Deal package in the United Kingdom, but of a shorter duration. In Canada, a range of multi-faceted programmes is offered by the various provinces. One example is Newfoundland's Linkages that targets social assistance recipients aged 18 to 24 years who have not completed post-secondary education. These people are offered the opportunity to engage in 26 weeks of career-related employment, participate in regular group career planning workshops and earn an allowance towards the cost of post-secondary education. No evaluations are available yet.

Short-term job-training programmes aimed at very disadvantaged youths have been operating in the United States over the past two or three decades. A number of careful evaluations, including random-assignment experiments, indicate that such targeted youth training programmes have achieved little to raise the long-term job success of disadvantaged youth participants. Lerman (1997) highlights the importance of poor attitudes towards work among disadvantaged youths as a factor in explaining the dismal record of such special youth measures. Grubb (see p. 363 in this volume) also points to the poor quality of teaching provided and to the fact that the duration of these programmes is too short to be able to overcome the major disadvantages of the groups targeted. He explores the nature of some "exemplary programmes" to see what lessons they hold for education and training policies for disadvantaged youths (see Box 9).

Box 9. **Factors that make for successful education and training programmes for disadvantaged youths**

Grubb (p. 363 in this volume) identifies five "precepts" for effective education and training:

1. Effective programmes for disadvantaged youths contain an appropriate mix of general (or remedial, or basic) education, occupational skills training, and work-based learning, in the best cases integrated with one another.

2. They provide a variety of support services, like counselling and placement services.

3. They maintain strong links to the local labour market and garner employer support for the programmes.

4. They provide their clients with pathways of further education opportunities, so that they can continue education and training if they wish.

5. They collect appropriate information about their results and use these to improve the quality of their programmes.

C. Policies to affect the demand for youth labour

Although education and training policies are central elements of any effective strategy for improving youth labour market prospects, a comprehensive policy framework has to pay attention to labour market arrangements and institutions and their impact on job and earnings prospects. Wage-setting institutions, employment protection legislation and fixed-term contract regulations are often deemed to affect the entry of youths into the labour market. This section reviews policies aimed at altering such institutions with a view to stimulating the demand for young workers. It will also examine policies aimed at creating new job opportunities for youths in the public or non-profit sector.

Reducing payroll costs

Reductions in payroll costs are intended to increase youth employment and work-based training. Youth payroll costs can be reduced in two ways: via the direct alteration of wage structures, *e.g.* through lower minimum wages; and via reductions in non-wage costs, whether through lower payroll taxes or wage subsidies to firms. Both approaches aim to induce employers to increase their demand for youth labour.

Section II.B above reviewed the countries where lower minimum wage rates for young workers are in place. Many countries have also allowed de facto sub-minimum wages for youths as a result of special employment programmes that allow employers to pay young workers wages at a lower rate than the minimum wage or the contractual minima. Typical examples are the apprenticeship contracts discussed above, the qualification and adaptation contracts in France, work-training contracts in Belgium and the New Workers' Scheme in the United Kingdom. Rather than abolish the statutory minimum wage or widen the gap between it and the rate applicable to young people, many countries, like France, Italy, Portugal and Spain, have preferred to cut employers' social security contributions significantly for young workers or pay wage subsidies tied to the hiring of young people. In many cases, the financial incentive is accompanied by relaxed employment protection regulations, as normally the jobs are temporary. Table 24 provides some examples of these types of contracts (excluding those that alternate training within the enterprise and in an education institution, described in Table 21).

So-called "atypical contracts" employ large numbers of young people in some countries. In France, in 1997, around 20% of young employees under 26 years of age were employed with one or another "atypical contract" in the private sector, accompanied or not by training. In Italy, approximately 38% of employees aged between 14 and 24 years old are employed either with a training-employment or apprenticeship contract. A further 7% in the age group 25-32 are employed with an employment-training contract.

Besides the obvious objective of raising employment rates among the targeted population, these programmes are also inspired by the hope that work experience alone will make disadvantaged young people more employable in the future.

It is not clear whether subsidies to employment create many net new jobs. Instead of increasing total employment, firms may simply substitute subsidised workers for unsubsidised ones (the "substitution effect"), or hire subsidised workers whom they would have hired even in the absence of the subsidy (the "dead-weight effect"). The available evidence shows that subsidies to employment can indeed suffer from large deadweight loss and substitution effects, and hence have small net employment gains. Substitution effects, however, may be justified on equity grounds, if they help provide the most disadvantaged groups with jobs.

Much of the impact of employment subsidies depends on their design and on the labour market context in which they operate. Firm take-up is partly a function of how much information is made available to employers about the subsidy and how easy it is to claim. There is also the question of how large the subsidies have to be to get firms to take-up such measures. High subsidies will be needed if demand elasticities for the targeted groups are low, which the empirical evidence suggests is indeed the case. Another relevant issue concerns the extent of targeting. On the one hand, the larger the group participating in the programme, the higher the cost and the lower the cost-effectiveness for disadvantaged workers. On the other hand, strict targeting can lead participants to experience the stigma of coming from a programme only for the weakest individuals, and may, therefore, be unable to overcome employers' reluctance to hire them. The most appropriate approach depends, among others, on the role played by labour market institutions and conditions. Lerman (see p. 419 in this volume) notes that broadly targeted programmes are most appropriate when unemployment is not concentrated on a hard-core of disadvantaged young people. In situations with high unemployment, targeted wage subsidy programmes may only reallocate, instead of reducing, unemployment.

Little evidence is available on the impact of subsidised employment on the subsequent jobs and earnings prospects of young people, but it appears that programmes that alternate subsidised work within the enterprise and training in a specialised institution are the most effective in aiding a smoother transition to the regular labour market. Therefore, the quality of the jobs provided and the presence of a training element are key features for the success of such demand-side programmes. The formal recognition in the labour market of the experience acquired through them can also help in making that experience transferable to other firms.

Employment protection regulations

Another aspect of labour market arrangements that is sometimes deemed to affect the entrance of youth into the labour market is employment protection legislation (EPL). A number of potential benefits have been evoked to justify EPL: enhanced job and income security for employees; increased incentives for employers to invest in firm-specific human capital and for employees to acquire the formal education or vocational qualifications which employers look for; increased job search prior to being laid off by imposing early notification of dismissal.

However, the potential benefits of strict EPL have to be weighed against potential costs. By imposing a tax on work-force adjustments, EPL is often claimed to lead to a more sclerotic labour market, that is unable to achieve the volume of workforce adjustment required in response to rapid changes in technologies and product market competition. Furthermore, EPL may exacerbate the dualism of the labour market between protected workers on the one hand and job seekers and temporary workers on the other, thus increasing the share of vulnerable groups in the stock of unemployment or the duration of their unemployment spells. In particular, it is claimed, young new entrants to the labour market may be particularly penalised by strict EPL.

The OECD *Employment Outlook* (OECD, 1999) explores these issues. Simple, cross-country comparisons suggest that EPL may affect the demographic composition of unemployment and employment. In countries where EPL is stricter, unemployment for younger workers tends to be higher, while their employment-to-population ratio tends to be lower. However, these findings are only very weakly confirmed in the multivariate regression analysis. Other empirical studies reviewed in Rogowski and Schöman (1996) focus on the effects of the introduction of more flexible rules in the use of fixed-term contracts in France, Germany, Spain[32] and the United Kingdom. The empirical evidence shows that the new rules have resulted in more young employees being recruited into fixed-term employment than before. This finding, however, is not surprising, since youths are over-represented among labour market entrants and new hires.

A key question is whether temporary contracts lead to stable employment or whether they become traps for some people who move from one such job to another interspersed by periods of unemployment. Italy, Portugal and Spain have introduced incentives to transform temporary contracts into permanent ones. These incentives take the form of fiscal benefits, subsidies and reductions in (or exemptions from) social security contributions. In Italy and Spain, for example, an insufficient number of conversions reduces the possibility for the firm of further hirings with youth contracts. Despite similar incentives, the proportion of conversions differs substantially. In Italy, 59% of trainee contracts were transformed into regular ones in 1996 (ISFOL, 1998). In Spain, only 12% of training contracts and 28% of learning contracts were so converted in 1997 (OECD, 1998b).

Conversion rates, however, do not tell us whether individuals who start with a fixed-term contract end up in a stable career path or not. Longitudinal data can help to answer this question. Bearing in mind data comparability problems,[33] evidence from France and Italy suggests that youths who start off on a temporary contract during their first year out of school do better in the longer term than those who start in unemployment. In particular, in Italy, starting off with a fixed-term contract is actually associated with a higher probability of being employed six years later compared with those on a permanent contract. There are two likely reasons for this. First, the Italian fixed-term contracts are designed for a rather select group of skilled youths. Second, the legal requirement on firms to transform at least one-half of these contracts into permanent ones may effectively help (OECD, 1998b), although issues of deadweight and substitution remain. In Spain, the picture is different: the likelihood of being employed 15 months after exit from school differs little by type of contract. Thus, the empirical evidence on traps or stepping-stones remains unclear.

Direct job creation schemes

Direct job creation schemes are often used as a complementary policy tool in the hope of giving youth work experience and contact with the labour market. These schemes are usually characterised by restrictions on the type of employer – traditionally, the public or non-profit sectors; the duration of the subsidy – normally, the jobs are temporary; and the type of job – often, it must be of social benefit. In general, the employment must be additional, *i.e.* it would not have existed without public intervention, and labour costs are shared between the public authority and the sponsor of the project. Although normally targeted at the long-term unemployed of any age with particular disadvantages on the labour market, youths are often included in these schemes. Many European countries, in particular Belgium, France, Italy, the Netherlands and the Scandinavian countries, have used such programmes. Outside Europe, Australia up to 1994, and New Zealand, have experimented with some job creation schemes.

Direct job creation measures have gone through several phases. They were very popular after the first oil shock and into the 1980s. But, as evaluations of such programmes yielded very poor outcomes, most countries moved away from their use in the late 1980s. Recently, they have seen a resurgence. These alternating fortunes reflect changes in the aims of this measure over the period.

In the past, job-creation programmes were often used as a counter-cyclical measure and their aim was primarily to get people into jobs, with little attention being paid to their impact on long-term employability. When participation in these programmes was used mainly as a vehicle to re-establish eligibility to unemployment benefits, they appeared to operate as a revolving door, with many of the same people moving in and out of them.

Recently, some governments have re-designed job-creation schemes with supply-side objectives in mind (Table 25). More attention is being paid to the quality of the jobs, by reinforcing the social benefit element or by requiring that they meet new or unsatisfied needs, and to support services provided to the participant in terms of career guidance and counselling. Ellwood and Welty (1998) note that, although displacement is potentially a very large problem in these programmes, it can be kept to a minimum when the programmes are targeted at workers who are very different from the traditional workforce, and when workers do distinct assignments, as opposed to doing work which is identical to that performed by regular workers. They argue that policy makers are faced with a trade-off when organising job-creation programmes. On the one hand, the more valuable the work is, the greater the apparent long-term benefit to recipients, and perhaps the greater the value of the work of the community. On the other hand, the more valuable the work is, the greater the risk of substitution, the greater the cost, and the greater the administrative complexity in generating the jobs and monitoring them.

Examples of programmes that lie at the extreme ends of this trade-off are the ambitious "New Services, Youth Jobs" programme in France, and workfare projects included in activation packages like the New Deal in the United Kingdom or the Mutual Obligation arrangements in Australia.

"New Services, Youth jobs" has been set up to provide State support for the development of activities designed to meet new or unsatisfied needs. Activities recognised by the local authorities as satisfying the criterion receive support in the form of financial aid for all the jobs they create for young people: the aid is equal to 80% of the minimum wage for the first five years of each job. To this cost must be added a large amount to allow for the start-up and monitoring of the planned activities. Between October 1997 and end-March 1999, 150 000 individuals were recruited through this programme. Nearly all the jobs created are full-time, more than one-half of them pay slightly above the minimum wage, and most of them are occupied by young people with no or little qualifications. This programme is ambitious since one of its prime objectives is the durability of projects in three respects: the activities need to ensure that unsatisfied needs can be met in the long term; the jobs created with State support for an emerging activity need to be given professional status; and the young recruit must be properly trained to ensure he/she stays in employment after the five years, possibly in a job other than the one held during the programme. Clearly, the responsibility of the government in ensuring that this programme succeeds is considerable: if it fails to create valuable and lasting job opportunities by fostering the emergence of a "third sector", there is the danger of locking the targeted youths into dead-end jobs (Gautié, p. 387 in this volume).

D. Mobilising labour supply

Removing barriers to work rooted in the tax and benefit system

This sub-section reviews the role of tax and benefit systems in providing financial incentives for young people to take part in training programmes and to look for work. It does so by comparing the income provided by unemployment and related welfare benefits to that which might accrue from work. If the former income is high compared with the latter, benefit recipients may have less incentive to search for and accept employment. However, the level of expected income when in work is not the only determinant for the labour supply decisions of young people. The stability of the job or its training content are other important factors (see Box 10 on the opinions of young Europeans on their likely attitude if they were confronted with unemployment).

Box 10. **Stylised facts on young Europeans confronted with unemployment in 1997**

What would young people be most likely to do if they were unemployed?

Answers to this question are available from the Spring 1997 Eurobarometer survey on young Europeans. Six of the options given were each selected by over 10% of those interviewed: most would accept any job, but with specific conditions. One youth in five specified stability of the job as their main criterion; one in six would accept any job whatever the conditions; one in seven would only take a job that is well paid; one in eight would try to do an apprenticeship or training course to prepare for a different career. Other options that very few young people would select in the event of unemployment were setting up their own business, take advantage of the situation by travelling and visiting different countries, working in the black-market economy or doing voluntary work.

Although youths tend to earn less than older workers, they also tend to receive lower social protection benefits, if any, especially when they have just left school and have not accumulated any work experience. Figure 10 shows net replacement rates for young people in case of joblessness. The numbers shown assume a twenty-year old unemployed single person with no employment record, living alone with no family responsibilities and whose expected earnings in any new job are at two thirds of the average production worker's level. The highest replacement ratios are found in the Nordic countries, Belgium and Germany. In France and Italy, young unemployed persons without work experience are not even entitled to any form of benefit. It must be noted that these calculations are based on rigid assumptions which are not always representative of reality. More evidence would be needed to verify whether the actual replacement rates differ from the simulated ones, and to check how many individuals are actually affected by them. In fact, many unemployed young people do not qualify for either joblessness-related compensation or other kinds of support. This is especially true for those young people who have no employment record, as most of them would still be living with their parents and their entitlement to social protection benefits would normally be conditional on a means test based on the family's income.

All the above considerations lead to the conclusion that the disincentive to look for work is particularly weak for young people. The concern in the case of young people is more about future benefit dependency. In some countries, eligibility conditions for unemployment insurance benefit have recently become more stringent. Increased efforts have been made in many countries to help the unemployed find a job, though this has been coupled with increased pressure on them to search actively for work and remain in contact with the labour market. On the one hand, public employment offices have tried to improve their placement services and the counselling and guidance given to the registered unemployed, which now often include assessment of skills and identification of suitable training courses to enhance these skills. For example, in New Zealand, the Youth Action initiative aims to help young people into employment by assisting them to search actively for appropriate employment, training or education. Young people are assigned a case manager to help them formulate an action plan and regular follow-up interviews are undertaken to provide ongoing assistance. On the other hand, continued payment of unemployment benefits has been made conditional on participation in active labour market programmes or the acceptance of a suitable job offer. It was noted above that, in countries like Australia, Denmark, Finland and the United Kingdom, policy measures have also been launched to combat youth unemployment by combining a shift to active policies with tighter rules on benefits as far as eligibility conditions and job-seeking requirements are concerned.

This new approach through which social protection is offered in exchange for personal commitment to integration, via participation in training, community service or work programmes can be seen as a positive development. It allows all the unemployed, including the most disadvantaged, to receive an offer that is adapted to their specific needs and inclinations. More importantly, it aims to prevent social exclusion rather than cure it. However, "activating social protection" also has some pitfalls, as discussed by Nicaise (p. 347 in this volume). A preventive approach may turn out to be less effective and much more expensive than a remedial one in serving the groups who most need help. Furthermore, those among the latter group who are not covered by social protection will not benefit from the policy measures. A further danger is that of increased exclusion from social protection for those who refuse the offer or drop out. The containment of such risks and the success of this approach in combating social exclusion will depend on the quality of the services provided and on the offer of customised programmes, positive support and sufficient freedom of choice.

Self-employment support

Another form of policy to help the unemployed find a job is support to start a business. Such programmes are offered only on a limited scale in OECD countries and normally they are not targeted exclusively at youths. Evaluation evidence suggests that they usually only work for a small subset of the population, notably higher educated prime-age workers (OECD, 1996c).

Evidence from the ISSP (International Social Survey Programme) survey of 1989 shows that young people have a higher probability of saying that they would choose to be self-employed compared with adults.[34] There appears to be some scope, therefore, for helping young people move into self-employment. Some countries are developing measures of this type specifically for youths, where the offer of entrepreneurial skills training is coupled with business start-up loans, loan guarantees and grants. In Sweden, Youth Start Projects are pilot projects that address youths aged less than 20 years and aim to help them find a job or create their own business. Most jurisdictions in Canada now offer entrepreneurial skills training as well as business start-up loans, loan guarantees and grants. One example is Nova Scotia's Centre for Entrepreneurship Education and Development, which acts as a catalyst in the areas of entrepreneurship education, research and programme design, professional development, and community entrepreneurship. The programmes, targeted at people under 30 years of age, have resulted in 25 to 30% of participants starting businesses. In 1997, there were 110 new business starts creating 200 new jobs. However, there has not been much systematic study of the effectiveness of this approach.

In Italy, a law introduced in 1986 aims at promoting youth entrepreneurship in the south by offering generous financial help towards the development of business plans elaborated by youths aged 18-29 years. They are also offered training courses on how to run a company. Some follow-up studies of this programme have yielded encouraging results, as they found that more than half the enterprises so formed have survived longer than three years, which is generally viewed as the necessary running-in time to solve start-up problems and move definitively into the productive economy. However, an evaluation study that uses a control group of non-subsidised enterprises found that the survival of the subsidised firms depends on the existence of the subsidies, and not on the ability of the screener to select good potential firms (Battistin *et al.*, 1998).

CONCLUSIONS

The economic state of the average young person in OECD countries falls short of what is desirable. Despite a decline in the relative numbers of youths and the proliferation of programmes aimed at young people in the past two decades, their employment and earnings position has worsened, in some countries substantially. Another worrying trend is that there has been an increase in the proportion of youths living in households where no other person is employed. On the positive side, more youths are enrolled in education for longer periods of time. This will have a potential pay-off in the future if the additional education increases their competencies and if OECD economies can provide sufficient jobs to absorb them. However, part of this extension of schooling is often a response to adverse labour market conditions.

As long as overall unemployment remains high, it is unrealistic to expect significant improvements in youth labour markets. Youth employment and unemployment are highly responsive to the economic cycle, and the effects of labour market slack are especially detrimental for out-of-school youths, particularly young men. Hence, a sound combination of macroeconomic and structural policies is needed to lay the ground for solving youth labour market problems. However, the large cross-country differences in the levels of, and changes in, youth employment and unemployment rates over the past two decades suggest that other factors are at work, and that more specific policies will be needed. These span over the domains of education, labour market and social policy.

Developing young people's employability is a key policy issue for ensuring their successful transition to the labour market and access to career-oriented employment. Policy in the domain of education can attempt to achieve this by augmenting the quality of initial education/training and by making school diverse, flexible and attractive enough to meet the interests and aspirations of the widest possible range of young people. A common thread in recent initiatives has been to develop more flexible and transparent pathways between education/learning and employment. Many of these initiatives are too recent to evaluate so it will be essential to carefully monitor them and gather the necessary information for proper evaluation. Enough evidence is available, though, on apprenticeship/dual-type systems in German-speaking countries and Denmark, which have been remarkably successful in giving non-university-bound young people a good start in the labour market. In spite of the challenges they currently face, dual systems provide an attractive model to other countries. However, establishing large-scale apprenticeship systems in countries lacking any such tradition of strong government/employer/union linkages is very difficult. These countries need to consider possibilities for developing solid programmes within their existing institutions and with the co-operation of all the main actors.

Of particular concern to policy makers is the relatively small group of young people who leave school with very limited skills and who find themselves particularly penalised in the labour market. This so-called "hard-core" group of young people is a key problem, some might even argue the problem, in youth labour markets. In the past, much optimism was expressed that short and well targeted active labour market programmes could do much to help these young people. But the impact of such programmes on disadvantaged youths has, to date, been disappointing. There is little evidence to show *why* these policies have not worked, but wisdom suggests that they were over-ambitious given the means they used to attempt to overcome the serious disadvantages of the targeted groups.

One key issue in dealing with the problems of at-risk youths is how best to identify them as early as possible, ideally both before and while they are still in the education system. A second key issue is when and how to effectively assist them. An effective strategy should help prevent at-risk youth from embarking on a vicious circle of cumulative disadvantages and hence from being subject to prolonged periods of joblessness. Reducing early exits from education must remain prime objectives. Outside the education system, the provision of a combination of specially tailored services ranging from remedial education and training to work experience, counselling, and social support seems a promising approach. Important dimensions to consider in the design and implementation of such specific programmes are the establishment of close contacts with the local labour market and co-operation between all levels of governments and between the education, social and labour market authorities. It is also important that these programmes collect information about their results and use them to improve their quality.

But greater success in these objectives, on their own, will not be sufficient. Tackling high and persistent unemployment and other aspects of inequalities are essential parts of any "youth-oriented" policy package. Broad and comprehensive reforms to reduce the large, and in some cases widening, educational and labour market inequalities youths face are urgently needed. Thus, to resolve the youth problem will require much more than a proliferation of youth-oriented programmes.

NOTES

1. OECD (1995) reported estimates of those at risk of failing in school of between 15 and 30%. OECD (1998c) shows drop-out rates from legal compulsory schooling to vary between a few per cent to just under 50%. One-half of the countries for which data are available report drop-out rates of over 10%.

2. In Finland, it is particularly easy to find a flat to rent and students are entitled to a 70% subsidy on normal rent (EUROSTAT, 1997).

3. In Canada and the United States the rise in the fraction of youths remaining with their parents has, in fact, forestalled a deterioration in their relative income (Card and Lemieux, 1997). The family has played an important role in dampening the effect of the decline of the economic status of youth. But even when they live away from home, young people are often not financially independent, e.g. when the dwelling is paid for by their parents.

4. In OECD (1998b), a very simple illustrative approach was adopted in order to compare labour market outcomes for those youths who did and did not work in paid employment during their last year in school. Employment rates in both the first and the fifth year after leaving school were computed – without differentiating by level of educational attainment – from longitudinal data sets in Germany and the United States. The proportion of the samples working during their last year in school was almost 80% in Germany and 53% in the United States. Although in both countries employment rates one year after leaving school were substantially higher for those youths who worked in their last year of school than for those who did not work, the most interesting results related to the employment rates five years later. In the case of the United States, there is considerable persistence in the gap between individuals who worked in their last year of school and those who did not work, whereas it was almost eliminated in Germany. This difference may suggest that Germany has a more structured set of institutions for integrating young people into the labour market than has the United States.

5. OECD (1998f) shows that it is difficult to obtain reliable data on pupils who leave education before finishing their studies. Three alternative measures of drop outs were presented: the proportion of young people who were not participating at the compulsory leaving age; the proportion not participating at the age of 17, when upper secondary education is normally underway; and the proportion not participating at the "expected" year of upper secondary completion.

6. Researchers have used the term "status zero" to describe young people aged 16 and 17 who are not in education, training or employment. The term highlights the relative obscurity of this group in official statistics. A study in an area of high unemployment in Wales suggests that between 16 and 23% of 16 and 17-year olds were at one time or another not in education, training or employment (Rees et al., 1996). They mainly consist of young people with low educational attainment who have rejected education, who survive on family hand-outs and are frequently involved with the informal economy.

7. Employers express concerns about inadequate education, work readiness or "personal" qualities of 16-year-old job seekers and find it hard to recruit 16-year olds of the required calibre (Hasluck et al., 1997).

8. As an illustration, the paths that young people in the United States take in pursuit of their education are less often like "pipelines" and more like "swirls". Students, by choice or necessity, "swirl" in and out of a variety of educational institutions at different times in their lives (OECD, 1998e).

9. A wide-ranging thematic review of the transition, involving in-depth country-specific studies, is currently being undertaken at the OECD. An interim report provides an initial account of the principal conclusions to emerge from the six countries reviewed in 1997 (OECD, 1998e). The six countries (Australia, Austria, Canada – the provinces of Nova Scotia and Quebec –, the Czech Republic, Norway and Portugal) were selected because they represent a diverse range of social and economic contexts as well as of policy approaches. Eight other OECD countries are in the process of being reviewed in a second round (Denmark, Finland, Hungary, Japan, Switzerland, Sweden, the United Kingdom, and the United States), and a report will be produced in autumn 1999.

10. The Spearman rank correlation coefficient between the two indicators is 0.35 for the 15-19 age group, 0.91 for the 20-24 age group and 0.82 for the 15-24 age group.

11. Incidence in Figure 6 is defined relative to the youth population not to the youth labour force or the total number of youth unemployed – the two more conventional definitions of incidence of long-term unemployment.

12. Difficulties in interpreting earnings data need to be noted in international comparison in general, and for youths in particular. First, the earnings measures and the time period covered are not uniform. For example, the data sometimes refer to annual, sometimes to weekly, and sometimes to monthly earnings. Second, earnings data refer to full-time workers. Ideally, one would prefer data on hourly wage rates, but these data are only available for a few countries.

13. Two caveats need to be given (see OECD, 1996a for more details). First, the measure of low-paid employment is a relative one. It implies that the absolute cut-off point for determining low pay differs across countries. Second, the measure of low-paid employment refers only to full-time workers who earn less than two-thirds of median earnings for all full-time workers.

14. A limitation of this analysis is that it was restricted to continuously employed full-time wage and salary earners. This limitation is particularly problematic for young workers, traditionally over-represented in part-time jobs and in intermittent work.

15. In France for example, the teenage employment-population ratio declined by over 18 percentage points between 1975 and 1996, but OECD (1998b) suggests that the rise in the minimum wage relative to average wages accounted for less than half a percentage point in the decline. An even more dramatic decline in teenage employment occurred in Spain, despite a fall in the relative value of minimum wages to average wages.

16. A minimum wage was introduced in the United Kingdom from April 1999. Youths aged 16 and 17 and all those on formal apprenticeships are exempt. A lower rate is applied to 18-21-year olds and to workers starting a new job with an employer and receiving accredited training. Similarly, in Ireland, a minimum wage is planned to be introduced from April 2000. Workers under the age of 18 will be paid at a lower rate as well as new entrants without experience.

17. The considerable diversity in the way in which minimum wages are set and operated in OECD countries suggests that the detrimental effect of minimum wages on youth employment can easily be exaggerated. Reduced minimum wages exist also for young people undergoing apprenticeship training in many countries and special employment programmes may also allow employers to pay younger workers less than the statutory minimum. Several countries have also used reductions in employer social security contributions to lower the cost of hiring young people while maintaining the real take-home value of the minimum wage.

18. See Tables 3.6 and 3.7 in OECD (1998b).

19. The different data sets preclude any uniformity in the timing of permanent entry. For example, the Australian data refer to labour market entry between 1989-1990, while the timing for American youth ranges between 1981-1988. No formal attempt has been made to determine whether or not the year of entering the labour market had any lasting impact on these young people. Finally, this sub-section measures the evolution of certain labour market outcomes from the date of permanent entry to the labour market. This puts individuals in a similar time frame with a similar exposure to the labour market. Another possibility would consider people at a given age and measure cumulative experience obtained at each age (Pergamit, 1995).

20. Blau and Kahn (1997) find similar American-German differences over the 1980s and 1990s using synthetic cohorts aged 18-29 and 25-36 years old.

21. OECD (1998b) also shows calculations for full- and part-time employment. In general, though the differences are often small, part-time working tends to mean less stable employment histories compared with working in a full-time job.

22. Three points need to be made. First, there can be a problem with retrospective questions in that some people may not accurately recall what their main activity was for each month (Germany and France) or each week (United States) between the annual surveys. Second, all the data are subject to right and left censoring. Finally, the calculations do not take account of the destinations of where the unemployed go to when they do leave unemployment i.e. it is not known whether they found a job or dropped out of the labour force. This limitation has implications for assessing welfare issues, especially if one assumes that getting any kind of job is better than remaining jobless. Some prior OECD work for the 1988 Employment Outlook suggested that unemployed Americans were somewhat more likely to find jobs compared with other countries, but were also considerably more likely to leave the labour force.

23. For the details of such a comprehensive strategy and an assessment of how countries' experiences in recent years have matched up to it (see OECD, 1997c, forthcoming).

24. There are different degrees to which the counterfactual component can be implemented. In highly experimental methods, eligible applicants are randomly assigned either to a treatment group or to a control group. The outcomes of the programme for the treatment group are judged against those for the control group. In quasi-experimental methods, the control group of non-participants is selected ex-post, with characteristics as similar as possible to those of the treatment group. In weakly experimental evaluations, outcomes for participants may be compared with those of participants in other programmes or with those of persons in nearby non-participant age groups, to prior experiences of the participants themselves or to comparable groups in other countries (Ryan and Büchtemann, 1996).

25. Five-year technical colleges qualify young people both for technician-level occupations and for entry to higher education. Students in their last two years are obliged to complete training periods in enterprises during holidays. Participation in these schools has been growing for many years and is currently close to 25% of the youth cohort, with their graduates continuing to have very good employment prospects.

26. In Austria, the five-year technical colleges qualify young people both for technician-level occupations and for higher education, and, as from the academic year 1997/98, those who have completed apprenticeship will be entitled to enter higher education on the basis of a vocational leaving certificate (Berufsreifeprüfung). Similarly, in Norway, the 1994 reform enables students in the vocational pathway to qualify for both work and tertiary study.

27. Modern Apprenticeship aims for a National Vocational Qualification (NVQ) at level 3 or above rather than level 2 typical under Youth Training. This latter programme consisted of two years training provided by employers and financed by government. The young persons are usually not apprentices with an employment status, but trainees with a government allowance. Although Youth Training did spread formal training beyond those who might have taken up apprenticeships, its quality was often poor, and the scheme acquired a bad reputation both among employers and young people (Gospel, 1998).

28. In 1991, 20% of migrant children left the education system without a school certificate compared with 30% in the early 1980s. In 1980, only 14% of 15- to 18-year-old foreigners participated in the dual system compared with 37% in 1991 (OECD, 1994).

29. Records from the follow-up service show that, in the school year 1996-1997, there were 7% of youths with a right to education who had a need for guidance and to be followed up. About 4% accepted an offer of education or work during the course of the school year; 1.5% were still being followed up by the counties; less than 0.5% had rejected help from the follow-up service; and about 0.3% proved impossible to trace (OECD, 1998e).

30. At the European Council meeting in Luxembourg on 20-21 November 1997, the European Council approved a number of guidelines for employment policies, which have become common lines of policy for EU member states. These guidelines rest on four main pillars: entrepreneurship; employability; adaptability; and equal opportunities.

31. From 1 January 1998, the Youth Work Guarantee plan has been replaced by the new "Jobseekers Employment Act" (WIW), which also covers older long-term unemployed persons.

32. In Spain, restrictions on the applicability of fixed-term contracts were largely reduced in 1984. However, during the 1990s the number of reasons for entering into such types of contract were again restricted. In Germany, fixed-term contracts without the obligation to specify an objective reason were introduced with the Employment Promotion Act of 1985. Restrictions on the maximum number and duration of such contracts were further relaxed during the 1990s. In France, there have been several attempts to introduce flexibility in the use of atypical employment since 1972: after a substantial relaxation of restrictions for fixed-term contracts in 1985/86, regulations were tightened again in 1989/90, in particular concerning the maximum duration and maximum number of successive contracts.

33. The Italian and Spanish data refer to all youths leaving education, while the French data refer to low-skilled youth with less than upper secondary education. The time over which individuals are observed also differs. It is a six-year period for France and Italy, but just 15 months for Spain. Finally, the Italian data cover only wage and salary workers.

34. The survey covers nine countries (Austria, West Germany, Hungary, Ireland, Italy, Netherlands, Norway, United Kingdom and the United States). On average, 54% of young people aged less than 30 years responded they would prefer to be self employed, against 47% of people aged 30 years or over. Young Italians had the highest probability (73%) of saying that they would like to set up their own business.

BIBLIOGRAPHY

BATTISTIN, E., GAVOSTO, A. and RETTORE, E. (1998), "Why do Subsidised Firms Live Longer? An Evaluation of a Program Promoting Youth Entrepreneurship in Italy", mimeo.

BÉDUWE, C. and CAHUZAC, E. (1997), "Première expérience professionnelle avant le diplôme. Quelle insertion pour les étudiants de second cycle universitaire", *Formation Emploi,* Centre d'Études et de Recherches sur les Qualifications (CEREQ), Marseilles, No. 58, April-June, pp. 89-108.

BERNHARDT, A., MORRIS, M., HANDCOCK, M. and SCOTT, M. (1998), "Work and Opportunity in the Post-Industrial Labour Market", Institute on Education and the Economy Brief, No. 19, February.

BLAU, F.D. and KAHN, L.M. (1997), "Gender and Youth Employment Outcomes: The US and West Germany, 1984-91", National Bureau of Economic Research, Working Paper No. 6078.

BOCK, K. and TIMMERMANN, D. (1998), "Education and Employment in Germany: Changing Chances and Risks for Youth", *Education Economics,* No. 1, pp. 71-92.

BYNNER, J., FERRI, E. and SHEPHERD, P. (1997), *Twenty Something in the 1990's,* Ashgate, Aldershot.

CARD, D. and LEMIEUX, T. (1997), "Adapting to Circumstances: The Evolution of Work, School, and Living Arrangements Among North American Youth", National Bureau of Economic Research, Working paper No. 6142.

CLARK, K. and SUMMERS, L. (1979), "Labour Market Dynamics and Unemployment: A Reconsideration", Brookings Papers on Economic Activity, No. 1, pp. 13-60.

DARES (Direction de l'Animation de la Recherche, des Études et des Statistiques) (1997), *La politique de l'emploi,* La Découverte, Paris.

DUSTMANN, C., MICKLEWRIGHT, J., RAJAH, N. and SMITH, S. (1996), "Earning and Learning: Educational Policy and the Growth of Part-time Work by Full-time Pupils", *Fiscal Studies,* pp. 79-104, February.

ELLWOOD, D.T. and WELTY, E.D. (1998), "Public Service Employment and Mandatory Work: A Policy Whose Time Has Come and Gone and Come Again?", Preliminary draft for the Conference on Labour Markets and Less-skilled Workers, Washington DC, November.

EUROPEAN COMMISSION (1997a), *Labour Market Study, All EU countries,* DG V, Brussels.

EUROPEAN COMMISSION (1997b), *Employment Observatory,* Mutual Information System on Employment Policies, Brussels.

EUROPEAN COMMISSION (1998), "Draft Joint Employment Report", SEC(1998) 1688 final, Brussels.

EUROSTAT (1997), *Youth in the European Union. From Education to Working Life,* Luxembourg, March.

EUROSTAT (1998), "From School-to-Working Life: Facts on Youth Unemployment", *Statistics in Focus,* Population and Social Conditions, No. 13, Luxembourg.

FRANZ, W., INKMANN, J., POHLMEIER, W. and ZIMMERMANN, V. (1997), "Young and Out in Germany: On the Youths' Chances of Labour Market Entrance in Germany", National Bureau of Economic Research, Working Paper No. 6212.

GALLAND, O. (1997), "L'entrée des jeunes dans la vie adulte", *Problèmes politiques et sociaux,* No. 794, La Documentation Française, Paris, December.

GARDECKI, R. and NEUMARK, D. (1997), "Order from Chaos? The Effects of Early Labour Market Experiences on Adult Labour Market Outcomes", National Bureau of Economic Research, Working Paper No. 5899.

GOSPEL, H. (1998), "The Revival of Apprenticeship in Britain?", *British Journal of Industrial Relations,* No. 3, pp. 435-457.

GREGG, P. and MACHIN, S. (1998), "Child Development and Success or Failure in the Youth Labour Market", Centre for Economic Performance, Working Paper No. 397.

HASLUK, C., HOGARTH, T., MAGUIRE, M. and PITCHER, J. (1997), "Modern Apprenticeship: A Survey of Employers", DfEE Research Studies RS53, The Stationery Office, London.

HAVEMAN, R. and KNIGHT, B. (1998), "The Effect of Labour Market Changes from the Early 1970s to the late 1980s on Youth Wage, Earnings, and Household Economic Position", Discussion Paper No. 1174-98, Institute for Research on Poverty, Madison, WI.

INSEE (1995), "Les trajectoires des jeunes: transitions professionnelles et familiales", *Économie et Statistique,* No. 283-284, Paris.

INSEE (1997), "Les trajectoires des jeunes: distances et dépendances entre générations", *Économie et Statistique,* No. 304-305, Paris.

ISFOL (1998), "Employment in Italy: Profiles, Paths, Policies", Rome.

LERMAN, R.I. (1996), "Building Hope, Skills, and Careers: Making a US Youth Apprenticeship System", *Social Policies for Children,* The Brookings Institute, Washington DC, pp. 136-172.

LERMAN, R.I. (1997), "Employment and Training Programmes for Out-of-School Youth", Urban Institute, Washington DC.

LYNCH, L. (1993), "The Economics of Youth Training in the United States", *Economic Journal,* September, pp. 1292-1302.

MARCHAND, O. and MINNI, C. (1997), "En mars 1997, un jeune sur neuf était au chômage", *Premières Synthèses,* Direction de l'Animation de la Recherche, des Études et des Statistiques (DARES), 97.12, No. 52.1, Paris.

MARQUARDT, R. (1998), "Labour Market Policies and Programs Affecting Youth in Canada", Paper provided to the OECD in the framework of the School-to-Work Transition review.

MCKECHNIE, J., HOBBS, S. and LINDSAY, S. (1998), "Part-time Employment and School: A Comparison of the Work Habits of 3rd, 4th and 6th year Students", Department of Applied Social Studies, University of Paisley.

MORISSETTE, R. (1998), "The Declining Labour Market Status of Young Men", in Corak, M. (ed.), *Labour Markets, Social Institutions, and the Future of Canada's Children,* Statistics Canada and Human Resources Development, Ottawa.

NEUMARK, D. (1998), "Youth Labour Markets in the U.S.: Shopping Around vs. Staying Put", National Bureau of Economic Research, Working paper No. 6581.

OECD (1978), "Youth Unemployment, A Report on the High Level Conference", 15-16 December 1977, Paris.

OECD (1984), *The Nature of Youth Unemployment,* Paris.

OECD (1994), *The OECD Jobs Study: Evidence and Explanations,* Paris.

OECD (1995), *Our Children at Risk,* Paris.

OECD (1996a), *Employment Outlook,* Paris, July.

OECD (1996b), *Education at a Glance - Analysis,* Paris.

OECD (1996c), *Enhancing the Effectiveness of Active Labour Market Policies,* Paris.

OECD (1997a), *Employment Outlook,* Paris, July.

OECD (1997b), *Literacy Skills for the Knowledge Society. Further Results from the International Adult Literacy Survey,* Paris.

OECD (1997c), *Implementing the OECD Jobs Strategy: Member Countries' Experience,* Paris.

OECD (1998a), *Pathways and Participation in Vocational and Technical Education and Training,* Paris.

OECD (1998b), *Employment Outlook,* Paris, June.

OECD (1998c), *Education Policy Analysis,* Paris.

OECD (1998d), *Education at a Glance - OECD Indicators,* Paris.

OECD (1998e), "Thematic Review of the transition from initial education to working life. Interim comparative report", DEELSA/ED(98)11 and Background papers from reviewed countries, Paris.

OECD (1998f), *Children and Families At Risk - New Issues in Integrating Services,* Paris.

OECD (1998g), *Benefit Systems and Work Incentives,* Paris.

OECD (1999), *Employment Outlook,* Paris, June.

OECD (forthcoming) *The OECD Jobs Strategy: Assessing Performance and Policy,* Paris.

OSWALD, A.J. (1997), "The Missing Piece of the Unemployment Puzzle", Department of Economics, University of Warwick.

PAYNE, J. (1987), "Does Unemployment Run in Families? Some Findings from the General Household Survey", *Sociology*, No. 21, pp. 199-214.

PERGAMIT, M.R. (1995), "Assessing School to Work Transition in the United States", *Statistical Journal of the United Nations Economic Commission for Europe,* No. 3-4, pp. 272-287.

PÉROT, Y. and SIMON-ZARCA, G. (1998), "Apprentissage - De Nouveaux Parcours de Formation", *Bref,* No. 139, CEREQ, Marseilles, February.

RAFFE, D. (ed.) (1988), *Education and the Youth Labour Market: Schooling and Scheming,* Falmer Press, London.

REES, G., ISTANCE, D. and WILLIAMSON, H. (1996), "Status Zero: A Study of Jobless School Leavers in South Wales", *Research Papers in Education,* No. 11, pp. 219-235.

ROBINSON, L. (1998), "The Effects of Part-time Work on School Students", Research Report, No. 9, Longitudinal Surveys of Australian Youth, Australian Council for Educational Research, October.

ROGOWSKI, R. and SCHÖMAN, K. (1996), "Legal Regulation and Flexibility of Employment Contracts", in Schmid, G., O'Reilly, J. and Schömann, K. (eds.), *International Handbook of Labour Market Policy and Evaluation,* Edward Elgar Press, Cheltenham, UK, pp. 623-651.

RUHM, C. (1997), "Is High School Employment Consumption or Investment", *Journal of Labour Economics,* October, pp. 735-776.

RYAN, P. (1998), "Is Apprenticeship Better? A Review of Economic Evidence", *Journal of Vocational Education and Training,* No. 2, pp. 289-325.

RYAN, P. and BÜCHTEMANN, C. (1996), "The School-to-Work Transition", in Schmid, G., O'Reilly, J. and Schömann, K. (eds.), *International Handbook of Labour Market Policy and Evaluation,* Edward Elgar Press, Cheltenham, UK, pp. 308-347.

SOLLOGOUB, M. and ULRICH, V. (1997), "Apprenticeship Versus Vocational School: Selectivity Bias and School to Work Transition: Evidence from France", Centre National de la Recherche Scientifique, Université de Paris I, Paris.

STANLEY, M., KATZ, L. and KRUEGER, A. (1998), "Impacts of Employment and Training Programs: The American Experience", mimeo.

WERQUIN, P. (1997), "1986-1996: dix ans d'intervention publique sur le marché du travail", *Économie et Statistique,* INSEE, No. 304-305, Paris, pp. 121-136.

WERQUIN, P., BREEN, R. and PLANAS, J. (eds.) (1997), "Youth Transitions in Europe: Theories and Evidence", Centre d'Études et de Recherches sur les Qualifications (CEREQ), No. 120, Marseilles.

Figure 1
Proportion of young people attending school by age, gender and labour force status[a]

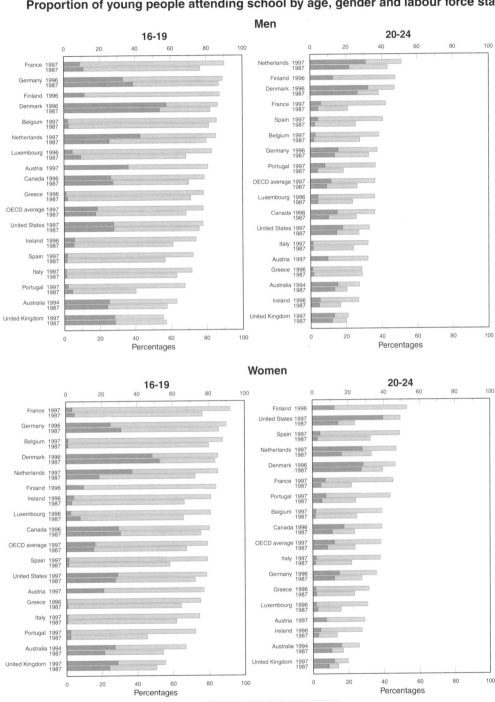

a) Countries are ranked in descending order of the total percentage of youth attending school in the latest available year.

Source: OECD School-to-work Database.

Figure 1 *(cont.)*
Proportion of young people attending school by age, gender and labour force status[a]

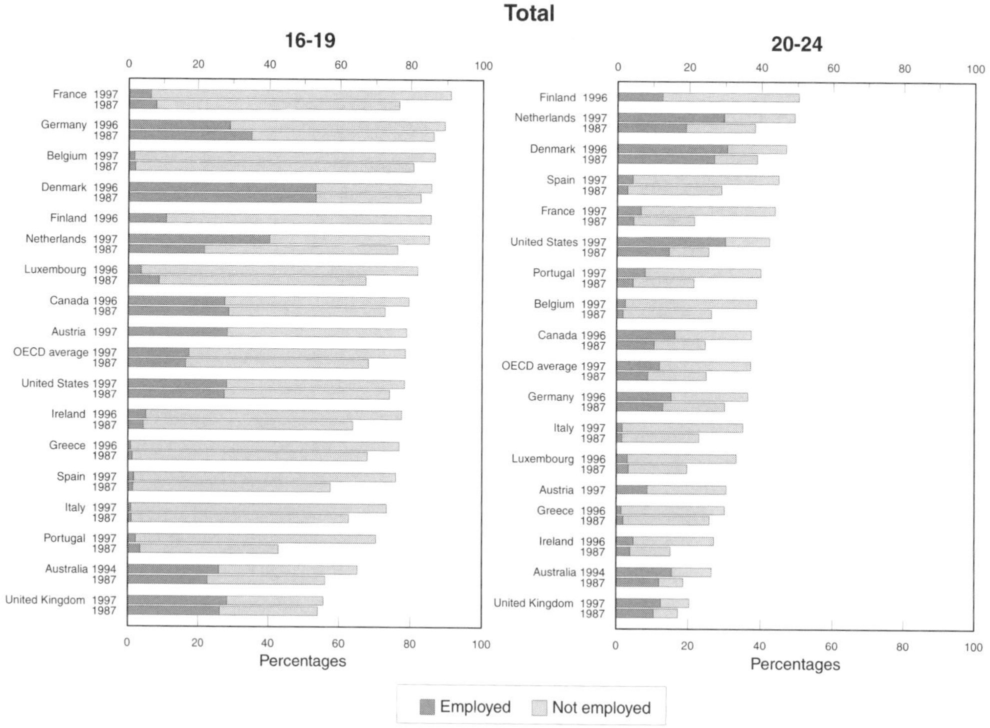

a) Countries are ranked in descending order of the total percentage of youth attending school in the latest available year.

Source: OECD School-to-work Database.

Figure 2

Proportion of teenagers not attending school by gender

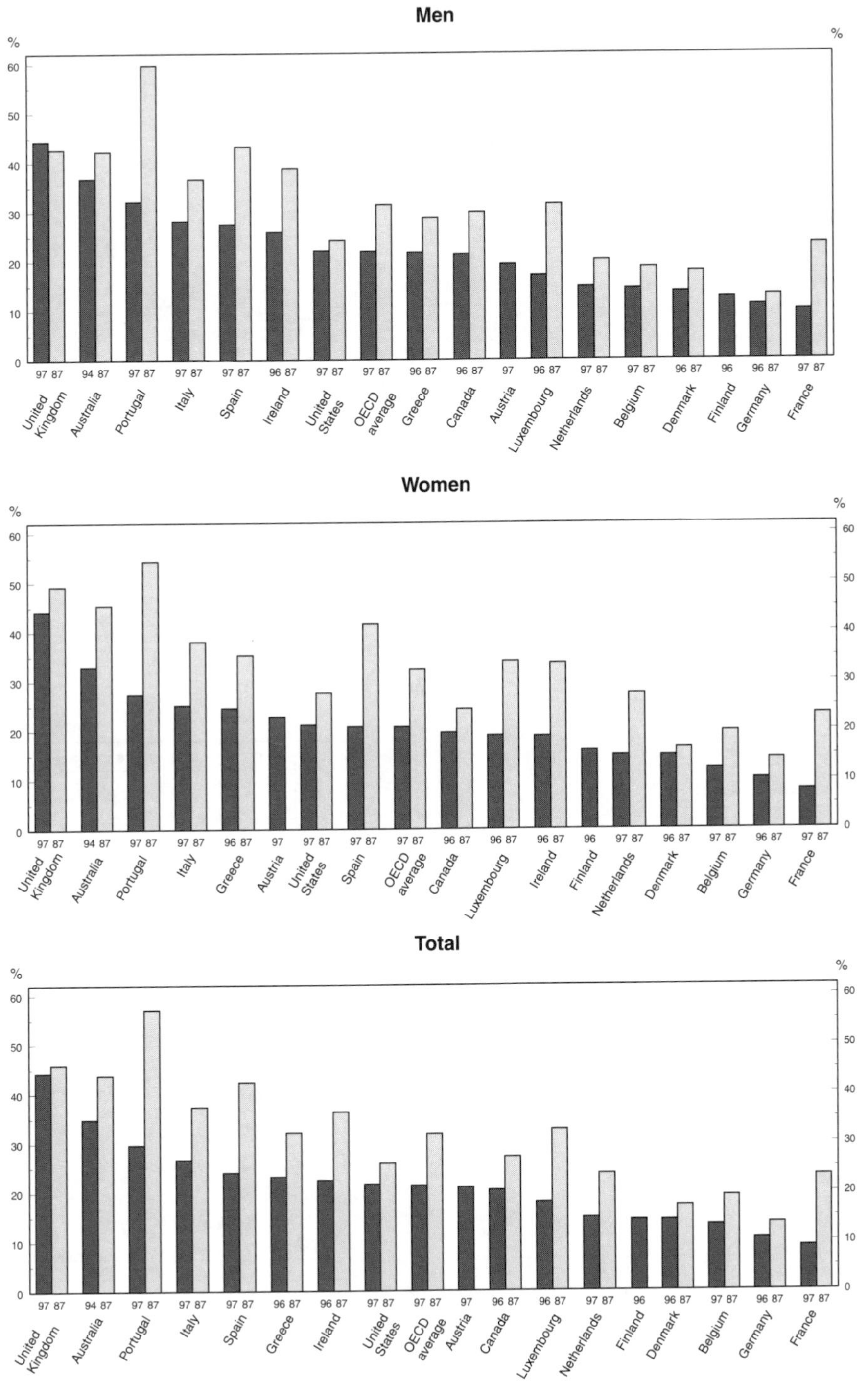

a) Countries are ranked in descending order of the total percentage of 16-19 not attending school in the latest available year.

Source: OECD School-to-work Database.

Figure 3
Proportion of young people not attending school and not employed by age and gender[a]

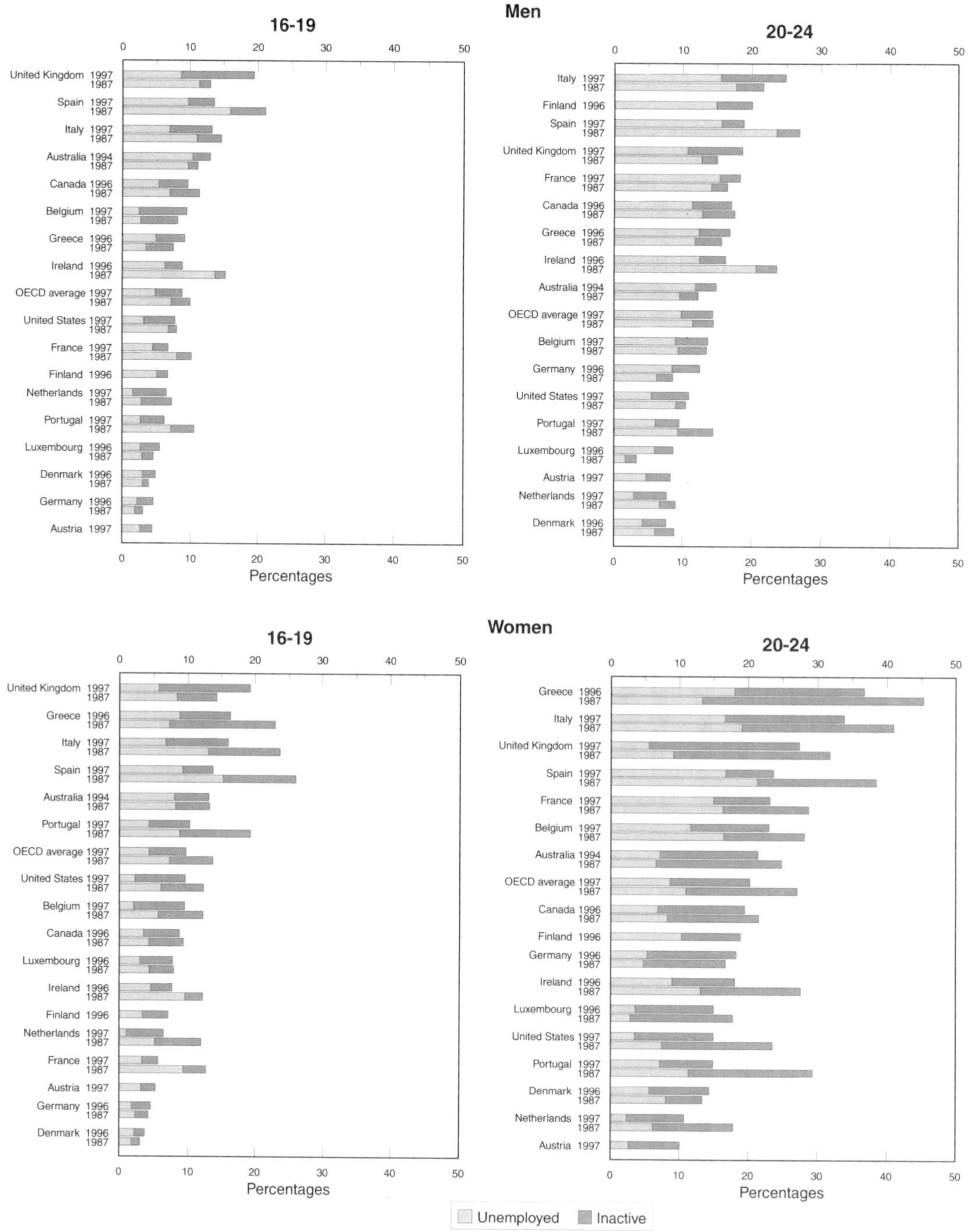

a) Countries are ranked in descending order of the percentage of youth not attending school and not in employment in the latest available year.
Source: OECD School-to-work Database.

Figure 3 *(cont.)*

Proportion of young people not attending school and not employed by age and gender[a]

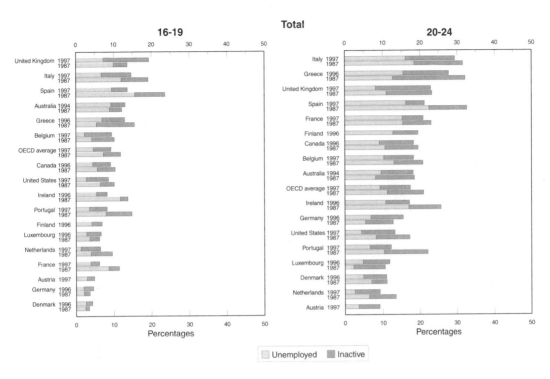

a) Countries are ranked in descending order of the percentage of youth not attending school and not in employment in the latest available year.

Source: OECD Schoo-to-work Database.

Figure 4
Young people aged 25-29 with low educational attainment by gender, 1996 *a, b*
As a percentage of all youth aged 25-29

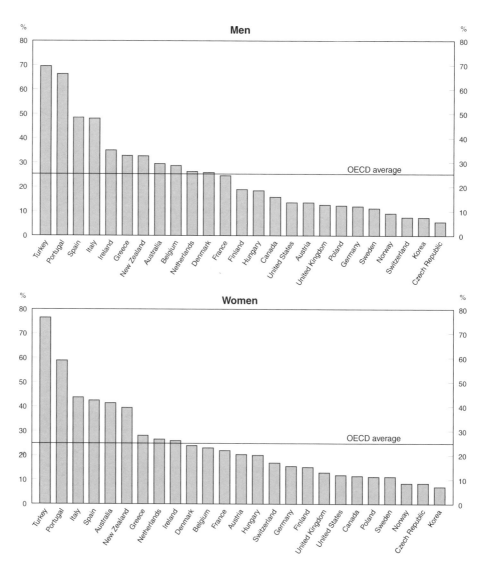

a) Low educational attainment corresponds to less than upper secondary. Data refer to 1995 for New Zealand, Poland and Turkey.
b) Countries are ranked from left to right in descending order of the proportion with low educational attainment.
Source: OECD Education Database.

Figure 5
Youth (15-24) share of the working age (15-64) population, 1997[a]

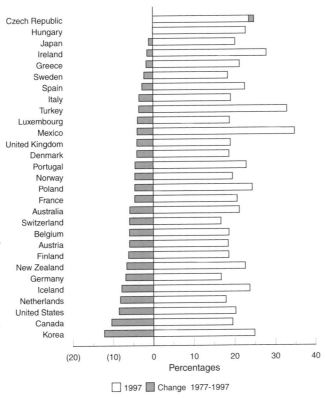

a) Countries are ranked from top to bottom in ascending order of the
absolute level of the percentage point changes over the period
1977-1997.

Source: United Nations projection demographic data, 1996.

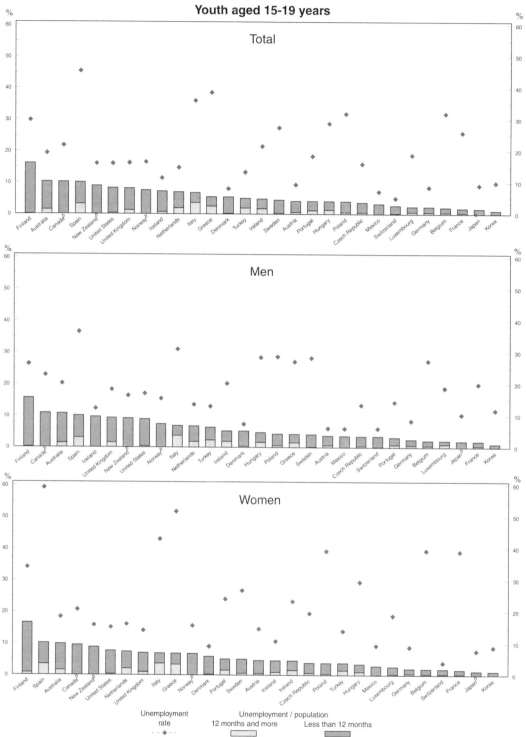

Figure 6
Unemployment indicators, 1997 [a]

a) Countries are ranked from left to right in descending order of the unemployment/population ratio.
b) No breakdown by duration of unemployment is available.
Source: OECD Database on unemployment duration and EUROSTAT.

Figure 6 *(cont.)*
Unemployment indicators, 1997 [a]

Youth aged 20-24 years

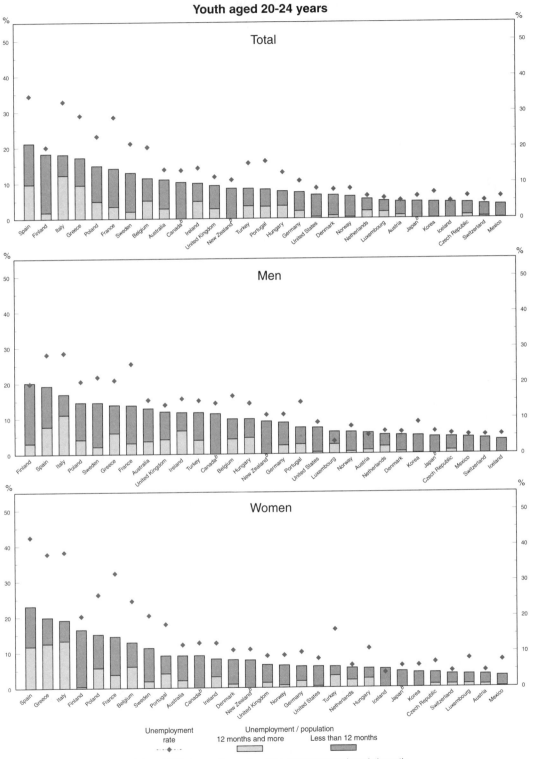

a) Countries are ranked from left to right in descending order of the unemployment/population ratio.
b) No breakdown by duration of unemployment is available.
Source: OECD Database on unemployment duration and EUROSTAT.

Figure 6 *(cont.)*
Unemployment indicators, 1997 [a]

Youth aged 15-24 years

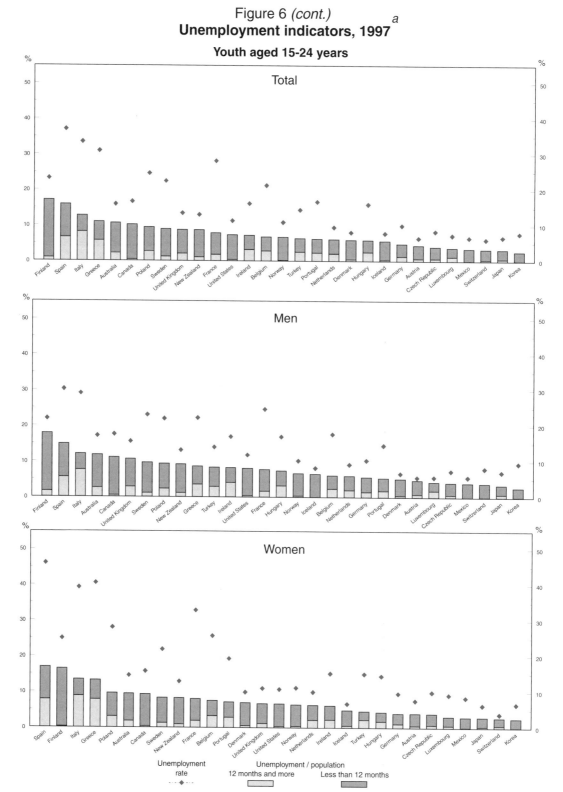

a) Countries are ranked from left to right in descending order of the unemployment/population ratio.
Source: OECD Database on unemployment duration and EUROSTAT.

Figure 7
Age-earnings profiles for different cohorts of workers by gender
Log of earnings in national currency at 1990 prices

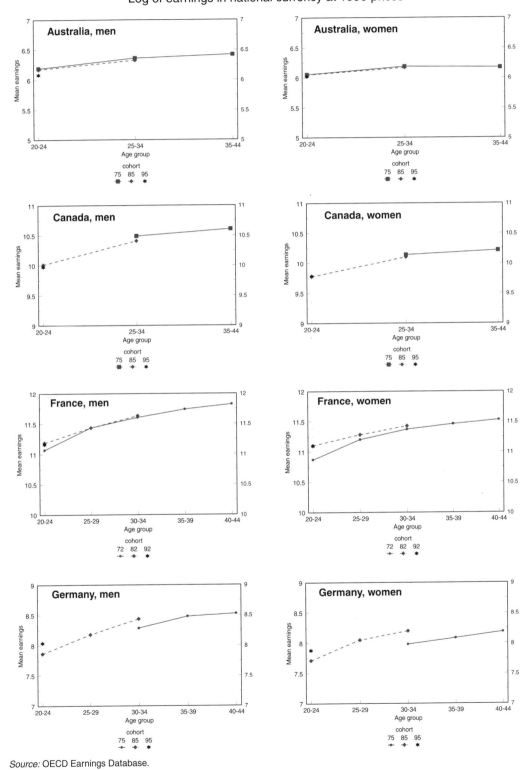

Source: OECD Earnings Database.

Figure 7 *(cont.)*

Age-earnings profiles for different cohorts of workers by gender

Log of earnings in national currency at 1990 prices

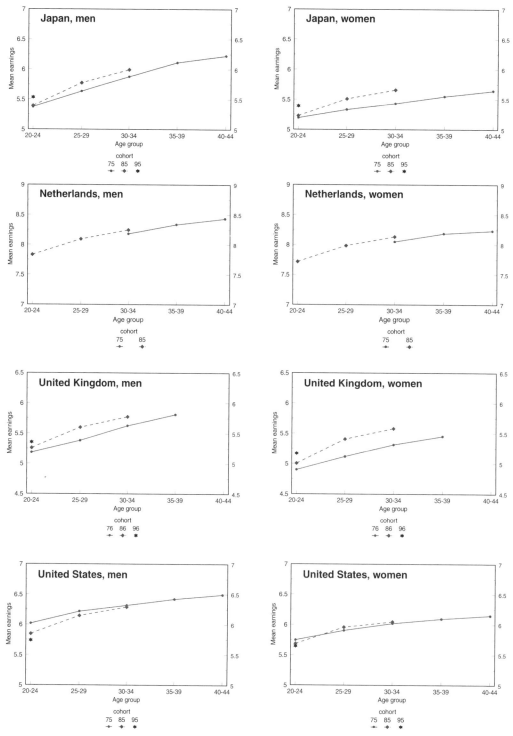

Source: OECD Earnings Database.

Figure 8

Mean earnings for youth aged 20-24 years relative to other workers aged 35-44 years, 1977-1997

Total

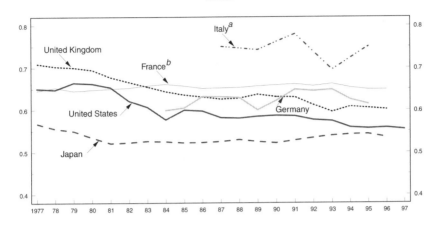

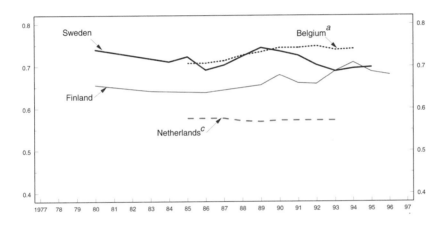

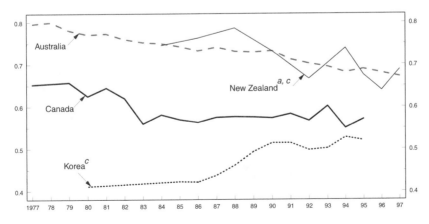

a) Data refer to median earnings.
b) Earnings for workers aged 21-25 relative to those aged 31-40.
c) Earnings for workers aged 20-24 relative to those aged 40-44.
Source: OECD Earnings Database.

Figure 9

Employment of new school-leavers aged 16-24 years one year after leaving school *a*

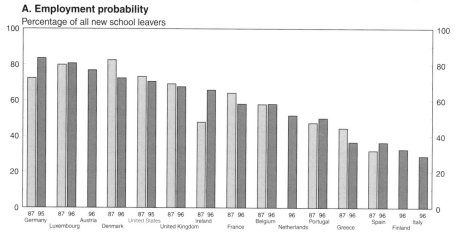

A. Employment probability

Percentage of all new school leavers

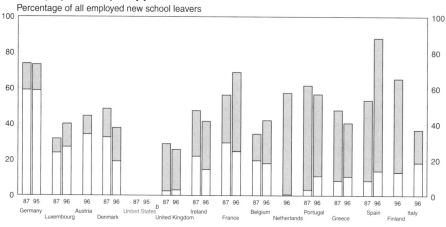

B. Employed in temporary jobs

Percentage of all employed new school leavers

☐ Contract covers a period of training   ☐ Other reasons

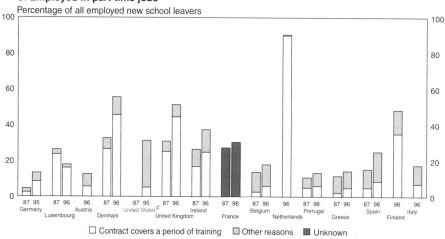

C. Employed in part-time jobs

Percentage of all employed new school leavers

☐ Contract covers a period of training   ☐ Other reasons   ■ Unknown

a) Countries are ranked in descending order the employment probability.

b) Data on temporary jobs are not available.

c) Data for 1987 are not available.

Source: OECD (1998*b*).

Figure 10
Net replacement rates[a] for young people,[b] 1995
Unemployment, housing benefits and social assistance benefits

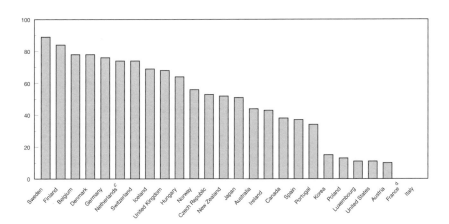

a) Net replacement rates at 66.7% of the average production worker (APW) level of earnings. The chart abstracts from the presence of waiting periods and compares the maximum obtainable benefit levels. For further details, see OECD (1998*g*).

b) Unemployed single person of 20 years of age, living alone without family responsibilities and without an employment record.

c) Benefit payable to a 21-years-old individual. Young unemployed job-seekers do not have any benefit entitlement in theory, unless they can demonstrate a real need.

d) People under 25 are not entitled to the social assistance benefit (RMI).

Source: OECD Database on Benefit Systems and Work Incentives.

Table 1. **Life satisfaction in European countries by age groups, 1975-1996**

	Employed	Unemployed	Not in the labour force	Employed	Unemployed	Not in the labour force
	Percentage of persons very or fairly satisfied			Percentage of persons not at all satisfied		
15-19 years	87	72	90	3	8	2
20-24 years	87	67	88	3	9	2
25-54 years	85	63	84	3	12	4

Source: Calculated from Eurobarometer surveys 1975-1996 by David Blanchflower, Dartmouth College, United States.

Table 2. **Opinions on the importance of work, 1989**
Percentage of persons who strongly agree or who agree

	Less than 25-years-old	25-years-old and over	All
Work is a person's most important activity			
Employed	39	46	45
Unemployed	55	52	53
Out of the labour force	33	55	52
All	38	50	48
Would enjoy having a paid job even if I didn't need the money			
Employed	67	67	67
Unemployed	72	68	69
Out of the labour force	51	66	68
All	67	60	61

Source: International Social Survey Programme dataset covering nine countries (Austria, West Germany, Hungary, Ireland, Italy, the Netherlands, Norway, United Kingdom and the United States).

Table 3. **Young people living with their parents by age and gender, 1985 and 1996/97**

	15-19				20-24				25-29	
	Men		Women		Men		Women		Men	Women
	1985	1996	1985	1996	1985	1997	1985	1997	1997	1997
Australia[a]	87.4	87.3	83.1	81.9	49.6	50.2	30.5	36.5	..	..
Austria	..	94.8	..	91.8	..	76.5	..	58.7	40.7	20.5
Belgium	97.1	92.6	94.8	93.5	76.3	68.7	57.7	58.6	23.5	13.5
Canada[b]	88.9	90.8	82.2	84.7	49.8	53.4	30.4	39.1	..	..
Finland	..	50.9	..	47.5	..	17.6	..	9.4	7.0	2.3
France	94.9	94.1	88.8	91.1	55.8	62.4	35.7	44.1	23.2	11.4
Germany	95.1	95.5	91.8	92.1	64.3	65.1	42.9	45.1	27.1	11.9
Greece	93.8	94.8	88.4	92.7	74.2	80.6	48.6	68.2	65.5	38.7
Ireland	95.3	91.1	93.4	88.0	73.0	66.3	56.0	49.5	39.3	25.2
Italy	97.2	96.6	95.9	95.8	87.4	92.7	67.7	85.1	72.5	51.8
Luxembourg	92.8	95.2	89.8	93.4	74.0	71.8	55.0	57.1	36.6	21.9
Netherlands[c]	95.6	96.7	92.4	93.3	64.0	61.3	39.6	37.2	19.5	6.1
Portugal[c]	93.7	92.9	90.3	89.5	80.6	87.9	68.1	76.3	65.9	50.3
Spain[c]	95.4	95.1	94.1	94.0	89.0	92.4	77.8	88.2	72.2	56.6
United Kingdom	94.4	92.9	87.2	87.3	56.9	55.0	33.8	35.8	22.5	11.9
United States[a]	89.9	87.9	85.4	83.7	49.5	50.0	36.3	38.0	..	..
OECD unweighted average	**93.7**	**93.1**[d]	**89.8**	**90.1**[d]	**67.5**	**68.4**[d]	**48.6**	**54.2**[d]	**39.7**	**24.8**

.. Data not available.
a. 1986 and 1996.
b. 1985 and 1996
c. 1988 instead of 1985.
d. To be compared with 1985, the OECD unweighted average does not include Austria and Finland.

Sources: OECD (1998b); EUROSTAT, Labour Force Surveys.

Table 4. **Why young people leave their parental home later?** [a, b]
by gender, 15-24 years old, in 1997
Percentages

	Can't afford to move out		Want all the home comforts without all the responsibilities		Want to save up to make a good start later		Not enough suitable housing available for young people		Parents don't impose such strict rules on young people in the home as they used to		Get married or move in with their partner later than they used to	
	Men	Women	Men	Women	Men	Women	Men	Women	Men	Women	Men	Women
Austria	54.4	61.1	27.7	30.7	28.0	33.4	46.9	43.0	26.7	26.6	29.3	27.0
Belgium	62.7	58.5	37.3	42.5	41.5	42.9	19.0	18.0	32.7	30.6	26.5	29.9
Denmark	65.4	61.9	35.3	34.0	36.6	40.1	39.9	49.3	27.1	34.0	18.6	22.4
Finland	75.2	81.9	35.8	31.1	41.0	43.0	32.2	35.2	32.6	31.4	18.9	20.8
France	86.2	86.1	32.1	30.2	32.5	37.6	22.0	16.3	32.5	28.8	27.5	34.6
Germany	62.7	61.6	33.7	35.3	30.9	34.1	30.3	28.2	35.7	34.4	32.4	37.0
Greece	62.9	73.7	39.1	36.5	36.2	31.7	8.1	8.5	21.2	30.7	20.8	23.9
Ireland	70.7	72.0	41.7	41.3	38.8	36.9	21.2	28.3	24.4	23.5	14.0	17.7
Italy	69.8	73.6	42.6	41.4	24.9	28.8	15.7	19.0	32.8	34.2	45.6	41.2
Luxembourg	56.3	47.4	40.8	37.1	44.7	49.5	18.4	25.8	24.3	41.2	32.7	25.9
Netherlands	69.6	75.2	42.5	40.5	36.3	44.2	32.7	41.5	27.1	24.5	28.9	27.0
Portugal	60.2	70.6	23.4	19.6	40.8	39.5	38.2	45.3	28.9	22.3	28.9	27.0
Spain	77.9	83.3	27.4	29.7	31.6	28.7	31.3	32.8	16.0	14.0	35.2	32.4
Sweden	94.5	96.2	30.3	22.5	47.2	51.5	28.3	38.9	14.3	14.3	20.2	24.6
United Kingdom	75.6	81.3	43.2	41.3	32.7	33.6	37.1	40.3	22.2	20.5	10.0	16.4
European Union	**72.6**	**75.7**	**35.8**	**35.3**	**32.1**	**34.4**	**27.4**	**28.3**	**28.0**	**27.0**	**25.9**	**28.8**

a. The question posed was: Some people say that, nowadays, adolescents and young adults tend to live longer in their parents' homes than they used to.
What do you think are the three main reasons for this?
1. Young people can't afford to move out.
2. Young people get married or move in with their partner later than they used to.
3. There's not enough suitable housing available for young people.
4. Young people want to save up so they can make a good start later.
5. Sharing accommodation with friends etc. isn't as popular as it used to be.
6. They want all the home comforts without all the responsibilities.
7. These days, parents don't impose such strict rules on young people in the home as they used to.
8. Parents need their children to help out financially.
9. Young people move out just as soon as they used to if not sooner (SPONTANEOUS).
10. Other reasons (SPONTANEOUS). Don't know.
b. Percentages can exceed 100 since these are multiple responses.
Source: Eurobarometer 47.2 on Young Europeans, Spring 1997.

Table 5. **Where do young people aged 15-24 years get most of their financial resources?**[a]

1997

	Parents or family	Partner	Regular job	Casual work	Work in the underground economy	Unemployment/ social security benefits	Training allowance/ educational grant
Austria	**41.0**	**3.2**	**45.5**	**8.2**	**1.7**	**4.7**	**13.5**
With a job	9.6	3.2	82.6	2.8	1.8	1.1	10.3
Students	77.5	1.1	11.4	12.5	0.7	1.8	18.5
Neither with a job nor studying	17.0	14.9	19.1	14.9	6.4	44.7	4.3
Belgium	**48.0**	**5.8**	**33.0**	**9.2**	**2.7**	**10.3**	**2.3**
With a job	12.6	6.9	78.8	6.1	0.0	1.3	0.0
Students	87.9	1.5	2.9	14.3	5.1	1.5	3.7
Neither with a job nor studying	20.6	16.5	9.3	2.1	2.1	56.7	4.1
Denmark	**18.7**	**1.7**	**64.8**	**3.5**	**4.2**	**8.5**	**28.2**
With a job	3.4	2.4	94.7	2.9	7.8	3.4	6.8
Students	29.2	0.6	54.9	4.1	2.4	3.2	45.7
Neither with a job nor studying	12.7	5.5	14.5	1.8	1.8	60.0	0.0
Finland	**40.5**	**2.7**	**24.7**	**19.5**	**0.8**	**15.2**	**25.3**
With a job	9.2	1.7	78.2	10.1	0.8	10.9	2.5
Students	52.7	1.7	12.9	23.8	1.0	6.3	35.0
Neither with a job nor studying	23.2	10.1	2.9	8.7	0.0	73.9	7.2
France	**47.8**	**8.3**	**40.2**	**14.7**	**7.0**	**5.7**	**5.3**
With a job	14.1	9.0	87.5	5.1	2.7	3.9	1.2
Students	83.2	2.7	3.9	22.7	9.8	1.2	11.3
Neither with a job nor studying	42.7	22.5	7.9	18.0	10.1	23.6	1.1
Germany	**37.8**	**4.9**	**51.2**	**15.8**	**2.4**	**7.8**	**5.8**
With a job	14.8	1.4	84.4	7.8	1.7	1.1	5.1
Students	80.1	2.7	13.9	30.3	2.5	1.0	8.7
Neither with a job nor studying	22.3	25.7	8.1	10.8	5.4	55.4	1.4
Greece	**50.8**	**5.3**	**40.5**	**5.3**	**0.3**	**1.7**	**0.0**
With a job	9.2	1.5	86.0	5.9	0.4	1.8	0.0
Students	94.0	0.5	2.5	5.0	0.0	0.5	0.0
Neither with a job nor studying	71.5	20.8	4.6	4.6	0.0	3.8	0.0
Ireland	**38.0**	**2.2**	**36.8**	**12.0**	**1.3**	**13.2**	**4.7**
With a job	6.5	0.5	89.7	3.8	0.5	2.2	0.5
Students	66.2	1.3	15.6	19.8	1.6	1.9	7.5
Neither with a job nor studying	10.3	7.5	6.5	4.7	1.9	64.5	3.7

Table 5. **Where do young people aged 15-24 years get most of their financial resources?**[a]
1997 (cont.)

	Parents or family	Partner	Regular job	Casual work	Work in the underground economy	Unemployment/ social security benefits	Training allowance/ educational grant
Italy	**67.5**	**2.3**	**26.2**	**15.5**	**3.5**	**0.2**	**1.3**
With a job	14.9	3.7	85.7	7.5	2.5	0.0	1.9
Students	91.4	0.6	3.7	16.3	3.1	0.3	1.5
Neither with a job nor studying	73.9	5.2	6.1	24.3	7.0	0.0	0.0
Luxembourg	**58.0**	**5.5**	**37.5**	**23.0**	**7.0**	**1.5**	**4.5**
With a job	16.7	4.2	91.7	8.3	5.6	1.4	0.0
Students	85.6	4.5	6.3	35.1	5.4	0.9	7.2
Neither with a job nor studying	52.9	11.8	5.9	0.0	23.5	5.9	5.9
Netherlands	**32.5**	**4.7**	**33.8**	**22.8**	**3.8**	**5.7**	**24.7**
With a job	5.9	5.0	71.7	15.1	2.3	3.7	2.7
Students	55.8	1.6	12.9	28.1	4.4	0.9	44.2
Neither with a job nor studying	7.8	18.8	6.3	23.4	6.3	35.9	3.1
Portugal	**50.7**	**3.3**	**47.0**	**5.0**	**1.0**	**1.3**	**1.7**
With a job	15.6	2.3	87.9	3.6	1.0	0.0	0.0
Students	93.0	0.4	3.0	6.1	1.3	0.9	4.3
Neither with a job nor studying	65.6	18.8	9.4	7.8	0.0	9.4	0.0
Spain	**62.3**	**2.8**	**35.8**	**10.8**	**1.5**	**2.0**	**1.5**
With a job	26.7	1.5	85.9	6.8	0.5	0.0	0.0
Students	91.9	1.2	6.5	9.6	1.2	0.4	3.5
Neither with a job nor studying	60.4	8.2	16.4	19.4	3.7	8.2	0.0
Sweden	**34.2**	**1.2**	**29.5**	**18.7**	**3.2**	**11.7**	**10.3**
With a job	3.4	0.0	82.7	10.6	5.0	8.4	7.3
Students	52.4	1.7	7.3	22.8	2.5	4.8	12.4
Neither with a job nor studying	21.2	1.5	4.5	18.2	1.5	59.1	9.1
United Kingdom	**17.4**	**6.1**	**56.8**	**6.3**	**0.5**	**18.3**	**2.8**
With a job	4.2	3.6	89.6	2.4	0.4	2.9	1.6
Students	58.3	0.6	29.2	17.3	0.0	3.0	7.7
Neither with a job nor studying	12.1	17.0	1.6	4.9	1.1	70.3	0.5
European Union	**45.0**	**4.7**	**41.5**	**12.6**	**2.9**	**6.8**	**5.2**
With a job	12.6	3.6	85.9	6.0	1.6	1.9	2.4
Students	79.9	1.6	9.7	18.7	3.5	1.3	9.9
Neither with a job nor studying	41.4	14.9	7.6	14.5	4.6	32.5	0.9

a. The question posed was: Where do you get most of your money from? (several answers possible) My regular job; Unemployment or social security benefits; Training allowance or educational grant; My parents or family; Casual work; My partner; Work in the underground economy; Others.
Source: Eurobarometer 47.2 on Young Europeans. Spring 1997.

Table 6a. **Proportion of unemployed young people in households where no other person is employed, 1985 and 1996** (Percentages)

	15-19		20-24	
	1985	1996	1985	1996
Australia[a]	26.4	22.8	37.1	36.3
Austria	..	18.4	..	21.6
Belgium	20.2	33.9	28.3	38.8
Canada	21.7	24.1	39.7	40.9
Finland	..	23.5	..	64.6
France	19.2	25.8	27.9	29.8
Germany[b]	17.5	36.3	36.6	45.5
Greece	18.6	16.1	25.7	23.6
Ireland	27.9	40.5	35.0	43.5
Italy	12.4	21.5	21.1	27.1
Mexico	..	8.5	..	8.5
Netherlands[c]	22.3	17.8	48.6	44.5
Portugal[c]	8.9	9.5	15.1	18.6
Spain[c]	20.0	22.6	24.1	26.2
Switzerland	..	4.8	..	22.5
United Kingdom	26.6	32.4	44.1	48.7
United States[a]	20.6	18.8	39.6	40.1
OECD unweighted average	**20.2**	**24.8[d]**	**32.5**	**35.7[d]**

.. Data not available.
a. 1986 instead of 1985.
b. Data for Germany relate to west Germany for 1985, but to the whole of Germany for 1996.
c. 1988 instead of 1985.
d. To be compared with 1985, the OECD unweighted average does not include Austria, Finland, Mexico and Switzerland.
   The averages are 22.2 and 34.2 for those aged 15-19 and those aged 20-24, respectively, when these four countries are included.
Source: OECD(1998b).

Table 6b. **Proportion of young people not in the labour force in households where no other person is employed, 1985 and 1996** (Percentages)

	15-19		20-24	
	1985	1996	1985	1996
Australia[a]	12.8	19.0	29.6	36.8
Austria	..	5.8	..	27.8
Belgium	11.0	14.0	16.3	20.1
Canada	17.4	19.4	34.8	36.8
Finland	..	17.6	..	57.3
France	11.4	12.7	29.2	37.2
Germany[b]	8.1	9.5	29.9	31.5
Greece	14.6	12.1	27.5	35.4
Ireland	14.5	18.7	36.6	44.0
Italy	6.9	11.0	11.9	18.3
Mexico	..	5.7	..	5.7
Netherlands[c]	13.7	12.8	38.3	38.3
Portugal[c]	7.2	6.8	12.5	15.3
Spain[c]	10.1	12.2	14.3	14.0
Switzerland	..	1.5	..	15.4
United Kingdom	16.1	19.5	45.8	54.9
United States[a]	15.2	15.0	30.7	35.3
OECD unweighted average	**12.2**	**14.1[d]**	**27.5**	**32.1[d]**

.. Data not available.
a. 1986 instead of 1985.
b. Data for Germany relate to west Germany for 1985, but to the whole of Germany for 1996.
c. 1988 instead of 1985.
d. To be compared with 1985, the OECD unweighted average does not include Austria, Finland, Mexico and Switzerland.
   The averages are 12.5 and 30.8 percent for those aged 15-19 and those aged 20-24, respectively, when these four countries are included.
Source: OECD (1998b).

Table 7. **Unemployment rates for young adults (25-29) by educational attainment and gender, 1996**

Percentages

	Men				Women			
	Less than upper	Upper secondary	University/ tertiary	Total	Less than secondary	Upper secondary	University/ tertiary	Total
Australia	13.4	6.6	5.6	8.3	10.4	7.8	4.1	7.5
Austria	8.6	3.4	3.9	4.2	8.5	2.8	7.6	4.3
Belgium	13.0	6.0	3.4	7.2	29.1	17.4	6.5	14.8
Canada	20.2	12.5	7.8	11.1	23.6	10.8	7.4	9.5
Czech Republic	17.6	1.9	0.9	2.5	18.2	5.6	1.4	6.0
Denmark	14.9	5.6	6.0	8.8	24.3	9.4	6.3	12.4
Finland	25.8	15.3	8.0	15.6	32.9	19.0	11.5	18.8
France	21.1	12.1	11.1	14.1	32.4	18.4	12.9	19.1
Germany	18.6	7.4	6.2	8.5	15.8	7.7	5.6	8.2
Greece	8.2	9.9	16.8	11.0	26.7	24.1	24.2	24.6
Hungary	20.5	8.7	2.7	10.0	21.4	12.5	5.3	12.4
Ireland	24.7	8.5	5.6	13.2	24.5	7.3	4.5	9.3
Italy	14.1	15.4	27.3	15.4	22.0	20.2	34.0	22.3
Korea	3.5	3.6	5.2	4.1	1.7	1.9	2.1	2.0
Netherlands	9.0	4.0	6.9	6.0	8.0	5.1	6.3	6.0
New Zealand	12.7	3.0	3.9	6.0	9.2	3.6	4.4	5.7
Norway	9.9	6.4	6.0	6.6	11.6	6.0	5.0	6.1
Poland	21.8	11.3	7.7	12.1	34.3	19.2	7.9	17.9
Portugal	8.2	7.9	11.2	8.6	10.3	9.8	7.5	9.6
Spain	26.3	19.9	24.7	24.4	41.3	30.9	32.7	35.5
Sweden	20.0	13.9	7.1	12.9	26.4	13.1	6.6	12.6
Turkey	8.2	10.0	7.0	8.5	7.4	20.1	8.9	10.0
United Kingdom	23.6	10.5	5.0	10.6	17.8	8.3	3.3	7.6
United States	15.7	7.6	4.1	7.4	17.3	6.6	1.3	5.1
OECD unweighted average	**15.8**	**8.8**	**8.1**	**9.9**	**19.8**	**12.0**	**9.1**	**12.0**

Source: OECD Education Database.

Table 8. **Education and employment activities of persons aged 18 and 22 years, 1984 and 1997**
Percentages

| | | In education or training | | | | Not in education and training | | | |
| | | In employment | | Not in employment | | In employment | | Not in employment | |
		1984	1997	1984	1997	1984	1997	1984	1997
Men	Australia[a]	27.5	23.6	17.0	30.0	38.5	30.1	17.0	16.4
18-year-olds	Austria	..	33.1	..	43.9	..	18.6	..	4.5
	Belgium	3.7	1.7	71.0	82.9	14.4	3.4	10.9	12.0
	Canada[b]	20.8	27.6	38.0	44.9	23.0	15.6	18.2	11.9
	Denmark[b]	44.8	57.8	27.3	22.9	21.5	13.3	6.4	6.0
	Finland[b]	..	14.2	..	71.9	..	5.8	..	8.1
	France	8.6	11.0	54.3	78.0	19.1	4.0	18.0	7.0
	Germany[b]	45.2	46.0	33.0	40.9	16.6	7.2	5.3	6.0
	Greece[b]	2.2	1.5	55.2	68.1	31.1	16.7	11.4	13.8
	Ireland[b]	8.7	4.8	39.1	61.1	34.8	22.4	17.4	11.7
	Italy	1.2	1.3	55.5	67.4	29.6	17.6	13.7	13.7
	Luxembourg[b]	22.2	4.2	43.5	74.6	28.1	12.1	6.2	9.1
	Netherlands[c]	10.0	45.5	61.4	34.5	16.4	11.2	12.2	8.7
	Portugal[d]	5.9	2.1	29.0	62.6	51.9	28.7	13.2	6.6
	Spain[d]	0.5	2.9	48.8	66.8	25.3	15.1	25.4	15.2
	United Kingdom	24.7	29.8	19.6	17.2	34.4	32.0	21.4	21.0
	United States	20.8	26.4	40.1	41.6	25.5	20.4	13.7	11.5
	OECD unweighted average	**16.5**	**19.6**	**42.2**	**53.5**	**27.3**	**16.1**	**14.0**	**10.8**
Men	Australia[a]	12.1	13.1	5.9	8.3	69.2	60.0	12.8	18.6
22-year-olds	Austria	..	10.2	..	24.0	..	59.0	..	6.7
	Belgium	4.9	2.6	33.7	36.3	46.9	44.1	14.6	17.0
	Canada[b]	8.4	15.9	14.9	21.5	54.0	46.7	22.8	15.9
	Denmark[b]	13.8	21.9	14.0	22.2	61.5	45.0	10.7	10.9
	Finland[b]	..	9.7	..	37.5	..	32.2	..	20.6
	France	4.3	5.7	11.0	39.5	68.5	36.6	16.2	18.3
	Germany[b]	6.7	13.6	22.3	21.5	61.6	52.9	9.5	12.0
	Greece[b]	1.3	1.6	20.7	28.4	63.1	53.4	15.0	16.7
	Ireland[b]	4.3	4.8	9.4	20.7	65.1	56.8	21.2	17.7
	Italy	1.9	1.4	22.8	28.4	56.8	44.6	18.5	25.7
	Luxembourg[b]	4.2	2.3	14.5	27.2	77.9	63.0	3.4	7.5
	Netherlands[c]	15.3	32.0	26.6	20.4	43.0	40.7	15.0	7.0
	Portugal[d]	5.6	8.1	14.0	28.3	65.3	54.5	15.1	9.1
	Spain[d]	0.3	4.8	18.2	33.6	46.5	44.5	35.0	17.1
	United Kingdom	8.8	13.1	7.1	8.6	67.3	59.7	16.8	18.5
	United States	13.7	20.0	11.8	15.2	62.4	53.2	12.1	11.6
	OECD unweighted average	**7.0**	**10.6**	**16.5**	**24.8**	**60.6**	**49.8**	**15.9**	**14.8**
Women	Australia[a]	12.9	26.4	22.1	32.5	46.4	24.6	18.6	16.6
18-year-olds	Austria	..	22.6	..	49.0	..	22.3	..	6.2
	Belgium	1.1	1.2	73.9	88.0	11.7	1.7	13.3	9.1
	Canada[b]	20.6	29.6	38.9	44.0	23.0	15.2	17.5	11.3
	Denmark[b]	36.7	44.5	34.7	39.9	20.6	9.9	7.9	5.7
	Finland[b]	..	13.2	..	71.3	..	9.0	..	6.4
	France	3.9	3.8	59.3	86.5	12.7	2.5	24.1	7.2
	Germany[b]	33.8	33.9	39.1	51.2	19.3	6.1	7.8	8.8
	Greece[b]	0.7	0.9	49.0	69.0	17.6	9.3	32.7	20.9
	Ireland[b]	3.9	5.1	48.1	72.9	33.2	11.7	14.9	10.4
	Italy	1.3	0.9	53.4	74.7	19.2	9.3	26.1	15.1
	Luxembourg[b]	9.0	2.6	43.8	80.5	41.3	12.8	5.9	4.1
	Netherlands[c]	7.4	44.6	59.3	38.7	20.1	9.3	13.1	7.4
	Portugal[d]	1.7	2.4	37.9	70.5	37.3	16.3	23.2	10.8
	Spain[d]	0.1	1.8	48.8	74.7	15.6	8.2	35.5	15.3
	United Kingdom	15.6	29.3	20.3	18.7	40.8	30.2	23.3	21.7
	United States	20.5	30.4	35.7	42.6	22.0	14.5	21.8	12.4
	OECD unweighted average	**11.3**	**17.3**	**44.3**	**59.1**	**25.4**	**12.5**	**19.0**	**11.1**

Table 8. **Education and employment activities of persons aged 18 and 22 years, 1984 and 1997** (*cont.*)
Percentages

		In education or training				Not in education and training			
		In employment		Not in employment		In employment		Not in employment	
		1984	1997	1984	1997	1984	1997	1984	1997
Women	Australia[a]	8.6	15.0	5.6	9.4	58.6	52.9	27.1	22.7
22-year-olds	Austria	..	7.2	..	23.9	..	58.7	..	10.1
	Belgium	2.5	1.9	24.5	33.4	47.6	42.0	25.4	22.7
	Canada[b]	9.1	19.8	9.4	19.1	55.1	40.6	26.5	20.5
	Denmark[b]	23.8	30.4	9.0	22.4	49.6	32.4	17.7	14.8
	Finland[b]	..	12.1	..	42.6	..	29.5	..	15.8
	France	5.3	8.2	11.7	37.6	53.8	30.5	29.2	23.7
	Germany[b]	5.8	14.4	17.3	18.6	57.5	45.1	19.4	22.0
	Greece[b]	2.2	2.2	12.3	28.5	33.1	32.5	52.4	36.7
	Ireland[b]	2.5	4.0	5.4	20.4	66.6	59.3	25.6	16.2
	Italy	1.3	2.5	18.3	37.7	40.0	27.7	40.4	32.1
	Luxembourg[b]	2.1	1.3	7.8	25.0	76.5	60.2	13.6	13.4
	Netherlands[c]	9.8	32.0	15.3	17.3	54.5	40.6	20.3	10.1
	Portugal[d]	3.6	7.3	20.5	38.1	41.9	44.7	33.9	10.0
	Spain[d]	0.3	4.9	24.6	45.7	28.0	28.2	47.1	21.2
	United Kingdom	4.6	11.1	5.3	8.7	54.7	52.6	35.3	27.6
	United States	11.0	21.7	8.8	14.3	54.5	47.3	25.7	16.7
	OECD unweighted average	**6.2**	**11.5**	**13.1**	**26.0**	**51.5**	**42.6**	**29.3**	**19.8**
Total	Australia[a]	20.2	25.0	19.6	31.2	42.4	27.4	17.8	16.5
18-year-olds	Austria	..	27.5	..	46.6	..	20.5	..	5.4
	Belgium	2.5	1.4	72.4	85.3	13.2	2.6	12.0	10.6
	Canada[b]	20.7	28.6	38.5	44.4	23.0	15.4	17.8	11.6
	Denmark[b]	40.8	50.6	31.0	32.1	21.1	11.4	7.1	5.8
	Finland[b]	..	13.7	..	71.6	..	7.4	..	7.3
	France	6.1	7.5	57.0	82.1	15.7	3.3	21.2	7.1
	Germany[b]	39.4	40.2	36.1	45.8	18.0	6.7	6.5	7.3
	Greece[b]	1.4	1.2	51.9	68.6	24.0	12.7	22.6	17.6
	Ireland[b]	6.3	4.9	43.6	66.6	34.0	17.4	16.1	11.1
	Italy	1.2	1.1	54.5	70.8	24.3	13.7	20.0	14.4
	Luxembourg[b]	16.0	3.4	43.7	77.6	34.3	12.5	6.1	6.6
	Netherlands[c]	8.7	45.1	60.3	36.7	18.3	10.2	12.7	8.0
	Portugal[d]	3.9	2.3	33.1	66.9	45.1	22.0	17.9	8.9
	Spain[d]	0.3	2.3	48.8	70.8	20.4	11.6	30.5	15.2
	United Kingdom	20.2	29.6	19.9	17.9	37.6	31.1	22.3	21.4
	United States	20.6	28.4	37.9	42.1	23.8	17.5	17.6	12.0
	OECD unweighted average	**13.9**	**18.4**	**43.2**	**56.3**	**26.3**	**14.3**	**16.5**	**11.0**
Total	Australia[a]	10.3	14.1	5.8	8.9	63.8	56.5	20.2	20.6
22-year-olds	Austria	..	8.7	..	24.0	..	58.9	..	8.5
	Belgium	3.8	2.3	29.4	34.9	47.2	43.1	19.6	19.7
	Canada[b]	8.7	17.8	12.1	20.3	54.5	43.7	24.6	18.2
	Denmark[b]	18.8	25.8	11.5	22.3	55.6	39.3	14.2	12.7
	Finland[b]	..	10.8	..	39.8	..	31.0	..	18.4
	France	4.8	7.0	11.4	38.5	60.5	33.3	23.3	21.2
	Germany[b]	6.2	14.0	19.8	20.0	59.5	49.0	14.4	17.0
	Greece[b]	1.8	1.9	16.1	28.5	46.6	42.3	35.6	27.3
	Ireland[b]	3.4	4.4	7.5	20.5	65.8	58.1	23.3	17.0
	Italy	1.6	1.9	20.5	33.1	48.2	36.0	29.8	28.9
	Luxembourg[b]	3.2	1.8	11.0	26.1	77.1	61.7	8.7	10.4
	Netherlands[c]	12.6	32.0	21.0	18.9	48.7	40.6	17.7	8.5
	Portugal[d]	4.5	7.7	17.6	33.5	52.4	49.3	25.5	9.5
	Spain[d]	0.3	4.9	21.3	39.4	37.8	36.7	40.7	19.1
	United Kingdom	6.8	12.1	6.3	8.6	61.2	56.2	25.8	23.0
	United States	12.3	20.9	10.2	14.7	58.2	50.2	19.3	14.2
	OECD unweighted average	**6.6**	**11.1**	**14.8**	**25.4**	**55.8**	**46.2**	**22.8**	**17.3**

.. Data not available.

a. 1994 ; *b.* 1996 ; *c.* 1983 ; *d.* 1986.
Source: OECD School-to-Work Database.

Table 9. **Labour market and schooling status of persons aged 18 and 22 years, 1984 and 1997**
Percentages

		Proportion attending school		Proportion in some form of apprenticeship		Proportion not attending school and not in the labour force		Employment/ population ratio		Unemployment/ population ratio	
		1984	1997	1984	1997	1984	1997	1984	1997	1984	1997
Men	Australia[a]	26.4	41.6	18.1	11.9	2.1	3.8	66.0	53.7	17.2	16.3
18-year-olds	Austria	..	42.8	..	34.1	..	2.1	..	51.6	..	5.0
	Belgium	72.6	82.5	2.1	2.1	4.2	7.9	18.1	5.1	8.1	4.3
	Canada[b]	58.8	72.5	..	..	6.1	5.6	43.8	43.2	15.3	12.3
	Denmark[b]	41.5	51.7	30.6	29.1	1.7	2.3	66.3	70.3	8.0	9.3
	Finland[b]	..	86.1	..	..	..	1.0	..	19.1	..	19.1
	France	54.8	80.7	8.1	8.3	3.2	2.6	27.2	15.0	15.3	5.2
	Germany[b]	37.1	41.1	41.1	45.8	1.0	3.4	61.8	53.0	5.0	2.8
	Greece[b]	56.8	69.1	0.6	0.5	5.5	6.0	33.4	18.1	7.1	8.3
	Ireland[b]	41.8	63.5	6.1	2.4	1.3	3.4	43.5	27.1	18.3	8.6
	Italy	56.4	68.7	0.4	0.0	2.9	6.4	30.8	18.9	12.2	8.1
	Luxembourg[b]	44.0	72.1	21.8	6.7	3.1	3.6	50.5	16.3	3.6	5.5
	Netherlands[c]	68.1	73.0	3.3	7.1	4.5	6.3	26.3	56.8	10.6	5.5
	Portugal[d]	34.9	64.7	-	-	3.8	2.7	57.9	30.2	11.9	6.0
	Spain[d]	49.3	69.7	-	-	1.6	5.0	25.8	18.0	23.8	13.9
	United Kingdom	29.2	34.6	15.1	12.4	2.4	11.4	59.0	61.8	21.0	12.4
	United States	60.9	68.0	..	..	1.1	6.6	46.3	46.8	17.9	9.0
	OECD unweighted average	**48.8**	**63.7**	**11.3**	**11.5**	**3.0**	**4.7**	**43.8**	**35.6**	**13.0**	**8.9**
Men	Australia[a]	10.2	17.2	7.8	4.3	1.9	4.3	81.3	73.1	12.2	16.7
22-year-olds	Austria	..	32.6	..	1.6	..	3.8	..	69.3	..	4.4
	Belgium	36.9	38.0	1.7	0.9	2.4	6.0	51.8	46.7	14.7	11.9
	Canada[b]	23.3	37.4	..	..	6.4	5.6	62.4	62.6	17.3	11.5
	Denmark[b]	20.0	33.2	7.8	10.9	3.7	6.7	75.3	66.9	8.4	8.1
	Finland[b]	..	47.2	..	..	..	1.9	..	41.3	..	29.1
	France	15.0	43.1	0.4	2.0	2.6	3.3	72.6	42.1	14.3	15.6
	Germany[b]	23.8	26.1	5.1	9.0	1.4	4.2	68.3	66.4	8.5	8.4
	Greece[b]	21.9	29.8	0.1	0.2	3.4	3.7	64.3	54.9	13.1	13.8
	Ireland[b]	11.9	22.4	1.8	3.1	2.4	4.0	69.4	60.7	20.1	14.4
	Italy	24.5	29.5	0.2	0.2	3.4	9.1	58.7	46.0	17.3	18.1
	Luxembourg[b]	16.8	28.2	1.9	1.3	1.0	1.7	82.2	65.3	2.9	5.9
	Netherlands[c]	39.6	48.5	2.4	3.9	2.8	4.9	58.2	72.7	16.0	3.6
	Portugal[d]	19.6	36.4	-	-	4.9	2.9	70.9	62.4	11.9	9.6
	Spain[d]	18.5	38.3	-	0.0	2.3	2.8	46.8	49.3	32.6	17.8
	United Kingdom	14.6	18.2	1.3	3.5	2.3	8.4	76.0	72.8	15.1	11.5
	United States	25.5	35.3	..	..	0.9	6.4	76.1	73.2	12.4	7.0
	OECD unweighted average	**21.5**	**33.0**	**2.3**	**2.9**	**2.8**	**4.7**	**67.6**	**60.3**	**14.4**	**12.2**
Women	Australia[a]	28.6	51.4	6.5	7.5	6.9	5.5	59.3	50.9	14.6	17.5
18-year-olds	Austria	..	49.4	..	22.2	..	2.0	..	44.9	..	5.8
	Belgium	74.3	88.1	0.7	1.0	5.9	6.0	12.8	2.8	9.6	3.4
	Canada[b]	59.5	73.6	..	..	7.9	5.6	43.6	44.8	11.8	10.3
	Denmark[b]	50.2	78.3	21.3	6.1	3.3	1.7	57.3	54.4	7.1	12.1
	Finland[b]	..	84.6	..	..	..	2.1	..	22.6	..	23.7
	France	61.0	86.5	2.3	3.8	4.4	2.7	16.3	6.3	20.5	5.7
	Germany[b]	43.3	49.4	29.6	35.6	2.5	5.5	53.1	39.6	6.6	4.1
	Greece[b]	49.5	69.8	0.2	0.1	22.4	8.8	18.3	10.1	14.4	14.6
	Ireland[b]	50.6	77.0	1.4	1.0	2.2	3.8	37.1	16.4	18.6	7.9
	Italy	54.3	75.3	0.4	0.2	11.9	9.0	20.5	10.3	16.6	7.2
	Luxembourg[b]	45.4	81.0	7.5	2.1	3.4	1.9	50.3	15.4	3.0	2.2
	Netherlands[c]	65.9	78.0	0.8	5.3	4.8	4.9	27.4	54.0	12.8	7.8
	Portugal[d]	39.5	72.9	0.1	-	11.8	6.4	38.9	18.6	14.5	6.3
	Spain[d]	48.9	76.5	-	-	15.2	4.3	15.6	10.1	20.3	15.2
	United Kingdom	31.5	41.9	4.4	6.1	10.8	16.2	56.4	59.5	14.9	7.2
	United States	56.2	73.0	..	..	8.6	9.2	42.5	45.0	17.7	6.6
	OECD unweighted average	**50.6**	**71.0**	**5.8**	**6.5**	**8.1**	**5.6**	**36.6**	**29.7**	**13.5**	**9.3**

Table 9. **Labour market and schooling status of persons aged 18 and 22 years, 1984 and 1997** (*cont.*)
Percentages

		Proportion attending school		Proportion in some form of apprenticeship		Proportion not attending school and not in the labour force		Employment/ population ratio		Unemployment/ population ratio	
		1984	1997	1984	1997	1984	1997	1984	1997	1984	1997
Women 22-year-olds	Australia[a]	10.8	20.3	3.4	4.0	20.5	13.5	67.2	67.9	7.7	11.8
	Austria	..	29.6	..	1.6	..	5.5	..	65.9	..	5.5
	Belgium	26.1	35.3	0.9	..	9.2	11.7	50.1	43.9	19.1	12.2
	Canada[b]	18.4	38.8	..	..	16.6	13.0	64.1	60.4	10.8	8.6
	Denmark[b]	17.4	38.8	15.3	14.0	7.5	6.5	73.4	62.7	11.1	11.6
	Finland[b]	..	54.7	..	..	..	5.6	..	41.4	..	23.6
	France	16.7	44.3	0.2	1.5	14.4	7.8	59.1	38.5	16.1	17.8
	Germany[b]	19.7	23.7	3.4	9.2	12.7	15.2	63.3	59.5	7.2	7.4
	Greece[b]	14.3	30.5	0.2	0.2	41.8	18.6	35.3	34.7	12.1	19.9
	Ireland[b]	7.1	22.0	0.7	2.4	16.0	7.6	69.0	62.5	10.4	8.9
	Italy	19.5	39.9	0.2	0.3	22.7	16.5	41.3	30.2	20.0	18.2
	Luxembourg[b]	8.7	24.5	1.3	1.8	13.0	9.6	78.6	61.5	0.5	3.9
	Netherlands[c]	24.0	48.2	1.1	1.2	14.0	8.6	64.3	72.6	9.3	4.8
	Portugal[d]	24.2	45.4	-	-	21.3	5.0	45.5	51.3	14.3	6.7
	Spain[d]	24.9	50.5	-	0.1	21.3	5.3	28.3	33.2	25.8	22.1
	United Kingdom	9.2	18.2	0.8	1.6	26.1	21.4	59.4	63.7	10.1	6.8
	United States	19.8	36.0	..	..	15.8	12.4	65.5	69.0	11.3	5.2
	OECD unweighted average	**17.4**	**35.3**	**2.1**	**2.9**	**18.2**	**10.8**	**57.6**	**54.1**	**12.4**	**11.5**
Total 18-year-olds	Australia[a]	27.5	46.4	12.3	9.7	4.5	4.6	62.6	52.3	15.9	16.9
	Austria	..	46.4	..	27.7	..	2.1	..	48.0	..	5.4
	Belgium	73.4	85.1	1.4	1.6	5.0	7.0	15.6	4.0	8.8	3.9
	Canada[b]	59.1	73.0	..	..	7.0	5.6	43.7	44.0	13.5	11.3
	Denmark[b]	45.8	66.1	26.0	16.6	2.5	2.0	61.9	61.7	7.5	10.8
	Finland[b]	..	85.4	..	..	..	1.6	..	20.8	..	21.3
	France	58.0	83.5	5.1	6.1	3.8	2.6	21.5	10.8	18.0	5.4
	Germany[b]	40.2	45.0	35.3	40.9	1.7	4.4	57.4	46.6	5.8	3.4
	Greece[b]	52.9	69.5	0.4	0.3	14.4	7.5	25.4	13.9	11.0	11.7
	Ireland[b]	46.1	69.8	3.8	1.7	1.7	3.6	40.3	22.1	18.4	8.3
	Italy	55.3	71.8	0.4	0.1	7.4	7.7	25.6	14.8	14.4	7.6
	Luxembourg[b]	44.6	76.7	15.0	4.3	3.2	2.7	50.4	15.8	3.3	3.9
	Netherlands[c]	67.0	75.6	2.0	6.2	4.7	5.6	26.9	55.3	11.7	6.7
	Portugal[d]	37.0	69.1	0.1	-	7.6	4.7	49.0	23.9	13.1	6.2
	Spain[d]	49.1	73.1	-	-	8.5	4.6	20.7	14.0	22.1	14.6
	United Kingdom	30.3	38.2	9.8	9.4	6.6	13.7	57.8	60.7	17.9	9.9
	United States	58.6	70.5	..	..	4.7	7.9	44.4	45.9	17.8	7.8
	OECD unweighted average	**49.7**	**67.4**	**8.6**	**8.9**	**5.6**	**5.2**	**40.2**	**32.6**	**13.3**	**9.1**
Total 22-year-olds	Australia[a]	10.5	18.8	5.5	4.1	11.5	8.9	74.1	70.5	9.9	14.3
	Austria	..	31.1	..	1.6	..	4.6	..	67.6	..	5.0
	Belgium	31.8	36.7	1.3	0.5	5.6	8.7	51.0	45.4	16.7	12.1
	Canada[b]	20.9	38.1	..	..	11.5	9.3	63.3	61.5	14.1	10.0
	Denmark[b]	18.7	35.7	11.5	12.3	5.6	6.6	74.3	65.0	9.7	9.7
	Finland[b]	..	50.7	..	..	..	3.6	..	41.3	..	26.6
	France	15.9	43.7	0.3	1.8	9.0	5.7	65.2	40.2	15.3	16.8
	Germany[b]	21.8	24.9	4.3	9.1	7.0	9.7	65.8	62.9	7.9	7.9
	Greece[b]	17.7	30.2	0.2	0.2	24.5	11.6	48.3	44.2	12.5	11.6
	Ireland[b]	9.7	22.2	1.3	2.7	8.8	5.8	69.2	61.6	15.5	11.6
	Italy	21.9	34.8	0.2	0.3	13.3	12.9	49.8	38.0	18.7	18.2
	Luxembourg[b]	12.6	26.4	1.6	1.5	7.2	5.5	80.3	63.5	1.7	4.9
	Netherlands[c]	31.9	48.3	1.8	2.6	8.4	6.7	61.2	72.6	12.7	4.2
	Portugal[d]	22.1	41.2	-	-	14.0	4.0	56.9	56.5	13.2	8.0
	Spain[d]	21.5	44.2	-	0.1	11.3	4.0	38.1	41.6	29.4	19.9
	United Kingdom	12.0	18.2	1.1	2.6	13.9	14.7	67.9	68.4	12.7	9.2
	United States	22.5	35.6	..	..	8.8	9.5	70.5	71.1	11.8	6.1
	OECD unweighted average	**19.4**	**34.2**	**2.2**	**2.8**	**10.7**	**7.8**	**62.4**	**57.2**	**13.4**	**11.8**

.. Data not available. - Nil lor less than half of the last digit used.
a. 1994 ; *b.* 1996 ; *c.* 1983 ; *d.* 1986.
Source: OECD School-to-Work Database.

Table 10. **Labour force participation rates by age and gender, selected years**

		1979			1989			1997		
		15-19 year-olds	20-24 year-olds	25-54 year-olds	15-19 year-olds	20-24 year-olds	25-54 year-olds	15-19 year-olds	20-24 year-olds	25-54 year-olds
Australia	Men	61.4	90.2	94.5	59.5	89.2	92.7	52.9	84.3	90.6
	Women	55.0	69.2	51.4	57.1	77.5	65.3	53.6	75.3	68.6
Austria	Men	..	..	..	..	..	..	46.3	71.5	89.9
	Women	..	..	..	..	..	..	31.2	67.7	71.0
Belgium	Men	..	..	..	10.0	64.4	92.4	7.9	60.6	92.1
	Women	..	..	..	8.2	56.8	60.3	5.1	52.6	69.7
Canada	Men	57.3	86.5	94.9	60.6	84.9	93.8	47.6	79.2	91.1
	Women	51.1	72.4	58.5	56.7	77.6	74.7	45.9	71.8	76.6
Czech Republic	Men	..	..	..	..	..	..	26.0	82.5	95.2
	Women	..	..	..	..	..	..	19.9	57.8	82.0
Denmark	Men	..	..	..	69.5	88.3	94.5	70.0	85.0	92.5
	Women	..	..	..	61.4	80.2	86.6	65.4	74.5	81.7
Finland	Men	45.9	81.5	92.3	45.8	82.5	93.5	34.3	72.0	89.6
	Women	36.2	69.1	81.2	39.5	70.6	87.2	29.6	58.2	84.0
France	Men	26.5	80.1	96.3	14.9	69.3	95.6	9.4	54.3	94.8
	Women	20.0	68.9	63.0	9.4	59.9	72.1	4.3	44.9	77.3
Germany	Men	48.0	79.4	94.9	41.6	78.3	92.1	34.6	76.5	92.5
	Women	44.3	71.8	55.4	36.6	73.5	62.6	26.7	67.5	73.7
Greece	Men	..	..	..	22.7	72.0	94.4	15.5	66.7	94.6
	Women	..	..	..	17.9	53.9	51.6	13.3	52.9	57.5
Hungary	Men	..	..	..	..	..	..	16.5	69.5	85.0
	Women	..	..	..	..	..	..	11.8	48.9	67.2
Iceland	Men	..	..	..	..	..	..	45.0	75.5	96.7
	Women	..	..	..	..	..	..	46.5	77.4	85.1
Ireland	Men	50.2	91.2	95.0	31.6	80.7	91.8	25.9	75.7	90.5
	Women	41.9	68.6	27.6	25.0	74.4	42.9	19.5	67.5	58.4
Italy[a]	Men	33.0	71.7	93.3	26.4	71.5	90.8	21.5	57.5	85.3
	Women	28.6	55.4	38.9	22.8	63.9	48.6	16.5	48.1	50.9
Japan	Men	18.0	70.1	97.2	17.0	71.2	97.0	18.9	75.0	97.6
	Women	18.6	69.9	56.2	17.3	74.3	63.2	16.8	73.4	66.7
Korea	Men	..	..	..	11.7	60.2	94.0	8.6	56.9	94.0
	Women	..	..	..	18.7	63.6	54.1	13.0	66.4	58.4
Luxembourg	Men	..	..	..	28.7	74.8	94.7	11.9	62.5	93.4
	Women	..	..	..	24.3	71.4	48.0	7.8	59.4	58.0
Mexico	Men	..	..	..	..	..	..	59.7	85.6	96.8
	Women	..	..	..	..	..	..	31.3	41.9	46.1
Netherlands	Men	..	..	..	42.9	78.4	93.3	55.4	81.5	93.1
	Women	..	..	..	39.2	75.5	56.3	52.7	78.1	69.4
New Zealand	Men	..	..	..	58.6	88.7	94.0	55.9	83.5	92.1
	Women	..	..	..	54.5	69.3	68.5	55.7	72.0	72.5
Norway[b]	Men	43.2	62.6	92.8	47.0	79.9	93.3	47.7	78.4	92.6
	Women	40.7	61.0	66.0	46.0	70.3	79.0	43.3	68.8	83.3
Poland	Men	..	..	..	..	..	..	14.9	71.2	89.4
	Women	..	..	..	..	..	..	9.8	57.5	76.5
Portugal[c]	Men	67.9	91.9	94.7	52.5	83.5	94.4	26.8	68.8	92.9
	Women	54.8	71.3	53.6	39.9	69.3	67.8	20.0	57.6	76.8
Spain[b]	Men	57.9	83.3	95.6	44.8	77.7	93.9	30.4	65.6	92.6
	Women	43.4	55.6	30.2	32.7	62.2	44.9	21.3	56.0	58.1
Sweden[b]	Men	57.9	83.9	95.4	49.4	84.0	94.7	26.2	69.7	91.0
	Women	58.0	80.1	81.2	53.6	82.2	90.6	29.5	62.9	86.2
Turkey	Men	..	..	..	60.7	87.3	95.2	48.6	77.9	92.1
	Women	..	..	..	41.3	41.9	37.8	27.7	35.9	29.5
United Kingdom[b]	Men	..	..	..	74.5	91.2	94.9	63.7	83.2	91.6
	Women	..	..	..	70.8	75.9	71.9	60.9	70.1	75.0
United States[b]	Men	61.5	86.4	94.4	57.9	85.3	93.7	52.3	82.5	91.8
	Women	54.2	69.0	62.3	53.9	72.4	73.6	51.0	72.7	76.7
OECD	**Men**	**48.4**	**81.4**	**94.7**	**42.2**	**79.2**	**93.8**	**34.8**	**73.3**	**92.2**
unweighted average	**Women**	**42.1**	**67.9**	**55.8**	**37.6**	**68.9**	**64.0**	**29.7**	**62.1**	**69.2**

.. Data not available.

a. The age group is 25-59 instead of 25-54 ; b. The age group is 16-19 instead of 15-19 ; c. 1996 instead of 1997.

Sources: OECD, Labour Force Statistics, 1977-1997. Data for Belgium, Denmark, Greece and Luxembourg were provided by EUROSTAT.

Table 11. **Employment/population ratios by age and gender, selected years**

		1979			1989			1997		
		15-19 year-olds	20-24 year-olds	25-54 year-olds	15-19 year-olds	20-24 year-olds	25-54 year-olds	15-19 year-olds	20-24 year-olds	25-54 year-olds
Australia	Men	52.5	82.6	91.7	51.9	82.1	89.0	42.2	71.3	84.6
	Women	43.8	63.6	48.8	48.8	71.4	62.3	43.7	66.2	64.1
Austria	Men	..	..	..	..	..	..	43.5	67.7	86.5
	Women	..	..	..	..	..	..	26.7	64.5	67.7
Belgium	Men	..	..	..	8.4	57.6	88.1	5.8	50.7	86.4
	Women	..	..	..	5.8	46.1	53.1	3.1	39.7	62.6
Canada	Men	48.0	77.0	90.4	51.8	75.7	88.0	36.8	67.8	83.9
	Women	43.0	64.9	54.2	50.2	70.6	69.1	36.4	62.8	70.5
Czech Republic	Men	..	..	..	..	..	..	22.6	77.8	92.3
	Women	..	..	..	..	..	..	16.1	53.7	77.9
Denmark	Men	..	..	..	64.0	77.1	87.9	64.9	79.9	88.7
	Women	..	..	..	55.6	68.7	79.7	59.5	66.6	77.0
Finland	Men	38.3	75.0	87.3	39.4	78.7	91.3	25.3	57.8	80.3
	Women	30.3	63.9	77.8	34.0	66.1	85.5	19.5	46.4	74.6
France	Men	22.8	73.8	93.3	12.9	59.0	89.8	7.5	40.5	85.6
	Women	13.5	59.0	59.5	7.0	45.5	64.0	2.7	30.4	67.3
Germany	Men	46.9	76.8	93.0	39.7	73.3	87.1	31.7	68.0	85.1
	Women	42.2	67.7	53.3	34.3	68.3	57.7	24.4	60.8	66.0
Greece	Men	..	..	..	19.5	58.9	91.3	11.3	52.8	89.9
	Women	..	..	..	10.9	36.6	46.9	6.4	33.0	50.7
Hungary	Men	..	..	..	..	..	..	11.8	59.5	78.0
	Women	..	..	..	..	..	..	8.4	43.5	62.7
Iceland	Men	..	..	..	..	..	..	39.4	71.4	94.6
	Women	..	..	..	..	..	..	41.6	74.2	81.8
Ireland	Men	43.8	83.6	88.8	22.4	65.1	78.8	20.6	63.9	81.7
	Women	36.8	65.2	26.3	18.2	63.5	36.6	15.0	59.0	53.0
Italy[a]	Men	24.3	58.9	91.5	17.4	53.6	86.4	14.8	41.1	79.1
	Women	17.2	41.9	36.2	11.6	40.3	42.3	9.4	29.7	44.2
Japan	Men	17.0	67.9	95.7	15.6	68.5	95.5	16.9	70.3	95.1
	Women	18.1	67.6	55.2	16.3	71.5	61.9	15.6	68.9	64.6
Korea	Men	..	..	..	10.8	54.5	91.5	7.6	51.8	91.8
	Women	..	..	..	17.2	60.7	53.6	11.9	62.3	57.5
Luxembourg	Men	..	..	..	27.8	73.4	93.9	9.7	60.3	92.0
	Women	..	..	..	21.6	70.0	47.0	6.4	54.6	56.3
Mexico	Men	..	..	..	..	..	..	56.1	81.1	94.8
	Women	..	..	..	..	..	..	28.4	38.7	44.4
Netherlands	Men	..	..	..	36.9	71.2	88.2	47.9	76.4	89.7
	Women	..	..	..	31.1	67.5	50.0	44.2	73.2	65.0
New Zealand	Men	..	..	..	49.4	77.1	88.9	46.8	74.3	87.3
	Women	..	..	..	45.9	62.7	64.9	47.0	64.3	68.5
Norway[b]	Men	39.4	59.5	92.1	38.6	72.4	89.7	40.4	72.3	89.7
	Women	35.8	58.4	64.9	39.7	63.6	76.2	36.5	62.5	80.4
Poland	Men	..	..	..	..	..	..	10.6	56.6	82.1
	Women	..	..	..	..	..	..	6.0	42.4	67.3
Portugal[c]	Men	58.8	82.9	92.1	48.2	76.2	92.0	23.0	58.8	87.7
	Women	38.4	54.1	49.6	33.6	59.3	63.6	15.2	47.3	71.1
Spain[b]	Men	44.2	71.9	90.1	33.7	58.9	84.5	19.3	47.2	80.1
	Women	31.5	45.7	28.9	17.8	36.6	35.3	8.7	32.3	43.4
Sweden[b]	Men	52.5	80.7	94.2	46.8	81.2	93.6	19.6	55.3	82.6
	Women	52.0	76.9	79.8	50.8	79.6	89.5	22.6	50.8	78.6
Turkey	Men	..	..	..	50.2	72.9	90.0	42.3	66.2	88.1
	Women	..	..	..	35.2	34.5	35.2	23.9	30.1	28.1
United Kingdom[b]	Men	..	..	..	65.8	81.6	89.2	52.1	71.6	85.4
	Women	..	..	..	64.3	69.2	67.3	52.4	63.9	71.3
United States[b]	Men	51.7	78.9	91.2	48.7	77.8	89.9	43.4	75.2	88.4
	Women	45.3	62.4	59.0	46.4	66.4	70.4	43.3	66.8	73.5
OECD unweighted average	**Men**	**41.6**	**74.6**	**91.6**	**36.4**	**70.3**	**89.3**	**29.1**	**63.8**	**86.8**
	Women	**34.5**	**60.9**	**53.3**	**31.7**	**59.9**	**59.6**	**24.1**	**53.2**	**63.9**

.. Data not available.

a. The age group is 25-59 instead of 25-54.

b. The age group is 16-19 instead of 15-19.

c. 1996 instead of 1997.

Sources: OECD, Labour Force Statistics, 1977-1997. Data for Belgium, Denmark, Greece and Luxembourg were provided by EUROSTAT.

Table 12. **Unemployment rates by age and gender, selected years**

		1979			1989			1997		
		15-19 year-olds	20-24 year-olds	25-54 year-olds	15-19 year-olds	20-24 year-olds	25-54 year-olds	15-19 year-olds	20-24 year-olds	25-54 year-olds
Australia	Men	14.6	8.4	2.9	12.9	8.0	4.0	20.2	15.3	6.6
	Women	20.4	8.0	5.1	14.6	7.9	4.7	18.4	12.1	6.6
Austria	Men	..	..	..	..	..	..	6.0	5.3	3.8
	Women	..	..	..	..	..	..	14.5	4.7	4.6
Belgium	Men	..	..	..	16.3	10.7	4.6	27.2	16.4	6.2
	Women	..	..	..	29.5	19.0	12.0	39.3	24.4	10.2
Canada	Men	16.3	10.9	4.7	14.5	10.9	6.2	22.8	14.4	7.9
	Women	15.8	10.3	7.3	11.4	9.0	7.5	20.7	12.6	7.9
Czech Republic	Men	..	..	..	..	..	..	13.3	5.6	3.1
	Women	..	..	..	..	..	..	19.4	7.1	5.1
Denmark	Men	..	..	..	7.9	12.7	7.0	7.3	6.1	4.1
	Women	..	..	..	9.5	14.4	8.0	9.0	10.6	5.7
Finland	Men	16.7	8.0	5.4	14.1	4.6	2.3	26.3	19.8	10.4
	Women	16.2	7.6	4.3	13.8	6.4	1.9	34.0	20.2	11.1
France	Men	13.8	7.8	3.2	13.9	14.9	6.0	19.9	25.4	9.7
	Women	32.6	14.4	5.5	25.2	24.0	11.2	38.9	32.2	12.9
Germany	Men	2.4	3.2	2.0	4.7	6.5	5.4	8.3	11.2	8.0
	Women	4.7	5.6	3.8	6.2	7.1	7.9	8.8	9.9	10.4
Greece	Men	..	..	..	14.0	18.1	3.3	27.0	20.8	4.9
	Women	..	..	..	39.3	32.1	9.1	51.6	37.7	11.9
Hungary	Men	..	..	..	..	..	..	28.4	14.3	8.2
	Women	..	..	..	..	..	..	29.3	11.0	6.7
Iceland	Men	..	..	..	..	..	..	12.2	5.4	2.3
	Women	..	..	..	..	..	..	10.6	4.2	3.9
Ireland	Men	12.7	8.3	6.6	29.1	19.3	14.2	20.2	15.7	9.7
	Women	12.3	5.0	4.5	27.2	14.6	14.8	23.2	12.5	9.3
Italy[a]	Men	26.5	17.9	1.9	34.0	25.1	4.9	30.9	28.4	7.3
	Women	39.7	24.3	7.1	48.9	36.9	13.0	42.9	38.2	13.1
Japan	Men	5.4	3.2	1.6	8.0	3.8	1.5	10.3	6.2	2.5
	Women	2.7	3.3	1.9	6.0	3.8	2.2	7.6	6.1	3.2
Korea	Men	..	..	..	7.7	9.5	2.7	11.6	8.9	2.4
	Women	..	..	..	7.9	4.5	1.0	8.7	6.2	1.7
Luxembourg	Men	..	..	..	3.0	1.9	0.9	18.7	3.5	1.5
	Women	..	..	..	11.1	2.0	2.1	18.7	8.1	2.9
Mexico	Men	..	..	..	..	..	..	6.0	5.2	2.1
	Women	..	..	..	..	..	..	9.3	7.6	3.6
Netherlands	Men	..	..	..	14.1	9.2	5.5	13.6	6.3	3.7
	Women	..	..	..	20.5	10.5	11.1	16.0	6.2	6.5
New Zealand	Men	..	..	..	15.8	13.1	5.5	16.3	11.0	5.3
	Women	..	..	..	15.8	9.5	5.2	15.8	10.7	5.4
Norway[b]	Men	8.8	4.9	0.7	17.7	9.4	3.9	15.4	7.8	3.2
	Women	12.0	4.3	1.6	13.8	9.5	3.5	15.6	9.1	3.5
Poland	Men	..	..	..	..	..	..	28.6	20.5	8.2
	Women	..	..	..	..	..	..	39.1	26.2	12.0
Portugal[c]	Men	13.3	9.8	2.7	8.1	8.6	2.5	14.2	14.6	5.6
	Women	30.0	24.1	7.5	15.8	14.4	6.2	24.0	17.9	7.3
Spain[b]	Men	23.6	13.7	5.7	24.8	24.2	10.0	36.5	28.1	13.5
	Women	27.4	17.7	4.6	45.6	41.2	21.2	59.3	42.4	25.4
Sweden[b]	Men	9.7	3.8	1.3	5.4	3.3	1.1	28.2	21.7	9.4
	Women	10.5	4.0	1.7	5.4	3.1	1.2	26.7	20.4	8.9
Turkey	Men	..	..	..	17.3	16.4	5.5	13.0	15.1	4.3
	Women	..	..	..	14.6	17.7	6.9	13.8	16.3	4.8
United Kingdom[b]	Men	..	..	..	11.7	10.4	6.0	18.2	14.0	6.7
	Women	..	..	..	9.2	8.9	6.5	14.0	8.9	4.9
United States[b]	Men	15.9	8.7	3.4	15.9	8.8	4.1	16.9	8.9	3.7
	Women	16.4	9.6	5.2	14.0	8.3	4.4	15.0	8.1	4.1
OECD	**Men**	**13.8**	**8.3**	**3.2**	**14.1**	**11.3**	**4.9**	**18.5**	**13.4**	**5.9**
unweighted average	**Women**	**18.5**	**10.6**	**4.6**	**18.4**	**13.9**	**7.3**	**23.0**	**15.4**	**7.6**

.. Data not available.

a. The age group is 25-59 instead of 25-54.

b. The age group is 16-19 instead of 15-19.

c. 1996 instead of 1997.

Sources: OECD, *Labour Force Statistics*, 1977-1997. Data for Belgium, Denmark, Greece and Luxembourg were provided by EUROSTAT.

Table 13. **Low-paid employment among young people less than 25 years old: incidence, distribution and concentration[a]**

		Incidence[b]	Distribution[c]	Concentration[d]
Australia	1995	34.5	46.6	2.5
Austria	1993	19.5	24.3	1.5
Belgium	1993	22.2	34.7	3.1
Canada	1994	57.1	22.9	2.4
Finland	1994	27.1	11.5	4.6
France	1995	49.5	26.1	3.7
Germany	1994	50.4	58.6	3.8
Italy	1993	27.0	60.9	2.2
Japan	1994	36.4	41.4	2.3
New Zealand	1994/95	41.3	41.0	2.4
Sweden	1993	18.7	25.9	3.6
Switzerland	1995	44.0	38.8	3.4
United Kingdom	1995	45.8	28.5	2.3
United States	1994	63.0	21.6	2.5
Unweighted average		**38.3**	**34.5**	**2.7**

a. The data refer to full-time employees only. Low pay is defined as less than two-thirds of median earnings for all full-time workers.
b. Percentage of workers under the age of 25 who are low paid.
c. Low-paid youths as a proportion of all low-paid workers.
d. Incidence of low-paid youths divided by the overall incidence of low-paid employment.
Source: OECD (1996a).

Table 14. **Measures of young people in low-paid employment, 1986-1991[a]**
Weekly/monthly earnings of continuously employed full-time workers

Incidence of low-paid employment (percentage of workers under 25 who are low paid)			
	Ever low paid 1986-1991	Low paid in 1986	Always low paid 1986-1991
Denmark	12.1	7.9	0.0
France[b]	27.0	14.5	1.5
Germany	53.7	45.4	1.8
Italy	25.6	18.0	0.7
United Kingdom	42.7	39.0	7.3
United States	61.2	47.0	14.4

Relative incidence of low-paid employment			
(incidence of low-paid employment among workers under 25 relative to overall incidence of low-paid employment)			
	Ever low paid 1986-1991	Low paid in 1986	Always low paid 1986-1991
Denmark	2.7	3.3	0.0
France[b]	2.2	2.8	1.9
Germany	3.4	4.3	1.2
Italy	2.6	3.2	1.4
United Kingdom	2.7	3.4	1.9
United States	2.0	2.2	1.9

Average cumulative years in low-paid employment for workers who were low paid in 1986			
	Under 25	25-34	35-49
Denmark	1.7	1.7	2.3
France[b]	2.6	2.8	3.0
Germany	2.4	3.0	3.5
Italy	2.5	2.7	3.5
United Kingdom	3.1	4.1	4.6
United States	4.0	3.9	4.2

a. Low pay defined as less than two-thirds of median earnings of continuously employed full-time workers.
b. Data refer to 1984-1989.
Source: OECD (1997a).

Table 15. **Employment rates[a] over the first three to five years after leaving initial education by gender and educational attainment**

	Men			Women		
	First year	Third year	Fifth year	First year	Third year	Fifth year
Less than upper secondary						
Australia	65.1	65.9	75.9	55.4	45.5	39.2
France[b]	77.5	81.3	78.1	68.3	73.0	69.0
of which in subsidised jobs	25.0	16.3	7.2	30.6	24.0	10.0
Germany	87.5	91.9	88.5	73.7	79.2	72.6
Ireland	75.9	81.0	78.4	62.7	64.9	61.2
United States	49.5	64.8	79.8	31.6	31.9	39.3
Upper secondary						
Australia	74.9	74.9	82.5	78.2	75.4	74.2
France	..	..	..	..	..	..
Germany	88.2	96.3	95.0	83.6	89.9	86.0
Ireland	68.1	90.3	87.1	62.0	87.6	88.5
United States	71.6	77.7	85.9	61.1	68.0	71.1
University/tertiary						
Australia	78.2	84.0	87.0	79.0	77.6	77.6
France[c]	80.4	94.4	95.5	77.6	91.2	91.2
Germany	85.9	87.7	99.7	75.4	82.7	86.9
Ireland	73.7	83.6	..	78.6	94.0	..
United States	87.1	94.7	95.4	81.0	86.9	81.8

.. Data not available.
a. Defined as the percentage of the sample with a job.
b. Subsidised jobs refers to *Travaux d'utilité collective, Contrats d'emploi solidarité, Contrats d'adaptation* and *Contrats de qualification*. Time spent in obligatory national service is excluded.
c. Data refer to the first, third and fourth year after leaving initial education at the university/tertiary level.
Source: OECD (1998b).

Table 16. **Unemployment rates[a] over the first three to five years after leaving initial education by gender and educational attainment**

	Men			Women		
	First year	Third year	Fifth year	First year	Third year	Fifth year
Less than upper secondary						
Australia	30.5	29.7	19.6	28.7	23.9	21.6
France	15.4	16.7	20.2	23.5	21.0	24.0
Germany	11.7	7.7	13.0	15.5	8.9	16.9
Ireland	22.4	18.7	21.4	30.9	25.6	25.7
United States	42.2	29.4	14.9	47.9	34.6	28.1
Upper secondary						
Australia	22.6	22.6	14.8	16.0	13.8	9.9
France	..	..	..	..	..	..
Germany	9.8	1.8	3.7	9.0	5.9	5.9
Ireland	17.4	6.8	11.3	19.7	6.7	5.4
United States	20.5	15.8	8.6	21.5	14.4	11.0
University/tertiary						
Australia	21.2	14.5	9.5	17.0	13.3	10.5
France	14.4	4.4	3.8	17.2	5.4	5.3
Germany	4.9	12.3	3.7	17.9	0.6	0.0
Ireland	9.2	7.5	..	8.5	7.5	..
United States	10.0	3.5	2.6	9.7	5.7	4.2

.. Data not available.
a. Defined as the percentage of the labour force who are unemployed.
Notes and Sources: See Table 15.

Table 17. **Average cumulative time employed over the first three to six years after leaving initial education by gender and educational attainment conditional upon labour force status in the first year**[a]

Proportion of time

	Men			Women		
	Employed the the first year (1)	Unemployed the the first year (2)	Not in labour force the first year (3)	Employed the first year (4)	Unemployed the first year (5)	Not in labour force the first year (6)
Less than upper secondary						
Australia	0.78	0.40	0.36	0.79	0.20	0.08
France[b]	0.86	0.50	0.61	0.79	0.49	0.42
of which in subsidised jobs	0.17	0.15	0.11	0.22	0.14	0.13
Germany	0.93	0.56	0.37	0.88	0.49	0.47
Ireland[c]	0.88	0.38	0.62	0.83	0.23	0.20
United States	0.86	0.50	0.37	0.64	0.23	0.19
Upper secondary						
Australia	0.83	0.51	0.56	0.84	0.42	0.40
France	..	..	..	..	..	..
Germany	0.98	0.58	0.37	0.88	0.67	0.66
Ireland[c]	0.90	0.60	0.64	0.89	0.59	0.65
United States	0.89	0.55	0.42	0.84	0.44	0.36
University/tertiary						
Australia	0.89	0.53	0.33	0.84	0.56	0.41
France	0.96	0.62	0.54	0.94	0.61	0.43
Germany	0.96	0.80	0.71	0.92	0.78	0.18
Ireland[c]	0.92	d	d	0.90	d	d
United States	0.97	0.69	0.65	0.92	0.56	0.45

.. Data not available.

a. The figures refer to the percentage of time employed over a four-year interview period for Australia and France (university/tertiary), a five-year interview period for Germany and the United States, and a six-year interview period for France (less than upper secondary). Labour force status is determined at the time of each annual survey. The first year is included in the average cumulative time.

b. Time spent in subsidised jobs is included, while time in obligatory national service is excluded.

c. The figures refer to the per cent of months spent mainly in employment over a five-year period (less than upper secondary and upper secondary) and over a three-year period (university/tertiary). The data are based on retrospectively constructing annual work histories.

d. The sample size is too small for reliable estimates.

Sources: See Table 15.

Table 18a. **Distribution of time spent employed over the first three to six years since leaving initial education by gender and educational attainment**

Percentages

			Men								Women				
	Total	Never employed	Employed					Total	Never employed	Employed				
			one period	two periods	three periods	four periods	five periods			one periods	two periods	three periods	four periods	five periods
Less than upper secondary														
Australia[a]	100	8.3	7.4	14.8	16.7	15.7	37.1	100	37.3	12.7	6.9	4.9	7.8	30.4
France[b]	100	2.9	6.1	9.7	12.4	21.6	47.4	100	5.4	9.1	10.5	11.9	15.4	47.7
Germany[a]	100	1.5	2.5	1.7	7.2	20.8	66.3	100	7.9	2.4	6.3	4.7	33.4	45.3
Ireland[c]	100	6.5	3.8	5.9	13.2	15.2	55.4	100	16.9	7.8	9.6	14.2	8.4	43.1
United States[a]	100	7.8	8.8	12.1	18.6	21.9	30.9	100	29.1	25.3	12.8	15.9	10.6	6.4
Upper secondary														
Australia[a]	100	4.4	5.0	6.3	15.0	16.9	52.4	100	6.4	5.6	6.0	10.3	18.9	52.8
France	..	..	..	..	..	..	..	..	..	..	..	..	..	63.1
Germany[a]	100	0.0	2.0	2.2	2.7	12.1	81.1	100	0.7	1.9	7.7	5.8	20.8	63.1
Ireland[c]	100	2.1	2.3	4.4	9.4	28.4	53.4	100	2.4	2.5	4.6	9.4	30.2	50.9
United States[a]	100	2.9	5.4	8.3	12.9	22.1	48.4	100	8.4	9.4	13.3	13.4	19.9	35.5
University/tertiary														
Australia[a]	100	5.2	3.9	3.9	7.8	13.0	66.2	100	2.0	11.2	8.4	13.3	13.3	51.8
France[d]	100	6.7	4.9	18.7	38.1	31.6	..	100	3.6	3.7	7.4	21.6	63.7	..
Germany[a]	100	0.0	0.0	0.0	4.5	25.2	70.2	100	5.2	2.1	0.0	9.0	27.8	55.9
Ireland[e]	100	12.3	5.3	16.2	66.2	..	..	100	1.7	3.0	15.5	79.8	..	..
United States[a]	100	0.5	0.7	1.8	3.5	17.2	76.3	100	3.1	2.7	5.4	9.9	18.7	60.2

.. Data not available.

a. Data refer to the first five-year interview period since leaving education.

b. Data refer to the first six-year interview period since leaving education. The column "five periods" reports values for five to six periods. Especially for men, these figures are underestimates of those with three or more periods employed because those going directly into obligatory national service are excluded.

c. Data refer to the first five years since leaving education.

d. Data refer to the first four-year interview period since leaving education. Especially for men, these figures are underestimates of those with three or more periods employed because those going directly into obligatory national service are excluded.

e. Data refer to the first three years since leaving education.

Sources: See Table 15.

Table 18*b*. **Distribution of time spent unemployed over the first three to six years since leaving initial education by gender and educational attainment**

Percentages

	Total	Never unemployed	Unemployed					Total	Never unemployed	Unemployed				
Men								**Women**						
			one period	two periods	three periods	four periods	five periods			one periods	two periods	three periods	four periods	five periods
Less than upper secondary														
Australia[a]	100	39.8	18.5	16.7	16.7	2.8	5.5	100	65.7	14.7	11.8	2.0	2.9	2.9
France[b]	100	52.3	23.1	12.4	7.7	2.7	1.8	100	37.2	23.5	15.8	13.3	6.4	3.9
Germany[a]	100	71.8	16.4	6.4	1.7	3.7	0	100	72.9	18.1	4.2	2.7	2.0	0.2
Ireland[c]	100	58.7	12.6	12.8	5.9	3.8	6.2	100	60.2	10.4	8.9	4.9	5.2	10.4
United States[a]	100	38.0	28.5	19.9	6.1	5.1	2.3	100	43.6	31.2	16.1	6.1	2.1	1.0
Upper secondary														
Australia[a]	100	58.1	15.0	13.8	4.4	5	3.7	100	68.2	14.2	6.4	3.0	2.6	5.6
France	..	..	..	..	..	..	..	..	..	..	..	..	..	..
Germany[a]	100	85.1	9.6	3.6	1.5	0.2	0	100	79.4	15.4	4.1	0.6	0.0	0.6
Ireland[c]	100	70.6	18.5	5.8	2.0	1.9	1.2	100	76.0	16.8	3.7	2.0	0.9	0.6
United States[a]	100	58.3	22.7	12.8	4.3	1.7	0.2	100	62.0	23.4	9.8	3.6	0.8	0.4
University/tertiary														
Australia[a]	100	68.8	13.0	7.8	5.2	3.9	1.3	100	62.9	21.7	7.7	5.6	2.1	0.0
France[d]	100	83.9	12.7	2.4	0.8	0.3	..	100	77.4	16.5	4.3	1.3	0.5	..
Germany[a]	100	79.5	20.5	0.0	0	0	0	100	81.6	17.9	0.5	0.0	0.0	0.0
Ireland[e]	100	82.2	13.1	0.0	4.7	..	..	100	89.5	7.8	1.8	0.9	..	..
United States[a]	100	82.2	14.6	2.0	0.6	0.4	0.2	100	80.3	14.8	3.3	1.4	0.1	0.0

.. Data not available.

a. Data refer to the first five-year interview period since leaving education.

b. Data refer to the first six-year interview period since leaving education. The column "five periods" reports values for five to six periods. Especially for men, these figures are underestimates of those with three or more periods unemployed because those going directly into obligatory national service are excluded.

c. Data refer to the first five years since leaving education.

d. Data refer to the first four-year interview period since leaving education. Especially for men, these figures are underestimates of those with three or more periods unemployed because those going directly into obligatory national service are excluded.

e. Data refer to the first three years since leaving education.

Sources: See Table 15.

Table 19. **How widespread is youth unemployment?**

Percentage of young people with any time unemployed over five years after leaving initial education

	France	Germany	United States
All persons	..	27.8	57.2
Men	..	27.1	56.4
Women	..	28.6	58.0
Level of education			
Less than upper secondary	82.1	38.2	84.1
Upper secondary	..	25.1	69.6
University/tertiary	..	22.4	47.0

.. Data not available.
Sources: See Table 15.

Table 20. **How concentrated is youth unemployment by educational attainment over the first five years since leaving initial education?**

	France	Germany				United States			
	Less than upper secondary	All	Less than upper secondary	Upper secondary	University/ tertiary	All	Less than upper secondary	Upper secondary	University/ tertiary
Unemployed as a percentage of the population:									
Less than 3 months	5.6	6.7	9.3	4.2	9.0	28.1	27.9	28.5	27.9
3 to 6 months	5.9	9.5	9.1	9.8	9.4	10.8	16.3	12.3	9.4
6 to 9 months	6.6	3.4	5.6	3.4	1.0	6.5	7.7	9.6	4.5
9 to 12 months	5.6	3.1	4.5	3.5	0.0	3.5	9.0	5.8	1.6
12 to 24 months	25.6	3.7	6.8	2.6	3.1	6.5	16.1	10.9	2.8
24 to 36 months	16.8	0.8	1.4	0.8	0.0	1.5	5.1	2.2	0.8
36 months and over	15.9	0.8	1.4	0.8	0.0	0.3	2.1	0.3	0.1
Unemployed as a percentage of all weeks of unemployed:									
Less than 3 months	1.1	4.8	3.8	3.2	16.0	9.7	4.6	7.1	16.7
3 to 6 months	2.7	17.3	9.7	19.1	37.1	13.4	8.7	10.8	20.0
6 to 9 months	4.2	11.1	10.8	12.4	5.7	13.7	7.0	14.0	16.4
9 to 12 months	4.4	14.2	13.4	17.5	0.0	10.9	10.8	11.7	9.5
12 to 24 months	24.9	27.6	31.4	22.4	41.3	33.1	34.5	37.8	24.4
24 to 36 months	25.2	10.2	11.9	10.9	0.0	15.2	22.4	15.8	10.6
36 months and over	37.5	14.8	19.0	14.5	0.0	4.1	11.9	2.9	2.3

Sources: See Table 15.

Table 21. **Main apprenticeship/training contracts aimed at youths**

	Description	Duration	Financial incentives for employers	Qualification	Scope
Australia Apprenticeship	The apprentice works for an employer (or a group of employers) and attends a training institution (TAFE college or private providers), normally one day a week.	4 years	Apprentice pay is set below that of a comparable worker. Wage subsidies to the employers.	Certificate issued by a State Training authority.	In 1996, there were 120 000 apprentices (7% of employees aged 15-24). 38 000 started in the year.
Traineeship	Operating in occupations other than traditional trades, such as in office-based and retail industries.	12 months	Same as above	Same as above	Around 47 000 started in 1996
Austria Apprenticeship	Training in state-recognised occupations, taking place both at the workplace (4/5) and in a vocational institution (1/5). Training is based on regulations. There are 244 listed apprenticeship trades.	3 or 4 years	Apprentice pay set below that of adult unskilled workers. Subsidies to apprentices or employers in gender-specific jobs and for disadvantaged young people.	The apprenticeship ends with an examination leading to a Journeyman's Certificate. Access to tertiary education through a special exam.	In 1996, there were 128 000 apprentices (24% of employees aged 15-24).
Denmark Vocational education and training	Education and training at school alternates with training in the enterprise. There are 86 courses in trade and technical fields, and more than 200 specialities.	3 to 5 years	Apprentice pay is lower than average wages. Wage subsidies were introduced in 1990, but are now being scaled down.	The programme ends with a vocational test, leading to a professional qualification.	In 1996, there were 114 000 apprentices (25% of employees aged 15-24).
France Apprenticeship Contracts	Training is undertaken in specialised centres. All employers can use these contracts. The apprentice works under the responsibility of a "master".	1 to 3 years, depending on the profession and the level of qualification.	The wage paid is lower than the legal minimum wage, and rises with age and tenure. Reduction of social security contributions. Premium paid to the employer according to the age of the apprentice and the duration of training.	Traditionally, the training is formally recognised by a certificate of vocational competence (CAP), but it is now being extended to diplomas of higher level.	In December 1997, there were 340 000 apprentices (14% of employees aged 15-25). (*Source:* DARES)
Skill Training Contracts (*Contrats de Qualification*)	Open to all employers with few exceptions. A minimum of 25% of the total duration of the contract must be spent in a general or vocational education institution.	6 to 24 months.	The wage paid is lower than the legal minimum wage, and rises with age and tenure. Reduction of social security contributions. Subsidies towards the cost of hiring and training.	Traditionally, the training is formally recognised by a certificate of vocational competence (CAP), but it is now being extended to diplomas at higher levels.	In 1997, 129 000 young employees had a qualification contract (5% of employees aged 15-25). (*Source:* DARES)

Table 21. **Main apprenticeship/training contracts aimed at youths (*cont.*)**

	Description	Duration	Financial incentives for employers	Qualification	Scope
Germany Dual system	1 or 2 days a week are spent in training colleges providing a combination of vocational and general education. There are some 375 state-recognised occupations. Training regulations for each occupation are set jointly by the employers and trade unions.	3 years	Apprentice pay is lower than the collectively-agreed wage.	Diploma	In 1996, around 1 590 000 apprentices (41% of employees aged 15-24). 574 000 started in the year.
Ireland Apprenticeship (reformed in 1996)	Modular approach allowing for flexibility and cross-skilling: 3 phases of off-the-job broad-based training (lasting 40 weeks in total) and 4 phases of on-the-job. Primarily concentrated in skilled craft trades.	4 years	Apprentice pay is set below that of a comparable worker. Wage subsidies to employers.	From 1996, based on standards achieved rather than time served.	In 1996, there were 10 800 apprentices (5% of employees aged 15-24 years)
Netherlands Apprenticeship contracts	Training is offered at the workplace and in an education/training institution one day per week. The number of contracts may be collectively agreed by the social partners.	2 or 3 years	Apprentice pay is set below that of a comparable worker. Wage subsidies to employers.	Certificate	In 1996, there were 148 000 apprentices (14% of employees aged 15-24).
Norway Apprenticeship within the "2+ model" (from 1994)	2 years of school + 2 years of apprenticeship with a firm. The content of education (both general and vocational) was broadened and new places were created in white collar and service occupations. Pupils who are not able to obtain an apprentice place can follow an advanced course at school.	2 years	The apprentice pay is stipulated in the wage agreement of the trade and is about half that of a skilled worker. Subsidies to enterprises and the training establishments.	Journeyman's qualification. Access to higher education by taking an additional half a year of general education.	The number of apprenticeship contracts has increased from 19 000 in 1993 to 28 000 in 1996.
United Kingdom Modern Apprenticeship (from 1994)	Written agreement between the employer and the apprentice, specifying the training content and qualifications to be attained. Offered in 76 sectors.	3 years	Apprentice pay is set below that of a comparable worker. The government contributes towards the cost of off-the-job training.	NVQ Level 3	In February 1998, there were 117 000 apprentices.
National Traineeships (from 1997)	Same as above, but limited to 39 sectors.	2 years	Same as above	NVQ level 2	..

Sources: Eurostat Vocational Education and Training data collection; European Commission (1997*a*, *b*); OECD (1998*e*).

Table 22. **Examples of recent educational reforms at the secondary level that reinforce the vocational stream, selected countries**

Country	Year	Description
Ireland	1995	The Leaving Certificate programme (senior secondary level), is being restructured into three components: - the established Leaving Certificate Programme, with emphasis on general academic education; - the Leaving Certificate Applied Programme; - the Leaving Certificate Vocational Programme. The latter two form part of the Vocational Preparation and Training Programme (VPT-1). The second component of VPT (VPT-2) consists of courses generally taken after completion of secondary education.
Norway	1994	The new system provides all young people with an entitlement to 3 years of upper secondary education, to be exercised within a 4-year period. The general education content of vocational courses has been increased and vocational study areas broadened to include wider occupational or industry groupings. The apprenticeship pathway has been strengthened.
Spain	Introduced in 1992, will be fully operational in 1999.	Compulsory education has been extended to 10 years and basic technical training will be included. The curricula are being designed by the education administration, employer organisations and unions in each province. Vocational training modules include work practice in local firms. The number of places available is currently being negotiated by firms, unions and schools.
Sweden	1991	Re-organisation of upper secondary schooling to provide 16 programmes, 2 theoretical and 14 vocational. All vocational programmes have been extended to 3 years. Vocational study programmes involve unpaid external work experience in structured work placements occupying 15% of the student's time.

Sources: European Commission (1997a); OECD (1998e).

Table 23. **Training and remedial education programmes aimed at unemployed and disadvantaged youths, selected countries**

Country	Target groups	Programme structure	Monitoring and/or evaluation results
Czech Republic Bridge Project	15-18-year-olds who have only basic or incomplete basic education.	Provision of a mix of counselling, training and job placements for a period of 4.5 months. Retraining is offered at a technical-vocational school and with an employer. The training is recognised with a certificate of basic vocational qualifications. Participants are then offered an internship with an employer; if this does not prove successful, the young person returns to the labour office for more guidance and training.	After 4 rounds of the programme since 1994, the labour office reports that of the 169 trainees concerned, 143 had successfully completed the programme, and, of these, 103 were employed.
Denmark Youth package	Youths aged under 25, in receipt of unemployment benefit for 6 months with little or no qualifications.	Right and obligation to take part in normal education or special courses for at least 18 months, earning an allowance corresponding to about half the unemployment benefit.	Survey analysis results: 1 1/2 years after the introduction of the package, 75% of unemployed youths had left unemployment, 12% were in activation programmes or on leave, and 13% were unemployed.
Ireland Youthreach Programme	Youths aged 15 to 18 who leave school without qualifications.	Regulated by the Dept. of Education. The first phase is spent in Youth Centres where basic skills are provided. In the second phase, skills needed in the labour market are taught in PES Community Training Workshops.	Poor outcomes: after completion, 30% of participants were at work; 57% were unemployed; 6% were attending education or a training scheme (O'Connell and Sexton, 1995).
United States Job Corps	Severely disadvantaged youths.	Highly intensive programme that provides basic education, vocational skills, and a wide range of supportive services, including job placement services after completion, in a residential setting.	JC participation appeared to increase educational attainment and earnings and to reduce welfare dependency and criminality. As these evaluation results are based on quasi-experimental methods carried out 20 years ago, DOL is now running a new random-assignment evaluation.
Job Start	Same as above.	Demonstration programme with the purpose to determine whether a programme with the intensity of Job Corps, but run in a non-residential setting, could be cost-effective.	JS raised educational attainment, but provided generally disappointing employment results.

Sources: European Commission (1997a and 1998); OECD (1998e); Stanley et al. (1998).

Table 24. **Special employment contracts for young people**

Country and title of the programme	Target group	Programme description	Other conditions for eligibility	Scope
Belgium Springboard jobs (suppressed in 1998).	Youths aged under 30 who have not previously worked for 6 months or more.	Indefinite-term work contracts. Wage reduced to 90% of the normal wage for the first 12 months of the contract. Shorter notice period for 3 years.		On 1/03/98, 2 685 contracts (*Source:* Ministère Fédéral de l'Emploi et du Travail).
Work-training contracts	Job-seekers under 30 years of age.	Each private or public sector employer employing at least 50 persons is obliged to engage, for at least 6 months (12 months in the public sector), youth from the target group in numbers equal to 3% (2% for the public sector) of the labour force.		In 1998, 16 414 young people were employed on these contracts (*Source:* Ministère Fédéral de l'Emploi et du Travail).
France Adaptation contracts	Youth aged 15 - 25 years.	Wage paid corresponds to at least 80% of the collectively agreed wage but cannot be lower than the legal minimum wage. The employer is supposed to provide training. Maximum duration: 1 year.		In Dec. 1997, 43 000 young people aged 15-25 were employed with an adaptation contract (*Source:* DARES).
Italy Work training contracts (CFL)	Registered youth aged 15-29 years with at least upper secondary education.	Reduction of social security contributions. Maximum duration: 1 year. The employer must impart the training.	Hiring on a CFL is conditional upon renewal of at least 50% of previous CFL in the last 2 years. Reductions of social security contributions are extended for a further 12 months if the contract is transformed into a permanent one.	In 1996, approximately 14% of employees aged 14-24 years. A further 7% among employees aged 25-32 (*Source:* ISFOL).
Portugal Employment subsidy	Youths aged 16-30 years and the long-term unemployed.	Exemption from social security charges to employers. Full subsidy rate only if the contract is permanent.	The number of employees in the firm must have increased in comparison to the end of the last calendar year	1995: 43 000 youth were hired under the programme.
Spain Practice contracts	Youth aged less than 30 years who have left the education system for no more than 2 years.	Maximum duration: 2 years. Reduction in social security contributions. Wages are set lower than the collectively agreed ones for a comparable worker.	If no renewal, the employer cannot fill the position with a fixed-term contract for one year. Further 2-years reduction in social security contributions if worker is given a permanent contract upon expiry of the practice contract.	2% of young workers aged <30 in 1997 (*Source:* INEM).
Training contracts	Unskilled youth aged 16-21.	Maximum duration: 2 years. Reduction in social security contributions.	Same as above.	10% of young workers aged under 25 in 1997 (*Source:* INEM).

Sources: European Commission (1997*a,b*); OECD (1998*b*).

Table 25. **Job creation programmes aimed at young people**

Type of programme	Countries	Examples
Programmes specifically aimed at youths.	Canada; France; Ireland; the Netherlands; New Zealand; the United States.	Canada, *Youth Service Canada*: work for non-student youth who face great barriers to entering the labour market in community service projects.
		France, *New Services, Youth Jobs* initiative: aims to create new jobs for young people in social services catering for unfulfilled needs.
		United States, *Job Corps*: team-work in service projects, usually lasting for 6-12 months, for highly disadvantaged youths. Accompanied by some training.
		The Netherlands, *Jobseekers Employment Act* (WIW) municipalities place youth aged below 27, threatened with LTU, in temporary jobs.
		New Zealand, *Youth Service Corps*: provides young school leavers with opportunities with work experience and work-skill acquisition through participation in community-oriented projects.
Programmes aimed at disadvantaged workers, including at-risk youths.	Austria; Belgium; Finland; France; Germany; Italy; New Zealand; Norway; the Netherlands; Poland; Hungary; and the United States.	Austria, *Aktion 8000*: temporary contracts (max 12 months). Pay corresponding to the local standard and the relative collective agreement. Subsidy corresponding to 66% of TLC for up to 12 months in the non-profit sector and 50% in case of PA.
		Italy, *Socially useful jobs*: work cannot exceed 80 hours a month for a maximum of 12 months. Projects can be sponsored by social co-operatives.
Workfare programmes	Australia; Denmark; Finland; the Netherlands; the United States; and the United Kingdom.	United Kingdom, *New Deal* arrangements: 6-month jobs with the Environment Task Force or in the voluntary sector for young people unemployed for at least 6 months.

Sources: European Commission (1997b); national submissions to the OECD.

PLENARY SESSION:

WHAT HAVE WE LEARNED OVER THE PAST TWO DECADES
ABOUT THE NATURE OF YOUTH LABOUR MARKET PROBLEMS

THE YOUTH JOB MARKET PROBLEM AT Y2K

by
Richard B. Freeman
Harvard University, United States
NBER and the Centre for Economic Performance, LSE

Introduction

If your local mad scientist or shaman offered you a Ponce de Leon Fountain of Youth potion that would restore you to age 25 you would almost certainly accept it. You'd be healthier, stronger, more able to party all night (...) and get up the next morning and do it again. You wouldn't have to worry about thinning hair, expanding waistline, and the other signs of senescence. Only one thing would worsen if you made the trade: your labour market prospects. As the OECD has pointed out in its rationale for this conference, as we approach Y2K the career employment and earnings opportunities for young workers are worse now in most OECD countries than they were 20-30 years ago.

In much of western Europe, youth unemployment is high, with young workers waiting long periods of time before they find a job and remaining in their parental home longer than the previous generation. Even in the full employment US, highly educated young persons in bio-medical science, the area most likely to produce the Ponce de Leon potion, have diminished opportunities, while an extraordinary proportion of the least educated young men end up in jail or prison.[1]

– What has gone wrong with the youth labour market?

– How have youths responded to the deteriorated job market facing them?

What, if anything, can we do to improve the youth labour market?

This paper examines these questions. If I give complete unassailable answers, our hosts could close the conference this morning and let us all go out and (...) see the tourist sites, party and do it again. But succeeding sessions will surely add considerable information and insight into the youth labour market problem at Y2K and some of my comments may prove controversial.

1. What has gone wrong with the youth labour market?

The facts for young men are simple. Along a variety of dimensions the economic position of male workers in the age bracket 20 to 24 has worsened relative to that of older workers (see Table 1).

– The age-earnings profile has twisted against young men, so that the earnings of the young, especially those with less than university training, are lower now relative to those of older workers than they were 20-30 years ago.

– The ratio of youth to adult unemployment has held roughly constant, implying that in high unemployment OECD countries, the absolute level of joblessness of young workers has risen relative to that of older workers.

– The rate of employment among youths no longer enrolled in school has fallen relative to that of prime age adults.

– An increasing proportion of young workers find employment in jobs which traditionally require less education than they have.

The situation among young women is less troubling, as young women have continued to move into the job market in increasing numbers and as female pay has improved relative to male pay. Still,

– Young women make less than seemingly comparable young men.

– The age-earnings profile has tilted against young women as against young men.

– The unemployment rate for young women workers has risen in most countries.

– Poverty has become increasingly concentrated among single parent female-headed households.

One simple statistic captures the overall change in the labour market position of young workers. This is the ratio of the young persons' share of personal income to the ratio of their share of the population of persons aged 15 and over. The share of personal income going to young workers is the multiplicand depends on both their relative earnings and relative employment (and any changes in their share of non-labour market income). Column 1 of Table 2 records the population share among men of two age groups – 15-24 and 25-34 – in the US. Column 2 gives the share of personal income going to those groups, while column 3 gives the ratio of shares. For both groups the share of income going to the young has fallen substantially more than the share of the population in the groups, producing a marked fall in the relevant ratios. The pattern among women in columns 4-6 is similar. In the US, the shift in income among age groups is also evinced in rates of poverty. The rate of poverty among the elderly has fallen substantially but the rate of poverty among children, who are invariably in households headed by young adults, has not. Since the relative pay of youths has fallen in other OECD countries as well as in the US and relative employment of youth has also trended downward, the findings in Table 2 should generalise to other countries. Young persons are getting a proportionately smaller share of income than they did 20 or so years ago.

– What makes the worsening of the job market for young workers in the 1980s and 1990s remarkable is that many of the basic economic forces that affect youth employment prospects went in the opposite direction.

– The youth share of the population fell. Many analysts and policy-makers expected that the demographic change would essentially eliminate the youth employment problem save for socially excluded groups.

– The composition of employment among industries shifted toward sectors that hire relatively many workers - retail trade and services like hotels and restaurants. This should have increased employment if not the wages of young workers.

– The technological factor that many analysts cite as underlying the long run rise of inequality and higher premium on skills – computerisation – should have benefited the young, who have grown up with computers, relative to older workers, who have not.

– The years of schooling attained by young workers relative to that of older workers increased in most countries. This should have raised their relative pay and employment.

In addition to the fall in the position of young workers relative to older workers, there has been a significant rise of inequality in earnings among young workers, at least in the United States. As Table 3 shows, the earnings of more educated workers relative to those of less educated workers has risen sharply – more so among the young than among older workers, particularly among men. Inequality within education groups has also gone up, though data for the US here tell a more mixed story about whether inequality rose more or less among the young than among the old. At the same time, the gender gap has declined most among young workers.

Why the deterioration?

If demographic factors and long term demand worked to improve the situation for young workers, why did their economic position deteriorate?

Table 4 presents a list of potential factors that caused the deterioration. One reason is that aggregate unemployment was relatively high in OECD countries in the 1980s-1990s. The demand for young workers is highly sensitive to aggregate economic conditions (Blanchflower and Freeman, 1996; Clark and Summers, 1982, pp. 199-235). As new entrants to the job market, young workers lack the specific training or seniority that buffers older workers from swings in market conditions. Their employment is highly dependent on the aggregate state of the labour market. High rates of unemployment in the EU thus go a long way to explaining the prevailing rate of youth joblessness, though an adverse trend remains for young men (but not for young women) [OECD (1996)]. The fall in joblessness in the US in the late 1990s produced some rise in youth wages, as well as employment, after two or so decades of decline. But it did not come close to restoring the relative position of young workers.

The influx of women into the job market may also have affected the economic position of young workers. Many women workers are new entrants or re-entrants into the job market who might fill jobs that younger workers would otherwise hold. But female pay has increased as the supply of women to the workforce has grown. Since we would expect the effects of an increase in the supply of women to be greater on women than on substitute young male workers, any "cherchez la femme" story is difficult to sustain.

Increased trade with third world countries might also have a negative effect on the economic position of young workers. The share of youths in the working age population worldwide is much larger than just the share in advanced countries. Thus, trade with Least Developed Countries (LDCs) might be expected to reduce the relative position of young workers. But again, the sectors which compete most with less developed countries are those such as apparel that traditionally employ women workers, so one would expect trade to have devastated their wages or employment rather than that of young men.[2]

All told, it is highly unlikely that much of the youth economic problem is due to supply side factors. The increased supply of competitive workers due to women or trade may have affected the position of young workers, but these forces do not seem sufficiently powerful to counteract the demographic and demand factors that favoured young workers. To explain the observed deterioration in terms of labour supply, we must argue that workers in the baby-boom generation are highly substitutable with younger workers so that the baby-boom cohort reduced not only their earnings but those in the ensuing smaller cohorts as well. As the baby-boom cohort gets older and older, however, and the economic position of young workers remains depressed, this becomes an increasingly tenuous claim.

But there is yet another supply side possibility that may resonate with those who need the Ponce de Leon potion. This is that young workers are simply not as good as older workers. Test scores for younger and older workers in the OECD international adult literacy survey reject this explanation save for the US and Ireland. This survey, conducted in 1994, gave adults in several countries the same test of their literacy skills – prose, document and literacy. Columns 1 and 2 of Table 5 record the proportion of young persons

(16-25) who scored high and low in document literacy, respectively. Column 3 shows the difference between the proportions of young who scored high and the proportion who scored low. A positive number in column 3 means that proportionately more younger persons were in the top category than in the lowest category, while a negative number means that more young persons are in the lowest category. The figures for all countries except the US and Ireland are positive. For contrast, column 4 records the analogous difference for workers aged 46-55 where the figures are generally negative, implying that there were considerably fewer "more skilled" workers than "less skilled" workers in the older cohort. With the striking exception of the US, the difference between columns 3 and 4 is positive, implying that the younger cohort is relatively more skilled than the older cohort. Even in the US, moreover, the difference in skills is modest.[3]

In sum, it is difficult to make a case for shifts in demand or supply or for deterioration of youth skills as causing the worsened job market for young workers. High unemployment explains some of the jobless problem among EU youths and some of the fall in relative wages of youths in the US.

2. How have youths responded to the deteriorated job market?

People respond to labour market developments in two ways: through individual actions, moving from areas of low or declining opportunity into areas of large or rising opportunity; and through collective action, protesting declines in income and seeking redress from the state. The 1980s-1990s deterioration in the youth job market has seen considerable individual responsiveness but little collective protest or action.

Individual supply responses have taken three forms:

- Greater enrolments in higher education, particularly outside the US. Among Americans, the proportion of young workers enrolled in college and university fell in the 1970s, then rose from the mid-1980s to the late 1990s. But the rise in enrolments has been larger in other OECD countries, so that the US has lost much of its edge in producing college/university graduates.

- Shifts in the fields of study and occupations that students choose. In the US students have shifted from sciences and liberal arts into business related areas. The flow of students toward relatively higher paying fields should have increased the earnings of young workers relative to the earnings of older workers.

- Longer times until marriage, family formation, and child-bearing. Between 1971 and 1994, the proportion of 16-24 year-old American men who were heads/spouses in their own family fell from 22% to 11%; while in Canada the proportions dropped from 16% to 8%. Among women the trends were similar: a drop from 36% to 24% in their own family in the US and a drop from 30% to 17% in Canada (Card and Lemieux, forthcoming).

Taken together, increased schooling and residence in parental homes has elongated the period of youthful preparation for the job market and family formation. The "young" are older than they were several decades ago.

By contrast, there has been little collective action by youths to improve their economic situation. With the sole exception of French youths who protested proposed youth sub-minimum wages in 1995 and low teacher-pupil ratios and school quality in 1998, there has been virtually no collective youth response to the worsened job prospects. High youth joblessness in Spain, Italy, and the UK, has not generated another Danny the Red (Daniel Cohn-Bendit), mass student movements, or the conflict of the generations that marked the 1960s. In the US the American Association of Retired Persons raises the battle cry for the old, but there is no countervailing force on behalf of young workers.

Why haven't youths protested? Table 6 lists some possible factors.

One possible explanation is that, economics aside, youths are happier than in the past. Blanchflower and Oswald (forthcoming) state that youths report greater happiness or life satisfaction than before. Perhaps sex, drugs, the end of the cold war, postponement of family responsibilities, and improved consumption have offset the fall in relative earnings and employment. But the increased happiness of youths is not evinced in one hard statistic: the relative number of suicides by young people, which have trended differently across countries. Suicide rates among young men rose between the 1970s and 1990s in English-speaking countries and Norway. They fell in Japan, Sweden, Austria and in the former Federal Republic of Germany, and show little change elsewhere.

Another explanation is that the worsened employment and earnings opportunities of young workers is a temporary state that simple ageing will eliminate. Perhaps an extra year to find a permanent job or a drop in starting pay are transitional glitches with little or no consequences for one's lifetime income prospects. What matters is permanent income – the discounted present value of lifetime incomes – not transitory incomes. In fact, the lifetime incomes of young workers are affected by their entering the world of work in a depressed job market. Cohorts who start off in worsened conditions historically do not recover from the initial adverse shock on their economic prospects. A cohort that enters the job market in a bad period will not "catch-up" to the position it would have had if it had entered in a good period. At best, the lifetime income profile of the cohort will follow a "normal" path, beginning at a lower starting point.

What is the comparison?

Even if young workers suffer a permanent loss in real income compared to what they might have made absent the depressed market, they are still likely to have higher lifetime incomes than earlier generations. In a world of rising per capita incomes, it would take an extraordinary shock for young cohorts to end up with lower incomes than older cohorts. Consider two groups of workers, parents and youngsters separated by 25 years. Both groups' income consists solely of labour market earnings. With a growth rate of real earnings of 1.5% per year due to technological change and human and physical capital accumulation, the younger generation will have a 45% higher discounted lifetime income than the older generation. Even a 20% permanent fall in the real earnings of the younger cohort relative to their parents will leave them with a 25% income advantage. Thus, if youths compare their lifetime income to that of older workers, the fact that they are better off (though less so than they might have been) may also dampen collective sentiments for protest.

Note also that the "rising tide" of growth argues against programmes designed solely to redistribute income toward younger people. As long as the older generation provides the young with education and physical capital, the young have higher lifetime incomes than the old. Your local 20-25 year-old may have problems in the job market today, but he or she will still enjoy a higher standard of living than your local 45-50 year-old.[4] In some situations, moreover, improvements in technology will make the lives of younger cohorts almost incommensurately better. Today, medicine cannot cure the wealthiest person with AIDS and certain cancers, but in the future, medicine will presumably cure the poorest person with those diseases. From this perspective, the drop in the relative earnings of the young is an egalitarian redistribution. If you had to choose to reduce the earnings of older or younger workers or to have older or younger workers jobless, it is better to have the burden fall on the young.

That each generation should (and will) do better than the previous generation is part-and-parcel of the modern economic world. To what extent has the depressed youth job market challenged this notion? Into the late 1990s, surveys in the US reported that a rising proportion of the population believed that their children would not enjoy the benefits of the rising tide. In 1997, 67% of Americans said that they thought the "economic situation" for their children would be worse than for their generation (Yankelovitch,

1997). Given trends in the real earnings of median workers in the US in the 1970s-1990s, this was not an unrealistic expectation for many Americans. I would expect Americans to have a more optimistic view as the economic boom of the late 1990s has continued. I do not know whether rising real wages or high unemployment in the EU creates more or less optimistic views toward the future than those expressed by Americans.

But there is another possible comparison. Perhaps youths do not compare themselves much with the older generation. Older persons may remember that they had a relatively better employment situation when they were young, but the young can hardly be expected to look at historical age-earnings ratios and take to the streets. Perhaps youths compare themselves largely with their peers. In this case, a fall in the ratio of incomes of the young to the old will not produce generational conflict. Everyone in a youth cohort may have a depressed income, but those at the top of the group might regard their situation as good rather than poor.

If the right comparison group are persons within a youth cohort, there are two telling statistics. First, for the US at least, inequality in earnings has, as noted, risen substantially among the young. Second, Table 7 shows that in 1996 there was a significant concentration of youth unemployment or inactivity in households where no other person is employed. In the majority of OECD countries for which trend data exist, moreover, the concentration of unemployed in jobless homes has increased. From this perspective, the "real problem" in the youth job market is that society is sorting young people into two groups – the educated, skilled, and well–paid; and the less educated, unskilled, and unemployed or low paid.

Lack of power

One additional explanation for the lack of youth protest about the falling relative income of young workers is that the weak labour market gives them little power to make demands on the rest of society. What can they do in politics or in the job market? The pre-baby boomers enjoyed a strong market that gives them a relatively good economic position. The baby-boom generation, whose incomes fell relative to older workers, has the strength of numbers. The post baby-boomers have neither numbers nor a strong labour market. They cannot readily strike against more senior workers. With severe competition in the job market, who wants to risk their future by engaging in disruptive protests? In addition, the more skilled and educated young persons may have more in common with the older generation than with the less skilled and educated of their own generation.

3. Improving the youth labour market

The preceding arguments suggest that the youth labour market problem should be viewed more as a problem of within-cohort inequality among young workers than as a problem of generational redistribution. The problem of less skilled, lower paid, and unemployed young workers is part-and-parcel of the broader problem of increased inequality in many advanced countries. Because societies have greater institutional authority over the young and because getting youths onto a good track early can prevent future economic problems for them and their families, there is good reason to focus some policies on the young, as all advanced countries have done.

Policies to improve the economic status of young workers take one of two forms. The policies either seek to improve the skills of youths or they seek to alter the labour market opportunities facing them. Table 8 breaks down these broad categories into five groups. Within each group there are a diverse set of specific programmes. Some countries have excelled in some programme areas but have done poorly in others, so there is much room for exchanging experiences and learning more about what works and what doesn't.

In terms of providing basic skills through schooling, the US, for example, has done relatively poorly equipping youths in the lower tiers of the skill distribution for the world of work, but it has had some success in improving outcomes for disadvantaged youths by relocating families from inner city areas to suburbs with its Moving to Opportunity programme. Australia has increased school enrolments among youths from poor families by offering a financial reward to remain in school. While the apprenticeship programmes of Germany, Austria and Switzerland have their problems, these programmes have produced a lower youth joblessness rate relative to adult rates than in many other countries.

Studies of post-school (second chance) training programmes show a diverse set of experiences. US JTPA and other programmes have failed to bring young men successfully into the job market but have been reasonably successful with young women. Sweden's extensive active labour market programmes do not appear to pass benefit-cost tests. Since post-school training programmes are generally quite short, even the most successful such programme cannot do all that much to raise the economic position of youths who face problems in the job market. Some prison education and training programmes seem to work, but others do not.

Once young workers are in the job market, governments have tried a variety of policies to improve their economic situation. On the one side are payments of income or benefits to the less advantaged. Under this group are negative income tax payments to low paid workers, child care subsidies, and child allowances. Since it is not that difficult to cut checks, these programmes tend to be relatively successful in improving the economic position of low income workers. While most such programmes cover workers of all ages, the main beneficiaries are in fact the young. When the programmes are tied to work, moreover, they increase the incentive to work as opposed to going on the dole. Another programme in this area are minimum wages, which if chosen judiciously can raise incomes with little effect on employment.

To deal with lack of employment as opposed to low incomes, countries have tried to move firms along demand curves in various ways, and to improve the job search procedure. There are work-sharing programmes that give incentives to companies that reduce hours and hire young workers, as in Belgium and France, which have not proven particularly successful. There are subsidies to employers to hire low-wage or disadvantaged youths, which seem to be marginally successful. School-to-work transition programmes vary widely, as do programmes designed to increase the speed at which young workers find jobs. One low cost programme which has had some success, at least in the US, has been creating job clubs and social networks that encourage young jobless persons to seek work and teach them how to go about this activity.

The ideal design for assessing all of these programmes is a random assignment experiment imbedded into a benefit-cost study. Absent the random assignment design, analysts use non-experimental techniques to try to assess how youths who had a programme experience might have fared had they not gone through the programme. As best we can tell, some programmes seem effective, meeting benefit-cost tests, while others may produce sufficient gain for the disadvantaged so as to be judged successful from redistributive grounds, even if they fail a benefit-cost test. But the fact that a particular programme fails does not mean that society should throw up its hands and prepare dole checks or prison cells for youths. Rather, we need a lot more experimentation to develop the appropriate programme.

It is unrealistic, however, to expect too much even from the best programme. If the huge drop in the relative supply of youths failed to improve the job market for young workers, and if the booming US job market still leaves many young less educated workers with low pay and employment prospects, it is hard to imagine how any modest government programme can bring more than a few of these youths into the mainstream economy. To resolve the problems facing less skilled low-wage young workers will require a broader attack on educational and economic disparities, and full employment as well, in addition to normal youth labour market policies. Programmes for disadvantaged and less skilled or educated youth that meet reasonable benefit-cost criterion, perhaps with benefits weighted to take account of distributional issues, can advance the public good, but they are not panaceas to the overall inequality problem in which the youth problem is imbedded.

NOTES

1. See Board on Biology, Commission on Life Sciences, National Research Council, *Trends in the Early Careers of Life Scientists* (1998) for an analysis of the job situation in bio-medical sciences. See Freeman (1996) for an analysis of the rise in crime and incarceration among young less educated men.

2. See Freeman (1998) and Freeman and Revenga (1995).

3. Since the adult literacy survey covers only a point in time, it does not tell us whether the skills of young persons have changed relative to older workers over time. But the fact that the young are more skilled than older workers in most countries suggests that skills have risen over time, just as has the years of schooling of young persons relative to older persons.

4. Does this imply that an egalitarian society should tax the young to compensate the old for their missing out on the rising tide? If economic growth were simply manna from heaven, this would seem justifiable. But the older generation gains from growth through its ownership of capital, and its decision to bequeath capital to the young underlies part of the growth. If the older generation wants to see its children progressing at the rising tide, and a young cohort suffers an exogenous negative shock, the appropriate policy will be to compensate the young in some fashion – to share the cost of the shock – even though the older group will be poorer in terms of lifetime income.

BIBLIOGRAPHY

BLANCHFLOWER, D. and FREEMAN, R. (1996), "Growing into Work", OECD, Paris.

BLANCHFLOWER, D. and OSWALD, A. (forthcoming), "Youth Unemployment, Wages and Wage Inequality in the UK and the US", in D. Blanchflower and R. Freeman (eds.), *Youth Employment and Joblessness in Advanced Countries,* University of Chicago Press for the National Bureau of Economic Research, Chicago.

CARD, D. and LEMIEUX, T. (forthcoming), "Comparisons of the Experience of Youth in the US and Canada", in D. Blanchflower and R. Freeman (eds.), *Youth Employment and Joblessness in Advanced Countries,* University of Chicago Press for the National Bureau of Economic Research, Chicago.

CLARK, K. and SUMMERS, L. (1982), "The Dynamics of Youth Unemployment", in R. Freeman and D. Wise (eds.), *The Youth Labor Market Problem: Its Nature, Causes and Consequences,* University of Chicago Press for the National Bureau of Economic Research, Chicago.

FREEMAN, R. (1996), "Why Do So Many Young American Men Commit Crimes and What Might We Do About It?", *Journal of Economic Perspectives,* Vol. 10:1, Winter, pp 25-42.

FREEMAN, R. (1998), "Will Globalization Dominate US Labor Market Outcomes?", in S. Collins (ed.), *Imports, Exports and the American Worker,* The Brookings Institution, Washington, DC.

FREEMAN, R. and REVENGA, A. (1995), "How Much Has LDC Trade Affected Western Job Markets", *CEPII Conference on International Trade and Employment: The European Experience,* September 26.

OECD (1986), *Employment Outlook,* Paris.

OECD (1996), *Employment Outlook,* Paris.

OECD (1997), *Literary Skills for the Knowledge Society,* Paris.

OECD (1998), *Employment Outlook,* Paris.

NATIONAL RESEARCH COUNCIL, BOARD ON BIOLOGY, COMMISSION ON LIFE SCIENCES (1998), *Trends in the Early Careers of Life Scientists,* National Academy Press, Washington DC.

US BUREAU OF THE CENSUS, *Census of Population, ORG files.*

US BUREAU OF THE CENSUS (1995), *Statistical Abstract of the United States, 1995,* US GPO, Washington, DC.

US BUREAU OF THE CENSUS (1999a), "Resident Population of the United States: Estimates, by Age and Sex", from www.census.gov/population/estimates/nation/intfile2-1.txt.

US BUREAU OF THE CENSUS (1999b), "Historical Income Tables - People", from www.census.gov/hhes/income/histinc/p08.html.

YANKELOVITCH PARTNERS (1997), *CNN Survey,* Feb 5-6.

Table 1. **Measures of the worsened youth job market**

	Male		Female	
Ratio of employment-population rates of 20-24 and 25-54 year olds	1979	1994	1979	1994
OECD unemployment average	81	72	112	87
France	79	49	99	49
Germany	83	82	127	103
Italy	64	52	116	79
Japan	71	74	122	111
US	87	86	106	90
Unemployment rates of 15-24 year olds	1990	1997	1990	1997
OECD	11.2	13.7	12.1	14.0
EU	13.8	19.7	18.3	22.4
US	11.6	12.6	10.7	10.7
Ratio of unemployment rate of 15-24 and 25-54 year olds	1990	1997	1990	1997
OECD	2.7	2.4	2.3	2.6
EU	2.6	2.3	2.2	2.1
US	2.5	3.2	2.1	2.1
Ratio of earnings of 20-24 year olds to 34-44 year-olds, in 1980s and 1990s	Male		Female	
Australia	**		**	
Canada	***		**	
Denmark	-		-	
France	**		**	
Italy	**		-	
Japan	*		**	
Norway	*		*	
Sweden	-		-	
UK	**		**	
US	***		**	

Note: *represents down around 5 points; **represents down around 10 points; ***represents down around 20 or more points; - represents little change. The figures for France are for 21-24 and 40-50 year-olds.
Sources: Employment-Population Rates, OECD (1986), Table 42; Unemployment Rates, OECD (1998), Table C in Statistical Annex; Earnings Ratios, OECD (1996), Chart 4.6.

Table 2. **The declining share of national income accruing to the young in the US**

	Men			Women		
	Share of population	Share of income	Ratio	Share of population	Share of income	Ratio
Ages 15-24						
1980	25.5	8.9	.35	23.0	13.1	.57
1990	20.2	5.3	.26	17.4	7.5	.43
1997	19.3	4.8	.25	16.5	6.4	.39
Ages 25-34						
1980	21.9	24.7	1.14	16.4	25.1	1.53
1990	23.0	22.1	.96	21.3	23.3	1.09
1997	18.9	17.9	.95	17.7	19.7	1.11

Sources: US Bureau of the Census, "Historical Income Tables - People", from www.census.gov/hhes/income/histinc/p08.html; US Bureau of the Census, "Resident Population of the United States: Estimates, by Age and Sex", from www.census.gov/population/estimates/nation/intfile2-1.txt; US Bureau of the Census (1995), *Statistical Abstract of the United States*, USGPO, Washington, DC, Table 14.

Table 3. **Earnings differentials by years of schooling for workers aged 25-29 and 45-54 for the period 1979-97**

Ratios of earnings of given school group to earnings of those with 12 years of schooling

Years of schooling	Ages 25-29		Ages 45-54	
	1979	1997	1979	1997
Men				
C4+	113	156	138	176
C4	112	138	143	150
C1-3	104	108	114	114
12	100	100	100	100
<12	84	76	81	72
Women				
C4+	143	188	167	200
C4	128	155	138	158
C1-3	112	116	117	120
12	100	100	100	100
<12	83	78	83	73

Source: Tabulated from the US Bureau of the Census, *Census of Population*, ORG files.

Table 4. **Explanations for the deterioration in youth economic position**

Explanation	Evidence
Aggregate economic conditions: high unemployment especially harmful for youths	Considerable
The influx of women: substitutes for youth workers	Not much
Increased LDC trade: young workers substitute for youth	Not much
Baby boomers are substitutes for younger cohort	Not much
Youth are less skilled	Not much
Composition of industrial demand	None

Source: Author.

Table 5. **Percentage of 16-25 year olds with high and low literacy skills and the difference between those in the highest and lowest groups for the age groups 16-25 and 46-55**

	16-25 year olds			46-55 year olds
	% in highest group	% in lowest group	% highest % lowest	% highest % lowest
Sweden	40.7	3.1	37.6	23.5
Canada	31.0	10.4	20.6	-0.6
Switzerland (G)	26.3	7.1	19.2	-10.8
Switzerland (F)	26.0	8.7	17.3	-8.3
Netherlands	26.0	6.1	19.9	1.1
Belgium (Flanders)	25.0	5.8	19.2	-10.2
Germany	22.8	5.2	17.6	7.1
UK	21.5	17.8	3.7	-8.3
New Zealand	20.6	18.3	2.3	-5.8
Australia	19.2	9.7	9.5	-9.1
US	16.1	24.7	-8.6	-4.1
Ireland	13.2	17.0	-3.8	-26.9

Source: OECD (1997), Table 1.6.

Table 6. **Why youths have not taken to the streets**

Explanation	Support
Youths are happier - more relaxed social conditions	Some from happiness surveys
No nuclear threat/draft	(Blanchflower and Oswald)
Youth problems are transitional	No
Youths do not compare themselves to older generations	??
Youths still on rising lifetime income trajectory	True for all but US
Youths are more heterogeneous	True
Youths have no power to protest	True

Source: Author.

Table 7. **Proportion of unemployed or inactive youth in households where no one is employed, 1996**

	Youths unemployed		Youths inactive	
	15-19 year olds	20-24 year olds	15-19 year olds	20-24 year olds
European Union	24.9	36.0	12.7	32.8
US	18.8	40.1	27.5	30.8

Source: OECD (1998) and information provided by the OECD Secretariat.

Table 8. **Programmes to help young persons succeed in work**

I. Policies to prepare youths for the job market	
Education and training during the school years	Schooling, apprenticeship, scholarship and fellowships, relocation programmes, juvenile delinquency prevention programmes
Post-school training and job finding programmes	Active labour market programmes, short term skill training programmes, prison training

II. Policies to open up the job market for youths	
Earnings or income supplements	Tax benefits for low income workers, minimum wages, child subsidies or allowances
Job-creation programmes	Employment subsidies to firms, reductions in social charges for young workers work-sharing, prison labour
Transition programmes	School-to-work transition, job clubs

Source: Author.

WORKSHOP 1

PROTECTING AT-RISK YOUTH FROM EDUCATIONAL FAILURE

IMPROVING EDUCATIONAL PERFORMANCE OF AT-RISK YOUTH

by
Peter Mortimore and Jo Mortimore
Institute of Education, University of London

Executive summary

Definition of at-risk youth

At-risk youths are those who are at serious risk of failing in school and who will probably be unsuccessful in making the transition to work and adult life and as a consequence are unlikely to be able to make a full contribution to active society.

Although, in the folklore and literature of most countries, examples can be found of famous people who failed in school but went on to extraordinary feats, the chance of failure in life is greatly increased by failure at school.

The causes of failure

Failure can be associated with many factors including:

– An *individual's* genetic or constitutional make up.

– His or her family's emotional climate and socio-economic status.

– The *community's* norms, values and pressures.

– The *school's* effectiveness at promoting positive or negative development.

– The characteristics of the *education system* in which the individual is educated.

– The employment opportunities of the *society*.

Thus, failure can be related to personal, familial and community effects – which, together, influence the self-esteem, sense of efficacy and resilience of individuals – or to factors within the school and society. Whilst we recognise the web of influences affecting every individual's life chances, our focus will be on just two factors – publicly funded schools and education systems.

Attempts to protect at-risk youth from the effects of failure

These have usually taken the form of:

– Special endeavours within particularly effective schools.

– Special intervention projects and programmes.

– System reform.

Although some progress has been achieved, the evidence from evaluations shows that few of these approaches have thus far proved to be as successful as has been hoped.

Lessons for policy and practice

This paper identifies eight lessons for policy and practice:

– There are no quick and easy panaceas; what seems to work in one setting may not transfer to another.

– Progress is more likely if the proposed solution fits well with the problem. This necessitates an appreciation of local circumstances, of the need for flexibility and of possible unintended consequences.

– The longer at-risk students can be protected from failure in school, the greater the chance of preserving their self esteem and keeping them in the system.

– Narrow views of school achievement need to be broadened to include the likely implications of lifelong learning.

– The role of the professional teacher, too often subject to denigration by politicians and the media, is crucial in implementing change and should be recognised as such.

– Developments in ICT will challenge current beliefs about learning and teaching but the schools of the 21st century, although different, are unlikely to be redundant since their social and custodial role will probably remain.

– There needs to be greater collaboration over planning and implementing strategies between the different individuals, communities, agencies and organisations whose roles impinge on at-risk students.

– Finally, the political will to persuade the advantaged to cede some of their advantages is crucial in the pursuit of a more inclusive, equitable and ultimately more harmonious society.

Introduction

We begin with a quotation from the American educator, Henry Adams, to remind us of the scope of the educational endeavour:

"A teacher affects eternity: he can never tell where his influence stops" (Adams, 1907).

The first part of this paper presents a definition of at-risk students. The second part examines the possible causes of their condition. The third section of the paper discusses what we know about the policies and practices which have been used to protect at-risk students. The fourth and final part endeavours to draw lessons from past experience and highlights the principles which need to underpin any policies or practices adopted by governments, school districts or individual schools.

1. The definition of at-risk students

During the early 1990s OECD countries discussed the concept of children "at risk" and advanced the following operational definition: "Children and youth 'at risk' are viewed as those failing in school and unsuccessful in making the transition to work and adult life and as a consequence are unlikely to be able to make a full contribution to active society (OECD, 1995, p. 21)."

This definition has subsequently been widely adopted in research activities and discussions around these students and is helpful, in that it focuses on the serious and long-term consequences of school failure, echoing the European Commission's view that "failure at school begets social failure" (European Commission, 1994, p. 9).

The following sections consider the causes of failure, discuss attempts to protect at-risk youth from the effects of failure, and identify lessons for policy and practice.

2. The causes of failure

The factors that have been associated with failure and with SAR – and are likely to be implicated in their causes – range from the individual to the societal (Kovacs, 1998). Their impact can be explained by both psychological and sociological theories. They are discussed in some detail here in the belief that it is necessary to understand them before being able to design policies or practices able to overcome their effects. One of the reasons why previous efforts to do so have failed is that insufficient attention has been paid to achieving a good match between the problem and its solution.

Individual factors

Individual causes include the lack of intellectual ability due to a poor genetic endowment; constitutional factors (such as a cognitive deficit caused by brain damage); or a perceptual or physical disability. (Few psychologists would support a predominantly genetic explanation though a number would be happy to see it included as one of several factors.) In addition to physical causes, individuals vary in temperamental and motivational styles. Some, for example, bring little energy or enthusiasm to their schooling. (Many educators will have come across students who, despite many advantages, lack the necessary motivation to achieve.) It is clear that in many countries a sizeable proportion of each age cohort of students fails to develop its potential and, unlike earlier days when unskilled jobs were plentiful, the individuals concerned face fewer opportunities to redeem themselves and to become independent, self-supporting citizens. Of course, it is difficult to be certain about any individual's potential. To an extent, we probably all fail to reach our own potential. (There are few who can boast of the achievements of a Mozart or a Yo Yo Ma.) Part of the problem is that potential cannot be viewed directly and has to be inferred from current attitudes and behaviour and from previous performance.

Only certain individual factors are open to change: genetic and constitutional factors are not; temperamental differences may be; motivation and the effective application of effort certainly are. For most people, therefore, there is considerable scope to develop potential to a far greater extent than currently happens.

In educational discussions of genetic and constitutional factors the issues of gender and sexuality are sometimes ignored, particularly issues of "at-riskness" for girls and young women. There appears to be a male bias in much of the literature. For example, many of the studies which discuss "students at-risk", in reality, are discussing "boys-at-risk" – probably because many of the assumptions made about the behaviours of at-risk youth tend to be based on boys' typical conduct. The needs of girls in programmes designed to assist "at-riskness" have not been adequately investigated, although a recent book by Epstein *et al.* (1998) attempts to address some of the issues.

The literature is also mainly silent about issues around sexualities. This is disappointing. Young lesbian women and gay men at school and in the community continue to be marginalised in the construction of their sexual identities and this contributes to these students being placed at-risk (see Epstein and Johnson, 1998).

There is, in contrast, a substantial literature on race and its impact on education. The issue of race *per se* will not be dealt with in here except through the recognition that people of colour and members of ethnic minority groups, many of whom are already at a disadvantage economically, may also have to confront the damaging impact of racism in their education and, subsequently, in their search for employment. These matters are explored in more detail in Wilson (1997); Ogbu (1997); and Heath and McMahon (1997).

Family factors

Family factors associated with SAR include both socio-economic and emotional elements. The socio-economic factors are themselves complex and operate in a variety of ways, many of them linked to the controversial concept of disadvantage (Rutter and Madge, 1976).

Disadvantage

"The concept of social disadvantage is not easy to define partly because it is a relative concept, tied to the social context of time and place" (Mortimore and Blackstone, 1982, p. 3).

Townsend (1996) defines poverty in the same relative way as: "(...) the absence or inadequacy of those diets, amenities, standards, services and activities which are common or customary in society".

A graphic account of what being poor is actually like has been reported by Oppenheim (1993): "Poverty means going short materially, socially and emotionally. It means spending less on food, on heating and on clothing (...). Poverty means staying at home, often being bored, not seeing friends (...) not being able to take the children out for a treat or a holiday (...)" (p. 4).

Despite the general improvement over recent years in the living standards of most people in the developed world, conditions have worsened for a significant minority. For instance, in England the number of people living in poverty (defined as living on 50% of average national earnings or less) has shown a threefold increase since 1979 and now stands at one quarter of the population (Walker and Walker, 1997). As a result, "Britain stands out internationally as having experienced the largest percentage increase in income inequality between 1967 and 1992" (Dennehy *et al.*, 1997, p. 280). This situation is largely due to the widening rift between what Howarth *et al.* (1998) term the "work rich" and the "work poor".

Research by Howarth *et al.* (1998) shows how, at every stage, the economic circumstances of the family are the major determinants of life chances – but nowhere more so than for children. The proportion of children living in poor households in England is now 32%, compared to a European Union average of 20% (Eurostat, 1997). Researchers from the Thomas Coram Research Unit estimate that about one third of children now live in households with no full-time earner (Brannen *et al.*, 1997).

Social disadvantage is also frequently associated with poorer health (Holtermann, 1997; Howarth *et al.*, 1998). Children from disadvantaged families tend to be of lower birth weight, physically weaker and have less energy for learning than their peers. They are also more likely to be emotionally upset by the tensions in their lives. For many such children, life is grim:

"Children from poor homes have lower life expectancy and are more likely to die in infancy or childhood; they have a greater likelihood of poor health (...) a greater risk of unemployment, a higher probability of involvement in crime and enduring homelessness" (Holtermann, 1997, p. 26).

Almost by definition, students from disadvantaged backgrounds are more likely than others to live in a worse environment. Of course, disadvantage exists in rural areas, as it does on the suburban fringes of many cities, but it is often in the inner city that the worst problems are found. High density living is not, in itself, a bad thing – many people choose to live in this way – but it tends to mean living in greater proximity to crime and drugs and it frequently means living in poor quality housing.

Emotional climates

In addition to material disadvantage, some families provide poor psychological environments for their children's emotional development or for their motivation to succeed in their schooling. In the most extreme cases this may be because of child abuse or some other manifestation of pathological behaviour by one or both parents. Brendtro and Long (1995), for instance, argue that children's emotional troubles mostly stem from what they term "broken social bonds" between adults and children. As a result, trust, competence, self-management and pro-social behaviour skills fail to develop. In other cases, hostile learning environments result from a parent's own negative experience of schooling. Children growing up in such environments are less likely to receive educational help at home.

In summary, absolute disadvantage can be reduced through improvements in life conditions although, as Acheson (1998) argues in relation to health issues, relative inequalities can remain. And it is inequalities which can lead to at-risk status. Most national tests and examinations set up students who have experienced the worst health, diet and housing in competition with other students who have enjoyed the best. Small wonder that there is such a high correlation between success rates and socio-economic status. The surprising thing is that so many individuals can defy this overall relationship and succeed in spite of their disadvantages. (Emotional climate is different and affects families across the socio-economic spectrum.)

Community norms, values and pressures

Where a large number of families with hostile attitudes to schooling live in proximity (for example, in run down public housing estates), there is a danger of the whole community developing negative attitudes to education. Whilst there is a danger of stereotyping families who do not fit this pattern, it has to be recognised that children need to be exceptionally highly motivated to be able to overcome the negative attitudes of such an environment. To stand out against peer and community pressure and strive to succeed in school, in such circumstances, takes a great deal of courage and determination.

School factors

Schools, despite the intentions of system administrators, are seldom uniform. They vary in their intakes of students, the attitudes of their teachers, the effectiveness of their principals and the efficacy of their influences on students. Over the last twenty or so years these differences have been examined in detail under the generic banner of Effective Schools research (Mortimore, 1998). This body of research has sought to find ways of judging schools which are independent of the quality of the students entering them and which concentrate instead on how well schools perform with the students they do receive.

The Effective Schools movement – strongly motivated by a moral concern for disadvantaged children and the seemingly limited opportunities available to them – led to a programme of investigations of schools inspired, in the United States, by the late Dr. Ron Edmonds's catch phrase "all children can learn" (Edmonds, 1979) and, in the United Kingdom, by the pioneering work of Rutter *et al.* (1979). The evidence from these studies shows that schools can make a measurable difference to the life chances of students, regardless of their ability. This is not to claim that schools *determine* outcomes (students, as we have noted, have varying degrees of talent, motivation and commitment) but rather to illustrate that schools which "promote" effective learning are likely to lift the attainments of their students above what would otherwise have been achieved.

At the same time, this research shows that some schools can *increase* the risk of failure for their students, whatever their initial ability. These schools have developed a non-rational approach to confronting evidence of failure; a fear of outsiders; a dread of change; a capacity for blaming environmental or familial conditions for failure; and a strong set of internal staff cliques (Reynolds, 1995). Furthermore some schools, as Stoll (1995) has noted, lack collective vision, have unfocused leadership, dysfunctional staff relationships and ineffective classroom practices. In a similar vein Myers has argued that such schools not only permit their students to make less progress than expected but may even have a retarding effect:

> "In other words it is possible that the students will do worse (...) by attending the school than they would have done if they had stayed at home" (Myers, 1995, p. 6).

Ineffective schools tend to be located in areas of high social disadvantage. The reasons for this are complex. They include the fact that students from such areas tend to perform worse than those from more advantaged districts in norm-based competitive tests and examinations (for a host of reasons already touched upon). The challenge for students and teachers in such schools is much greater – whilst the tangible rewards may be far fewer.

SAR also tend to be concentrated in the same schools. This is becoming increasingly so in systems where parents can exercise choice (the best informed can avoid schools with high proportions of SAR) and where schools (with an eye on the published examination results) can select their students or exclude those who are "hard to teach" (Bentley, 1998). As a consequence, the problems are increased for the staff in those schools which have to cope with high proportions of students who see little value in schooling – and for the students, whose opportunities to overcome their disadvantages are inhibited by the "context effect".

The students and teachers in such schools are less likely to be able to maintain the energy levels needed for outstanding performance. They become discouraged that their results – in comparison with other schools – look poor. With time, this discouragement spreads to other aspects of school life and a spiral of decline gets underway. Expectations of staff and students are lowered. Students feel that they are unlikely to succeed and so reduce their effort. Some "act out" and lower still further their teachers' morale. Parents lose confidence in the school and try to remove their children. Teachers lose confidence in themselves. In times of teacher shortages such schools often have difficulty in recruiting and retaining high quality teachers who are tempted to work in less demanding and more satisfying schools. There are of course exceptions which we describe later in the paper where outstanding principals and staff "buck the trend".

Currently in the English system, about half of all those entered for the national examinations for all sixteen-year-olds (the General Certificate of Secondary Education – the GCSE) fail to obtain any of the three top grades. In 1998, 46% achieved these top grades in five separate subjects and thus gained access to an assured route to higher education with the scope to move on to the most prestigious employment opportunities. Does this mean that 54% of their peers are at-risk of failure? The situation is not exactly that severe or clear cut because some of this group will repeat examinations and improve their credentials either in schools or in further education colleges specialising in courses for young adults. For many, however, failure at age 16 will be a negative experience which will inhibit later learning ventures. Learning after school – in adult life – is beyond the remit of this paper but Bentley (1998) has described many projects directed at engaging disaffected young adults.

Characteristics of the education system

Individual schools can only operate within the context of their national systems of schooling, the growth of which, over the last hundred years, has been uneven (Green, 1990). Systems have arisen from quite different motivations related to a nation's history and context. The aims of the education system of the newly established Soviet Union during the 1920s were quite different, for instance, to those of many of the post colonial African countries established during the 1950s and 1960s (Levin and Lockheed, 1993; Connell, 1998) or to the newly-independent island state of Singapore in 1965 (Gopinathan, 1996).

Systems also vary in their propensity to distribute success and failure – although valid international comparisons are notoriously difficult to draw and interpret (Alexander, 1996). The pitfalls of selecting which samples to use; the problems of obtaining reasonable translations of tests; the challenge of achieving adequately reliable and valid measures all make drawing comparisons a difficult task. To reject the results of all comparisons on grounds of their methodological weaknesses, however, would be foolish. There are clear messages – even though they are made up of imperfect fragments – that some nations, despite starting school at a later age, are exceptionally successful in mathematics and manage to achieve high levels of fluency in several languages. Furthermore, many educational systems in developed countries seem to create longer tails of underachievers than elsewhere.

While the factors contributing to this situation are complex and involve national temperaments, cultural attitudes, capacities for work, historical decisions about calibrating assessment levels, social attitudes and employment possibilities, the consequences are clear. For instance, an average student in England has a high chance of relative failure – as we have already shown. This is considerably higher than a similar student in Singapore. Traditionally, the United States has led the world in the proportion of its young people graduating from high school. Now, however, it lies 22nd out of the 23 OECD countries reporting this measure (OECD, 1998a, p. 31). Although American rates have declined (from 77% in the late 1950s to 72% in 1996), most of the difference is due to other countries catching up (Cornwell, 1998).

Structural factors

Systems differ in whether they are comprehensive – made up of "common" schools catering for the full range of students – or selective. Selective systems either provide different types of schools for what are seen as different types of academic or vocational students (as in some of the German *Länder*, in the former German Democratic Republic) or assign students to a hierarchy of schools on the basis of competitive test scores (Singapore). Systems vary in how much choice they allow parents to have over which school their child attends. They also differ in whether students who fail end-of-year courses are "retained" and forced to repeat the same year alongside younger students. How great a part any of these factors actually plays in increasing or reducing SAR is difficult to estimate, given the countless other influences at work.

International tests

In future, it might be possible to compare actual, rather than relative, failure rates between different countries. Currently this is possible only in the somewhat exceptional circumstances when standard tests, such as the Third International Tests of Maths and Science (TIMSS), have been used (OECD, 1998a). Using data on mathematics performance from TIMSS, it can be seen that Japanese and Korean fourth grade students score significantly higher than all other participating groups. In fact, the average fourth grader in these two countries outperformed even the average eighth grader in the lowest performing countries. However, there is concern within the Korean system that "passing examinations" dominates life in schools which have, as a result, become "mere training camps to pass examinations" (Korean Ministry of Education, 1996, p. 86). The outcome of the intense competition in Korea has been a growth in private tuition and the widespread disappointment of all the students who do not – despite the enormous efforts and costs expended – obtain sufficiently high marks to enter the most prestigious universities.

The latest TIMSS tests included practical "performance" tests taken by samples of students in a number of the participating countries (TIMSS, 1997). Students in Singapore topped the eighth graders and those in Canada, the fourth graders. As such tests become more commonplace it will be possible to gauge whether the differences in failure and success rates between country systems reflect real differences or whether these are mainly the result of inappropriate calibrations of pass and fail levels.

The structure of the national education system, therefore, is a key factor both in the way it helps to define SAR – and even to create them – and in the solutions it offers for their problems.

Employment opportunities

A common feature of most countries during recent years has been the widespread incidence of youth unemployment. In OECD countries the current unemployment rate for young people aged 20-24 with less than upper secondary education attainment is, on average, just more than 21%. This average, however, conceals a range of 40% – between countries such as Poland, Sweden and Spain (with levels as high as 51%) and Austria, Brazil and Korea (with levels as low as 11%) [OECD, 1998a]. These large differences are bound to affect students' motivation, though they do so in complex and contradictory patterns. In those countries with high levels of youth unemployment, school students of average or above average ability may be inclined to remain in school rather than joining the ranks of unemployed. Although, as Hummeluhr (1997) has argued in relation to youth unemployment in Nordic countries, young people's decisions will also be affected by the level of social security payments and the existence (and size) of training grants. At the same time, students of less than average ability may lose their motivation for schooling on the grounds that the competition for jobs will be such that they will have little chance of finding employment. It is, therefore, quite difficult to judge the direct impact of unemployment on youth attitudes to schooling, as Merkens (1996) points out.

Commentary

These six factors do not operate exclusively. We know from studies of educational priority programmes in England that the effects of socio-economic disadvantage are cumulative (Sammons *et al.*, 1983). We also know that individual, familial and societal factors interact in multiplicative ways. The actual impact of a bad school on a particular student's education will depend mostly on the resilience of the individual and on his or her willingness to continue learning. But the potential impact – in conjunction with the other factors – is daunting. Added to this is the effect of those national school systems that place more students at-risk of failure. For the most disadvantaged, each new factor adds considerably to the problems faced by those least able to compete – with any possibility of success – and so increases the probability of their failure. This became starkly evident in an English study of the educational consequences of homelessness (Power *et al.*, 1995).

3.   Attempts to protect at-risk youth from the effects of failure

Three separate categories of different approaches have been identified in the literature:

- Special endeavours within particularly effective schools.

- Focused intervention projects and programmes.

- System reform.

It is important to stress, however, that there will be frequent overlaps between these categories. At a more basic level, problems will be encountered in judging the efficacy of any programme. The somewhat naive approach to "what works" needs to be extended to "what works *for whom* and under *which circumstances*".

Special endeavours within particularly effective schools

The school effectiveness studies undertaken over the last twenty years have enabled researchers in various countries to study schools extensively and to judge their outcomes in relation to their student intakes. Only after the relative progress has been estimated have any judgements of efficacy been made. A number of what have been termed "key factors" – concerned with both whole school and classroom processes – have been identified. These factors have been much debated and formed part of a review of the characteristics of effectiveness drawn from 60 separate studies (Sammons *et al.*, 1995). The factors include:

– A strong learning culture within the school.

– High expectations of teachers and students.

– A shared vision and one set of goals for the whole school community.

– Extensive teamwork amongst the students and the staff.

– Recognition of the rights and responsibilities of students.

There are few surprises in this list. A culture of learning in which students can try hard sounds eminently reasonable – yet it is by no means a characteristic of all schools – nor of all societies (Barber, 1996). High expectations of both parties are also vitally important – although it takes a brave staff to ask the student body to make its expectations explicit. If this level of trust does exist within the school community, however, it is relatively easy to develop a single vision and related goals. Teamwork within the school also appears essential. Allied to this is the sense of equity which ensures that both staff and students recognise the double-sided nature of their implicit contract.

A recent study of differential effectiveness also identified a number of similar factors associated with effective *departments* in secondary schools (Sammons *et al.*, 1997). The study found that particularly effective departments tended to promote:

– A consistent approach between teachers in the same discipline.

– High departmental expectations across all classes.

– Teamwork between staff and students.

– Continuous monitoring of the progress of students.

– A commitment to continuous improvement in both teaching and learning.

– Support and monitoring by senior management.

As with the school factors, effective departments also appeared to thrive on high expectations, consistent approaches and teamwork. What became clear from the study was support for Fullan's view that both pressure (in the form of monitoring) and support are necessary for high performance (Fullan, 1993). The commitment to improvement also proved to be essential at the departmental level.

We also know something about effective classrooms from Australian research (Hill and Rowe, 1996). The researchers found that teachers in effective classrooms promote:

– A concentration on learning.

– Purposeful teaching.

– The monitoring of individuals' progress.

– Active involvement and attentiveness of students.

– A variety of teaching methods.

– A consistency of approach.

– The value of role modelling.

The classroom factors focus mostly on the essential business of schools: learning and teaching. But the power of modelling and the social psychology of the teacher-student relationship also appear important.

The characteristics of schools, departments and classrooms should not be seen as a blueprint for effectiveness at any level. They have not been conclusively proved to be essential but, given the consistency of their identification by researchers working in different developed and developing countries and employing different methods, the probability of their importance is clear (Levin and Lockheed, 1993). The ways in which they are created and enacted, however, will vary not only between teachers and between schools but between cultures (Bennett, 1993; Little and Sivaithambaram, 1993).

Evidence from a recent English study of "value added" results shows that – once all background factors have been taken into account – some schools are able to "lift" their students' results in national tests by the equivalent of two grades (Thomas and Mortimore, 1996). MacGilchrist (1997) also argues forcefully that some of the special interventions (noted earlier) which have been mounted to support the learning of students with special difficulties – and, in many cases, disadvantaged backgrounds – demonstrate that more schools, given adequate resources, can help such students.

In theory, researchers should be able to estimate fairly precisely how many individual students have been helped by their schools to overcome the effects of personal disadvantage. By addressing the results of secondary schools and noting their intake information from five years earlier, it should be possible to estimate some "value added" scores for some schools in relation to others. Those which had raised the achievement of SAR significantly beyond what had been achieved by similar students in other schools, could be assumed to have succeeded. The results could be aggregated to provide an estimate of the likely total number of SAR that have been helped by the efforts of school improvement. Retrospective investigations could then attempt to explore how the schools had helped these students and, in particular, whether improvement had been the result of a planned programme or whether it had occurred seemingly spontaneously. Other information, such as whether the SAR group had been a particularly high or low proportion of the total, could also be collected so as to inform us about the importance of the educational context in which students learn.

Unfortunately, such an investigation remains a theoretical possibility. Not only would it be difficult to ensure that one really was "comparing like with like" but there are few countries with suitable national databases which bring together accurate intake and outcome data. Moreover, it is worth noting that attributing causal effects to particular initiatives in complex organisations like schools is always likely to be difficult. Analyses of American statistical evidence suggest that achievement gains are often too readily attributed to a particular initiative when there may well be entirely different explanations, such as a change of an intake (Henig, 1994). Without appropriate data and suitably robust analytical techniques, therefore, the evidence for the ability of schools to help individual SAR has to rest on theory and on the historical evidence of those institutions which, in the absence of alternative explanations, do appear to have bucked the trend.

The English National Commission on Education (NCE, 1996) undertook a project designed to uncover how some schools with disadvantaged students had improved and succeeded "against the odds". Eleven teams (each consisting of an educational researcher and two representatives from the business world or the community) carried out fieldwork to identify why particular schools were successful in the face of disadvantage. In one case study the quality of the leadership team and the way it had trusted the majority of the staff to create a set of school aims focused on achievement was particularly impressive (Mortimore *et al.*, 1996). Students were committed to learning and staff held high expectations for students' examination performance and social behaviour.

The findings from all the case studies in the project emphasise the importance of: a leadership stance which builds on and develops a team approach; a vision of success which includes a view of how the school can improve; the careful use of targets; improvement of the physical environment; common expectations about students' behaviour and success; and an investment in good relations with parents and the community. The authors note how a crisis in the life of the school can become a catalyst for successful change.

The project demonstrates that committed and talented principals and teachers can improve schools even if such schools contain a proportion of disadvantaged students. In order to achieve improvement, however, such schools had to exceed what could be termed "normal" efforts. Members of staff have to be more committed and work harder than their peers elsewhere. What is more, they have to maintain their efforts year after year so as to sustain the improvement. There can be no switching on the 'automatic pilot' if schools are aiming to buck the trend.

What makes the school factor different from individual or family factors is that it should be more amenable to the possibility of change. Whilst individual traits and family characteristics are "givens", schools are not. Schools are national institutions supported by public funds. Their accountability provides scope for development and change. This is why, in many different countries, school effectiveness research and the related field of school improvement have been seen as an important area of social science (Levin and Lockheed, 1993). However, whilst particularly effective schools can make a difference to the life chances of their students they cannot, by themselves, overcome the problems facing SAR, as Barber (1996) has argued.

Moreover, schools are affected by their role within a wider society which still maintains social divisions and a powerful sense of hierarchy. A particular criticism of school improvement work is that it has tended to exaggerate the extent to which individual schools can challenge such structural inequalities (Whitty, 1997). Whilst some schools can succeed against the odds, the possibility of them all doing so, year in and year out, still appears remote, given that the long-term patterning of educational inequality has been strikingly consistent in most countries throughout the history of public education.

Doubts have even been cast on whether Sweden, usually seen as a shining exception, has actually succeeded in bucking this particular trend in recent years (Erikson and Jonsson, 1996). Although there are different theories about how the social and cultural patterning of educational outcomes occur (Goldthorpe, 1996), these patterns reflect quite closely the relative chances of different groups entering different segments of the labour market. Accordingly, whilst it might be possible, for example, for the ethos of a particular school to help transform the aspirations of a specific group of its students, it seems highly unlikely that, in the absence of more substantial social changes, all schools could do so.

As noted earlier, a depressing research finding is that the *relative* performance of the disadvantaged has remained similar even when the *absolute* performance of such groups has improved. Just as poverty is a relative concept, educational success also appears to be partly relative. A large-scale longitudinal study of primary schools (Mortimore *et al.*, 1988) found that no school reversed the usual "within school" pattern of advantaged students performing better than SAR. However, some SAR in the most effective schools made more progress than their peers in the least effective schools and some even did better in absolute terms.

The problems and dilemmas facing schools with large numbers of at-risk students, compared with those with advantaged intakes, are much greater than current policies recognise (Proudford and Baker, 1995; Thrupp, 1995; 1997). Robinson, rather pessimistically, claims that no educational measures are likely to alleviate the impact of disadvantage. He sees the tackling of social and economic disadvantage as imperative, arguing that "a serious programme to alleviate child poverty might do far more for boosting attainment and literacy than any modest interventions in schooling" (Robinson, 1997, p. 17). This suggests a continuing need for positive discrimination and the effective targeting of human and material resources.

Smith *et al.* (1997) recommend three sets of actions to support schools in disadvantaged areas. They argue that, because of the competitive market that has been created in many countries, education in poor areas must not be considered in isolation. Given the competitive market between schools, they recommend a stronger interventionist role for the system and suggest that "choice" is too blunt an instrument for improvement.

Intervention projects and programmes

The choice of examples

Ideally, the only examples of projects and programmes provided in this paper would be those which had been shown – beyond reasonable doubt – to be highly effective with SAR. This is not possible for a number of reasons. First, there has not been a tradition of closely monitoring educational projects and programmes and even where such monitoring has taken place it has been more likely, in general, to consist of descriptive rather than hard-nosed evaluative comments. This is not because educational researchers are unwilling to come to hard judgements but, rather, because of the difficulties of undertaking evaluation in real-life situations. Unlike, for instance, medical research, which deals with controlled clinical trials, most educational projects are not susceptible to "blind" or "double-blind" procedures or placebos but depend on the human interaction between learners and teachers.

Second, the status of "exemplary programmes" and their utility have become a focus for debate in the columns of the American Educational Research Association's journal *Educational Researcher*. The debate began with Slavin proposing a design competition for instructional programmes "capable of significantly raising students achievement on tests linked to national standards" (Slavin, 1997a, p. 22). Klein responded by proposing the establishment of a system of expert panels "to find, develop, and share promising and exemplary products and programmes" (Klein, 1997, p. 12). These two articles were followed by a third in which Pogrow (1998) argued that the issue was more complicated than either Slavin or Klein implied. According to Pogrow, "there is no such thing as a programme that is universally successful" (p. 23). Pogrow also challenges the methodology of selecting any such exemplary programmes and points to the danger of giving too much power to a small "in group".

> "It is not healthy for our profession for (...) any individual to be the developer of a programme, the arbiter of proper methodology for determining programme effectiveness, the arbitrator of which programmes are effective and promising, and the operator of a federally funded centre" (Pogrow, 1988, p. 27).

Slavin and Pogrow agree over the lack of programmes which are exemplary in that, for instance, they "can increase learning to a surprising extent with a great deal of consistency" (Pogrow, 1998, p. 22). Slavin reports that he and Fashola found only 17 which had been evaluated in comparison to matched control groups and replicated beyond their original sites (Fashola and Slavin, 1998). Furthermore he states that, if the replication had been by a third party, the list would have been reduced to three or four (Slavin, 1997b). Pogrow (1998) found only one math and one science programme that he felt adequately matched the criteria.

In a similar vein, Herman and Stringfield (1995) caution that:

– "What works" will be situational and may not be able to be transferred to another setting.

– Cost data for most projects are imprecise and schools and districts are often unable to quantify "opportunity costs" (a point corroborated in an English study about the efficacy of support staff: Mortimore *et al.*, 1994).

– Projects tend to evolve and change (for example, Slavin's "Success for all" developed into "Roots and Wings").

Evidence of the paucity of evaluated programmes comes from Hermann and Stringfield's (1995) study which identified ten "promising" programs for educating disadvantaged students. These programmes possess what, in their judgement, is "reasonably strong evidence of effectiveness" (p. 2). Bearing in mind the limited number of robust evaluative studies available, the following section will include examples of projects and programmes which appear, on grounds of face validity, to fit Hermann and Stringfield "promising" category.

Early childhood projects and programmes

The following descriptions of potentially useful approaches have been drawn from Siraj-Blatchford (in press). It should be noted that only the first of the five programmes has been evaluated.

High/Scope

The High/Scope approach is based on the practice of Sara Smilansky. Weikart, Rogers, Adcock and McClelland (1971), working in the United States in the early 1970s, developed Smilansky's approach into what they termed the Cognitive Orientated Curriculum. It starts from the Piagetian principle that "children learn actively and construct their own knowledge" (Macleod, 1989, p. 33) and that this knowledge comes from their personal interaction with the world. These principles of social constructivism result in a curriculum that emphasises children learning through direct experience with real objects and from applying logical thinking to this experience.

Daily routines consist of the cycle of "plan, do and review". The children's progress is assessed around 58 key experiences, which are grouped around the eight categories of active learning, language, experiencing and representing, classification, seriation, number, spatial relations and time (Hohmann *et al.*, 1979). The adult's role is to participate as a partner in the children's activities and there is an emphasis on positive interaction strategies, allowing children to share control and form authentic relationships with other children. The adult supports children's learning and extends it by helping them to find solutions to problems. The approach claims to develop learning dispositions of independence, questioning and reasoning in the child as the foundations of other subsequent learning.

The High/Scope programme has been reviewed regularly through the study of a cohort of 123 African Americans born in poverty and identified as being at high risk of failing in school. When these children were aged three and four, they were randomly divided into three groups. One group received a "traditional" pre-school programme based on formal instruction. Another group followed a High/Scope programme and the last group had no programme. At the age of 27, the participants were interviewed and other data were analysed. The High/Scope group was found to have performed better academically, have had a higher economic status, a greater commitment to marriage and fewer arrests (Schweinhart *et al.* 1993). The evidence suggests, therefore, that a pedagogy that enables children to construct their own understandings may lead to positive outcomes in the long-term.

Reggio Emilia

Reggio Emilia is a district in Northern Italy where, over the last 35 years, the municipality has developed an extensive network of early childhood services for children from birth to six, providing for more than a third of the children less than three and nearly all children aged three to six. Providers of the early childhood services in Reggio understand the young child to be a co-constructor of knowledge and identity, a unique, complex and individual subject, engaging with and making sense of the world from birth, but always doing this in relationship with both adults and other children.

Reggio pre-schools develop close relationships between staff and parents and they employ some important "pedagogical tools". These "tools" include: the pedagogical documentation procedure, thematic work, the role of specialist staff (such as "atelierista" and "pedagogista" – or child development specialists) and the time built into the pedagogues' working week to analyse, debate and reflect on their pedagogical practice. Each pre-school consists of three classrooms (one each for three year olds, four year olds and five year olds) and an art studio. Two co-teachers and a resident art specialist, who all play an integral role in the children's learning, are assigned to each room. A pedagogista co-ordinates the teachers from several schools.

"Documentation" procedures are considered important for the children's learning and are focused on children's experiences and thoughts that may arise in the course of their work. Children are encouraged to express their understanding through symbolic representation such as drawing, sculpture or writing. These are then discussed and displayed and the displays form an important part of the documentation.

The Movimento da Escola Moderna (MEM) Curriculum

The MEM curriculum was initially heavily influenced by Frinet, the French educationalist whose work centred around the use of a printing press and community education. More recently, with the introduction of personal computers (Nabuco, 1997) and the growing influence of Vygotsky, the emphasis has remained on literacy and democracy but the practices have altered. The MEM was first introduced in Portuguese pre-school settings in the 1960s. According to Niza (1991), the educational aims of MEM are threefold: an initiation into democratic life; the re-institution of values and social meanings; and the co-operative reconstruction of culture.

The learning focus within MEM is on the group rather than either the teacher or on individual children. Communication, co-operation and negotiation are considered central in supporting the child's social, intellectual and moral development. The children are introduced to empowering "instruments" and institutional routines that include the compilation of attendance charts and classroom diaries, attendance and involvement in council meetings.

Students are encouraged to reflect upon and evaluate their experiences and to make collective decisions regarding their future activities in the "co-operative council". According to Folque (1995), "didactic tricks" and simulations are rejected in favour of using the "real" instruments of learning applied in wider society. In terms of science, for example, scientific investigation is encouraged as early as possible (see Siraj-Blatchford and MacLeod-Brundenell, 1999).

Te Whariki: The Woven Mat

In New Zealand, the metaphor (taken from the Maori language) of Te Whariki (woven mat) has been used to describe a curriculum framework in which each early years centre weaves its own curriculum and creates its own pattern from features and contexts unique to them, their children and their community (Carr and May, 1993). The curriculum framework includes four principles: empowerment; holistic development; family and community; and relationships. In addition there are five strands: well-being; belonging; contribution; communication; and exploration. Goals give clear directions for learning programmes and describe learning outcomes which identify the knowledge, skills and attitudes children should have the opportunity to develop (New Zealand Ministry of Education, 1996, p. 43).

Quality in Diversity in Early Learning (QDEL)

The Quality in Diversity framework has been formulated in the UK over the last four years. Grounded in principles drawn from Te Whariki, it emphasises the need to achieve quality provision for children of "different abilities, dispositions, aptitudes and needs", in a range of settings that cater for the diverse needs of a multi-cultural, multilingual and multi-faith society.

The framework provides guidance on three main elements: foundations; goals; and entitlements. While the foundations and goals relate most closely to policy and curriculum practice, the area of entitlement relates most closely to pedagogy. The framework emphasises parental partnership and play, which is considered crucial to early learning. There is also a clear recognition of the need for adults to support and extend children in their play. Children are considered to have an entitlement to have their learning planned, their resources organised and their progress understood and recorded. The importance of teachers observing children in their play and of evaluating and adapting what they do to maximise learning is emphasised.

Whilst, as noted, only the impact of the High Scope Project on SAR has been evaluated, the other four programs appear to justify the title "promising". Moreover, these innovative approaches are in line with OECD commitment to good early years education (OECD/CERI, 1982).

Elementary years

The projects include: an American project – Success for All; British parent involvement schemes designed to encourage children and parents to read together; English national literacy and numeracy schemes; planned reductions in class size; and an experimental project on Accelerated Schools.

Success for All

The Success for All (SFA) program began in Baltimore in the late 1980s under the leadership of Slavin (see Slavin *et al.*, 1993). It is now followed in hundreds of schools in many large systems in a number of American states. Basically, SFA is a school-wide restructuring which combines many different approaches identified in research studies as effective. Some of the features of the programme are whole-day kindergartens, beginning reading programs which combine a phonic and a whole language approach, subsequent student reading groups which are assessed and reconstituted every eight weeks, one-to-one tutoring for those experiencing difficulties and co-operative projects in writing/language arts and mathematics. The goal of the program is to keep each group of students progressing together and experiencing success in learning.

The program has been evaluated using matched control groups and superior progress has been identified in the experimental groups over follow-up periods of up to five years (Slavin *et al.*, 1994). Successful replications show that the program is transferable and not dependent on a particular school structure. Herman and Stringfield (1995) maintain that SFA is a highly successful program and it has been adopted as the model in the State of New Jersey. More critical views, however, have been produced by Jones *et al.* (1997) and Walberg and Greenberg (1998).

In Canada, Chambers *et al.* (1997) examined the implementation of SFA in elementary schools in Montreal. More than 500 SAR from four elementary schools participated, with three schools serving as controls and one as the experimental site. The SFA intervention was introduced in two stages, beginning with students in kindergarten through grade three and, later, including students up to grades six. All students were pre and post-tested. Despite some attrition of the sample, data on 128 experimental and 136 control students were analysed. Students in the SFA intervention programme performed significantly better than control students on both reading and self-concept measures. Students with learning disabilities also performed better on reading measures than students with similar needs in the control group.

Reading Recovery

Reading Recovery was devised in New Zealand by Professor Marie Clay of Auckland University. For twenty years she worked on the development of a scheme which would help those six-year olds who were experiencing difficulties with the early stages of reading and writing to catch up with their peers – before the onset of psychological problems, before the gap became too large and before the task became well nigh impossible (Clay, 1985). Children are given intensive help for a specific period (usually more than one school year) with the expectation that most will be able to progress within the mainstream by the end of that time – and that those who still need specialist help will be identified early. Reading Recovery adopts no particular reading method. Rather, it relies on the meticulous training of teachers to recognise reading problems and to design and deliver, on a daily basis, a personal programme tailored for each child.

The approach has been used in New Zealand, Australia, the United States and in the UK. In England, for example, between 1990 and 1995, 10 000 children received the programme from 900 teachers trained in Reading Recovery methods. Detailed evaluations of the project have been undertaken. The results indicated that almost three-quarters of the children who completed the programme reached the average literacy level of their class and that the programme was as effective for children whose first language was not English as it was for indigenous speakers. Moreover, "the Reading Recovery intervention was particularly effective for socially disadvantaged children ..." (Sylva and Hurry, 1995, p. 22) Although the programme was often described as expensive (in fact, average cost per child was about the same as the *administrative* costs of "statementing" [assessing] an individual child for special provision), it showed itself to be highly cost effective (Reading Recovery National Network, 1995).

Reading Recovery was introduced in the United States in 1985. Mounts (1996) examined the effectiveness of the Reading Recovery programme in the Midwest. Mount's findings suggested that gains in reading made by the Reading Recovery students were maintained in the third grade. However, when Reading Recovery programs in the US were reviewed by Herman and Stringfield (1995) they reported mixed findings on who benefits and for how long. Reading Recovery students outperformed controls on most measures (Pinnell, 1988) but those who did not succeed in the programme remained well below their class and the controls (Deford *et al.*, 1988). Some students outperformed the controls on oral reading but not on comprehension (Hiebert, 1994). For some, the benefits visible in second grade "washed out" by third grade – due, Hiebert suggests, to the characteristic of inner city, low income schools. Herman and Stringfield (1995) had reservations over the tendency of Reading Recovery teachers to "blame" those who did not benefit. Teachers also, unintentionally, invited the jealousy of other non-project teachers over the resources being devoted to the project. Herman and Stringfield acknowledge, however, that Reading Recovery provided a high quality staff development model which was faithfully applied.

In Australia, Center and Freeman (1996) found that Reading Recovery students initially outperformed students in the School Wide Early Language and Literacy (SWELL) programme (a whole-class interactive compensatory programme based on "Success for All") but that, within two years, there were no differences between Reading Recovery, SWELL or control children.

Parental involvement in reading

A number of projects around the world have sought to involve parents with the education of their children and, in particular with reading. Freire's work in Brazil, for instance, has been highly influential (see Fine, 1997 for a sociological review of the impact of parental involvement on US schools). One of the first studies to be closely evaluated took place in Haringey (England). Tizard *et al.* (1982) compared the reading progress of elementary pupils whose parents had agreed to read with them each evening with the progress of a group of similar children whose class had the benefit of an extra teaching assistant and a control group who received no extra help. In the carefully controlled study the results showed that the experimental group – the first group – made more progress than either group of their peers. The Haringey study resulted in several home-school reading "pacts" and the practice is now widely emulated in the UK. A further study undertaken in Sheffield (England) combined a distribution of special resources into the homes of young children with home visits by special project workers. An evaluation of the project shows that it had an impact on children's experience of early writing and the use of books (Hannon *et al.*, 1991).

Literacy hour

Also in England, the new Labour government, as one of its strategies to raise standards of literacy, has introduced a literacy hour in all publicly funded primary schools. For one hour each day all the students and their teachers engage in a variety of whole-class, group and individual oral and written work. Although the programme is – in theory – not mandatory, detailed and highly prescriptive guidelines have been produced, which schools are expected to follow. The initiative is being evaluated in order to judge its efficacy over time.

Numeracy hour

A similar initiative by the government, announced at the time of writing, is the numeracy hour. Additional funds are to be made available for maths summer schools, family numeracy projects and in-service training for teachers in mathematics. Reports from the National Foundation for Educational Research, which has evaluated the numeracy hour pilot study of eleven year olds, indicated promising gains in mathematics (Minnis *et al.*, 1999).

Reduction of class size

There has long been professional interest in the impact of different class sizes – and the contentious and related questions of class size and resources. Internationally, class sizes vary widely – from an average of 11 pupils to one teacher in Sweden to classes of 60 or over in some states of the Indian subcontinent. Early research tended to be inconclusive (Burstall, 1979). A more recent review of the research also indicates how difficult it is to reach firm conclusions on the educational effects of different sized classes (Blatchford and Mortimore, 1994).

In the United States, School Wide Compensatory education projects (SWPs) have frequently used Chapter I funds in order to reduce class size (Herman and Stringfield, 1995). Evaluation has proved difficult, however, due to the enormous variation in kind and degree of implementation. Doss and Holley (1982) reported encouraging results in their study in Texas of SWPs which had reduced class size. However, a follow-up study five years later found no differences in achievement (Christener, 1987).

In Tennessee, the Student Teacher Achievement Ratio (STAR) Project took place from 1985 to 1989 and involved more than 7 000 students and 328 classes in 79 primary schools in an experiment designed to ascertain the effects of different sized classes (Nye *et al.*, 1993). The results of this experiment showed statistically significant benefits of reduced class size from kindergarten through to the end of grade Three. The research team also found that students from minority ethnic groups benefited most from the smaller class environment. The actual size of the benefits, although consistent across types of schools and types of pupils, were relatively modest.

Given the very high cost of reducing classes to the levels found effective in Project STAR, the value of small classes has been questioned by, amongst others, Slavin (1990). He argues that, for an equivalent amount of money, more students could receive better learning support through the use of Reading Recovery or similar programmes focused on individual learners.

A subsequent interpretation of the evidence on this topic concluded that there was sufficient evidence to justify the reduction of classes in the first two years of schooling (Mortimore, 1995). This could mean having to "pay for" the smaller classes with this age group by tolerating larger classes for older pupils. Moreover, it was argued that the needs of teachers, as well as pupils had to be taken into account. Even if, for older students, clear gains could not be identified in the direct measures of student achievement, the difficulties of managing, monitoring and providing adequate feedback for large groups of learners had to be acknowledged. This is especially true in areas of social and economic disadvantage, where students need additional support if they are to have any chance of achieving at the same levels as their more advantaged peers.

A consortium of English local education authorities (LEAs) is currently funding a large scale study designed to explore: whether those in smaller classes show better achievement and relationships with teachers and peers; whether additional training in getting the most out of smaller classes helps; and whether the independent effect of training is greater than that of size.

In the meantime, some LEAs have endeavoured to reduce the size of classes for the youngest students, in line with the research findings. The British government pledged to reduce the size of infant classes in its pre-election manifesto and, in the first full Budget of the new administration, provided extra money to enable infant classes to be reduced to no more than 30. Although this move has been welcomed, concerns are now emerging that the implementation of the policy, at a time of low teacher recruitment, is having unfavourable unintended consequences. These include schools being less likely to be able to afford classroom assistants (despite the extra funding for teachers), to more mixed-age classes, larger classes further up the school or schools turning away children once they have the requisite 30 in a class (Johnson and Jamison, 1998).

Accelerated schools

Accelerated schools are usually transitional elementary schools that provide a period of catching up for students moving from elementary to secondary schools. The characteristics of the programme are that parents are involved with the management of the schools, clear targets are agreed upon and back up is provided from health professionals. Direct instructional styles are used, as are peer tutoring, co-operative learning and an extended school day. "The goal (...) is to bring all children up to grade level, rather than limit interventions for the disadvantaged to "pull out" sessions..."(Levin, 1987).

Even though there are a number of projects implementing these ideas (Finnan et al., 1996; Boyd and Shouse, 1996), there does not appear to have been a large-scale systematic evaluation of them.

Secondary years

Projects and programmes in this section include high school academies and Magnet and other models of schools in the United States. Examples in England include City Technology colleges and the Cognitive Acceleration in Science (CASE) scheme.

High school academies

A number of high school academies have been established in various states. These generally take the form of mini schools-within-schools of about 100 students. Academic and vocational courses, supported by industrial and commercial sponsors, are delivered within these units. The characteristics of the academies are small classes, individual tuition and opportunities for mentoring by representatives of the sponsors' organisations. Evaluations have shown improved attendance and completion rates. College application rates have also increased. However, the costs – and opportunity costs – for the sponsors and the college staff are high (Archer and Montesano, 1990).

Magnet and other new kinds of schools

Another American initiative is the Magnet Schools movement whose genesis lies in the anti-segregation policies of the 1960s and 1970s. The aim of the movement is to ensure that schools in predominantly black areas are so popular that white students voluntarily enrol in them. Magnet schools specialise in different aspects of the curriculum. They frequently enjoy enhanced funding. Restructured "Charter" schools – such as those in Philadelphia; Louisville (Kentucky); Hammond (Indiana); Dade County (Florida); and Southern Maine – appear to be successful not only because of their resources but because of staff involvement in learning, evaluating their own work and inventing new practices (Darling-Hammond, 1997). Whilst there is evidence of the success of such schools in the inner city, there is also concern about their impact on neighbouring "non-specialist" schools. The new schools are able to attract those parents most able to support the school and those students most likely to succeed academically. Stuart Wells and Serna (1997) point to the problem:

> "As long as elite parents press the schools to perpetuate their status through the intergenerational transmission of privilege that is based more on cultural capital than "merit", educators will be forced to choose between equity-based reforms and the flight of elite parents from the public school system" (p. 734).

City Technology Colleges

A similar initiative in England, directly influenced by Magnet schools, was the pilot project of 15 City Technology Colleges (CTCs) (Department of Education and Science, 1986). The aim of the pilot scheme was to provide technology-rich secondary schools in areas of social disadvantage in order to provide a scientifically and technologically biased curriculum for students with an aptitude in those subjects. The intention was to develop partnerships between central government and industry, with the latter bearing a considerable proportion of the costs of the schools. In the event, less money than was expected came from sponsors for capital costs and central government bears all the running costs (Edwards *et al.*, 1992). Like their American counterparts, CTCs have been well-resourced and are sited in new or extensively refurbished premises. Most of the CTCs operate with an extended day (for enrichment programmes) and a five-term school year. Some have a longer school year. They enjoy greater freedom over the employment and deployment of staff and have the scope to develop flexible and innovative staffing practices (Mortimore, 1997).

The CTCs have attracted considerable hostility, however, mainly due to the disproportionate amount of public resources they received, their demoralising effect on other schools in their localities (not always the most deprived areas) and their admission procedures (Edwards *et al.*, 1992; Murphy *et al.*, 1990). The pilot programme was not extended and the scheme has now been altered so that funding is spread more widely across publicly-funded secondary schools who apply for, and are granted, technology school status. Schools use the extra funding for technology equipment and expertise.

Cognitive Acceleration through Science Education (CASE)

The CASE project originated at Kings College in the University of London in 1990 (CASE, 1990). Operating with secondary students, the project was designed to improve students' ability to learn. Based on a set of principles drawn from the work of Piaget, Fuerstein and others, the project's method enables students to learn to think in different ways (including the ability to reflect on how they are thinking). Through systematic in-service work with teachers and with specially prepared materials, the project team piloted its methods in science lessons in comprehensive schools in various parts of England. In comparison with the carefully selected sample of control classes, the students who had experienced the CASE approach gained considerably higher grades in science, mathematics and English in the 1990 national public examinations taken by sixteen year olds – the General Certificate of secondary education (GCSE).

All *phases of schooling*

The examples include: the Comer Programme; the Paideia model; the Coalition of Essential Schools; and Education Action Zones.

The *Comer Program*

The Comer Program addresses children's health and social needs, as well as their educational needs (Comer, 1980). The program developed out of work undertaken over the last thirty years in New Haven (Connecticut). It is based on the generation of a master school development plan designed to meet the whole needs of children. The Program has nine components: three guiding principles (positive, no fault decision making; collaborative styles of working; and high expectations for student work and development); three mechanisms for development (parental involvement; a school planning team; and a professional mental health team); and three operations (a comprehensive school plan; staff development; and an assessment and modification facility). All are deemed essential to the work of the program.

The program has been evaluated in a number of different ways including the use of randomly selected students in matched schools (Cauce *et al.*, 1987). Positive evaluations show better attendance and fewer suspensions of troublesome students. There have also been a number of more critical evaluations, however, showing levels indistinguishable from control groups.

Paideia Model

The Paideia model, developed by Adler (1984), aims to improve the quality of education for all students, whatever their background. The Paideia program has three goals: knowledge acquisition; the development of intellectual skills; and a greater understanding of ideas and values. The goals are pursued via three strategies: didactic instruction; coaching; and small-group "Socratic" seminars with an emphasis on question and discussion. Ideally, staff are trained in the strategies and some school-wide restructuring is desirable in order to accommodate the three approaches which may a need longer day or smaller classes for part of the day.

In Chicago the Paideia programme reached 5 000 students (K-12) in 23 schools and was evaluated by Wallace (1993). Students showed improvements in attendance, reading, maths and science and in expressing their ideas and were positive about the three approaches. Teachers remarked on students' improved reading and vocal skills, respect for teachers and appreciation of reading. Parents were pleased about their children's more positive attitude to school.

Herman and Stringfield (1995) reviewed four Paideia programs and found inconsistent implementation. The seminars were the program component most likely to be implemented and, moreover, teachers adopted the questioning strategies in their other classes. The level of implementation was affected, however, by the scheduling demands of the program, the desirability (and attendant costs) of having a trained co-ordinator, the degree of ownership teachers had for the program and the costly effect of high staff turnover and accommodating new staff who were ill-informed about Paideia. Parent involvement waned except in one project which had a special volunteer co-ordinator. Some administrators thought the program was too abstract and needed too much investment to make it workable. Herman and Stringfield concluded that the loose structure of the programme was both an advantage and a disadvantage but that to succeed, it needed committed staff, a trained co-ordinator and support from the school administration.

Coalition of Essential Schools

The Coalition of Essential Schools (CES) was founded by Ted Sizer in 1984 (the same year as Paideia) as a basis for school restructuring. Sizer and colleagues avoid suggesting a "blueprint" suitable for all schools. Rather, their nine Common Principles are deliberately ambiguous so as to encourage schools to develop context-specific strategies. Some of the principles, however, match some of the features of effective schools discussed in the school effectiveness literature (Sammons *et al.*, 1995). For example, schools should have an intellectual focus; simple, universal goals; and high (but realistic) expectations. In addition, the principles stress a maximum teacher load, increased costs per student of no more than 10% and individualised active learning (Meier, 1997). The latter is facilitated by means of longer than usual timetabled blocks of time, some integration of subjects and the Socratic method of question and discussion (noted in relation to the Paideia program).

The CES is hard to evaluate because each example is unique and, as Herman and Stringfield (1995) note, does not necessarily view success in terms of increased scores on norm-based tests. In some instances the CES program has been introduced as a kind of "school within a school". Some evaluations, however, have been positive with regard to students' participation in school and changes in teaching practices (Herman and Stringfield, 1995). Thus, Desmond (1992) found that CES teachers had internalised student-centred approaches and that they concentrated more on performance assessment and collaborated more with professional colleagues over it. Some of the implementation efforts have encountered problems already noted in connection with other interventions. These include inconsistent or ill-planned implementation; resentment over the time or resources allocated to the project from teachers not involved in it; teacher resistance to subject integration; waning or wavering commitment by teachers, principals or district administrators; staff turnover; priority having to be given to state mandates; and excessive effort directed at planning which left little energy for implementation. Consequently, the CES recommended that programmes be operationalised more quickly and become school-wide sooner. CES is currently undertaking a longitudinal evaluation. The pilot study for that work found lower drops out rates and improved attendance and achievement (Cushman, 1991).

Information and communication technologies (ICT) and computer assisted learning (CAL)

It is sometimes suggested that the print-based culture of schools is in itself an obstacle for disadvantaged students and that this might be overcome by the new information technologies. It is too early to know whether ICT will provide dramatic new opportunities. So far, few schools have had the resources to invest in adequate equipment and too few teachers have been fully trained in its use. In the UK, for example, Pascoe (1999) claims that "eighty per cent of computer equipment is located in only 20% of schools". Pascoe does not say – but it is unlikely that the concentration is in the more disadvantaged schools. Experiments in particular schools in the United States and in Australia in CAL need further evaluation before we would know whether the technology will provide radically more powerful ways of learning. Herman and Stringfield (1995) comment on how the variety and rapidly changing hardware and software "defies efforts to evaluate computer-assisted instruction as a single intervention type" (p. 77). Evaluations that have been carried out have been of variable quality and have come up with inconsistent positive effects. CAL seems to be motivating for students and more effective when used as a supplement to, rather than a replacement for, the teacher (Roberts and Madhere, 1990). Herman and Stringfield (1995) suggest that schools might involve parents more in their CAL and that "parents who understand the system may be a useful resource for their children" (p. 83). However, we have to remember that ICT is shaped by the same social forces as other more obviously social phenomena. For example, any potential benefits for disadvantaged students may be offset by the fact that those from advantaged families are more likely to have access to IT equipment in the home and thus to develop the relevant "know how" sooner. Furthermore, the Internet, often proclaimed as a democratic medium which eradicates social distinctions, is actually used mainly by white middle class males and this has consequences for the material available on it (Kenway, 1996).

Education Action Zones

The British Government has created a pilot programme of up to 25 Education Action Zones in areas with a mix of under-performing schools and high levels of disadvantage (Department of Education and Employment, 1997). The main aim of the initiative is to try out new approaches which bring together partners from across society, rather than seeing problems as solely in the realm of the education service (an approach in accord with OECD, 1998c). Education Action Zones will have at their centre a forum of local parents and representatives from local business and community interests in which an action plan and targets will be formulated, implemented and monitored. It remains to be seen how these develop and whether their existence does indeed channel more help and energy into the target areas whilst avoiding the pitfalls, noted below, of the old Educational Priority Areas (Halsey, 1972; Smith, 1987). Nevertheless, the idea seems worth pursuing, provided that each zone's forum includes all relevant constituencies, there is a significant redistribution of resources into these areas and the initiative is fully evaluated.

Support beyond statutory schooling

The emphasis of this paper, as we have noted, is on statutory schooling. It is worth commenting briefly, however, on efforts to improve educational opportunities for those who have become marginalised. Support may be in the form of further education courses, organised youth clubs or off-site learning and outreach projects in the community, many of which aim to reduce social exclusion.

In England, further education provision, long held to be the "Cinderella" of the education system, was reviewed by a Committee chaired by Baroness Kennedy. The Kennedy Report (Kennedy, 1997a) lists a number of detailed recommendations for government, the Training and Enterprise Councils and individual further education colleges. These include: the launching of a lottery-funded government campaign for the creation of a "learning nation"; the redistribution of public resources towards those with less success in earlier learning; the encouragement of company-funded learning centres for adult workers; and the creation of a unitised system for recognising achievement (the Pathways to Learning Project).

Commenting on the report, Kennedy argues that drawing more people into the learning community is not only central to economic prosperity but also "(...) one of the most effective ways of tackling social exclusion" (Kennedy, 1997b, p. 3). She claims that "(...) we have been seeing the most terrible separation between rich and poor over the past decades and education has a vital role in redressing the consequences of that division". This requires "(...) a redistribution of public resources towards those with less success in earlier learning".

Changes such as these would ease the financial costs for those who needed to make up in their own time for an unsatisfactory experience of schooling. Such opportunities are necessary if more people are to continue their education and, in particular, if the disadvantaged are to play any part in the formation of a learning society. They are only likely to succeed, however, in the context of a culture – as well as a structure – of inclusiveness. Yet much of the previous history of education in many different countries has been built on a culture of exclusiveness. It is how to change this culture that probably represents education's greatest challenge.

Furlong *et al.* (1997) reported a research project that studied the effectiveness of youth work with vulnerable young people in Scotland. The research, carried out in six distinct geographical areas characterised by disadvantage, focused on young people aged 13 to 16. In each neighbourhood, the project examined the experiences of young people and youth work service providers. Questionnaires were completed (nearly 1 200 in all) and focus groups were held with students in local secondary schools. It was evident from the way that young people used their leisure time that the transition from organised activities for groups to more casual leisure activities can increase vulnerability.

Organised youth work had the greatest appeal for those under age 14; older adolescents tended to "hang around" with friends. About half the girls and six out of ten of the boys were currently involved in some sort of youth club or activity, with participation decreasing with age. The most vulnerable youth were the least likely to participate in organised activities. Moreover, current membership of a youth group was not, in itself, associated with a reduction in risk. Attending a youth club, however, meant less time spent on the street which, in turn, could indirectly reduce risk.

Bentley (1998) has written about the educational and social needs of those young people who are not interested in organised youth provision or who may even have been excluded from it, for the same reasons many of them will have been excluded from school. He describes several projects which involve co-operation between schools; further education colleges; social services; community groups; sports organisations and voluntary organisations concerned with crime prevention, drug abuse and young offenders. There are many interesting and imaginative ideas being tried out but, as yet, none appear to have been subject to rigorous evaluation. An on-going evaluation of a government programme to support disruptive and disaffected students in England shows that, whilst it is difficult to reduce exclusions from school, this can be done in exceptional circumstances although the chances of the students being re-integrated into mainstream schooling are low (Hallam and Castle, 1999).

The Social Exclusion Unit

Also in England, the government has created an inter-departmental Social Exclusion Unit. The purpose of the unit is to bring together the various strands of government whose responsibilities impinge on, for example, education, employment, the family, social services, housing and the law. The unit aims to develop co-ordinated approaches to social problems and to reduce the likelihood of the development of a socially, culturally and politically excluded underclass, described by Demos (1997). Though still a relatively new initiative, the unit has the potential to further the kind of integrated provision that OECD (1998c) calls "the most promising solution (...) by working together, human services can provide more effective and appropriate services – and at a reduced cost to governments" (p. 13).

Student support mechanisms

Student support mechanisms are an approach which has been used widely in the United Kingdom. It is characterised by the use of compensatory mechanisms. These include individual benefits, such as free school meals, uniform grants and other special measures for low income families. The problems with individual benefits, however, are that the levels of funding have always been relatively modest and thus have been unable to compensate for the major differences in the conditions of children's lives (Smith and Noble, 1995). Other compensatory mechanisms have included the allocation of additional resources to particular schools, such as in the Educational Priority Area (EPA) programmes of the 1960s and 1970s, when extra payments were made to schools with high proportions of disadvantaged students (Halsey, 1972; Smith, 1987).

The major drawback of such schemes is that targeting is necessarily inefficient. Some advantaged students will gain access to extra resources within the chosen schools, whilst many disadvantaged students, in other schools receiving no extra resources, will not have the chance to do so (Acland, 1973; Plewis, 1997). However, there may still be cost-effective benefits, as shown by work concerned with the development of "at risk" registers of birth disorders, carried out more than twenty years ago (Alberman and Goldstein, 1970). Later versions of the EPA idea, adopted by the (former) Inner London Education Authority, provided extra resources on a sliding scale rather than on an all-or-nothing basis (Sammons et al., 1983).

System reform

In discussions of the problems which beset schooling today the complex and multifaceted nature of the problems is often ignored or, at best, insufficiently explored. As a result, discussions tend to result in outbursts of blame directed at teachers by government or the media or, alternatively, complaints by teachers about parents, students or the pressures of reforms and their reversals. Clearly, different participants may be expressing valid points but there is a tendency in public debate to generalise overmuch from these "grains of truth".

Debate – often acrimonious – between those occupying opposing positions rarely leads to agreed definition of problems and, even less, to the identification of solutions. Yet, paradoxically, schooling is seen by many non-educationists as a simple matter. Because all have experienced it, there is a widespread belief that everybody understands its processes. This belief is coupled with a "golden age phenomenon" according to which many older people believe that those who attended school today are subject to fewer taxing demands and, as a result, achieve lower standards.

Despite the fact that in many countries in the OECD teachers are working even harder than before, many feel less confident in their role and less assured of the value of their contribution to society. In some countries, new bureaucracies are consuming resources which would otherwise go to schools. Where school choice has been promoted, the market has often created a two-class system to the detriment of students from disadvantaged homes and putting even greater numbers at risk of educational failure.

It is probably easier to design from scratch a school system suitable for a modern society than it is to reform an existing one. It would be unrealistic, however, to attempt to do so. No government would risk throwing overboard something as fundamental as its system of schooling. Changes, therefore, will have to be built on the existing platform of provision. Most school systems are complex; one realises just how complex they are as soon as one tries to analyse what is wrong with them and how they could be improved. The systems have multiple interwoven strands – historical, sociological, political and financial. They include many players with different, sometimes competing, interests and agendas. As a result, most systems have been remarkably stable in their structure over the last 100 years and most changes made have been relatively superficial (Cuban, 1990; Sarason, 1990). The school day remains fairly inflexible, for example. The process of teaching and learning is largely determined by the timetable and the structure of subject domains. Children progress in age cohorts, often divided by ability; and summative learning outcomes are assessed by national examinations (Hallam and Ireson, in press).

Some systemic changes have been undertaken but these rarely tackle the underlying problems which have been noted. According to the OECD, most countries have opted to deal with the question of at-risk students through remedial rather than preventive measures (OECD, 1998b). Five aspects of educational systems which have been subject to systemic change are: the extension of compulsory schooling, provision for early years education, curriculum reform, decentralisation and the accountability of individual schools.

Extension of compulsory schooling

The modal age for the end of compulsory education in the OECD countries is 15 – although it is still as young as 14 in four countries and as old as 18 in Belgium. Those countries with the highest school leaving age appear to keep a higher proportion of its young people in the system than do others with lower limits.

Provision for early years education

Provision has increased in most OECD countries although there are still unresolved issues about how best it should be organised. The tension between education and care has not been satisfactorily resolved – even though the integration of health, education and social services is considered the obvious sensible course (OECD, 1998c) – and many families with two working parents are forced to pay greater attention to the care rather than the educational issues. There are also continuing tensions over the principle of funding and whether private provision (often by untrained volunteer parents) can match that of the state.

Curriculum reform

A major reform has taken place in England with the introduction of the National Curriculum in 1988. (The difficulties of finding sufficient time for all the possible components have not yet been settled.) Less dramatic change has also occurred in Finland, Norway, Portugal, Japan and Sweden, as well as in a number of East European countries following the fall of communism (OECD, 1998b). Most countries are still grappling with the challenge of how best to include ICT. Singapore, meanwhile, has announced that it is reducing the content of its curriculum by 30% so as to allow sufficient time for more creative, problem solving approaches.

Decentralisation

In recent years, many governments have endeavoured to reduce the powers of the state whilst preserving their own strategic role. Different national initiatives in delegating powers from the centre share many common features and each owes a lot to the ideas about the desirability of a market in education and to the pioneering work of the Edmonton School District in Alberta (Canada). In Sweden, for instance, municipalities have had full responsibility for education since 1991. In Spain, regional authorities have been increasing their powers and a number now have full responsibility for education. In France, regions have been given fuller responsibilities but many powers remain centrally controlled.

Other governments have gone further in delegating responsibilities to individual schools. In New Zealand this has led to the abolition of the regional education boards. In Victoria (Australia), England and parts of the United States, local management policies stem from the theory that moving the decision making power to schools will lead to higher standards of achievement. Thus, in Australia, the drive for change came from the "Schools of the Future" project. It was designed to shake up the system through the delegation of power to the school and, incidentally, reduce the power of the teachers' unions. Some commentators see it as possibly leading to greater privatisation of schooling. There appears to be a strong focus on student outcomes and data are seen as crucial to good management. It is also recognised, however, that the stresses of the initiative had taken their toll, particularly as they had been compounded by the cuts in provision which had to be delivered – under the new arrangements – by the schools.

In England, delegation was introduced to increase the power of both "hub and rim" – government and individual school governing bodies – and, simultaneously, to reduce the power of the local education authorities. The hope was that such a move would not only make schools more efficient as businesses but would also raise standards. Delegation has altered considerably the job of the school principal and schools are probably more efficient. But the negative impact of delegation on local services which, in certain cases reduces the capabilities of local services by transferring resources to schools, also has to be recognised.

In the US, a number of private groups – including the National Alliance for Restructuring Education and the National Centre for Education and the Economy – also believe that delegation is necessary to raise standards. They have been working with a national sample of school districts in an experimental restructuring project involving site-based decision making. In the majority of the schools involved in the experiment there was less complacency about the achievement levels of their students. There was also a greater awareness of the need for strategic thinking and a developing sense that a set of common achievement measures across the country would be helpful.

So far, however, there is no evidence that delegation has actually altered students' patterns of learning or improved achievement. Summers and Johnson (1996) report that "there is little evidence to support the notion that School-based Management is effective in increasing student performance "(p. 80).

A number of lessons about the introduction of systemic change – many of them reiterating previous findings of Fullan (1991) – have emerged from the experience of delegation:

– Involving participants in planning is a wise investment.

– Genuine consultation (and subsequent amendments) convinces teachers of the value of change.

– Change takes time.

– Innovation works best if it is both "top-down" and "bottom-up".

– Combining cuts with innovations hinders their acceptance.

– Moving the point of decision-making closer to the point of implementation increases efficiency but may have unintended side effects.

– The needs of the disadvantaged may be given less consideration in a market driven system.

– There is a danger that an increasing concern with the efficiency of single schools could lead to neglect of the system as a whole.

– It is easier to change systems than to improve student outcomes.

Accountability of individual schools

Underpinning many of the changes of recent years is an acceptance of the importance of the individual school. This policy has probably been taken furthest in New Zealand and in England. New methods of inspection make public the inspectors' criticisms of schools and the authorities set targets for improvement. Ultimately, schools which fail to make sufficient progress are closed. These somewhat dramatic interventions are rare (in England, one school has been compulsorily closed and three New Zealand schools have had the powers of their school board handed over to a commissioner) but they serve to make the point to other schools. Similarly, in the state of Kentucky, a fall of more than 5% in a school's test scores can lead to designation of "crisis status" with implications for the tenure of all staff.

It is too early to tell if these somewhat draconian measures are likely to raise standards and they may never provide a clear answer. At the same time as governments are taking these steps to increase the accountability of schools, school improvement is emerging as a dynamic area in social policy. Whilst governments, the local education authorities or school districts, and consultants from higher education all have their parts to play, the main thrust for improvement must come from the school community itself. There is a growing body of knowledge about the ways in which schools do "turn themselves around" which illustrates the need for effective leadership and management, improved teaching skills and enhanced self-confidence in the establishment of a positive learning culture.

Principals have faced a number of challenges as they have sought to improve their individual schools at a time of such accountability. They have had to try to sustain the dedication of colleagues at a time when there has been widespread criticism of schools; develop new ways of teaching which will tap into new ways of learning; exploit as fully as possible the opportunities afforded by developments in ICT; and find new ways of supporting at-risk students. As the earlier discussions and the OECD (1998*b*) recognise, there are no "quick fix solutions" to these challenges.

In terms of the big picture, it is clear that the systemic changes involving an increase in years spent in compulsory schooling or the liberalisation of the curriculum in countries that were previously part of the Soviet bloc have been good. They continue the trend established in most Western countries in the 20th century. This big picture includes a trend towards less differentiated (more comprehensive) schooling and takes account of the rising expectations of the general population about education. It also indicates a move towards a more inclusive education for those with special needs. The emphasis on scientific education and the increasing use of technology is also likely to increase in the future.

The smaller picture, dealing with some of the more recent trends which have affected some countries, is more difficult to discern. The changes to do with increased accountability and the loss of autonomy have succeeded in unsettling the world of education. As a result, there has been a radical change of attitudes amongst some teachers. In England, for instance, there is probably a greater emphasis on achievement now and many more schools are now imbued with a more positive spirit than before the reforms. Delegation has brought a new sense of ownership over resources, property and school planning. Many of the schools which were already successful when the reforms were introduced, have improved still further. Some have received considerable extra funding and some have increased their capacity to select incoming students. These schools and their teachers have benefited considerably from the changes.

For other schools, however, the picture may be different. Hours of precious time have been wasted by practitioners dealing with bureaucratic demands which they feel have added little to their core activities of learning and teaching. A National Curriculum and its allied assessment system have been created and frequently revised – at considerable public expense. The former system of school inspections has been replaced with one which is harsher and less trusted. Morale in much of the profession has fallen and many experienced and talented teachers and head teachers have chosen to leave teaching. Many aspects of schooling have been made subject to market pressures and a clear pecking order of schools has been established. For those schools at the bottom of the pecking order, life has become much harder as their proportion of "hard to teach" students has increased. Such pressures have not necessarily benefited the at-risk students with whom this paper is concerned. Such students may be better divided between a greater than a smaller number of schools.

4. Lessons for policy and practice

In this paper we have spelled out our interpretation of the educational problems faced by at-risk students. We have shown that, with some notable exceptions, school students with disadvantaged backgrounds do not do as well as their advantageous peers – hardly a surprising finding in a competitive system. Moreover, some governments have failed to exploit fully what knowledge there is about how to combat these problems and a number of the initiatives and intervention strategies that appear to have had some success in some countries have not been taken up in others. Furthermore, some of those that have been adopted and shown to have benefits have inexplicably been allowed to wither. Reading Recovery in England is a notable example.

Meanwhile, the advantaged have sometimes gained even more than the disadvantaged from those initiatives that have been pursued. The consequence is that the disadvantaged – without the help and support of focused extra help – slip further behind. Thus the conventional pattern of outcomes is maintained – with the advantaged at the top and the disadvantaged (with some exceptions) at the bottom. So can there be ever a solution to this set of problems?

Like OECD (1998b) we believe that there cannot be a simple solution:

"No single or overarching explanation can account for it; no simple or universally applicable measures can be found to address it. Overcoming failure requires a sustained and long-term effort to meet the needs of all students, especially of the low-achievers"(p. 56).

The OECD goes on to argue for the need to pursue solutions "through different combinations of three main approaches – systemic, institutional and programmatic" (OECD, 1998b, p. 56). We prefer to conceptualise the problem in terms of actions by individuals, schools and systems.

Individual factors

Westfall and Pisapia (1994) undertook a study of resilient at-risk students in order to identify factors that the students believed contributed to their academic success. They found that positive use of time and meaningful involvement in school or other activities helped, as did clear and specific long-term goals. The students had an internal locus of control and accepted personal responsibility for both successes and failures. Younger students thought that teachers and counsellors played a more important role in their successes while older students were less enthusiastic about this. Almost all of these students had come from what the researchers termed "dysfunctional homes" but most could name one or more persons who had been significant in helping them.

Johnson (1997) has also written about the concept of resilience, drawing on the work of Garmezy (1985). She defines resilience as the ability to overcome social and personal disadvantages, often through protective or compensatory strategies. Similarly, Grosset (1997) undertook a study of why some at-risk students are able to beat the odds and achieve educational success while others are not. Aspects of personality such as confidence, discipline, and perseverance, as well as encouragement from faculty and other students, greatly influenced them – as did support from their families.

Smith (1997) carried out a qualitative analysis of the literature on self-esteem from the standpoint of urban youth education. He defines and describes elements of self-esteem and links it to self-worth, learners' social environmental cues, teacher attitudes and other variables. In Smith's view, at-risk youth carry the additional burden of internalising disapproval based on race and poverty. Smith stresses the importance of self-esteem to academic achievement and suggests specific classroom strategies which, by increasing co-operation and social responsibility, build positive self-esteem in at-risk students. He also argues that teachers must first consider their own self-esteem because those with high self-esteem are more effective teachers.

We do not yet know enough about resilience and how it may be fostered. It appears, however, to be a crucial characteristic in the explanation of why some individuals succeed in situations where they are at considerable risk of failure. Certainly this is a characteristic which all schools should seek to promote amongst their most vulnerable students.

School factors

Whilst exceptional schools, against the most unequal odds, can help their SAR to succeed, many more need some extra component if they are to flourish with the most at-risk students. This component might be additional resources; supplementary professional help (such as a school social worker or extra classroom assistants); employing the most gifted teachers; or allowing extra time (such as an additional year of secondary schooling). One way or another schools need to find ways of nurturing their at-risk students and of bringing them up to the same starting line from which more advantaged students begin their schooling.

The notion of measuring schools on the basis of students' progress – rather than just on their end attainment – may not sound very radical but it underpins many of the ideas of this paper. It is impossible to make a fair judgement of a school without taking into account the nature of its student intake. With such information it becomes possible to estimate the progress a school has promoted amongst its students. It is this measure which is the most likely to reveal something about the school's effectiveness.

Much of the research cited here shows that it is more difficult to turn around a school which has a student body made up predominantly of those at-risk of failure. It is possible – and there are some striking examples of this achievement – but it is foolish to pretend that the social background of students makes no difference. We know from many international studies that middle-class families are able to extract more out of any educational situation than their less-advantaged peers. The benefits of economic and social advantage, as well as the "cultural capital" of knowing how the system works, mean that middle-class children have a head start in any competitive educational system. Ways of helping the children of the disadvantaged so that the gap between them and their more affluent peers is reduced are always likely to be difficult to identify. Some aspects of parental involvement are illustrative of this fact. Parental involvement, introduced with a central, if not prime, aim of helping disadvantaged children, was taken up with great enthusiasm by the middle-classes. The result was that the gap between their children and other children – far from reducing – actually grew. This leads to a dilemma. Is it ethical and practicable for the state to help *only* the children of the disadvantaged? Ethical because those not getting extra help will feel that they are also entitled to it and may cite equal opportunities, policies or legislation in order to get it; practicable, because once an idea becomes known, ambitious – and advantaged – parents will find ways to use it to their further advantage. There is no clear solution to such a dilemma and each country has to decide on its own policy about how far it is prepared to go down the path of positive discrimination.

The research on school differences shows clearly that schools which have a reasonable academic balance of ability in their intakes have great advantages over those which do not (Rutter *et al.*, 1979; Mortimore, 1998). Replication in New Zealand of this important finding has recently been reported by Thrupp (1997). Having a balance of ability in a school's intake does not guarantee that schools always succeed. Some schools with advantaged students still fail to challenge their learners and, as a result, underachieve. Yet because their students can fairly easily achieve what appear to be reasonable results, they are seldom seen as failing and, as a consequence, many remain complacent. In contrast, other schools – provided they receive a minimum of students for whom successful schooling is possible – can exceed all normal expectations. Having a balance is important but if, as in some countries, parents expect to be able to choose their child's school, this situation is hard to achieve.

For advantaged parents, choosing schools has become one of the ways in which they can perpetuate their own privileged status for their children. Of course, it has always been the case that those with sufficient resources could ensure an exclusive set of peers for their children – either by moving house to an appropriate school's catchment area or by paying for private schooling. This is one of the options where private schools coexist alongside the publicly-funded system. By instituting parental choice for publicly-funded schools policy makers no doubt hoped to capture the motivation of ambitious parents. This they did – but they also created the opportunity for the advantaged to consolidate their position without paying fees.

In making these points, we are not condemning parents for doing the most natural thing – trying to improve the life chances of their children. We are simply pointing out that in choosing a school a parent is also choosing his or her children's companions and that if some schools attract more than their share of advantaged – and generally easier to teach – students, then other schools will suffer the loss of such students.

The research findings on school differences must bear some responsibility for increasing the desire of parents to choose schools. Researchers did, after all, tell parents that the school could make a significant difference to a child's academic results. The research also suggested a solution to the problem – creating schools with balanced intakes. A situation in which increasing numbers of parents demand – and expect to gain – access to the first school of their choice is bound to cause disappointments. In England, for example, parents gain information from published performance tables ("league tables"), in which every school in the country is ranked by performance in national tests or results in public examinations. This leads inexorably to more and more people desiring access to fewer and fewer schools and results in an increasingly unsatisfactory situation. Unlike material goods, the production of places in favoured schools cannot be increased *ad infinitum* (the most prestigious English independent schools have not expanded greatly nor sought to produce duplicate institutions). A better solution surely is to try to raise the standard of as many schools as possible so that "choice" becomes less of an imperative and balance is easier to achieve.

In England in the early days of comprehensive schools a proportion of relatively advantaged parents, committed to the comprehensive ideal, voluntarily renounced the opportunity to have their children educated exclusively with children from similar backgrounds and opted for all-ability schools in order to improve the system as a whole. These parents accepted that their own children's subsequent attainments might be slightly lower than they would have been in a more select or selective environment. But they doubtless hoped that their children's experience of growing up with a cross-section of the population would bring its own benefits and that their participation would improve the system overall. That sense of private contribution to the public good has been much reduced in the 1980s and 1990s during which time individualism and the education market have held sway. We suggest that clear leadership from governments is needed in order to "mobilise public opinion" (OECD, 1998, p. 7) on the need for an equitable distribution of school places.

Systemic factors

It is apparent from many of the initiatives discussed in this paper that disadvantaged students need more help than individual schools can provide if they are to overcome the obstacles they face. For these students to reach the national average (an average made up predominantly of those who are not disadvantaged) represents an enormous challenge. Given that any average represents a central point in a wide spectrum of attainment, at-risk students achieving this level will have had to leapfrog over many of their more advantaged peers. It is a pious hope to assume that this can be achieved by the majority of at-risk students in many countries' systems.

This is not to be patronising about such students, but simply to recognise that they have to compete with their peers in what amounts to a schooling race in which they begin from way behind the starting line.

As we have already argued, disadvantage and underachievement present deep-seated problems which require systemic change. Such change involves the advantaged groups ceding some of their privileges (Bennett, 1993). It is widely recognised that democratic governments which pursue such a course of action are vulnerable to loss of support. The lesson of this paper, however, is that, without such actions, the disadvantaged groups will stay locked behind the advantaged groups and their children will be unlikely to break out from this pattern. This is not only unacceptable for individuals but economically wasteful for today's societies which need to raise the general levels of learning capabilities across their populations and to create what Lassnig (1998) calls "learning economies". Moreover it is politically unwise if social exclusion, in which may grow the seeds of civil unrest, is to be avoided (Eurydice, 1994).

As all the empirical evidence reported in this paper has made clear, labelling schools and their students (and by implication, their teachers) as failures is likely to be unproductive (Kovacs, 1998). Fragile confidence will be damaged by such actions and parents will choose (if they can) to send their children elsewhere. Furthermore, teachers who choose to work with those who lack the natural and material resources of the advantaged – and may be amongst the hardest to teach – need support not blame. Otherwise they will take the easy way out and forsake the needs of the disadvantaged – by seeking to attract "easier to teach students" to their schools – or simply by moving to a school with "easier to teach" students. We have come across a number of schools which have successfully taken the first course. Their school results improve but not as a result of changes in their teaching or in the management of the school. It is simply the effect of a changed – and more advantaged – intake. As Gewirtz (1997) argues in relation to England:

> "Within the current educational regime governed by the discourses and technologies of the market and performativity, "good management" is in large part defined as the ability to transform the socio-economic and linguistic make up of a school (...) what it is effectively doing is producing a redistribution of students amongst schools. It cannot address the root causes of educational underachievement".

If teachers have to operate in a hostile climate in which they feel they are being blamed for the shortcomings of social and economic situations beyond their control it is likely that: the gap between successful (and perhaps effective) schools serving advantaged communities and those schools perceived to be unsuccessful (even though some may be effective in relative terms) will increase; astute principals will seek to improve simply by attracting "easier to teach" students through careful marketing and publicity; and the opportunities for at-risk students will further decline.

5.   Key lessons

We noted, at the beginning of this paper, the multiple and interrelated factors associated with the pattern of poor educational performance of at-risk students – many of which are addressed by other contributors to the seminar. Our focus has been on the role of schools and education systems. With that caveat in mind, what are the key lessons for improving the educational performance of at-risk students?

First, there are no easy panaceas, no holy grail. There is, however, scope for each nation to learn from those interventions which have been evaluated in other countries and whose good practice has been disseminated (OECD, 1998b). The many initiatives that have been noted in this paper are, in the main, promising – but no more. They are also limited in that it is questionable whether they would transfer easily to other environments. That said, it is worth encouraging innovation. Governments which have the courage to trust their systems to explore new ways of better supporting those who might otherwise fail may reap considerable rewards.

Second, and closely related to the first lesson, is the need to achieve a good match between the problem and its solution. An understanding of the factors contributing to a problem, a recognition of local circumstances and of the need for a flexible approach, and an awareness of the possible intended and unintended consequences of proposed actions may help in identifying appropriate solutions.

Third, if it is possible to protect at-risk students from failure in the educational system for as long as possible they will have a greater chance of developing and progressing at their own pace. This is not an argument for retention policies, with their attendant negative social effects. Rather, it is a plea for experiments with individualised learning and flexible age and ability grouping practices in which students may try out different learning styles and modes. They may be able to make up at later stages for earlier losses and, most important of all, maintain a positive self image of themselves as potential learners. It has to be recognised that, even so, the gap in achievement may still not be narrowed, merely delayed. But we believe that the longer students can be encouraged to stay in the system and achieve (albeit probably still less, as group, than their advantaged peers) the less damaged will be their self-esteem and the better equipped will they be to cope with adult life.

Fourth, unless there is a systematic move away from narrow views of school achievement – in which only a few can succeed – towards broader views of lifelong learning in which all can progress, the opportunities for those at risk are unlikely to change very much. They will remain "at the bottom of the pile". The implications of lifelong learning need to be worked through. Summative school assessments (which anoint some students and stigmatise others) become less important if citizens are continuing to study and to develop new skills all their working lives.

Fifth, as Delors (1996) argues "The importance of the role of the teacher as an agent of change, promoting understanding and tolerance, has never been more obvious". Yet in a number of countries, teachers are not considered a high status group. Pay is low in comparison to other professional groups and recruits have – with exceptions – not come from the most highly qualified students. In some countries, teaching has been an all-graduate profession for comparatively few years. Phrases such as "those who can do – those who can't teach" are used to characterise a group which, whilst being generally seen as worthy, is not rated highly and, in some countries, is subject to denigration by politicians and the media. Where this is the case, there is less chance of the education system coping with the type of changes that have been proposed in this paper for, as an ILO/UNESCO Committee of Experts (1988) declared: "When teaching as a profession is ill-regarded in a society, that ill-regard reflects itself on the entire system of organised education" (paragraph 16).

Sixth, it is not enough to restrict our thinking to the present, to schooling as we know it. Effective schools in the 20th century may be less effective in the 21st. New systems, better able to cope with economic uncertainties and the growth of lifelong learning, may be needed. ICT promises to challenge much of what we know about learning. We do not think that schools will become redundant – too much depends on their social and custodial roles – but they are likely to change considerably.

Seventh, it is imperative that those concerned with education act in concert with parents and community and with those in other fields, such as the social and health services and the business sector, and that those most closely involved play an active part in planning and implementing the proceedings so that peoples' lives are not fragmented by contradictory pressures.

Eighth, last and probably most important of all, those with power need to question whether they are prepared to invest adequate resources (diverted if necessary) and to use their power to persuade the advantaged to cede some of their freedom to preserve the privileges they cherish, in pursuit of a more inclusive, equitable and harmonious society. As Bennet reminds us, "The political dimensions are crucial in any attempt to provide effective education for the disadvantaged. In almost every society it is the middle class who reap the greatest benefits from schooling, and consume the largest share of governmental educational resources" (Bennett, 1993, p. 51).

BIBLIOGRAPHY

ACHESON, D. (1998), *Independent Inquiry into Inequalities in Health Report*, The Stationery Office, London.

ACLAND, H. (1973), "Social Determinants of Educational Achievement: An Evaluation and Criticism of Research", Ph.D. Thesis, University of Oxford.

ADAMS, H. (1907), *The Education of Henry Adams*, Chapter 20.

ADLER, M. (1984), "Paideia Proposal: An Educational Manifesto", cited in R. and S. Stringfield (1995), *Ten Promising Programs for Educating Disadvantaged Students: Evidence of Impact*, Center for Social Organisation of Schools, Baltimore MD.

ALBERMAN, E.D. and GOLDSTEIN H. (1970), "The 'At Risk' Register: A Statistical Evaluation", *British Journal of Preventative Medicine*, 24, 3, pp. 129-135.

ALEXANDER, R. (1996), *Other Primary Schools and Ours: Hazards of International Comparisons*, CREPE Occasional Paper, Warwick, UK, Centre for Research in Elementary and Primary Education, University of Warwick.

ARCHER, E. and MONTESANO, P. (1990), "High School Academies", *Equity and Choice*, pp. 16-17.

BAKER-GRAHAM, A. (1994), "Working with Girls and Women At Risk", ERIC Accession, No. ED 378021, EDRS Microfiche.

BARBER, M. (1996), *The Learning Game: Arguments for an Educational Revolution*, Gollancz, London.

BENNETT, N. (1993), "How Can Schooling Help Improve the Lives of the Poorest? The Need for Radical Reform", in H. Levin and M. Lockheed (eds.), *Effective Schools in Developing Countries*, Falmer, London and Washington, DC.

BENTLEY, T. (1998), *Learning Beyond the Classroom: Education for a Changing World*, Routledge, London.

BLATCHFORD, P. and MORTIMORE, P. (1994), "The Issue of Class Size for Young Children in Schools: What Can We Learn From Research?", *Oxford Review of Education*, 20, 4, pp. 411-428.

BOYD, W. and SHOUSE, R. (1996), "The Problems and Promise of Urban Schools", in O. Reyes, H. Walberg and R. Weissberg (eds.), *Children and Youth: Interdisciplinary Perspectives*, Sage, Washington, DC.

BRANNEN, J., MOSS, P., OWEN, C. and WALE, C. (1997), *Mothers, Fathers and Employment: Parents and the Labour Market in Britain, 1984-1994*, DfEE/Institute of Education, London.

BRENDTRO, L. and LONG, N. (1995), "Breaking the Cycle of Conflict", *Educational Leadership*, February, pp. 52-56.

BURSTALL, C. (1979), "Playing the Numbers Game in Class", *Education Guardian*, 7 April.

CARR, M. and MAY, H. (1993), "Choosing a Model: Reflecting on the Development and Process of Te Whariki: National Early Childhood Curriculum Guidelines in New Zealand", *International Journal of Early Years Education*, 1, 3, pp. 7-21.

CASE (1990), "Better Learning: A Report from the CASE Project", Kings College, University of London, London.

CAUCE, A., COMER, J. and SCHWARTZ, B. (1987), "Long-term Effects of a System-Oriented School Prevention Program", *American Journal of Orthopsychiatry*, 57, 1, pp. 127-131.

CENTER, Y. and FREEMAN, L. (1996), *The Use of a Structured Literacy Program to Facilitate the Inclusion of Marginal and Special Education Students into Regular Classes*, ERIC Accession, No. ED405673, EDRS Microfiche.

CHAMBERS, B. et al. (1997), *The Challenges of Implementing Success for All in a Canadian Context*, ERIC Accession, No. 409095, EDRS, Microfiche.

CHRISTENER, C. (1987), "Schoolwide Projects: The Almost Revolution Six Years Later", paper presented at the AERA Annual Meeting, Washington, DC.

CLAY, M. (1985), *The Early Detection of Reading Difficulties*, Heinemann, London.

COMER, J.P. (1980), *School Power: Implication of an Intervention Project*, Free Press, New York.

CONNELL, H. (1998), *Reforming Schooling – What Have We Learnt?*, UNESCO, Paris.

CORNWELL, R. (1998), *Times Educational Supplement*, 4 December, p. 18.

CUBAN, L. (1990), "A Fundamental Puzzle of School Reform", in A. Leiberman (ed.), *Schools as Collaborative Structures: Creating the Future now*, Falmer Press, New York.

CUSHMAN, K. (1991), "Taking Stock: How Are Essential Schools Doing?", *Horace*, 8, 1, pp. 1-12.

DARLING-HAMMOND, L. (1997), "Restructuring Schools for Students' Success", in A. Halsey, H. Lauder, P. Brown and A. Wells (eds.), *Education: Culture, Economy, Society*, Oxford University Press, Oxford, pp. 332-337.

DEFORD, D., PINNELL, G., LYONS C. and YOUNG, P. (1988) *Reading Recovery*, Volume IX, Report of the Follow-up Studies, Ohio State University, Columbus OH.

DELORS, J. (1996), "Learning: the Treasure within", *Report of the International Commission on Education for the 21st Century*, UNESCO, Paris.

DEMOS (1997), *The Wealth and Poverty of Networks: Tackling Social Exclusion*, Demos, London.

DENNEHY, A., SMITH, L. and HARKER, P. (1997), "Not to be Ignored: Young People, Poverty and Health", in A. Walker and C. Walker (eds.), *Britain Divided: the Growth of Social Exclusion in the 1980s and 1990s*, Child Poverty Action Group (CPAG), London.

DEPARTMENT FOR EDUCATION and EMPLOYMENT (DfEE) (1997), *Excellence in Schools*, Cm 3681, HMSO, London.

DEPARTMENT OF EDUCATION and SCIENCE (DES) (1986), *A New Choice of School*, DES, London.

DESMOND, C. (1992), "A Comparison of the Assessment of Mastery in an Outcome-Based School and a Coalition of Essential Skills School", paper presented at AERA Annual Meeting, San Francisco.

DOSS, D. and HOLLEY, F. (1982), *A Cause for National Pause: Title I Schoolwide Projects*, Austin Independent School District Office of Research and Evaluation, Austin, Texas.

EDMONDS, R. (1979), "Effective Schools for the Urban Poor", *Educational Leadership*, 37, 1, pp. 15-27.

EDWARDS, T., GEWIRTZ, S., and WHITTY, G. (1992), *Researching a Policy in Progress: the City Technology Colleges Initiative*, Research Papers in Education, 7, 1, pp. 79-104.

EPSTEIN, D. and JOHNSON, R. (1998), *Schooling Sexualities*, Open University Press, Buckingham and Philadelphia.

EPSTEIN, D., ELWOOD, J., HEY, V. and MAW, J. (1998), *Failing Boys? Issues in Gender and Achievement*, Open University Press, Buckingham and Philadelphia.

ERIKSON, R. and JONSSON, J. (eds.) (1996), *Can Education be Equalized? The Swedish Case in Comparative Perspective*, Westview Press, Boulder, CO.

EUROPEAN COMMISSION (1994), *The War Against School Failure: A Challenge for European Construction*, Office of the Official Publications of the European Union, Luxembourg.

EUROSTAT (1997), Reported in the Guardian, 28 April.

EURYDICE (1994), *Measures to Combat Failure at School: A Challenge for the Construction of Europe*, European Commission, Brussels.

FASHOLA, O. and SLAVIN, R. (1998), "School-wide Reform Models: What Works?", *Phi Delta Kappan*, 79, 5, pp. 370-378.

FINE, M. (1997), "(Ap)Parent Involvement: Reflections on Parents, Power and Urban Public Schools", in A. Halsey, H. Lauder, P. Brown and A. Wells (eds.), *Education: Culture, Economy, Society*, Oxford University Press, Oxford.

FINNAN, D., ST. JOHN, E., MCCARTHY, J., and SLOVACEK, S. (eds.) (1996), *Accelerated Schools in Action: Lessons from the Field*, Corwin Press, Thousand Oaks, CA.

FOLQUE, M. (1995), "The Influence of Vygotsky's Work in the Modern School Movement: Early Childhood Education Curriculum Model", unpublished paper.

FULLAN, M. (1991), *The New Meaning of Educational Change*, Cassell, London.

FULLAN, M. (1993), *Change Forces: Probing the Depths of Educational Reform*, Falmer Press, London.

FURLONG, A., CARTMEL, F., POWNEY, J. and HALL, S. (1997), *Evaluating Youth Work with Vulnerable Young People*, Scottish Council for Research in Education, ERIC Accession, No. ED415292, EDRS Microfiche.

GARMEZY, N. (1985), "Stress-Resistant Children: The Search for Protective Factors", in J. Stevenson (ed.), *Recent Research in Developmental Psychopathology*, Pergamon Press, Oxford, pp. 213-233.

GEWIRTZ, S. (1997), "Can all Schools be Successful? An Exploration of the Determinants of School Success", paper presented at the British Educational Research Association Annual Conference, York.

GOLDTHORPE, J. (1996), "Class Analysis and the Reorientation of Class Theory: The Case of Persisting Differentials in Educational Attainment", *British Journal of Sociology*, 47, 3, pp. 482-505.

GOPINATHAN, S. (1996), "Globalization, the State and Education Policy in Singapore", *Asia Pacific Journal of Education*, 16, 1, pp. 74-87.

GREEN, A. (1990), *Education and State Formation: The Rise of Education Systems in England, France and the USA*, St. Martin's Press, New York.

GROSSET, J. (1997), *Beating the Odds: Reasons for At-Risk Student Success, Institutional Research Report*, No. 93, Philadelphia Community College, Philadelphia PA.

HALLAM, S. and CASTLE, F. (1999), Personal Communication.

HALLAM, S. and IRESON, J. (in press) "Pedagogy in the Secondary School" in P. Mortimore (ed.), *Understanding Pedagogy and its Impact on Learning*, Sage, London.

HALSEY, A.H. (ed.) (1972), *Educational Priority, EPA, Problems and Policies*, 1, HMSO, London.

HANNON, P., WEINBERGER, J. and NUTBROWN, C. (1991), "The Sheffield Early Literacy Development Project", *Current Issues in Early Childhood*, 44.

HEATH, A. and MCMAHON, D. (1997), "Education and Occupational Attainments: The Impact of Ethnic Origins", in A. Halsey, H. Lauder, P. Brown and A. Wells (eds.), *Education: Culture, Economy, Society*, Oxford University Press, Oxford, pp. 646-662.

HENIG, J. (1994), *Rethinking School Choice: Limits of the Market Metaphor*, Princeton University Press, Princeton.

HERMAN, R. and STRINGFIELD, S. (1995), *Ten Promising Programs for Educating Disadvantaged Students: Evidence of Impact*, Center for Social Organisation of Schools, Baltimore, MD.

HIEBERT, E. (1994), "Reading Recovery in the United States: What Difference Does It Make to an Age Cohort?", *Educational Researcher*, 23, 9, pp. 15-25.

HILL, P. and ROWE, K. (1996), "Multilevel Modelling in School Effectiveness Research, School Effectiveness and School Improvement", *Multilevel Modelling Newsletter* 7, 1, pp. 1-34.

HOHMANN, M., BARNET, B. and WEIKART, D. (1979), *Young Children in Action*, High/Scope Press, Ypsilanti, MI.

HOLTERMAN, S. (1997), *All Our Futures: The Impact of Public Expenditure and Fiscal Policies on Children and Young People*, Barnados, Barking, Essex.

HOWARTH, C., KENWAY, P., PALMER, G. and STREET, C. (1998), *Key Indicators of Poverty and Social Exclusion*, New Policy Institute, London.

HUMMELUHR N. (1997), *Youth Guarantees in The Nordic Countries*, Background Paper Commissioned by OECD.

ILO-UNESCO (1988), *Committee of Experts on the Application of the Recommendation Concerning the Status of Teachers*, ILO/UNESCO, Geneva.

JOHNSON, F. and JAMISON, J. (1998), *The Impact of Class Size: An Interim Research Summary*, National Foundation for Educational Research, Slough, Buckinghamshire.

JOHNSON, G. (1997), "Resilient At-Risk Students in the Inner-City", *McGill Journal of Education*, 32, 1, pp. 35-49.

JONES, E., GOTTFREDSON, E., and GOTTFREDSON, D. (1997), "Success for Some: An Evaluation of the Success for All Programmes", *Evaluation Review* 21, 6, pp. 643-670.

KENNEDY, H. (1997a), *Learning Works: Widening Participation in Further Education (The Kennedy Report)*, Further Education Funding Council, London.

KENNEDY, H. (1997b), "The Report", *Guardian Education*, July 1, pp. 2-3.

KENWAY, J. (1996) "The Information Superhighway and Post-Modernity: The Social Promise and the Social Price", *Comparative Education*, 32, 2, pp. 217-231.

KLEIN, S. (1997), "Response: A System of Expert Panels and Design Competitions: Complementary Federal Approaches to Find, Develop and Share Promising and Exemplary Products and Programs", *Educational Researcher*, 26, 6, pp. 12-20.

KOREAN MINISTRY OF EDUCATION (1996), "The Development of Education, National Report of the Republic of Korea", Ministry of Education, Seoul.

KOVACS, K. (1998), "Combatting Failure at School: An International Perspective", in L. Stoll and K. Myers (eds.), *No Quick Fixes: Perspectives on Schools in Difficulty*, Falmer, London, pp. 222-241.

LASSNIG, L. (1998), "Youth Labour Market Policy in Austria", *Consultancy Report for the OECD*, Draft Version.

LEVIN, H. (1987), "Accelerated Schools for Disadvantaged Students", *Educational Leadership*, 44, 6, pp. 19-21.

LEVIN, H. and LOCKHEED, M. (1993) (eds.), *Effective Schools in Developing Countries*, Falmer, London and Washington, DC.

LITTLE, A. and SIVASITHAMBARAM, R. (1993), "Improving Educational Effectiveness in a Plantation School: The Case of the Gonakelle School in Sri Lanka", in H. Levin, and M. Lockheed (eds.), *Effective Schools in Developing Countries*, Falmer, London and Washington, DC, pp. 87-107.

MACGILCHRIST, B. (1997), "Reading and Achievement", *Research Papers in Education*, 12, 2, pp. 57-176.

MACLEOD, F. (ed.) (1989), *The High/Scope Project, School of Education*, Exeter, UK.

MEIER, D. (1997), "Can the Odds be Changed?", *Educational Policy*, 11, 2, pp. 194-208.

MERKENS, H. (1996), "Youth at Risk: Attitudes and Value Concepts among Young People in Europe at Time of Social Change", in D. Benner and D. Lenzen (1996) (eds.), *Education for the New Europe*, , Berghahn Books, Providence, RI and Oxford, England, pp. 43-68.

MINNIS, M., FELGATE, R. and SCHAGEN, I. (1999), *The National Numeracy Project: Technical Report for 1998*, National Foundation for Educational Research, Slough, Bucks.

MORTIMORE, J. (1997), *Innovatory Staffing Practices in City Technology Colleges*, Unpublished Ph.D. thesis, University of London, London.

MORTIMORE, J and BLACKSTONE, T. (1982), *Disadvantage and Education*, Heinemann, London.

MORTIMORE, P. (1995), "The Class Size Conundrum", *Education*, September.

MORTIMORE, P. (1998), *The Road to Improvement: Reflections on School Effectiveness*, Swets and Zeitlinger, Lisse, The Netherlands.

MORTIMORE, P., DAVIES, H. and PORTWAY, S. (1996), "Burntwood School: A Case Study", in National Commission on Education (NCE) (1996), *Success Against the Odds: Effective Schools in Disadvantaged Areas*, Routledge, London, pp. 146-174.

MORTIMORE, P., MORTIMORE, J. and THOMAS, H. (1994), *Managing Associate Staff*, Paul Chapman Publishing, London.

MORTIMORE, P., SAMMONS, P., STOLL, L., LEWIS, D. and ECOB, R. (1988), *School Matters: The Junior Years*, Wells, Somerset, Open Books, Reprinted 1995, Paul Chapman Publishing, London.

MOUNTS, J. (1996), *What is the Effect of Reading Recovery on the Reading Achievement of At-Risk Students?*, ERIC Accession, No. ED416448, EDRS Microfiche.

MURPHY, R., BROWN, P. and PARTINGTON, J. (1990), "An Evaluation of the Effectiveness of CTCs' Selection Processes", Report to the Department of Education and Science.

MYERS, K. (1995), "Intensive Care for the Chronically Sick", paper presented at the European Conference on Educational Research, University of Bath, Bath, UK.

NABUCO, E. (1997), "The Effects of Three Early Childhood Curricula in Portugal on Children's Progress in the First Year of Primary School", unpublished Ph.D. Thesis, Institute of Education, University of London, London.

NATIONAL COMMISSION ON EDUCATION (NCE) (1996), *Success Against the Odds: Effective Schools in Disadvantaged Areas*, Routledge, London.

NEW ZEALAND MINISTRY OF EDUCATION (1996), *Te Whariki: Early Childhood Curriculum*, Learning Media Ltd, Wellington, NZ.

NIZA, S. (1991), *Sentido do acto pedagogico B Uma prespectiva pedagogica de Desenvolvimento Funcional* (The meaning of pedagogical action: A Functional Developmental Perspective), Unpublished paper.

NYE, B., ACHILLES, C., ZAHARIAS, J., FULTON, B. and WALLENHORST, M. (1993), "Tennessee's Bold Experiment: Using Research to Inform Policy and Practice", *Tennessee Education*, 22, 3, pp. 10-17.

OECD (1995), *Our Children at Risk*, OECD, Paris.

OECD (1998a), *Education at a Glance: OECD Indicators*, OECD, Paris.

OECD (1998b), *Overcoming Failure at School*, OECD, Paris.

OECD (1998c), *Co-ordinating Services for Children and Youth At Risk*, OECD, Paris.

OECD (1982), *Caring for Young Children: An Analysis of Educational and Social Policies*, Paris.

OGBU, J. (1997), "Racial Stratification and Education in the United States: Why Inequality Persists", in A. Halsey, H. Lauder, P. Brown and A. Wells (eds.), *Education: Culture, Economy, Society*, Oxford University Press, Oxford, pp. 765-778.

OPPENHEIM, C. (1993), *Poverty: the Facts*, Child Poverty Action Group (CPAG), London.

PINNELL, G. (1988), "Sustained Effects of a Strategy-Centered Early Intervention Program in Reading", paper presented at AERA Annual meeting, New Orleans.

PLEWIS, I. (1997), "Letter to the Times Educational Supplement", 9 May.

POGROW, S. (1998), "What is an Exemplary Program, and Why Should Anyone Care? A reaction to Slavin and Klein", *Educational Researcher*, 27, 7, pp. 22-29.

POWER, S. WHITTY, G. and YOUDELL, D. (1995), *No Place to Learn: Homelessness and Education*, Shelter, London.

PROUDFORD, C. and BAKER, R. (1995), "Schools that Make a Difference: A Sociological Perspective on Effective Schooling", *British Journal of Sociology of Education*, 16, 3, pp. 277-292.

READING RECOVERY NATIONAL NETWORK (1995), *Reading Recovery in England*, Institute of Education, London.

REYNOLDS, D. (1995), ndon "Failure Free Schooling", *IARTV Series 49*, IARTV, Melbourne.

ROBERTS, V. and MADHERE, S. (1990), Chapter 1 Resource Laboratory Program for Computer Assisted Instruction (CAI) 1989-90, Evaluation Report, District of Columbia Public Schools (ED334299), Washington, DC.

ROBINSON, P. (1997), *Literacy, Numeracy and Economic Performance*, Centre for Economic Policy, London School of Economics, London.

RUTTER, M. and MADGE, N. (1976), *Cycles of Disadvantage*, Heinemann, London.

RUTTER, M., MAUGHAN, MORTIMORE, P. and OUSTON, J. (1979), *Fifteen Thousand Hours: Secondary Schools and their Effects on Children*, Paul Chapman Publishing, London.

SAMMONS, P., HILLMAN, J. and MORTIMORE, P. (1995), "Key Characteristics of Effective Schools: A Review of School Effectiveness Research", Report commissioned by Ofsted, Institute of Education and Ofsted, London.

SAMMONS, P., KYSEL, F. and MORTIMORE, P. (1983), "Educational Priority Indices: A New Perspective", *British Educational Research Journal*, 9, pp. 27-40.

SAMMONS, P., THOMAS, S. and MORTIMORE, P. (1997), *Forging Links: Effective Schools and Effective Departments*, Paul Chapman Publishing, London.

SARASON, S. (1990), *The Predictable Failure of Educational Reform: Can We Change Before It's Too Late?*, Jossey Bass, San Francisco.

SCHWEINHART, L., BARNES, H. and WEIKART, D. (1993), *Significant Benefits: The High/Scope Perry Preschool Study through Age 27*, High/Scope Educational Research Foundation, Michigan.

SIRAJ-BLATCHFORD, I. (in press) "Early Childhood Pedagogy: Practice, Principles and Research", in P. Mortimore (ed.), *Understanding Pedagogy and its Impact on Learning*, Sage, London.

SIRAJ-BLATCHFORD, I. and MACLEOD-BRUDENELL, J. (1999), *Supporting Science, Design and Technology in the Early Years*, Open University Press, Buckingham.

SLAVIN R. (1990), "Class Size and Student Achievement: Is Smaller Better?", *Contemporary Education*, 62, 1, pp. 6-12.

SLAVIN, R. (1997a), "Design Competitions: A Proposal for a New Federal Role in Educational Research and Development", *Educational Researcher*, 26, 1, pp. 22-28.

SLAVIN, R. (1997b), "Design Competitions and Expert Panels: Similar Objectives, Very Different Paths", *Educational Researcher*, 26, 6, pp. 21-22.

SLAVIN, R., KARWEIT, N., DOLAN, L., WASIK, B. and MADDEN, N. (1993), "Success for all: Longitudinal Effects of a Restructuring Program for Inner City Elementary Schools", *American Educational Research Journal*, 30, pp. 123-148.

SLAVIN, R., MADDEN, N., DOLAN, L., WASIK, B., ROSS, S. and SMITH, L. (1994), "Success for All: Longitudinal Effects of Systemic School-by-School Reform in Seven Districts", Paper presented at the Annual Meeting of the AERA in New Orleans.

SMITH, G. (1987), "Whatever Happened to Educational Priority Areas?", Oxford Review of Education, 13, 1.

SMITH, G., SMITH, T. and WRIGHT, G. (1997), "Poverty and Schooling: Choice, Diversity or Division?", in A. Walker and C. Walker (eds.), Britain Divided: The Growth of Social Exclusion in the 1980s and 1990s, Child Poverty Action Group (CPAG), London.

SMITH, T. and NOBLE, M. (1995), Education Divides: Poverty and Schooling in the 1990s, CPAG, London.

SMITH, V. (1997), Self-Esteem and Urban Education, ERIC Accession Number ED411351, EDRS Microfiche.

STOLL, L. (1995), "The Complexity and Challenge of Ineffective Schools", paper presented at the European Conference on Educational Research, University of Bath, September.

STUART WELLS, A. and SERNA, I. (1997), "The Politics of Culture: Understanding Local Political Resistance to Detracking in Racially Mixed Schools, in A. Halsey, H. Lauder, P. Brown and A. Wells (eds.), Education: Culture, Economy, Society, Oxford University Press, Oxford, pp. 718-735.

SUMMERS, A. and JOHNSON, A. (1996), "The Effects of School-Based Management Plans", in E. Hanushek and D. Jorgenson (eds.), Improving America's Schools: The Role of Incentives, Washington, DC.

SYLVA, K. and HURRY, J. (1995), "Early Intervention in Children with Reading Difficulties: An Evaluation of Reading Recovery and a Phonological Training", report prepared for the School Curriculum and Assessment Agency (SCAA), Thomas Coram Research Unit, University of London, Institute of Education/SCAA, London.

THOMAS, S. and MORTIMORE, P. (1996), "Comparison of Value Added Models for Secondary School Effectiveness", Research Papers in Education, 11, 1, pp. 5-33.

THRUPP, M. (1995), "The School Mix Effect: The History of an Enduring Problem in Educational Research, Policy and Practice", British Journal of Sociology of Education, 16, pp. 183-203.

THRUPP, M. (1997), "The Art of the Possible: Organising and Managing High and Low Socio-Economic Schools", paper presented to the annual meeting of the AERA in Chicago, pp. 24-28.

TIMSS (1997), Performance Assessment in IEA's Third International Mathematics and Science Study, Center for the Study of Testing, Evaluation and Educational Policy, Boston MA.

TIZARD, J., SCHOFIELD, W. and HEWISON, J. (1982), "Symposium: Reading-Collaboration between Teachers and Parents in Assisting Children's Reading", British Journal of Educational Psychology, 52, 1, pp. 1-15.

TOWNSEND, P. (1996), Quoted in H. Richards, "Perspectives", Times Higher Educational Supplement, August 30, p. 13.

WALBERG, H., and GREENBERG, R. (1998), "The Diogenes Factor: Why it's Hard to Get an Unbiased View of Programs like 'Success for All'", Education Week, 52, 36.

WALKER, A. and WALKER, C. (eds.) (1997), Britain Divided: the Growth of Social Exclusion in the 1980s and 1990s, Child Poverty Action Group (CPAG), London.

WALLACE, T. (1993), "Chicago Public Schools: Evaluation of the 1987-88 Paideia Program", in D. Waldrip, W. Marks and N. Estes (eds.), Magnet School Policy Studies and Evaluations, IRIEC, Houston, TX.

WEIKART, D., ROGERS, L., ADCOCK, C. and MCCLELLAND, D. (1971), The Cognitively Oriented Curriculum: A Framework for Pre-School Teachers, University of Illinois, Urbana IL.

WESTFALL, A. and PISAPIA, J. (1994), Students Who Defy the Odds: A Study of Resilient At-Risk Students, ERIC Research Brief #18.

WHITTY, G. (1997), Social Theory and Education Policy: The Legacy of Karl Mannheim, Karl Mannheim Memorial Lecture, Institute of Education, London.

WILSON, J. (1997), "Studying Inner-City Social Dislocations: The Challenge of Public Agenda Research", in A. Halsey, H. Lauder, P. Brown and A. Wells (eds.), Education: Culture, Economy, Society, Oxford University Press, Oxford, pp. 750-764.

THE KORSØR PRODUCTION SCHOOL
AND THE DANISH PRODUCTION SCHOOLS

by
Gert Moeller and Verner Ljung
Korsør Production School, Denmark

1. Background and legislation

The Danish production schools arose out of a number of pilot projects initiated by the Ministry of Education at the end of the 1970s. The background was increasing youth unemployment and far too great a number of youngsters who did not continue their education after compulsory school.

The production schools have since developed into an independent school form. In 1985 the first independent legislation was passed within this area. This legislation has been revised a couple of times since, the last time in 1998.

The legislative framework consists of broad descriptions that regulate the activities of the schools. Within this framework and with a background of the special practice and profile that this school form has developed over the years, each school has extended freedom to arrange its activities so that they suit local conditions and so that local involvement is maintained and developed.

The revision of 1998 decreed that production schools be part of the national society's strategy for education of all youngsters and that they should, to a large part, be geared towards those having the greatest difficulty in continuing their education after compulsory education.

Denmark has invested heavily in educational strategies for the last decade. Great improvements have been made, but even today about 20% of those who finish compulsory school each year either do not begin or do not successfully complete further studies.

2. Student capacity

Today there are 108 production schools, scattered all over the country. In 1998 the schools had a total capacity of about 5 700 places per year (corresponding to 240 000 student weeks). The capacity of the schools vary greatly: 11% of the schools have less than 25 places per year, 38% have from 25-50 places, 20% have from 51-100 places, 23% have from 101-200 places, and 8% have from 201-250 places per year (figures from 1997).

Korsør Production School, which represented the production schools at the OECD conference, was established in 1984 by Korsør Municipality – a municipality with slightly more than 20 000 inhabitants situated at the western coast of the island Zealand.

Today the school has a capacity of about 80 places per year, and the majority of the almost 200 students admitted each year come from the local municipality. The school has had continuous co-operation with its southern neighbouring municipality, from where approximately one quarter of the students are recruited, for many years.

The production schools have continuous admission and school-leaving all year round, and the stay is consequently of individual duration with an estimated average of 5-6 months. In 1998 all production schools combined had a throughput activity or total in-take of about 11-12 000 youths, meaning short or long-term contacts with just under 2% of the total population of the age group between 16 and 24.

3. The relationship of production schools to the legislation concerning the combating of youth unemployment and its place within the educational framework

The Danish legislation concerning the combating of youth unemployment is today arranged in such a way that all youths under 30 who are unemployed, have the right to get and the duty to receive an offer of activation from the municipality of residence. The activation can either be supported work or education, of at least 30 hours a week.

The production schools were formally closely related to these municipal initiatives for the combating of youth unemployment, but as of 1996 all youths with no education beyond compulsory schooling could freely be admitted to a production school, whether employed or not.

As a result of this change, the production schools are no longer primarily an activation offer for unemployed youths, but must be considered an ordinary offer of education for those who have a need for an alternative access to further education and work, compared with the traditional youth education, namely vocational training and higher secondary education.

As a school form the production schools are not an integrated part of the traditional education, but placed as an independent institution at the fringe of the total Danish youth education picture.

Today 90% of the production school students are admitted freely. The production schools may still, however, be used by the municipalities as part of the statutory activation, but it is only about 10% of the students who are referred to the schools in this way.

4. The target groups of the schools

Applicants to production schools must be under 25 and, as a rule, have competed the obligatory 9-year basic general education. Youths admitted to the production schools are usually not sure about career or education paths. They are students whom the educational system has been unable to motivate or maintain. Even though about 95% of those who finish compulsory schooling each year begin a programme of youth education, a substantial number of those will drop out of the programme they have chosen. In 1994/95 the drop-out rate within vocational training was about 27% (10 800 persons) while it was about 32% (8 400 persons) within higher secondary education (the figures are from the Educational Memorandum of the Ministry of Education, 1998).

– With regard to Korsør Production School, 52.4% of a total of 187 youths enrolled had dropped out of vocational training prior to admission at Korsør during 1998. Another 8% had dropped out of secondary higher education (see Table 4).

– Approximately 10% of the 187 student admitted in 1998 had not completed the 9-year obligatory education and had thus left the basic general school without the school-leaving certificate (see Table 5).

– 14% of the 84 students who were registered at the school as of January 11th 1999 stated that they had attended a local alternative school for pupils with special difficulties. Seven per cent stated that they had attended a foreign language class, and 33% stated that they had either attended a special class or received remedial instruction or other special tuition (see Table 6).

– In 1998 8.6% were under the age of 15 upon their admission to the school; 43.9% were between the ages of 15-17, 44.9% between the ages of 18-22, and only 2.6% were age 23 or more (see Table 2).

– In the last 2 years, enrolees have been divided equally between men and women (see Table 1).

It is the experience of the production school that it is important to mix the single student group at the school and at each workshop in such a way that youths with widely different backgrounds and difficulties are represented.

These very often vast differences in the profiles of the youths contribute to securing both the dialogue and the balance necessary to create the coherence and dynamics of the school.

5. Organisation

A production school is established as an independent institution through local initiative by one or more municipalities. The local authorities approve the regulations and give a modest statutory basic grant (a fixed amount irrespective of the student capacity of the individual school).

As from 1996, the greater part of the production school finances comes from activity-derived state grants, fixed by the annual state budget. The state grants constitute 90-95%. Added to this is the revenue from the sale of the manufactured goods from the school workshops. The boards of the schools must have representatives appointed by the trade unions and the employers' union, and there must not be a majority of members appointed by the public authorities on the board.

Only a very few production schools are housed in modern buildings. In most cases the production schools have taken over older or run-down buildings, which the school itself – in co-operation between students and teachers – has renovated and later rebuilt or extended when possible. In this way the students often participate in establishing, furnishing, and influencing the settings of the schools.

6. Creating a school on the move

From the beginning production schools have sought to develop an extremely flexible framework. Production schools are constantly on the move, with positive energy, and continuously capable of integrating youths who have been rejected by the traditional educational system. They must not assume a character of being a socio-educational arrangement or a therapeutical institution.

At Korsør Production School we have students continuously registering and leaving, which means that the training at a production school may be mixed into the youth's own educational development when he or she wants and/or needs it. Youths may be admitted from day to day all year round, and there is no limit in advance as to how long the stay at the school may last.

At Korsør Production School a total of 105 youths completed the training in 1998. Of these, 48.6% had a stay at the school between 1 and 7 months, 21.9% between 7 and 12 months, and 14.3% for more than 12 months. An additional 15.2% were registered for less than 1 month (see Table 7).

As something relatively new the schools have – as already mentioned – free admission. All youths under 25 who have not already finished a youth education (typically higher secondary education or vocational training etc.) may be freely admitted to a production school anywhere in the country.

At Korsør Production School nearly 90% of the 187 students who were registered in 1998, were freely admitted, that is after the youths' own enquiry to the school for admission. Nearly 10% were referred from the municipalities as part of an activation duty (see Table 3).

All our students have the right to a "fresh start", a new opportunity – to be admitted to the production school without our demanding – or maybe even in all secrecy obtaining – all kinds of information from the local authorities about his or her former behaviour within the established system. The schools are independent institutions, which as a rule have no obligation to deliver or obtain information to or from authorities outside the schools about the student's personal and social affairs.

A considerable part of the work of the schools is concerned with the youth's personal and social situation, which is often a precondition for the youth's presence and active participation in the training. The fact that the schools are not diploma-oriented means that each student may explore both his strong and weak points. The individual programme is flexible, creating unanticipated links and no student will consequently participate in totally mapped-out educational programmes. Student guidance at the production schools is integrated into the training. The guidance takes place daily and is integrated in social and work processes at the workshops, and the responsibility is basically placed with all the teachers of the school. Moreover regular formal guidance talks about the training take place to secure the continuous evaluation of the educational and personal development of each student. Finally, guidance about educational and professional prospects takes place.

- The individual training process must be documented, to which end Korsør Production School uses the following tools:

- When the student starts at a workshop a personal file is created, containing a description of the aims and goals of the workshop.

- The file also contains an agreement form, which is worked out in co-operation between student and teacher, with a plan for educational as well as personal development. This plan is followed-up continuously (at least every three months) with a talk that leaves sufficient time for the student and the teacher to discuss the youth's educational and personal development.

- The file also contains a description of the tasks that the student participates in or has finished. It may be in the form of for example drawings, pictures, CD-ROMs, tapes, products, etc.

- The file finally contains safety instructions since no student uses tools, machines, or materials without these having been studied, understood and signed by the student.

All youths admitted to the production schools receive a school grant which is subject to tax and paid out every fortnight. The school grant is to be seen partly as payment for the work which the youths carry out at the workshops of the schools, partly as an amount that entails independence from the public benefit systems. The school grant is at present DKK 1 070 per week (corresponding to about USD 170) for youths of over 18 and DKK 440 per week (corresponding to about USD 70 for youths under 18). The expenses for the school grant are paid by the production schools and reimbursed by the state.

A small number of students, usually six to eight, works with each workshop instructor. Seen in relation to the total permanent staff (including management and administration) the average number of students is approximately five per staff member.

To ensure a social, secure, and inspiring environment where the youths can develop, the production schools are dependent on committed teachers who have a professional background, who can take on responsibility for the instruction and guidance they practice, who are fond of youths and have special insight into them, and who can motivate and inspire them. These teachers receive good wages.

The majority of the teachers are not educated as proper teachers, but come from practical working life, as a rule with a vocational background and with widely different forms of educational experience.

Besides, it is characteristic of the production school instructors that they are all hired under the same working conditions and work according to the same set of rules – no matter what their educational backgrounds are.

7. Objectives and tasks

The production school education is based on the idea of creating training that integrates or unites production, theoretical education, guidance and personal development.

All education at the production schools thus has two closely connected objectives: to strengthen the personal development of the students, and to qualify them for the general educational system or the labour market.

The personal development – also called life skills – is about the individual's own acquisition of and adjustment to social rules and values.

The qualification is about acquisition of knowledge, competence, and skills, which means more target-oriented education and attachment to the labour market. It is characteristic that – while personal development or life skills are not easily taught – the training may be organised to restore an ascertained lack of qualification in the youth.

The task of the production schools is to organise the training of each student in order to create a fruitful inter-action between personal development and acquiring qualifications. This double approach, with which the student picks up knowledge, is of great importance to our understanding of and attitude to what happens to the young students during their stay.

We do not only talk about their professional, technical qualifications, but also their social orientation, their belief in their own manoeuvring skills and their basic navigation ability.

8. Workshop training

The principal element of the education is that youth learn by doing, gaining experience, building on it, and gradually extending the range of action, both as a human being and professionally.

The training at each school is centred around a number of various workshops with youths participating in the accomplishment of real production assignments, including larger complex tasks or projects.

- The workshops of Korsør Production School work *i*) independently with assignments; *ii*) with projects together with other workshops; or *iii*) with the whole school. Each student is always attached to a particular workshop.

- The assignments are integrated into an educational framework. As part of this, order sheets of all assignments are worked out, and in this connection, use of materials, consumption per hour, etc. are calculated.

All products are manufactured with intent of being sold. This means that the products must be of a sufficiently professional standard and quality. The fact that goods and services are used and sold is experienced by the youths as acknowledgement of a real piece of work. They feel needed.

Whether it is ordinary product manufacturing, services, or, for example, music or theatre performances, etc., production is the most visible activity.

Korsør Production School has the following permanent workshops:

- Metal workshop,

- Sailor and wood workshop,

- Textiles/design and shop,

- Painter's/signmaker's workshop,

- EDP/multimedia,

- Office,

- Music workshop,

- Pedagogical workshop,

- Kitchen/canteen.

Workshops offer assignments of varying difficulty so as to foster professional development. For each student, tasks must be found which at the same time contain challenges and the possibility of independent solutions.

- The educational activities of Korsør Production School are organised round single workshops or projects whose basis is the production/services, e.g. real productions or projects like metal production, sign production, supply of food, a musical band, a folder in English.

- The training must drop "would-be" situations and be close to reality: the food is served and eaten, the metal product is sold, the sign is put up, the band tours, the folder in English is distributed to the world.

- The school meets the youths' demand for practical and concrete challenges in the shape of participation in realistic production processes in which built-in educational possibilities and challenges are used and met.

During their training the students will get a chance to test themselves at one or more workshops, and through the practical, independent work they learn how to learn. They gain experience, acquire skills and new knowledge – real qualifications which may be difficult for the youths to obtain these days when many unskilled job possibilities disappear.

The practical work on the production assignments means that there are many things that must be done – many duties that must be carried out. These duties are part of the pedagogical agenda of the workshops. They are both the source and the centre of a good, practicable environment of learning. It is the youths' inclination that motivates – and this inclination is also connected to the discipline inherent in the necessary work.

The production schools are also related to the craftsman's culture that does not teach through theory, but through concrete motivation. Problems, when encountered, are resolved. During their stay at the school the students inevitably develop personally, and as they experience that they can produce within one or more practical fields, they regain the belief that they can learn something new.

This motivates them to accept the schools' offer of training in Danish, math, foreign languages, information technology, etc. The offer aims at filling the educational gaps which each student has within these fields.

– Korsør Production School works out documentation for the students' participation in this training. The documentation is kept in the student's personal file.

Moreover, it is our task to acquaint the students with social and cultural matters. For that purpose we arrange a number of activities across the workshops for parts of or the whole school.

– Korsør Production School arranges among other things: common activities with social subjects, net café, common meals, daily common briefing about large and small activities, various arrangements/parties in connection with festivals and our own traditions, excursions and school camps, and international co-operation and exchanges.

An extremely important aspect of the activities of the production schools is to create a coherent youth environment. At the production school the youths become part of a binding, social, working community where they meet other youths – friends, acquaintances and equals. The whole training is not oriented towards a specific education and thereby also becomes a sanctuary from the pressure of expectation and the cliques that often characterise youth education in general. A school environment where it is possible to test one's self individually and socially.

9. Results

The results are often measured by where the youths go when they leave. Consequently, it is expected that the youths actually continue an education or get a job after the stay at the school.

As already mentioned, the schools have an obligation also to admit those youths who have the most trouble completing their education. Statistics cannot always accurately reflect the remarkable progress the students have made, when compared to their state upon admission. The Ministry of Education currently only measures the youths' work and educational situation at the time of leaving without factoring in their situation upon admission and without following up on the situation some time after their leaving. In addition to this, other conditions, such as the local employment situation and local educational possibilities, etc. (which will always influence the results of the measuring), must be taken into consideration.

The results of the production schools for 1997 were as follows: slightly more than 37% continued in a proper education and roughly 20% obtained an ordinary job. Approximately 9% continued in municipal job programmes, while 20% followed other activities, including conscription, maternity leave, journey abroad, etc. (see Table 8).

The remaining 15% were directly unemployed. This last group consists of:

– Youths who left the production school but who quickly received and were obliged to accept a new offer of activation from the municipality if *i*) they had not found a job; *ii*) were not continuing their education; *iii*) did not return to the production school.

– Youths with major social, health and/or behavioural problems (serious mental or drug problems for example) who thereby fell outside the target group of the production schools as well as the municipal activation projects.

For 1998, the results were as follows: 43.8% of 105 youths who left Korsør Production School that year started an education programme, and 20% got a job. Another 3.8% continued in a municipal activation programme, 14.3% became unemployed and 18.1% continued in other activities.

10. Pedagogical attitudes and methods

While the framework and times have changed, the attitudes and the methods of the production schools are no new invention. They are a continuation of pedagogical attitudes and methods which have been described and practised ever since Antiquity. To talk about a particular pedagogical trend within the production schools would therefore be incorrect. It is rather a pedagogy rooted in common sense and the obligation to create the framework and the conditions that meet the students' needs to be active – especially at the workshops of the school, where the instructors' credibility depends on their own good example.

The starting point of the development of the pedagogical activities of the production schools has thus been our acknowledgement that the actual learning lies elsewhere, and not where many people expected. The most important thing is that we listen to, and are receptive to, the students.

11. A crossbreed within education

We have thus far tried to describe the special combination of craftsman's skills, integrated theoretical training, personal development, student guidance, cultural education, and coherent youth environment that characterise the Danish production schools. This combination makes the production school particularly capable of realising wide-ranging training offers for a great variety of youths, irrespective of qualifications and social background.

We are talking about a small field compared to the traditional youth education – but also a school model which has in the last years achieved considerable recognition nationally and aroused interest internationally.

In this connection it must be emphasised that on the one hand the description of the school form – as it is outlined in this paper – often verges on ideal reflections, which cannot always and in all respects correspond completely with the reality of each school, but that on the other hand we have experience and faith in the potential of this school form.

The art of realising this potential – to create and maintain a school form on the move – is certainly not without great difficulties and with inherent dangers of institutionalisation. Compared with traditional school forms everything has to be evaluated – and continuously re-evaluated – and mixed in a new way so that each element turns out differently.

The production school is constantly performing a difficult balancing act between

– social policy

• because the schools continuously pick up youths who are threatened with rejection

• because the school grant received by the youths makes them independent of the social benefit system

• because the schools take an interest in their social situation and help them outside the official welfare system

– educational policy

• because the schools go easy on teaching youths who have other ways of learning than the majority

- because the schools challenge the established educational system

- because the schools fill gaps from the basic general school when the student is motivated,

– and labour market policy

- because the youths get job training through their participation in real production tasks

- because the school grant received by the youths compensates for a piece of work and for active participation in the training

Throughout the almost 20-year history of the production schools there have been several political attempts at categorising the form, thereby limiting our manoeuvrability. At present, there is a closer relation with the educational field which is probably preferable if it does not tip the balance. For the production schools are linked to education, social fields and the labour market and in our opinion these links must be maintained and further developed if the schools are to serve those youths whose needs are the greatest. To conclude: in our experience, the following criteria must be met when organising training for the youths in the production schools:

– The student groups must be mixed with youths of widely different backgrounds and qualifications.

– The training must have a practical basis and must be ruled by duty, necessity and in a working community.

– There must be continuous admission and school-leaving and individual training programmes.

– The teachers must be characterised by personal involvement in the youth group.

– There must be a coherent youth environment at the school.

Table 1. **Breakdown by sex of the registered students for 1997 and 1998**
(Percentage of the total number of registered students)

	Female	Male
1997	49.5	50.5
1998	49.7	50.3

Table 2. **Age at admission**
(Percentage of the total number of registered students)

	1996	1997	1998
under 15	7.6	10.5	8.6
15 to 17	42.1	42.1	43.9
18 to 22	46.2	42.1	44.9
23 or older	4.1	5.3	2.6

Table 3. **How students were recruited to the school**
(Percentage of the total number of admitted students)

	1996	1997	1998
Freely admitted	84.2	90.5	89.8
Activated by the municipality	15.2	8.4	9.6
Activated by the job center	0.6	1.1	0.5

Table 4. **Students who had dropped out prior to admission**
(Percentage of the total number of admitted students)

	1996	1997	1998
Dropped out of vocational education	45.1	47.5	52.4
Dropped out of higher secondary education	8.2	8.9	8
Non drop-out	46.7	43.6	39.6

Table 5. **Basic educational background of students**
(Percentage of the total number of admitted students)

	1996	1997	1998
Not completed[a]	12.9	10.5	9.6
9th form[b]	46.2	47.4	47.6
10th form[c]	40.9	42.1	42.8

Notes:

a. Have not completed the 9-year basic obligatory education and don't have certificate.

b. Have completed the 9-year basic obligatory education and have certificate.

c. Have completed optional 10th year with certificate.

Note for Tables 1 to 5: 171 registered students in 1996; 190 in 1997; 187 in 1998.

Table 6. **Percentage of students having special arrangements in basic general school on January 11 1999**[a]

Special arrangement	Percentage
A class[b]	14
Foreign language class[c]	7
Remedial instruction class etc.[d]	33
Other classes[e]	46

Notes:

a. The table is based on information collected on January 11 1999 from a total of 84 students registered on that day at the production school.

b. Alternative municipal school for basic general school pupils with special difficulties.

c. Special class within basic general school for children of immigrants and fugitives.

d. Students who have attended a remedial instruction class or who have received remedial instruction or who have received other special training offers.

e. Students who stated that they have not participated in special educational arrangements.

Table 7. **Duration of stay at school for those students who left[a] between 1996-98**
(Percentage of the total number of school-leavers)

	1996	1997	1998
Less than 1 month	12.1	15	15.2
1 to 4 months	45.5	29.9	28.6
4 to 7 months	20.2	14.2	20
7 to 10 months	12.1	16.5	9.5
10 to 12 months	3	7.9	12.4
More than 12 months	7.1	16.5	14.3

Notes:
a. The figures for students leaving the school are as follows: 99 people in 1996; 125 people in 1997; 105 people in 1998.

Table 8. **Students' situation upon leaving[a] for the years 1996-98**
(Percentage of the total number of school-leavers)

	1996	1997	1998
Education	30.3	37.8	43.8
Wage earners	26.3	20.5	20
Activation[b]	6.0	8.7	3.8
Unemployment[c]	21.2	14.2	14.3
Other activities[d]	17.2	19.7	18.1

Notes:
a. The figures for students leaving the school are as follows: 99 people in 1996; 125 people in 1997; 105 people in 1998.
b. Students in municipal activation projects.
c. Includes:
 • youths who have left the production school but who will quickly receive and be obliged to accept a new offer of activation from the municipality if *i*) they have not found a job; *ii*) are not continuing their education; *iii*) do not return to the production school.
 • youths with major social, health and/or behavioural problems (serious mental or drug problems for example) who thereby fall outside the target group of the production schools as well as the municipal activation projects.
d. Including, for example, conscription, maternity leave, changing address.

Source for all tables: Author.

WORKSHOP 2

INNOVATIVE PRACTICES IN LINKING INITIAL EDUCATION TO THE WORLD OF WORK

IMPROVING PATHWAYS IN THE UNITED STATES FROM HIGH SCHOOL TO COLLEGE AND CAREER*

by
David Stern
Professor of Education, University of California, Berkeley
Director, National Center for Research in Vocational Education

Summary

This paper describes the development of new pathways in the United States that prepare high school students both for further education and for work. By combining work-related applications with rigorous academic studies, these new pathways are intended to improve on both traditional vocational and traditional academic education. Traditional vocational education has been criticised for not providing a sufficient theoretical foundation for graduates to continue learning and adapting throughout their working lives. Pure academic education, on the other hand, seems irrelevant or incomprehensible to many students. Combining the two may improve students' academic performance and develop work-related capabilities at the same time. If successful, these new pathways will improve students' chances of completing university studies because they will have not only the necessary academic background but also a better understanding of how their schooling relates to a desired career. Students who do not go directly into tertiary education after high school will have the option to do so at a later time. Those who start college but do not finish will have some employment-related knowledge and experience to fall back on.

These new pathways combine three key elements (Benson, 1997). First, the curriculum includes both academic and vocational studies. Second, explicit links between secondary and tertiary education are created through course sequences that bridge the two levels. Third, work-based learning tied to classroom instruction helps students develop a range of work-related skills and abilities, and leads to deeper understanding of academic concepts by engaging students in their practical application.

Trends and issues. The rationale for these integrated pathways derives from a set of pervasive trends, discussed in Section 1. As in nearly all OECD countries, US students are staying in school longer. The great majority of US high school students aspire, and their parents aspire for them, to attend a four-year college or university and complete a bachelor's degree at least. These aspirations are based in part on the fact that university graduates generally are more successful in finding jobs, and the jobs they find are generally better paid. The additional earnings associated with a university degree are relatively high in the United States compared to other OECD countries, and they have continued to increase in the 1990s. Conversely, individuals who leave high school without a diploma are at an increasingly serious disadvantage in the labour market. New pathways are therefore designed to promote high school completion, and preserve the option of attending university for as many students as possible.

---

* Some of the accounts and analysis in this paper of developments in the United States have benefited from collaborations with a number of people, including Charles Dayton, Carolyn Dornsife, Mayo Tsuzuki Hallinan, Ilana Horn, Shannon Nuttall, James R. Stone III and Miguel Urquiola. Endnotes in the text mark sections to which particular individuals have contributed. Despite these contributions, responsibility for any error of fact or interpretation is mine alone.

At the same time, combining work and school is becoming more common. While labour force participation of 15-24 year-olds has been declining overall in most OECD countries including the United States, the proportion of employed teenagers and young adults who are students has grown dramatically. Studies of working students in the United States have found that those who work a moderate number of hours per week actually perform better in school than those who do not work at all, but academic performance suffers among students who work more than about 15 to 20 hours per week. School supervision of students' work appears to mitigate the negative effects. Linking students' part-time employment with their classroom studies therefore may contribute to educational achievement, while still allowing students to gain valuable work experience.

In the relatively unregulated labour markets of the United States, mobility among jobs and movement in and out of unemployment are relatively common, especially for recent school leavers. Researchers have debated about the extent to which employment instability reflects productive search for jobs that best match workers' interests and capabilities. Recent studies suggest that, notwithstanding such benefits, the net effect of instability for recent school leavers is to reduce their subsequent employment and earnings. Creating coherent pathways that lead from school to more stable employment therefore would provide lasting benefits.

Combining academic and vocational curriculum in high schools. New pathways are designed to permit a smoother transition to college and career, by satisfying academic course requirements for admission to a four-year college or university, while also including vocational instruction and work-based learning. The point is to combine work and school in a coherent way in order to keep students' options open during and after high school. By helping students acquire work experience related to their studies, these pathways make it easier for them to work their way through college, as most US students do. The work experience and skills acquired in high school also provide a built-in safety net for students who start college or university but do not finish.

Several different versions of these pathways are described in Section 2. Excerpts from first-hand accounts by researchers at the National Center for Research in Vocational Education (NCRVE) are included to give readers a clear impression of what students actually do.

– Career clusters or majors are sequences of academic and vocational courses related to broad fields of work such as health sciences, industrial and engineering systems, natural resources, arts and communication, or social and human services. Students usually go through a process of career exploration and guidance to decide which field to select. Courses in academic subjects are not specialised by career field, but include students from different clusters or majors.

– Urban career magnet schools or programs draw students city-wide who are interested in a field such as aviation, fashion, or tourism.

– Career academies are a rapidly spreading form of integrated pathway. They are self-contained groupings of students and teachers within a larger high school, focused on a theme such as health occupations, business and finance, manufacturing, engineering, or computers. The teaching of academic subjects is to some extent related to the academy theme.

– Whole high schools are now being divided into subschools, like academies, each with its own theme.

Proponents of integrated pathways hope to avoid the problem of unequal esteem that has hurt traditional vocational education. However, parents and teachers of students in existing advanced academic courses often resist merging them into a combined academic-vocational curriculum.

Connecting secondary and tertiary education. Section 3 discusses attempts to form more direct linkages. In 1990 a federal law provided money for states and localities to develop "Tech Prep" programs, which link the last two years of high school to the first two years of tertiary education, usually in a two-year community college. Sequences of courses leading from high school to community college culminate in two-year associate degrees in various technical or office-related occupations. Beyond these so-called "2+2" sequences, some localities have negotiated "2+2+2" agreements with four-year colleges or universities, leading to a bachelor's degree. According to some of these agreements, students who enter a two-year or four-year college are supposed to be given credit for courses they have already taken at a lower level, but in practice this option is reported to be seldom used, because faculties in the receiving institutions are reluctant to recognise coursework in the sending institutions as equivalent to their own. Such difficulties may frustrate students who aspire ultimately to transfer to a four-year institution.

Work-based learning (WBL) is discussed in Section 4. Traditionally, the main purpose of school-supervised work experience for students has been to help them acquire knowledge or skill related to employment in particular occupations or industries. This is the chief aim of co-operative education, the most common traditional form of school-supervised work experience for students in the United States. In recent years, however, the proposed purposes of WBL have expanded to include career exploration and planning, learning all aspects of an industry, increasing personal and social competence related to work in general, and enhancing students' motivation and academic achievement. Examples of WBL that address each of these purposes are drawn from direct observations by NCRVE researchers.

Although it is possible to find such examples, the general practice of WBL does not address most of these purposes in any systematic way. The most common form is brief visits to worksites, or job-shadowing to observe the process of work. Less common are the potentially more demanding experiences of paid or unpaid internship, service learning, or school-based enterprise. Even in these more intensive experiences, there is usually little explicit connection with what students are doing in their classes, especially in academic subjects. Strengthening the WBL component of integrated pathways will require greater involvement by teachers of academic subjects, who may sometimes be unwilling to invest the necessary time.

A ***brief summary of evaluation results*** is presented in Section 5. Career academies have been evaluated more often than the other approaches, because they are relatively well-defined and have been in existence for a number of years. Studies comparing students in career academies with similar students in the same schools have generally found that academy students improve their academic performance and are more likely to graduate from high school. Graduates from career academies have been found by some studies to be more likely to enrol in tertiary education, including four-year colleges and universities. Evaluations have not found much difference in the labour market performance of academy and non-academy graduates in the first few years after high school, except that some studies have found academy students working more hours per week.

A study of career magnet schools and programs, in which students were randomly assigned either to magnets or to regular high schools, found that magnet students performed no better academically, and were somewhat less likely to graduate from high school. This is attributed to great variation among magnet programs, and the fact that some explicitly discourage students who are not deemed ready for internships placements with employers. Analysis of a subsample of graduates from career magnets and regular high school programs found that the magnet graduates earned higher wages, completed more college credits after two years, and reported less high-risk behaviour such as smoking or drinking. This is attributed to more successful construction of a positive identity and sense of direction among the magnet graduates.

Two comparison studies of youth apprenticeship have found that apprenticeship students perform better in high school, are more successful in the labor market after graduation, and are at least as likely as other graduates to attend college.

Concluding comments are offered in Section 6. It may seem paradoxical that programs with work-related themes have improved students' academic performance and enrolment in tertiary education. The explanation seems to be that students become more confident in the ability to understand academic concepts when they see how to apply them in practical contexts. Integrated pathways may therefore help to resolve the dilemma for educational policy, of how to respect students' university aspirations, while recognising that most will not, in fact, complete university degrees. The logic of integrated pathways is similar to the "double qualifying" vocational pathways that have been described in many other OECD countries. The fact that attempts to create such pathways have been so widespread in the United States, where such initiatives must be taken locally, indicates that many people see a need for them.

1. Trends and issues in the transition from school to work

Like most other OECD countries, the United States in the 1990s has been redesigning institutional pathways that lead young people from secondary school to work and further education. This section briefly reviews some of the trends that have given rise to these initiatives.

More years of initial schooling

In the broadest historical perspective, current efforts can be seen as a continuation of developments that began with the industrial revolution, which removed production from the control of households and altered the economic and educational relations between adults and children in two fundamental ways. First, the value of children's time as participants in economic production diminished as young children were barred from factory work. Instead, young children became a drain on the productive time of adults, who could no longer work and supervise children simultaneously. Second, the separation of production from households made it more difficult for parents to teach children how to make a living. These changes eventually contributed to the rise of mass schooling and with it the basic life-cycle pattern of the industrial age: a transition from family to school in early childhood, followed by a transition from school to work sometime after puberty, and in old age a transition to retirement for those who could afford it. Each of these transitions – as well as the adult task of juggling work and child-raising – can be stressful, and failure is not uncommon. Institutional frameworks for managing and supporting these transitions have therefore been subject to continual reform and redesign.

The average number of years of initial schooling, after growing slowly but steadily for the past one or two centuries, has increased rapidly in the recent past. The *Employment Outlook* (OECD, 1996, Table 4.6) shows the proportions of 18 and 22 year-old men and women enrolled in school in 1984 and 1994, for 15 countries including the United States. At age 18, school enrolment of both men and women rose in all 15 countries: the unweighted average for men grew from 49% in 1984 to 64% in 1994, and from 50 to 66% for women. Completion of upper secondary education has now become the norm in many countries. At age 22, enrolment also increased in all 15 countries for females, and in all but one country (Belgium) for males: the unweighted averages rose from 20 to 28% for men and 16 to 29% for women. Tertiary education is becoming common, as secondary education did earlier in the twentieth century and primary education in the nineteenth.

Schooling is generally valued because it can enhance membership in a civilised culture, in part by improving access to work that is relatively prestigious and well rewarded. In the United States and a number of other countries, the monetary payoff to higher education continued to increase in the first half of the 1990s. OECD's *Education at a Glance* (1998a) reports the ratio (multiplied by 100) of the mean pre-tax earnings of university graduates to those of upper secondary graduates. At the beginning of the 1990s and in 1996, Table 1 shows that male and female university graduates in most countries had earnings at least 50% greater than upper secondary graduates. In the United States the ratio increased substantially for men, and slightly for women, between the beginning and the middle of the decade. The earnings advantage of US university graduates over secondary graduates grew from 64 to 83% for men, and from 74 to 75% for women. Of the other 10 countries in the table, five showed an increasing ratio for men (and one country showed no change), though only three reported an increase for women. With regard to men, but not women, the US trend was shared by a majority of these countries.

Although the earnings of university graduates relative to upper secondary graduates did not grow across the board in the early 1990s, longitudinal data from 15 countries in 1996 show that new university graduates in all but two countries were more likely to be employed than were new graduates from upper secondary school (OECD, 1998*b*, Chart 3.2). Evidently, the transition from initial schooling to work is smoother for graduates at the university level than at the upper secondary level. During the first five years after leaving school, the differences between university and upper secondary graduates narrow but do not disappear: university graduates continue to have higher rates of employment and lower rates of unemployment (Tables 3.8, 3.9). The labour market in most OECD countries gives its warmest welcome to university graduates.

The rising trend in educational attainment does create problems, however. In many countries a majority of secondary school students aspire to attend university. In the United States, 52% of young people entered university-level education in 1996, more than in any other OECD country (OECD, 1998*a*, Table C3.1). However, US colleges place large numbers of students in remedial courses after they are admitted (Kirst, 1998), and only about two-thirds of the students who enrol in four-year degree programs actually receive a bachelor's degree by the age of 30 (Adelman, 1998). The survival rate in university-level education is lower in the United States than in most other OECD countries (OECD, 1998*a*, Table C4.1). Those who start college but do not finish may experience disappointment, disorientation, and difficulty in finding desirable employment. Therefore, one of the key aims of new pathways at the secondary level in the United States is to combine more rigorous academic studies with work-related applications and work-based learning, so that high school graduates will be better prepared both to succeed in higher education and to find desirable jobs if they do not go to, or finish, college.

Fewer young people work, and more of those who work are students

As young people have stayed in school longer, their participation in paid employment has generally diminished. The *Employment Outlook* (OECD, 1996, Table 4.2) revealed a pervasive decline in employment rates among 15-19 and 20-24 year-olds from 1979 to 1994, in the United States and most other countries. It should be noted, however, that youth employment in many countries is strongly influenced by the business cycle, and many OECD countries were at a relatively low point in the cycle in 1994. Nevertheless, reports on individual countries also confirm a widespread trend toward lower employment rates among young people (Stern and Wagner, 1998; OECD, 1998*c*).

At the same time, more young people are working while enrolled in school. The *Employment_Outlook* (OECD, 1996, Table 4.10) compares the proportion of employed 18 and 22 year-old men and women who were students in 1984 and 1994 for 15 countries. For 18 year-old men, the proportion increased in all countries but one (Greece), and the unweighted average across countries rose from 16 to 25%. Similarly, the proportion of 18 year-old employed women who were students also rose in all countries but one (Italy), with the unweighted average increasing from 14 to 30%. Students did not comprise a majority of the employed 18 year-olds in any country in 1984, but they became a majority in 1994 in three countries for men and four countries for women. The increase in the proportion of employed 22 year-olds who were students was equally pervasive, although the fractions are lower than for 18 year-olds: the unweighted average across countries in 1994 was 10% for men and 11% for women. The United States had higher than average proportions of students among employed 18 and 22 year-old males and females in both 1984 and 1994, but not as high as Canada, Denmark, or the Netherlands. The United States also shared in the generally rising trend. Zemsky *et al.* (1998) provide additional detailed data on the growing tendency for US youth to pursue school and work simultaneously.

This trend also may have some adverse effects. In the United States participation of students in paid work unconnected with their schooling has raised concern that working may undermine their academic performance.[1] Previous research on working students has revealed a curious pattern: students who work a moderate number of hours per week, usually less than 15 or 20, actually perform *better* in school than students who do not work at all, and they also perform better than their peers who work longer hours per week. A 1995 review by Stern *et al.* (pp. 41-44) summarised the research up to 1993 on the academic performance of working high school students. Ten studies found that students who worked more than 15 or 20 hours a week had lower grades, did less homework, were more likely to drop out, or were less likely to complete postsecondary education, compared to other students. Three studies found no significant differences associated with working long hours. As for students working less than 15 or 20 hours a week, five studies found they had better grades, test scores, or likelihood of going to college than students who did not work at all, although three studies found that students who worked moderate hours did worse in school than students who were not employed.

Three more recent studies have found additional evidence that the association between hours of work and performance in school follows an inverted-U pattern, with students who work moderate hours performing at a higher level than students who work more, and also higher than those who do not work at all. Light (1997) analysed high school transcript data from the NLSY 1979 cohort and discovered that students who worked 1-20 hours per week on average completed more course credits – with a larger share of those credits in math and science – and still received better grades than students who did not work at all, or those who worked more than 20 hours a week.

Mortimer and Johnson (1997, 1998) also found some evidence of the inverted-U pattern in their longitudinal study of high school students in St. Paul, Minnesota. When they examined academic performance in high school, the researchers found that "seniors who limited their hours of work had higher grade point averages than those who worked more than 20 hours per week and those who did not work at all. However, the fact that this pattern occurred in only one year detracts from the argument that moderate employment has pervasive achievement-related benefits" (Mortimer and Johnson, 1998, pp. 200-201).

The inverted U is somewhat more pronounced in the St. Paul data on enrolment in postsecondary education, especially for young men. Unlike previous studies, the St. Paul study distinguished between the duration and intensity of employment: that is, between how many months a student worked during the high school years, and the student's average number of hours worked per week. In theory, long duration might indicate steadiness and ability to hold a job, while high intensity might signal a disinterest in school. Therefore, a student who accumulated a total of, say, 1 000 hours of employment over a four-year period by working in short bursts of 30 or 40 hours a week might be quite different from a student who worked steadily at a pace of 8 to 10 hours a week. Dividing students into four groups classified as high or low on duration and intensity according to their work pattern while in high school, Mortimer and Johnson (1997) found that young men in the high duration, low intensity category completed more months of postsecondary education in each of the four years after high school, compared to the other three categories of working students, and also compared to students who did not work at all in high school. The difference remained statistically significant in each year even when socio-economic background was controlled, although it became non-significant in the first and fourth year after high school when differences in ninth grade grades, educational goals, and intrinsic motivation toward school were also controlled (p. 29). For young women the pattern was less consistent, but by the fourth year after high school those who had worked less than 20 hours a week during high school were completing more months of postsecondary schooling than those who had worked more than 20 hours a week and those who had not worked at all (p. 32).

A third source of recent evidence is the longitudinal survey conducted by the National Center for Research in Vocational Education (NCRVE). This survey followed students in high schools and two-year colleges from autumn 1988 through spring 1992. A complete description of the sample and survey procedures is given in Cagampang and others (1993). Study sites were chosen because they offered co-operative education (co-op) programs that created relatively strong connections between the worksite and the school by means of written training plans, visits by school personnel to the students' workplaces, and participation by job supervisors in awarding students' grades. One purpose of the survey was to compare the experiences of co-op students with that of other employed students who were not in co-op, and with students who were not employed at all. The inverted-U relationship between high school grade-point average and hours worked per week on the current job was replicated in the NCRVE data. Students who were not working had lower average grades than those who were working in non-co-op jobs. Co-op students, who on average worked longer hours than non-co-op students, had the lowest average grades (Stern *et al.* 1995, pp. 45-47). Within both the co-op and non-co-op groups, longer hours were associated with lower grades.

However, the association between working long hours and getting low grades was weaker within the co-op group (Stern *et al.*, 1997, p. 221). This and other evidence that school supervision may mitigate the adverse effects of students' work provides part of the rationale for efforts in the 1990s to link students' work more closely to school. As discussed later in this paper, work-based learning tied to the school curriculum has been one of the main elements of new, integrated pathways for high school students in the United States.

Stabilising early employment

The interim report from the OECD thematic review of school-to-work transition (OECD, 1998c, pp. 18-20) distinguished between countries with open, flexible labour markets and countries where labour markets are organised by occupations with well-defined systems of qualification and governance. The United States is possibly the most extreme example of the first type, with little legal or institutional regulation of wages, benefits, working conditions, training, skill requirements, or procedures for hiring and firing. The possibility for many American students to find part-time jobs is one result of these relatively unregulated labour markets.

Another feature of unregulated labour markets is that people move around a lot, from one job to another, or between work and unemployment. In particular, studies of the labour market experience of young people in the US have found that high school leavers often spend several years floundering, flip-flopping from job to job without much sense of purpose or career direction (Hamilton, 1990; Osterman and Iannozzi, 1993). Compared to other industrialised countries, young Americans are less likely to be in jobs they have held for five years or more, even after reaching age 35 (Stern *et al.*, 1995, p. 7). Instability in the youth labour market has been seen as harmful to young people, especially from low-income and minority groups.

As opposed to these concerns, a different theory holds that instability may reflect productive investment in job shopping, by which employers and employees eventually find "good matches" that raise their mutual productivity for an extended period thereafter (Johnson, 1978; McCall, 1990; Heckman, 1994). As Heckman (1994) put it, "Job shopping promotes wage growth. Turnover is another form of investment, not demonstrably less efficient than youth apprenticeships (p. 105)". The models motivating this view generally involve situations in which people and jobs differ in various respects, and therefore some people are more productive than others in certain jobs. No workers or firms have prior information on what the best matches are, however, and in order to obtain such information people must take different jobs and switch when they find others for which they are better suited (Mincer and Jovanovic, 1981; Flinn, 1986). High turnover may be positive in this perspective, not only because individuals make higher wages as they make better matches, but also because aggregate productivity is increased. The implication is that policies or programs aimed at reducing job shopping would be detrimental to young people and society in general.

Three recent studies shed new light on this dispute. One, by Klerman and Karoly (1995), found that the transition from school to work is smoothest for four-year college graduates and roughest for high school dropouts, compared to high school graduates or those with "some college." This result is more consistent with the view of instability as a negative experience that people try to avoid, because if job shopping were a form of positive investment it is not clear why people with more schooling would get less of it. Furthermore, a second study, by Gardecki and Neumark (1995), revealed that people who experienced more unstable employment in the first year or two after leaving school tended to continue having more unstable employment three or four years later. Again, this seems more consistent with the idea that unstable employment is a bad thing, because if it led to better job matches it should not be expected to go on for so long. Finally, Neumark (1997) reanalysed the same data, using local unemployment rates in the first five years after individuals left school as econometric instruments for early job stability. The results indicate that more stable employment in the first five years after leaving school does in fact lead to higher wages in subsequent years.

Although Neumark cautions that this finding does not necessarily indicate a market failure which would warrant intervention, this and other evidence does imply that there may be lasting benefits from offering more stable and coherent pathways for young people. The next three sections of this paper describe some of the recent attempts to build new pathways for young people in the United States.

2. Combining academic and vocational curriculum in high schools[2]

Given the high and rising monetary rewards for university graduates in the United States, the great majority of high school students aspire (and their parents aspire for them) to attend a four-year college or university and earn a bachelor's degree or more. As of 1996, however, only 35% of young Americans were earning bachelor's degrees at the normal age of graduation (OECD, 1998a, Table C4.2b). Although this is a larger percentage than in most other OECD countries, it raises a difficult question: how to respect the college aspirations of high school students (and their parents), and at the same time prepare for the fact that almost two out of three will not earn a bachelor's degree?

Traditionally, vocational education has been a distinct alternative to preparation for college or university. By law, vocational education in the United States has been defined as preparation for occupations not requiring a bachelor's or advanced degree. This limitation was reaffirmed by the 1998 amendments to the Perkins Act, which provides federal money for vocational education. By definition, therefore, traditional vocational education cannot satisfy the aspirations of students and parents who want bachelor's degrees.

Instead, high schools in the United States have been developing new, integrated pathways that are designed to keep students' options open by providing academic courses of study that satisfy entrance requirements for four-year colleges, and at the same time preparing students for employment through new forms of work-based learning linked to the school curriculum. By combining work-related applications with rigorous academic studies, these new pathways are intended to improve on both traditional vocational and traditional academic education. Vocational education, as will now be explained, has been criticised for not providing a sufficient theoretical foundation for graduates to continue learning and adapting throughout their working lives. Pure academic education, on the other hand, seems irrelevant or incomprehensible to many students. Combining the two may produce an alloy that is stronger than either of the separate elements by itself. If successful, these new pathways will improve students' chances of completing university studies because they will have not only the necessary academic background but also a better understanding of how their schooling relates to a desired career. Students who do not go directly to a four-year college or university after high school will have the option to do so at a later time. Those who start college but do not finish will have some employment-related knowledge and experience to fall back on.

For the most part these innovations have been initiated locally, although they have also received support from federal and state legislation, and from non-governmental agencies financed by private foundations (the various sources of support are described in Urquiola *et al.*, 1997). Conspicuous examples of this approach include the High Schools That Work project of the Southern Regional Education Board, which included more than 800 high schools as of 1998 (Bottoms, Presson and Johnson, 1992), and several networks that support career academies (Stern, Raby and Dayton, 1992), which will be described further below.

The idea of combining academic and vocational education is not new. When the creation of separate vocational and academic streams was first being considered in the United States, John Dewey (1916) was among those who argued in favour of keeping them together. But Dewey lost the argument, and the 1917 Smith-Hughes Act created federal support for a separate kind of vocational education that became well established in subsequent decades. While students in the academic track were prepared for further education, those in vocational classes were made ready for work.

The recent push to combine, or recombine, academic and vocational education in the United States began during the 1980s, when influential spokesmen for the nation's employers started to complain that graduates from high school vocational programs lacked the academic knowledge and thinking skills to participate in the newly emerging economy where incessant change requires continual learning and problem solving (National Academy of Science, 1984; Committee for Economic Development, 1985; Kearns and Doyle, 1988). Since employers had been the most politically important backers of vocational education for most of this century, these statements had a decisive effect on the debate in Congress when the federal law authorising support for vocational education came up for its periodic renewal. The 1990 amendments to the Carl Perkins Act turned vocational education 90 degrees, requiring that the basic federal grant to the states for vocational education be spent only on programs that "integrate academic and vocational education." This idea was subsequently reinforced and elaborated by the 1994 School-to-Work Opportunities Act. And the 1998 amendments to the Carl Perkins Act again mandated "integration of academics with vocational and technical education programs through a coherent sequence of courses to ensure learning in the core academic, and vocational and technical subjects" [Section 135(b)(1)].

Integrating academic and vocational education changes what students are given to learn in school, and how they go about learning it. Whether the change is superficial or fundamental depends on the meaning attached to the idea of integration. The American tradition of local control over education leaves local districts and schools free to adopt very different practices under the very same banner of "integrating academic and vocational." Some innovative practices have been developed by individual teachers, or by groups of teachers within schools. Other innovations have affected entire schools or districts. Various curricular and pedagogical approaches to academic-vocational integration are described in Grubb (1995) and in Urquiola *et al.* (1997). Here the discussion focuses on structural changes which can be said to alter the pathways leading through high school to further education and work.

Four main types of structural modification can be distinguished: 1) career clusters or majors; 2) urban career magnet schools; 3) career academies; and 4) dividing an entire high school into self-contained subunits. These terms have not been defined by statute, and their usage varies considerably. The definitions used here seem to be the most prevalent, however.

Career clusters or majors

Both the Perkins Act and the School-to-Work Opportunities Act require a coherent sequence of academic and vocational courses for students. Such a sequence is said to be vertically aligned and constitutes a career major or cluster (Grubb, 1995). Students usually begin the career cluster sequence in the tenth grade, after a career exploration class or experience has given them a basis for choosing a major. Students in the same cluster may have very different goals after high school. For example, a business cluster may include students wanting to become office support workers as well as those wishing to pursue managerial positions or to become entrepreneurs.

In practice, clusters do not always create such heterogeneous groupings. Sometimes more academic groupings are distinguished from more vocational concentrations. For example, a school may distinguish between an automotive and an engineering major, where the automotive students are less likely to be college-bound. Additionally, schools sometimes maintain a separate college preparatory track because they feel no need to eliminate it, or because some members of the community want to preserve it.

The cluster approach does not require teachers of academic subjects to change what they do. Academic departments may remain intact and continue to control course content. Students in any given academic class may come from various majors or clusters. Vocational teachers, on the other hand, must create a coherent sequence of elective courses and co-ordinate their scheduling with relevant academic courses, in order to form the backbone of a career cluster.

The state of Oregon has adopted the career cluster model statewide. NCRVE researchers visited one of the state model high schools in 1996. Box 1 describes major elements of that school's approach at the time.

Box 1. **Career clusters in Oregon, 1996**

Located in east Portland, David Douglas High School (DDHS) serves 1 852 students. The student body consists of a largely Caucasian population (89%), as well as Asian/Pacific Islanders (6%), Hispanics (2%), African Americans (2%), and American Indian/Alaskan Natives (1%). Though relatively homogenous in terms of race or ethnicity, the school represents a diverse population in terms of special needs and interests. In response to this, David Douglas High School offers a comprehensive program of study while at the same time preparing students for an increasingly competitive job market.

In the autumn of 1993, David Douglas High School and the Oregon Business Council (OBC) joined in a partnership to design a comprehensive high school program that would meet the expectations of the Oregon Education Act for the 21st Century and successfully develop a model that could be used by other districts and communities. Their vision was an eight-point plan of action which included both the David Douglas Model District Partnership (a K-12 plan) and the site-based Project STARS (Students Taking Authentic Routes to Success), a high school effort to prepare students for the future and the world of work. What resulted from this partnership was a multi-faceted long-term strategy for whole-school restructuring that involved community and business leaders, parents, students, school administrators and teachers.

All DDHS students participate in one of seven broad career areas, called "constellations," which reflect the six career areas embodied in the state legislation and an additional Hospitality cluster created at the school. In a document prepared for NCRVE, DDHS defines career constellations as "a personalised educational program. Broad areas with both academic and technical orientations, flexible and overlapping in nature." These are:

Social and Human Services.

Health Sciences.

Business and Management.

Industrial and Engineering Systems.

Natural Resources.

Arts and Communications.

Hospitality, Tourism and Recreation.

The state clusters were developed in conjunction with the Oregon Business Council, which has adopted David Douglas as a pilot site for its school-to-work involvement.

The 9th and 10th grades are devoted primarily to general study, and the 11th and 12th to working within major areas of study. All students must complete 25 credits to graduate. Required courses that fulfil state requirements for graduation amount to 16 credits, including four years of English, three years of social studies, two years of mathematics and of science, and one year of health education, foreign language, and physical education. Students must also complete nine credits of elective courses, which are designed to "build skills in areas of study that meet the student's needs for vocational training *and* college admission as well as the pursuit of individual interests."[3] Meeting minimum graduation requirements does not by itself qualify students to enter a four-year college or university, however.

Each individual student works with a counsellor to determine the best sequence of courses for that student's learning and postsecondary educational objectives. Due to the individualised nature of the constellation program, David Douglas High School has been able to accommodate all students' first choices with regard to constellation area. Students can also change from one constellation to another after meeting with their counsellor.

Students begin preparing to choose career majors through initial career exploration in middle school, followed by an intense career exploration class and selection of career cluster in grade 9. At this time an individual education plan is developed for the remainder of the high school career, as well as the steps beyond – to college or university, community college, military service, apprenticeship, or entry into the work force. All individual student career pathways developed during career exploration classes and counselling examine postsecondary training requirements and attempt to leave students prepared for postsecondary education. Every student has a faculty mentor, a teacher in the student's area of career interest, who works closely with both the individual student and guidance counsellors to ensure the student's path of success. Additionally, David Douglas staffs a Career Resource Center, available to students before, during, and after school hours for students who wish to do independent career exploration. This planning process also allows students to work with teachers and counsellors to tailor enhancement courses to career choices.

A number of articulated pathways exist between David Douglas and local community colleges. Formal articulation agreements are currently in place with Mt. Hood Community College. Specified courses in which students can earn both high school and college credit are taught at David Douglas High School by DDHS faculty. These include: Advanced Placement Math, Math Analysis and Trigonometry, Advanced Placement US History, Advanced Writing IV, French, Spanish, Keyboarding II and III, and Electronic Calculator.[4] In order to participate, students must complete a Mt. Hood Community College application and pay half tuition.

In addition, students may participate in a 2+2 Tech Prep course of study which "helps students develop work-based skills without duplicating classes from high school to college."[5] This program combines elective courses in the junior and senior years of high school with a planned two-year program of study at a community college. Opportunities for 2+2 Tech Prep are offered in Keyboarding, Accounting, Marketing, Office Tech, Electronic Calculator, Hospitality, Early Childhood Education, Small Engines, Metals, Industrial Mechanics, Electronics, Journalism, and Video Technology. The DDHS Curriculum Guide for students states that "the 2+2 Tech Prep Program may result in employment directly out of high school, a certification program, an associate degree, or an additional two years at a four-year college."[6]

Urban career magnets

Another school structure that supports integrated curriculum is the single-theme high school. In particular, some big cities have created specialised magnet high schools with career themes. Katz *et al.* (1995) found that the single-theme configuration resulted in increased student investment in school, reflected in part by high attendance and low drop-out rates in successful career magnets in New York City. Teachers often have extensive experience in their schools' fields, lending an authentic insider's view into the industry. The schools' individual themes create a natural focal point for integrated curricula, and many teachers have the expertise and the desire to do so. With the skills and industry connections of the teachers and the common interests of the students, some of the most elaborate project-based integration occurs at such schools (Katz *et al.*, 1995). Results from an evaluation of career magnet schools in New York City are summarised later in this paper.

In 1996 NCRVE researchers visited the Chicago High School for Agricultural Sciences, which weaves a college-preparatory curriculum around the theme of agricultural science and related commerce. The excerpts in Box 2 illustrate some of the curricular integration that occurs in career magnet schools.

Box 2. **Chicago High School of Agricultural Science, 1996**

Chicago High School for Agricultural Sciences (CHAS) is a surprising place, located on 77 acres of farmland in the outlying Mount Greenwood section of the city. Students study in close proximity to the school greenhouse, where the horticulture students conduct lab experiments and plants and flowers are grown for numerous public sales and special events. The equipment garage also houses rabbits, chickens, and turkeys. Yet in spite of the school's numerous opportunities for hands-on agricultural study, no one attends CHAS to prepare for a farming career.

Instead, students and parents are attracted by the school's rigorous college preparatory curriculum which is supplemented with seven to eight full-year courses of agriculture-related science courses, ranging from horticulture to agricultural mechanics to food science. Principal Barbara Valerious is quick to clarify the school's mission to visitors. "We do not train kids to be farmers. We're basically a math and science high school with an agricultural emphasis."

The concept for an agricultural sciences high school was conceived in the early 1980s when the Chicago Board of Education was faced with financial difficulties and pressure from the state to increase its desegregation efforts. When the tenant of the city-owned Mount Greenwood property decided to leave farming, the city considered selling the land. However, activists convinced officials to save this last open space area located within the city's limits, and the city decided instead to use it for an agricultural magnet school where students could practice what they learned in an open-air lab. Such a facility, they reasoned, might help attract and keep both black and white students from leaving the public schools. In 1996, the school's student body was as follows:

Total number of students:	469
Eligible for free or subsidised lunch:	47.3%
Limited in English proficiency:	1.1%
African-American:	62.5%
Caucasian:	19.2%
Hispanic:	17.3%
Asian/Pacific Islander:	0.9%
Native American:	0.2%

CHAS opened its doors in 1985, and since then has been preparing students for college and a vast range of agriculture-related careers. As principal Valerious often explains to prospective students and their parents, "Only 2% of the country is involved in agricultural production, but about 20% of Illinois is involved in the non-production side of agriculture." This non-production sector includes horticulturists, veterinarians, futures traders, agricultural engineers, and everything in between.

The school has acquired a reputation for its strong program in academics and career preparation, and each year more and more students have applied. Now prospective students must apply through a lottery system. Each year the demand for spots at CHAS greatly exceeds the number of openings. Last year, for example, nearly 1 200 students from all over the city applied for the 150 openings in the freshman class. Some students travel up to two hours each way by train, bus, or car to get there.

Once at the school, students spend more time each day than their peers at any of the city's other public high schools. The longer school day is required so that students can meet CHAS's graduation requirements of 32 credits. (In contrast, Chicago only requires that its high school students complete a minimum of 20 credits in order to graduate.) Required courses include four years of English, two years of foreign language, and three years of mathematics (algebra through trigonometry). In addition, students must complete an ambitious agricultural science curriculum, as well as the traditional biology-chemistry-physics (and often Advanced Placement biology) sequence. With Tech Prep programs in food science and agricultural finance, CHAS has formalised articulation agreements with two postsecondary institutions.

All senior science classes require a research project, and the best of these are entered in the state science fair competition. Many of the students' award plaques decorate the walls of the school. Science teacher Dan Martin described several award-winning projects. "The majority of our projects are agriculturally-based. For example, one student's project was involved with Armor Foods where he looked at the fat content and taste of different meat samples. A second student worked on a four-year project on poinsettia development. Another student studied surface water management as it relates to irrigation, erosion, and drainage."

In many ways the school's agricultural focus helps students bring relevance to what might otherwise – in a more traditional high school – seem a disconnected, difficult curriculum. Students frequently point out how teachers make connections to agriculture, not only in science and agricultural science classes, but also in other classes. For example, the French teacher asks students to report on the farming industry in France. Math students analyse production charts. English teachers ask students to research and write about careers in agribusiness. The food science class combines chemistry with a challenging lab assignment to try to make Reese's candy without looking at the ingredients on the candy wrapper. Then students use geometry skills to design packaging that would meet certain capacity and shelf space requirements.

Business partners have also supported professional development efforts at the school. American Cyanamid and Monsanto have both sponsored 30 faculty each for extended in-service at their facilities in New Jersey and St. Louis, Missouri. Other business partners such as Kraft General Foods have sponsored individual "teacher externships" in which teachers learn how their subject is actually used at successful workplaces.

In addition, the faculty's small size helps to remove any barriers between agriculture and non-agriculture teachers. A food science teacher explains. "From the beginning of the school, agriculture was considered as important as English. My class is just as academic as the chemistry class that goes on next door. I don't think we, as a faculty, see the school as being either vocational or academic.

We just try to integrate subjects across the board." Agricultural finance teacher Lucille Shaw agrees. "It was never like 'here's the agriculture staff and here's the academic staff and never the two shall meet.' We've always been encouraged to mingle, and one of the advantages is the small faculty size. It's very easy to get to know someone here. When someone new comes in, within a week or two they're feeling at home because they're included in meetings and activities where you get to share ideas."

There is a feeling among faculty, students, and parents that CHAS is in many ways unique. Valerious explains the guiding philosophy of the school this way: "CHAS has always been different from most vocational schools or schools that have a vocational program. It was always designed to be both academic and vocational, and one was never considered to be better than the other. This is a community partnership that still believes in developing a youngster who can think and a youngster who can do: the true Renaissance person."

Some statistics indicating what CHSAS has accomplished are:

80% of graduating seniors go on to two- or four-year colleges

Graduating seniors earn more than USD 1 million in college scholarships each year

90.5% attendance rate

85.1% graduation rate vs. 61.7% district average

6.6% dropout rate vs. 15.5% district average

8.4% student mobility rate vs. 29% district average.

Career academies

Career academies[7] are partially self-contained subschools within larger high schools, usually enrolling 100 to 200 students from grade 9 or 10 through grade 12. Like career magnet high schools, these schools-within-schools use an occupational or industry theme to organise a whole course of study, including academic subjects. Frequently occurring academy themes are health careers, business and finance, natural resources, graphic arts, communications media, and manufacturing or engineering technology. Keeping students together with the same group of teachers for three or four years allows teachers and students to build strong personal relationships.

Career academies differ from traditional vocational education because they prepare high school students for both work *and* college. They provide broad information about an industry, showing students the variety of careers in a given field, and providing a foundation on which they can build with more advanced and specialised postsecondary preparation. They combine this with a rigorous academic curriculum that qualifies students for admission to a four-year college or university.

The first career academy was established in 1969 in Philadelphia, PA. It was an "Electrical Academy" at Edison High School, supported by the Philadelphia Electric Company. This gradually spread to other fields (business, automotive, health, environmental technology, law, horticulture, tourism, aviation) and other high schools, growing to a network of 28 academies today. In 1982 the separate non-profit organisations that had mobilised employer support came together in the Philadelphia High School Academies (PHSA), Inc. Financed by corporate contributions and foundation grants, PHSA continues to manage and finance these programs, while the city school district retains jurisdiction and supplies teachers and classrooms. Although the Philadelphia academies began as vocational training programs, today they send most of their graduates to college.

In 1981 the academy idea was introduced in California, starting with a "Computer Academy" at Menlo-Atherton High School and an "Electronics Academy" at Sequoia High School, just north of Palo Alto. Based on a series of evaluations that demonstrated improved student performance, California passed legislation in 1984 that supported ten replications of the model. Evaluations of these academies continued the pattern of encouraging results, and in 1987 a second state bill was passed, supporting approximately 40 additional replications. The pattern was repeated again in 1993, and with support provided under this legislation, California will provide approximately USD 14 million for 200 career academies in 1998-99. These academies range over some 25 career fields. Many others have begun on their own, and in many districts there are now several non-funded academies for every one receiving a state grant. The California Academies formalised the involvement of three academic courses as part of the model, along with one career-related course, in grades 10-12. They also advanced the notion of preparing students for college and careers at the same time.

Also in the 1980s, New York City created the first "Academies of Finance," sponsored by the American Express Company. American Express subsequently joined with other companies, which now number more than 100, to create the National Academy Foundation (NAF). NAF added the field of "Travel and Tourism" in 1987, and "Public Service" in 1990. As of 1998 it provides curriculum and technical support for nearly 400 academies in more than 30 states. The NAF Academies usually include only grades 11-12, but some individual NAF academies are moving toward the Philadelphia and California models, adding both earlier years of high school and more co-ordination with academic classes. NAF academies have been college-oriented since their inception.

In the early 1990s the Illinois State Board of Education became interested in the career academy model, and during the 1994-95 school year began 20 California style academies in that state. Most of those continue to operate, and with 18 new academies beginning in the autumn of 1998, Illinois will have 35 in operation during the 1998-99 school year. A request for proposals in autumn 1998 will offer planning grants to additional sites, with the expectation of adding at least another 20 or so, bringing the total by the year 2 000 to more than 50. Illinois has also replicated California's evaluation system with similar results – a pattern of improved performance among students enrolled in academies there.

Another site with a growing network of career academies is the city of Baltimore. Since 1990 Baltimore has started several kinds of academies, including NAF academies and California-style academies, and operates 13 academies as of 1998. Patterson High School received help from the Center for Research on the Education of Students Placed at Risk (CRESPAR) to restructure itself entirely into academies, and CRESPAR is now helping other schools, in Baltimore and elsewhere, to emulate this model, which it calls the Talent Development High School (LaPoint *et al.*, 1996).

Other examples could be cited, both cities and states. Several cities in California, including Bakersfield, Pasadena, Riverside, and Sacramento have developed extensive networks of academies. Oakland, California is aggressively expanding its career academies, enrolling students in 33 different academies in 1998-99. Other cities with developing networks include Atlanta, Chicago, Denver, Seattle, and Washington, D.C.

Although no one has an exact count, the number of academies around the country that exhibit the characteristics outlined above is probably more than 1 000 and growing. In the first two decades after their 1969 inception, the growth of career academies was steady but gradual. Since 1990, growth in the number of academies has accelerated (see Table 2), in part because some places have begun to apply the concept schoolwide.

Prior to 1990, it was unusual for a high school to contain more than a single career academy. Within a high school enrolling 1 500 students, for example, perhaps 150 would belong to the academy. In recent years, however, a growing number of high schools have started multiple academies.[8] In these schools, every student now belongs to an academy, starting in grade nine or ten. This development significantly expands the academy concept from a program serving a small number of students to a whole-school reorganisation strategy. As mentioned, CRESPAR is advancing this approach under the name of the Talent Development High School.

A precise count of career academies is impossible because there is no single, authoritative definition. The term "career academy" was coined in 1992 to encompass the Philadelphia academies, California partnership academies, and the NAF academies (Stern, Raby and Dayton, 1992). Only the California academies are defined in legislation. Nevertheless, these and other career academies generally share three basic features, as identified by researchers at the Manpower Demonstration Research Corporation (MDRC) (Kemple and Rock, 1996, p. ES-3). Box 3 encapsulates this definition.

Box 3. **Defining features of career academies**

First, academies are *small learning communities*. An academy comprises a cluster of students who have some of the same teachers for at least two years, and who share several classes each year. A group of teachers from academic and vocational disciplines are scheduled to have only or mostly academy students in their classes, meet with each other on a regular basis, and share in decision-making related to administrative policies, curriculum content, and instruction. One of these faculty members assumes lead responsibility for administrative tasks and usually serves as a liaison to the school principal and other building administrators, school district officials, and employer partners.

Second, academies combine a *college-preparatory curriculum with a career theme*. Examples of common themes are health care, business and finance, communications media, and transportation technology. Academic courses that meet high school graduation and college entrance requirements are linked with technical courses that focus on the academy's field of work. Teachers sometimes have shared planning time to co-ordinate course content and instructional strategies. Employability skills may be taught in the vocational courses and in one or more academic courses. Work-based learning opportunities for students tie classroom activities to work internships with local employer partners. College and career counselling informs students about options and planning for employment and further education, which may or may not be related to the academy career theme.

Third, academies embody *partnerships with employers*. An advisory group for the academy includes representatives from the local employer community, academy faculty, and the school district. Employer representatives give advice on curriculum, appear as guest speakers in classes, supervise student internships, provide financial or in-kind support, and sometimes serve as mentors for individual students.

The appeal of career academies is based in part on evidence of positive effects for students and teachers. Results for students are summarised later in this paper.

Because of their autonomous structure, academies offer greater opportunities for integrated curricula (Stern, Raby and Dayton, 1992). Of special importance for curricular integration is the fact that academic courses can be modified to reflect the academy's career theme, because each academy normally has its own classes in core academic subjects. Most academy programs also can draw on business partnerships, which provide job-shadowing sites, mentors, and/or internship sites for students, and expert advice for teachers. Sometimes teachers share a common preparation period and receive paid release time to create new curricula. These inducements were found to be critical in creating integrated curricula (Andrew and Grubb, 1995; Ramsey *et al.*, 1995).

Whole schools divided into subschools

As mentioned, some high schools and districts have recently announced their intention to remake themselves entirely as career academies. The idea of dividing a high school into "wall-to-wall" academies, where every student and teacher is affiliated with one, has been put into practice at Encina High School in Sacramento, California, and at Patterson High School in Baltimore, among others. Now Baltimore, Oakland, and other districts are beginning to implement this strategy districtwide. These efforts are beginning to transform career academies from a special program for a few students into a strategy that can be used for organising entire high schools.

The experience at Patterson High School has been described by LaPoint *et al.* (1996) and McPartland *et al.* (1996). In 1994 the school was deemed eligible for reconstitution by the Maryland State Department of Education because of poor attendance, high dropout rates, and low scores on achievement tests. A new leadership team, with help from the Center for Research on the Education of Students Placed at Risk (CRESPAR), reorganised the school into self-contained academies. One is for freshmen. The other four are career academies for students in grades 10 through 12. The themes are Arts and Humanities, Business and Finance, Sports Studies and Health/Wellness, and Transportation and Engineering Technology. Comparison of measures for 1994-95 with 1995-96 shows a complete turnaround in teachers' perceptions of school climate. For example, the number of teachers in grades 10-12 who said the learning environment was not conducive to school achievement for most students fell from 86.7 to 4.5%! Student attendance rose to 77.7% in 1995-96, compared to a 71.6% average in the three previous years. Promotion rates also increased. The schoolwide career academy structure and curriculum, along with other supports for student achievement, appear to be making substantial improvements at Patterson.

This strategy draws on school-reform initiatives that were not career-oriented, in particular the "house" system developed by the Coalition of Essential Schools. Little (1995) examined the impact of house systems on teachers' work. She found that subschool systems force teachers to give more attention to students' cognitive and social development while multiplying teachers' responsibility. But teachers' work can become more demanding because, when subject teachers must instruct students across grade levels within a subschool, their number of class preparations increases. Additionally, a subject-matter teacher's individual passions and interests in the subject may be given less scope. For example, a science teacher with extensive experience in chemistry may reluctantly end up teaching biology and physics. Worse yet, if teachers are not allowed to select their houses, resistance and conflict may ensue (Siskin, 1994; Little, 1995). Some sites have addressed these dangers by adopting a hybridised structure that groups some subject-matter teachers, while others "float" among the subschools. Little emphasises the importance for teachers of maintaining contact with their disciplinary colleagues and of being assured some stability in their groupings.

Potentially, dividing entire schools into subunits can multiply the opportunities for students to experience horizontally and vertically integrated curriculum. This configuration may also be more stable than an individual academy within an otherwise conventionally organised high school because the special arrangements for scheduling an individual academy tend to be problematic (Stern, Raby and Dayton, 1992). In addition, the small-school format in itself reduces the impersonality of large high schools (National Association of Secondary School Principals, 1996). Care must be taken, however, to ensure that teachers and students are not coerced and that students can transfer from one subschool to another if they so decide.

The excerpts in Box 4 from a 1996 field report by an NCRVE researcher provide a glimpse inside one school that is organised as a set of subschools for the purpose of promoting curricular integration.

Box 4. **Fenway Middle College High School, 1996**

Fenway Middle College High School is a Pilot School within the Boston Public Schools, serving approximately 250 students who have chosen Fenway as an alternative to their neighbourhood schools. Fenway's program was initially designed as a "last chance" for students at-risk of dropping out, either because they were disaffected or because they were not being served by the traditional system. Recently, it has attracted a range of students, from those who attend under a court order to those who have transferred from Boston's prestigious exam schools. As a member of the Coalition of Essential Schools, the Center for Collaborative Education, Boston Educators for School Reform, and the Middle College High School consortium, Fenway draws ideas from a variety of sources.

All Fenway students belong to one of three houses. There, they work with the same set of teachers for the duration of their high school career. The Houses are: The Children's Hospital Collaborative (partnered with Boston Children's Hospital), the CVS Pharmacy House (partnered with CVS Pharmacies), and Crossroads (partnered with Boston Museum of Science).

Every teacher is a member of two teams: academic and house team. Because Fenway is a pilot school in the Boston system, teachers sign a special contract which differs from the other public schools. Among the conditions they agree to are: a weekend faculty retreat, a longer working year, a curriculum week or workshop that is organised during the summer, and three required weekly meetings, which are full staff, within-house, and within-curriculum. Thus, the school fosters intensive collaboration among the teachers.

The House meetings provide time for teachers to discuss curriculum, projects, as well as specific concerns about students. The teacher who serves as the Cross-Roads House co-ordinator described these meetings as "the glue" that holds the faculty together. The subject-matter meetings allow for exchange on subject-specific issues, which one teacher reported, "makes a huge difference on your teaching, yourself as a teacher and yourself as a learner." In addition, there are mandatory faculty retreats in which curriculum is designed and issues of assessment are addressed.

One of the outcomes of this collaboration among teachers is the development of a thematic question to be addressed by all students in all classes every year. For example, the question that the teachers posed for this year is "What does it mean to be human?" Students seek an answer to this question across the grade levels and across academic subjects. A school-wide assembly was held to introduce the question.

Some new curricula have been developed specifically to integrate academic and vocational education. As the most established house at Fenway, the Children's Hospital Collaborative has the most extensive curriculum. In eleventh grade, during advisory class period, students take an innovative health curriculum that was developed in the summer of 1991. One of Fenway's teachers interviewed hospital staff to find out what students needed to know before working in the hospital. The curriculum is constantly revised and updated, and currently is divided into six units: What is a Hospital?, Introduction to Medical Ethics, Adolescent Health, Technology, Child Development, and The Environment. The curriculum seeks to increase students competency in five major areas: Work-Related Skills, Communication Skills, Reading/Vocabulary/Writing, Problem-Solving Skills, and Math/Science Related Skills. The program has received two major awards: The National Alliance for Business awarded its Outstanding Partnership Award to one program, and the US Department of Labor chose the collaborative program as one of the fifteen most outstanding job training programs in the nation.[9] For their Junior Project, this year's Children's Hospital Juniors did a research project on homelessness, going to different shelters and agencies.

The Museum of Science Collaborative (or "Crossroads House") requires students to work as assistants in the Eye-Opener Project, designed to introduce all of Boston's second graders to the museum. Students work with adult volunteers and help take groups of second-graders around the museum. On the vocational side, this experience helps teach students some of the people skills needed in the workplace. Additionally, it helps teenagers make the transition from child to adult. Lynn Baum, school program manager at the museum, says, "High school kids really benefit from thinking of themselves as role models." On the academic side, the Crossroads science teacher finds that the museum provides a "giant research lab" for students and professional development for her. She seeks ways to bring their experiences in the museum back to the classroom. For example, when the students created a bog environment in a plastic dish and grew plants in it at the museum, the teacher took the simulated swamp back to school where the students performed tests for acidity and lighting.[10] In 1995-96, the Crossroads Junior Project was on the subject of culture.

The CVS Collaborative curriculum starts in the ninth grade and requires students to take intensive science classes. Additionally, the school did a "gap analysis" of what students were lacking in mathematics, science, interpersonal and organisational skills. The ninth grade writing teacher created her curriculum specifically to build up the targeted skills so that students would perform better on the work-site. Students also have an opportunity to work with all aspects of the organisation. This year's Junior class researched demographic and regulatory information in order to open a store in Dorchester for their class project. The company will be opening the new "CVS/Fenway Store" soon.

Much learning is organised around projects and internships. All students participate in Project Week. Students are asked to wrestle with a large topic such as "What makes Boston a good place in which to live?" or "What makes a good museum?" Information is gathered by exploring the city with the guidance of Advisors so that Boston becomes a giant classroom. Students must write a concise report on their perspective and understanding of the topic.[11] In addition, every senior must do a six-week internship in which they work thirty hours a week. Juniors do intensive shadowing to observe different types of jobs within their partnered organisation.

An essential part of Fenway's program is promotion by exhibition. In other words, students must demonstrate that they have achieved the necessary level of competency in order to be promoted. In the individual classes, this means that all teachers use portfolios as one instrument of assessment. This means that credit is not awarded merely on the basis of seat time. Students must demonstrate competency in their classes and then prove a wide-range of competencies to graduate. Major milestones are the "Junior Review" exhibition and the presentation of a Senior portfolio to a graduation committee.

Junior Review is an assessment vehicle used to determine the structure of the student's remaining time at Fenway High School at the end of the Junior year. The outcome of the Review differs from student to student, but the general process is the same. Students meet with a Junior Review Committee to examine their academic record and their Junior Review Portfolio. As a result of the review, a student may be asked to take extra courses during the summer or may be encouraged to spend senior year taking college courses. It is also possible that the committee will determine that the student needs a two-year Senior Institute to meet the graduation requirements. This serves to normalise the reality that some students need five years of high school to meet graduation standards.[12]

The goal of Senior Institute is to prepare students for life after high school and to assure that each student has the necessary skills for success. The different parts of Senior Institute are: course work and portfolios, planning for after high school, a Senior Graduation Project, standardised tests, a senior internship, and an advisory portfolio. Students who succeed in completing all these areas and who persuade their Graduation Committee of their competency will receive a Fenway diploma. Students who do not complete all of these requirements re-enter Fenway in the autumn.[13]

One student commented on the value of portfolio assessment as preparation for college: "When I came here, they showed us how to do portfolios which are all your best papers... You have to do your best research on them, you have to type them up and make them your best pieces, which is what's required in college... [Fenway] prepares you for college so when you go there, that you'll be able to know how to manage your time, to be able to do your papers on time (...) I went to visit [a local college], and there's lots of freedom just like this school, but you also have to know how to manage your time in order to be able to pass."

Fenway staff are constantly assessing their program, their students, and themselves. They monitor both quantifiable and qualitative progress of their students. The following statistics for 1995-96 were provided by the school:[14]

Average Daily Attendance:	Fenway: 95.2%	Boston Public Schools: 84%
Advance to next grade:	Fenway: 96%	Boston Public High Schools: 85%
College enrolment:	Fenway: 81%	Boston Public Schools: 60%
Faculty Average Daily Attendance:	Fenway: 99%	Boston Public Schools: 95%

Trends and obstacles

Although the absence of comprehensive data makes it impossible to draw precise empirical conclusions about prevailing trends, there does appear to have been some progression in the development of approaches to integrating academic and vocational curriculum in high schools. The concerns about under-prepared vocational graduates that prompted the 1990 Perkins amendments led first to efforts aimed at upgrading the academic content of vocational curricula, by enriching vocational courses and offering vocational students access to more rigorous academic classes. The initial focus on upgrading vocational instruction was logical, given that the Perkins Act applied specifically to federal funds for vocational education. The High Schools That Work initiative, which began in the late 1980s and grew to include some 800 high schools by the late 1990s, was also targeted on improving academic preparation for "vocational completers," though it later evolved to include all students who were not being served by the college-prep curriculum (Bottoms, Presson and Johnson, 1992; Bottoms and Presson, 1995).

The 1994 School-to-Work Opportunities Act challenged states and localities to broaden their view beyond vocational or work-bound students, by creating career majors that would be available to "all students," including the "academically talented." This meant thinking school-wide, about changing not only curricular content but also the structure of the school. This added impetus to developments that had already been occurring For example, some high schools had been trying to generalise career academies as a school-wide model. Others were blending integrated academic-vocational education with the principles and practices promoted by the Coalition of Essential Schools (Cushman, Steinberg and Riordan, 1997). By the mid-1990s, numerous high schools were exploring how STW reform might fit with broader conceptions of school restructuring (Goldberger and Kazis, 1995).

Efforts to incorporate the ideas of academic-vocational integration into school-wide restructuring have met with major problems, including active resistance by some parents and teachers who see it as a threat to the college-preparatory curriculum. This has been confirmed by the first report of the evaluation of partnerships funded by the 1994 School-to-Work Opportunities Act. The authors of that report suggest that some of the resistance stems from stigmatisation of "applied" academic courses as "remedial," and the concern over whether colleges will accept them (Hershey *et al.*, 1997, pp. 86-88). Scepticism of parents and teachers that the integrated approach has something to offer to college-bound students remains a major barrier to implementing these new pathways in the United States.

3.   Connecting secondary and tertiary education[15]

An important part of the strategy for creating new pathways in the United States involves keeping open the options of advanced training and education at the postsecondary level. The Tech Prep program launched by the 1990 Perkins Act was a major new initiative intended to facilitate the transfer of high school students to college, reduce or eliminate remediation at the college level, and prevent duplication of course work and credits. Most Tech Prep consortia required students to develop educational plans that include potential postsecondary choices.

The goal of linking secondary and postsecondary education was strongly reaffirmed by the 1994 School-to-Work Opportunities Act. While the 1990 Tech Prep law had focused on linking high schools with two-year colleges, however, STWOA explicitly stipulated that a high school career major "may lead to admission to a two-year or four-year college or university" [Section 4(5)(F)]. As a result, the four-year college and university is increasingly included in the discussion of how to build a school-to-work system (Zemsky and Oedel, 1995). Renewal of the Tech Prep program in the 1998 Perkins amendments explicitly added "a baccalaureate degree" as one of the objectives [Section 202(A)(3)(E)], where the original 1990 law had specified only "an associate degree or certificate" [Section 344(b)(2)]. Despite growing federal support for linking secondary and tertiary education more closely, observations and surveys reveal barriers that continue to confront practitioners. Here we examine the roles of secondary schools, community colleges, and four-year institutions in the linkage process.

Linking high school with two-year colleges

A central feature of Tech Prep is the articulation of courses or course sequences between high school and community college, so that students may earn college credit while still in high school. The most comprehensive research study related to this topic was done by Mathematica Policy Research, Inc., as part of the multi-year, federally sponsored investigation of Tech Prep.[16] Based upon the results from their 50-state survey, Silverberg and Hershey (1994) report that curriculum articulation agreements existed in many communities before Tech Prep implementation. These results substantiated similar findings by the National Assessment of Vocational Education (1994).

> "In 17 states, at least 80% of the consortia reported having articulation agreements before Tech Prep. In 38 states, more than half of the consortia had pre-existing agreements (Silverberg and Hershey, 1994, p. 98)."

Following the receipt of Tech Prep funding, consortia made further efforts to develop or update articulation agreements, mainly in occupational fields related to business and mechanical/industrial trades (Silverberg and Hershey, 1994, p. 101). Approximately 30% of consortia have agreements with more than one postsecondary institution, and the goals of most agreements are to grant college credit (p. 102).[17] In the 46 consortia that reported data on numbers of high school Tech Prep students entering different kinds of college programs in autumn 1993, the majority were enrolled at a community, junior, or technical college (p. 122), and 70% of these students entered articulated occupational programs (p. 123). In their follow-up survey, Silverberg (1996) found that students entering articulated occupational programs rose to 76% of all Tech Prep students entering community college in the autumn of 1994 (p. 55).

Despite these survey findings, site visits to ten local consortia revealed that many students do not take advantage of articulated courses.

> "Students fail to take advantage of opportunities to obtain college credit for high school course work and instead retake the articulated course at the college level rather than jump ahead to more advanced course work (Hershey, Silverberg and Owens, 1994, p. 140)."

The lack of secondary student enrolment in articulated courses is also noted by Pedraza, Pauly and Kopp (1997), and by Grubb *et al.* (1996). These findings seem to suggest a lack of confidence that high school courses really can substitute for courses at the community college level. Such substitutions become even more difficult when community college courses are intended to count toward transfer to a four-year college or university.

Linking two-year colleges to four-year colleges

Community colleges have become the major provider of education and training for occupations that do not require a bachelor's degree (Hansen, 1994; Grubb, 1996). At the same time, they retain the function of preparing students who wish to transfer to four-year colleges or universities. They also serve other purposes including general, remedial, and community education. Garland (1994) illustrates the diversity among two-year colleges by listing the different kinds that exist in the State of Pennsylvania.

> "There are thirteen public community colleges, twenty-five two-year branch campuses of senior public institutions, nine independent junior colleges, one technical institute, and one state technical school administered by the Department of Education. In addition, there are some 330 private career schools at the postsecondary level (p. 298)."

Other states also sponsor diverse sets of two-year institutions.

The fact that most Tech Prep students who enter community college enrol in vocational-technical departments, where they receive instruction and support services geared toward securing job placements, may imply that they have less probability of transferring to four-year institutions (Grubb, 1996). However, in certain fields such as nursing and the engineering technologies, where accrediting and professional bodies have encouraged upward educational mobility, Prager (1993) reports that occupational-technical students in community colleges continue their education beyond the first two years at the same or a greater rate and number than their so-called "transfer" peers. Furthermore, a study by Cohen and Ignash (1993) compared the transferability of liberal arts and non-liberal arts (mainly technical and vocational) courses from two-year to four-year colleges. Their study included 164 colleges in three states: California, Texas, and Illinois. Generally, they found a high rate of transferability of non-liberal arts courses, and that students who take these courses are not "cooled out" of baccalaureate degree programs (p. 35). They concluded that, since the non-liberal arts courses do transfer, the concept of "terminal education" should be laid to rest (p. 42).

A more recent study of 395 community colleges by Cohen and Brawer (1996) sought to discover the "underlying causes of differing transfer rates" to four-year colleges or universities (p. 3). When asked "What in the curriculum hinders transfer?", faculty at institutions with low transfer rates gave "students who change from vocational education to transfer education curriculum" more than any other response. The authors explained that respondents from low-transfer colleges stated during interviews that "half of the students have to take a remedial course, and colleges resist the transfer of students who have changed their majors from vocational to transfer" (p. 16). The implication is that these students may need remediation once they have transferred.

Just as high schools and two-year colleges have created course articulation agreements, so have two-year and four-year colleges. Such agreements are supposed to give students at the sending institution credit for certain courses at the receiving institution. However, as already noted, the existence of such agreements between high schools and two-year colleges does not guarantee that students actually benefit from them. The same is true of agreements between two-year and four-year colleges.

A study of the Maricopa County Community College District in Arizona illustrates why articulation agreements may be illusory (Wright *et al.*, 1996). Although Arizona public baccalaureate degree-granting institutions have designated certain community colleges courses as acceptable for meeting General Studies/Liberal Studies requirements, specific departments often impose additional demands. In recent years, these departments' decisions have led to a loss of direct course equivalent transfer. Since departmental policies are subject to sudden change, transferability cannot be assured more than one year in advance.

Cho (1994) also found similar results in the State of Illinois. In her investigation of articulated art programs between the community colleges and four-year university she reported that, "in spite of having the articulation compact, course-equivalency-related problems still persist in Illinois. Many 4-year institutions continue to require their own lower division courses by citing "major" deviations in the general education curriculum at community colleges" (p. 558).

Linking high school to four-year college or university

High school students can gain access to baccalaureate programs either by going to a two-year college and transferring, or by going directly from high school to a four-year institution. An example of the community college strategy was 1986 legislation in California, which directed governing boards of high school and community college districts to collaborate with the trustees of the California State University and the University of California to extend "2+2" education[18] to the baccalaureate level, by establishing "2+2+2" educational pathways for students. In 1983 California had enacted Senate Bill 851, which required the California Postsecondary Education Commission to develop a plan for a course number system to be used in public postsecondary institutions. As a result, the California Articulation Number System (CAN) began in 1985 as a cross-reference course numbering system designed to identify courses which are most commonly presented by students who transfer from one school and system to another. Students who take CAN designated courses do not have to provide receiving schools with course syllabi or justification for course content. The system is equally funded by the three public segments: California Community Colleges, the California State University and the University of California. Articulated courses will be accepted as equivalent by programs which articulation agreements. The CAN system served a key component for beginning the 2+2+2 system.

The 1986 legislation directed the California Postsecondary Education Commission to study the feasibility of extending career-oriented programs to the baccalaureate degree. Twenty-one model projects were funded in 1988-89, and again in 1990-91 (Ramer, 1991). One project was the "Connecting Link" between East San Gabriel Valley Regional Occupational Program – which serves students in their last two years of high school – with the two-year Los Angeles Trade-Technical College and the four-year California State University at Los Angeles (Tuntland, 1995). The first articulation agreements for "Connecting Link" were signed in 1990. Students participate in a series of learning experiences including workplace assignments, and complete courses where work-related applications are infused throughout the curriculum. They develop career decision-making skills, academic basic skills, technological skills, information skills, and interpersonal skills.

As of 1993, the completion rate for East San Gabriel high school students was 95%. Nine students who finished the business/marketing/fashion merchandising program enrolled at Los Angeles Trade Tech, four earned the two-year associate of arts degree, and one student completed the four-year baccalaureate degree at California State University-Los Angeles in June, 1995. Many new systems and administrative procedures had to be put in place to achieve even these small numbers.

On a much larger scale, many high schools throughout the United States have adopted applied academic courses such as those produced by the Center for Occupational Research and Development (CORD) in Waco, Texas. Although these courses have been designed to fit into 2+2 or Tech Prep sequences leading from high school to community college, subsequent transferability to four-year institutions has been problematic. The most comprehensive examination of the transferability of these courses to date has been conducted by McCormick, Alt and Geis (1998) based on a survey of admissions staff at "flagship" campuses of state public universities. They concluded:

> "Despite the promise that many educators believe applied courses hold, some universities, particularly ones that are highly selective in admissions, viewed the academic rigor of integrated courses with scepticism. Some admissions counsellors thought that the courses represented a "dumbing down" of college-prep materials; thus, we found that 12 flagship schools did not accept any integrated courses toward meeting the subject requirements. In other states, universities accepted applied courses but gave them less than full credit; a common example of this was accepting CORD's Applied Math 1 and 2 (two years), but as only one year of math. Another approach was to count applied courses only if students demonstrated their learning through some external means (p. 5)."

A second strategy for assuring that integrated academic-vocational course sequences can lead to a four-year college or university is to bypass the two-year college. Bailey and Merritt (1997) describe purposes and examples of "school-to-work for the college-bound" with little attention to the two-year link. An important initiative in this regard is the development of new procedures and standards for admissions to four-year institutions. Some of these institutions are explicitly intended to recognise student learning from integrated vocational-academic courses and work-based learning.

In Oregon, for example, legislation passed in 1991 requires all secondary schools to offer Certificates of Initial Mastery (CIM) and Certificates of Advanced Mastery (CAM). These certificates will be performance-based, and students progress as they demonstrate mastery of defined intellectual skills and content knowledge. The K-12 system is being redesigned to allow students to move from level to level. To respond to these changes, the Oregon State System of Higher Education is developing compatible new admission procedures. The Proficiency-Based Admission Standards System (PASS), is a completely new approach to admissions, which will require students applying for admission to public universities in Oregon to demonstrate proficiency in six content areas and nine process areas (Houghton, 1997). Proficiency will be determined by three types of assessments: criterion-referenced tests, prescribed assessment tasks, and teacher verification of performance according to consistent state-wide standards. Students will receive a numerical score for each proficiency as well as an overall score. Although the overall score will be similar to a grade point average for admission purposes, it is expected to be a more accurate tool for comparing students across the state because it will be based upon state-wide assessment standards. The PASS transcript will be easy for university personnel to process because it is based on a proficiency score (from one to five), rather than a portfolio of student work.

Wisconsin has developed and adopted a competency-based admission procedure as an alternative to traditional criteria for admission to the public universities in that state. A pilot of the competency-based admission policy was conducted in eight Wisconsin high schools during the 1995-96 school year. Two admission procedures were established and compared – traditional vs. competency-based. Both groups of applicants presented their ACT scores, letters of recommendation, and statement of interest; however, in the latter group the students included a competency-based admission profile form (University of Wisconsin System, 1997, 1998). This form is completed by high school teachers and includes five content areas (English, mathematics, science, social studies, and foreign language) with various competency items listed under each. For example, under mathematics the competencies include the following: use of constants, use of variables in linear situations, use of variables in algebraic situations, use of variables in transcendental situations, geometry. Each competency is rated on a five-point scale. Findings from the pilot study indicate that, because each University of Wisconsin campus sets its own minimum admission requirements, with UW-Madison having the highest requirements, admissions of competency-based applicants tended to be more prevalent at certain campuses. For instance, most students in the competency-based applicant pool tended to be accepted at other campuses than the UW-Madison branch. Nevertheless, the new procedure has the potential to facilitate entrance into four-year universities for students who have pursued career-related courses of study in high school.

Barriers to creating closer connections

Creating academic-vocational pathways that link high school to two-year and four-year postsecondary institutions requires active collaboration of faculty and administrators at different education levels. But resistance of high school and postsecondary faculty members to establishing integrated courses and articulated curriculum has been noted by several studies (National Assessment of Vocational Education, 1994; Bragg, Layton and Hammons, 1994; Grubb, 1995; Honeycutt, 1995). A study by Sorensen (1993) found that administrators in community colleges and high schools had different perceptions regarding ideal and actual practices of curriculum articulation.

Honeycutt (1995) surveyed community college personnel in North Carolina and found considerable confusion on the part of the respondents regarding their understand of the concept, purpose, and target student for Tech Prep. The longer community colleges had been participating in Tech Prep, however, the less their administrators and faculty believed Tech Prep students needed remediation. This suggests that initial resistance to linkages can be overcome with persistent collaborative efforts.

Whether sufficient effort will be exerted depends on incentives. These would seem to vary at different levels of the educational system. Selective four-year degree-granting institutions set standards that sending institutions – high schools and two-year colleges – must observe. Because they are selective, these four-year liberal arts colleges and universities do not usually view sending institutions as their "customers." They assume that sending institutions will make the effort to understand admission requirements and comply with them, and are not constantly seeking ways to simplify requirements, make them more transparent, or adapt them in response to changing curricula in high schools or two-year colleges.

On the other hand, many four-year postsecondary institutions are not in a position to be very selective. In their eagerness to recruit students, they already offer undergraduate majors in applied fields including business, health occupations, and engineering. These institutions are more likely to be interested in collaborating with high schools and two-year colleges to create clearer admission pathways and to transfer credits. It is possible, therefore, that access to four-year institutions from integrated academic/occupational programs in high schools and two-year colleges in the United States will be limited largely to four-year colleges that offer occupational majors. This would be similar to the pattern in other industrialised countries, where vocational secondary graduates increasingly are given the option to continue in postsecondary education, but only in polytechnics or other institutions for applied studies, rather than the humanities and sciences.

4. Work-based learning

A renewed emphasis on work-based learning (WBL) has been central to recent US initiatives to create integrated academic-vocational pathways. In the relatively unregulated US labour market, where formal statements of skill requirements have not been defined for most jobs, employers rely heavily on job applicants' records of previous work experience to decide who is qualified. WBL therefore can help students begin to acquire work experience that will help them enter a desired career field. Hershey *et al.* (1997) confirmed that local partnerships funded by the School-to-Work Opportunities Act have placed high priority on developing WBL opportunities for students.

The 1990s initiatives are reminiscent of the work experience movement of the 1970s, when the President's Science Advisory Committee (1973), headed by James Coleman, articulated the view of many experts that giving young people responsibilities outside of school would help them make the transition to adulthood. Experience and research since then, however, have clarified that not all work experience is necessarily beneficial (Greenberger and Steinberg, 1986). Quality matters (Stern and Nakata, 1989; Stern *et al.*, 1990*b*). Connecting students' work more closely with school might improve quality, enhancing the educational and developmental value of work experience. Research on co-operative education (co-op), the most prevalent form of school-supervised work experience in the United States, has demonstrated that co-op students in high school and college generally do give more positive reports about their work than students employed in jobs that are not school-supervised (Stone *et al.*, 1990; Stern *et al.*, 1995, 1997). But co-op in high schools and two-year colleges has been used mainly as an adjunct to vocational education leading to specific occupations, and has not been tied to the academic curriculum or to preparing students for a four-year college or university. Except for some research on the Experience-Based Career Education program of the 1970s (Owens, 1980), WBL's potential value for purposes beyond acquiring specific job skills was not explored very much before the 1990s.

The new interest in WBL as a possible means to achieve more general educational or developmental objectives raises fundamental questions. What does "work-based learning" actually mean, and how does it relate to learning in classrooms? This section explains the different purposes for which WBL is being tried, describes the most common formal structures for arranging WBL, and discusses some of the key issues that arise in trying to make WBL serve more purposes for more students.

Purposes of work-based learning, and examples

WBL has been both pushed and pulled into the public policy limelight. The push has come from concern about chronically high levels of youth unemployment, declining numbers of high-wage manufacturing jobs for high school graduates, and a general lack of coherent career-entry paths for young people who do not attend college (William T. Grant Foundation, 1988). The idea of making WBL available to large numbers of youth, as in Germany (Hamilton, 1990), attracted widespread attention in the early 1990s among policy makers and politicians. It was a conspicuous theme in Bill Clinton's 1992 Presidential campaign.

At the same time, WBL has been pulled into discussions of an emerging learning-based economy (Stern *et al.*, 1990*a*; Berryman and Bailey, 1992; Marshall and Tucker, 1992). Computers and telecommunications, globalisation of markets for labour and capital, deregulation and the spread of "lean" production have obliged workers at all levels to become increasingly flexible. Whether employed by a high-performance work organisation or forced to move from one employer to another, people at work must continue to learn and adapt at a faster rate than in the past. WBL is a logical strategy to prepare young people for work that is more learning-intensive. In short, "workplaces are part of the education system of the future" (Hamilton and Hamilton, 1997, p. 1).

Several distinct possible purposes of WBL for students emerge from a review of the literature and observation of efforts in the United States. These may be classified as follows:

1. Acquisition of knowledge or skill related to employment in particular occupations or industries.

2. Career exploration and planning.

3. Learning all aspects of an industry.

4. Increasing personal and social competence related to work in general.

5. Enhancing students' motivation and academic achievement.

These purposes are not mutually exclusive. To some extent they may even be mutually reinforcing: for example, learning all aspects of an industry may promote career awareness and planning. Given that students have limited time, however, it is not possible to maximise all of these purposes simultaneously. Therefore, in practice, different programs emphasise different purposes.

Acquisition of knowledge

Acquisition of knowledge or skill related to employment in particular occupations or industries is the main purpose of traditional apprenticeship, co-op, and other forms of on-the-job training. Learning by doing, under the guidance of an experienced supervisor, is intended to develop knowledge and facility with specific equipment and procedures that are necessary to do the job.

In the 1990s, however, this traditional practice is being placed in a lifetime career perspective. Preparation that is limited to a particular entry-level job is increasingly regarded as insufficient, because the job is likely to change soon. New skill standards for various industries and occupational clusters therefore include "core competencies" or "foundations" that should enable people to progress and adapt as conditions change (Klein, 1996; Tucker, 1995). Hamilton and Hamilton (1997), in proposing "technical competence" as the first of seven "principles for work-based learning," explain it this way:

> "Work-based learning teaches young people how to perform work tasks (...). Technical competence includes not only mastering procedures but also understanding fundamental principles and concepts underlying procedures, increasing capacity for analytical judgement, and, in most occupational areas, becoming computer literate (p. 10)."

The observation[19] in Box 5, by an NCRVE researcher in a St. Louis career magnet high school indicates the range of occupationally related knowledge and skill that students may develop through WBL.

Box 5. **Acquisition of knowledge or skill related to employment in particular occupations or industries**

Marilyn, a senior who is double majoring in pre-nursing and pre-medicine, has an internship at a university laboratory and at a hospital out-patient clinic. Both locations are part of large medical complex that includes several speciality hospitals, a medical school and research laboratories. Marilyn drives herself to the internship every Thursday beginning at 7 a.m. at the hospital. After approximately 3 to 3.5 hours there, she makes her way by a series of enclosed tunnels and overhead walkways to the university research laboratory in cell biology.

The work at the hospital is directly linked to Marilyn's high school class in Ambulatory Care, which has provided an introduction to terms, human biological systems and treatment processes. In class, students have practised the series of questions to ask an incoming patient to elicit the symptoms and descriptions of pain or conditions that would help a medical practitioner make a diagnosis, such as, "What hurts," "How long has it been hurting," or, "Have you had previous injuries?" At the hospital, Marilyn, dressed in hospital "blues," interviewed patients who were arriving for out-patient surgery. She checked with her supervisor and an in-out board to determine which patients would be arriving at what times, for what kinds of surgeries, and with what prior conditions. That particular day, for example, there were several dental surgeries for adults with severe mental disabilities that required anaesthesia and prevented the patients from being able to have normal dental care at a dentists' office. These patients are particularly difficult to interview and prepare for surgery and are accompanied by adult "handlers." Marilyn has also observed various surgical procedures along with medical students and done research for her science project at the hospital library.

At the university research lab, Marilyn and her "mentor researcher" discussed the series of experiments they had been conducting in search of a particular protein believed to be involved in the development and loss of elasticity in the skin. They described the findings and directions the experiments were leading. The mentor-mentee relationship began during a summer in which Marilyn was selected as one of 10 "Summer Scientists" in a partnership between the university and the city's high schools. Although the program ended at the end of the summer, the research project was to continue, and Marilyn worked out an agreement with the researcher to serve as her mentor for her senior project, which she plans to enter in the Science Fair for the next school year. The research uses samples of skin from calves and cows obtained on trips to the nearby stockyards where Marilyn accompanies the university researchers. The lab is full of expensive equipment, and Marilyn moves comfortably from the walk-in refrigerator containing her samples to the various lab stations where she conducts her research. Marilyn continues the kind of question-and-answering with her mentor that she began with her Advanced Biology teacher the previous day to continue preparing for the Science Fair.

New forms of "youth apprenticeship" that have appeared in the 1990s use WBL outside of schools to teach knowledge and skill for particular occupations or industries, while keeping students' career options open. An example was described by Pauly, Kopp and Haimson (1995) in Wisconsin, one of the first states to develop youth apprenticeship. This particular case is a printing program located in the small town of West Bend.

West Bend's workplace instruction is designed to expose youth apprentices to many occupations and specialities in the printing industry. Youth apprentices are grouped in pairs and assigned to line-level trainers as they rotate through several divisions during the first semester. In subsequent semesters, students spend more time at each work station. The curriculum is made up of competencies that are broken down into specific steps that the student learns to perform. Examples of competencies that youth apprentices are expected to learn during the first semester include using job cost estimating software, performing basic electronic publishing operations, producing paste-up sheets, producing a diffusion transfer line print, producing a metal offset plate and an electrostatic plate, and performing a lithographic offset duplicator setup. Trainers are responsible for determining when students have achieved a specific competency and for rating overall performance. Students develop portfolios from their work-based experience that include checklists of their competencies, test results from training they have received, and samples of their work. Grades are determined jointly by classroom instructors and workplace staff (Pauly, Kopp and Haimson, 1995, p. 142).

Two-year colleges, as the largest civilian providers of advanced vocational and technical education (Grubb, 1996), offer various kinds of WBL to help students prepare for work in particular occupations or industries. Examples are given by Bragg and Hamm (1996), who describe how this kind of WBL can be offered through traditional apprenticeship, new-style youth apprenticeship, Tech Prep, co-op, clinical internship, and school-based enterprise.

Career exploration and planning

A broader aim, career exploration and planning, has become an increasingly important purpose of WBL in the 1990s as high schools are offering students more choice among distinctive pathways leading to college and careers. As noted earlier, the effort to create these pathways has been prompted in part by concern that young people in the United States often spend several years "floundering" in the labour market before they find steady, long-term jobs (Hamilton, 1990). If a young person's journey through school and various kinds of early work experiences could be more connected and purposive, the chances of eventually finding enjoyable and rewarding work might be better. The idea of "career majors" in the 1994 School-to-Work Opportunities Act was intended as a structure for students to create a coherent sequence of learning and work experiences.

In this context, WBL allows students to taste and sample different kinds of work, to understand what is going on and how they might fit in, but without necessarily making any long-term commitment.

Many local programs are now sequencing WBL for high school students to start with brief job shadowing visits, and lead to longer experiences later. Based on observations in 1992-93, Pauly, Kopp and Haimson (1995) noted:

> "The widespread use of career exposure activities is particularly striking. Career academies, occupation-academic cluster programs, and restructured vocational programs have worked with employers to create career-exposure opportunities that appear to go far beyond those available to most high school students. There are numerous examples of these activities among the case studies. The co-op placements in Fort Collins include opportunities to participate in several community service activities for short periods so that students can try several different jobs. Job shadowing is used in the Los Angeles, Central Point, and Portland programs to enable students to observe the range of activities of an adult worker during a typical workday. The students participate in job shadowing several times in order to compare the tasks and responsibilities of different jobs. Some employers have developed summer internship programs that expose students to high-skill tasks that are normally reserved for senior employees; working with skilled staff members, Baltimore finance academy students help prepare reports on loan applications and Oakland health academy students have assisted in delivering babies. Borrowing the concept from medical training, some employers rotate students among all of their major production centers; for example, Socorro health academy students spend time in each of the main departments of the largest hospital in El Paso."

Students use journals to record and reflect on their workplace experiences in some school-to-work programs, including the Socorro health academy and the Cambridge vocational restructuring program, which also includes a seminar for students to discuss their workplace experiences and journal entries. Since many young people have virtually no knowledge about the world of work, these career-exposure activities can widen their horizons dramatically – a particular benefit for students who have no vision of a productive future life (*op. cit.*, pp. 139-140)

Revisiting these same programs in mid-1996, the researchers found that WBL sequences and options were being further elaborated. Job shadowing was being used more frequently, sometimes sandwiched between internships. One program required students in grade 10 to complete a job shadowing experience in each of four career paths before choosing one path the next year. Since job shadowing requires less effort than internships on the part of employers, larger numbers of employers are willing to participate in this way. In addition to acquainting students with a variety of work settings, job shadowing provides a way for employers and school staff members to start building a relationship that can lead to more intensive kinds of WBL (Pedraza, Pauly and Kopp, 1997).

Students interviewed by NCRVE on the topic of their WBL experiences readily talk about career exploration and decision-making. Excerpts are given in Box 6.

Box 6. **Career exploration and planning**

A health academy student in Oakland, California reflected:

"I think it's beneficial because I think with a lot of careers there's misconceptions about what really goes on, how things really work and function. So when you're there you get to see it, you get a complete understanding of it as opposed to reading about it in books. I think it helps you make a better decision."

Occasionally, students feel they have found their true calling as a result of their WBL. One student at Roosevelt High School in Portland explained:

"I knew I wanted to work with people but I really wasn't sure what I wanted to do. And then I was able to go on an internship at an elementary school nearby and work with third graders, and through that experience I made my full decision that I wanted to be a teacher and it really helped me. It just clicked right there. I'd been on several job shadows, which is one-day thing, and nothing really – I kind of went all over the place with my job shadows and finally with that internship I was able to really see what I wanted."

Other students describe how their experiences changed their ideas of what they wanted to do. In a small town in South Carolina, a Medical Science student shadowed an emergency room nurse, realising that she was not cut out for the high pressured and gory work when she passed out. She then began a shadowing experience with a Physical Therapist, first thinking she would just want to be an assistant. "He had a lot of paperwork," she explains. "I didn't want a lot of paperwork. [...] Then watching this Physical Therapist that I'm watching now, she has just set my mind that that's what I want to do. [...] You see different people every day. You do different routines with every person you do. So it's not a job I'm going to get bored with."

An Academy of Finance student at the same school reported similar clarity as a result of a work experience. "At first I wanted to be a Real Estate agent and I expressed that interest. The Academy of Finance director offered me the job as a receptionist at a Real Estate office. [...] I found that Real Estate is not my thing – I'm not that competitive. That really helped a lot because that eliminated it." A field trip to the Federal Reserve with a Banking and Credit class helped her find a new direction. "I loved it down there and I thought, well gosh, I know I want to work in a bank!" She has requested an internship placement at a bank.

Some students say they have not yet settled on any particular kind of work, but their WBL placement has helped them clarify what they do *not* want. For instance, a student in Oakland declared, "At first when I joined the Media Academy I thought I wanted to go into broadcasting, but once I had my internships, I realised that's not what I want to do."

At the postsecondary level, an elaborate structure for work-based career exploration and planning has developed at LaGuardia Community College in New York City (Grubb and Badway, 1995). "Every full-time day student – including those majoring in Liberal Arts – is required to enrol in three 12-week internships or co-op placements, varying from 15 to 40 hours per week..." (p. 4). Students become eligible for co-op after completing all the prerequisites for a major, at least one course in their major, and the co-op preparation course. Each student meets with a co-op faculty adviser to find an appropriate placement. In conjunction with each of their three internships, students also enrol in a six-week seminar. Generally, the seminars provide "a framework for analysing and evaluating students' internship experiences, linking work experience with critical analysis and reflection." (p. 11) The second in this series of three seminars, titled "Fundamentals of Career Advancement," focuses specifically on career planning.

"Using short practical exercises, research activities and case studies, students gather and analyse information about career options and about four-year colleges. An important element in this second seminar is a "map" for extracting the greatest potential learning from any work experience, by replicating strategies used by successful executives: seeking challenging assignments; coping with hardships; observing key people; and getting feedback on strengths and areas for improvement (Grubb and Badway, 1995, p. 13)."

This description illustrates how advanced forms of school-supervised work experience for older students can merge with and enhance the process of lifelong learning at work.

Learning all aspects of an industry

Learning all aspects of an industry is an explicit objective in the 1990 Perkins Amendments, the 1994 School-to-Work Opportunities Act, and the 1998 Perkins Amendments. This stipulation was intended to ensure that vocational education or school-to-work programs teach more than the skills needed for specific entry-level jobs. According to the Center for Law and Education, a chief proponent of the concept, providing students with understanding and experience in all aspects of an industry or industry sector is essential to integrating academic and vocational education, empowering students to make career choices, preparing them to adapt to technological change, and equipping them to play an active part in economic development of their local communities (Jacobs, 1995, p. 9). Hamilton and Hamilton (1997) add that broader knowledge and skill enables students to participate in flexible work teams, which are becoming more prevalent in many settings. The official definition of "all aspects" is given in Box 7.

Box 7. **Learning all aspects of an industry**

The 1994 law, with only minor changes from 1990, specified eight "aspects." Jacobs (1995) explains them as follows:

Planning: examined both at the industry level and at the firm level; various forms of ownership, including co-operatives and worker ownership; relationship of the industry to economic, political, and social context.

Management: methods typically used to manage enterprises over time within the industry; methods for expanding and diversifying workers' tasks and broadening worker involvement in decisions.

Finance: ongoing accounting and financial decisions; different methods for raising capital to start or expand enterprises.

Technical and production skills: specific production techniques; alternative methods for organising the production work, including methods which diversify and rotate workers' jobs;

Underlying principles of technology: integrated study across the curriculum of the mathematical, scientific, social, and economic principles that underlie the technology.

Labour issues: worker rights and responsibilities; labour unions and labour history; methods for expanding workers' roles.

Community issues: the impact of the enterprise and the industry on the community, and the community's impact on and involvement with the enterprise.

Health, safety, and environmental issues: in relation to both the workers and the larger community (p. 8).

Goldberger, Kazis, and O'Flanagan (1994) describe three ways in which work experiences have been structured to promote this learning agenda. Rotating students through departments "is a powerful antidote to narrow occupational training" (p. 46). If students are paid, it helps if their wages are billed to a central budget, not to their work units or departments. In addition to spending relatively long periods of time in department-based training, a second strategy for teaching "all aspects" is to provide shorter experiences in a variety of different settings within the organisation or industry. Third, students are sometimes paired with worksite mentors who have broad organisational responsibilities, and who can help students understand the bigger picture.

Hamilton and Hamilton (1997) also advocate rotation through different placements. They also mention two additional approaches to teaching all aspects of an industry through WBL. One is straightforward: give students an initial orientation to the organisation, provide literature, and include them in events like company picnics. The second is more difficult: structuring projects for students to plan and carry out at the worksite. They give an example of project activities undertaken by a participant in their youth apprenticeship demonstration project in Broome County, New York. This young man was learning Manufacturing and Engineering Technology through WBL at The Raymond Corporation, a manufacturer of electrically powered fork lift trucks. In his fourth year of the program, while enrolled in community college, he was assigned to:

> "write plans; work on design and drafting; order and process requisitions for materials for special material handling carts; assemble and weld the carts; update a computer database for welders and their qualifications; complete a time study and product flow analysis of various work stations and present results and recommendations; report on active usage of fixtures to assess storage status and recommend dispositions; further develop welding and cutting torch skills (p. 20)."

These strategies for helping students understand and experience multiple aspects of work all focus on participants as individuals. Another kind of approach is to bring together students as a group to reflect on their different work experiences. This was a feature of Experience-Based Career Education in the 1970s. Conventional co-op programs also include a related class where students discuss various aspects of their different work experiences; this is particularly well developed at LaGuardia Community College (Grubb and Badway, 1995). Groups such as these give students a chance not only to reflect on their own experiences, but also to hear about other students' situations.

School-based enterprises offer some advantages as work settings in which students can learn about all aspects of an industry. Because their main purpose is educational, school enterprises can give students more room to experiment and make mistakes than a non-school enterprise usually can do. Students working both in school enterprises and in outside jobs have reported that school enterprises provide more opportunities for learning, doing a range of tasks, and working in teams (Stern, 1984; Stern et al., 1994). Numerous testimonial statements from students in high school and community college enterprises were reported in Stern et al. (1994), including descriptions of how some school enterprises even engage students in designing or redesigning job structures and organisational procedures. Recent examples of school enterprises teaching many aspects of an industry come from Sebastian River High School in Sebastian, Florida, where:

> "(…) the school's restaurant provides hands-on experience in a school-based enterprise. The restaurant, Sharky's Cafe (…) is open to the public several days each week and for special breakfast and lunch events by local community organisations. According to a school brochure, "Students will be equipped to handle every phase of the business of running a restaurant, and they will be taught the skills for commercial food preparation. Upon completion of the culinary arts program, students will be ready for many phases of commercial restaurants as well as for further culinary arts training.

> The Environmental Science Academy uses both school and state property to extend learning from the classroom to the outside world. There is a greenhouse and aquaculture project on campus, and the academy students are landscaping a section of the school grounds to support an outdoor teaching facility complete with open-air theatre and sample flora from around the state. In addition, the academy participates in a partnership with the local water management district in which, according to the school brochure, students "help implement a management plan... The students take an extremely active role, including surveying the habitat, inventorying species and designing nature trails to allow public use of the land."

In community colleges, Bragg and Hamm (1996) give recent examples of college-sponsored enterprises, including a fruit tree orchard and a child care center, where students can learn many aspects of their chosen field.

Increasing personal and social competence related to work in general

Beyond technical skills, career awareness, and learning all aspects of an industry, many contemporary discussions of WBL also point to a broader set of capacities that are assumed to be desirable in most or all work situations, not only in particular occupations or industries. Sometimes termed generic work skills, core competencies, or transferable skills, they encompass two basic dimensions that Hamilton and Hamilton (1997) call personal and social competence.

Making up lists of these generic capacities has become a popular activity in the 1990s, and many public and private groups of employers or educators have produced frameworks (see Klein, 1996). The one that has had the most influence in the United States so far was the SCANS report (US Department of Labor, 1991). The Secretary's Commission on Achieving Necessary Skills, appointed by the Secretary of Labor, proposed a way for schools to conceive of knowledge and skill beyond the traditional academic disciplines. The SCANS framework consists of a three-part foundation, then five general competencies. The three-part foundation consists of:

- *Basic skills*: reading, writing, arithmetic/mathematics, listening, and speaking.
- *Thinking skills*: creative thinking, decision making, problem solving, seeing things in the mind's eye, knowing how to learn, and reasoning.
- *Personal qualities*: responsibility, self-esteem, sociability, self-management, and integrity/honesty.

Over and above this foundation, SCANS sketched competencies along the following five dimensions:

- *Resources*: time, money, materials and facilities, and human resources.
- *Interpersonal*: participates as member of a team, teaches others new skills, serves clients/customers, exercises leadership, negotiates, and works with diversity.
- *Information*: acquires and evaluates, organises and maintains, interprets and communicates, uses computers to process information.
- *Systems*: understands systems, monitors and corrects performance, improves or designs systems.
- *Technology*: selects technology, applies technology to task, maintains and troubleshoots equipment.

A more parsimonious list was proposed by Murnane and Levy (1996), based on their observation of hiring practices by employers who screen new applicants carefully.

In addition to things that employers have always looked for – reliability, a positive attitude, and a willingness to work hard – these employers now look for hard and soft skills that applicants wouldn't have needed 20 years ago:

- The ability to read at the ninth-grade level or higher.
- The ability to do math at the ninth-grade level or higher.
- The ability to solve semi-structured problems where hypotheses must be formed and tested.
- The ability to work in groups with persons of various backgrounds.
- The ability to communicate effectively, both orally and in writing.
- The ability to use personal computers to carry out simple tasks like word processing.

These are the New Basic Skills, the minimum skills people now need to get a middle-class job (*op. cit.*, pp. 31-32)

Both SCANS and Murnane and Levy meant their lists to guide curriculum and instruction in schools generally, including regular classroom teaching as well as work-based learning. As Stasz *et al.* (1990) have demonstrated, generic work skills can indeed be learned in classrooms, and it would be wrong to assume that they can only be acquired at worksites.

Hamilton and Hamilton (1997) offer a list of skills that is specifically tailored to WBL. Developed by the "workplace teachers" at the various companies that participated in their demonstration project, the "Guide to Evaluating Personal and Social Competence" consists of two separate lists. Major headings under "Social Competence: Participate in an organisation" are:

– *Systems*: understand the organisation.

– *Rules*: adhere to professional norms.

– *Teamwork*: cooperage with others.

– *Communication*: give clear messages.

Under "Personal Competence: Act responsibly," the major headings are:

– Self-confidence.

– Initiative.

– Motivation.

– Continuous improvement.

– Career planning.

Stasz and Kaganoff (1997) use a slightly different set of categories to analyse what students learn through WBL. Under "generic skills" they include problem solving, communications, and teamwork. They also propose a separate category of "work-related attitudes," which "include work habits and personal qualities that are crucial for success on the job." (p. 61). Working hard and taking responsibilities seriously are examples. Stasz and Kaganoff also consider "personal and social skills" as distinct from generic skills or attitudes. Being generally friendly, feeling confident, respecting themselves and other people are examples of these.

Plausible and insightful as these lists of skills are, they have been subjected to very little empirical validation. The most stringent validation would demonstrate that people who possess the stipulated skills or capacities actually perform better than those who do not. This would involve measuring the skills, measuring performance, and demonstrating that more skill causes better performance. For example, Murnane, Willett and Levy (1995) have shown that math skills were a more potent predictor of wages for recent high school graduates in the 1980s than in the 1970s. Such studies are rare, however. Another approach is to watch people at work and observe the skills and capacities they are using. For example, Stasz *et al.* (1996) used this method to understand the role of teamwork, communication skills, and certain general "dispositions" or attitudes in several different technical occupations.

Despite considerable uncertainty about whether and how these personal and social skills actually affect performance at work, it is not difficult to find testimonial evidence from young people who participate in WBL. Examples are given in Box 8.

Box 8. **Increasing personal and social competence related to work in general**

One obvious effect of WBL is to confront students with the expectations and demands of customers or clients who are depending on them. Even for older students, this can spur personal and social development. A co-op student at LaGuardia Community College was quoted as saying: "It's something other than sitting in a classroom or even in a lab. It's the real world. You drew it, you just put it together, and it still doesn't work. But we're on a deadline, we've got to have this done because we've got a real customer that's screaming for it. You know. So here is the real world" (Grubb and Badway, 1995).

Working engages students in social interactions they would not otherwise have. For example, a high school intern working with the East Manhattan Chamber of Commerce in New York City was responsible for soliciting new membership to the Chamber, which involved "pounding the pavement" and approaching store owners in person. She described this experience as new and challenging, and was extremely proud that her supervisor had the confidence to allow her to represent the Chamber to the public. It was this kind of empowerment that was preparing her for a future in business, and she was well aware that this internship would look very good on her resume in the future.

A young woman who had recently graduated from a high school in Boston explained to an NCRVE interviewer how the social skills she developed in her internship helped her get her present job.

> "Basically, I wouldn't have a job if I didn't have my internship... Where I come from, if you talk to me in the wrong way, I'm going to address you back in that same manner. I'm not going to be nice to you and try to get you to calm down or whatever... But because I've worked, I've learned how to tolerate things, I've learned how to deal with people and their attitudes and I've learned how to, you know, thank people when they're nice to me, when they give me my forms on time, you know, things like that."

More systematic attention to how WBL can develop personal and social competence is a major advance over the more limited, traditional focus on WBL as a means to acquire specific technical skills. As personal and social dispositions become part of the curriculum, however, educators and program designers will have to face some difficult questions.

One fundamental question is whether WBL is intended merely to adapt young people to jobs, or whether it is also intended to develop their capacity for creative and critical thinking about work (Simon, Dippo and Schenke, 1991). Obviously, an employer's interest sometimes conflicts with the interests of employees. The basic fact that employees' pay and benefits are costs to employers is a perpetual cause of conflict, though it may not be overt. Health and safety, the division of work responsibilities, and lack of participation in decision making are other sources of conflict between employers and employees. One way or another, WBL designers and teachers have to deal with these contentious issues. Confronting them openly might help students better understand what their options are. Rather than run the risk of stepping into a political minefield, however, most programs seem to be keeping silent.

A more subtle kind of conflict may also arise between the interest of employers and the well-being of customers or clients. Here the basic issue is that it costs money to make a product or service better. Product specifications or service contracts may state what customers or clients have the right to expect, but buyers generally have less information than sellers about what they are getting. How many customers are able to judge whether their cars have been properly serviced, X-rays have been properly read, or computers have been properly built? Even though a company's long-run success depends on keeping customers satisfied, resources are always limited, which means that people at work face a perpetual trade-off between keeping down employers' costs and making clients or customers better off. Since WBL is being supported by public funds, program designers and teachers would seem to have some obligation to make sure that students understand their responsibility at work to protect the interests of the public.

Enhancing students' motivation and academic achievement

Farthest removed from the goal of teaching skills and knowledge related to particular occupations is the objective of improving students' academic performance in school. It may even seem too great a stretch: Why should experience on a job be expected to improve achievement in the classroom? The answer has a negative and a positive part.

First, on the negative side, students' work experience might be redesigned so that working long hours does less damage to achievement in school. As noted earlier, most students in the United States already hold jobs while they attend high school or college, and those who work long hours often get lower grades. A possible explanation is that working long hours actually causes students' academic performance to decline. If so, then connecting students' work experience more closely to school might do less harm to academic motivation and performance.

Second, more positively, research in the 1980s on learning outside of school stimulated new interest in the idea that providing some kind of "contextual" or "situated" learning opportunities for students would improve their understanding and retention of academic subject matter (Resnick, 1987; Raizen, 1989; Lave and Wenger, 1991). American educational authorities in the past, notably Dewey (1916) and Whitehead (1929), have argued that education should confront students with problems that matter to them, including practical problems that arise in the context of productive activity. In the United States, however, debates have tended to oscillate between the ideological poles of "relevance" and "rigor." The advocates of work experience in the 1970s, for example, were clearly tilting toward relevance, and the "excellence" movement of the early 1980s was in part a reaction against that. Cognitive scientists in the late 1980s and 1990s offered the possibility that "applied learning" or "cognitive apprenticeship" might achieve rigor through relevance. And there is evidence that engaging students in activities which have value beyond the classroom contributes to academic achievement. even as measured by conventional tests (Newmann and Wehlage, 1995). This research has prompted educators to take another look at WBL as a possible means to improve academic performance.

Hamilton and Hamilton (1997) list "academic achievement" as one of their seven principles for work-based learning. Their demonstration project revealed, however, that WBL by itself was not sufficient to raise students' academic achievement.

> "We conclude that neither grades nor course enrolments will improve as an indirect result of work-based learning; improved academic performance must be a central focus of school-to-work systems and specific steps taken to foster it. The most critical need is for a variety of learning options and instructional approaches, for explicit links between knowledge and application, and for new school structures (p. 54)."

Nevertheless, they provide testimonial evidence illustrating how WBL can enhance academic study in the classroom. A math teacher who had visited students' worksites explained,

> "When material can be made meaningful to their everyday life as it is in the workplace, it has some relevance. I had a couple of good examples this year where apprenticeships were a factor in my classroom instruction, and that would not have happened if I had not been familiar with the work environment. One was teaching standard deviation with a student who was doing very poorly in math. I was able to say, "Gee, I think we use standard deviation in the workplace. I wonder if someone could tell us what that means?" And sure enough [finger snap], it came to life and he explained exactly what a standard deviation was, why it was important to the statistical research of the company, and how was using it on a regular basis. No problem whatsoever because it was in a meaningful context for him. So that was application for the whole class. But he would not have volunteered if I hadn't known enough to go for it. It was my familiarity with what they were doing and what he was doing that made me able to use that kind of knowledge. Unfortunately, few teachers have had those opportunities (p. 58)."

This story shows how WBL can enliven an abstract concept not only for the particular student who uses it at work, but also for other students who hear about the application.

Teaching academic concepts through WBL is not a new idea. In health-care occupations, clinical internship traditionally has been part of the curriculum. When Bragg, Hamm and Trinkle (1995) surveyed community colleges around the country asking for exemplary WBL programs, most of the programs nominated were in the health field. Pauly, Kopp and Haimson (1995) give an example of a high-quality WBL program in that field for high school students.

"At the King-Drew Medical Magnet High School in Los Angeles, all students take a curriculum that includes work experience linking learning in school and at the workplace. Students learn biological, chemical, and physiological concepts, as well as methods and ideas of scientific research. Students work in ten different medical settings over the course of three years (...).

Los Angeles program and hospital staff work together to create training plans that specify experiences and outcomes for each student placement. Close co-ordination between workplace supervisors and school staff maximises learning opportunities at the workplace and their connection to classroom instruction. Workplace objectives are designed to help students understand scientific aspects of their work experience in the context of the division or department to which they are assigned. For example, during the rotation in gastroenterology, students learn the parts of the stomach and their functions, why biopsies are performed and how they are used, and procedures for gastric analysis. Grade 11 and 12 students who select a research laboratory as a placement are expected to learn how to set up a scientific investigation, how to perform laboratory techniques and procedures, and the procedures for conducting a scientific investigation. Hospital staff prepare reports that students have learned specified topics.

Each semester, students in the Los Angeles program take a course related to their work experience... As part of these courses, students must show that they have completed the learning objectives specified for their work placements... Students are also given assignments that require research efforts at the workplace, and grade 12 students must write two research papers based on investigations completed at their workplaces... Students' academic courses also draw on their workplace experiences; for example, English assignments and vocabulary words draw on students' work-based experiences, and eleventh graders write a term paper related to the workplace as part of their history course. Teachers spend some of their planning periods at workplaces to gain a better understanding of students' experiences (pp. 140-142)."

Some high schools and community college have been able to take the internship-based teaching model from the health field and apply it elsewhere. Examples are given in Box 9.

Box 9.
Enhancing students' motivation and academic achievement

At a high school in Boston visited by an NCRVE researcher, internships have become a central part of the junior and senior curriculum. The school's internship handbook states: "The goal of the (...) internship is to provide students an opportunity to demonstrate the application of their acquired academic skills to real work situations. First-hand experiences will give students greater insights about the career which they believe they would like to pursue. The experience enables students to research a complex and in-depth question within their field." While at their internship, the handbook states that students must do the following: keep a daily log, keep a weekly list of skills that are being acquired, write or draw a diagram of the internship site after touring the facility, conduct at least two interviews with persons at the internship site, design a flow chart of how decisions are made and communicated at the site, write a one-page site policy manual, research and write an in-depth paper that probes the major internship question, read two books (...) and participate in the evaluations.

The culminating piece of the internship is the Senior Project, described as "a personalised independent learning experience that demonstrates in an interdisciplinary fashion skills and knowledge. Students will investigate a topic of interest with the assistance of their Advisor, House and Senior Institute Co-ordinator... The final project should include technology application, math application as well as an oral and visual presentation with a written conclusion. The senior project will be presented and defended to students' graduation committees." The handbook suggests that there are basically two kinds of questions that can be addressed by the Senior Project: Experimental (e.g. "How does reading aloud to pre-school children affect their reading ability in kindergarten?") or Ethical (e.g. "Should cameras be allowed in courtrooms?").

Similarly, LaGuardia Community College in New York City has connected WBL with course content through its co-op seminars. As explained in the discussion of career exploration, LaGuardia requires students to engage in a series of three co-op placements. Along with each placement, students participate in a seminar. The second seminar in the series focuses on career exploration; the first and third relate to students' majors. According to Grubb and Badway (1995), five major-specific seminars were available at the first level: Accounting Information Systems; Application of Computer Information Systems Concepts in the Workplace; Management Principles: Theory and Application; and Introduction to Teaching. "At this initial phase, topics include information gathering, data organisation, quality standards, maintaining currency in technical skills, and other issues specific to the major." (p. 13) The third-level seminars related to majors were: Accounting Information Systems for Decision-Making by Objectives; What Do Managers Do: An Advanced Approach; Advanced Computer Information Systems; and School Food Service Management. At this advanced level, "seminars demand the use of systematic research skills in an independent and professional way (...) [S]tudents are expected to review theory while applying complex knowledge to their fieldwork experience." (p. 14).

As these accounts suggest, bringing out the academic content of students' work experience is mainly done by the school or college, though worksite supervisors must collaborate and support the effort. To the extent that WBL is intended to promote students' academic achievement rather than teach specific job skills, enterprises sponsored by schools and colleges themselves become more advantageous.

For example, Stasz (1996) describes an urban high school enterprise that began in 1993 as a community garden: students sold produce at local farmers' markets. The student-owners decided to create a product that they could successfully market on a wide scale, and "Food from the Hood" salad dressing was born. While the business creates a focus and motivation for student learning, nearly as much time and effort is spent on academics. The calendar posts both business-related events and SAT test dates. Volunteer mentors work closely with students to help them study for the SAT and to complete college applications. Student conversation is often about school, grades, classes, and college. And nearly all the student-owners go on to college, as compared to fewer than half of the students enrolled in the same high school (p. 2).

In addition to creating a cognitive connection between academic concepts and their practical application, WBL also can strengthen students' motivation. For example, in a South Carolina high school where the curriculum has been organised into career clusters with extensive WBL, students told NCRVE interviewers of changes in their attitude toward school as a result of their participation in the Clusters. A self-described average student explained the motivation she found: "I never excelled in science, I never excelled in English, I never excelled in math... I never found my thing. But this, it really gave me a focus. I totally know what I want to do... I'm not ignorant to the fact that I may change my mind because everyone changes their mind, but I think that I will stay in this general area and it really has given me assurance." She went on to imagine what her high school experience would have been without the opportunity to participate in a Cluster: "I would probably go through the basic classes and just do the routine." In actuality, she reported that before, "I was discouraged because I couldn't do well. Now I'm doing okay in the business and I'm striving – it's given me more self-esteem that I can do this, when I was falling behind in Chemistry and science." Her grades have improved to all A's and B's.

It may seem paradoxical that WBL and work-related curricula can increase students' desire for schooling, but this is not an uncommon finding (e.g., Phelps *et al.*, 1996). Apparently, students gain confidence in their ability to master school subjects when they connect them to activities they understand and value.

As the WBL revival of the 1990s has gained momentum, however, there is still controversy about whether it can benefit students who are already performing well in school, or whether it should mainly be reserved for the "non-college-bound." Few would object if students who were performing poorly in school become encouraged by WBL and a related curriculum to continue their studies after high school. But there is definitely opposition to the idea of adding WBL to the college-prep curriculum (Bailey and Merritt, 1997; Vo, 1997). As a result, students in career-related programs featuring WBL sometimes express mixed feelings. Pauly, Kopp and Haimson (1995) reported:

> "In several schools, students complained that other students who are not part of their program see it as being for "dumber kids and dropouts who can't handle academics." One student said, "It's like they all think we're the stupid ones, and we're dropouts. And that we're only good for working, not for learning." These students pointed out that many of their program's graduates attend college, and students in more than half of the programs characterised their courses as more demanding than the regular high school courses. Nevertheless, they were aware that the stigma attached to programs with a workplace component or an occupational theme remains strong (p. 152)."

Although some high schools have committed themselves to preparing all students for college *and* careers (*Business Week*, 1996), the traditional division between academic and vocational education is still strongly ingrained in the minds of many students, teachers, administrators, policy makers, and parents. If the established mind-set is to change, it will probably require some evidence that adding WBL can in fact improve understanding and retention of academic knowledge by students who are already succeeding in conventional classroom and lab instruction. That evidence can come only after WBL is actually tried with such students. And trying out WBL as a means to improve the academic performance of college prep students requires the existence of curriculum materials or ideas for using the workplace as a laboratory in a rigorous way. Examples of such materials do exist (Vickers, 1996) and will be described below. Until instructional ideas like these are adopted and tested on a wide scale, the academic benefits of WBL are likely to remain restricted in many schools to students who are not deemed academically most promising.

Methods and challenges

Implicit in this discussion of purposes has been a description of methods for WBL. To make that explicit, the most common forms can be listed:

– *Paid work experience*: students receive training in the context of a paid job. This is traditional in co-operative education, and is viewed as desirable in STWOA.

– *Unpaid internship*: students learn while they carry out productive responsibilities in a work setting outside of school, but they are not compensated. This is standard practice in certain industries, particularly health care.

– *Service learning*: unpaid internship, usually in a government office or non-profit agency, with primary focus on serving the community rather than building students' skills, though considerable learning may occur.

– *Job shadowing*: students visit worksites for the purpose of observing, but are not responsible for carrying out any of the work there, and are not paid.

– *School-based enterprise*: students produce goods or services for other people, in connection with a school class or other school activity.

Hershey *et al.* (1998), in the second report from their official evaluation of the School-to-Work Opportunities Act, found that 51% of high schools involved in local partnerships were said to sponsor job shadowing in the 1996-97 school year. School-based enterprises and service learning were next in reported frequency, with 32 and 31% of high schools offering them, respectively. Paid internships during the school year were said to be available in 27% of high schools, and unpaid internships in 24% of them (p. 84). Interviews with students in grade 12 in eight states revealed that the percentage who had participated in job shadowing rose from 62% in spring 1996 to 67% in spring 1998, while the percentage who had participated in school-based enterprise went from 26 to 25%, and those in paid or unpaid internships remained constant at 28% (p. 85).

The challenges to making high-quality WBL available to large numbers of students are formidable. The first report on the evaluation of STW partnerships funded through the states found that the great majority of WBL placements were obtained by students themselves, not by the school. Although it is possible to convert students' part-time jobs into powerful learning experiences, students' responses suggested that this was not usually happening. Links between students' work experience and the classroom were infrequent and generally tenuous. Only 16% of the seniors responding to the 1996 survey indicated that they had completed a classroom assignment using information or skills gained from an intensive work-based activity, and had their performance in that activity count toward a grade at school (Hershey *et al.*, 1997, Chapter V). That fraction fell to 13% in the 1998 survey (Hershey *et al.*, 1998, pp. 93-94). Pedraza, Pauly and Kopp (1997) conclude that a trade-off exists between scale and intensity: involving more students will mean offering less intensive experiences.

If WBL is intended not only to expose students to the workplace and give them an opportunity to acquire specific procedural know-how, but also to accomplish any of the broader purposes we have discussed, then it must be carefully planned and monitored by people who understand both the work setting and what is to be learned there. Steinberg (1997) spells out "six A's": questions to ask when designing projects in general, including projects at the work site:

– *Authenticity*. Does the project emanate from a problem or question that has meaning to the student? Is it a problem or question that might actually be tackled by an adult at work or in the community? Do students create or produce something that has personal and/or social value, beyond the school setting?

– *Academic rigor*. Does the project lead students to acquire and apply knowledge related to one or more discipline or content areas? Does it challenge students to use methods of inquiry central to one or more disciplines (*e.g.* to think like a scientist)? Do students develop higher order thinking skills and habits of mind (e.g., searching for evidence, taking different perspectives)?

– *Applied learning*. Are students solving a semi-structured problem (*e.g.* designing a product, improving a system, or organising an event) that is grounded in a context of life and work beyond the school walls? Does the project lead students to acquire and use competencies expected in high performance work organisations (*e.g.* teamwork, appropriate use of technology, problem-solving, communications)? Does the work require students to develop organisational and self-management skills?

– *Active exploration*. Do students spend significant amounts of time doing field-based work? Does it require students to engage in real investigation, using a variety of methods, media, and sources? Are students expected to communicate what they are learning through presentations?

– *Adult connections*. Do students meet/observe adults with relevant expertise and experience? Does the work of adults become more visible to students? Do adults from outside the classroom help students develop a sense of the standards for this type of work?

– *Assessment practices*. Do students have opportunities to review exemplars of similar work products? Are there clear milestones or "deliverables" at the completion of each distinct phase of the work, culminating in an exhibition, portfolio, and/or presentation? Do students receive timely feedback on their works-in-progress and also engage in periodic, structured self-assessment using clear project criteria that they have helped to set?

These questions echo and elaborate on the definition of authentic pedagogy developed by Newmann and Wehlage (1995).

Vickers (1996) and her team have produced outstanding examples of project designs that meet these criteria and are expressly intended to be carried out at worksites by high school students. By addressing practical questions that arise in specific work settings, students can master certain concepts that are included in current curricular standards for high school science. One unit focuses on the human cardiovascular system, a second on water testing and aquatic ecology, and a third on heating, ventilating, air conditioning and heat flow. Each unit involves students in a set of common workplace experiences, complemented by lessons and exercises in the school classroom and laboratory. Exposing all students to the same events in the workplace is necessary to ensure that they all have the same experience to analyse. This is a deliberate departure from the typical practice of WBL in the United States, where individual students usually do different things. It is more similar to German apprenticeship, which is designed to ensure that all trainees acquire a common core of knowledge.

Another example of a program creating group experiences for students at worksites is the Rindge School of Technical Arts in Cambridge, Massachusetts. As part of a learning sequence that integrates various kinds of classroom instruction and school-based enterprise with workplace internships, Rindge sent some of its academic teachers out to conduct classes for student interns at some of the host companies. Rosenstock (1997) points out that these classes serve the purpose of "connecting activities" as specified by STWOA, by physically and intellectually joining instruction in academic subjects with students' workplace experience.

Even without trying to ensure that a whole group of students experience something in common, extracting valuable learning from students' work experience takes a lot of doing. Packer and Pines (1996, pp. 53-54) describe what it takes to produce "learning-rich work experience." Managers at the worksite have to support the idea. Sufficient lead time must be allowed for preparation. Job supervisors have to be trained in their new role, then matched with students. Students need time and help to reflect on what they are doing at work and what they are learning from it. Students' learning should be documented so that school credit can be awarded. Program operators have to be alert for unexpected problems and opportunities that occur along the way, and everyone involved should participate in continuously improving the process. Obviously, all of this takes someone's time, which has to be budgeted.

One additional feature is needed to ensure that WBL becomes an integral part of the curriculum: teachers of academic subjects have to be involved. Traditionally, co-operative education has linked structured WBL with instruction in vocational subjects, and has been supervised by vocational teachers. If WBL is to serve broader educational purposes and a broader cross-section of students, it will have to be linked to instruction in the core academic subjects of English, math, science, and social studies. This is possible, as we have seen. But it will not happen on a large scale unless and until academic teachers are persuaded that it is worthwhile for themselves and their students. Resistance may be strongest on the part of teachers in college-prep courses. Whether WBL helps students prepare for the Advanced Placement examination in calculus or history, for example, still remains to be seen. Sending non-vocational teachers to spend some time in workplaces outside the school may help them find practical applications of their subject matter, and STW partnerships have been providing this kind of opportunity through summer internships and other arrangements.

There may be a chicken-and-egg problem here, however. Teachers who do not believe WBL has anything to offer their students are unwilling to spend the time looking at workplaces themselves. If they believe that good instruction in academic subjects builds intellectual skills which are useful in work settings – which is true – they may also believe that school-supervised work experience for students has little to add and is not worth the trouble. Cracking this resistance may be essential to making WBL an option for large numbers of students.

5. Brief summary of evaluation results

The examples described in the preceding three sections are not isolated instances. To the contrary, thousands of US high schools have been engaged in this kind of innovation to some extent. Much of this innovation predated the 1994 School-to-Work Opportunities Act and will presumably survive its expiration in 2001, but the funding provided by that Act did accelerate the spread of some new practices (Visher *et al.*, 1998). The survey by Hershey *et al.* (1998) of 998 local school-to-work partnerships in 34 states found that 46% of high schools were reported to be offering "career majors" of some kind (p. 68).

Since these are mainly local initiatives, however, there is a great deal of variation in practice. For instance, a 1998 survey of high school seniors in eight states found that 65% of seniors whose schools were involved in school-to-work partnerships reported participating in career development activities; 18% said they had a career-related academic class[20] ; and 13% had paid or unpaid work experience linked to school; but only 3% of students had experienced all of these conditions (Hershey *et al.*, 1998, p. 97).

This variation complicates the task of evaluation. In theory, it would be possible to observe all the different programmatic options each student experienced, and to compare the performance of students who had participated in different combinations of options. Leaving aside the issue of how to control for non-random selection of students, the number of different combinations becomes very large if there are more than a few distinct programmatic elements. Furthermore, the most important question, at least initially, is whether or not the program makes a difference when taken as a whole.

Career academies

Because of these complications, the most revealing evaluations of new, integrated pathways in US high schools have involved career academies. As described earlier, a career academy is a reasonably well-defined package of three main elements: small learning community, combined academic-vocational curriculum, and partnerships with employers who provide internships and other services for students. Since academies usually have served only a fraction of the students within a given high school, other students in the same school can comprise a comparison group for purposes of evaluation. Career academies have been developing and spreading since 1969, providing numerous opportunities for evaluation. The remainder of this subsection, culminating in Tables 3-6, summarises the results of evaluations of career academies.[21]

Several studies in California have found that academy students perform better than a comparison group of students in the same high schools with similar demographic characteristics and similar ninth grade records of low grades, high absenteeism, and disciplinary problems. An evaluation of the first two academies in California in the early 1980s found that academy students in grades ten through twelve had better attendance, earned more credits, obtained higher grades, and were more likely to graduate (Reller, 1984; additional citations in Stern, Raby and Dayton, 1992; see also Raby, 1995). From 1985 through 1988 a similar evaluation of the ten initial state-funded academies in California showed substantial and statistically significant advantages for academy students in attendance, credits earned toward graduation, grade point averages, and retention through high school (Dayton *et al.*, 1989; Stern *et al.*, 1989).

Annual data collected from state-funded academies in California continue to show improvement after students enter an academy and while they are in it (Dayton, 1997). High school dropout rates in academies average about 7 or 8% over three years – about half the rate in the general population of California students, despite the fact that state-funded academies are required to recruit a majority of students who are economically or educationally disadvantaged. Although these data describe only the performance of academy students, without comparison groups, they are consistent with the comparison-group evaluations.

The California comparison-group evaluations also followed students after they graduated from high school. Academy graduates were at least as likely to be enrolled in postsecondary education as their non-academy schoolmates one or two years after high school. At the same time, they had more hours of paid employment. Additional details are given in Stern, Raby and Dayton (1992).

More recently, Maxwell and Rubin (1997) surveyed former high school students from a large California school district one or two years after their graduating year. They found that students who had attended career academies were at least as likely to be enrolled in four-year colleges as students who identified themselves as having been in the academic track in high school. Both the career academy and academic track graduates had significantly greater likelihoods of enrolling in four-year college than graduates who classified themselves as having been in the high school general track. Yet academy students had lower average scores on sophomore reading tests in high school, and they were less likely to be native English speakers, compared to students in the general track.

Maxwell and Rubin (forthcoming) also analysed school district records on academy and non-academy students. They found that students in career academies obtained significantly better grades. This was not due to easier grading standards within the academies: Maxwell and Rubin found that courses within most of the academies actually awarded *lower* grades than non-academy courses in the same subjects. Furthermore, when Maxwell and Rubin divided students into high, middle, and low groups according to tenth grade math and English test scores, they found in each group that academy students obtained higher grades than non-academy students. The higher grades of academy students appear to be the main reason for their higher rate of college attendance, compared to non-academy students.

Outside of California, an earlier evaluation of business academies in Philadelphia (Snyder and McMullen, 1987*b*) found a higher graduation rate compared to the city-wide average, but a lower rate of postsecondary enrolment for academy graduates than for the general student population, and no significant differences in employment after graduation compared to graduates of other business programs. On the other hand, an early study of a NAF academy in New York City found high rates of postsecondary enrolment (Academy for Educational Development, 1990). The difference apparently reflects the origin of the Philadelphia academies in traditional vocational education, while the NAF academies were designed as college preparatory from the outset. A subsequent study by Linnehan (1996) found that graduates from Philadelphia business academies reported better attendance while in high school, and that this carried forward into less absenteeism in their post-high school jobs.

Hanser, Elliott and Gilroy (forthcoming) analysed data from three career academies affiliated with the Junior Reserve Officers' Training Corps (JROTC). They found positive effects on attendance, credits earned, grades, and the likelihood of staying in high school.

Ten career academies in different parts of the country are currently being evaluated by MDRC. The evaluation uses an experimental design in which students who apply to the academy in each school are randomly assigned either to the academy or to a control group that remains at the same school but does not enrol in an academy. This procedure is an improvement over previous evaluations, where it is possible that academy students have some unobserved prior characteristic, such as ambition or planfulness, which causes them both to enter a career academy and to perform better in school and afterward. Randomisation minimises the average differences, observed or unobserved, between academy students and those in the control group.

Student performance results from the MDRC evaluation have not yet been published, but early findings on the experiences of students and teachers show that academies "provide their students and teachers with a greater degree of institutional support than is available to their non-Academy counterparts in the same comprehensive high schools" (Kemple, 1997, p. ES-1). More specifically, after one or two years in an academy, students gave significantly more positive responses to questions about teacher support, peer support, intrinsic motivation, and the perceived relevance of schoolwork. The overall index of engagement, however, was the same for both academy and control students.

Teachers in the academies, compared to colleagues at the same schools, expressed significantly more positive views of teacher collaboration, resource adequacy, influence over their work, degree of community among teachers, emphasis on personal attention to students, and job satisfaction. They also rated themselves higher on effectiveness, but the difference was not statistically significant.

Poglinco (1998) analysed interviews with students, teachers, and administrators from three of the academies in the MDRC study, to see whether academies were supporting students' college goals. One of the themes running through students' comments is that the atmosphere of trust and encouragement created within the academy, and with workplace mentors, bolstered their general self-confidence. College aspirations were seldom mentioned as a reason for entering the academy in grade nine or ten, but they became more explicit by junior year.

McPartland *et al.* (1996) have produced the first reported results of converting an entire high school to academies. Patterson High School in Baltimore was slated for reconstitution because "it was one of the two worst high schools in the state of Maryland in 1994 (p. 1)". For example:

> "Small groups of unruly students were constantly roaming the halls and stairways, and repeated faculty efforts to bring order to the building were unsuccessful. Teachers, unable to maintain peace in the halls, retreated to their classrooms where they tried to do their best with the students in their rooms. They kept the doors of their rooms closed, and many papered over their door windows to shut out the outside confusion (p. 2)."

With help from CRESPAR, Patterson reorganised itself into a set of academies: one for ninth graders, and four career academies for students in grades ten through twelve. Results in the first year included better student attendance and a turnaround in teachers' ratings of the school climate.

Tables 3-6 summarise the quantitative evidence that has been published to date, or is about to be published. Table 3 briefly describes the studies, including those already mentioned. As shown in Table 4, eight of these studies produced evidence on academic performance in high school and the likelihood of graduating, with results consistently indicating better performance by career academy students. Table 5 lists five studies with data on enrolment in postsecondary education: two found that career academy graduates are more likely than non-academy graduates to attend college, one found very high rates of college-going for academy graduates but lacked a non-academy comparison group, one found no difference between academy and non-academy graduates, and one – the early study in Philadelphia already mentioned – found less college-going by business academy graduates. Finally, Table 6 lists four studies with data on employment in the first year or two after high school: here the Philadelphia study found business academy graduates were more likely to be working, one other study found academy graduates had more hours worked than non-academy graduates, and two studies found no differences between the two groups.

The evidence to date therefore indicates that students in career academies have been more academically successful while in high school. The evidence on enrolment in postsecondary education is more limited, but on balance suggests that academy graduates are more likely than non-academy graduates to attend college. There is little evidence that career academies give their graduates any immediate advantage in the labour market. In other words, entry-level job training is not what career academies seem to be delivering. Instead, they appear to be helping students strengthen their academic performance, which may improve their career options some years later.

Career magnet programs[22]

Crain *et al.* (1998) analyse unusual data from a natural experiment in New York City, which has established academic career magnet programs either as schools-within-schools in comprehensive high schools or as totally separate schools called total academic career magnets, of which there are eight. These programs generally stress careers like pre-law, business, and computer science.

The natural experiment arises from a random selection process that operates as follows. Each program is required to accept students from three different groups according to their seventh grade scores on a test of reading. One sixth of magnet students come from the group with reading scores in the top sixth of the distribution, one sixth come from the bottom sixth, and the remaining two thirds come from the middle of the reading distribution. Since 1987 the magnets are required to accept one half of students within each reading group through a random lottery. Thus, each program generates three natural experiments, since students who are chosen at random (the treatment group) can be compared with their lottery-losing counterparts (the control group) within their reading level.

Unfortunately, as in some other random-assignment studies, this experiment is not as clean as it initially appears, because of leakage from the treatment and control groups. About one-third of the lottery winners did not attend the career magnet to which they randomly won admission, choosing instead to remain in their neighbourhood high school or to go somewhere else. Conversely, 18% of the students who lost the lottery nonetheless ended up attending their first-choice program, as part of the group chosen by the magnet program non-randomly (Crain *et al.*, 1998, p. 11).

After attempting to take into account this degradation of the experimental design, Crain *et al.* (1998) find that career magnet programs do not produce higher graduation rates than traditional comprehensive schools: after the fourth year of high school, 14% of the lottery winners had dropped out of high school, compared to 11% of the lottery losers (p. 23). Career magnet students also had slightly lower math test scores than their counterparts in comprehensive high schools, and there were no significant differences in reading test scores, absenteeism, or the proportion taking advanced (New York State Regents') graduation tests (p. 59).

Crain *et al.* (1998) provide various possible explanations for these negative and null findings. First of all, the career magnets are a very diverse array of programs and schools. They were created at local school sites without much central direction or control. The quality and design therefore vary a great deal. Within the career magnets, furthermore, not all students are treated equally. Some programs are geared to providing employers with well-trained juniors and seniors who can serve as productive interns, and they deliberately recruit more students in grades nine and ten than they will want to keep, so that they can select the best for internships (p. 39). A chapter by Sullivan and Little also finds that there is often a "bad fit" between the magnet program and individual students' interests.

On the other hand, analysis of a sample of graduates found more positive results. Specifically, a chapter by Zellman and Quigley compared 51 lottery winners who graduated from career magnet programs and 59 lottery losers who attended and graduated from comprehensive high schools. The two samples were matched on their first choice of career magnet, on age, and on school performance in grades seven and eight. All respondents in this subsample took part in semi-structured interviews lasting several hours. Zellman and Quigley found that:

> " (…) career magnet students were significantly less likely to engage in a variety of behaviours that are associated with reduced school performance. Career magnet graduates were significantly less likely than comprehensive high school graduates to have ever been in a fight during or since high school, to have ever smoked, to drink alcohol at least weekly, every used drugs, or ever become pregnant or made someone else pregnant. In sum, 41% of career magnet graduates reported no risk behaviours, while only 19% of comprehensive high school graduates fell into the 'no reported risk behaviours' category. Indeed, the reduced incidence of these high-risk behaviours constituted the biggest differences between career magnet and comprehensive graduates.

> The substantially lower incidence of a wide range of at-risk behaviours might well be due to the higher attrition rates in career magnet programs, discussed earlier. They may also reflect the impact of the institutional setting on career magnet students. An academic core curriculum for all students, shared beliefs in the importance of work, and the legitimacy of workplace socialisation led to the enforcement of many behaviours such as punctuality, appropriate attire, and personal responsibility that are incompatible with high-risk behaviour. The teaching of career skill may have led as well to a sense that work and a career could be attained, beliefs that are incompatible with taking high risks.

> Better behaviour and skills acquisition appeared to pay off. Career magnet graduates indicated a starting hourly wage that was one dollar higher than that for comprehensive students [USD 7.27 compared to USD 6.28]. Current hourly wage also varied in the same way for the 61 interviewees who were currently working [USD 8.00 compared to USD 7.01.] (p. 164)."

Zellman and Quigley also found that the career magnet graduates were more likely to say that their parents were willing to make financial sacrifices in order for them to attend college (p. 173), despite the lack of socio-economic differences between the career magnet and comprehensive high school groups. Moreover, Crain *et al.* (1998) discovered that, in the first year or two after graduating from high school, the lottery winners completed more postsecondary credits and were more likely to have declared a college major, compared to the lottery losers who had graduated from comprehensive high schools, even though the two groups spent about the same amount of time working (pp. 181-182).

Allen's chapter in Crain *et al.* (1998) sheds more light on these results, based on additional six-hour life-history interviews with 26 members of this subsample. Among these 26, the process of constructing a positive and coherent personal identity seems to have gone further for the career magnet graduates. Students' own explanations indicate that the process of achieving a positive identity was helped by features of career magnets including participation in a community of practice, sustained-caring relationships with adults and peers, immersion in an occupation, opportunities to acquire work-related skills, and school-supervised work experience.

Despite the negative or null findings for the whole population in a highly variable set of magnet schools and programs, the more in-depth studies by Crain and associates of 110 graduates from career magnets and comprehensive high schools help explain how career-related pathways sometimes do produce positive effects for high school students. Building students' self-confidence and a sense of direction enables them to avoid high-risk behaviours and make a more successful transition to college and career.

Youth apprenticeships[23]

In the early 1990s there was much discussion in the United States about trying to emulate the kind of apprenticeship system found in Germany and neighbouring countries (Hamilton, 1990). Formal apprenticeships do exist in the United States, but they are limited to a few industries, serve a very small fraction of the labour force, and mainly enrol individuals older than 25 (Stern *et al.*, 1995). Several states initiated new youth apprenticeships for students starting in grade 11 and 12 and extending for two or three years, combining paid employment with related schooling, and leading to an industry-recognised credential. In a 1996 national survey of high schools, 20% reported that they offered some kind of apprenticeship option, in which 4% of students were said to participate (Visher *et al.*, 1998).

Only a few evaluations of these new programs have been published to date. Orr (1996) reports on a longitudinal, comparison-group evaluation of youth apprenticeship in the printing industry at five sites in Wisconsin, which was one of the first states to create a youth apprenticeship program. This particular program includes: a competency-based curriculum and assessment system; required two-year (part-time) paid training and work experience at a printing company; a work-based mentor; technical college instruction in printing technology and some academic subjects; integrated academic and vocational instruction; and collaborative school and industry oversight. In order to identify the program's effect on students, the evaluation identified two comparison group of students: in conventional vocational printing programs, and in regular classes at the same high schools. The three groups appear to be similar on a number of dimensions, but there are some important differences. The apprenticeship program does not serve very poorly performing students or those who are educationally at risk, because employers would be reluctant to offer them training placements. Orr also reports that the youth apprenticeship program enrols relatively few females and non-white students.

Orr finds significant positive results for students in the youth apprenticeship program compared to the other two groups. Between sophomore and senior year, the students in apprenticeships showed greater improvement in their average grades, fewer disciplinary problems, and better attendance. Six to eight months after graduating from high school, the apprenticeship students were more likely to be employed in the printing industry, experienced less unemployment, worked more hours per week, and had higher average hourly earnings.

Phelps and Fulton (1997) also provide data on youth apprentices in Wisconsin, though without any comparison group. Responses to a July 1997 survey from 98 of the 170 graduates who had received Certificates of Occupational Proficiency in the summer of 1996 indicated that 48% were working full time and planned to continue doing so, 28% were working full time but planned to work only part time in the autumn, and 22% were working part time. All but 13% said their jobs were at least somewhat related to their apprenticeship training, and 90% felt the apprenticeship program had been at least somewhat helpful in finding their current jobs. Furthermore, 40% had enrolled in a four-year college or university, and 35% had enrolled in some other kind of postsecondary education or training.

Another youth apprenticeship evaluation that uses a comparison group is a report on Project ProTech in Boston (Jobs for the Future, 1998). Based on 107 responses from 163 students who had graduated from the program between 18 and 42 months prior to the survey in June 1997, and 124 responses from a comparison group of 460 former students, the study found 78% of the ProTech graduates attended college the year after finishing high school, compared to 72% of the other former students. Among young African-Americans, the difference was more pronounced. At the same time, more of the ProTech students were working: 87%, versus 75% of the comparison group.

6. Concluding comments

In the United States and many other OECD countries, a large majority of young adolescents would like to go on to university or other forms of higher education, but in fact only a minority will actually obtain university degrees. This gap between aspiration and current reality is a problem for individuals and policy makers alike. Particularly problematic in the United States is the fact that low-income and minority groups are far less likely to attend a four-year college or university, and if admitted they are much less likely to finish a bachelor's degree, compared to their affluent, non-minority peers (Gladieux and Swail, 1998).

Evidence summarised in this paper suggests that new pathways in US high schools are leading to increased university enrolment among low-income and minority students by combining academic and vocational courses with work-based learning. Studies of career academies, career magnet programs, and youth apprenticeships have found that graduates from these integrated high school pathways are going on to four-year colleges and universities at higher rates than similar students who follow a traditional high school curriculum. This finding may seem paradoxical. Why are graduates from pathways with work-related themes more likely to stay in school? Part of the explanation seems to be that students gain confidence in their ability to master abstract, academic concepts when they understand how these ideas can be applied in practice. This encourages them to attempt what most people want to do at their age: go on to college or university.

There are also reasons to expect that graduates from these integrated pathways will be more successful in completing their bachelor's degrees. As noted earlier, dropout rates from tertiary education are high in many OECD countries, and US non-completion rates are higher than most. Graduates from secondary school programs that have combined academic and vocational courses with work-based learning may be more likely to finish the next stage of their education because they have a clearer sense of purpose, based in part on a better understanding of how their schooling relates to their desired careers. The vocational courses and work-based learning these students experienced in high school will also make it easier for them to find high-wage jobs while they work their way through college, as most US students now do. Although no evidence has yet been collected to test whether these favourable results are actually occurring, relevant data will become available within the next few years.

Some educators and analysts worry that it may be a mistake to prepare more young people for tertiary education by expanding these integrated high school pathways. Even though the proportion of jobs that require a bachelor's degree has grown, most jobs still do not. And not all high school students are interested in, or capable of, going to college.

These assertions are factually correct, but they do not reduce the value of integrated pathways, because the purpose of such pathways is to leave students' options open. If young people choose to work full-time after leaving high school, they will be better off for having had vocational courses and work-based learning while in school. Those who find sufficiently rewarding work right out of high school will be off to a good start. Those who decide at some point that they would like to return to further education will have the academic basis for doing so. In the relatively unregulated US labour market, integrated pathways offer built-in safety nets. Furthermore, they spare high school staff from having to make highly error-prone decisions about who is and who is not college-bound at age 14 or 15.

This kind of logic may also explain the development of similar kinds of pathways in other countries. Despite the differences in history and institutional frameworks, there is a pronounced similarity between the new, integrated courses of study in the United States and the "double qualifying" vocational pathways which are appearing or expanding in numerous other OECD countries (OECD, 1998c, pp. 68-69; also OECD, 1998d; Stern, Bailey and Merritt, 1996). Examples include the five-year vocational programs in Austria, upper secondary technical schools in the Czech Republic and in Denmark, the General National Vocational Qualifications in England and Wales, vocational high school diplomas in France and Switzerland, integrated courses in Japanese vocational high schools, Norway's 1994 reform of upper secondary education, Sweden's upper-secondary reform a few years earlier, and the merging of academic and vocational qualifications into a single framework in Scotland.

Unlike most other OECD countries, however, the United States leaves most educational decisions to local authorities, with no control by the federal government (OECD, 1998a, Charts E5.1 and E5.3). On the positive side, this means that some local districts and schools are always trying something new, resulting in the kinds of innovation described in this paper. On the negative side, local control also means that it is very difficult to create changes which require many separate institutions to work together. For instance, as noted earlier, creating coherent pathways from high school to college and career requires some degree of co-ordination among secondary and tertiary educational institutions, which are controlled by separate authorities, as well as employers who often lack formal channels through which to communicate with schools. The new pathways also still have to be rationalised in terms of new academic standards which many states are currently in the process of implementing, and new occupational skill standards which the federal government is developing in concert with industry groups (see Hershey *et al.*, 1998, pp. 73-78). Much work remains to be done before these new options are available for a majority of high school students. Nevertheless, in the relatively disorganised policy-making environment for US education, it is remarkable that coherent new pathways for young people have been created in so many different localities. Evidently, many Americans believe that creating such pathways is worth the effort.

NOTES

1. Historically, concerns about child labor have emphasised risks to children's health and safety. For a recent comprehensive review of the effects of work on children, including academic performance as well as health and safety, see Committee on the Health and Safety Implications of Child Labor (1998).

2. Mayo Tsuzuki Hallinan, Ilana Horn, Shannon Nuttall, and James Stone contributed to the writing of this section.

3. *Curriculum Guide,* p. 2 (emphasis added).

4. *Curriculum Guide,* p. 34.

5. *Curriculum Guide,* p. 35.

6. *Curriculum Guide,* p. 35.

7. Charles Dayton contributed to the writing of this subsection.

8. Examples are Belleview H.S. in Belleview, Florida; Encina H.S. in Sacramento, California; Patterson H.S. in Baltimore, Maryland; and William H. Turner H.S. in Miami, Florida.

9. From the documents "The Children's Hospital Fenway Collaborative Curriculum" by Scott W. Eddelman and *Jobs for the Future* article entitled "New Models of Work-and-Learning in Health Care."

10. From the *Boston Globe,* July 17, 1994, "Science museum weaves dreams," by Marie C. Franklin.

11. Student handbook.

12. *Junior Review Handout,* January 1996.

13. Student handbook.

14. From Fenway Middle College High School Statistics 1995-96.

15. Carolyn Dornsife contributed to the writing of this section.

16. The primary publications provide data on students enrolled during the fall of 1993, when 94 consortia reported a total of 12 265 high school Tech Prep graduates, with 250 consortia reporting a total of 172 822 enrolled Tech Prep students. From their 1994 follow-up survey, Silverberg (1996) reported 238 consortia had a total of 43 623 Tech Prep graduates, while 459 consortia had 432 067 Tech Prep students enrolled (p. 40).

17. The authors defined postsecondary institutions as community, junior, and technical colleges or four-year colleges and universities (Silverberg and Hershey, 1994, p. 102, footnote 5).

18. "2 + 2" is common shorthand for a course sequence that connects the last two years of high school with the first two years of postsecondary education, usually at a two-year college.

19. In this and other excerpts from NCRVE field observations and interviews, students' real names are not used.

20. Defined by Hershey *et al.* (1998, p. 69) as satisfying three conditions: the student had selected a career for which to plan, had taken an academic class related to that interest, and had completed work-related assignments in one or more academic classes.

21. Only results that have been published, or are about to be published, are summarized here. Several unpublished dissertations also contain descriptions and evaluations of academies.

22. Miguel Urquiola contributed to the writing of this section.

23. Miguel Urquiola contributed to the writing of this section.

BIBLIOGRAPHY

ACADEMY FOR EDUCATIONAL DEVELOPMENT (1990), "Employment and Educational Experiences of Academy of Finance Graduates", Academy for Educational Development, New York.

ADELMAN, C. (1998), "What Proportion of College Students Earn a Degree?", *AAHE Bulletin* (published by the American Association of Higher Education), pp. 7-9.

ANDREW, E. N. and GRUBB, N. (1995), "The Power of Curriculum Integration: Its relationship to other reforms", in W. N. Grubb (ed.), *Education Through Occupations in American High Schools,* Teachers College Press, New York, NY.

BAILEY, T. and MERRITT, D. (1997), *School-to-Work for the College Bound,* MDS-799, National Center for Research in Vocational Education, University of California, Berkeley, CA.

BEHN, W.H., CARNOY, M., CARTER, M.A., CRAIN, J.C. and LEVIN, H.M. (1983), "School is Bad, Work is Worse", *School Review,* 83, pp. 49-68.

BENSON, C. (1997), "New Vocationalism in the United States: Potential problems and outlook", *Economics of Education Review,* 16(3), pp. 201-212.

BERRYMAN, S.E. and BAILEY, T. (1992), *The Double Helix: Education and the Economy,* Teachers College Press, New York, NY.

BOSTON GLOBE (1994), "Science Museum Weaves Dreams", July 17.

BOTTOMS, G. and PRESSON, A. (1995), "Improving High Schools for Career-bound Youth", in W.N. Grubb (ed.), *Education through Occupations,* Vol. 2, Teachers College Press, pp. 35-54, New York, NY.

BOTTOMS, G., PRESSON, A. and JOHNSON, M. (1992), *Making High Schools Work through Integration of Academic and Vocational Education,* Southern Regional Education Board, Atlanta, GA.

BRAGG, D., LAYTON, J. and HAMMONS, F. (1994), *Tech Prep Implementation in the United States: Promising trends and lingering challenges,* The National Center for Research in Vocational Education, University of California, Berkeley, CA.

BRAGG, D.D. and HAMM, R.E. (1996), *Linking College and Work: Exemplary policies and practices of two-year college work-based learning programs,* MDS-795, National Center for Research in Vocational Education, University of California, Berkeley, CA.

BRAGG, D.D., HAMM, R.E. and TRINKLE, K.A. (1995), *Work-based Learning in Two-year Colleges in the United States,* MDS-721, National Center for Research in Vocational Education, University of California, Berkeley, CA.

BUSINESS WEEK (1996), *New American High Schools,* McGraw-Hill, New York.

CAGAMPANG, H. (1993), *Learning from School-based Work Experience Programs, Codebook: Merged data files for high school and two year college students,* National Center for Research in Vocational Education, University of California, Berkeley, CA.

CHO, M. (1994), "Articulation and Transfer Issues in Community College Art Programs in Illinois", *Community College Journal of Research and Practice,* 18(6), pp. 557-567.

COHEN, A. and BRAWER, F. (1996), *Policies and Programs that Affect Transfer,* American Council on Education, Washington, DC.

COHEN, A. and IGNASH, J. (1993), "The Total Community College Curriculum", *Probing the Community College Transfer Function. Research on curriculum, degree completion, and academic tasks,* National Center for Academic Achievement and Transfer and the American Council on Education, pp. 9-44, Washington, DC.

COMMITTEE FOR ECONOMIC DEVELOPMENT (1985), *Investing in our Children,* New York.

COMMITTEE ON THE HEALTH AND SAFETY IMPLICATIONS OF CHILD LABOR (1998), *Protecting Youth at Work,* National Academy Press, Washington, DC.

CONCHAS, G. (1998), "Structuring Opportunity: Cultural community and Latino high school success", Draft July 8, Department of Sociology, University of Michigan, Ann Arbor, MI.

CRAIN, R.L., ALLEN, A., THALER, R., SULLIVAN, D., ZELLMAN, G.L., LITTLE, J.W. and QUIQLEY, D.D. (1998), *The Effects of Career Magnet Education on High Schools and their Graduates,* MDS-779, (draft), National Center for Research in Vocational Education, University of California, Berkeley, CA.

CUSHMAN, K., STEINBERG, A. and RIORDAN, R. (1997), "Connecting School and Work as a Means to Whole-school Change", Coalition of Essential Schools, Brown University, Providence, Rhode Island.

DAYTON, C. (1997), *California Partnership Academies: 1995-96 evaluation report,* Foothill Associates, Nevada City, CA.

DAYTON, C., WEISBERG, A. and STERN, D. (1989), *California Partnership Academies: 1987-88 evaluation report,* Policy Analysis for California Education (PACE), University of California, Berkeley, CA.

DEWEY, J. (1916), *Democracy and Education: An introduction to the philosophy of education,* Macmillan, New York.

EDUCATION COMMISSION OF THE STATES (1997), *Profiles in Connecting Learning and Work: State initiatives,* Education Commission of the States, Denver, CO.

FLINN, C. (1986), "Wages and Job Mobility of Young Workers", *Journal of Political Economy,* (94)3.

GARDECKI, R. and NEUMARK, D. (1995), *Early Labor Market Experiences and their Consequences for Adult Labor Market Outcomes,* Office of Technology and Assessment, US Congress, Washington, DC.

GARLAND, P. (1994), "Understanding the Many Contexts of the Two-year College", in G. Baker (ed.), *A Handbook on the Community College in America,* Greenwood Press, Westport, CT.

GLADIEUX, L.E. and SWAIL, W.S. (1998), "Postsecondary Education: Student success, not just access", in S. Halperin (ed.), *The Forgotten Half Revisited: American youth and young families 1988-2008,* American Youth Policy Forum, Washington, DC.

GOLDBERGER, S. and KAZIS, R. (1995), *Revitalizing High Schools: What the school-to-career movement can contribute,* American Youth Policy Forum, Institute for Educational Leadership (with Jobs for the Future and the National Association of Secondary School Principals), Washington, DC.

GOLDBERGER, S., KAZIS, R. and O'FLANAGAN, M.K. (1994), *Learning through Work: Designing and implementing quality worksite learning for high school students,* Manpower Demonstration Research Corporation, New York.

GREENBERGER, E. and STEINBERG, L.D. (1986), *When Teenagers Work,* Basic Books, New York.

GRUBB, W.N. (1995), *Education through Occupations in American High Schools. Volume 1, Approaches to integrating academic and vocational education. Volume 2, The challenges of implementing curriculum integration,* Teachers College Press, New York.

GRUBB, W.N. (1996), *Working in the Middle: Strengthening education and training for the middle-skilled labor force,* Jossey-Bass, San Francisco.

GRUBB, W.N. and BADWAY, N. (1995), "Linking School-based and Work-based Learning: The implications of LaGuardia's co-op seminars for school-to-work programs", paper prepared for the US Congress, Office of Technology Assessment, School of Education, University of California, Berkeley, CA.

GRUBB, W.N., BADWAY, N., BELL, D. and KRASKOUSKAS, E. (1996), *Community College Innovations in Workforce Preparation: Curriculum integration and Tech Prep,* League for Innovation in the Community College, National Center for Research in Vocational Education, and National Council for Occupational Education.

HAMILTON, M.A. and HAMILTON, S.F. (1997), *Learning Well at Work: Choices for quality,* Cornell Youth and Work Program, Cornell University, Ithaca, NY.

HAMILTON, S.F. (1990), *Apprenticeship for Adulthood: Preparing youth for the future,* The Free Press, New York.

HANSEN, J. (ed.) (1994), *Preparing for the Workplace. Charting a course for federal postsecondary training policy,* National Academy Press, Washington, DC.

HANSER, L.M., ELLIOTT, M.N. and GILROY, C.L. (forthcoming), *Career Academies: Evidence of positive student outcomes,* (draft), RAND Corporation, Santa Monica, CA.

HAYWARD, B. and TALMADGE, G. (1995), *Strategies for Keeping Kids in School,* US Department of Education, Washington, DC.

HECKMAN, J. (1994), "Is Job Training Oversold?", *The Public Interest,* 115, pp. 91-115.

HERSHEY, A.M., HUDIS, P., SILVERBERG, M. and HAIMSON, J. (1997), *Partners in Progress: Early steps in creating school-to-work systems,* MPR 8292-650, Mathematica Policy Research, Inc, Princeton, New Jersey.

HERSHEY, A.M., SILVERBERG, M., HAIMSON, J., HUDIS, P. and JACKSON, R. (1998), *Expanding Options for Students: Report to Congress on the national evaluation of school-to-work implementation,* MPR 8292-660, Mathematical Policy Research, Inc, Princeton, New Jersey.

HERSHEY, A.M., SILVERBERG, M. and OWENS, T. (1994), *The Diverse Forms of Tech-prep: Implementation approaches in ten local consortia,* US Department of Education, Office of Planning and Evaluation Service, Washington, DC.

HONEYCUTT, F. (1995), *An Investigation of Tech Prep as Perceived by Community College Faculties and Administrative Staff,* Doctoral dissertation, Ed.D., North Carolina State University.

HOUGHTON, M. (1997), *School Reforms and Higher Education,* National Governors' Association, Washington, DC.

JACOBS, L. (1995), *The School-to-Work Opportunities Act of 1994: A guide to the law and how to use it,* Center for Law and Education, Washington, DC.

JOBS FOR THE FUTURE (1998), *School-to-Career Initiative Demonstrates Significant Impact on Young People,* Jobs for the Future, Boston, Massachusetts.

JOHNSON, W. (1978), "A Theory of Job Shopping", *Quarterly Journal of Economics,* 92, pp. 261-278.

KATZ, R.H., JACKSON, L.J., REEVES, K. and BENSON, C. (1995), "Urban Career Magnet High Schools", in W. N. Grubb (ed.), *Education through Occupations in American High Schools,* Vol. 1, Teachers College Press, New York.

KEARNS, D.T. and DOYLE, D.P. (1988), "Winning the Brain Race: A bold plan to make our schools competitive", Institute for Contemporary Studies, ICS Press, San Francisco, CA.

KEMPLE, J.J. (1997), *Career Academies: Communities of support for students and teachers: Emerging findings from a 10-site evaluation,* Manpower Demonstration Research Corporation, New York.

KEMPLE, J.J. and ROCK, J.L. (1996), *Career Academies: Early implementation lessons from a 10-Site evaluation,* Manpower Demonstration Research Corporation, New York.

KIRST, M. (1998), "Bridging the Remediation Gap", *Education Week,* September.

KLEIN, S.G. (1996), *Skill Standards: Concepts and practices in state and local education. A synthesis of literature and alternative conceptual frameworks,* MPR Associates, Berkeley, CA.

KLERMAN, J. and KAROLY, L. (1995), *The Transition to Stable Employment: The experience of youth in their early labor market career,* National Center for Research in Vocational Education, University of California, Berkeley, CA.

LAPOINT, V., JORDAN, W., MCPARTLAND, J.M. and TOWNS, D.P. (1996), *The Talent Development High School: Essential components,* Center for Research on the Education of Students Placed at Risk, Johns Hopkins University and Howard University, Baltimore, MD.

LAVE J. and WENGER, E. (1991), *Situated Learning: Legitimate peripheral participation,* Cambridge University Press, Cambridge, U.K.

LIGHT, A. (1997), "High School Employment, High School Curriculum, and Post-school Wages", unpublished manuscript, US Bureau of Labor Statistics, Washington, DC.

LITTLE, J.W. (1995), "Subject Affiliation in High Schools that Restructure", in L.S. Siskin and J.W. Little (eds.), *The Subjects in Question: Departmental organization and the high school,* Teachers College Press, New York.

MARSHALL, R. and TUCKER, M. (1992), *Thinking for a Living,* Basic Books, New York.

MAXWELL, N. and RUBIN, V. (1997), *The Relative Impact of a Career Academy on Post-secondary Work and Education Skills in Urban Public High Schools,* the Human Investment Research and Education Center (HIRE), School of Business and Economics, California State University, Hayward, CA.

MAXWELL, N. and RUBIN, V. (forthcoming), *Improving the Transition from School to Work: Assessing the impact of old and new strategies* (draft), the Human Investment Research and Education Center (HIRE), School of Business and Economics, California State University, Hayward, CA.

MCCALL, B. (1990), "Occupational Matching: A test of sorts", *Journal of Political Economy,* 98(1), pp. 45-69.

MCCORMICK, A.C., ALT, M.N. and GEIS, S. (1998), *The View from Higher Education: Public universities respond to educational reform,* MDS-913, National Center for Research in Vocational Education, University of California, Berkeley, CA.

MCPARTLAND, J., BALFANZ, R., JORDAN, W. and LEGTERS, N. (1998), "Improving Climate and Achievement in a Troubled Urban High School Through the Talent Development Model", *Journal of Education for Students Placed at Risk*, 3(4), pp. 337-361.

MCPARTLAND, J., LEGTERS, N., JORDAN, W. and MCDILL, E.L. (1996), *The Talent Development High School: Early evidence of impact on school climate, attendance, and student promotion*, Center for Research on the Education of Students Placed at Risk, Johns Hopkins University and Howard University, Baltimore MD.

MINCER, J. and JOVANOVIC, B. (1981), "Labor Mobility and Wages", in S. Rosen (ed.), *Studies in Labor Markets*, The University of Chicago Press, Chicago, IL.

MORTIMER, J.T. and JOHNSON, M.K. (1997), "Adolescent Part-time Work and Post-secondary Transition Pathways: A longitudinal study of youth in St. Paul, Minnesota (US)", Unpublished manuscript, revised March 4, Life Course Center, University of Minnesota, Minneapolis, MN.

MORTIMER, J.T. and JOHNSON, M.K. (1998), "Adolescent Part-time Work and Educational Achievement", in K. Borman and B. Schneider (eds.), *Youth Experiences and Development: Social influences and educational challenges*, National Society for the Study of Education 1998 Yearbook.

MURNANE, R.J. and LEVY, F. (1996), *Teaching the New Basic Skills*, The Free Press, New York.

MURNANE, R.J., WILLETTT, J.B. and LEVY, F. (1995), "The Growing Importance of Cognitive Skills in Wage Determination", *Review of Economics and Statistics*, 77(2), pp. 251-266.

NATIONAL ACADEMY OF SCIENCES, PANEL ON SECONDARY SCHOOL EDUCATION AND THE CHANGING WORKPLACE (1984), *High Schools and the Changing Workplace: The employers' view*, National Academy Press, Washington, DC.

NATIONAL ASSESSMENT OF VOCATIONAL EDUCATION (1994), *Interim Report to Congress*, US Department of Education, Office of Educational Research and Improvement, Washington, DC.

NATIONAL ASSOCIATION OF SECONDARY SCHOOL PRINCIPALS (1996), *Breaking Ranks*, National Association of Secondary School Principals, Washington, D.C.

NEUMARK, D. (1997), *Youth Labor Markets in the US: Shopping around vs. staying put*, National Center for Postsecondary Improvement, Stanford University, Stanford, CA.

NEWMANN, F.C. and WEHLAGE, G.G. (1995), *Successful School Restructuring*, Center on Organization and Restructuring of Schools, University of Wisconsin, Madison, WI.

OAKES, J. (1985), *Keeping Track: How Schools Structure Inequality*, Yale University Press, New Haven, CT.

OECD (1993), *Education at a Glance: OECD Indicators*, Paris

OECD (1996), *Employment Outlook*, Paris.

OECD (1997), *Education at a Glance: OECD Indicators*, Paris.

OECD (1998a), *Education at a Glance: OECD Indicators*, Paris.

OECD (1998b), *Employment Outlook*, Paris.

OECD (1998c), *The Transition from Initial Education to Working Life: Interim comparative report*, DEELSA/ED(98)11, Paris.

OECD (1998d), *Pathways and Participation in Vocational and Technical Education and Training*, Paris.

OLSON, L. (1997), *The School-to-Work Revolution*, Addison-Wesley, Reading, MA.

ORR, M. (1996), *Wisconsin youth Apprenticeship Program in Printing: Evaluation 1993-1995*, Jobs for the Future, Boston, MA.

OSTERMAN, P. and IANOZZI, M. (1993), *Youth Apprenticeships and School-to-Work Transitions: Current knowledge and legislative strategy*, National Center on the Educational Quality of the Workforce, University of Pennsylvania, Philadelphia, PA.

OWENS, T. (1980), *Experience-based Career Education: Summary and implications of research and evaluation findings*, National Institute of Education, Washington, DC.

PACKER, A.H. and PINES, M.W. (1996), *School-to-Work*, Eye on Education, Princeton, NJ.

PAULY, E., KOPP, H. and HAIMSON, J. (1995), *Home-grown Lessons: Innovative programs linking school and work*, Jossey-Bass, San Francisco.

PEDRAZA, R.A., PAULY, E. and KOPP, H. (1997), *Home-grown Progress: The evolution of innovative School-to-Work programs*, Manpower Demonstration Research Corporation, New York.

PHELPS, L.A. and FULTON, D.V. (1997), *Follow-up Survey of 1996 Youth Apprenticeship Graduates,* Center on Education and Work, University of Wisconsin, Madison, WI.

PHELPS, L.A., SCRIBNER, J., WAKELYN, D. and WEIS, C. (1996), *Youth Apprenticeship in Wisconsin: A stakeholder assessment,* Department of Workforce Development, State of Wisconsin, Madison, WI.

POGLINCO, S.M. (1998), *Career Academies as a Support for Students' College Goals: Perceptions of students, teachers, and administrators in three academies,* Paper prepared for the annual meeting of the American Educational Research Association, San Diego, Manpower Demonstration Research Corporation, New York.

PRAGER, C. (1993), "Transfer and Articulation Within Colleges and Universities", *Journal of Higher Education,* Vol. 64(5), pp. 537-554.

PRESIDENT'S SCIENCE ADVISORY COMMITTEE (1973), *Youth: Transition to Adulthood,* US Government Printing Office, Washington, D.C.

RABY, M. (1995), "The Career Academies", in W.N. Grubb (ed.), *Education Through Occupations in American High Schools,* Vol. 1, Teachers College Press, New York.

RAIZEN, S.A. (1989), Reforming Education for Work: A cognitive science perspective, MDS-024, National Center for Research in Vocational Education, University of California, Berkeley, California.

RAMER, M. (1991), *Community College/High School Articulation in California: 2+2 program definition and barriers to implementation,* California Community College Administrators for Occupational Education, Sacramento, CA.

RAMSEY, K., EDEN, R., STASZ, C. and BODILY, S. (1995), "Integrating Vocational and Academic Education: Lessons from early innovators", in W.N. Grubb (ed.), *Education through Occupations in American High Schools: The challenges of implementing curricular integration,* Vol. 2, Teachers College Press, New York.

RELLER, D. (1984), *The Peninsula Academies: Final technical evaluation report,* The American Institutes for Research, Palo Alto, CA.

RELLER, D.J. (1985), *The Peninsula Academies: Interim evaluation report, 1984-85 school year,* American Institutes for Research, Palo Alto, CA.

RELLER, D.J. (1987), *A Longitudinal Study of the Graduates of the Peninsula Academies: Final report,* American Institutes for Research in the Behavioral Sciences, Palo Alto, CA.

RESNICK, L.B. (1987), "Learning in School and Out", *Educational Researcher,* 16, pp. 13-20.

ROSENSTOCK, L. (1997), "The New Urban High School", Address given to the annual meeting of the California Partnership Academies, Anaheim, CA, April 21.

SILVERBERG, M. (1996), *Building School-to-Work Systems on a Tech Prep Foundation. The status of school-to-work features in tech-prep initiatives,* US Department of Education, Office of Planning and Evaluation Service, Washington, DC.

SILVERBERG, M. and HERSHEY, A.M. (1994), *The Emergence of Tech-Prep at the State and Local Levels,* US Department of Education, Office of Planning and Evaluation Service, Washington, DC.

SIMON, R.I., DIPPO, D. and SCHENKE, A. (1991), *Learning Work: A critical pedagogy of work education,* Bergin and Garvey, New York.

SISKIN, L.S. (1994), "Is the School a Unit of Change? Internal and external contexts of restructuring", in P.P. Grimmett (ed.), *Teacher Development and the Struggle for Authenticity: Professional growth and restructuring in the context of change,* Teachers College Press, New York.

SNYDER, P. and MCMULLAN, B.J. (1987a), *Allies in Education, A Profile of Philadelphia High School Academies,* Public/Private Ventures, Philadelphia, PA.

SNYDER, P. and MCMULLAN, B.J. (1987b), *Allies in Education, Schools and Businesses Working Together for At-risk Youth,* Public/Private Ventures, Philadelphia, PA.

SORENSEN, J. (1993), *Secondary and Postsecondary Vocational Education Curriculum Articulation as Perceived by Community Colleges and High School Administrators,* Doctoral dissertation, Ed.D., University of Northern Iowa.

STASZ, C. (1996), "What Do Students Learn in Work-based Learning?", *CenterWork* 7(4): 2, National Center for Research in Vocational Education, University of California, Berkeley, CA.

STASZ, C. and KAGANOFF, T. (1997), *Learning how to Learn at Work: Lessons from three high school programs,* DRU-1697-NCRVE/UCB, RAND, Santa Monica, CA.

STASZ, C., MCARTHUR, D., LEWIS, M. and RAMSEY, K. (1990), *Teaching and Learning Generic Skills for the Workplace,* National Center for Research in Vocational Education, University of California, Berkeley, CA.

STASZ, C., RAMSEY, K., EDEN, R., MELAMID, E. and KAGANOFF, T. (1996), *Workplace Skills in Practice: Case studies of technical work,* Report for the National Center for Research in Vocational Education, RAND Corporation, Santa Monica, CA.

STEINBERG, A. (1997), "Making Schoolwork More Like Real Work", *The Harvard Education Letter,* 13(2), pp. 1-6.

STEINBERG, A. (1998), *Real Learning, Real Work,* Routledge, New York and London.

STERN, D. (1984), "School-based Enterprise and the Quality of Work Experience: A study of high school students", *Youth & Society,* 15(4), pp. 401-427.

STERN, D. and NAKATA, Y. (1989), "Characteristics of High School Students' Paid Jobs, and Employment Experience after Graduation", in D. Stern and D. Eichorn (eds.), *Adolescence and Work: Influences of social structure, labor markets, and culture,* Erlbaum, Hillsdale, NJ.

STERN, D. and WAGNER, D. (eds.) (1998), *International Perspectives on the School-to-Work Transition,* Hampton Press, Cresskill, NJ, in press.

STERN, D., BAILEY, T. and MERRITT, D. (1996), *School-to-Work Policy Insights from Recent International Developments,* MDS 950, National Center for Research in Vocational Education, University of California, Berkeley, CA.

STERN, D., RABY, M. and DAYTON, C. (1992), *Career Academies: Partnerships for Reconstructing American High Schools,* Jossey-Bass, San Francisco.

STERN, D., DAYTON, C., PAIK, I. and WEISBERG, A. (1989), "Benefits and Costs of Dropout Prevention in a High School Program Combining Academic and Vocational Education: Third-year results from replications of the California Partnership Academies", *Educational Evaluation and Policy Analysis,* 11(4), pp. 405-416.

STERN, D., FINKELSTEIN, N., URQUIOLA, M. and CAGAMPANG, H. (1997), "What Difference Does it Make if School and Work are Connected? Evidence on co-operative education in the United States", *Economics of Education Review,* 16(3), pp. 213-226.

STERN, D., MCMILLION, M., HOPKINS, C. and STONE, J.R. III (1990a), "Work Experience for Students in High School and College", *Youth & Society,* 21(3), pp. 355-389.

STERN, D., STONE, J.R. III, HOPKINS, C. and MCMILLION, M. (1990b), "Quality of Students' Work Experience and Orientation toward Work", *Youth & Society,* 22(2), pp. 263-282.

STERN, D., DAYTON, C., PAIK, I., WEISBERG, A. and EVANS, J. (1988), "Combining Academic and Vocational Courses in an Integrated Program to Reduce High School Dropout Rates: Second-year results from replications of the California Peninsula Academies", *Educational Evaluation and Policy Analysis,* 10(2), pp. 161-170.

STERN, D., FINKELSTEIN, N., STONE, J.R. III, LATTING, J. and DORNSIFE, C. (1995), *School to Work: Research on programs in the United States,* Taylor and Francis, Falmer Press, Washington and London.

STONE, J.R. III, STERN, D., HOPKINS, C. and MCMILLION, M. (1990), "Adolescents' Perception of their Work: School supervised and non-school-supervised", *Journal of Vocational Education Research,* 15 (2), pp. 31-53.

TUCKER, M. (1995), *On Occupational Clusters: Early thoughts on organizing the work of the National Skill Standards Board,* National Center on Education and the Economy, Washington, DC.

TUNTLAND, C. (1995), *The Challenge of Articulation: "The connecting link" a case study,* Doctoral dissertation, Ed.D., Graduate School of Education and Psychology, Pepperdine University, Malibu, CA.

US CONGRESS, OFFICE OF TECHNOLOGY ASSESSMENT (1995), *Learning to Work: Making the transition from school to work,* OTA-HER-637, US Government Printing Office, Washington, DC.

US DEPARTMENT OF LABOR, SECRETARY'S COMMISSION ON ACHIEVING NECESSARY SKILLS (SCANS) (1991), *What Work Requires of Schools,* US Department of Labor, Washington, DC.

UNIVERSITY OF WISCONSIN SYSTEM, OFFICE OF ACADEMIC AFFAIRS (1997), *University of Wisconsin System Competency-based Admission Pilot Project,* Author, Madison, WI.

UNIVERSITY OF WISCONSIN SYSTEM, OFFICE OF ACADEMIC AFFAIRS (1998), *The University of Wisconsin System Competency-based Admission Pilot Project - Spring 1998: Final report,* Author, Madison, WI.

URQUIOLA, M., STERN, D., HORN, I., DORNSIFE, C., CHI, B., WILLIAMS, L., MERRITT, D., HUGHES, K. and BAILEY, T. (1997), *School to Work, College and Career: A review of policy, practice, and results 1993-97,* MDS-1144, National Center for Research in Vocational Education, University of California, Berkeley, CA.

VICKERS, M. (1996), *Working to Learn,* TERC, Cambridge, MA.

VISHER, M.G., LAUEN, D., MEROLA, L. and MEDRICH, E. (1998), *School-to-Work in the 1990s: A look at programs and practices in American high schools,* United States Department of Education, Office of Educational Research and Improvement, Washington DC.

VO, C.D. (1997), "Not for My Child", *Techniques,* 71(9), pp. 20-23.

WHITEHEAD, A.N. (1929), *The Aims of Education,* Mentor Books edition, 1949, MacMillan, New York.

WILLIAM T. GRANT FOUNDATION (1988), *The Forgotten Half: Non-college youth in America,* Youth and America's Future, The William T. Grant Foundation Commission on Work, Family and Citizenship, Washington, DC.

WRIGHT, M., BRIDEN, M., INMAN, A. and RICHARDSON, D. (1996), *Articulation and Transfer: Definitions, problems, and solutions,* ERIC Document, ED 390 512.

ZEMSKY, R., BAILEY, T., CAPPELLI, P., IANOZZI, M. and SHAPIRO, D. (1998), *Thematic Review of the Transition from Initial Education to Working Life,* National Center for Postsecondary Improvement, Stanford University, Stanford, CA.

ZEMSKY, R. and OEDEL, P. (1995), *Challenge: To better understand the central role higher education has come to play in the preparation of a skilled workforce* (EQW Issue No. 8), National Center on the Educational Quality of the Workforce, University of Pennsylvania, Philadelphia, PA.

Table 1. **Ratio (times 100) of mean annual earnings of university graduates to mean annual earnings of upper secondary graduates, age 25-64, 1990* and 1996**

Country	Men		Women	
	1990	1996	1990	1996
Australia	158	161	175	139
Canada	146	152	165	172
Denmark	146	138	135	132
Finland	187	187	177	173
Netherlands	140	135	135	143
New Zealand	144	171	146	148
Norway	161	143	159	146
Portugal	175	182	185	175
Sweden	155	158	158	144
Switzerland**	152	146	164	161
United States	164	183	174	175

* Base year is 1989 for the Netherlands, and 1991 for Australia, New Zealand, Norway, and Portugal.
** Data for Switzerland are monthly not annual.
Sources: OECD (1993, Table R10A); OECD (1998a, Table F7.1).

Table 2. **Growth of career academies**

Year	Philadelphia	California*	National Academy Foundation
When founded	1969: 1 academy	1981: 2 academies	1982: 1 academy
1980	Approximately 5	–	–
1985	Approximately 10	12	8
1990	Approximately 20	29	54
1995	28	45	167
1998	28	200	289
Projected 2000	28	300	400

* Includes only state-funded academies. As a rough approximation, these numbers would need to be doubled to estimate the full number in California in 1998.

Table 3. **Published quantitative evidence on performance of students who participated in career academies**

Author(s) and date(s)	Data source
Reller (1984, 1985, 1987)	Data collected 1981-86 on students in two Peninsula Academies in California, and individually matched comparison groups in each school. Follow-up surveys 15 and 27 months after graduation.
Snyder and McMullen (1987a,b)	1981 sophomores entering business academies in three Philadelphia high schools traced to graduation. Graduates surveyed late 1986-early 1987, and compared to random sample of all graduates, and all business program graduates, from those three high schools.
Stern et al. (1988, 1989)	Data collected 1985-90 on students in 10 academies funded by state of California, and individually matched comparison groups in each school.
Academy for Educational Development (1990)	Follow-up of academy of finance students who graduated 1984-89. No comparison group.
Stern, Raby and Dayton (1992)	Follow-up surveys 10 and 22 months after graduation, of graduates from 10 state-funded California academies and comparison groups.
Hayward and Talmadge (1995)	1989-92 data from 10 different programs using vocational education to promote high school success. Two of the sites are career academies. Evaluation used random control groups in some sites, non-random comparison groups in others, including the academies.
McPartland et al. (1996 and 1998)	Reorganization of Patterson H.S. in Baltimore in 1995 included creation of four career academies for grades 10-12. Data analyzed from 1993 to 1998.
Kemple (1997)	Ten career academies included in an experimental evaluation since 1993. This is the only evaluation of career academies so far with students randomly assigned to academies and control groups.
Maxwell and Rubin (1997 and forthcoming)	1991-95 school records for three cohorts of students in grades 10-12 in an urban district, including nine career academies. Also a follow-up survey in mid-late 1996.
Hanser, Elliott and Gilroy (forthcoming)	1994-96 data from three Junior ROTC career academies in large cities were compared with data from other career academies or magnets in the same or similar schools, JROTC students not in academies, and students not participating in any academy or magnet.

Table 4. **Findings on academic performance and high school completion Students in career academies compared to other students**

Author(s) and date(s)	Main findings
Reller (1984, 1985)	Academy students earned more course credits than comparison group. One-year dropout rates 2 to 6% in academies, 10 to 21% in comparison group.
Snyder and McMullen (1987b)	Graduation rate for 1981 sophomores in three business academies was 77%, compared to city-wide average of 67% for freshmen.
Stern et al. (1988, 1989)	earned, average grades, and likelihood of staying in school. 3-year dropout rate for cohort entering 1985 was 7.3% in academies, 14.6% in comparison group.
Hayward and Talmadge (1995)	Academies showed generally better results than other programs, improving students' attendance, credits, grades, and likelihood of completing high school.
McPartland, Legters, Jordan and McDill (1996 and 1998)	Attendance in first implementation year rose from 71 to 77% at Patterson, compared to districtwide decline from 73 to 70% in grades 9-12. Survey of teachers found big improvement in reported school climate.
Kemple (1997)	Academy students report significantly more support from teachers and peers, more intrinsic motivation, and greater perceived relevance of schoolwork.
Maxwell and Rubin (1997 and forthcoming)	District records show academy students received higher grades. Follow-up survey found higher grades increased the likelihood of graduation; result was 92% graduation rate for academy students, 82% for non-academy.
Hanser, Elliott and Gilroy (forthcoming)	Students in JROTC career academies, and in other career academies or magnets, generally received higher grades, had better attendance, completed more credits, and were less likely to drop out, compared to statistically similar students not in academies.

Table 5. **Findings on enrolment in postsecondary education**
Students in career academies compared to other students

Author(s) and date(s)	Main findings
Reller (1987)	15 months after graduation, postsecondary enrolment rate 62% for academy graduates, 47% for comparison group. 55% of academy graduates, 22% of comparison group expected to complete bachelor's degree or more.
Snyder and McMullen (1987*b*)	18% of business academy graduates said school was main activity in 1986-87, compared to 35% of city-wide sample. Of those enrolled, 14% of academy graduates, and 43% of city-wide sample, intended to get bachelor's degrees.
Academy for Educational Development (1990)	89% of finance academy graduates said they had attended 4-year college or university, 58% majored in business or finance, and 67% planned to complete a master's or doctorate.
Stern, Raby and Dayton (1992)	1989 and 1990 follow-up surveys found no consistent differences between academy and comparison graduates in postsecondary attendance or degree aspirations.
Maxwell and Rubin (1997 and forthcoming)	Analysis of follow-up survey found higher grades for academy students increased their probability of going to college, and two of nine academies gave an extra added boost to college-going, resulting in 52% of former academy students going to 4-year colleges, compared to 36% of non-academy.

Table 6. **Findings on employment after high school**
Students in career academies compared to other students

Author(s) and date(s)	Main findings
Reller (1987)	No significant differences between academy and comparison students 27 months after graduation, in employment status, wages, or hours worked.
Snyder and McMullen (1987*b*)	64% of business academy graduates said work was main activity in 1986-87, compared to 42% of city-wide sample. Academy graduates employed a larger fraction of time since graduation.
Stern, Raby and Dayton (1992)	1989 and 1990 follow-up surveys of academy and comparison graduates found academy graduates working three more hours per week, but no consistent overall difference in hourly earnings.
Maxwell and Rubin (1997 and forthcoming)	Analysis of follow-up survey found no significant differences in wages or hours worked between former academy and non-academy students, but former academy students more often said their high school program had prepared them well for further education and work.

THE CONTRIBUTION OF EDUCATION AND TRAINING TO THE EMPLOYABILITY OF YOUTH: CHANGING CONCERNS, DEBATES AND MEASURES

by
Ulrich Teichler
Centre for Research on Higher Education and Work,
University of Kassel, Germany

1. Major debates and preoccupations

About two decades ago, the OECD (1977) published the report *Entry of Young People into Working Life*. The report documents a major paradigmatic shift which had occurred in the educational and employment policies of many industrial societies and in the international debates around the mid-1970s. Employment problems became a major concern, and vocational training was viewed as one of the potential means to redress or alleviate the problems observed.

The OECD, serving as a think-tank and mutually advising agency of major industrial societies as regards economic and various social policies, clearly changed its focus in the mid-1970s (Papadopoulos, 1994; Lutz, 1994). The preceding perspectives might be characterised as follows:

- Initially, in the early and mid-1960s, OECD studies and recommendations tended to advocate educational expansion in general as a means of economic growth. In this period, often characterised as "golden age of educational growth" (Papadopoulos, 1994), emphasis was placed on the expansion of general upper secondary education and higher education.

- In the late 1960s and early 1970s, efforts were made to consolidate the imperatives of contributing by educational measures to economic growth to that of reducing inequality of opportunity. Concurrently, various needs were felt to restructure the expanding system of education. As a result, a soft, permeable, expanding system of education – again with a strong general curricular emphasis – was viewed as the optimal way to serve both economic growth and equality of opportunity.

The employment problems triggered the so-called "oil shock" in 1973 contributed to a re-thinking of education and its societal role. Papadopoulos (1994) described the OECD educational activities during the period of the mid-1970 until the early 1980s under the heading of "recession and its consequences". "Employability" became a major educational objective, and special attention was paid to vocational and technical education and training. This shift is clearly visible, for example, in the educational statistics of the OECD. Whereas educational growth and educational attainment were measured before this period in terms of full-time school and higher education enrolment, work and school-based training were eventually treated as more or less equal to schooling.

It should be noted, though, that critique of a strong emphasis on general education, academic competencies and educational expansion in general was by no means completely new in the mid and late 1970s. Notably, views were widely held in continental European countries during the 1960s and early 1970s that the OECD studies and policy documents were too strongly shaped by specific educational traditions of the Anglo-Saxon countries. According to the dominant continental European perspectives, substantial components of post-secondary education in the United States served the same purposes as vocational and technical education outside higher education in continental European countries, and the large proportion of unskilled labour in the United Kingdom tended to be considered as economically and socially unwise. Also, one should not forget that suggestions to expand and to create comprehensive patterns of secondary education and to expand higher education triggered very controversial debates and policy processes in most continental European countries from the outset.

One could assume that the growing interest in Europe in the 1970s to seek a strengthening of the role of vocational and technical education might have been reinforced by the fact that joint educational activities of the European Economic Community were initially confined to vocational training and activities aimed at facilitating the recognition of professional qualifications (Neave, 1984). This might be misleading, though, because the EC widened its involvement in education beyond vocational training – initially towards higher education, and subsequently towards all areas of education – just when the OECD began to get involved in analyses and policy statements on vocational training. And the EC was far more successful in putting its mark on higher education in the European Member countries – through the ERASMUS programme for promoting student mobility – than it ever has been as regards vocational education and training.

The youth unemployment spreading in the mid and late 1970s could have been redressed by various measures. Any means of retaining youth in the educational system would have been welcomed, and any type of learning could have been considered as contributing to the individuals' abilities to cope with the increasing demands of the employment system. And, in fact, we note a mixture of proposals and measures at that time. The interest in post-compulsory vocational training notably grew, because countries with an elaborate training system – Germany and some of its neighbour countries – faced the lowest youth unemployment ratio relative to the overall unemployment ratio. This supported the hypothesis that the work and partly school-based apprenticeship system might serve the employability of youth better than any other educational feature.

The 1977 report *Entry of Young People into Working Life* clearly demonstrates that the concern about youth unemployment had become a prime focus in the search for new relationships between education and employment. It also shows that an awareness had grown of the complexities of the relationships between education and employment: we do not note any inclination to put all the faith on simple explanatory models and single measures. Many of the observations at that time still seem to be true today.

Two decades later, the issue of the possible contribution of education and training to the employability of youth still ranks highly in the educational and employment policies of industrial societies. In one respect, this weight has even grown: youth employment problems are not viewed anymore as concerns of a recession period, but rather as a secular phenomenon. And vocational and technical training has become a regular area of analysis and recommendation in the domain of OECD activities (OECD, 1994a, 1998d). It would be misleading, however, to suggest that the focus of the debates about the relationships between education and employment had not changed at all over the last two decades.

Rather, the preoccupation with the contribution of education and training to the employability of youth was complemented by renewed concern about education's contribution to economic growth, whereby the rhetoric shifted toward "competitiveness". Also, the mix of targeted educational, training and labour market measures prevailing in the majority of continental European countries, not the least based on concern for equity and social cohesion, was challenged by neo-liberal economic thought. This approach which obviously dominated in the United States and played a significant role there influenced the so-called OECD *Jobs Strategy* according to which wage flexibility and a reduction of public labour market measures were preferable (OECD, 1997b).

Two decades of search for the best ways of strengthening employability through education and training have not led to a widespread consensus of an optimal model. On the one hand, the value of work-based learning was widely acknowledged, and we note a spread of apprenticeships systems, insertion of work experience into school and higher education curricula and the strengthening of co-operation between the education system and the world of work in many countries. On the other hand, pressures for a more general approach of the upper secondary stage grew as a consequence of rapid change of work tasks, problems of matching skills and work tasks, a growing weight of the transitory function of upper secondary education in the wake of expansion of post-secondary education, and an increasing importance of life-long learning. The Japanese model, often described as a combination of general schooling and varied on-the-job training, *i.e.* as the absolute contrast to the German model, was most popular in public debates in OECD Member countries during the 1980s and only lost some of its glamour, when economic problems grew in Japan during the 1990s. Finally, the growing sophistication of knowledge about the complex relationships between education and employment and the insight about different conditions between the various OECD Member countries did not facilitate sweeping statements about optimal solutions altogether.

This does mean, however, that the last two decades of debate and experience can be characterised merely by socio-political dissension and persistence of national idiosyncrasies of educational and training systems and of the relationships between education and employment. Noteworthy changes occurred, some of which will be summarised here with an emphasis on the European scene. First, a short overview should be provided about the major changes of the structures of education and training and of participation in upper secondary and higher education. In addition, a short discussion is in place of two key indicators of the external impacts of education and training: differences of unemployment and of income according to educational and training background. Further, the search for improved relationships between education and employment will be illustrated with the debate on the German and the Japanese "model" and some of the issues involved. Finally, some current approaches in education and training shall be illustrated which obviously play a role in many OECD Member countries.

2. Quantitative trends

Expansion of education seems to be an perennial trend since World War II. The OECD *Job Study* (1994*b*, p. 95) demonstrates this with the help of data of the educational attainment of the population. On average of the OECD countries, 32% of the population over 25 years of age in 1960 had at least some (upper) secondary education (and possibly also higher education), 41% in 1970, and 59% in 1985. According to a recent study, on average 62% of the adult population of the OECD countries in 1995 had completed upper secondary education or higher education (OECD, 1998*c*). In comparison: of the adult population in developing countries in 1960, 6% had experienced secondary education. The respective figures were 8% for 1970 and finally 19% for 1985 (*ibid.*).

Up to about the mid-1970s, when a need for expansion of general and full-time education was widely felt and advocated, the OECD educational statistics presented the ratio of full-time upper secondary education as a key indicator of education beyond compulsory schooling. The OECD report *Entry of Young People into Working Life* (1977) offered data on the full-time enrolment rates of 15-25 year-olds around 1970. As Table 1 shows, less than 40% of 17 year-olds on average in the European OECD Member countries were enrolled in full-time schooling in 1970. We note a substantial variety ranging from 61% in Sweden to 20% in Germany. Except for Australia, the non-European members of the OECD reported substantially higher ratios of full-time enrolment in upper secondary education: three quarters or more.

Average years of schooling were highest in the U.S. labour force in 1975 according to such an approach (11.3 years). In Europe, a relatively high average of years of schooling was reported (Graff, 1996, p. 285) for: United Kingdom (10.9 years); the Federal Republic of Germany and the Netherlands (9.6 years each); Switzerland (9.5 years); and Norway (9.1 years). In contrast, the average period of schooling had been relatively low in France, Spain (5.6 years each) and Portugal (4.2 years).

In the late 1970s, the OECD changed its computation of enrolment in upper secondary education. It presented overall enrolment rates, *i.e.* including those in part-time enrolment and in apprenticeship training. The revised interpretation already shaped the text, but not the statistics of the 1977 OECD study. This presentation of aggregate data of upper secondary education including combined work and school-based training still prevails today as, for example, quotations from OECD Jobs Study might show. Under the heading of "Why some countries do better than other countries in reducing early school-leaving" the Jobs Study identified three groups of countries:

– Countries which "developed relatively open access to post-secondary education, thus motivating many young people to finish secondary education, especially since they could not offer work-based qualification alternatives" (OECD, 1994c, p. 130). Canada, Japan, Sweden and the United States represent this group.

– "European countries with very different sorts of provision of upper secondary education, including both entirely school-based provision and dual systems... What these countries have in common is a long and continuing tradition of highly organised systems of education and training, with clearly defined and collectively organised and accepted responsibilities" (ibid.).

– "Countries that have not had a strong apprenticeship tradition (France, Ireland and Spain), and (...) countries which – in addition to lacking a strong apprenticeship tradition – also had education systems that tended to use upper secondary education exclusively to identify and prepare candidates for university education (Australia, New Zealand and the United Kingdom)" (ibid.).

The OECD Jobs Study points out that the third group of countries, including some Nordic countries, experienced the highest increase of enrolment rates in upper secondary education from the mid-1970s to the 1990s. As Table 2 shows, some of these countries reached or surpassed the 80% level (France, Norway and Denmark almost 80%). In contrast, the enrolment rate of the 17 year-olds remained below 60% in 1990 in the United Kingdom, New Zealand and Turkey.

In 1996, the average upper secondary education rate was 85% on average of the 23 OECD Member countries for which information was available (OECD, 1998a, p. 41). It should be noted, though, that the majority of the countries not providing information are known for below-average enrolment in upper secondary education. This notwithstanding, we might estimate that the proportion of young people with "low educational qualifications" (OECD, 1998b, p. 45, i.e. lower secondary school as highest level of educational attainment) was not substantially higher than 20% on average. In 1995, the proportion of persons with "low educational qualifications" among the 20-24 year-olds – 24% on average of the OECD countries (for which information was made available) – varied substantially among European OECD Member countries: 65% in Turkey; 57% in Portugal; 41% in Spain; 34% in Denmark; 31% each in Italy and the Netherlands; 26% each in Greece and Ireland; 21% in Finland; and 7-13% in the Czech Republic, France, Norway, Poland, Sweden and the United Kingdom. The respective figures for OECD Member countries outside Europe were 6% in Korea, 15% in the United States, 16% in Canada and 32% in Australia (OECD, 1998b, p. 98).

Difference of the varied educational and training options cannot be demonstrated validly anymore by statistics on full-time and part-time enrolment, because the OECD Education Database also counts apprenticeship training as full-time, if schooling and training in the company together comprises full-time activity (OECD, 1998a, p. 169). Table 3 shows the ratios of general upper secondary graduates on the one hand and on the other the vocational and apprenticeship graduates. Only in a minority of European OECD Member countries do the graduates from general programmes outnumber those from vocational and apprenticeship programmes: in Ireland, Portugal, Greece, Spain and Denmark among the countries for which information is available. In the one extreme, 77% of young Irish complete general upper secondary education while only 2% complete vocational education. In the other extreme, 71% of young Czechs complete apprenticeship training or vocational schools, while only 11% complete general upper secondary education.

According to recent studies, the proportion of young people entering apprenticeship training after full-time compulsory education was highest in the mid-1990s in Denmark (more than 50%). In other EU

Member countries, the ratios were more than 40% in Austria and Germany, around 30% in the UK and about 20% in the Netherlands (Tessaring, 1998, p. 130).

Entry rates to post-secondary education increased substantially during the period discussed. It is difficult to provide a time series, because the definitions of post-secondary versus higher education and non-university versus university-level have been changed and because many institutions have been upgraded over time. Moreover, we have to pay attention to the differences of entry ratios, overall enrolment ratios of the respective age groups and graduations, because the completion rates ("survival rates", *i.e.* the number of graduates of the new entry students some years earlier) vary substantially among the OECD countries, *i.e.* between 35% and 90% (OECD, 1998*a*, p. 198).

The ratio of new entry students at institutions of higher education in OECD countries rose from about 20% around 1960 to more than 50% in the 1990s. Similarly, UNESCO reports an increase of the enrolment quota of students in developed countries among the 18 to 23 age group from 15% in 1960 to 40% in 1990 (UNESCO, 1995, pp. 15-16). OECD statistics on educational attainment of the population showed average higher education ratios of: 7% in 1960; 10% in 1970; 16% in 1980 (OECD, 1994*b*, p. 95); and 21% in 1995 (OECD, 1998*c*, p. 98). Graduation ratios from tertiary education seem to have about doubled from the mid-1970s to the mid-1990s. The OECD statistics, however, allows us to establish a time series only for a few European countries, as shown in Table 4. Whereas the graduation ratio in Italy increased marginally, the respective ratio in Spain almost quadrupled.

The change of graduation quota over time can be also demonstrated indirectly with the help of data on the educational attainment of the labour force. One should bear in mind, though, two major limitations of Table 5. First, persons are not included who have obtained a non-university tertiary qualification (*e.g.* completion of two-year study programmes or of vocational tertiary programmes not considered part of higher education). Second, the age group of 25-34 year-olds tends to provide too small ratios of recent graduates, because in a substantial number of European countries the majority of university graduates are awarded a university degree at the age of 25 and higher (OECD, 1998*a*, p. 201). On average of the 20 European countries for which information is provided in Table 5 for the year 1996, the proportion of university-level graduates among the 55-64 age population was 7%, and the respective ratio was 13% among the 25-34 age population. Even if we take into account the late timing of graduation in a substantial number of European countries, the ratio did only slightly more than double within 30 years.

As for the 1990s, the OECD also publishes a "first-time university graduation rate" (OECD, 1998*a*, p. 31), thereby excluding as far as possible a double counting of persons obtaining a first and subsequently an advanced degree. The figures for 1996 were: 34% in the United Kingdom; 28% in Denmark; 27% in Norway; 26% in Spain; 25% in Ireland; 24% in Finland; 22% in Hungary; 20% in the Netherlands; 19% in Sweden; 16% in Germany and Portugal; 15% in Iceland; 13% in the Czech Republic, Greece and Italy; 10% in Austria; and 9% in Switzerland.

In looking at the career paths of youth, it might be more appropriate to compare the number of secondary education graduates to those entering tertiary education or possibly an advanced stage of upper secondary education. The most recent OECD statistics allow us to compare the upper secondary graduation ratios of 1996 with the entry rates to tertiary education in 11 European OECD Member countries in the same year. The data presented in Table 6 suggest that the proportion of secondary school leaver eventually enrolling in higher education has surpassed more than half on average. In addition, about one tenth of upper secondary school leavers eventually completed a second (advanced) level of secondary education (OECD, 1998*a*, p. 173).

For many years, in most of the OECD Member countries, only a minority of secondary school leavers eventually transferred to tertiary education. In many countries, most of those having completed general secondary education traditionally transferred to tertiary education, whereas vocational upper secondary education or training tended to be terminal. In the meantime, however, the trend of transformation towards "universal higher education" proceeds, and some kind of tertiary education seems to "become the norm" for the majority not only of the upper secondary school leavers, but even the age group (OECD, 1998e). At present, the majority of those opting for vocational schooling or apprenticeship training still expect this to be the final stage of pre-career education. One might ask, though, whether the trends of increasing "technical" training, i.e. training between the traditional skilled worker training and higher education, the blurring of boundaries between technical training at upper secondary and post-secondary level, and the further expansion of higher education will make vocational upper secondary schooling and training an option also which is predominantly neither viewed as terminal nor as transitory from the outset.

Altogether, enrolment in all types of upper secondary education and training in OECD Member countries seems to have grown from an average of almost 60% in the late 1970s, to almost 80% in the late 1990s. There was no clear trend as regards the growth of the general or the vocational sector of upper secondary. However, the transitory function of upper secondary education clearly grew in the wake of increasing enrolment in tertiary education from about 20% to almost 50%.

3. Changing patterns of educational institutions and programmes

In comparative policy debates about the role education and training play for the preparation for the world of work, differences in employment sector and income according to levels of educational attainment are often referred to. One has to keep in mind, though, that substantial differences exist between industrialised societies, as far as structures of educational institutions and programmes as well as the typical educational pathway are concerned. Therefore, the major differences which are usually considered relevant for the relationships between education and employment shall be briefly summarised (also the overviews in Postlethwaite, 1988; Johnson, 1987; EURYDICE and CEDEFOP, 1993; European Commission, 1997; Jablonska-Skinder et al., 1992).

In the last two decades the public debate on issues of preparing youth for employment and work has focused on young people of the age of about 15 to 20 years. Terms employed in characterising this stage of education, training, work and living conditions vary: "post-compulsory", "upper secondary", "16-19 year-olds", etc. Actually, the typical starting age of various upper secondary education programmes ranges, in different European countries from 13 to 17 years, according to an overview provided by OECD (1998a, pp. 366-367). The typical graduation age ranges from 17 to 22 years of age. There was a clear trend towards a higher starting and completion age of upper secondary education on average in OECD Member countries during the last two decades.

Lower secondary education

Before concern about employment and work of youth began to grow in the 1970s, a more or less unified system of lower secondary education and requirements of 8-10 years of schooling had become the dominant pattern in most European countries. Some differentiation of curricula persisted in lower secondary education, but this was significantly reduced in the 1960s and early 1970s in various European countries in order to improve opportunities of all youth and in order to provide a basis for a presumed increasing demand of middle-level and high-level occupations.

In the countries strongly emphasising apprenticeship training, such as Austria, Germany, the Netherlands and Switzerland, lower education continued to be divided into distinct tracks or programmes, as a rule, provided by separate institutional types. Various measures were taken, though, to soften the division according to tracks, e.g. the establishment of some comprehensive schools, the increase of common elements of curricula, the establishment of rules which facilitate the transition between the tracks, etc. The division according to the traditional school tracks also was strongly challenged in the subsequent decades as a consequence of the growing social demand for advanced levels of education. For example, the German *Hauptschule* showed more and more signs of becoming merely a residual school (*Restschule*) where basic problems of social adjustment overshadowed the process of teaching and learning which in turn increased pressures to opt for advanced educational tracks.

The dominant trend towards a unification of lower secondary education in the majority of European countries did not persist over the 1980s and 1990s, as far as curricula were concerned. In summarising the trends of secondary education in Europe from the 1960s to the 1990s, and in depicting recent developments both in lower and upper secondary education Kallen (1995, p. 458) points out: "The principle of an all-inclusive common curriculum is being challenged and there is a trend to reintroduce a certain degree of diversity and choice. The difference from the earlier situation is often minor. The change is more of perspective: curriculum differentiation is no longer seen as anathema. Diversity has regained importance in the wake of the high value that is now attached to widened programme choice. These developments must be seen in the context of the new thinking about the role of education in society and about the place of the individual that has become the new credo of policy makers and of public opinion: that of the primacy of the individual and of free choice, of the right to diversity corresponding to individual needs and wishes, of competitiveness and of performance, whereas goals that were highly valued until the 1970s, such as equality, solidarity and co-operation, have lost esteem. Such ideas are no longer held just by a few, politically at the right end of the spectrum, but have been interiorised by many educators who in the past considered such 'mercantile' concepts as incompatible with education's high mission."

The moderate curricula differentiation under the umbrella of unified schools in the majority of western European countries and the persistence of tracks in some western European countries was reflected in the schools reforms in the central and eastern European countries: most countries introduced some diversification of lower secondary education in the early 1990s (Koucky, 1996; Kotasek, 1996).

Restructuring of education and training at upper secondary level

At the level of upper secondary education, we noted a clear trend towards increased overall participation in education and training in the European OECD Member countries from the 1970s to the 1990s. This was most pronounced in those countries characterised by relatively low participation up to the 1970s. Of the countries already reporting participation ratios of 80% or more in the 1970s, some experienced a further increase, whereas in others, the high ratio remained more or less constant thereafter.

Various typologies were established both in order to characterise the programmes and the overall patterns of educational and training provisions notably on the upper secondary level in the various countries as well as the nature of education and occupational training received (Tessaring, 1998, p. 16). The OECD Education Database divides upper secondary programmes into three types:

- general programmes;
- school-based vocational and technical programmes;
- combined school and work-based vocational and technical programmes.

According to this classification we note that, among European countries (Table 7):

- The majority of students are enrolled in general programmes in Greece, Iceland, Ireland, Portugal and Spain.
- School-based vocational options prevail in Belgium and Italy and are also relatively the most frequent option in Austria, Luxembourg and the Netherlands.
- In contrast, combined school and work-based training is the most frequent option in Germany, Poland and Switzerland.

As regards the national patterns of educational and training provisions, it is easier to establish somewhat clear types for the 1970s than for the 1990s. In OECD Member countries, we could observe, by somewhat modifying the above quoted typology of the OECD *Jobs Study* (OECD, 1994c, p. 130) four types:

a) Almost universal upper secondary schooling prior to high enrolment ratios in higher education. Enrolment in general programmes, the prestigious part of which clearly preparing for higher education, outnumbered that of vocational schooling. This enrolment exists notably outside Europe: in Canada, Japan and the United States. Some experts expected Sweden to move in that direction or already classified Sweden as one of the countries belonging to this type.

b) Almost universal upper secondary education and training in diverse types of education and training provisions. Apprenticeship training outnumbered vocational schooling and enrolment in general education programmes. This was true for Austria, Germany and Switzerland.

c) A substantial component of vocational schooling alongside general upper secondary programmes. France and various Nordic countries represent this type.

d) A dominance of general education programmes in upper secondary education alongside a high proportion of youth not attending post-compulsory education or training at all. This could be observed in Ireland, the United Kingdom and the majority of Mediterranean OECD Member countries.

Of course, some countries are located somewhat between the different types. For example, the upper secondary system in the Netherlands could be viewed as a mix of the types (*a*) and (*c*).

In the 1990s, various countries might be viewed as mixed types or as countries predominantly belonging to a certain type but also comprising elements typical for other types. Obviously, however, the changes emerging do not suggest any new typology. For as will be discussed below, most countries did not substantially revamp the system of upper secondary education and training – Norway (OECD, 1997d) and – outside Europe – Australia (OECD, 1997d; Department of Employment, Education and Training, 1998) might be the exceptional cases) – but rather supplemented and modified their traditionally prevailing options. This led to a greater diversity of options in most European countries. As a consequence, differences of enrolment in the various types of upper secondary education and training were somewhat reduced. It would be misleading, however, to claim a clearly convergent trend.

In a recent OECD study, the French expert Pair (1998) presents a hypothetical framework according to which high participation in vocational and technical education is most likely, if, among other things:

– The number and diversity of possible programmes increase.

– Educational pathways diverge at a relatively late stage.

– Various opportunities exist for transfer.

– Possibilities exist to increase the level of qualification both at secondary and post-secondary education.

This hypothetical framework obviously does not take into account the option above. A high participation in education and training on upper secondary level already existed in countries with a strong apprenticeship system at a time, when both opportunities of transfer between these types of upper secondary provisions as well as opportunities to transfer from vocational training to post-secondary education were very limited.

It should be noted that these typologies focus on the main options of education and training at upper secondary level. In addition, two types of post-compulsory training measures were employed in various countries:

– Short vocational training programmes which do not lead to any "complete" occupational qualification.

– Training programmes as part of measures for unemployed youth.

As regards the latter, the OECD shows that public expenses for these types of programmes vary substantially between the European OECD Member countries. According to 1995 data (OECD, 1998c, p. 39):

– More than 0.10% of the gross domestic product (GDP) was spent on public measures for unemployed youth in Italy (0.28 in 1992), Denmark (0.17), Portugal (0.15) and Sweden (0.11). A sizeable proportion was also spent in Spain (0.09), Finland and Norway (each 0.08), the Netherlands (0.06) as well as Germany and Luxembourg (each 0.05).

– In Austria, the Czech Republic, Greece, Hungary, Poland, Switzerland and the United Kingdom, marginal or no funds were spent for these purposes.

As regards the nature of educational and occupational training received by the individuals, a typology similar to that presented in the OECD report *Entry of Young People into Working Life* (1977, p. 14) might be appropriate (the final two categories presented here were taken as a single category in the OECD report):

– compulsory schooling with no vocational training;

– basic occupational training, either within the educational system or through Ministry of Labour programmes;

– quasi-apprenticeship training or apprenticeship training for basic occupations;

– solid occupational training as highly skilled craftsmen or technicians' training;

– completion of general secondary education;

– first-level short higher education (*e.g.* the English and Irish bachelor) or short professional programmes in higher education (*e.g. hoger beroepsonderwijs* in the Netherlands, *Fachhochschulen* in Germany or *ammattikorkeakoulu* in Finland);

– long first university degrees (*e.g.* Italian *laurea* or the Austrian M*agister*) or –advanced – master degrees as second degrees.

Altogether, we noted four major trends from the mid-1970s to the mid-1990s, as far as participation in various types of education and training programmes beyond compulsory schooling are concerned:

– As already noted, the attendance rates in upper secondary education increased, *i.e.* the proportion of persons leaving the education and training system without qualification was reduced. Notably, basic occupational schemes, apprenticeship systems and vocational schools served the increase of the "retention" rate.

– In the majority of European countries, in which the overall attendance in upper secondary education had been already relatively high in the 1970s, the participation in apprenticeship system or in basic-level full-time vocational schools declined thereafter or was less often the terminal pre-career training, because an increasing proportion of the respective age group opted for high-level vocational and technicians' training.

– In the majority of European countries, the proportion of youth in the typical age of upper secondary education opting for general programmes grew (Kallen, 1997).

– In most European countries, the proportion of upper secondary graduates who continued study on post-secondary level increased. Thus, the transitory function of upper secondary education gained importance.

Education and training on the upper secondary level cannot only be classified according to institutional, programme and curricular types on that stage. In addition, we note classifications referring to the relationships between this educational stage and the subsequent one. Accordingly, education and training on upper secondary level might be either:

– A "track" or a "segmented" system, in which some institutions or programmes are clearly viewed as preparatory for higher education and others clearly as work-preparatory, or

– A differentiated system, in which some institutions or programmes are more likely to lead to higher education than others but all provide some chance of enrolment in higher education.

It does not come as a surprise to note that such a typology hardly was employed in the public debate on education and training at the upper secondary level in Europe, because – in contrast to Japan and the United States – all European countries provide some education or training schemes on post-secondary level which do not allow application to higher education.

Finally, one might classify the patterns of education and training on the secondary level (including possibly other levels) according to its relationships to employment:

– First, we note that the final pre-career stage of education might be, in one extreme, clearly "coupled" with respective occupational levels and areas, thus underscoring the relevance of credentials, and, in the other extreme, at most "loosely coupled" or "de-coupled", thus leaving the selection and allocation at the time of transition from education to employment to relatively open market processes. The terms employed for this distinction differ widely; many studies refer to the distinction made by Maurice, Sellier and Silvestre (1982) between a qualification oriented system (*e.g.* in Germany) and an organisation oriented system (*e.g.* France) or to distinction between professionally oriented and a market oriented system (*e.g.* the United States).

– Second, the education and training systems might be, in one extreme, highly standardised, as far as curricula, modes of instruction and learning, learning sites, assessment and certification are concerned, and, in the other extreme, highly diverse and not standardised.

The United States is often named as the OECD country with the least "coupled" and the least standardised system. Education and training in most European countries seem to be clearly standardised, but vary to the extent to which a "coupling" to occupational levels and individual occupations are concerned. As a rule, the German speaking countries are viewed as those which have developed and preserved the closest "coupling" as well as a high degree of standardization (Hannan and Werquin, 1998).

Tertiary education

In Europe, no consensus emerged as regards a classification of tertiary education:

– A distinction between "undergraduate" and "graduate" education did not make sense in intra-European comparison, because regular university programmes in the majority of western European countries, as a rule, lead to a first degree which is considered equivalent to a U.S. or English "master", thus combining "undergraduate" and the first "graduate" levels in Anglo-Saxon terms in a single programme.

– A distinction between "higher education" and other "post-secondary", "tertiary" or "third-level" education is feasible in the European context because all countries employ some mechanisms of formally recognising institutions of higher education in charge of certain types of programmes and credentials. Such a dividing line, however, was seldom employed because programmes outside higher education programmes were conceived in most European countries as advanced stages of secondary education or vocational training, not as "post-secondary".

– A demarcation between "short-cycle" and long programmes of tertiary education, as initially suggested by the OECD (1973), did not gain popularity because the contrast between the "vocational" approach of the relatively short programmes and the "academic" approach of university programmes was generally viewed as more salient. The vocational programmes in some European countries, however, required as many years or in a few cases even more years than university programmes. Notably, British polytechnics, established in the 1960s and eventually upgraded to universities in 1992, required the same length of study and awarded the same first degree as universities.

In the 1970s and 1980s, a distinction between university programmes on the one hand and of occupationally oriented programmes on the other hand – others than those leading to the traditional professions of medical doctors, lawyers, etc. – was generally viewed as the most important one (Williams, 1985). Because the English language provides a terminology which is widely viewed as irritating as far as advanced occupational levels are concerned ("vocational" viewed as derogatory and "professional" as linked to the traditional professions), typologies employed in the 1970s and 1980s tended to underscore the distinction between university education and "non-university higher education" (the overview in Teichler, 1988a):

– In England, Wales, Ireland and, for some subjects in Sweden, university programmes comprised three years of study. In other European countries it is between four to six years.

– Non-university higher education was provided in most western European countries by a distinct institutional type ("polytechnics", *Fachhochschulen*, *institut universitaire de technologie*, *hoger beroepsonderwijs*, etc.) comprising courses of mostly two to four years of study (including possibly practical work periods) which were considered to be more applied than those provided by universities.

France was generally viewed as an exception, because the *grandes écoles* – a "non-university" institution – had more demanding entry standards and a higher professional value than the French universities.

The distinction between a university sector and an occupationally oriented non-university sector was somewhat blurred in the 1980 and 1990s (Jallade, 1991; Meek *et al.*, 1996; Teichler, 1998b). On the one hand, an "academic drift" was widespread in non-university education. On the other hand, the increased employment problems led many universities to seek for a closer link of their programmes to the world of work – sometimes called "vocational drift". Governments of various European countries decided to strengthen the status of non-university institutions and programmes in order to make them more attractive as compared to university education and to reinforce efforts to raise the employability of graduates.

As a consequence of these trends and policies, the European Community defined in 1988 the successful completion of three years of study at institutions formally recognised as higher education institutions in a member state as the typical entry qualification to occupations requiring highly educated people. All member countries were obliged to recognise three-year qualifications of persons wishing to be professionally mobile within Europe; if higher levels of qualifications were mandatory in the respective country, provisions had to be made which allowed individuals from other Member countries to acquire the additional qualification through short periods of study or internship as well as through examination.

Recent classifications by UNESCO (the upgrading of various programmes from ISCED 5 to ISCED 6) and by OECD reflect this state of affairs. Recent OECD data now consider students of the occupationally oriented colleges in Europe, often labelled as "non-university higher education" in the past, as students in "university-level" programmes, if the programmes require at least three years of study. The OECD (1997a, pp. 389-398) now classifies tertiary programmes and degrees as:

– non-university tertiary programmes;

– short first university degree programmes (e.g. English bachelor);

– long first university degree programmes (e.g. German Diplom or Italian Laurea);

– second university degree programmes (e.g. English Master);

– Ph.D. or equivalent.

According to this classification, in 1996 the ratio of graduates of the respective age group was, on average of the 18 European OECD Member countries for which information was available, 12% from non-university tertiary programmes, 7% from short and 11% from long first university programmes, 3% from second degree programmes and 1% from Ph.D.'s or equivalent programmes (OECD, 1998a, p. 200). However, we note such a variety between European countries that average figures are hardly revealing (Teichler, 1998a). Therefore, Table 8 presents examples of the distribution of graduates in various European countries according to the classification employed nationally.

It is interesting to note that the EU policies as well as the restructuring of the UNESCO and OECD data classification are hardly viewed as relevant by scholars who undertook classifications of higher education systems in Europe in the 1990s (Scott, 1996; Teichler, 1998b; cf. also various contributions in Meek et al., 1996). Rather, recent typologies agree in making a distinction between:

– "Unitary or "unified" systems, i.e. clearly dominated by a single, university-type institution characterised by "academic" approaches and at most comprising small segments of other institutions and programmes. This traditionally holds true for Austria, Italy and since the 1990s also for the United Kingdom.

– "Binary", "dual", "two-type" or "multi-type" systems which are characterised by a duality of academically oriented programmes and institutions on the one hand and on the other, institutions and programmes emphasising a "vocational" or "applied" nature of their programmes. Germany, the Netherlands and recently Finland are considered typical examples, though the programmes of German Fachhochschulen and Dutch hogescholen now require altogether four years of study and practical work experience and therefore are counted as long university-level programme in the OECD database.

As in the case of upper secondary education, one cannot observe a clear convergent trend of the structures and major curricular approaches of higher education in Europe from the 1970s to the 1990s. While some countries moved towards or preserved a unitary system, others established or reinforced a two-type structure. Thus, it does not come as a surprise to note that the central and eastern European countries in restructuring higher education did not consider a single option to be clearly superior and thus opted for different solutions (Hennessey et al., 1998).

There were signs, though, that the policies of the higher education institutions themselves drifted towards a blurring of the distinction between academic and applied or "vocational" approaches; it depended on the governments whether they yielded to these pressures and reinforced them or whether they aimed to stabilise the dual structure (Van Vught, 1996). There are also indications that the emphasis placed in higher education policies in many European countries, since the 1980s, on competition between individual institutions and on the evaluation of institutions or programmes, has underscored and steepened a hierarchy among individual higher education institutions and departments according to academic "quality" compared to which the distinction between major types of institutions or major curricular types looses relevance (Scott, 1996).

It should be noted that no new common notion of non-university tertiary education has emerged in Europe since the European Union, UNESCO and OECD determined that three-year or longer higher education programmes of an applied nature belong to the same category as academic university programmes. Rather, the definition "non-university tertiary education" in the OECD data base comprises a mix of one or two-year programmes at higher education institutions (for example the French programmes at the *Instituts universitaires de technologies* which were not extended to three-year programmes as a consequence of the EU decision) or advanced vocational training programmes which are not considered in the respective countries as "tertiary" or "post-secondary" (for example German training of *Techniker* or *Meister*).

In many European countries, the boundaries between higher education, under pressure to diversify in the wake of expansion, and advanced vocational education, under pressure to improve its quality as a consequence of perceived changing job requirements and as a trend towards the upgrading of this sector for various reasons, seem to become blurred. This holds true for many central and eastern European countries, among others, where both the political consensus and resources which would be needed for a standardised restructuring are lacking (Hennessey *et al.*, 1998). Finland can be viewed as a rare exception: almost all of the advanced vocational education is expected to be absorbed by the newly established three-year vocational college system (*ammattikorkeakoulu*).

In contrast to upper secondary education, the view is widely held in higher education in Europe that a global compatibility of credentials would be desirable in the wake of rising international student and professional mobility. In response, some countries move towards the establishment of a short university degree equivalent to an English bachelor. This was implemented in Denmark at almost all institutions and programmes in the late 1980s and in Finland in the mid-1990s at some institutions and programmes. It continues on an experimental basis in Germany. In Denmark and Finland, however, only a small minority of students consider the bachelor as terminal pre-career education, and up to the present, these reforms do not seem to challenge the dominant view in most European countries that the short higher education programme should be more directly work-preparatory in nature than most of the long university programmes.

A *comparison across levels of education*

Altogether, we note a larger number of cases of a substantial restructuring of tertiary education in OECD Member countries during the last two decades than of corresponding restructuring of upper secondary education. A substantial number of new institutional types of higher education and post-secondary institutions were introduced in some European countries. Additionally, new levels of programmes and degrees were introduced or previously existing non-university institutions were upgraded to universities. Major structural changes were nonetheless seldom implemented in the upper secondary education even though the increase of vocational and apprentice programmes as well as the extension of "double qualification" in some countries are worth noting (cf. the development in Australia, Norway and the Netherlands).

We might speculate why upper secondary was less often structurally revamped than testing education though it seemed to be more strongly affected by the grown employment problems of youth and by the concern about employability. One of the major reasons might have been that tertiary education experienced higher growth rates during that period. In addition, uncertainty about possible future directions might have been higher with respect to upper secondary education than with respect to tertiary education.

4. Relationships between education and employment

Growing complexity of analysis

The employment value of education was already a major theme of analysis before the growing employment problems in the mid-1970s changed the focus of attention. Up to the early 1970s, studies aiming to assess the relationships between education and career took the occupational group, the status, and income as employment measures and work assignments or job satisfaction as work measures. Since about the mid-1970s, however, the range of employment and work measures to be analysed was extended substantially. In addition to the previously customary measures, attention was paid to the minimum conditions of employment, notably:

– unemployment or employment of school leavers and graduates;

– the length of the search period for employment;

– provisional versus "normal" or "regular" employment;

– part-time versus full-time employment;

– short-term contract etc. versus indeterminate employment;

– employment inappropriate or appropriate to the level and type of education.

In addition, studies more often included more refined categories of educational attainment and of the types of educational programmes and institutions. Whereas many previous studies often only compared the educational value of the major educational levels (compulsory education, upper secondary education and higher education), many subsequent studies differentiated according to subjects and fields as well as to types of institutions and programmes of the same level.

Moreover, awareness grew about the relevance of measuring the relationships between education and work at various stages of the career, for the process of transition from education to work turned out to be a complex and protracted affair, possibly lasting even more than ten years (Gensbittel and Mainguet, 1995; OECD, 1996c). It is generally assumed that the process of transition has become longer notably as the consequence of greater employment problems, increasing flexibility and diversity of educational and training provisions, a decreasing "stability" or increasing "flexibility" of careers, and finally of a greater inclination on the part of young persons to accept trial and error as well as occupational mobility in search, provisional employment and various phases of education and training in order to reach position and work assignments which match their expectations. Moreover, the growing life-long learning activities and other factors could restructure the relationships between pre-career education and employment. Consequently, any recent attempt of measuring the relationships between education and employment has to take into account the extended transition period, *e.g.* through measuring at various points in time after completion of pre-career education, and thus to examine the extent to which initial and early employment and work have a lasting impact on subsequent career stages.

Measuring the relationships between education and employment in order to establish the impact of education and training on subsequent employment and work turned out to be most complicated (Rumberger, 1994). The most easily available data, *i.e.* those on the relationships between education level, type and subject on the one hand and on the other hand on employment status, occupational category and income, are also the crudest ones: they allow us only to infer in an indirect way the extent to which the knowledge acquired in education is actually utilised on the job. Studies asking the employed persons to assess the links between education and employment or to measure competence and work assignments tend to be undertaken only in single countries and for select educational and occupational areas. They are seldom repeated at various historical and career points in time. Moreover, the links between education and employment actually observed are not *per se* measures of the impact of education on employment or of the utility of knowledge, because various other factors come into play, for example, the employers' inclination to recruit skills primarily internally or externally, the employers' attitudes towards presumed over-education, the extent to which training tends to be provided in-career or pre-career, or the traditions and regulations of rewarding credentials. The conceptual, methodological and data issues involved have led to a state of information which leaves ample room for varied interpretations, and many of these interpretations mirror the major public philosophical and political controversies regarding education and its economic, social and political functions.

Education and equality

Before major employment problems emerged in market-oriented industrial societies in the mid-1970s, two aspects of the relationships between education and employment were most frequently the focus of research and related policy debates: the relationships between educational expansion and demand of the employment system and the relationships between socio-biographic background, education and subsequent occupational and life chances.

Research on the relationships between socio-biographic background, education and subsequent employment and life course (OECD, 1975; Shavit and Blossfeld, 1993) suggests, first, that the traditional influence of parental education and occupation on the educational attainment of the subsequent generation was only moderately reduced in the process of educational expansion and reforms striving to counteract inequality of opportunity. Notably, children of least educated and low-status parents moved upward educationally less often than tended to be hoped for by many key actors of educational reforms. Second, research on the relationships between educational attainment and occupational opportunities showed – across a range of diverse findings – neither a clear trend of a closer "coupling" between educational attainment – both vertically and horizontally – and level and type of employment and work nor of a "de-coupling". Frequent claims of rising "credentialism" on the one hand, as well as a growing irrelevance of education for status-attainment on the other, were true at most for individual sectors or countries, but did not prove to be appropriate for describing the general changes in the relationships between education and employment in industrial societies in the course of educational expansion. What happened, though, as a consequence of educational expansion seemingly surpassing the immediate demands of the economy in most industrialised societies already before the employment crisis and the declining growth rates since 1973, is a change in the role of educational credentials vis-à-vis high-level occupations: consensus among experts grew that educational credentials more often became a necessary but not a sufficient condition for entry into high-level and middle-level occupations.

Continued research on these topics in the 1980s and 1990s kept some of the basic questions. The modes of analysis became more complex, not the least due to the rapid computerisation of social science research. Recent studies take into account more in detail the pathways and stages in the relationships between background, education and life chances. In addition, they often address problems of "social exclusion" of the most disadvantaged groups.

Educational attainment, career and demand

Research on the relationships between education, employment and demand for graduates notably comprised studies on trends of graduate employment and projections of demand for graduates, on the relationships between educational attainment and income and on the changing whereabouts of graduates from higher education in occupational categories (see the overviews in Teichler *et al.*, 1980; Psacharopoulus, 1987; Levin and Rumberger, 1988). Most studies came to the conclusion already around 1970, as stated above, that the supply of graduates from higher education tended to surpass the demand and to lead to an increased proportion of graduates active in occupations for which a degree was not an undisputed requirement. Findings remained varied as regards the "returns" for educational investment.

A controversial debate began as to whether the educational expansion leads to "over-education", whether employers continue to prefer highly-educated persons, even if they are not required, for purpose of optimal "screening" of talents, whether perceptions of demand and recruitment practices were largely supply-driven, whether the supply beyond immediate demand served long-term demands and innovation in the employment system (Collins, 1979; Suda, 1980; Teichler et al., 1980; Lutz, 1981; Rumberger, 1981; Boli, Ramirez and Meyer, 1985; Spenner, 1985; Teichler, 1992; Psacharopoulus, 1993; Alpin, Shackleton and Walsh, 1998; Teichler, 1998c). Also, the questions were raised whether supply beyond immediate demand served a democratisation or a stricter hierarchisation in the distribution of job responsibilities and life chances, and how it could be assessed in wider economic and social terms: as "wastage", as economically affordable social and cultural enrichment, etc.

The paradigmatic shift

When, after the so-called "oil shock" in 1973 concern about youth employment problems became a major issue of both labour market and educational policies, research on the relationships between education and work did not abandon the previously dominant themes, but the themes were supplemented, and, as already mentioned, the focus changed:

– Relevant employment indicators addressed shifted toward the negative side of employment and work: unemployment, extended job search, precarious employment and under-utilisation of competencies.

– As regards the educational system, emphasis moved from advanced levels towards the lower and middle levels of education and their relationships to employment as well as the interrelationships between different levels.

– Exclusive, or almost exclusive attention was no longer paid to full-time or general schooling and higher education, but only to vocational schooling and training, including part-time educational arrangements.

– Finally, studies were undertaken which tried to establish the impact of various educational and employment measures aiming to enhance the employability of youth.

Concurrently, a broader range of competencies was taken into account: knowledge, social skills and various competencies for coping with the world of work. Also views became more cautious as far as convergent trends in industrial societies are concerned.

Many prior studies and related policy documents implicitly or explicitly had appreciated the expansion of full-time schooling and higher education as likely to contribute to economic growth, social and cultural enhancement, and to a fair, open, welfare oriented achievement society. Others, in challenging these views, still underscored the paradigmatic relevance of these views. Beginning in the mid-1970s, however, views spread that the expansion of general upper secondary education and higher education might harm those not successfully climbing the educational ladder. For example, expansion was claimed to cause a "displacement" of opportunities and to lead to less complex and responsible work assignment for those with lower levels of education (Lutz, 1981). Also, vocational training as well as close ties between education and the economy were criticised less often than in the past for their limited scope of enhancement of talents and reduced opportunity for upward educational mobility and praised more often for their positive impact on fostering vocational competencies, increasing employability, reinforcing vocational pride, etc.

Education, training and unemployment

Many studies and many information-summarising policy reports on educational issues address unemployment, its causes, measures to redress as well as possibly the impact of those measures. The overall unemployment ratio of the European OECD Member countries rose on average from marginal levels in the early 1970s towards about 5% in the late 1970s. After various ups and downs, it increased to about 8% in the mid-1990s (OECD, 1997*b*).

Theories aiming to explain the persistently high unemployment rates in market economies since the mid-1970s point out a broad range of factors, *e.g.* specific economic and political incidences (such as the "oil shock"), increased frictions on the labour market as a consequence of rapid change, demographic trends and increased labour force participation of women, mismatches between skills and demand, restructuring of the economy, aggregated impacts of public interventions in the economy, etc. (Schettkatt, 1996). Most experts continue to agree, however, that educational and training policies can play a role not only in the redistribution of unemployment risks among youth, but also in reducing the overall level of youth unemployment to some extent.

Youth unemployment has been a major policy concern since the mid-1970s in Europe. In the European Union in 1995, the average youth unemployment rate (percentage of unemployed among the 15-24 year-olds in the labour force) averaged 22% in the Member countries (European Commission, 1997). It varied substantially:

– Highest youth unemployment rates were reported in Spain (43%), Finland (38%) and Italy (33%).

– Various other countries experienced sizeable youth unemployment rates as well: Greece (28%), France (27%), Belgium (24%), Ireland (21%), Sweden (19%), Portugal (17%) and the United Kingdom (16%).

– The unemployment rates were lowest in the Netherlands (12%), Denmark (10%), Germany (9%) and Austria (6%).

Whereas youth unemployment in many European countries was about twice as high as unemployment in the overall labour force, the youth unemployment rates in Austria, Germany, Switzerland and the Netherlands hardly differed from that of the overall labour force. This pattern did not change substantially from the late 1970s to the late 1990s.

The OECD comments on the available statistics in the following way: "Apprenticeship systems in the German-speaking and some other countries have a good record of keeping youth unemployment (...) at comparatively very low levels and at ensuring that these labour market benefits persist for young people." (OECD, 1998*b*, p. 53). One has to bear in mind, however, that youth unemployment is also comparatively low in the Asian OECD Member countries, *i.e.* Japan and Korea, where many young persons take up regular employment without any prior vocational training. Obviously, other factors might contribute to low youth unemployment as well: placement procedures, low starting salaries as well as the employers' intention to shape the occupational skills primarily through on the job-training within the company.

Actually, however, only about 10% of the total age group were registered as unemployed on average in the EU Member countries in the mid-1990s, notably because more than half of the respective age group were active in education and training. The trend towards educational expansion as well as the measures to provide additional programmes of training and education and to create employment opportunities for unemployed youth and for youth at risk had the combined effect of keeping the ratios of those unemployed among the 15-24 year-old population at that level. Again, we note substantial differences among countries, ranging from 20% in Finland and 18% in Spain to 5% in Germany and 3% in Austria (European Commission, 1997).

Available information clearly shows that the risk of unemployment is inversely proportional to educational attainment. We note, however, substantial differences between countries and noteworthy variations over career stages.

The OECD calculated expected years of unemployment over the working lifetime on the basis of 1996 unemployment statistics (OECD, 1998c, p. 110). Accordingly, on average of 20 European countries, persons:

– trained below upper secondary level expected 3.7 years;

– trained on upper secondary level 2.3 years;

– trained on tertiary level 1.4 years of unemployment.

Examples of quite distinct unemployment periods according to educational attainment are the Czech Republic and Ireland. In contrast, unemployment differs only to a very moderate extent in Italy and Portugal, and is more or less equal according to the various educational levels in Greece. There was no clear correlation between level of educational expansion and variation of unemployment according to educational attainment.

Available statistics show that the differences of unemployment ratios according to educational attainment grew in many OECD countries during the 1980s; notably the risk of unemployment increased for persons without education and training beyond the typical level of compulsory schooling. In the 1990s, however, no substantial change can be observed in the relative risk of unemployment according to the level of educational attainment on average of the OECD Member countries (OECD, 1994b, pp. 38-41; OECD, 1998a, p. 345).

Recent data show that, in many European countries, unemployment of youth without upper secondary education during the first few years after entry into the labour force is not much higher or about as high as early unemployment of secondary school graduates (OECD, 1998a, pp. 253-259). In Denmark, the unemployment rate of youth below 20 years of age, i.e. mostly of persons without upper secondary education credentials, is even lower than the rates of all age groups. Measures of retaining persons in education, of providing employment-oriented short training or in a few countries even of guaranteeing employment of young persons often focus on youth not trained beyond compulsory education.

On the other hand, the unemployment rates of the 25-29 year-olds not trained beyond lower secondary education are in most European Member countries – except for some Mediterranean countries – substantially higher than of those trained in upper secondary and possibly higher education (see Table 9). This finding suggests, as some experts point out, that measures for alleviating the career start of youth "at risk", as a rule, do not have lasting impacts. Many research projects provide evidence that, even if the career had a precarious start, most of those completing upper secondary education or training or higher education succeed after a few years, to enjoy relatively stable employment and satisfying work.

In the majority of European OECD Member countries, the unemployment rate among young women was clearly higher in 1996 than among young men. In Austria, Germany, Ireland and Sweden, however, the unemployment rates of women and men younger than 30 years were more or less equal, and in the United Kingdom it was substantially lower than that of men. As regards the relationships between educational attainment and unemployment in Europe, the patterns for women were on average similar to those of men (OECD, 1998a, p. 257).

It might be added here that young women (younger than 25 years) in all EU member countries more often take over part-time employment than young men. Notably in the Nordic countries, but also in France and Greece, the proportion of young women employed part-time is higher than among women of all ages (Beduwé and Giret, 1998, pp. 7-8).

The OECD publications do not provide data on differences of unemployment quota according to type of upper secondary education and training received. Most data available show differences according to countries. For example, those having completed vocational training and schooling in France, Germany and the Netherlands are less likely to be unemployed than those having completed general upper secondary education. In the United Kingdom, the level of education seems to count primarily, whereas the type of education and training plays a lesser role (Brauns, Müller and Steinmann, 1997, pp. 19-36; Dronkers, 1993).

Altogether, the data on the relationships between education and unemployment tend to be viewed as only moderately supporting the view that raising the educational attainment of the population can serve as a tool of reducing unemployment. There is of course the immediate "retainment" effect, but this is partly counterbalanced by the fact that higher education levels lead to higher labour force participation. As a whole, the effect of education in reducing the unemployment often is conceived as "more long-term than short-term" (Bovin, 1995, p. 80).

Transition

Altogether, the transition period from education to employment changed significantly in the European Member countries during from the 1970s to 1990s (OECD, 1998*f*; Stern and Wagner, 1999):

- The average age of leaving pre-career education grew as a consequence of educational expansion. As already discussed, access to the employment system immediately after completion of lower secondary education declined substantially, and notably enrolment in higher education continued to grow. In 1996, 90% of the 16 year-olds, 84% of the 17 year-olds, 73% of the 18 year-olds, 53% of the 19 year-olds, and 42% of the 20 year-olds on average of 21 European Member countries were enrolled in education and training institutions (OECD, 1998*a*, p. 161).

- The search period between completion of education and the start of employment became longer.

- The extent to which "mixed statuses" occur in the early years, *i.e.* part-time employment, short-contract employment, provisional employment, choice of additional full-time or part-time education and training, etc. grew significantly.

- Youth unemployment increased (more or less along a general increase of unemployment).

Altogether, the process of transition became longer. Thereby, differences between countries remained substantial. In the process of educational expansion, the differences in enrolment rates in upper secondary education declined over time, whereas differences in tertiary enrolments remained relatively stable.

Available statistics show that the occurrence of "mixed statuses", *e.g.* part-time employment, short-term employment also varies substantially between the European countries (Béduwé and Giret, 1998). One should bear in mind, though, that these data cannot be merely interpreted as indicating market-driven employment problems, but also as results of policies of counteracting unemployment.

In addition, measures of facilitating the transition between higher education and employment differ substantially:

- In Japan, educational institutions and companies co-operate closely in the transition process, thereby ensuring that most graduates get employed immediately after completing schooling and study and that the reputation of the school or university but also achievement in upper secondary education have a strong and visible effect on career opportunities (Kariya, 1991; Teicher and Teichler, 1997).

– In the Anglo-Saxon countries, schools and institutions of higher education are strongly active in occupational guidance and institutions of higher education in particular, in the placement of graduates as well.

– In the Nordic countries, in France, Germany, the Netherlands and some of their neighbour countries, large public employment systems are established which are expected to provide occupational guidance and also to play a major role in the placement of youth.

– In Austria, Germany and Switzerland in particular, the apprenticeship facilitates transition to employment, because employers employing apprentices on a provisional basis like to keep the successful ones, thus utilising the apprenticeship systems successfully as a screening device.

– Notably, Nordic countries but also some other European countries opted for various public employment measures in order to keep youth unemployment within bounds.

While data on the overall pathways and their characteristics as well as the overall duration of the transition period exists, it is difficult to provide an overall picture with comparable data across the various countries.

In combining information on ratios of unemployment, duration of unemployment as well as various measures of reduced and precarious employment conditions (part-time employment, short-term contracts, etc.), two French scholars created a typology of transition from education to employment (Béduwé and Giret, 1998, pp. 11-12):

– In Austria, Germany and Luxembourg, both youth unemployment and youth unemployment of long duration are relatively infrequent. Also part-time employment of youth is fairly uncommon, but short-term is relatively frequent.

– In Denmark, Sweden, the United Kingdom and the Netherlands, youth unemployment is somewhat higher, but of relatively short duration. Part-time employment, encouraged by policy measures, and short-term contracts for youth are widely spread.

– In Belgium, France, Ireland and Portugal, the youth unemployment rates are higher than in the previous two groups of countries, and in various of these countries, the duration of unemployment is often high. Part-time employment is not very frequent, and short-term contracts in the majority of these countries are very pronounced among young people.

– Italy, Greece and Spain report the highest quota of youth unemployment. Long-term unemployment is frequent both among youth and the adult labour force. In the majority of these countries, part-time employment and short term contracts are seldom.

– In Finland, youth unemployment is very high, but often short-term. Many young persons are employed part-time and on short-term contracts.

These findings clearly reflect that the more active youth employment policies in the northern European countries lead to a reduction of long-term unemployment. Often unemployment is successfully reduced at the expense of stable and full-time employment. In most southern European countries, employment measures to cope with youth unemployed are less common. Often, the families are expected to provide a shelter for youth not employed.

Education and earnings

In all industrialised societies, persons having successfully completed higher levels of education are also likely to receive higher income. According to 1996 OECD data (OECD, 1998a, p. 358), on average in 16 European countries, persons aged 25-64:

– with an upper secondary education had an income 1.31 times as high as that of persons without an upper secondary education;

– with a non-university tertiary education 1.52 times as high;

– with university education 2.06 times as high.

The substantial differences by country in the relationships between educational attainment and earnings can neither be explained by major structures and curricular approaches in upper secondary and higher education nor by the level of educational expansion. It is interesting to note in this context that the income differentials by educational attainment did not change substantially in most European countries for which information is available, from the early 1970s to the early 1990s (see Table 10). Also, recent analyses suggest that income difference according to educational attainment did not change substantially either during the 1990s in most European countries (Hannan and Werquin, 1998). The income differences, however, grew over the past decades in the United States and continued to increase in the 1990s. They also began to grow in the late 1980s in the United Kingdom and continued to rise in the 1990s, i.e. in those countries in which the income dispersion in the work force, i.e. the ratio of the 9th decile to the 1st decile of income, rose substantially over this period, whereas it remained more or less constant in most continental European OECD Member countries (ILO, 1996, pp. 58-64).

In all OECD Member countries for which information is available, income differences by educational attainment widen in the course of the career. At the age of 25-29 years, income differences by educational attainment are very small in almost all countries with the notable exception of the United States and the United Kingdom. In all countries, the gaps widen at least until the age of 55-59 years. Thereby, the income advantages of university graduates to upper secondary education graduates increase strongly more in the course of the career than the income advantages of upper secondary graduates to those of persons without upper secondary education. In the Nordic countries, the income difference between graduates of upper secondary education and that of persons without secondary education even remains marginal over the course of their career (OECD, 1998a, pp. 357).

Altogether, the income of women is substantially lower than that of men for all levels of educational attainment. The available data, however, suggest that income differences by educational attainment are larger for women than for men in most countries (Pole, 1995; OECD, 1998a, p. 353; OECD, 1998c, pp. 68-73 and 112-113).

The OECD calculated "rates of returns" in the various OECD Member countries (ibid.). Accordingly, the individual rate of return for investment in upper secondary education is often higher than that for investment in university education. Among the eleven European countries, for which respective data are provided, returns for advanced education surpass returns of business capital in five countries (Finland, Ireland, Norway, Switzerland and the United Kingdom). They are about equally high in three countries (Denmark, France and the Netherlands) and they are clearly lower than capital returns in three countries (Germany, Italy and Sweden). Again, these differences can neither be explained by the types of educational and training institutions and programmes nor by the level of educational expansion.

Available research in various European countries suggests that the growing supply of workers with high levels of education continued to surpass the growth of occupations for which those levels of education traditionally were required (OECD, 1993; Werquin et al., 1997). The number of graduates from higher education increasingly surpassed the number of positions traditionally held by graduates, and the number of school leavers from the lower secondary level declined faster than the number of low skilled jobs.

This led some researchers to speculate about "over-education" or about major supply-driven changes of the relationships between education and employment. On the other hand, many experts argue that changes of the work assignments within occupational categories have increased the chances of applying higher level of skills and knowledge in occupations traditionally not filled by persons with these levels of skills. As a consequence, most graduates from higher education are asked in many surveys about the appropriateness of their educational level to their position and the extent to which they utilise on the job the competencies acquired in the course of study. The results of these surveys show that substantial proportions of graduates taking over assignments traditionally not requiring a degree consider their education useful and appropriate. The surveys, however, differ so much in methodology between countries and over time that hardly any general conclusions can be drawn (cf. the summaries in Teichler, 1988b; OECD, 1992; Teichler, 1996). They obviously indicate, however, that studies claiming an oversupply on the basis of links between educational attainment and occupational categories provide a too static picture of job requirements. The proportions of those considering themselves as inappropriately employed do not substantially grow over time, and also studies on the rate of return cast doubt that the supply increasingly surpasses the real demand. It is impossible thought to disentangle the extent to which the survey finding of relative constant proportions over time of graduates perceiving appropriate employment is based on some lowering of expectation on the one hand and on the other on rising job requirements.

Most comparative data presentations on the relationships between educational attainment and employment do not differentiate between different types of education and training on upper secondary level. As far as data are available, they show striking differences between the various European countries. The less vocational training is traditionally provided on that level, the more likely graduates from general upper secondary education continue to have more favourable job prospects. In reverse, graduates from vocational training are likely to fare as well, if not better, than graduates from general upper secondary education in those countries in which vocational training or vocational schooling are traditionally well established.

A recent comparative study shows that graduates from countries with a highly selective school system and a strong tradition of vocational training (*e.g.* Germany and Switzerland) are likely to experience the greatest congruence between education and work both horizontally and vertically. Also phenomena of social exclusion seem to be less pronounced in these countries. On the other hand, the inequalities in these countries by socio-biographic background are most substantial (Müller and Shavit, 1998).

Altogether, the available findings first suggest in fact that general upper secondary education, vocational schooling and predominantly work-based vocational training do not differ so strikingly on average across Europe in terms of the employment opportunity they provide as was widely believed up to the early 1970s. The value of vocational training for enhancing competencies, securing employability and contributing to careers proved to be so high that it seems justified to consider them to be more or less at the same educational level. Second, the differences between European countries as regards the employment and career value of various types of upper secondary education and training remained so substantial that any general claim of an unquestionable superiority of a single model in those respects is likely to be challenged.

5. Substantive and organisational links between education and employment

Alternating learning at school and at work: apprenticeship systems

In the "golden age" of educational expansion and reform, as some experts retrospectively characterise the 1960s and early 1970s, vocational education tended to be taken into consideration only as far as it was linked to general education in upper secondary and higher education. Systems of vocational training which were primarily work-based and only supplemented by vocational schooling, were often viewed as coming to an end, for they seemed to be closely linked to traditional occupations bound to shrink. Moreover, demands of the occupation system seemed to call less and less for induction into specific operations and more and more for abilities to master "conceptual, planning, supervisory and monitoring functions" (Lutz,

1994, p. 19). Consequently, the German education system was strongly criticised as backward in the only OECD review of the national educational policy of the Federal Republic of Germany in the early 1970s notably due to its track structure in secondary education, limited links between vocational and secondary education, lack of permeability and slow expansion of academic secondary and higher education.

When the focus of debate shifted to a considerable extent towards the employment value of education after 1973, the system of education and training in the Federal Republic of Germany and some of its neighbours – notably Austria and Switzerland and in some respects the Netherlands (OECD, 1994e) – were viewed very favourably because the rates of youth employment more or less matched those of the unemployment in the overall labour force. Most other OECD Member countries experienced over-proportionate youth unemployment. The question was on the agenda, whether the German system could serve as a model for other countries. "Within a few years (1975-1980), the education systems of the German-speaking countries which had up to then been perceived to be archaic and socially unjust, suddenly found themselves taken as 'models' as far as the vocational training was concerned. Since then, numerous studies and visits by foreign delegations to these countries have confirmed and reinforced this positive image, at the risk of sometimes over-simplifying and glorifying a reality which is both complex and changing" (Durand-Drouhin and Romani, 1994, p. 10).

In characterising the German system of education and training (cf. the overviews in OECD, 1994e; Koch and Reuling, 1994; Stratmann and Schlösser, 1990), it is often pointed out that the countries with the strongest emphasis on vocational training of youth have preserved a track system of lower secondary education. In most German *Länder*, the pupils are allocated after four years of schooling to three different types of secondary schools: the Gymnasium comprising nine years is viewed as preparatory to university education, the *Realschule*, comprising six years, is considered to prepare for the more demanding levels of training and to intermediate-level occupations and the *Hauptschule* leading within four years either to early entry into the labour force or the skilled labour apprenticeships. However, there are no formal entry requirements to most sectors of the apprenticeship system.

The training capacities are determined by the individual companies which hire the apprentices, employ them on a special apprentice status, and provide financial support for living expenses which, as a rule, is higher than the maximum need-based public scholarship for university students. The apprentices learn and work during the period of two to 3.5 years mostly 3-4 days per week in the company – in large companies often for some period in training workshops but otherwise in a normal work setting. The remaining time is spent at a public vocational school the programmes of which are structured according to the different occupational areas for which the training prepares. Enrolment in vocational schools is mandatory during the whole training period, but also up to the age of 18 for youth transferring to regular employment.

Regulations about the training and certification (*Ausbildungsregelungen*) have to be established through a process of consultation and agreements between employers, unions and government. The regulations are set up for individual "training occupations" and have a strong occupational focus: apprentices should acquire a more or less standardised set of competencies and skills and should eventually be prepared to be occupationally mobile.

The responsibility for the work-based training rests with the individual company. Committees for vocational training and examinations at chambers of crafts, industry and commerce, with representatives of employers, unions and government agencies, have some supervisory functions on the basic conditions for work-based training and are in charge of undertaking the qualifying exams at the end of this "dual" process of learning and of awarding the vocational qualification.

Those having completed apprenticeship might upgrade their training at later stages. In some areas, special schools are established for training towards a "technician's" etc. level. Moreover, the skilled workers, craftsmen etc. might participate after some years of professional experience in training programmes for a *Meister* examination which in the area of crafts qualifies for heading a firm and for training future apprentices.

The system of vocational training in Germany, though preserving principles which developed around 1900 and having become quasi-mandatory in the 1930s, was by no means static. It was the topic of controversial debates and underwent various substantial changes (Lipsmeier, 1994; Liesering, Schober and Tessaring, 1994; cf. also various articles in Arnold and Lipsmeier, 1995; Euler, 1998). For example, the number of "training occupations" was reduced from about 900 after World War II to less than 400 in the 1990s. Various curricular regulations were elaborated requiring a sequence of training and learning in order to ensure a basic training from which subsequent steps of specialisation might depart. Various measures were established in guaranteeing a certain quality everywhere, for example through establishing minimum qualification requirements of the supervisors of the training within the company. On the other hand, the traditional divide between demanding training programmes (*Lehre*) and other somewhat less demanding programmes (*Anlernen*) was discontinued, and short (one-year) training programmes were established for persons not accommodated in the apprenticeship system. Reform proposals for the creation of stronger links with the upper secondary school system and thus for the increase permeability of the educational paths did not succeed as far as the mainstream of vocational training is concerned. But the critique of the apprenticeship system had the beneficial effect of triggering measures to improve the pedagogical basis and to reduce inequities of quality of the work-based learning conditions.

When in the mid-1970s concern grew about employment problems and demographic problems (rising number of youth cohorts at a time of stagnant training places), politicians, experts and stakeholders in the Federal Republic of Germany eventually agreed to preserve the basis features of the vocational training system. At the same time, the decision was taken to strive for an expansion of the dual system of vocational education beyond presumed demand. Ideally, everybody should be at least trained on a skilled-worker level, because vocational training was assumed not only to prepare well for the work assignment in the respective occupation but also to provide the typical competencies for employability and for coping with basic civilisatory requirements.

The system of vocational training in Germany often was praised in comparative assessments for the following features:

– It creates strong vocational competencies in the respective occupational areas and reinforces a professional pride in one's proficiencies as well as a professional identity in those occupations which are not a top of class and status structures.

– It successfully makes use of learning in and experience of real work settings without making youth too dependent of the peculiarities of the individual firms and employers.

– It increases employment opportunities for youth, among other things through its *de facto* character of provisional employment.

– It seems to contribute to a relatively close match of competencies and work assignments, even though about half of the young workers transfer to other occupations within a few years of regular employment.

– It is embedded in a setting of close co-operation of government, educational experts and representatives of the employment system, thus ensuring permanent processes of deliberation and negotiation in order to accommodate the various views and demands. This creates a high degree of consensus and stability on core elements of the system.

– It leads to a relatively high degree of standardisation of vocational skills.

The increased attention paid to the "dual" system, *i.e.* the predominantly work-based and additionally school-based training system, in the German-speaking countries had a substantial impact on the reform of education and training at upper secondary education in many European countries, but never was more or less completely "imported". Even though apprenticeship training was generally accepted as a successful measure to increase employability (Ryan, 1998), obviously, a substantial range of barriers, reservation and critique remained. Four major points are worth mentioning:

1. Doubts were widespread whether the German "model" of dual vocational training could be a promising means of enhancing employability in different educational, employment and societal contexts. A dual system might be less successful, if not embedded in a highly "occupationalised" labour market, in a tradition of employers sharing the costs of training as risk investments in the future based on the trust that others will do so as well, in certain consensus-creating political settings and in a mood favourable for standardisation of skills. Also, the employment conditions of apprentices – being provisional employees – were often viewed as more important for enhancing their employment opportunities than the vocational training and learning as such.

2. The provision of training places in the German-speaking countries is at the mercy of the employers. Just at times, when unemployment grows, the number of training places tends to decline.

3. The vocational training system in the German-speaking countries is often viewed as too specialised and placing too much emphasis on the operational skills. In the majority of the other European countries, a stronger need is widely felt for enhancing general competencies, to train socio-communicative skills and to prepare for life-long learning. It is obvious, though, that opinions widely diverge among politicians, experts and practitioners, within as well as between countries, as to whether predominantly vocational training is bound to be "narrow" or whether it is in the position to contribute to broad and transferable skills and personality development in a similar way as general education is expected to do.

4. The critique continued that a system with little emphasis on permeability and mobility does not only fail, as other systems do, in striving for a parity of esteem between various types of education and training provisions as well as occupations (Parkes, 1993), but also precludes talented youth from opportunities of personality enhancement and social mobility.

Controversial debates could be observed in the German-speaking countries as well. One might argue that in the long run, however, the system was viewed as relatively flexible to change training programmes in the face of changing job requirements and to incorporate more elements of flexible learning. On the other hand, concern grew in Germany in the 1990s as regards the employers' readiness to provide training places. Also, the pattern of unemployment changed substantially during the 1990s. The unemployment rates of the unskilled increased from 13% in 1991 to 24% in 1997 and that for vocationally trained persons from 4 to 7% whereas the unemployment rates for those having completed advanced levels of vocational training, *Fachhochschulen* and universities remained more or less constant in the range of 3 to 5% (Reinberg and Rauch, 1998, p. 3).

The divide between schooling and in-company training

In the 1980s, the relationships between education and the world of work in Japan (cf. the overviews in Dore and Sako, 1989; Lequerc, 1989; Georg and Sattel, 1992; Münch and Eswein, 1992; Demes and Georg, 1994; Yoshimoto, 1996; Takanashi and Teichler, 1998) became very popular in international debates. It was not only obvious that the youth unemployment rate in Japan, as in the German-speaking countries, did not substantially differ from that of the overall unemployment rate in the labour force, but also that the youth unemployment rate, as well as the overall unemployment rate in Japan were clearly lower than in Europe and the United States. In addition, economic growth was by far more impressive in Japan during the 1980s, substantial technological innovation seemed to take place in industry, and interesting human resource and personnel policies in Japan challenged the traditions in the West. Moreover, Japan was the only major industrial society in which the transition processes from education to employment were, as a rule, very smooth across all levels of educational attainment. Last not least, the results of comparative studies on school achievement (Husén, 1991) along rumours of a low quality of higher education in Japan (cf. the summary in Teichler, 1997) contributed to the view that high general competencies of the intermediate-level work force might be the key to economic progress in Japan.

After nine years of schooling, about 95% of youth in Japan continue study in upper secondary education: among them more than 70% in general programmes and the others in vocational programmes which also comprise large proportions of general school subjects. In the mid-1970s, the proportion of the age-group enrolling at universities or two-year junior colleges was about 35%; this ratio increased since the late 1980s to almost 50% in the late 1990s. In addition, almost 20% enrol at post-secondary vocational schools and programmes (*senshû gakkô*) lasting up to three years. Thus, in the late 1990s, about one quarter of young persons employed for the first time are university graduates and more than one quarter graduates from non-university tertiary education. Only about one quarter transfers to employment after completion of upper secondary education.

Japanese schools as well as private institutions of higher education co-operate closely with employers in order to ensure that most upper secondary students and students at institutions of higher education know several months in advance where they will be employed (Yoshimoto, 1996; Teicher and Teichler, 1997). In the case of upper secondary education, firms largely base their recruitment decisions on the recommendations made by the schools (Kariya, 1991). These practices obviously reinforce the prestige hierarchy of schools and institutions of higher education.

The majority of school leavers and graduates from institutions of higher education seem to be hired as "raw material" eventually trained in the company according to the presumed needs and the prevailing human resource philosophy. The in-company training of upper secondary school graduates might vary from two to three years of apprenticeship-like training to merely occasional on-the-job training. On average, little emphasis is placed on formal off-the-job training (Umetani, 1980; Muta, 1994). Even if work assignments change little in the course of the career, the ideal is held in high esteem of the flexible company employee who identifies himself or herself with the firm and not with a profession and who is ready to change work assignments regularly or at any time where the need arises. It would be misleading, though, to assume that training within the company predominantly serves merely the preparation of immediate job assignment. Metzler (1999) came to the conclusion that initial in-company training in Japan rather can be characterised as provisional (*vorläufige Qualifizierung*). Yano (1997, p. 212) argues that Japanese firms are inclined to invest substantially into education because employees are likely not to change the company and because competencies are not understood in Japan as an individual asset, but rather "jointly held" by the company and the individual "through human relationships among members of the company".

The arrangements of education and training in Japan were widely praised internationally during the 1980s (Jallade, 1989). Japan seemed to be most successful in:

– Making the workforce flexible for change of assignments, innovation and constant learning on the job, thus serving well the needs of a changing economy more and more relying on flexible skills, while ensuring as well a good preparation for immediate work assignments.

– Facilitating a smooth transition from education to employment and contributing to low rates of youth unemployment.

– Reinforcing the impression that strong successful efforts in upper secondary education resulting in admission to higher education will be rewarded. This ensured a highly competent worforce.

In the 1980s, the relationships between education and employment in Japan seemed to be more unanimously admired in the international debates than within Japan, where certain features had remained controversial. The international admiration of the social context of the Japanese economy also seems to have declined since the economic recession starting in 1991. In Japan, many features of the employment system and of the relationships between education and employment seem to be undergoing rapid changes in the 1990s. Among others, the proportion of young persons not continuing education who do not transfer immediately from education to employment increased from almost 10% around 1990 to almost 20% in 1997.

The following critical arguments of the pattern prevailing in the 1980s in Japan are widely spread:

– Competition for success in pre-career education is by and large a self-serving process (Takeuchi, 1997) with various detrimental consequences like discouragement of individuality and creativity (National Council of Educational Reform, 1987).

– The development of vocational skills and the chances for in-career learning are very much left to the mercy of the individual company. The chances are limited to counteract individually the status one is assigned to at entry into the labour force. Also, career chances of women continue to be more restrained than in other industrialised societies (Weber, 1998).

– The strong company-orientation in occupational guidance, information and hiring practices as well as reinforcement of company loyalty create a substantial frustration notably among the young employees. Surveys undertaken in the early 1990s show that the Japanese workforce is on average less satisfied with its work than that of other industrial societies (Ministry of Labour, 1994, pp. 50-52). Also, in spite of the mechanisms of reinforcing company loyalty and lifelong employment, mobility during the first few years of employment in Japan has reached the level of most European countries (Teicher, 1995).

– The various measures ensuring a process of smooth transition from education to employment turned out to function well under smooth labour market conditions. However, when unemployment problems grew, those not fairing well in the dominant system faced more serious problems than youth in other countries where more individual initiative is expected from youth in that process and where public employment agencies play a stronger role (cf. various contributions in Takanashi and Teichler, 1998). Also, employers, when turning away from the ideal of life-long employment, were less inclined than in the past to keep the traditional modes of recruitment.

– Finally, the ideals of the skills required modified during the 1990s. Partly due to a change of perceived job requirements and partly as a consequence of the declining ideal of life-long employment, specialised training and specialists' careers are now held more in esteem than in the past. Currently, though, Japan does not seem to shift towards a "skilled labour" and an "occupationalised" system, specialised training and specialists' careers are now viewed as an important secondary pattern alongside the still dominant traditional pattern (Nihon Keieisha Dantai Renmei, 1995).

The Japanese "model" of the relationships between education and employment certainly had a lasting impact on the debates in Europe in reinforcing the view that a reinforcement of flexible competencies is compatible with a preparation of the workforce to function well as far as the immediate job tasks are concerned. Doubts, however, remained widespread whether the bulk of the basic preparation for the world of work should be largely left to the individual companies and work settings.

Beyond the varied model: the search for common approaches

Various efforts have been undertaken to assess the strengths and weaknesses of various educational systems. Chart 1, for example, shows the assessment of the vocational training system in five OECD Member countries. In the 1990s, however, we note less of a common belief in the strength of a certain "model" in the relationships between education and employment. This does not mean, however, that issue has lost momentum and that faith in the value of learning from international comparison has substantially eroded (Georg, 1997). For example, we note that both the OECD and the European Commission undertook various activities in the 1990s to sort out the experiences of different countries and to recommend some common approaches. It is obvious, though, that reflections and recommendations published by these two supra-national bodies do not aim to identify the best model. Rather, they try to explore some commonly appreciated components of education and training, *i.e.* common among or somewhere between the extremes of a large, highly standardised, predominantly work-based training system clearly separated from academic secondary education and preparing for an "occupationalised" labour market on the one hand and on the other hand a predominantly general upper secondary system leaving occupational preparation largely to the diverse employers and work settings.

This search for some common ground certainly reflects a disillusion in the previous search for major solutions. For the experiences and analyses of the late 1970s and of the 1980s had shown that the various national options are often rooted in specific contexts and that the structures, the content and the modes of education and training are embedded in a broad range of factors shaping youth employment and the productive utilisation of knowledge. More importantly, it is almost impossible to identify clearly the major factor contributing to success and failures in individual countries. Is the low unemployment of German youth due to work-based learning or is it more a question of the provisional employment of apprentices and thus on the screening system? Or do young Japanese meet favourable employment conditions primarily due to high general competencies or low wages or the provisional character of in-company training which reinforces the need for lifelong learning? Moreover, unemployment grew in many OECD Member countries during the 1990s. Finally, faith had decreased in the virtue and strength of governmental planning and steering on national level.

The European Commission's White Paper on "Growth, Competitiveness and Employment" (1993) advocated moving from a "once-and-for-all" full-time education and training system to a more open one as a response to an increasingly more knowledge-based economy. Co-operation between the education and employment systems should be improved in order to ensure a greater responsiveness and flexibility of education and training to the changing economic and employment needs. On the subsequent summit in Essen in December 1994, suggestions were made to promote investment in vocational training, to increase the flexibility of the labour, to encourage decentralised activities for job creation, to reduce labour costs and wage increase, and to switch further to active public employment policies (Hannan and Werquin, 1998).

In the White Paper "Teaching and Learning: Towards the Learning Society", the European Commission (1995) suggested that "in the EU Member countries:

- A broad knowledge bases and training for employment are no longer contradictory or separate things.

- There is increasing recognition of the importance of general knowledge in using vocational skills.

- Bridges are being built between schools and business sectors.

- These show that the ideological and cultural barriers which separated education and enterprises are breaking down, benefiting both.

- In lie with the traditions of the Member States, this co-operation is reflected in initial and continuing training.

- The principle of equal rights in education is being applied increasingly in the context of equality of opportunity.

- The drawing of the information society, which initially caused misgivings within the teaching profession, has now revealed new demands for education and training and has started to renew teaching approaches." (summarised by Parkes, 1993, p. 235).

The OECD report *Vocational Education and Training for Youth: Towards Coherent Policy and Practice* (McFarland and Vickers 1994) argued that vocational and technical education (VOTEC) was frequently ill-equipped to meet national demands for higher level skills in response to heightened international competition. In the eyes of many parents and students it remained a rigid, low-level track in which participation was falling in many countries. The report focused upon three key strategies to address the problem:

– Improved links between VOTEC and other sectors of education, in order to ensure that pathways and choices for young people are kept open as long as possible and VOTEC ceases to be a dead-end.

– Better relationships between theory and practice, between the classroom and the workplace, both to ensure that the relevance of classroom learning is heightened and to ensure that changes in technology and work organisation can be integrated into programmes quickly.

– Better co-ordination across different sectors and levels of education, and improved working relationships between education and the social partners.

The OECD *Jobs Study* concurrently undertaken led to different recommendations for individual countries with respect to the various areas of education. The joint rationale as regards vocational education and training, however, was, as already reported, to:

– expand and improve;

– standardise qualifications;

– strengthen links with business;

– improve integration with academic education (OECD, 1997*b*).

Finally, the OECD study on the *Transition from Initial Education to Working Life* (OECD, 1998*f*) underscored that economic restructuring and technological changes had contributed, in all countries analysed, to the blurring of occupational profiles. Also, a need was felt to provide youth with the skills, knowledge and attitudes to cope with unpredictable labour market changes throughout their working life. This was viewed to imply broad-based and qualifying initial and training along "the existence of genuine systems of lifelong learning". Finally, a need was felt to "introduce truly integrated forms of practical and theoretical learning on a large scale". A consensus was observed that work-based learning should be provided for everybody in combination with classroom learning.

In summarising the various comments and recommendations and in also considering national policies (Lipsmeier and Münk, 1994; CEREQ and OECD, 1994; Bertrand *et al.*, 1994; OECD, 1994*a*), we might identify the following major trends in education and training policies at upper secondary level in Europe during the 1990s:

– The belief in the pedagogical virtue of work-based learning has substantially grown. In a working setting, youth seem to be more motivated to learn, get accustomed to the typical conditions and ways of problem-solving of future work and combine cognitive and sensu-motoric learning with the acquisition of socio-communicative competencies and with the understanding of norms and values relevant to employment and work (Bertrand *et al.*, 1994, pp. 50-61; Koch, 1994; Bundesinstitut für Berufsbildung, 1998).

– Many activities were undertaken to counteract the divide between vocational and general or "academic" education on the upper secondary level. They might strive for:

  • a change of the programmes and educational career path, for example the establishment programmes leading towards a "double qualification" of preparation of entry to higher education and vocational qualification;

- a growing permeability between the programmes;

- competencies neither viewed as general nor as vocational in the traditional sense, for example "key qualifications" – a popular term for basic skills to prepare people for societal tasks, core skills for most or all occupations, specific but transferable skills or hybrid skills, based on a combination between skills usually needed for distinct occupations, a stronger emphasis on socio-communicative competencies and personality enhancement, etc. (Nijhof and Streumer, 1998).

It should be noted, though, that upper secondary education in many European countries moved towards a strengthening of a broad and general emphasis (Kallen, 1997). The uncertainty of predicting future employment, the dynamic change of work tasks, the growing need for life-long learning and the expansion of post-secondary education seem to favour such an approach.

– As the importance of life-long learning was more strongly advocated than ever before, for example in reports published or commissioned by major international organisations (Delors *et al.*, 1996; European Commission, 1995; OECD, 1996*b*), upper secondary education is expected to change in terms of envisaging less to prepare in a targeted way for a long period in life and more to lay the foundation for subsequent learning. It is often stated, however, that this remained a claim in the 1990s, while the actual processes of initial education have not changed substantially.

– In order to measure the efficiency of education, often the introduction of new means or the extensions of existing ones of assessing skills are advocated or actually implemented. For example, we note:

- a continuation of comparative studies on school achievement;

- the development of measurements of manual skill precision;.

- the international comparison of different levels or literacy (OECD and Statistics Canada, 1997);

- the introduction of measures of assessing basic vocational skills.

Overall, however, we find that assessment of competencies with the help of testing or other measurement not integrated into the processes of examinations closely linked to the regular processes of learning and feedback are most strongly advocated in countries characterised by lack of standardisation, or little emphasis on specific vocational training.

In most continental European countries, the introduction of new means of testing and assessment is less strongly advocated than for example in Australia, the United Kingdom or the United States. On the other hand, we observe efforts to improve the system of certification of occupational qualifications (OECD, 1996*a*). Among other things, systems of certification are sought, which facilitate the recognition of modular learning and the recognition of the qualification of persons who are mobile within Europe. It should be noted, though, that a need is widely felt to strike a balance between standardisation of training and flexibility in response to technological rationality or economic change (cf. the comparative study by Standaert, 1993).

– The expansion of upper secondary education and other phenomena of a move towards a "middle-class society" have led in many countries to more visible signs of a social demarcation between the middle class and less favoured persons or between those being trained beyond lower secondary education and those only completing secondary education and less. The term "social exclusion" became widely accepted to depict the inherent dangers.

In most industrial societies, "over-education" is thought desirable to prevent social exclusion. Efforts are made to prevent an early exit from initial education even if advanced schooling and training will not lead in more or less all cases to jobs requiring at least skilled worker qualification. During the last two decades, however, awareness grew that measures to integrate the majority of youth into the mainstream of education, training and subsequent employment and work are not necessarily the most suitable ones for youth at risk. Rather, specific measures, possibly starting at a much earlier age might be needed for the latter, even though any specific measures run the risk of stigmatising those addressed.

Changes in tertiary education

In the 1990s, the debate about the extent to which tertiary education should take into consideration its potential for "utility on the market place" or focus on the "advancement of knowledge" (OECD, 1998*e*) certainly did not emerge newly, as a view on the debates and policies from the 1960s to the 1980s shows (Teichler, 1996), but certainly intensified. We note warnings of a "business valuing in academia" (Lutz and Field, 1998) on the one hand and on the other, efforts to establish close ties between higher education and industry (cf. the overview in Kirkland, 1992). Some hope that a stronger entrepreneurial spirit might strike a balance between responsiveness to society and pursuit of knowledge for its own sake (Clark, 1998).

The changing conditions to which higher education is being exposed and the efforts to reorganise the connections between higher education and the world of work are best illustrated by contrasting them with the traditional self-concept of the university. According to Husén (1994, p. 13), the "Western university", which served as a model throughout the world, "has been characterised by the following:

– It made a more or less sharp distinction between theory and practice.

– It has put a premium on autonomy and aloofness to the extent of complete irrelevance.

– It has been both socially and intellectually an élite institution.

– It has tried to be an 'ivory tower', as an institution whose main purpose is to 'seek the truth'."

Even if this characterisation plays down the strong professional emphasis in some fields and even if academic emphasis and professional preparation for the public or publicly supervised sectors of the employment system have not been understood as contradictions in the past, experts agree in observing a growing pressure on higher education during the last two decades to provide evidence of its relevance for the world of work. As already has been pointed out above, some European countries kept or even introduced newly two-type or multi-type structures, thus underscoring the applied nature of teaching and learning in separate sectors, whereas others blurred the distinctions, abolished a divide according to the type or never had embarked on it. This observation suggests to refrain from sweeping generalising statements as far as the impact of the growing pressures for professional relevance on tertiary education is concerned.

It might be justified, though, to state five major changes in the relationships between higher education and employment in Europe in the 1980s and 1990s:

1. We note a move towards the establishment and extension of systematic processes of evaluation in higher education. This, among other things, leads to increased information on graduate employment and work and makes the actors in the higher education system more aware of the relevance of such a feedback (Brennan *et al.*, 1995) – whatever conclusions they might draw on that basis.

2. The variety of trends as regards patterns of institutions and programmes notwithstanding, diversity among institutions and programmes seems to grow both within individual sectors and the higher education system in general. In this context, many institutions and departments seek to promote their specific profile through strengthening the employment and work relevance of study.

3. More emphasis is placed on learning processes which allow the students to anticipate the world of work and the confrontation between academic knowledge and problem-solving on the job (Teichler, 1996, pp. 89-104). Internships, other short phases of work experiences and problem-based learning seem to gain popularity in Europe (Boezeroy et al., 1998) and are obviously a major issue in many parts of the world as well (Lynton and Elman, 1987; Rao and Wright, 1991). Besides, the number of students in higher education in many European countries who spend a substantial part of their time on part-time employment – in order to cover their living expenditures, gain work experience and establish contacts which might facilitate the process of transition from study to employment – seems to be growing.

4. As already stated, an increasing number of institutions of higher education establish and extend contacts with representatives of the world of work.

5. Tertiary education institutions, programmes and career paths, which are not considered in the respective European countries as part of "higher education" seem to have grown. They might be conceived as being advanced stages of vocational education for those having completed initial vocational training or vocational training programmes, notably for graduates from general upper secondary schools not as academically demanding as those at universities and applied higher education institutions such as *Fachhochschulen* and *Hogescholen* which had moved close to universities. It is still premature to assess whether this is likely to be a sector or institutional type of its own or just a transient phenomenon.

Altogether, the enormous expansion of post-secondary education suggests that many issues discussed in the past with respect to upper secondary education will be brought up in the future with respect to some sectors of tertiary education.

The paradigmatic shift in the mid-1970s meant to move the attention from the positive to the negative side of educational impacts, from the higher and intermediate to the lower levels of education, from full-time general schooling to any kind of education and training, from knowledge and skills to coping with the world of work. In this context, the belief declined in a convergence of education and its relationships to the world of work in industrialised societies.

6. Concluding observations

The employment crisis emerging in the market-oriented industrial society as of 1973 contributed to a substantial paradigmatic shift as regards the relevance of different sectors of and approaches to higher education. During the 1960s and early 1970s, the international discussion about the future developments of education and their contribution to societal change had paid attention to full-time schooling, academic and general approaches in secondary education and the expanding higher education system. Educational expansion was largely viewed as contributing to economic growth, the reduction of inequality of opportunity and personality enhancement. Since about the mid-1970s, the employment value of education has been more strongly emphasised, and work-based vocational training appeared as a valuable means to serve this goal.

The dominance of the apprenticeship system in the German-speaking countries, previously viewed as bound to be phased out, was widely admired in Europe – not the least because youth unemployment rates in these countries, in contrast to most other countries, does not surpass the overall unemployment rates. Reinforcement of professional identity and pride in professional work were viewed as impressive feature of a strong emphasis on work-based training combined with part-time vocational schooling.

The "German model" was not spread *in toto*. It seemed to be too closely embedded into an "occupationalised" labour market, specific traditions of employers' views and specific conditions of establishing consensus among the key actors. In addition, belief was widespread in many European countries that a strong emphasis of work-based vocational training might contradict the need to prepare for uncertainty, rapidly changing work tasks, new technologies and life-long learning. On the other hand, neither did we observe a strong inclination in Europe in the 1980s to copy the "Japanese model" of a relatively clear divide between a strong general approach of initial education and in-company training according to the prerogatives of the individual firm.

Rather, a policy gained momentum to spread enrolment in upper secondary education through a diversity of options of general upper secondary education, vocational schooling and predominantly work-based vocational training, reinforced by efforts to reduce the disparity of esteems of the various sectors and programmes. Moreover, the value of work-based learning became generally accepted – irrespective of the continuing divergence as far as beliefs in the personality-enhancing value of strongly general and strongly vocational approaches of education are concerned.

Altogether, changes in the relationships between education and employment and related policies have been relatively small in the last few decades, once the paradigmatic shift in the mid-1970s occurred. It is worth noting, though, that the policy arena experienced some changes: the notion of a cyclical crisis of the labour market was substituted for by that of a structural crisis. The belief in macro-structural policies faded, and more emphasis was placed on the institutional and individual actor as well as on competitiveness. In some countries, neo-liberal thoughts gained popularity thus reinforcing the view that widened income gaps and job security might help to mobilise youth. Finally, the growing sophistication of knowledge as regards the impacts of targeted social action led to a spread of more cautious views.

During the last two decades, enrolment in upper secondary increased from less than 60% to almost 80% on average in OECD Member countries, and enrolment in tertiary education grew from about 20% to approximately 50%. Substantial restructuring could be more often observed in tertiary education than in secondary education, where additions to previously existing structures prevailed.

During the last two decades, the relationships between educational attainment and type of education on the one hand, and on the other, unemployment, transition to employment and income did not change enough to call for a reconsideration of the prevailing paradigms. Available information suggests that a strong vocational approach in upper secondary education might be rewarded in some countries, but not in others. The findings caution against expecting employment miracles from educational measures. Still, they nourish the widespread belief in Europe that retention, learning and training in upper secondary serves the purpose of counteracting social exclusion. Available information finally also call for reconsideration of the frequent claim that vocational training is bound to limit the flexibility of the work-force. Instead, pedagogical options gained importance in Europe which try to combine the strengths of the seemingly contradicting general and vocational approaches, *e.g.* through the fostering of "key qualifications".

While claims lost momentum over the years that factors such as the employment problems, the rapid change of work tasks or new technologies favour certain types of upper secondary education, the character of upper secondary education might be most strongly changed in the future by the renewed rapid expansion of tertiary education. While the debates from the mid-1970s to the mid-1990s on the tasks and functions of upper secondary education had strongly focused on its "terminal" function, and many observations on the relationships between education and employment had disregarded the role higher education and graduate employment played, the "massification" of tertiary education might turn out to be the most powerful force for a paradigmatic shift in the near future. At present, steps towards such a shift are more clearly visible than those usually expected on the way towards a life-long learning society.

BIBLIOGRAPHY

ALPIN, C., SHACKLETON, J.R. and WALSH, S. (1998), "Over- and Under-education in the UK Graduate Labour Market", *Studies in Higher Education*, Vol. 23, No. 1, pp. 17-34.

ARNOLD, R. and LIPSMEIER, A. (eds.) (1995), *Handbuch der Berufsbildung*, Leske and Budrich, Opladen.

BÉDUWÉ, C. and GIRET, J.F. (1998), *Analyse comparative des modes d'intégration des jeunes aux marchés du travail européens*, Université des Sciences Sociales, LIRHE, Toulouse.

BERTRAND, O., DURAND-DROUHIN, M. and ROMANI, C. (1994), "Issues, Problems and Perspectives: Lessons from an International Debate", *Apprenticeship: Which Way Forward?*, CEREQ and OECD, Paris, pp. 41-88.

BOEZEROOY, P., KAISER, F., KLEMPERER, A. and DE LANGE, S. (1998), *Combining Learning and Working in Higher Education*, University of Twente, Centre for Higher Education Policy Studies, Enschede.

BOLI, J., RAMIREZ, F.O. and MEYER, J. (1985), "Explaining the Origins and Expansion of Mass Education", *Comparative Education Review*, Vol. 29, No. 2, pp. 145-170.

BOVIN, B. (ed.) (1995), "Education, Employment and Unemployment", *Education and Employment*, OECD, Paris, pp. 69-81.

BRAUNS, H., MÜLLER, W. and STEINMANN, S. (1997), *Educational Expansion and Returns to Education: A Comparative Study on Germany, France, the UK, and Hungary*, Mannheimer Zentrum für Europäische Sozialforschung, Mannheim.

BRENNAN, J., KOGAN, M. and TEICHLER, U. (eds.) (1995), *Higher Education and Work*, Kingsley, London.

BRENNAN, J.L., LYON, E.S., McGEEVOR, P.A. and MURRAY, K. (1993), *Students, Courses and Jobs*, Kingsley, London.

BUNDESINSTITUT FÜR BERUFSBILDUNG (ed.) (1998), *Lernen im Prozeß der Arbeit*, BIBB, Berlin and Bonn.

CEREQ and OECD (eds.) (1994), *Apprenticeship: Which Way Forward?*, OECD, Paris.

CLARK, B.R. (1998), *The Entrepreneurial University*, Pergamon, Oxford.

COLLINS, R. (1979), *The Credential Society: An Historical Sociology of Education and Stratification*, Academic Press, New York.

COMMISSION OF THE EUROPEAN COMMUNITIES (1993), *Growth, Competitiveness, Employment: The Challenges and Ways Forward into the 21st Century*, Office for Official Publications of the European Communities, Luxembourg.

DELORS, J. et al. (1996), *Learning: the Treasure Within*, UNESCO, Paris.

DEMES, H. and GEORG, W. (1994), "Bildung und Berufskarriere in Japan", in Demes, H. and Georg, W. (eds.), *Gelernte Karriere: Bildung und Berufsverlauf in Japan*, Iudicium, München, pp. 13-31.

DEPARTMENT OF EMPLOYMENT, EDUCATION AND TRAINING (1998), "Australia", *Pathways and Participation in Vocational and Technical Education and Training*, OECD, Paris, pp. 27-80.

DORE, R. and SAKO, M. (1989), *How the Japanese Learn to Work*, Routledge, London.

DURAND-DROUHIN, M. and ROMANI, C. (1994), "The Issues", *Apprenticeship: Which Way Forward?*, CEREQ and OECD, Paris, pp. 9-18.

DRONKERS, J. (1993), "The Precarious Balance between General and Vocational Education in the Netherlands", *European Journal of Education*, Vol. 28, No. 2, pp. 197-207.

EULER, D. (1998), *Modernisierung des dualen Systems: Problembereiche, Reformvorschläge, Konsens- und Dissenslinien, Materialien zur Bildungsplanung und zur Forschungsförderung No. 62*, Bund-Länder-Kommission für Bildungsplanung und Forschungsförderung, Bonn.

EUROPEAN COMMISSION (1995), *Teaching and Learning: Towards the Learning Society*, Office for Official Publications of the European Communities, Luxembourg.

EUROPEAN COMMISSION (1997), *Key Data on Education in the European Union,* Office for Official Publications of the European Communities, Luxembourg.

EUROPEAN COMMUNITY, DIRECTORATE GENERAL INFORMATION, COMMUNICATION AND CULTURE (1989), *The European Community and the Recognition of Diplomas,* Office for Official Publications of the European Communities, Luxembourg.

EUROSTAT (1997), *Youth in the European Union: From Education to Working Life,* Luxembourg.

EURYDICE and CEDEFOP (1993), *Structures of the Education and Initial Training Systems in the European Union,* Office for Official Publications of the European Communities, Luxembourg.

GENSBITTEL, M.-H. and MAINGUET, C. (1995), "La transition entre l'école et l'emploi", *Education and Employment,* OECD, Paris, pp. 55-67.

GEORG, W. (1997), "Zwischen Tradition und Moderne: Berufsbildung im internationalen Vergleich", in Arnold, R., Dobischat, R. and Ott, B. (eds.), *Weiterungen der Berufspädadogik,* Steiner, Stuttgart, pp. 153-166.

GEORG, W. and SATTEL, U. (eds.) (1992), *Von Japan lernen?,* Deutscher Studien Verlag, Weinheim.

GRAFF, M. (1996), "Zur Bedeutung der Bildung im Prozeß der wirtschaftlichen Entwicklung", *Kölner Zeitschrift für Soziologie und Sozialpsychologie,* Vol. 48, No. 2, pp. 274-295.

HANNAN, D.F. and WERQUIN, P. (1998), "Transitions from Education to Work", unpublished manuscript.

HENNESSEY, M.A., LAMPINEN, O., SCHRÖDER, Th., SEBKOVA, H., SETÉNYI, J. and TEICHLER, U. (1998), *Tertiary Professional and Vocational Education in Central and Eastern Europe,* European Training Foundation and Council of Europe, Torino and Strasbourg.

HUSÉN, T. (1991), "Japanese Education in a Comparative Perspective: A European View", *Education in Japan and in Europe in a Comparative Perspective,* International Association of University Presidents, Guadalajara, pp. 5-21.

HUSÉN, T. (1994), "The Idea of the University: Changing Roles, Current Crisis and Future Challenges", in Husén, T. (ed.), *The Role of the University: A Global Perspective,* United Nations University, Tokyo, pp. 7-31.

INTERNATIONAL LABOUR OFFICE (1996), *World Employment 1996/97,* Geneva.

JABLONSKA-SKINDER, H., TEICHLER, U. and LANZENDÖRFER, M. (1992), *Handbook of Higher Education Diplomas in Europe,* Saur, Munich.

JALLADE, J.P. (1989), "Recent Trends in Vocational Education and Training: An Overview", *European Journal of Education,* Vol. 24, No. 2, pp. 103-125.

JALLADE, J.P. (1991), "L'enseignement supérieur en Europe: vers une évaluation comparée des premiers cycles", *La Documentation Française,* Paris.

JOHNSON, R. (1987), "Transition from School to Work in Western Europe", in Twining, J., Nisbet, S. and Megarry, J. (eds.), *Vocational Education,* Kogan Page, London (World Year of Education 1987), pp. 30-40.

KALLEN, D. (1995), "Thirty Years of Secondary Education", *European Journal of Education,* Vol. 30, No. 4, pp. 457-466.

KALLEN, D. (1997), "Editorial", *European Journal of Education,* Vol. 32, No. 1, pp. 3-13.

KARIYA, T. (1991), *Gakkô shokugyô senbatsu no shakaigaku: Kôsotsu shûshoku no nihonteki mekanizumu,* Tokyo Daigaku Shuppankai, Tokyo.

KIRKLAND, J. (1992), "Co-operation between Higher Education and Industry in the European Community: An Overview", *European Journal of Education,* 1992, Vol. 27, No. 4, pp. 325-331.

KOCH, R. (1994), "Pedagogical Objectives and the Organisation of Alternating Learning at School at Work", *Apprenticeship: Which Way Forward?,* OECD and CEREQ, Paris, pp. 121-126.

KOCH, R. and REULING, J. (1994), "The Responsiveness and Regulation of Training Capacity and Quality", *Vocational Training in Germany: Modernisation and Responsiveness,* OECD, Paris, pp. 69-122.

KOUCKY, J. (1996), "Educational Reforms in Changing Societies: Central Europe in the Period of Transition", *European Journal of Education,* Vol. 31, No. 1, pp. 7-24.

KOTÁSEK, J. (1996), "Structure and Organisation of Secondary Education in Central and Eastern Europe", *European Journal of Education,* Vol. 31, No. 1, pp. 25-42.

LEQUERC, J.M. (1989), "The Japanese Model: School-Based Education and Firm-Based Vocational Training", *European Journal of Education*, Vol. 24, No. 2, 1989, pp. 183-190.

LEVIN, H. and RUMBERGER, R. (1988), *Education, Work and Employment: Present Issues and Future Challenges in Developed Countries*, UNESCO, IIEP, Paris.

LIESERING, S., SCHOBER, K. and TESSARING, M. (1994), *Die Zukunft der dualen Berufsausbildung*, BeitrAB No. 186, Institut für Arbeitsmarkt- und Berufsforschung der Bundesanstalt für Arbeit, Nürnberg.

LIPSMEIER, A. (1994), "The Historical Context of the Vocational Training System", *Vocational Training in Germany: Modernisation and Responsiveness*, OECD, Paris, pp. 11-26.

LIPSMEIER, A. and MÜNK, D. (1994), *Die Berufsausbildungspolitik der Gemeinschaft für die 90er Jahre: Analyse der Stellungnahmen der EU-Mitgliedsstaaten zum Memorandum der Kommission*, Studien zu Bildung und Wissenschaft No. 114, BMBW, Bonn.

LUTZ, B. (1981), "Education and Employment: Contrasting Evidence from France and the Federal Republic", *European Journal of Education*, Vol. 16, No. 1, pp. 73-86.

LUTZ, B. (1994), "The Difficult Rediscovery of 'Professionalism'", *Apprenticeship: Which Way Forward?*, OECD and CEREQ, Paris, pp. 19-28.

LUTZ, F.W. and FIELD, R.W. (1998), "Business Valuing in Academia: The American University as a Center for Profit or Inquire", *Higher Education*, Vol. 36, No. 4, pp. 383-419.

LYNTON, E.A. and ELMAN, S.E. (1987), *New Priorities for the Universities: Meeting Society's Needs for Applied Knowledge and Competent Individuals*, Jossey-Bass, San Francisco, CA.

MAURICE, M., SELLIER, F. and SILVESTRE, J.J. (1982), *Politique d'éducation et organisation industrielle en France et en Allemagne*, Presses Universitaires de France, Paris.

MCFARLAND, L. and VICKERS, M. (1994), "La réforme de l'enseignement technique et la formation professionnelle: contexte et enjeux", *La formation professionnelle des jeunes: pour des politiques et des pratiques cohérentes*, OECD, Paris, pp. 7-19.

MEEK, V.L., GOEDEGEBUURE, L., KIVINEN, O. and RINNE, R. (1996), *The Mockers and Mocked: Comparative Perspectives on Differentiation, Convergence and Diversity in Higher Education*, Pergamon Press, Oxford.

METZLER, M. (1999), *Die vorläufige Qualifizierung: Betriebliche Erstqualifizierung von Hochschulabsolventen in Japanischen Großunternehmen*, Leske and Budrich, Opladen.

MINISTRY OF LABOUR (1994), *White Paper on Labour 1994*, Japan Institute of Labour, Tokyo.

MÜNCH, J. and ESWEIN, M. (1992), *Bildung, Qualifikation und Arbeit in Japan: Mythos und Wirklichkeit*, E. Schmidt, Berlin.

MÜLLER, W. and SHAVIT, Y. (1998), "Bildung und Beruf im institutionellen Kontext", *Zeitschrift für Erziehungswissenschaft*, Vol. 1, No. 4, pp. 501-533.

MUTA, H. (1994), "Zur Situation und Problematik betrieblicher Erstbildung in Japan", in Demes, H. and Georg, W. (eds.), *Gelernte Karriere: Bildung und Berufsverlauf in Japan*, Iudicium, Munich, pp. 191-215.

NATIONAL COUCIL ON EDUCATIONAL REFORM (1987), *Report on Educational Reforms*, Government of Japan, Tokyo.

NEAVE, G. (1984), *The EEC and Education*, Trentham, Stoke-on-Trent.

NIHON KEIEISHA DANTAI RENMEI (1995), *Shinjidai no "nihonteki keiei" – chôsen subeki hôkô to sono gutaisaku*, Tokyo.

NIJHOF, W.J. and STREUMER, J.N. (eds.) (1998), *Key Qualifications in Work and Education*, Kluwer, Dordrecht.

OE, A. (1994), "Arbeitsvermittlung durch Bildungsinstitutionen", in Demes, H. and Georg, W., *Gelernte Karriere: Bildung und Berufsverlauf in Japan*, Iudicium, Munich, pp. 93-122.

OECD (1973), *Short-Cycle Higher Education: A Search for Identity*, Paris.

OECD (1975), *Education, Inequality and Life Chances*, 2 vols., Paris.

OECD (1977), *Entry of Young People into Working Life*, Paris.

OECD (1990), *Education in OECD Countries 1987-88 – A Compendium of Statistical Information*, Paris.

OECD (1992), *From Higher Education to Employment*, 4 vols., Paris.

OECD (1993), *Education in OECD Countries 1988–90 – A Compendium of Statistical Information*, Paris.

OECD (1994a), *Vocational Education and Training for Youth – Towards Coherent Policy and Practice*, Paris.

OECD (1994b), *The OECD Jobs Study: Evidence and Explanations. Part I: Labour Market Trends and Underlying Forces of Change*, Paris.

OECD (1994c), *The OECD Jobs Study: Evidence and Explanations. Part II: The Adjustment Potential of the Labour Market*, Paris.

OECD (1994d), *Vocational Training in Germany: Modernisation and Responsiveness*, Paris.

OECD (1994e), *Vocational Training in the Netherlands: Reform and Innovation*, Paris.

OECD (1995), *Education and Employment*, Paris.

OECD (1996a), *Assessing and Certifying Occupational Skills*, Paris.

OECD (1996b), *Lifelong Learning for All*, Paris.

OECD (1996c), "The Transition from Initial Education to Working Life. Thematic Review: Scope, Purposes, Analytical Framework and Procedures", DEELSA/ED(96)14, Paris, mimeo.

OECD (1997a), *Education at a Glance: OECD Indicators 1997*, Paris.

OECD (1997b), *Implementing the OECD Jobs Strategy: Lessons from Member Countries' Experience*, Paris.

OECD (1997c), "The Transition from Initial Education to Working Life. Country Note: Australia", Paris, mimeo.

OECD (1997d), "The Transition from Initial Education to Working Life. Country Note: Norway", Paris, mimeo.

OECD (1998a), *Education at a Glance: OECD Indicators 1998*, Paris.

OECD (1998b), *Education Policy Analysis 1998*, Paris.

OECD (1998c), *Human Capital Investment: An International Comparison*, Paris.

OECD (1998d), *Pathways and Participation in Vocational and Technical Education and Training*, Paris.

OECD (1998e), *Redefining Tertiary Education*, Paris.

OECD (1998f), "Thematic Review of the Transition from Initial Education to Working Life: Interim Comparative Report", DEELSA/ED(98)11, Paris, mimeo.

OECD and STATSTICS CANADA (1997), *Literacy Skills for the Knowledge Society – Further Results from the International Adult Literacy Survey*, Paris.

PAIR, C. (1998), "Synthesis of Country Reports", *Pathways and Participation in Vocational and Technical Education and Training*, OECD, Paris, pp. 9-26.

PAPADOPOULOS, G. (1994), *Education 1960-1990: The OECD Perspective*, OECD, Paris.

PARKES, D. (1993), "Editorial: Parity of Esteem for Vocational Education?", *European Journal of Education*, Vol. 28, No. 2, pp. 131-134.

POLE, N. (1995), "Gender Disparities in Labour Market Outcomes of Education", *Education and Employment*, OECD, Paris, pp. 111-123.

POSTLETHWAITE, N. (ed.) (1988), *The Encyclopaedia of Comparative Education and National Systems of Education*, Pergamon Press, Oxford.

PSACHAROPOULOS, G. (1987), *Economics of Education: Research and Studies*, Pergamon Press, Oxford.

PSACHAROPOULUS, G. (1993), "Returns to Investment in Education: A Cost-Benefit Analysis", *Policy Research Working Papers*, No. 1067, World Bank, Washington, DC.

RAIZEN, S.A. (1994), "Les études et le travail: bases de recherches", *La formation professionnelle des jeunes: pour des politiques et des pratiques cohérentes*, OECD, Paris, pp. 79-127.

RAO, T.V. and WRIGHT, C. (1991), "Entrepreneurial Skills Development Programmes in Fifteen Commonwealth Countries", Commonwealth Secretariat, London.

REINBERG, A. and RAUCH, A. (1998), *Bildung und Arbeitsmarkt: Der Trend zur höheren Qualifikation ist ungebrochen*, IAB Werkstattbericht No. 15, Institut für Arbeitsmarkt- und Berufsforschung der Bundesanstalt für Arbeit, Nürnberg.

RUMBERGER, R.W. (1981), *Over-education in the U.S. Labour Market*, Praeger, New York.

RUMBERGER, R.W. (1994), "Labour Market Outcomes as Indicators of Educational Performance", *Making Education Count: Developing and Using International Indicators*, OECD, Paris, pp. 265-286.

RYAN, P. (1998), "Is Apprenticeship Better? A Review of the Economic Evidence", *Journal of Vocational Education and Training*, Vol. 50, No. 2, pp. 289-325.

SCOTT, P. (1996), "Unified and Binary Systems of Higher Education", in Burgen, A. (ed.), *Goals and Purposes if Higher Education in the 21st Century*, Kingsley, London and Bristol, PA, pp. 37-54.

SHAVIT, Y. and BLOSSFELD, L. (1993), *Persistent Inequality: Changing Educational Attainment in Thirteen Countries*, Westview Press, Boulder, CO.

SCHETTKAT, R. (1996), "Das Beschäftigungsproblem der Industriegesellschaften", *Aus Politik und Zeitgeschichte*, No. B26, pp. 25-35.

SPENNER, Kenneth I. (1985), "The Upgrading and Downgrading of Occupations: Issues, Evidence, and Implications for Education", *Review of Educational Research*, Vol. 55, No. 2, pp. 125-154.

STANDAERT, R. (1993), "Technical Rationality in Education Management: A Survey Covering England, France and Germany", *European Journal of Education*, Vol. 28, No. 2, pp. 159-175.

STERN, S. and WAGNER, D.A. (eds.) (1999), *International Perspectives on the School-to-Work Transition*, Hampton Press, Cresskill, NJ.

STRATMANN, K. and SCHLÖSSER, M. (1990), *Das Duale System der Berufsbildung*, A.M. GAFB, Frankfurt.

SUDA, Z. (1980), *Occupational Satisfaction of Graduates under Conditions of "Over-qualification"*, European Centre for Work and Society, Maastricht.

TAKANASHI, A. and TEICHLER, U. (eds.) (1998), *Berufliche Kompetenzentwicklung im Bildungs- und Beschäftigungssystem in Japan und Deutschland*, Nomos, Baden-Baden.

TAKEUCHI, Y. (1997), "The Self-Activating Entrance Examination System – Its Hidden Agenda and Its Correspondence with the Japanese 'Salary Man'", *Higher Education*, Vol. 34, No. 2, pp. 183-198.

TEICHER, K. (1995), "Zwischenbetriebliche Mobilität in Japan im Kontextpersonalpolitischen Wandels", unpublished doctoral dissertation, Kassel.

TEICHER, K. and TEICHLER, U. (1997), "Der Übergang vom Bildungs- in das Beschäftigungssystem", *Bildung und Erziehung*, Vol. 50, No. 4, pp. 409-429.

TEICHLER, U. (1988a), *Changing Patterns of the Higher Education System*, Kingsley, London.

TEICHLER, U. (1988b), "Higher Education and Work in Europe", in Smart, J.C. (ed.), *Higher Education: Handbook of Theory and Research*, Vol. IV, Agathon, New York, pp. 109-182.

TEICHLER, U. (1992), "Occupational Structures and Higher Education", in Clark, B.R. and Neave, G.R. (eds.), *The Encyclopaedia of Higher Education*, Vol. 2, Pergamon Press, Oxford, pp. 975-992.

TEICHLER, U. (1996), *Higher Education and Graduate Employment: Select Findings from Previous Decades*, Wissenschaftliches Zentrum für Berufs- und Hochschulforschung der Universität Gesamthochschule Kassel, Werkstattberichte No. 52, Kassel.

TEICHLER, U. (1997), "Higher Education in Japan: A View from Outside", *Higher Education*, Vol. 34, No. 2, pp. 275-298.

TEICHLER, U. (1998a), "Higher Education and Employment in Europe", Bundesministerium für Wissenschaft und Verkehr, Vienna, mimeo.

TEICHLER, U. (1998b), "The Changing Roles if the University and Non-University Sectors in Higher Education", *European Review*, Vol. 6, No. 4, pp. 475-487.

TEICHLER, U. (1998c), *The Requirements of the World of Work*, ED-98/CONF.202.7.1, UNESCO, Paris

TEICHLER, U., HARTUNG, D. and NUTHMANN, R. (1980), *Higher Education and the Needs of Society*, NFER Publ., Windsor.

TESSARING, M. (1998), *Training for a Changing Europe: A Report on Current Vocational and Training Research in Europe*, CEDEFOP, Tessaloniki.

UMETANI, S. (1980), *Vocational Training in Japan*, Institut für Asienkunde, Hamburg.

UNESCO (1995), *Policy Paper for Change and Development in Higher Education*, Paris.

VANVUGHT, F. (1996), "Isomorphism in Higher Education? Towards a Theory of Differentiation and Diversity in Higher Education Systems", in Meek, V.L., Goedegebuure, L., Kivinen, O. and Rinne, R. (eds.), *The Mockers and Mocked: Comparative Perspectives on Differentiation, Convergence and Diversity in Higher Education*, Pergamon Press, Oxford, pp. 42-58.

WEBER, C. (1998), *Chancengleichheit auf Japanisch: Strukturen, Reformen und Perspektiven der Frauenerwerbsarbeit in Japan*, Leske and Budrich, Opladen.

WERQUIN, P., BREEN, P. and PLANAS, E. (1997), *Youth Transitions in Europe: Theories and Evidence*, CEREQ, Marseille.

WILLIAMS, G. (1985), "Graduate Employment and Vocationalism in Higher Education", *European Journal of Education*, Vol. 20, pp. 181-192.

YANO, M. (1997), "Higher Education and Employment", *Higher Education*, Vol. 34, No. 2, pp. 199-214.

YOSHIMOTO, K. (1996), "Transition from School to Work in Japan", Planning Meeting for the Thematic Review of The Transition from Initial Education to Working Life, OECD, Paris, mimeo.

Table 1. **Full-time enrolment rates of 17 year-olds, 1970**

Country	Enrolment rate
Austria (1969)	23.6
Belgium (1966)	47.0
Denmark	31.8
Finland (1967)	43.5
France	45.1
Germany (1969)	20.4
Greece (1969)	45.8
Ireland (1973)	44.2
Italy (1966)	27.4
Luxembourg	30.2
Netherlands	41.5
Norway	59.8
Portugal	22.0
Spain	22.8
Sweden (1972)	60.8
Switzerland	54.8
United Kingdom	26.2
Australia	37.2
Canada	77.2
Japan	74.8
United States	86.2

Source: OECD (1977), p. 18.

Table 2. **Trends in enrolment rates for 17 year-olds, 1975-90**

	Percentage of all 17 year-olds				
	1975	1980	1984	1986	1990
Canada	m	m	75.9	78.5	80.2
United States	m	m	87.7	89.0	80.0
Australia	m	m	m	49.8	91.9
Japan	83.9	92.6	m	90.5	90.4
New Zealand	38.4	41.3	m	54.4	56.9
Belgium	m	m	81.7	86.4	m
Denmark	44.6	75.5	m	75.4	78.2
France	m	m	75.3	79.7	85.6
Germany	90.7	98.4	96.4	100.0	95.8
Ireland	m	m	63.3	64.7	72.7
Netherlands	72.4	80.1	m	86.8	89.5
Portugal	35.5	m	39.2	m	m
Spain	m	m	48.8	53.1	62.8
United Kingdom	m	m	46.3	49.4	58.7
Finland	65.5	76.8	m	90.6	m
Norway	65.1	72.4	75.7	76.2	82.8
Sweden	55.4	m	m	86.0	84.7
Switzerland	77.9	86.0	82.8	83.4	85.9
Turkey	m	m	m	31.5	30.2

m = Data not available

Sources: OECD (1990, 1993, 1994c, p. 130).

Table 3. **Ratio of upper secondary graduates to population at typical age of graduation (times 100) by type of programme**

First educational programmes (1996)

	Total			General			Vocational and apprenticeship		
	M + W	Men	Women	M + W	Men	Women	M+W	Men	Women
Australia	m	m	m	m	m	m	m	m	m
Austria	86	88	84	15	13	18	71	76	66
Belgium (Fl. Community)	117	104	130	34	30	39	82	74	90
Canada	73	70	77	x	x	x	x	x	x
Czech Republic	83	81	85	11	9	14	71	72	70
Denmark	81	76	87	46	38	55	35	38	32
Finland	98	93	104	48	40	57	50	53	47
France	85	85	86	34	29	40	51	56	46
Germany	86	86	86	25	22	29	61	64	58
Greece	80	75	86	54	46	63	26	29	23
Hungary	86	m	m	25	18	33	59	m	m
Iceland	m	m	m	m	m	m	m	m	m
Ireland	79	75	83	77	72	82	2	2	2
Italy	79	76	82	19	16	22	59	59	59
Japan	99	96	102	73	69	76	26	27	26
Korea	91	91	91	54	57	50	37	33	41
Luxembourg	m	m	m	m	m	m	m	m	m
Mexico	26	m	m	22	m	m	4	m	m
Netherlands	81	m	m	33	m	m	48	m	m
New Zealand	93	86	99	63	59	67	30	27	33
Norway	117	133	101	49	43	56	68	90	45
Poland	94	m	m	25	m	m	69	m	m
Portugal	91	115	66	79	99	58	17	22	12
Spain	73	65	81	44	m	m	27	25	29
Sweden	81	80	82	27	21	34	54	59	48
Switzerland	81	86	76	20	18	23	61	68	53
Turkey	m	m	m	m	m	m	m	m	m
United Kingdom	m	m	m	m	m	m	m	m	m
United States	72	69	76	x	x	x	x	x	x
Country mean	**85**	**86**	**88**	**40**	**39**	**45**	**46**	**49**	**43**
WEI Participants									
Argentina	34	31	36	15	10	20	18	21	16
Brazil	34	21	47	x	x	x	x	x	x
Chile	49	45	54	28	24	32	21	21	22
China	37	43	30	14	16	11	23	27	19
India	m	m	m	m	m	m	m	m	m
Indonesia	30	32	27	19	20	18	11	12	9
Jordan	69	66	73	54	47	62	15	20	11
Malaysia	41	35	48	37	29	45	5	7	2
Paraguay	m	m	m	16	14	18	m	m	m
Philippines	63	61	65	63	61	65	a	a	a
Russian Federation	88	82	94	49	47	52	38	35	40
Thailand	46	44	48	32	29	35	14	14	14
Uruguay	m	m	m	m	m	m	14	13	14

WEI programme: World Education Indicators programme (OECD/UNESCO).

a = Data not applicable because the category does not apply.

m = Data not available.

x = Data included in another category/column of the table.

Brazil: Data refer to 1995. Russian Federation and Thailand: Data refer to 1997.

Sources: OECD Education Database. OECD (1998a, p. 172)

Table 4. **Ratios of tertiary education graduates in selected European OECD Member countries**

Country	1975[a]	1987[a]	1996[b]
Austria	3	7	9
Finland	24	30	38
Italy	9	8	11
Norway	52	54	75
Spain	8	16	30

a. Proportion of the age group obtaining a short non-university qualification and university education.
b. Net graduation rates of non-university tertiary programmes, short first university degree programmes and long first university degree programmes.
Sources: OECD (1990, pp. 81-83, 113); OECD (1998a, p. 195).

Table 5. **Percentage of the population that has attained a specific level of education, by age group, 1996**

	At least upper secondary education					At least university-level education				
	Age 25-64	Age 25-34	Age 35-44	Age 45-54	Age 55-64	Age 25-64	Age 25-34	Age 35-44	Age 45-54	Age 55-64
Australia	57	62	60	54	46	15	16	18	14	8
Austria	71	82	75	67	53	6	7	7	5	4
Belgium	53	70	58	47	31	11	14	11	10	6
Canada	76	85	81	73	56	17	20	18	17	11
Czech Republic	84	92	87	84	71	10	11	12	10	8
Denmark	66	74	70	65	50	15	16	17	16	11
Finland	67	83	76	60	40	12	13	13	12	7
France	60	74	64	56	38	10	12	10	10	5
Germany	81	86	85	81	71	13	13	16	14	9
Greece	44	66	52	36	22	12	16	14	11	6
Hungary	63	80	75	62	28	13	14	15	15	9
Ireland	50	66	54	38	30	11	14	11	9	6
Italy	38	52	46	31	17	8	8	11	8	5
Korea	61	88	63	41	25	19	30	18	11	7
Luxembourg	29	32	33	28	20	11	11	14	12	6
Netherlands	63	72	66	57	47	23	25	25	21	16
New Zealand	60	65	64	56	49	11	14	13	10	6
Norway	82	91	87	78	62	16	19	17	14	8
Poland	74	88	82	68	47	10	10	10	12	8
Portugal	20	32	24	15	9	7	11	9	6	4
Spain	30	50	34	20	11	13	19	15	10	6
Sweden	74	87	80	70	53	13	11	15	16	10
Switzerland	80	87	82	78	71	10	11	10	9	6
Turkey	17	23	19	14	7	6	7	7	7	3
United Kingdom	76	87	81	71	60	13	15	15	12	8
United States	86	87	88	86	77	26	26	26	28	20
Country mean	**60**	**72**	**65**	**55**	**42**	**13**	**15**	**14**	**12**	**8**
WEI Participants										
Argentina	27	36	29	21	15	5	5	6	4	3
Brazil	25	31	27	19	11	9	9	11	9	4
India	8	11	9	6	3	5	6	5	3	2
Indonesia	19	28	17	13	7	2	3	2	1	1
Malaysia	33	48	32	18	8	m	m	m	m	m
Paraguay	33	43	31	26	19	11	13	11	9	6
Thailand	13	19	14	7	4	6	9	7	3	1
Uruguay	27	36	30	22	14	10	14	12	8	5

WEI programme: World Education Indicators programme (OECD/UNESCO).
m = Data not available.
Poland: Year of reference 1995.
Turkey: Year of reference 1997.
Sources: OECD Education Database; OECD (1998a, p. 44).

Table 6. **Ratios of upper secondary graduates and net entry rates to tertiary education in European OECD Member countries, 1996**

| Country | Upper secondary graduates | | | Entry rates to tertiary education | | |
	General	Vocational apprenticeship	Total	Total	Non-university tertiary	University level
Austria	18	66	84	29	-	29
Denmark	46	35	81	45	10	35
Finland	48	50	98	67	22	47
Germany	25	61	86	27	-	27
Greece	54	26	80	31	13	18
Hungary	25	59	86	35	-	35
Ireland	77	2	79	53	24	29
Netherlands	33	48	81	34	-	34
Norway	49	68	117	55	29	26
Poland	25	69	94	65	17	48
Switzerland	20	61	81	46	30	16
Average	**36**	**50**	**86**	**44**	**13**	**31**

Source: OECD (1998*a*, pp. 172 and 183).

Table 7. **Distribution of enrolment in public and private upper secondary education by type of programme and percentage of upper secondary students enrolled in part-time programmes, 1996**

	Distribution of enrolment in upper secondary education by type of programme						Part-time enrolment as a percentage of total enrolment			
	Men + Women				Women		Students at the typical age		Students older than the typical age	
	General programmes	Vocational and technical programmes	of which school-based	of which combines school and work based	General programmes	Vocational and technical programmes	General programmes	Vocational and technical programmes	General programmes	Vocational and technical programmes
Australia	33	67	x	x	36	64	n	84	n	94
Austria	24	76	42	34	26	74	n	n	25	24
Belgium	32	68	65	3	35	65	a	4	a	74
Canada	m	m	m	m	m	m	m	m	m	m
Czech Republic	16	84	37	47	18	82	n	n	19	38
Denmark	47	53	5	48	53	47	n	n	n	n
Finland	48	52	47	5	50	50	m	m	m	m
France	46	54	43	11	52	48	n	n	n	n
Germany	24	76	24	52	28	72	n	1	n	1
Greece	68	32	32	n	74	26	2	7	6	9
Hungary	32	68	42	26	38	62	4	1	39	9
Iceland	57	31	26	4	75	25	m	m	m	m
Ireland	80	20	15	5	80	20	n	13	10	51
Italy	28	72	72	a	32	68	m	m	m	m
Japan	72	28	28	a	75	25	2	1	87	1
Korea	58	42	42	a	55	45	n	n	n	n
Luxembourg	35	65	50	15	39	61	n	n	n	n
Mexico	84	16	16	a	82	18	n	n	n	n
Netherlands	30	70	47	23	35	65	2	4	71	24
New Zealand	62	38	30	8	62	38	1	42	47	37
Norway	42	58	x	x	50	50	n	n	4	2
Poland	31	69	m	69	42	58	m	m	m	m
Portugal	74	26	26	a	77	23	m	m	m	m
Spain	61	39	37	2	62	38	m	m	m	m
Sweden	46	51	x	x	51	46	n	n	82	50
Switzerland	31	69	9	60	39	61	m	m	m	m
Turkey	m	m	m	m	m	m	m	m	m	m
United Kingdom	43	57	x	x	39	61	n	32	n	83
United States	m	m	m	m	m	m	m	m	m	m
Country mean	**46**	**53**	**35**	**19**	**50**	**50**	**1**	**10**	**20**	**26**
WEI participants										
Argentina	67	33	33	a	71	29	n	n	n	n
Chile	58	42	42	a	61	39	n	n	n	n
China	43	57	x	x	38	62	n	n	n	n
India	97	3	x	x	98	2	m	m	m	m
Indonesia	61	39	a	39	63	37	n	n	n	n
Jordan	77	23	15	8	85	15	n	n	n	n
Malaysia	78	22	22	a	84	16	n	n	n	n
Paraguay	91	9	9	a	92	8	n	n	n	n
Philippines	100	a	a	a	100	a	m	m	m	m
Russian Federation	57	43	43	a	63	37	n	n	n	n
Thailand	72	28	27	1	75	25	n	n	98	2
Uruguay	80	20	20	a	84	16	n	n	n	n

WEI programme: World Education Indicators programme (OECD/UNESCO).
a = Data not applicable because the category does not apply.
m = Data not available.
n = Magnitude is either negligible or zero.
x = Data included in another category/column of the table.

Russian Federation and Thailand: Data refers to 1997.
Sources: OECD Education Database; OECD (1998a, p. 169).

Table 8. **Distribution of graduates in selected European countries
according to national categories of degrees**

France (1994/95)	IUT	37 380
	STS	81 852
	Licence universitaire	126 831
	Maîtrise universitaire	80 903
	Grandes Écoles	41 335
	Teaching qualifications	24 279
	DEA-DESS à l'université	46 511
	Doctorat universitaire	8 963
Germany (1995)	Diplom (FH)	75 082
	Diplom, Magister, Staatsexamen (universität)	**105 703**
	Teaching qualifications	26 748
	Doktor	**22 387**
Italy (1995)	Diploma	7 511
	Laurea	**104 877**
Spain (1991)	Short courses	44 000
	Long courses	**74 000**
Finland (1995)	AMK (1997)	4 974
	University Bachelor	1 453
	University Master	9 819
	University Licentiate	**793**
	University Doctorate	**765**
Netherlands (1993/94)	Hbo	48 056
	University	24 789

Source: Unpublished data of the TSER Research Project "Higher Education and Graduate Employment in Europe".

Table 9. **Unemployment rates of youth by level of educational attainment, age and gender, 1996**

		Below upper secondary education			Upper secondary education			Non-university secondary education		University-level education	
		Age 15-19	Age 20-24	Age 25-29	Age 15-19	Age 20-24	Age 25-29	Age 20-24	Age 25-29	Age 20-24	Age 25-29
Australia	Men	24.3	23.4	13.4	16.6	9.1	6.6	8.9	7.9	8.9	4.2
	Women	20.8	15.1	10.4	16.5	11.5	7.8	7.8	3.9	5.2	4.2
Austria	Men	5.7	12.8	8.6	3.4	5.0	3.4	9.3	1.1	m	4.4
	Women	10.4	8.3	8.5	8.2	4.2	2.8	15.4	5.6	m	9.1
Belgium	Men	19.3	23.6	13.0	21.0	15.1	6.0	10.5	3.2	9.6	3.7
	Women	30.3	41.5	29.1	36.0	24.1	17.4	9.2	5.7	19.7	7.9
Canada	Men	24.7	25.7	20.2	16.0	13.7	12.5	11.6	9.6	10.1	4.9
	Women	20.3	23.4	23.6	15.8	11.6	10.8	11.4	8.0	8.3	6.5
Czech Republic	Men	17.6	13.9	17.6	11.0	3.6	1.9	x	x	4.0	0.9
	Women	27.4	10.7	18.2	12.1	3.2	5.6	x	x	11.4	1.4
Denmark	Men	2.0	12.1	14.9	4.4	6.6	5.6	11.2	5.5	6.1	6.2
	Women	2.8	18.7	24.3	5.8	7.4	9.4	11.0	6.4	7.4	6.3
Finland	Men	27.0	40.3	25.8	42.9	24.4	15.3	19.2	10.3	14.3	6.3
	Women	22.6	38.1	32.9	29.8	23.1	19.0	21.1	13.9	18.2	9.1
France	Men	20.8	33.6	21.1	18.0	18.1	12.1	13.7	10.7	11.7	11.5
	Women	32.5	42.1	32.4	44.7	30.0	18.4	23.0	9.6	23.1	17.3
Germany	Men	6.7	16.7	18.6	7.9	8.7	7.4	m	4.5	m	7.3
	Women	6.8	13.7	15.8	9.1	8.0	7.7	m	5.5	m	5.6
Greece	Men	23.0	13.6	8.2	40.5	22.2	9.9	33.7	14.4	33.8	19.2
	Women	45.8	32.8	26.7	61.5	40.1	24.1	42.2	23.9	43.4	24.4
Hungary	Men	46.8	25.0	20.5	25.1	13.1	8.7	x	x	4.3	2.7
	Women	33.4	16.6	21.4	24.0	9.8	12.5	x	x	2.7	5.3
Ireland	Men	29.4	28.9	24.7	17.6	14.1	8.5	8.6	6.0	8.4	5.1
	Women	37.5	34.5	24.5	21.8	12.0	7.3	8.2	4.4	5.1	4.7
Italy	Men	29.4	26.2	14.1	35.0	33.1	15.4	x	x	20.0	27.3
	Women	38.9	34.3	22.0	54.5	40.1	20.2	x	x	47.4	34.0
Korea	Men	10.0	9.1	3.5	8.3	7.3	3.6	x	x	13.5	5.2
	Women	9.6	3.2	1.7	5.9	3.9	1.9	x	x	6.2	2.1
Luxembourg	Men	10.4	11.1	6.0	m	9.6	5.5	x	x	m	1.2
	Women	20.6	7.7	5.7	m	1.6	n	x	x	m	n
Netherlands	Men	15.9	10.7	9.0	m	6.8	4.0	x	x	12.2	6.9
	Women	22.5	13.7	8.0	m	6.4	5.1	x	x	11.1	6.3
New Zealand	Men	19.7	14.4	m	14.2	7.5	3.1	m	m	m	2.1
	Women	14.0	15.4	m	8.7	7.8	4.1	12.9	m	m	2.6
Norway	Men	20.6	15.5	9.9	10.8	9.7	6.4	6.7	5.5	4.5	6.3
	Women	17.1	16.8	11.6	18.4	9.8	6.0	7.9	6.0	12.8	4.4
Poland	Men	24.8	27.0	21.8	47.8	25.3	11.3	16.7	7.7	27.3	7.7
	Women	43.8	42.0	34.3	54.2	28.5	19.2	27.7	9.2	11.1	7.1
Portugal	Men	13.2	12.5	8.2	28.8	19.6	7.9	28.6	18.0	17.9	9.8
	Women	21.7	15.8	10.3	43.9	21.2	9.8	13.2	4.5	29.8	8.4
Spain	Men	44.0	33.2	26.3	44.1	33.9	19.9	30.9	20.3	47.3	28.2
	Women	59.1	43.3	41.3	59.6	47.3	30.9	42.3	31.2	53.8	33.3
Sweden	Men	23.0	29.6	20.0	22.9	20.8	13.9	12.9	9.2	20.2	3.6
	Women	21.6	32.8	26.4	24.7	19.5	13.1	8.9	6.8	8.2	6.5
Switzerland	Men	(17.1)	m	m	m	(4.9)	(3.8)	m	m	m	m
	Women	(9.9)	m	(23.5)	m	(4.3)	7.1	m	m	m	m
Turkey	Men	10.1	11.2	6.4	27.0	22.7	8.9	x	x	28.9	9.6
	Women	6.4	6.7	7.4	44.1	34.4	20.7	x	x	29.3	11.9
United Kingdom	Men	34.1	32.7	23.6	16.9	14.3	10.5	10.9	2.7	14.0	6.1
	Women	26.4	19.2	17.8	12.8	8.3	8.3	4.7	3.0	8.5	3.4
United States	Men	23.9	16.8	15.7	12.4	11.2	7.6	4.5	3.9	6.8	4.1
	Women	18.2	23.5	17.3	10.2	7.7	6.6	5.9	0.6	4.3	1.6
Country mean	**Men**	**21.1**	**20.8**	**15.5**	**21.4**	**14.6**	**8.6**	**14.9**	**8.3**	**15.4**	**7.8**
	Women	**24.4**	**22.8**	**19.7**	**27.1**	**16.9**	**11.4**	**16.1**	**8.7**	**17.5**	**8.9**

United Kingdom: Data for 15-19 refer to 16-19 year-olds.
m = Data not available. x = Data included in another category/column of the table. ( ) Figures in brackets are subject to high sampling variability.
Sources: OECD Education Database; OECD (1998a, p. 257).

Table 10. **Ratios of earnings by educational qualification from the early 1970s to the early 1990s in selected European countries**
(1.00 = persons with lower secondary education)

Country	Years	Men				Women			
		General upper secondary	Vocational upper secondary	Short/ vocational higher education	University educ.	General upper secondary	Vocational upper secondary	Short/ vocational higher education	University education
Denmark	Early 1970s	-	-	-	-	-	-	-	-
	Late 1970s	-	-	-	-	-	-	-	-
	Early 1980s	1.14	1.15	1.20	1.58	1.10	1.08	1.27	1.46
	Mid/late 1980s	1.12	1.14	1.21	1.59	1.09	1.09	1.19	1.39
	Early 1990s	1.23	1.13	1.20	1.61	1.12	1.08	1.18	1.36
France	Early 1970s	2.05	1.25	2.21	3.85	1.86	1.32	2.14	3.11
	Late 1970s	1.77	1.22	1.72	4.23	1.58	1.26	1.81	3.20
	Early 1980s	-	-	-	-	-	-	-	-
	Mid/late 1980s	1.57	1.19	1.62	3.81	1.46	1.25	1.82	3.11
	Early 1990s	-	-	-	-	-	-	-	-
Netherlands	Early 1970s	-	-	-	-	-	-	-	-
	Late 1970s	-	-	-	-	-	-	-	-
	Early 1980s	1.26	1.17	1.46	1.96	1.10	1.16	1.47	2.20
	Mid/late 1980s	1.22	1.13	1.51	1.86	1.14	1.14	1.47	1.87
	Early 1990s	-	-	-	-	-	-	-	-
Sweden	Early 1970s	1.17	1.09	1.32	1.68	1.05	1.11	1.34	1.76
	Late 1970s	-	-	-	-	-	-	-	-
	Early 1980s	1.12	1.05	-	1.37	1.02	1.06	1.20	1.49
	Mid/late 1980s	1.20	1.12	1.40	1.57	1.01	1.10	1.20	1.36
	Early 1990s	1.14	1.16	1.37	1.55	.98	1.10	1.30	1.55
United Kingdom	Early 1970s	1.20	1.21	1.50	1.83	-	-	-	-
	Late 1970s	1.28	1.09	1.31	1.69	-	-	-	-
	Early 1980s	-	-	-	-	-	-	-	-
	Mid/late 1980s	1.27	1.13	1.47	1.87	-	-	-	-
	Early 1990s	1.33	1.14	1.56	2.04	-	-	-	-

Source: Adapted from OECD (1994c, pp. 160-161).

Chart 1. **Performance of national VET systems and the wage-labour nexus for intermediate qualifications in five countries**

	Germany	Japan	France	United Kingdom	United States
	Effectiveness of the national training systems				
Organisation and functioning of the school system	– Effectiveness of general school education – Effectiveness of higher technical training	– High degree of homogeneity in general school education – Weakness of technical school training	– Good level of general school education – Poor adaptation of technical training to companies' needs	– Low level of general education achieved by the majority of pupils – Almost complete lack of technical education	– Major participation in higher education but low level of the "forgotten half" – Low level in technical channels
Organisation and functioning of in-company training	– Effectiveness of apprenticeship system – Major commitment by companies to initial and continuing training	– Intensity of initial and continuing training in the company – Compensates for the weakness of technical education	– Weakness of apprenticeship. Continuing training does not balance out the gaps in technical training	– Major crisis in apprenticeship not compensated by the creation of YT programmes – Weakness of continuing training	– Very low development of apprenticeship – Low investment by companies in continuing training
Funding of training	– Funds allocated to vocational training by the federal State, Länder and companies	– Weakness of public funding – Compensated by the contribution from companies and households	– Considerable public financing of general and technical schools	– Public financing of education and YT programmes – Reduction of funds since 1980	– Low volume of funds allocated to primary and secondary education – Large volume of funds allocated to higher education
Degree of institutionalisation of training	– High degree of institutionalisation and codification of qualifications	– Low degree of institutionalisation and codification of qualifications	– High degree of institutionalisation and codification of qualifications	– Very low degree of institutionalisation and codification of qualifications	– Very low degree of institutionalisation and codification of qualifications
	Wage-labour nexus				
Organisation of work	– Based on co-operation and participation	– Strongly based on participation	– Very hierarchical and little participation	– Very hierarchical – Major division of labour	– Very hierarchical – Major division of labour
Forms of mobility	– Strongly based on vocational qualifications	– Closely linked to the evaluation of salaried employees within the company	– Major role of seniority and little recognition of qualifications	– Mobility difficult for salaried employees who do not have the status of skilled workers	– Limited recognition of vocation qualifications
Nature of industrial relations	– Stabilised	– Stabilised	– Somewhat adverse	– Very adverse	– Very adverse
Determining factors of salary income	– Influence of seniority and vocational qualifications	– Major influence of seniority and vocational qualifications	– Main influence of seniority and experience	– No direct influence of qualifications except for skilled workers	– Weak influence of vocational qualifications on salaries
Nature of wage-labour nexus	– Mainly participatory	– Mainly participatory	– Poorly participatory	– Very poorly participatory	– Very poorly participatory

Source: Tessaring (1998, p. 28), based on a study by E. Caroli.

WORKSHOP 3

**TRANSITION FROM INITIAL EDUCATION TO THE LABOUR MARKET:
WHAT MAKES FOR BETTER TRANSITIONS?**

YOUTH LABOUR MARKET ENTRY IN FRANCE

by
Patrick Werquin
Centre d'Études et de Recherches sur les Qualifications (CEREQ), France

Introduction

Until the early 1970s, France, in common with most other European countries, experienced full employment. The growth generated by post-war reconstruction had brought thirty years of economic success. It seemed that the market or market-related mechanisms ensured equilibrium of labour supply and demand and hence full employment. The eminently complex nature of the relationships among all the actors in the labour market was not a primary subject of economic research. Once the difficulties emerged, most of the mechanisms were questioned in turn and new areas of research became preponderant.

France was one of the first countries (immediately after the events of May 1968) to set up institutions (the Centre d'études de l'emploi, CEE, and the Centre d'études et de recherches sur les qualifications, CEREQ). whose purpose was to study the transition from school to working life (Balazs, Faguer and Laroche, 1997). The movement that uses microeconomic data with statistical models also began very early (Salais, 1974b) but was not taken up systematically until later (Courgeau, 1984; Florens, Gérard-Varet and Werquin, 1989; Moreau and Visser, 1991; Fougère and Kamionka, 1992). Where youth as such were concerned, they were treated at first as a single category – persons aged under 25 – in the same way as women, manual workers (Salais, 1974a, Tables 1 to 3) and, already, the long-term unemployed (Salais, 1977, Table 2), or else as a subject of central interest (UNEDIC, 1974; Delcourt, 1970; Capdevielle and Grapin, 1976). The data used in the first instance were those of the Institut national de la statistique et des études économiques (INSEE, labour force survey and training and skills survey; see, for example, Salais, 1974a, 1974b and 1977), and the demographic data collected by the Institut national des études démographiques (INED; see Courgeau, 1984). The problem of youth employment and unemployment, together with youth education and training, was clearly defined very early on, and terms that may appear new, like employability[1] and long-term unemployment[2], already existed then. Finally, this movement, which combined scientific research with policy concerns, also utilised administrative data collected by the Union nationale pour l'emploi dans l'industrie et le commerce (UNEDIC) and the Agence nationale pour l'emploi (ANPE).

To sum up, studies on youth employment in the broad sense were not as numerous in 1970 as they are now (Werquin, Breen and Planas, 1997) but they already existed and even examined problems comparable to today, though on a smaller scale (Bastide and Girard, 1966). This paper thus draws a little on the past in order to describe certain mechanisms and put the present problems of youth employment in France, into a time frame.

Given the wide difference in labour market performance in France between higher education graduates and the others, and above all in order to make use of a now very comprehensive collection of data pertaining specifically to the latter group, this paper concentrates on young people leaving initial education at the lowest levels. Section 4, in particular, deals with a survey on young persons entering the labour market without the general baccalauréat. Section 2 shows that the problems for this category of youth are special and much more marked than for the other categories. Section 3 describes and analyses youth employment policy in France. But first of all, a few institutional facts are given in Section 1.

1. The institutional context

The issue of the data underpinning most of the arguments put forward to explain or describe the functioning of the youth labour market is of undoubted relevance to a retrospective study of developments in France. The *Centre d'études et de recherches sur les qualifications* (CEREQ), established in 1970, is essentially concerned with studying the education-employment relationship (Romani and Werquin, 1998). Unemployment, although featured in certain pioneering studies, has not been the major concern. Only with the present course of events and worsening circumstances is data collection shifting towards more specific targets and focusing on unemployment. In any case, though, the fact that researchers want to obtain fuller and better information, and recognise the need for tighter sampling, means that they are moving over to targeted surveys and dispensing as far as possible with administrative data. CEREQ has been part of this movement since the beginning, with its longitudinal surveys on youth labour market entry.

In this regard, France does not always have the monitoring tools necessary for a proper understanding of the long-term mechanisms involved. Some foreign surveys cover a period of more than ten years (German Socio-Economic Panel – GSOEP) or even much longer (30 years for the American survey of household resources, the Panel Study of Income Dynamics – PSID). Although the idea of a long track is not unanimously accepted in France, location-specific experiments[3] are being carried out, and the introduction of the European households panel (ECHP of the European Union, or Europanel) likewise reflects this concern for long-period monitoring. As regards youth and labour market entry, CEREQ has conducted longitudinal surveys by education level[4] up to a recent date, followed by a survey on all education levels at the same time[5]. In addition to these monitoring projects, which have now become permanent, there are case-specific exercises such as surveys on certain higher education graduates and the three panels on school-leavers without the general *baccalauréat*. However, even though the usefulness of follow-up surveys seems to be recognised, there are not very many of them in France (with six years' monitoring from 1989 to 1995, the second *panel téléphonique* of CEREQ appears to have been one of the longest on its particular theme). The difficulty of obtaining sustained participation from persons questioned by telephone and the difficulties of data collection would seem to outweigh the inherent interest of the exercise.

Still on the subject of data collection, it rapidly became essential to cover all the processes described. Researchers were confronted with the paradox of having to deal urgently with problems – to meet social and/or institutional demand – at the same time that observation periods needed to be lengthened because school-to-work paths were becoming more complicated.

Research of this kind, with its bearing on youth integration, is therefore highly sensitive and relevant to policy-making. Consequently, they are closely inter-linked. Inasmuch as they cannot provide workable solutions to furnish jobs for people who have lost theirs or are seeking one for the first time, the main concern is to identify the groups at risk and make a diagnosis of potential exclusion. In this context, labour market strains do not affect all population groups equally, and certain problems are tackled more often than others. Young persons, women and immigrant populations are thus the subject of numerous studies.

Once the at-risk groups were identified, public policy action became inevitable: the transition from school to employment had to be institutionalised. This was done fairly rapidly by large-scale intervention in the youth labour market[6], but monitoring instruments were still needed, and with the creation or development[7] of data collection tools in the form of longitudinal surveys, the transition was further institutionalised, as it were: the public policy measures institutionalised the transition and the surveys instrumented it. There is still room for progress, given effects which may combine or cancel one another out, the presence of determinants that cannot be observed because they are not measurable, or the fact that no question can be formulated which will guarantee veracity of the answer and validity of the calculations[8].

In this context, although young people are often treated as an individual entity, they do not constitute a homogeneous category as regards entry into employment. For instance, there is the widely differing probability of unemployment based on the criteria habitually used to identify at-risk groups and hence to define the populations targeted by public policy: gender, educational attainment, possession of a formal credential, skill learned, etc. Furthermore, the existence of a "youth labour market" as such still remains to be proved. Admittedly, the normal workings of the market are considerably altered by public policy action, which introduces employer tax reliefs or subsidies to bring down the cost of youth labour, but the implications still have to be evaluated.

For purposes of economic analysis, the wide range of young people – in terms of social background, educational attainment, motivation and other personal characteristics affected by the job shortage situation – clearly indicates the extent of the problem. Discrimination between individuals should not be ruled out of the analysis, but it can be considered only as a contributory element when attempting to understand the mechanisms at work. Rarely does it explain the essential mechanisms.

Since the problem of job shortage and youth differentiation clearly differs in severity across countries, it has to be acknowledged that the macroeconomic context and sluggish activity have much to do with the employment crisis. Section 2 therefore sets out a few stylised facts that have been determined for France.

2. Youth and the labour market in France

In the mid-1970s employment declined in France. The number of job vacancies for young people leaving initial education and arriving on the labour market in search of a first job therefore began to decline also. The employment crisis had two particularly important consequences for young people. First, they remained in initial education for an increasing length of time. Second, the government intervened heavily in the labour market, designating youth as a target public.

The question of the existence of a specific labour market for youth is not addressed here. However, this government intervention, which in some years attained massive proportions (DARES, 1996) can be likened, in some respects, to a form of regulation of the new generations' entry into working life (Werquin, 1997). From a practical standpoint and for the case which concerns us here, government action on the youth labour market created a vast number of intermediate situations between initial education or training and regular employment[9], which made every pathway to employment unique. All the surveys show that the multiplicity of alternatives to regular employment is such that if one monitors young people month by month when they are first in the labour market, one finds as many possible pathways as there are individuals. One of the characteristics of youth's transition from school to work is that it is very complex, indeed even chaotic.

The sections that follow deal with the key figures for youth labour market entry, the characteristics of those who obtain a job, and the role of employment policy.

Longer education and entry of young people into working life

The numbers of young people leaving initial education give an idea of the labour skills offered to employers (Tables 1 and 2). It is important to note that the level of CAP or BEP (vocational education credentials) – Level V[10] – which for a long time was the principal school-leaving level in France, has now been superseded numerically by the level immediately above – Level IV – which corresponds to the *baccalauréat*[11]. This rise in the level of attainment on leaving initial education is shown also in Table 3: the proportions of students or participation rates for example, show that increasing numbers of students are staying in education and training, with ever fewer entering the labour market.

The lengthening of initial education has had two consequences. First, the level of educational attainment of young people has automatically risen (Tables 1 and 2). The number of those leaving school with no more than the *baccalauréat* has steadily declined. Even if they do not all attain the first recognised diploma level in higher education – Level III: diplomas like the BTS (advanced technician's diploma), DUT (university diploma of technology) or DEUG (diploma of general university studies) – a constantly growing proportion of young people are embarking on higher studies. In the space of five years the proportion of young higher-education graduates has risen from 30 to 39%.

The second consequence is equally automatic: fewer young people are in the labour force. However, this is true only of persons aged under 25 (Table 3). The participation rate has become so low in some age groups – for example, those under 20 – that the very notion of an unemployment rate should be questioned, and probably discarded in certain analyses (such as cross-country comparison[12]), in favour of the proportion of individuals unemployed. An unemployment rate is the number of job-seekers expressed as a proportion of the total of themselves plus those who are actually working (*i.e.* the labour force). There are so few young people in the labour force, however, because of longer studies, that the denominator of the youth unemployment rate is no longer significant. The rate is thus artificially amplified.

The proportion of unemployed persons, on the other hand, relates the number of jobless to the entire age group or population. It is thus a more transportable indicator when the participation rate is low. For example, if the unemployment rate for persons aged under 30 was 20.7% in 1994, this does not mean that one young person in five was unemployed that year. Only one in ten was (10.3%), since many were not seeking or did not want a job (Table 3).

Similarly, although very large numbers of young people are without jobs, their representation in the job-seeker total declined from 38.3% in March 1975 to 22.3% in March 1991 - another sign that young people are decreasingly present in the labour market. While the under-25s are undeniably a central subject of concern, the fact remains that their presence among total job-seekers has diminished markedly since the mid-1970s. This can be explained by the fact that when unemployment is at a comparatively low level and simply reflects the time taken for supply to adjust to demand, first-job-seekers are preponderant among the unemployed. Such was the case in 1975 (if less so today), and this is an indication of unemployment that is very present even beyond the age of 25, and especially in the age groups approaching retirement.

Lastly, one of the possible consequences of the decline in the youth participation rate is also the decrease in the proportion of youth in employment. Since fewer young people are looking for work, because they are prolonging their studies, it is logical that there should be fewer young people, proportionately, in employment (Table 3). Again, this applies particularly to the under-25s.

In conclusion, a feature specific to France would seem to be that the uppermost and lowest age groups have to bear the brunt of unemployment while those in between fare much better. Unemployment is therefore an almost unavoidable transit for young people now entering the labour market – to a greater or lesser degree depending on the credentials they have obtained. The section that follows gives some orders of magnitude.

Unemployment: an unavoidable transit

For those leaving the education system, a spell of unemployment seems inescapable. But the unemployment experience differs widely according to the educational standard reached. The diploma continues to be an effective defence against unemployment, and it would certainly be wrong to automatically attribute the residual, or frictional, unemployment of some higher-education graduates to the uselessness of their credentials. For example, the second CEREQ panel survey shows that among those who finished initial education without the *baccalauréat* in 1989, the proportion of unemployed ranged from 15 to 20% each month between September 1989 and January 1995, when the survey period ended. The third CEREQ panel, which is still ongoing, shows that between September 1994 and March 1997 the proportion of unemployed in the same category ranged from 25 to 30% each month (Werquin, 1997). Over the same period, the CEREQ surveys on higher education show a proportion of unemployed graduates that at no time exceeded 10%, and in fact was hardly ever more than just over 5%.

Martinelli, Zarca and Werquin (1999) find that long-term unemployment is virtually absent among graduates at the highest levels (II and I): 2% of them remained unemployed for up to three years in the five years following their labour market entry in 1992. By contrast, at the lowest levels (VI and V bis), the proportion was nearly 20%. Nearly half the former group never experienced unemployment, compared with only one-fifth of the latter group.

Apart from the number of young persons unemployed, it is also important to consider the intensity of this unemployment. Young people, when they are unemployed, do not necessarily remain so for very long, even though the average duration of unemployment is increasing. The notion of long-term unemployment – 12 consecutive months – does not really apply to young people who are out of work for a long time cumulatively but not continuously. Multiple-spell unemployment is very frequent among young persons, who alternate inactivity with periods of insecure employment. The unemployment observed is therefore composed of short repeated spells, and the notion of 12 months' unemployment over the last 18 months seems more appropriate.

By way of concluding this section, attention is therefore drawn to the increasing inapplicability of conventional concepts, like the unemployment rate and long-term unemployment, to the situation of French youth. Instead it would be preferable to use the proportion of young persons unemployed and either very long-term unemployment or, better still, the number of months' unemployment in the last 18 months.

Labour market programmes for youth introduced by the government are a consequence of the difficulties encountered by young people in finding and keeping a job. In addition to the problems of evaluation generated by their existence, they have considerably complicated the education-employment pathways, which are becoming increasingly complex and difficult to model.

3. Employment policy – Bridges between initial education and secure employment

Government intervention on the labour market in France began in the mid 1970s. The earliest decree, introducing the employment-training contracts, is dated 4 June 1974. Youth employment policy in France has gone through a number of important stages (DARES, 1996). The past 20 years can be divided into four periods. The 1970s saw an employment policy which accommodated macro-economic policy – symbolised by the "strong franc" policy in the second half of the decade, etc. – followed by a policy of direct entry into employment regardless of other considerations. Towards the middle of the 1980s, the focal points of employment policy shifted to education/training and reduction of labour costs. More recently, this same policy has concentrated on the low-skilled jobs sector.

Employment policy in France has, to varying degrees in these different periods, been partly responsible for the fact that the youngest and oldest age groups have to bear the brunt of employment shortage. This is especially true of older workers, who are encouraged to take early retirement. It is not so much the case with entry into working life, where several factors, including longer studies, are involved. Here it must be emphasised that French employment policy, by creating numerous intermediate statuses – between education and employment, and also between employment and unemployment – makes the integration pathways very complex and difficult to describe. Before this problem is discussed in detail (see p. 273), a few general principles of public intervention in France are considered in the following section.

Public intervention – Labour market programmes for youth

Labour market programmes for youth integration are central to the debate on the training-employment relationship, while revealing the absence of a natural theoretical link between education and training and employment. On the one hand, they are central to the debate because youth programmes in France are almost systematically inserted between the end of initial education and employment. This, incidentally, makes the employment-entry mechanisms very complex to describe, since young persons are confronted with a multitude of possible situations and most of the pathways observed alternate between various types of insecure jobs, youth schemes and unemployment. On the other hand, these programmes negate, in a sense, the existence of a relationship between education and employment, since they highlight the failure of initial education to lead directly to a first job, if that was ever its role.

Youth schemes in France are for the most part permanent and long-standing. The main schemes still in operation today date from the mid-1980s (Table 4): the *contrat de qualification* or CQ (skill formation contract); the *contrat d'adaptation* or CA (employment contract conditional on reskilling), and the *travaux d'utilité collective* or TUC (community work schemes) which have since become the *contrat emploi solidarité* or CES. France has had, and continues to have, up to ten or so major schemes operating at the same time. All the programmes have been regularly redesigned according to the economic or social needs of the moment or in light of operational experience. Their volume has been relatively stable over recent years (Table 5).

The employment-entry difficulties encountered by youth over a 20-year period therefore made it necessary to institutionalise the school-to-work transition. All the present schemes reflect, to a greater or lesser extent, two principles: reduction of labour cost and improvement of education. Labour cost reduction is generally obtained by tax reliefs or lump-sum inducements for employers. Improved education is taken here in its broadest sense – interfacing with the labour market. It involves skill adjustment if the skill possessed is not directly usable, or skill acquisition where either an obsolete skill or no skill at all is possessed. In some schemes like the CES, the education element, which in theory must be there, is in fact seldom present.

The French youth schemes are placed between the end of initial education and entry into employment. This zone, which has often been described (Demazière and Verdier, 1994; Whul, 1994) is currently the focus of government action. But public intervention could take place upstream[13] – in training to increase the number of teachers or costly education courses, etc. – or downstream – on-the-job training for purposes of job retention and to strengthen the employer/employee attachment through the acquisition of job-specific skills, etc. If in France it is located in the "border zone" (an area somewhere between the two), it is probably because of the diagnosis that has been made concerning the problems of first-job entry – a maladjustment in the transition from education to work. Two major ideas have developed which, in addition to the labour cost question, underlie public policy programmes: "work socialisation" (putting young people in a work environment), and "qualification" (imparting the skills necessary to convince an employer).

A considerable number of studies (Bouder, Cadet and Demazière, 1994; Bonnal, Fougère and Sérandon, 1994; Werquin, 1996 and 1997) have attempted to evaluate the social and labour market programmes for youth. These have produced the following findings.

Early, massive, varied and selective participation in youth schemes

Youth integration schemes begin very early on, at all education and training levels below the *baccalauréat*. Their use diminishes over time, however, and the number of repeats in the same scheme rapidly declines. For example, 70% of girls and 55% of boys in the cohort that left secondary education in 1989 went through one of the various schemes in the five years that followed; some youngsters even participated in as many as seven programmes, but there were no significant numbers for participation in more than three. Finally, there was a marked consistency between the level of educational attainment, the presumed quality of the scheme and the rate of job entry.

Access to skill-formation schemes (CA, CQ) is conditioned by the selectivity of the labour market. The most employable individuals (diploma holders, persons who have received some specialist training or have served apprenticeships) are the first served and soon find regular employment thereafter. Those who fail to do so return to unemployment, essentially in the case of women, or engage in temporary activities (another scheme, national service) in the case of men. The less employable individuals have to make do with lower-performance schemes (TUC-CES) which integrate them professionally less often and for shorter periods of time, while still giving them a first work experience.

The education credential/youth scheme combination conforms to a U-curve in its power of integration. The highest likelihood of employment is for the very few individuals who leave school early to undergo a skill formation scheme (CA, CQ) and for those who have been in a good scheme and also have high-level credentials. At the bottom of the U-curve are the young persons of Level V with a scheme of the TUC-CES type (Aucouturier and Gelot, 1994). The overall strategy is still very much slanted towards longer initial education, but it would seem that the formal credential is no longer an exhaustive indicator of a young person's capacities: additional information now has to be obtained as a means of assessing his or her integration potential.

Along this typical pathway a second scheme is frequently added to the learning process, and the rate of transition to employment is good for the most employable of those who stay the course. Males and females fare equally well employment-wise after one or two schemes although far more women than men become unemployed. On the other hand, the pathway that takes females from inactivity (non-labour market) to unemployment (labour market) via a non-commercial type of scheme is frequent, which suggests a closer relationship to employment through some schemes than through others (Sigot and Werquin, 1993).

Youth programme evaluation is complex

Two findings emerge from knowledge to date:

1. Mechanical effects do not prove the success of youth schemes. Young people who go through a programme are not officially unemployed during that whole period, so they experience shorter or fewer spells of unemployment; the longest programmes (CES) may appear artificially effective in reducing the duration of unemployment, but they seldom lead to employment. However, it should not be forgotten that France does not have long-run surveys that would make it possible to observe whether longer run effects are important.

2. The existence of these youth schemes has created a hierarchy or confirmed the one which the education system has established. There is a selection process whereby some of the schemes cater for individuals who are more "employable" than others, thus making evaluation all the more difficult (Lechene and Magnac, 1995).

From the standpoint of paths to and from one or more schemes, the major inference might well be that evaluation of youth programme effectiveness is contingent on the question of the decision to participate or not. Is participation in a youth scheme a voluntary act or does it result from a direct constraint imposed by the labour market? In other words, does each individual decide to participate in light of his or her personal situation and the benefit which hopefully will be derived from the scheme, or is it the employers associated with all these programmes who select the entrants?

Two different hypotheses exist in this connection. One is that those who go into a scheme have a handicap at the outset and the scheme therefore represents their only chance of ultimately finding employment. With this hypothesis, the natural baseline for evaluating the usual parameters of entry into employment is the group formed by those individuals who have never participated in youth schemes because they have not needed to. However, a significant proportion of non-participants are still without jobs three and a half years after finishing initial education (in December 1993, 17% of all women never having participated in a scheme were unemployed, although 61% had permanent work contracts; the figures for men were 15 and 65% respectively). This inevitably suggests the selection of individuals who are already employable to take part in these schemes, or conversely the exclusion of those who are not sufficiently employable.

The other, less prevalent, hypothesis is supported by a number of empirical findings. One of these is a disturbing similarity in credential level, educational attainment and skill acquisition between those who have been through at least one scheme and have obtained employment immediately afterwards, and those who have found employment without going through a scheme. This would suggest a group of individuals who are highly employable in that they possess specific assets which appeal to employers. Some of them have direct entry into employment. The others need one or perhaps two schemes in order to obtain jobs. Here the scheme acts as a catalyst and appears effective. In this context the most natural baseline is the group of individuals who have entered employment with or without first going through a scheme.

This reduces the problem of programme evaluation to the single criterion of entry into employment. On the other hand, the quantitative approach has to be supplemented by a more qualitative one that considers employment situations (status, contract, duration, pay). Hence the need to propose a different mode of evaluation.

Mention must also be made of the very different profiles found once the number of schemes gone through exceeds two. The individuals concerned have lower levels of formal credentials and initial skills. Furthermore, their scheme experience is much less productive in terms of employability.

There remains the question of why those who have not found employment have never taken part in a youth scheme. It could be due to a fear of being stigmatised (personal choice) or inability to gain access to a scheme (rationing by the market). Here it must be said that although France has many youth programmes, they do not all have equal credit with the different actors in the labour market. A plausible intermediate hypothesis would therefore be that young job-seekers willingly accept a market-sector scheme (CQ and CA), but are much more reluctant to enter a non-market scheme like the CES. Be that as it may, France does not provide youth with a homogeneous system of labour market programmes but with an assortment of very different schemes. Consequently, it is necessary to do more than just model a choice to take part or not in a youth programme. Because they are all different, the schemes are diversely rated by young people and by employers. Schemes differ in terms of effectiveness and also in the manner in which they are evaluated. This individuality is probably at the root of certain misunderstandings about the youth schemes. In particular, there is some confusion as to what it is plausible to assume concerning the initial characteristics (credential, skill learned, motivation, etc.) of young people entering a scheme. Thus, evaluation or even just analysis presupposes a clear identification of each scheme.

Lower initial pay for ex-participants in youth schemes

Two findings emerge from a construction of the path to failure (non-integration) based on observation of young persons' pay and their transit through youth employment programmes (Balsan, Hanchane and Werquin, 1994). The first is that young people who have gone through programmes receive lower starting salaries immediately afterwards than those who have not. This may be interpreted as an indication that youth schemes may be a barrier to entry into regular jobs.

The second finding is that the wage spread in immediate post-scheme employment faithfully reproduces the spread of in-scheme remuneration. In other words, the young people who receive the biggest allowances under a scheme receive the highest pay in first employment. This implies the existence of barriers to youth scheme entry, as well as suggesting that participation in a scheme causes young people to scale down their wage expectations.

Some youth schemes stigmatise participants, who then have difficulty integrating into the regular jobs sector. Others facilitate integration, while yet others lower wage expectations. Youth schemes are central to the process of integration and to the process of non-integration in that their great variety signifies differentiated treatment of problems. They also create differences: a hierarchy that puts youth on different paths, including the path to failure. Yet this hierarchy simply reproduces the one which initial education and social conditions created beforehand and which sufficed for selection for employment when the job shortage was not so severe as it is now.

It is not infrequent for certain authors, starting from the unavoidable premise of a general shortage of jobs, to equate youth schemes with "redistribution of poverty" or "equalisation of opportunities for potential 'outcasts'". It is clear that if public policy action is targeted at the young people most exposed to the risk of non-integration, problems might result for those who are at the level immediately above, but ineligible for such assistance. This does not apply in all cases, for several reasons:

- Programmes are constantly being redesigned to match youth needs as closely as possible. For example, the skill formation schemes used to be reserved for young persons who were very disadvantaged with respect to their initial level of education, so competition was very severe for youth of Level III (BTS, DUT essentially). They have now been given access to the *contrat de qualification*.

- The wide range of schemes (and these are likely to develop with the decentralisation of education funds) serves to meet a great number of wants.

- There have even been major extensions. For example, in becoming *contrats emploi solidarité*, the *travaux d'utilité collective* have been extended to the long-term unemployed, even over the age of 25.

All together, evaluation of labour market programmes for youth is complex and difficult, because there is no consensus on the effects they have. It is very clear that conclusions are radically different according to the point of view adopted. To sum up, youth programmes help young people to stay out of unemployment and ultimately to find jobs, but not to find good or stable jobs. Their position on the pathways to employment relates logically to occupational mobility and the acquisition of job experience. These subjects will be discussed in the section that follows.

Initial occupational mobility

Important issues to be addressed in analysing youth's entry into employment are those of the respective functions of outset conditions – known when leaving initial education – and experience acquired in the labour market. On the basis of cross-sectional data or even with longitudinal data, but with only estimates for the heterogeneity not observed[14], it is possible to predicate the central importance of labour market experience relative to education credentials or skills learned as an explanation for entry into employment over the medium term (6 years). But such data and methods cannot accurately portray employment entry and initial mobility in the labour market. In fact, the debate opened in recent literature in France concerns the extent to which labour market entrants profit from their educational credentials and attainment – their initial human capital – in order to obtain labour market or job experience.

This is not the right approach, for at least four reasons. First of all, the studies which are quick to put job experience, or rather labour market experience, at the forefront of the determinants of longer-lasting initial employment, count the very first months in the labour market as experience. But this period, which immediately follows the exit from initial education, can only be caused by the credential obtained or by other fixed characteristics known at the outset, since the individual concerned has no experience of the labour market as yet. When an individual seeks a job for the first time, his résumé cannot possibly contain a period of employment or other forms of experience, since he has only just entered the labour market!

If the first experiences thereafter result in longer-lasting first employment, it is fairly logical to suppose that a credential effect is involved.

Second, these questions are investigated more often than not with unsuitable data and inadequate methods. Because integration into the labour market is such a complex process in reality, the mechanisms of causality at work have to be approached with the right tools. If successful integration is defined as a relatively stabilised situation in employment (Vernières, 1993), then explaining this position – with a limited dependent-variable model[15] on cross-sectional data – by path variables on the labour market works well but proves only one thing: the near-endogenous character of the path variables as independent variables in a model where the dependent variable is itself a path variable a little further on in time. Even if this is the last point observed, because the survey goes no further, one is still in the middle of a path. The almost tautological nature of these models is never really addressed. It is rather going against reason to try to analyse a process which, by definition, is random and varies over time with descriptive tools and statistical specifications that are independent of time.

Third, to return to the subject of labour market experience, the studies which single out experience as the only constant determinant of entry into employment over the medium term use a definition of employment entry that tends to overlook the quality and durability of the jobs held. All the discussions on youth integration err by not taking account of all its dimensions.

Fourth and last, to omit outset conditions as a determinant of employment entry is to deny the existence of acquired skills which are very specialised and replete with know-how and technique, and which nearly always lead to jobs in appropriate sectors (Kirsch and Werquin, 1995).

Using limited dependent-variable models – of the logit or probit type – in a longitudinal context, Balsan, Hanchane and Werquin (1996, 1998 a and b) find that the outset variables, especially the education level/credential and acquired skill, cannot be displaced by experience variables in explaining job-holding, even up to six years after exit from initial education. The use of panel data which really track youth over time, and control of the non-observed heterogeneity among individuals, which is not described but which can be controlled on the hypothesis that an individual has the same non-observed characteristics at each questioning, leads to more refined findings on the opposition between outset conditions and labour market experience. The latter apparently does not overcome the former. Thus the youth employment crisis and youth unemployment cannot be resolved solely by youth's adjustment to the labour market: there is also the knowledge acquired in initial education to be considered. Not too surprisingly, therefore, the solution would seem to lie in a compromise between initial education and preparation for employment.

Given the marked deterioration in the youth labour market, many studies are concentrating on the paths to exclusion, work-related or even social. The idea fairly often is to measure the extent to which an individual characteristic is associated with, and therefore predictive of, exclusion from the labour market. The reverse point of view is taken here. What is needed is to identify as accurately as possible the characteristics associated with successful integration into the labour market, which will help towards an understanding of the whole integration process and thus assist policy-making. A few original findings on the situation of non-holders of the *baccalauréat* entering the French labour market are therefore analysed in the section that follows. Data are presented first and then some descriptive statistics.

4. Employment of French youth not holding the general *baccalauréat*

Among the difficulties encountered when attempting to describe integration pathways and evaluate youth schemes, the actual definition of employment is one of the most critical. For example, in the case of young people entering the labour market without the general *baccalauréat*, the time taken to obtain a first paid job continues to be only a few months. On the other hand, the time required to find a job with some aspects of stability (Atkinson and Micklewright, 1991) is two or three years depending on gender and the manner of reckoning national service. Thus it can legitimately be supposed that what has changed in France is not the duration of access to employment but the type of employment to which access is gained. This section therefore attempts to model the characteristics of employment. For this purpose, a job is defined as a set of components: pay, social status, number of hours worked, etc. Hence it is essentially the question of job quality and the personal success record which is addressed.

The emphasis is once again on those groups with the greatest difficulties, as indicated above, and those at the centre of policy making concerning youth employment. Moreover, limiting the study to those youths with a level inferior to the general baccalauréat, allows for the use of a CEREQ survey designed to determine what kind of jobs youth accessed.

The studies on transition to the labour market and entry into employment all seem to agree that the notion of unsuccessful integration should henceforth be defined as a process. It is no longer shocking or surprising, in France, that at certain educational levels a young person remains unemployed for several months, even years, before finding a job. What is truly surprising is that six years after leaving initial education, 20% of a generation is still jobless. It has not been out of work continuously, but the fact remains that one-fifth of that generation is still not integrated after six years; nor are the remainder all in regular jobs (Werquin, 1997).

Data – The third CEREQ "Panel Jeunes"

To permit a better insight into the role of the labour market programmes for youth introduced in the mid-1980s and augmented with complementary or supplementary measures since, CEREQ has conducted, three times over ten years, a survey by repeated observation (panel) of young people liable to be concerned by one or another of the integration programmes: from 1987 to 1989 for those having left initial education in 1986, from 1990 to 1995 for leavers in 1989, and from 1996 to 2000 (ongoing) for leavers in 1994.

The data used here are taken from the last of the three surveys. About 3 500 young persons who left secondary education or a *Centre de formation d'apprentis* (CFA) (apprentice training centre) in 1994 were questioned twice. This represents 42 months' follow-up, between October 1993 – to identify early leavers – and March 1997. The survey is representative of the 370 000 individuals who left initial education in France in 1994. The sample is heavily concentrated on the CAP or BEP level (Level V – ISCED 3). There are slightly more men than women. The two possible routes of initial education are represented: school, with the vocational skill identified, and apprenticeship.

Two figures indicate the magnitude of the employment problem for this particular group: only 4.3% of these young persons were continuously employed during the three years of tracking, while 6.3% had had no employment whatever. All the others were somewhere between these two extremes, and Table 6 shows how complex and varied their pathways were: in barely three years' on the labour market they experienced many different situations. A sizeable proportion of them alternated short spells of employment with unemployment.

Table 6 gives a breakdown but, globally, 56.7% of these young persons participated at least once over the 42 months in one of the public policy youth programmes (columns 3, 4 and 5). At the other extreme, 30.7% never had any employment (columns 6 and 7 plus a residual category of jobs).

Two pictures of the situation of these young people, three years apart, offer a different perspective. Table 7 shows the situation immediately following school – in December 1994 for the cohort that left initial education at the end of the 1993-1994 academic year – and two and a half years later. Unemployment has by no means disappeared: one-fifth of the cohort is still out of work. One-fifth, too, is in stable employment.

It is thus a population with very difficult and complex integration paths which is analysed in the section that follows on the subject of access to adequate employment.

Modelling access to a "good job"

A first hypothesis submitted here is that the quality of employment is better when a number of factors are present. Thus, on the basis of the survey findings on conditions offered at the time of hiring, a quality score is calculated. Each individual is assigned a value according to pay, type of work contract, number of hours worked weekly, and social status of the job. The higher the score, the better the quality of the job. Two other variables enter into the score: the fact that there is no trial period involved other than the statutory period, and the fact that the employee ceases to seek employment upon being hired. These last two items of information are used because they obviously say something about how the worker perceives his or her job status. The quality score is normed to a scale of between zero and one.

Only the first job is used here (37% of all the jobs covered, or 3 166 first jobs). There are several reasons for this. To begin with, it is the very first job (or jobs) which is regarded as decisive in the building of job experience. More technically, many fewer individuals have had two jobs and the econometric problems of endogenousness when incorporating past employment in the second-job score are not simple. Finally, since no information is as yet available concerning the macroeconomic context – levels of activity, local unemployment rates, etc. – it is difficult to treat jobs accepted at intervals of several years in the same way.

Two questions are tackled below. The first is whether a longer job search is needed in order to obtain a good job. The second is whether good jobs last longer. In both cases, a couple of ideas can be verified. First, there is the employer-employee relationship, which is materialised by this quality score. Thus defined, the score may also be seen as an index of matching between the employer, the employee and the job, since it is hard to imagine an employer recruiting a young person to a high-level, high-paying job under an indefinite-term contract, without the employer's making it quite clear to the employee that he or she is being recruited on a trial basis, and without the employer's recognising a potential for high productivity. The second idea is more general. It represents the premise that it is probably unwise for a young person to rush into a job immediately upon leaving school. This is not desirable for the young person, who may soon become demotivated if the job does not suit, or for the employer and the economy as a whole, since initial mismatches lead to efficiency losses.

The problem of employer-employee matching is approached, but not addressed directly in this section, for this would involve the measurement of matching, an exercise more complex than that which is taken here.

Obtaining a good job

Once the job quality score has been calculated, two types of variables are used to explain it. The first comprises all the initial characteristics known upon exit from initial education, such as the educational credential and the skill learned. The second consists in fact of one variable only: the duration of access to the job.

One of the hypotheses to be tested, therefore, is that there is a cost in terms of job quality when an individual takes the first job available. It may be thought that too rapid a match is necessarily a bad thing. Alternatively, it might be contended that the individuals who are the quickest to find employment are also the best, in which case the best jobs fall to them "naturally".

Table 8 shows a small but significant effect that argues in favour of the second hypothesis. The individuals who find employment quickly also tend to obtain good jobs. The model takes account of the selection bias that causes some young persons to have had no employment at all (6.3%). Above all, the model takes account of the fact that the duration of access to employment is almost certainly linked to the same individual characteristics as those causing the score. The duration of access to employment is therefore an instrumented model (not reproduced here) to rid that variable of its endogenous component. Variables like the number of job applications submitted, the number of siblings or the fact of having children seem to be good instruments: they govern access to a job but not the job itself. Furthermore, one of the advantages of the quality score as calculated is that it describes employment at the time of hiring and hence the outcome of worker/employer negotiation, with relatively little inclusion of all the rest. It may be argued, however, that the time spent by the young person in searching for a job is information which the employer will use. So this variable is instrumented all the same.

The way in which the credential-level variables are used needs some explanation. In France, at the pre-*baccalauréat* stage, a young person may have reached a given level of education without obtaining the formal credential corresponding to that level. This is one of the reasons why the French surveys never include the grades obtained in examinations: that information is represented well enough by possession or not of a credential. To allow for possible interactions, these two variables are therefore crossed in the models estimated, and those who have attained *baccalauréat* level and actually hold the *baccalauréat* are differentiated from those who have reached the same level but hold a lower credential (a BEP and/or a CAP) or no credential at all. The same applies to the level immediately below – BEP or CAP – where an individual may attain the final year of the course he or she is taking but fail the examination: the individual possesses the level but not the credential. It so happens that, in France, possession of a credential, especially in the very professionalised sectors, is an all-important reference. It is a determinant of pay scales, for example. It should also be pointed out that individuals who fail the final examinations may repeat. The variables for educational attainment therefore make it possible to measure this "lagging behind" or, possibly, an advance on the others.

The results given in Table 8 show that educational attainment is positively correlated with job quality but that things are not entirely linear. Holders of the *baccalauréat* have one of the best quality scores. More surprisingly, young persons leaving education at the BEP and CAP levels are those with the best score, *ceteris paribus*. This may be due to the manner of calculating the quality score – which might incline towards a dimension more frequent at this level – or quite simply to the fact that, since the baseline is absence of any qualification, everyone is distinguishable from that base, in many cases very widely relative to the others used in empirical studies (Martinelli, Zarca and Werquin, 1999). This argument is strengthened by the fact that young people of *baccalauréat* level but without any diploma, are difficult to distinguish from the baseline.

Making spontaneous applications for a job is seen to pay off. This may be interpreted as employer recognition of a young person's drive or as a proxy for certain non-observed variables such as sense of initiative.

It is only possible to know whether an individual possesses a particular skill if he has gone through normal (academic) schooling. This information can not be obtained about apprentices (from a CFA), with this group therefore constituting the baseline. The result is fascinating in that it strengthens a hypothesis rarely established empirically. Apprenticeship is often vaunted in France as a fast route to first employment, other things being equal. This is so, but the jobs obtained are apparently of lesser quality according to the score criteria.

Possession of a driving licence is one of the few variables it was possible to retain among all the peripheral variables available in the survey. Having written a résumé, working in the informal economy, having had a job while still at school, or even being a female, are variables which are not significant in this model. It will be seen later on that they explain the duration of the job found but not its quality. This leaves the driving licence as a help towards rather better jobs. It remains to be seen whether this is because the licence holders are enabled to seek employment more effectively, *i.e.* over longer distances, or because the jobs requiring use of a vehicle are of better quality. Alternatively, the fact of holding a licence might be read as a disguised gauge of personal initiative and forcefulness, or even as an indication of the financial status of the young person and his or her family.

Finally, age on leaving school yields nothing. It has been discarded in favour of scholastic lag and school-leaving before the end of the French academic year, which is in June. The result is clear: other things – like a high level of education and credential being equal – it is better to be a little older for employers seem to prefer maturity.

The natural question that now arises is the relationship between the duration of the employment obtained and job quality at the time of hiring.

Job quality and duration

Once job quality and the main characteristics associated with it have been defined, it has to be determined whether better jobs last longer. Table 9 suggests that this is so: the estimated coefficient of the score is positive and significant (0.095), which indicates that, measured thus, the better the quality of the job, the longer it will last. The hypothesis that a good initial match, shown here by a good quality rating, lengthens the employer-employee relationship is verified.

Here again, the results may suffer from a statistical bias due to the fact that the length of the observation window is very small. In such a case, the longer the duration of access to employment, the shorter the duration of that employment, even though it may last well beyond the end of the observation period. But the duration of access is linked to the quality score, as shown in the previous section. A first instrumental equation has therefore been developed in order to remove this problem. In addition to a few instruments mentioned earlier, the means of job search and the young person's birthplace or the birthplace of his parents are used. The effect measured can therefore be regarded as a pure effect.

Women tend to stay in better jobs for longer periods of time than men. This is an unusual result for France, where men are often found to have an advantage in most matters. Hence, again, the relevance of job quality approach. Neither the educational level nor the credential appear to count in this particular regard: they determine job quality but not job duration.

The school route, whatever the skill learned, leads to shorter employment than apprenticeship. Given the findings mentioned earlier concerning these variables, no overall conclusion seems possible. Apprenticeship leads sooner to longer-lasting jobs, but of lesser quality. This line of investigation needs to be developed, probably as to the relationship that is established between the prospective employer, or the apprentice master, and the apprentice.

Certain variables – having produced a résumé, having had a vacation job, having engaged in some paid work on an informal basis – probably indicate a chaotic transition period and difficulty in obtaining a regular, more stable job. These variables can be connected more with the consequence of successive failures than with the source of durable first employment. They probably concern that portion of the population which alternates short spells of employment with periods of unemployment. Finally, the variables "using youth programmes as a means of approaching employers" and "scholastic lag or lead" do not have any significant effect on employment duration.

There are many lines along which this work could be developed. One would be to investigate the occurrences of employment after the first job, and then to analyse the process of change of employer or employee and isolate the determinants of change in the quality score over time. This would mean extending the number of observations so as to have a longer time frame. The survey would then record all changes within the same place of employment. A method that makes it possible to measure movement in the quality score and change in matching by employer or employee is absolutely necessary in order to understand the mechanisms of integration.

Last, and most important, one should consolidate the composition of the quality score and construct a new, more neutral index based on the match frequencies of this or that event. The idea would then be to see which profiles are recruited in France at the different levels of education and investigate the mechanisms of access to these standard jobs.

5. Remarks and suggestions

Even when job shortage is taken as a given, it seems worthwhile to describe the mechanisms of successful entry into employment. This does not imply that it is necessary to increase the number of solutions, because the constraint of vacancy shortage imposed by the state of the economy would still remain. One of the ideas underlying the work presented in Section 4 is to make it possible for young people who can gain access to good jobs to keep them.

In conclusion, the following are some suggestions as regards development of the research but also strategies for dealing with the problems described:

– The mechanisms of employment entry should be separated as between speed of access and job quality. Movements back and forth between different situations in and outside the labour market must be minimised and reduced to problems of adjustment.

– The evaluation of rapid integration pathways should go beyond the first job. The quality of match between employer, employee and job should be monitored over time.

– The evaluation of youth employment programmes shows that they should focus on two aims:

  • To keep youth out of unemployment and inactivity because these can destroy skills, abilities and knowledge very rapidly. Public policy action can and must maintain young people at an adequate level of potential productivity so that they will not be definitively excluded from employment if a sustainable upturn in economic growth occurs.

  • To augment initial education, which should be general. Education schemes of a much more substantial kind can be imagined. Since the nature of skill demand is not known, even within a short time frame, young people must be educated for as long as possible and adjusted very rapidly thereafter to employment, with this adjustment taking place in a work environment.

– Youth employment programmes can and must be made highly specific in terms of the population targeted. This still leaves room for schemes to provide work for youth who have been inactive for too long. In sum, there needs to be as wide a variety of programmes as possible, in order to meet demands of all kinds.

– Long schemes, like the new *emplois jeunes*, should be so designed as to encourage crossovers along the way and not only at the end of five years.

– In this context, the end of compulsory schooling could be determined by the attainment of a required minimum level of education instead of the age reached, as at present. School leaving could be conditional on elementary tests, even if this were to pose the problem of dealing with youth of very low attainment and all the cases that require special or even social treatment.

NOTES

1. For INSEE, the employability of a group of unemployed persons is the mean instant probability of one member of that group finding a (or another) job. The term "employability" is much used, although definitions must certainly vary.

2. Currently defined as a period of unemployment exceeding 12 months. Here, too, the definition is shifting to a total of 12 months' unemployment during the last 18 months, in order to take account of multiple spells of unemployment. The concept of very long-term unemployment, in excess of three years, also exists.

3. Panel lorrain, CEREQ panels téléphoniques, DARES panels loupes.

4. Three groups of young people leaving initial education are covered: those who do not have the general baccalauréat, those registered as having obtained the baccalauréat in a given year, and those having finished tertiary education.

5. Survey introduced in the second half of 1997 (Martinelli, Zarca and Werquin, 1999).

6. The existence or specificity of which still remains to be proved.

7. CEREQ was set up before the first major shocks on the labour market.

8. For example, talent, taste, preference for the present, drive, a particular inability, chance or a handicap.

9. Regular employment is defined as a job having, at a minimum, an indefinite-term contract, and a full time wage at least equal to the minimum wage (SMIC).

10. The first vocational level in France. In theory these credentials are obtained at the age of 17, but in practice one to two years later. They correspond to levels 2 and 3 on the ISCED scale.

11. This credential is normally obtained at age 18 and gives entry to higher education. It may be academic or general – in which case the rate of continuation into higher education is 95% – or vocational – with a 30% rate of continuation.

12. For example, UK youth enter the labour market much earlier and Italian youth much later than French youth.

13. It is clear that in Germany, for example, the existence of the dual system and the natural link between the end of apprenticeship with a firm and hiring by that firm shifts the focus of concern upstream: to the time of seeking an apprenticeship.

14. These estimates are used, for example, in Balsan, Hanchane and Werquin (1996) to calculate initial values in iterative procedures.

15. Of the binomial logit type, for example.

BIBLIOGRAPHY

ATKINSON, A.B. and MICKLEWRIGHT, J. (1991), "Unemployment Compensation and Labour Market Transitions: A Critical Review", *Journal of Economic Literature*, No. 4, pp. 1679-1727.

AUCOUTURIER, A.L. and GELOT, D. (1994), "Les dispositifs pour l'emploi et les jeunes sortant de scolarité: une utilisation massive, des trajectoires diversifiées", *Économie et Statistique*, No. 277-278, Vol. 7/8, pp. 75-93.

BALAZS, G., FAGUER, J. P. and LAROCHE, F. (1997), *Bilan des travaux sur les jeunes et l'emploi*, Centre d'études de l'emploi, dossier 9.

BALSAN, D., HANCHANE, S. and WERQUIN, P. (1994), "Analyse salariale des dispositifs d'aide à l'insertion des jeunes", *Formation Emploi*, No. 46, June.

BALSAN, D., HANCHANE, S. and WERQUIN, P. (1996), "Mobilité professionnelle initiale: éducation et expérience professionnelle – Un modèle *Probit* à effet aléatoire", *Économie et Statistique*, No. 299, volume 9.

BALSAN, D., HANCHANE, S. and WERQUIN, P. (1998a), "Sub-minimum Wage Employment, Earnings Profiles and Wage Mobility in the Low Skill Youth Labour Market: Evidence from French Panel Data 1989-95", in S. Bazen, M. Gregory and W. Salverda (eds.), *Low Wage Employment*, Edward Elgar publisher.

BALSAN, D., HANCHANE, S. and WERQUIN, P. (1998b), "Analyse longitudinale de l'insertion professionnelle des jeunes en France: exemple des statuts d'emploi et des salaires", submitted to *Annales d'économie et de statistique*.

BASTIDE, H. and GIRARD, A. (1966), "Les tendances démographiques en France et les attitudes de la population", *Population*, No. 1, January-February.

BONNAL, A., FOUGÈRE, D. and SÉRANDON, A. (1994), "Une évaluation de l'impact des politiques d'emploi françaises sur les transitions individuelles sur le marché du travail", in M. Ourtau and P. Werquin (eds.), *L'analyse longitudinale du marché du travail*, CEREQ, Documents Séminaires, No. 99, September.

BOUDER, A., CADET, J.P. and DEMAZIÈRE, D. (1994), "Évaluer les effets des dispositifs d'insertion pour les jeunes et les chômeurs de longue durée – Un bilan méthodologique", CEREQ, Documents Synthèse, No. 98, December.

CAPDEVIELLE, Y. and GRAPIN, P. (1976), "L'insertion professionnelle à la sortie du système scolaire: quelques exemples sur la période récente", *Économie et Statistique*, No. 81-82, pp. 57-72.

COURGEAU, D. (1984), "Relations entre cycle de vie et migrations", *Population*, pp. 483-513.

DARES (1996), *40 ans de politique de l'emploi*, La Documentation française, December, 367 pages.

DELCOURT, C. (1970), "Les jeunes dans la vie active", *Économie et Statistique*, No. 18.

DEMAZIÈRE, D. and VERDIER, É. (eds.) (1994), *Évaluation des aides publiques à l'insertion et à la réinsertion*, CEREQ, Documents Séminaires, No. 94, May.

DIRECTION DE LA PROGRAMMATION ET DU DÉVELOPPEMENT (1998), *L'état de l'école – 30 indicateurs sur le système éducatif français*, Ministère de l'Éducation Nationale, Direction de la Programmation et du Développement, No. 8, 78, October.

FLORENS, J.-P., GÉRARD-VARET, L.-A. and WERQUIN, P. (1989), "L'impact de l'indemnisation sur la durée et l'ancienneté au chômage", *Économie et Prévision*, No. 87, Vol. 1, pp. 93-104.

FOUGÈRE, D. and KAMIONKA, T. (1992), "Un modèle markovien du marché du travail", *Annales d'Économie et de Statistique*, No. 27, pp. 149-188.

KIRSCH, J. L. and WERQUIN, P. (1995), "Quelque part... une relation formation – emploi. Spécialité de formation et emploi occupé: le cas du BEP", *Formation Emploi*, No. 52, pp. 29-47, December.

LECHENE, V. and MAGNAC, T. (1995), "L'évaluation des politiques publiques d'insertion des jeunes sur le marché du travail: questions microéconomiques", Rapport à la Délégation interministérielle à l'insertion des jeunes, April.

MARTINELLI, D., ZARCA, G. and WERQUIN, P. (1999), "Le suivi des jeunes de l'enquête Génération 92 – premiers résultats", *CEREQ – Bref*, No. 149, January.

MERON, M. and MINNI, C. (1995), "Des études à l'emploi: plus tard et plus difficilement qu'il y a vingt ans", *Économie et Statistique*, No. 283-284, Vol. 3/4, pp. 9-31.

MOREAU, A. and VISSER, M. (1991), "Durée du chômage des jeunes en France", *Annales d'économie et de statistique*, No. 20-21, pp. 257-278.

MINNI, C. and POULET, P. (1998), "L'évolution récente de la scolarité et de l'insertion professionnelle des jeunes", *Premières informations – Premières synthèses*, DARES, 98.12, No. 52.1, December.

ROMANI, C. and WERQUIN, P. (1998), "Alternating Training and the School-to-Work Transition: Programs, Assessment, Prospects", in D. Wagner and D. Stern (eds.), *School-to-Work Transition in OECD Countries: a Comparative Analysis*, Hampton Press, Cresskill, New Jersey, pp. 187-235.

SALAIS, R. (1974a), "La mesure du chômage dans l'enquête Emploi", *Économie et Statistique*, numéro 54, pp. 3-17, March.

SALAIS, R. (1974b), "Chômage: fréquences d'entrées et durées moyennes selon l'enquête Emploi", *Annales de l'INSEE*, No. 16-17, pp. 163-228, May-December.

SALAIS, R. (1977), "Analyse des mécanismes de détermination du chômage", *Économie et Statistique*, No. 93, pp. 21-37, October.

SIGOT, J.C. and WERQUIN, P. (1993), "Les mesures d'aide publique dans la dynamique de l'insertion des jeunes", *CEREQ – Bref*, No. 93, December.

UNEDIC (1974), "Enquête sur le chômage des jeunes", *Bulletin de liaison*, No. 51, March.

VERNIÈRES, M. (1993), *Formation Emploi*, édition Cujas, collection Théories, Paris.

WERQUIN, P. (1996), "De l'école à l'emploi: les parcours précaires", in S. Paugam (ed.), *L'exclusion: l'état des savoirs*, édition La Découverte, collection Textes à l'appui, Paris, February.

WERQUIN, P. (1997), "Dix ans d'intervention sur le marché du travail des jeunes en France, 1986-1996", *Économie et Statistique*, No. 304-305, Vol. 4/5, pp. 121-136.

WERQUIN, P., BREEN, R. and PLANAS, J. (eds.) (1997), "Youth Transitions in Europe: Theories and Evidence", CEREQ, Documents Séminaires, No. 120, March.

WHUL, S. (1994), "Chômage d'exclusion et politiques d'insertion", in G. Ferréol (ed.), *Intégration et exclusion dans la société française contemporaine*, Presses universitaires de Lille, Chapter 6, pp. 157-188.

WOLPIN, K.I. (1987), "Estimating a Structural Search Model: the Transition from School-to-Work", *Econometrica*, No. 4, volume 55, pp. 801-817.

Annex 1
ACRONYMS AND ABBREVIATIONS

ANPE	*Agence nationale pour l'emploi* (National Employment Agency)
APP	Apprenticeship
BAC	*Baccalauréat*
BEP	*Brevet d'études professionnelles* (Diploma of vocational studies)
BREF	*Bulletin de recherche sur l'emploi et la formation*
BTS	*Brevet de technicien supérieur* (Advanced technician's diploma)
CA	*Contrat d'adaptation* (Employment contract conditional on reskilling – from 1985 onwards)
CAP	*Certificat d'aptitude professionnelle* (Certificate of vocational competence)
CDD	*Contrat à durée déterminée* (Fixed-term contract)
CDI	*Contrat à durée indéterminée* (Indefinite-term contract)
CEC	*Contrat emploi consolidé* (Subsidised employment contract)
CEE	*Centre d'études de l'emploi*
CEF	*Contrat Emploi Formation*
CEP	*Certificat d'études primaires* (Certificate of primary studies)
CEREQ	*Centre d'études et de recherches sur les qualifications*
CES	*Contrat emploi solidarité* (Part-time community work for job-seekers)
CEV	*Contrat emploi de ville* (Urban job contract)
CFA	*Centre de formation d'apprentis* (Apprentice training centre)
CO	*Contrat d'orientation* (Work experience contract)
CQ	*Contrat de qualification* (Skill formation contract – from 1985 onwards)
DARES	*Direction de l'animation, de la recherche, des études et de la statistique*
DEUG	*Diplôme d'études universitaires générales* (Diploma of general university studies)
DP&D	*Direction de la programmation et du développement*
DUT	*Diplôme universitaire de technologie* (University diploma of technology)
ECHP	European Community Household Panel
FQP	*Formation et qualification professionnelle* (Survey by Insee)
GSOEP	German Socio-Economic Panel
INED	*Institut national des études démographiques*
INSEE	*Institut national de la statistique et des études économiques*
ISCED	International Standard Classification for Education
J2550	25 to 50% welfare contribution relief for employers hiring young persons (from 1986 to 1988)
OECD	Organisation for Economic Co-operation and Development
OLS	Ordinary Least Squares
PPAJ	*Pactes et plan avenir jeunes* (Youth employment agreements – from 1977 to 1983)
PSID	Panel Survey of Income Dynamics
SIVP	*Stage d'initiation à la vie professionnelle* (Work experience programme)
SMIC	*Salaire minimum interprofessionnel de croissance* (Statutory minimum wage – since 1970)
TUC	*Travaux d'utilité collective* (Community work schemes)
UNEDIC	*Union nationale pour l'emploi dans l'industrie et le commerce*

Annex 2.

RECOGNISED SKILL LEVELS IN FRANCE

Level	Definition
VI	Persons holding jobs not requiring education beyond the end of compulsory schooling.
V bis	Persons holding jobs requiring short-course training of one year maximum, leading to the Certificat d'éducation professionnelle (certificate of vocational education) or other similar credential.
V	Persons holding jobs normally requiring a level of education corresponding to the BEP or CAP.
IV	Persons holding supervisory jobs or possessing a qualification equivalent to the vocational Bac or the technician's diploma.
III	Persons holding jobs normally requiring education to the level of BTS, DUT or end of the first cycle of higher education.
I and II	Persons holding jobs normally requiring education to a level equal to or higher than the licence (bachelor's degree) or graduation from an *école d'ingénieurs* (engineering school).

Annex 3.

DESCRIPTIVE STATISTICS ON THE VARIABLES USED IN TABLES 8 AND 9

Variables used in Table 8	Proportion
Duration of access to the job	
Level and credential (baseline: no qualification)	15.7
Bac. level and holding bac.	21.1
Bac. level and holding at most a CAP and/or BEP	4.5
Bac. level and holding neither CAP nor BEP	1.6
BEP and/or CAP level and duly credentialled	38.3
BEP and/or CAP level but uncredentialled	18.8
Reason for choice of employer in cases of spontaneous application (baseline: not applicable)	78.1
Family and professional connections	0.5
Personal reason(s), such as motivation	0.2
Other reason(s), such as job location	20.9
Chance	0.2
Skill acquisition (baseline: apprenticeship)	14.2
Industrial by school route	33.9
Tertiary by school route	36.5
General tertiary by school route	15.3
Possession of a driving licence	71.9
Left school before end of academic year	7.2
Scholastic lag (in years)	
0	21.9
1	26.5
2	26.9
3	16.8
4	5.9
5	1.6
6 and +	0.4
Scholastic lead (yes/no)	5.8
Probability of obtaining a first job	93.7

Supplementary variables used in Table 9	Proportion
Being a woman	39.7
Knowing someone in the firm	18.2
Having produced a résumé	10.9
Earning money on the side	4.4
Performing voluntary work	1.6
Using youth schemes to approach employers	3.1
Having already had a vacation job	38.3
Having already had a weekend job	14.7
Having already had a fill-in job	29.5
Having already done a work experience course	69.5

Table 1. **Exits from initial education according to credential held** (in thousands)

Credential obtained (corresponding level)	1980	1990	1994	1995	1996
No credential, or CEP (VI)	202*	133	102	97	93
Vocational certificate only (V bis)	80	61	52	51	55
CAP, BEP or equivalent (V)	220	129	111	119	120
General *baccalauréat* (IV)	81	50	66	74	78
Technological or vocational *baccalauréat* or equivalent (IV)	32	65	94	90	93
BTS, DUT or equivalent (III)	29	60	85	103	93
Other bac+2, DEUG, paramedical, social (III)	36	37	29	32	34
Long-cycle higher ed. (II+I)	45	87	128	138	160
Total exits	**725**	**622**	**667**	**704**	**726**

* For exemple, 202 000 young persons entering the labour market with no credential, or with a CEP, in 1980.
Source: DP&D (1998).

Table 2. **Exits from initial education by level of attainment** (in thousands)

Level attained	1990	1994	1995	1996
Primary, no studies	7	5	3	2
No qualifications (VI and V bis)	76	53	53	58
CAP, BEP (V)	195*	162	172	166
Final year secondary ed. (IV, lower)	87	115	109	109
Non-graduate higher ed. (IV, upper)	73	90	94	104
Total bac-level (IV)	**160**	**205**	**203**	**213**
Graduate bac.+2, BTS, DUT, DEUG etc. (III)	97	114	135	127
Graduates of long-cycle higher ed. (II+I)	87	128	138	160
Total exits	**622**	**667**	**704**	**726**

* For exemple, 195 000 young persons entering the labour market after exiting from the final year of the CAP or BEP course, in 1990.
Source: DP&D (1998).

Table 3. **Distribution of youth from 1975 to 1994** (per cent)

	1975	1980	1985	1990	1994
Proportion of students					
age 15-29	29.6	33	35.3	41	44.6
age 15-19	70.9*	76.3	81.8	87.4	91.9
age 20-24	15.8	17.6	20.7	32.7	43
age 25-29	2.4	3.1	2.6	3.5	4.4
Labour force participation rate					
age 15-29	60.7	59.2	57.2	53	50
age 15-19	27.1	22.1	16.2	11.4	6.7
age 20-24	74.6	74	71.8	61.3	51.9
age 25-29	80.1	83	84.3	85.8	86.2
Proportion employed					
age 15-29	57.2	52.8	46.6	45	39.7
age 15-19	23.8	16.7	10.7	9.2	4.9
age 20-24	69.9	63	54.8	49.5	37.5
age 25-29	77.4	78.1	74.8	75.9	72.3
Proportion unemployed					
age 15-29	3.5	6.4	10.6	8	10.3
age 15-19	3.3	5.4	5.5	2.2	1.8
age 20-24	4.7	9	17	11.8	14.4
age 25-29	2.7	4.9	9.5	9.9	13.9
Unemployment rate					
age 15-29	5.8	10.9	18.6	15	20.7
age 15-19	12.1	24.5	34	19	26.2
age 20-24	6.3	12.2	23.7	19.2	27.7
age 25-29	3.3	5.9	11.2	11.6	16.1

* For example, of the young persons aged 15 to 19 inclusive in 1975, 70.9% were students.
Source: Enquêtes Emploi (Meron et Minni, 1995).

Table 4. **Youth schemes from 1976 to 1998**

(average annual numbers of participants in thousands, followed by numbers in December)

Year	PPAJ	J2550	1st job	App.	CEF	CO	CA	CO	PPAJ Work experience programmes	SIVP	TUC-CES	Other
1976					7.9							
1977	43.7			16.8	14				17.6			
1978	127.4			108.8	21.2				64.9			
1979	97.6			173.5	31.8				11.7			
1980	137.9			144.0	37.8				24.3			22.7
1981	142.4			201.5	36.2				71.2			16.8
1982	115.2			198.8	62.1				26.8		7.5	35.5
1983	9.4			180.1	82.1	0.4					7.5	53.0
1984				172.9	83.8	1.7					7.6	56.0
1985				169.2	75.8		5.8	0.7		9.7	122.8	51.8
1986		126.1		174.1	28.8		67.4	8.5		37.2	194.7	50.1
1987		222.2		198.7	2.2		203.8	33.4		103	195.2	37.6
1988		29.8		224.8			93.7	61.2		107	185.6	49.0
1989			35.0	235.6			81.7	99.3		41.9	155.9	44.3
1990			83.2	235.3			85.0	131		20.0	123.0	68.9
1991			109.0	227.8			72.7	142		12.8	106.2	66.5
Monthly number			1er, 2e				**Total CO, CA, CO**			**CES, CEC, CEV**		
Dec. 1995			37	292			154			118		
Dec. 1996			30	316			140			91		
Dec. 1997			28	340			149			84		
March 1998			27	330			155			83		

See abbreviations in Annex 1.

Sources: Meron and Minni (1995), followed by Minni and Poulet (1998).

Table 5. **Youth programme participants from 1995 to 1998** (in thousands)

	Dec. 95	Dec. 96	Dec. 97	Mar. 98
Work experience/formal training contracts (CO, CA, CO and apprenticeship)	446	455	489	485
Market employment (other than training-alternated)	294	309	299	na
Non-market employment	118	91	105	121
of which " emplois jeunes"	0	0	21	38
Total	**858**	**855**	**893**	**na**
Total less apprenticeship	566	540	553	na

na: Data not available.

Source: Minni and Poulet (1998).

Table 6. **Occurrences of various labour market situations**
from October 1993 to March 1997

No. of periods	1 Unemployment	2 Apprenticeship	3 Market progs.	4 Non-market progs.	5 Other progs.	6 CDD	7 CDI
0	27.8*	79.8	76.8	91.5	85.1	45.7	68.6
1	33.6	19.1	20.8	8.1	12.4	30.3	27.8
2	24.3	1.1	2.2	0.4	2.4	15.2	3.3
3	9.7	0	0.1	0.0	0.1	6.1	0.3
4	3.5	-	-	-	0.0	2.1	-
5 and +	1.2	-	0	-	-	0.6	-
Number of individuals	3 469	3 469	3 469	3 469	3 469	3 469	3 469

* For example, of the 3 469 individuals making up the sample, 27.8% never experienced unemployment, while 33.6% experienced it just once.

Table 7. **Situation of the 1992 cohort on leaving school and situation 3 years later**

	December 1994	March 1997
C_{DD}	**16.4***	**15.5**
C_{DI}	7.4	19.0
Non-standard employment	1.2	0.5
Apprenticeship	16.3	6.1
Market employment scheme	8.3	8.4
Non-market employment scheme	1.2	2.4
Other type of scheme	4.4	3.4
Studies	1.5	1.3
National service	7.0	3.4
Inactivity	4.6	1.4
Unemployment	**31.7**	**19.0**
Unknown (persons lost track of)	0	19.5
Number of individuals	3 469 (100%)	3 469 (100%)

* For example, of the 3 469 individuals making up the sample, 16.4% were employed under a fixed-term contract in December 1994. Three years later, in March 1997, 15.5% were similarly employed.

Table 8. **Explaining job quality**
Dependent variable = job quality score
Method: OLS

Variables	Coefficient	t and probability $> \lvert t \rvert$	
Constant	-0.002422	-0.600	0.5483
Duration of access to the job	-0.003520***	-2.707	0.0068
Level and credential (baseline: no qualification)			
Bac. level and holding bac.	0.010706***	3.173	0.0015
Bac. level and holding at most a CAP and/or BEP	0.008949**	2.110	0.0349
Bac. level and holding neither CAP nor BEP	0.004986	0.867	0.3861
BEP and/or CAP level and duly credentialled	0.005263*	1.717	0.0860
BEP and/or CAP level but uncredentialled	0.011629***	3.206	0.0014
Reason for choice of employer in cases of spontaneous application (baseline: not applicable)			
Family and professional connections	0.005461	0.638	0.5237
Personal reason(s), such as motivation	0.025917*	1.947	0.0516
Other reason(s), such as job location	0.003158**	2.033	0.0421
Chance	-0.004540	-0.341	0.7331
Skill acquisition (baseline: apprenticeship)			
Industrial by school route	0.005445**	2.080	0.0376
Tertiary by school route	0.007297***	2.616	0.0089
General tertiary by school route	0.007252*	1.858	0.0633
Possession of a driving licence	0.003449**	2.135	0.0328
Left school before end of academic year	0.006119**	2.393	0.0168
Scholastic lag	0.001758***	3.417	0.0006
Scholastic lead	-0.005453*	-1.774	0.0762
Probability of obtaining a first job	-0.007553	-0.573	0.5664

Observation: 3 166 first jobs (93.7% of the individuals had one).

*** 1% error to reject the null hypothesis.
** 5% error to reject the null hypothesis.
* 10% error to reject the null hypothesis.

Table 9. **Job duration and quality**
Dependent variable = Log(job duration)
Maximum Likelihood Method

Variables	Coefficient	t and probability > | t |	
Constant	1.48908437	66.69523	0.0001
Quality score	0.09528133***	74.30401	0.0001
Being a woman	0.14762674***	10.31199	0.0013
Level and credential (baseline: no qualification)			
Bac. level and holding bac.	0.08063353	0.480249	0.4883
Bac. level and holding at most a CAP and/or BEP	0.05417439	0.141	0.7073
Bac. level and holding neither CAP nor BEP	0.16906224	0.904599	0.3416
BEP and/or CAP level and duly credentialled	0.12200059	1.435178	0.2309
BEP and/or CAP level but uncredentialled	-0.0430164	0.147733	0.7007
Reason for choice of employer in cases of spontaneous application (baseline: not applicable)			
Family and professional connections	1.44432213***	12.14314	0.0005
Personal reason(s), such as motivation	0.22196627	0.230508	0.6311
Other reason(s), such as job location	0.05250519	1.355456	0.2443
Chance	-0.3187201	0.575644	0.4480
Skill acquisition (baseline: apprenticeship)			
Industrial by school route	-0.345376***	20.18093	0.0001
Tertiary by school route	-0.3326448***	16.09401	0.0001
General tertiary by school route	-0.1402576	1.42398	0.2327
Knowing someone in the firm	-0.236504***	23.36912	0.0001
Possessing a driving licence	-0.0142189	0.0875	0.7674
Having produced a résumé	-0.3453208***	19.8294	0.0001
Earning money on the side	-0.1813227*	2.673104	0.1021
Performing voluntary work	0.13956122	0.680827	0.4093
Using youth schemes to approach employers	-0.0703655	0.312041	0.5764
Having already had a vacation job	-0.0709775*	2.761457	0.0966
Having already had a weekend job	0.02757378	0.264551	0.6070
Having already had a fill-in job	-0.0232653	0.304284	0.5812
Having already done a work experience course	0.03082982	0.494614	0.4819
Left school before the end of the academic year	0.09117816	1.423036	0.2329
Scholastic lag	0.00391657	0.070094	0.7912
Scholastic lead	-0.1292322	1.764373	0.1841

Size of sample: 3 078 uncensored durations and 89 censored durations.
Log Likelihood = -5 156.

THE TRANSITION FROM INITIAL EDUCATION TO THE LABOUR MARKET: RECENT EXPERIENCE IN THE UNITED STATES

by
Lisa M. Lynch
Fletcher School of Law and Diplomacy, Tufts University, United States

Introduction

Twenty years ago as baby boomers entered the labour market in force, the functioning of the youth labour market in the US, as well as many other advanced industrialised economies was a major focus of policy makers and economists alike. In a comprehensive edited volume on the youth labour market Freeman and Wise (1982) summarised the nature of the youth problem in the US at the time as follows. First, the traditional distinction between being unemployed and out of the labour force was much less appropriate for youths than perhaps for other demographic groups in the labour market. As a result, analysis of the transition from school to work should examine not only unemployment rates but also employment and jobless rates of young workers. Second, youth joblessness was concentrated primarily among a small group of youth who experienced extended periods out of work. Consequently, the nature of the youth unemployment problem was more of long spells of unemployment for a minority of youth rather than many spells of unemployment for the majority of youth. Third, the young workers having the greatest difficulties in the labour market were most likely to be high school dropouts and minorities.

This paper will briefly summarise the similarities and differences in the youth labour market today compared to twenty years ago, and then examine recent empirical evidence on the consequences of early joblessness for those who have left school on subsequent labour market experience. The paper will go on to discuss some critical issues in the area of basic skills competencies of young new entrants into the labour market in the US, and then conclude with a final summary of the findings. Given length constraints, this paper can hardly begin to do justice to all of the empirical work that has been done over the past twenty years on the US youth labour market. Instead this paper seeks to highlight some of the major trends, consequences, and changes that have occurred in the US as young people make the transition from initial education into the labour market.

1. A comparison of the transition from school to work – the 1970s versus the 1990s

In some respects the current unemployment situation of US youths as they transit from school to work looks remarkably similar to the one facing US youths twenty years ago. In December 1978 the unemployment rate for teenage males was 16.6% while in December 1998 the rate was 16.4%. As reported in Freeman and Wise (1982), 1.56 million teenagers were classified as unemployed in 1978, but only 5% of teenage boys were unemployed, out of school and looking for full time work. The picture has not changed much over the past twenty years for males. As shown in Table 1, in 1997, only 4.3% of 16-24-year-old males were unemployed, out of school and looking for work.

Other aspects of the US youth labour market also do not appear to have changed much over the last twenty years. For example, in 1978 approximately 10% of young workers age 16-24 years of age were unemployed for six months or more, while in 1998 this number was 9%. In addition, twenty years ago 20-24-year-olds who had not completed high school had nearly twice the probability of experiencing unemployment as those who did complete high school. Twenty years later the Bureau of Labor Statistics, BLS (1998) found a similar pattern using the data from the National Longitudinal Survey of Youths (NLSY). This survey has followed 9 964 young men and women who were 14 to 22 years of age in 1979. In data collected from a 1996 survey of this cohort the BLS found that for those persons 31-38 years of age in 1995 who were high school dropouts, over half had experienced at least one period of unemployment during 1991-95. College graduates were only half as likely to have had a spell of unemployment.

Job shopping is as alive and well today for young workers in the United States as it was twenty years ago. Hall (1982) and Topel and Ward (1992) estimated that twenty years ago males by the age of 29 would hold an average of ten jobs. A shown in Table 2, using data from the NLSY, the average young male in the 1990s held close to nine jobs between the ages of 18 to 32 and the average young female held 8.3 jobs with the majority of the job switches occurring between the ages of 18 and 27. There is strikingly little difference in the average number of jobs held by race, gender or even educational background for youths in the 1990s in the United States.

As was true twenty years ago, there are still distinct differences in the labour market experience of youths by race and educational background. Tables 3 and 4 present some information on the nature of the employment experience of young workers using data from the 1996 interview of the NLSY. In 1995 the NLSY cohort was aged 31-38 years old. Therefore, by examining the percent of weeks employed and unemployed over the period 1991-1995 it is likely that most of this cohort will have "completed" their formal education and this period could be considered the early years following the transition from school to work. As shown in Table 3, male high school dropouts spend four times more time unemployed in their early years in the labour market than college graduates. The percentage of time spent unemployed is approximately twice as much for Blacks than Whites for all educational levels except college. When we look at weeks in employment in Table 4 we see that male(female) high school dropouts spent only 75(49)% of their early years in the labour market employed. Male (female) college graduates spent 95(81)% of their time employed. Staying on in school significantly increases the percentage of time spent in employment after leaving school, especially for women and Blacks.

But the acquisition of skills does not just occur in formal schooling; it can also take place in the workplace in the form of training. However, studies by Lynch (1992), Mincer (1988), Brown (1989), Lillard and Tan (1986), Bishop (1994), Barron et al. (1987) have all shown that education begets training. Firm provided training is much more likely to be obtained by more educated employees. This results in the creation of both a "virtuous" and a "vicious" circle of human capital accumulation. Individuals who acquire more schooling are also more likely to receive post-school employer provided training, while those with minimal education find it extremely difficult to make up this deficiency in human capital once they enter the labour market. For example, as shown in Blanchflower and Lynch (1994), by the age of twenty five high school graduates in the US are twice as likely as high school dropouts to have received any type of employer provided on-the-job training.

While there are some similarities in the youth labour market today with that of twenty years ago there are some important differences. For example, the unemployment rate for female teenagers has dropped from 16.8% to 11.3% over the last twenty years. More generally, as shown in Figure 1, the overall unemployment rate for 16-24 year olds has fallen from 12.1% in December 1978 to 9.8% in December 1998. In addition, if we look, as Freeman and Wise (1982) concluded we should, at the trends in employment rates for youths, more differences emerge. As shown in Table 5 the employment rate for teenagers has fallen from 48.3% in 1978 to 45.1% in 1998. The only group with a significant gain in employment is black teenagers, although their employment rate remains dramatically lower than the employment rate of Whites at 30.1% in 1998 versus 48.9% for white teenagers.

But before we conclude that the overall employment situation has deteriorated for youths over the past twenty years in the US another important trend must be noted. One of the largest differences between 16-24-year-olds today and the same age group twenty years ago is the proportion of youth in school. As shown in Figures 2a and 2b there has been a sharp increase here. This is due both to more youths, especially young women, staying on in postsecondary education, and declines in high school dropout rates. As shown in Figure 2b, in 1997, 70.3% of female and 63.5% of male high school graduates enrolled in college or university. In 1980 the enrolment rates were 51.8% and 46.7% respectively. In terms of race and ethnicity, from 1980 to 1995 high school graduates' college enrolment rates rose for Whites from 49.9 to 65.8%, for Blacks from 41.8 to 51.4%, and for Hispanics from 49.9 to 51.1%. While the rates rose for all race/ethnicity groups, they rose the most for Whites but barely changed for Hispanics. In addition, as shown in Figure 2a, high school dropout rates declined across all demographic groups, especially for black non-Hispanic males (from 22.3% in 1972 to 13.5% in 1996).

So part of the decline in the employment rate simply reflects the fact that young people are staying in school, and delaying their entry into the labour market. Since the ratio of median earnings of women(men) college to high school graduates rose from 1.44(1.29) to 1.69(1.67) from 1979 to 1995 this seems like a very wise decision. Rates of return to remaining on in school are large in the United States. For example, Kane and Rouse (1995) found that a year of post high school education in the US increases earnings by 5-10% after controlling for family background and test scores in high school. Work by Ashenfelter and Krueger (1994) on identical twins found that each year of additional schooling raised later earnings of the more educated twin by 13%.

While, as shown in Table 1, 55% of 16-24-year-olds are in school, many of those in school are also active in the labour market making it increasingly difficult to date the moment when a young worker transits from school to work. For example, a third of young people enrolled in high school also work, almost two-thirds of those enrolled in 2-year colleges are also employed, and almost one-half of those in 4-year colleges are also employed. Over 15% of those in college (2 or 4-year college programs) are part time students and of this group the vast majority are working (84.4%) while attending college. So in many respects what we see in the US today is that the transition between school and work is becoming just as blurred (if not more so!) as the transition between unemployment and out of the labour force for youths. Some students transit from school to work, others do both school and work for an extended period, and finally still others transit from work to school.

Finally, twenty years ago 50% of the unemployed were under 25 years of age while today only a bit more than a third of the unemployed are under the age of 25. This change in the overall composition of the unemployed is perhaps one of the greatest differences between today's youth labour market and that of twenty years ago. As discussed in Korenman and Neumark (forthcoming) this change in the proportion of the unemployed who are young is driven in large part by demographic changes. Twenty years ago the ratio of the youth population to the adult population in the US was 43% while today it is close to 30%.

2. The role of individual characteristics versus demand conditions for the duration of joblessness

In spite of the decline in the proportion of the overall unemployed in the US who are under the age of 24, young workers still represent a disproportionately high percentage of the unemployed. As shown in Table 6, while the overall unemployment rate in the United States may have been only 4.3% in January 1999, the unemployment rate for teenage males was almost four times as high. The unemployment rate for black teenage males is over 34% and a quarter of black teenage females are unemployed. While the unemployment rate for young workers age 20-24 is less than half the rate for those 16-19 years of age, it is still high at almost 7%. If one were to include the number of young workers who were out of the labour force but not in school these percentages would become even higher.

But unemployment rates do not tell us much about the dynamics of unemployment. For example, is the current unemployment rate of black teenagers high because there has been a large inflow into unemployment by black youth or is it high because of a marked decrease in the outflow from unemployment (*i.e.* longer duration of unemployment) by black teenagers? Table 7 provides some insight into the dynamics of youth unemployment today. In 1998 less than 10% of unemployed teenagers were in a spell of unemployment that was six months or longer. There is a large difference, however, in the average duration of a spell of unemployment and the median duration of youth unemployment. The median duration of a spell of unemployment for 16-19-year-olds was 4.4 weeks while the average duration was more than twice as long at 9.5 weeks. A similar pattern applies for young workers 20 to 24 years of age. The data in Table 7 suggest that while much of youth unemployment in the US is relatively short in duration, there is a small group of workers stuck in long spells of unemployment.

Perhaps we should not be particularly concerned about these youth unemployment rates or even durations of unemployment because youth unemployment is simply part of a productive and efficient job search process. In other words, time spent unemployed for young people is time spent accumulating valuable knowledge about the labour market. However, early periods of joblessness in a worker's career may have long term employment consequences for two primary reasons. First, the loss of valuable work experience, especially if this experience includes investment in on-the-job training, may make it more difficult for youths to find employment later on and depress their entire earnings profile. In addition, early periods of joblessness for young workers who are no longer in school may lead to poor work habits, weak labour force attachment and general alienation from society. Being without work for an extended period of time could alter the attitudes of youth if they then become discouraged about their chances of successfully finding work and this may spill over into their job search behaviour. Finally, employers who have great difficulty in distinguishing among new entrants into the labour market may use employment records as a signal of potential productivity. In this context, even a one time demand shock which raises overall unemployment could have long term consequences on the equilibrium level of unemployment.

Traditionally economists have used two distinct empirical research strategies to examine the consequences of unemployment. Macro economists have explored how changes in employment and unemployment duration over time affect changes in aggregate unemployment rates. The question of interest in most of this work is: Are changes over time in the aggregate unemployment rate driven by changes in the rate at which jobs end or are destroyed or by changes in the average duration of unemployment? But as discussed in Imbens and Lynch (1995), relatively little of this work, with the exception of Baker (1992), controls for changing characteristics of the unemployed over the business cycle. If the characteristics of the inflow into unemployment change over the cycle, one could confound pure business cycle effects with demographic effects.

An alternative empirical strategy pursued by micro economists (using detailed information on the employment history of young workers from data sources in the US such as the National Longitudinal Surveys) has been to estimate the determinants of the length of an individual's spell of unemployment or joblessness using longitudinal data. But these studies typically observe labour market transitions over a limited period of time making it difficult to tease out the effect of changes in the overall economy on the duration of joblessness. Specifically it may appear that a particular characteristic reduces re-employment probabilities when in fact individuals with that characteristic are just more likely to lose their jobs during periods of low average re-employment probabilities.

The distinction between the impact of individual characteristics versus macroeconomic demand conditions to explain fluctuations in the unemployment experience of workers in general or youth in particular has important policy implications. If individual differences are the main component of variation in re-employment probabilities, policies should be targeted at those with characteristics associated with low re-employment probabilities. If instead, changes in macroeconomic conditions are the main source of variation then more attention should be place on policies that affect labour demand conditions.

Twenty years ago it would have been exceedingly difficult to examine an issue such as this with the data that was available at the time. However, in Imbens and Lynch (1995), using data from the NLSY over the period 1978-1989, we construct a sample of approximately 5 000 men and women who have just entered the labour market and observe their labour market transitions in the first four years after they "permanently" leave school. We created seven "waves" of school leavers and pooled data on youth who finished school (completed and did not return for four years) in 1979 and their labour market experience through the 1983 interview date; those who finished school in 1980 and their labour market experience through 1984, etc. up to school leavers in 1985 and their labour market experience through 1989. In this way we were able to merge a wealth of information on the employment history of workers, their individual characteristics, and local labour demand conditions, and examine how the early labour market experience of these youths is affected by the two business cycles that occur over this period of time. We estimated the determinants of the duration of non-employment spells for these youths using a Cox regression or proportional hazard model that allows for a flexible time dependence that can incorporate both seasonal and business cycle effects.

It would take up too much space in this paper to go through all of the modelling issues involved but a short summary of our findings follows:

– Human capital significantly reduces the duration of a spell of joblessness. More educated workers have shorter spells out of work as do those workers who have received employer provided training. Government training does raise the re-employment probabilities for young women but appears to have little impact on young men.

– Young black males and young women have lower re-employment probabilities even after controlling for a wide range of characteristics. For women the number of children they have also increases the expected duration of a spell of joblessness.

– Unemployment compensation actually reduces the spell of joblessness for young workers in their early years in the labour market after school. This effect, however, may be just picking up greater attachment to the labour market since eligibility requirements for unemployment insurance require substantial labour market experience which these new entrants to the labour market are just acquiring.

– There is evidence of negative duration dependence: the longer the current spell of joblessness the lower the re-employment probability. In addition, while the number of past spells of joblessness has little impact on the duration of a current spell of joblessness, we find some evidence of lagged duration dependence in that those individuals who have had long previous spells of joblessness have longer So having experienced some unemployment as a young worker does not necessarily seem to have harmful effects later on, as long as this spell was short in duration.

– Poor local current spells of joblessness. labour market conditions reduce the re-employment probabilities for all young workers. But individuals in a long spell of unemployment in an area with a high unemployment rate do not appear to be as stigmatised by their joblessness as individuals who have long unemployment spells in low unemployment areas.

– While there are some changes in the characteristics of those young workers who become unemployed over the business cycle, a great deal of the variation in the re-employment probabilities seems to be driven by business and seasonal cycles, not just individual characteristics of job losers.

3. Knowledge gaps of young US workers in the 1990s

In Imbens and Lynch (1995) we conclude that there are significant differences in the labour market transitions from joblessness to employment of young workers by race, gender and human capital. But while investments in human capital matter in terms of the subsequent labour market experience of young workers, a successful transition from initial school to work is facilitated by both an individual's accumulated stock of human capital and overall demand conditions. At the moment, we are experiencing in the US a record peacetime expansion of the economy and historically low unemployment rates. In addition, as shown in Figure 2b, the proportion of young people staying on in postsecondary education has increased dramatically over the past twenty years. This would suggest that all must be terrific in the youth labour market, especially compared with twenty years ago.

But why are so many employers complaining about the quality of young workers and the quality of schools, especially high schools? In a recent nationally representative survey of US employers, almost one in five employers rated the quality of their local high school as unacceptable while less than 5% of employers rate their local community or 4-year colleges as unacceptable. Two-thirds of employers never use transcripts in hiring and one in four view academic performance as having no value. What is it that they are looking for in new young hires and what has happened to the capacity of youths and schools to meet these employer skill needs over time?

One of the big differences in the labour market today compared to that of twenty years ago can be found in this same survey of US employers. More and more employers today expect that non-managerial employees will be working in teams or participating in problem solving groups than was true in the past. Over 40% reported that three-quarters of their front line workers use computers. As a result of these changes most employers in the US report that their skill requirements are rising and that they are looking for workers with excellent communication skills and a positive attitude. As more employers adopt what are called "high performance workplace practices" they say that they need more workers who not only can do a specific task but are also able to problem solve, work in teams, be math and computer literate and have learned how to learn – the so-called "knowledge worker".

But when we look in Figure 3 at trends in knowledge as measured by reading achievement by age in the US we see that for pre-college youth there has not been a dramatic change in these scores since the early 1970s. Findings for math are especially surprising since recent work by Levine and Zimmerman has found that an additional half-year of math in high school for young women would increase their wages by 3-5.5%, and raises their probability of attending and graduating from college.

Figure 4 presents the average reading achievement for 17-year-olds by different demographic groups over the past 25 years. Here we see sharp differences by demographic background. In particular, average reading skills have actually worsened for males, improved and then worsened for Hispanics, and stagnated for Whites. At the same time there has been some slight improvement for females and a dramatic improvement in average reading skills for black non-Hispanics especially during the 1980s. However, a large part of the gains achieved by non-Hispanic Blacks in the 1980s was eroded in the late 1980s and early 1990s.

The picture, however, gets bleaker when we compare the basic skill competencies of young workers in the US to their counterparts in other advanced industrialised economies using data from the recent OECD Adult Literacy Survey. As shown in Figure 5 one in five employed workers age 16-24 in the US can barely add two numbers together compared with less than 10% in Canada and less than 5% in other European countries. In addition, those countries in the International Adult Literacy Survey that had higher variation in skills also experienced more inequality growth over the period 1979-1990. Why are there such large differences in the basic skill levels of youth across these countries? Nickell and Bell (1996) argue that the educational system in a country such as Germany system produces a much more compressed distribution of human capital than the US system. In Germany, basic educational standards are set for all students to attain and students know that their performance will be a critical factor in the probability that they attend university or obtain a good apprenticeship. In other words, the educational system sets high minimum standards for all, and there are incentives in place for all, and not just for those going on in higher education, to do well in school.

When youths complete their schooling in Germany as many as three quarters continue on in apprenticeship training. This school-to-work transition results in a very different level of skills attainment for new entrants in the labour market in Germany than in the US, especially for those in the bottom half of the ability distribution. For example, Buechtemann *et al.* (1993) followed two cohorts of youths leaving compulsory schooling in Germany and the US in 1978/1979. They found that after 12 years, 80% of the German youths had attained a vocational training certificate or university degree after leaving school while only 54% of their US counterparts had obtained a certificate or degree. Nickell and Bell conclude that a school system that sets and achieves a high level of performance for those in the bottom half of the ability range combined with a comprehensive post schooling leaving vocational training system can help minimise many of the negative consequences of a relative demand shift away from the unskilled.

One solution to this problems of inadequate skills of new entrants into the labour market is to get more students into higher education or to have more employers provide basic skills training if this is what they say they need. But recent work by Bishop and Kane has argued that the rising costs of tuition in the face of imperfect capital markets in the United States has had an adverse effect on college completion. In addition, a recent study by the US General Accounting Office (1996) shows how tuition at 4-year public colleges and universities has risen three times faster than the median household income between 1980 and 1995. Student aid has not kept pace with tuition levels so students and their families are relying more heavily on loans and working while in school. More federal financing of higher education now comes in the form of loans rather than grants. In 1970 loans made up 40% of federal aid while by 1990 they made up 65% of federal aid. In 1970 about one-third of college students worked full time while now almost half of all students work full time. So students are taking on greater debt to attend school and fewer can afford the luxury of being just a student and concentrating entirely on their studies. Given these rising costs, some are forced to not enter college, delay entry, not concentrate as much on their studies because of the need to work, or drop out of school in spite of the wage premium associated with acquiring more education.

4. Conclusion

If economists can agree on anything it is probably that returns to investments in human capital are large and real. More years of schooling are associated with higher earnings, lower unemployment, and higher productivity. In addition, surveys of employee benefits show that those with more years of schooling are also more likely to receive employer provided health insurance and pension benefits. In many respects current labour market conditions for youth in the US could not be better. Overall unemployment is low, the proportion of youth in the labour market has shrunk, and education levels have risen, especially for women. But if a young person enters the labour market today with a high school degree or less, they are unlikely to find much demand for their skills, or that employers are willing to invest in their human capital formation. The combined effects of a booming economy and a shrinking percentage of the workforce that is young may provide an opportunity to address the basic skills gap that we see in a disturbingly large proportion of young workers today. The challenge however will be to develop policies and programs that not only raise the proportion of youth who stay on in school but also raise the skill levels of those one in five young workers who can not perform simple arithmetic and who are already out in the labour market.

BIBLIOGRAPHY

ASHENFELTER, O. and KRUEGER, A. (1994), "Estimates of the Economic Returns to Schooling from a Sample of Twins," *American Economic Review*, December.

BARRON, J., BLACK, D. and LOEWENSTEIN, J (1987), "Employer Size: The Implications for Search, Training, Capital Investment, Starting Wages and Wage Growth", *Journal of Labor Economics*, January.

BISHOP, J. (1994), "The Impact of Previous Training on Productivity and Wages," in L. Lynch (ed.), *Training and the Private Sector: International Comparisons*, University of Chicago Press, Chicago.

BLANCHFLOWER, D. and LYNCH, L. (1994), "Training at Work: A comparison of US and British Youths" in L. Lynch (ed.), *Training and the Private Sector: International Comparisons*, University of Chicago Press, Chicago.

BROWN, J. (1989), "Why do Wages Increase with Tenure?", *American Economic Review*, December.

BUECHTEMANN, C., SCHUPP, J. and SOLOFF, D. (1993), "Roads to Work: School-to-Work Transition Patterns in Germany and the US", *Industrial Relations Journal*, June 24(1), pp. 97-111.

BUREAU OF LABOR STATISTICS (1998a), "Number of Jobs, Labor Market Experience, and Earnings Growth: Results from a Longitudinal Survey", news release, June 24.

BUREAU OF LABOR STATISTICS (1998b), Current Population Survey.

FREEMAN, R. and WISE, D. (eds.) (1982), *The Youth Labor Market Problem*, University of Chicago Press, Chicago.

HALL, R. (1982), "The Importance of Lifetime Jobs in the US Economy", *American Economic Review*, pp. 716-724.

IMBENS, G. and LYNCH, L. (1995), "Re-employment Probabilities Over the Business Cycle", Harvard and Tufts University, mimeo, July.

KORENMAN, S. and NEUMARK, D. (forthcoming), "Cohort Crowding and Youth Labor Market: A Cross-National Analysis", in Blanchflower and Freeman (eds.), *Youth Employment and Joblessness in Advanced Countries*, University of Chicago Press, Chicago.

KANE, T. and ROUSE, C. (1995), "Labor Market Returns to Two-Year and Four-Year College", *American Economic Review*, June.

LYNCH, L. (1992), "Private Sector Training and the Earnings of Young Workers," *American Economic Review*, March, pp. 299-312.

MINCER, J. (1988), "Job Training, Wage Growth and Labor Turnover", National Bureau of Economic Research, Working Paper No. 2690, August.

NICKELL, S. and BELL, B. (1996), "Changes in the Distribution of Wages and Unemployment in OECD Countries," *American Economic Review*, May, pp. 302-308.

TOPEL, R. and WARD, M. (1992), "Job Mobility and the Careers of Young Workers", *Quarterly Journal of Economics*, May.

US GENERAL ACCOUNTING OFFICE (1996), "Higher Education: Tuition Increasing Faster than Household Income and Public Colleges Costs," August.

Table 1. **Labour market and schooling status of 16-24 year olds**
(Percentage)

October 1997

Status	All	Men	Women
In school	55	55	56
- and working	24	23	26
- and unemployed	3	3	2
- and not in labour force	28	29	28
Working but not in school	33	36	30
Unemployed not in school	4	4.3	3.5
Not in labour force and not in school	8	5	11

Source: Bureau of Labor Statistics (Oct. 1997), Current Population Survey supplemental questions on school enrolment and high school graduation status of persons 16-24 years of age.

Table 2. **Average number of jobs between the ages of 18 and 32 by individuals aged 31-38 in 1995**

	Total[a]	18-22 years	23-27 years	28-32 years
Men	8.9	4.5	3.4	2.8
Women	8.3	4.3	3.1	2.4
White	8.8	4.6	3.3	2.6
Black	7.9	3.6	3.1	2.6
Hispanic	7.9	4.0	3.0	2.5

a. Note that jobs that were held in more than one of the 5-year age periods were counted in each column but only once in the total column.
Source: Bureau of Labor Statistics (1998a).

Table 3. **Percent of total weeks unemployed 1991-95 by individuals aged 31-38 in 1995**

	Men	Women	White	Black	Hispanic
High school drop-out	7.9	4.2	5.5	9.8	5.7
High school graduate only	4.8	4.1	3.6	8.4	4.9
Some college	3.8	2.9	2.8	5.6	3.4
College graduate	1.8	1.8	1.7	2.6	1.8

Source: Bureau of Labor Statistics (1998a).

Table 4. **Percent of total weeks employed 1991-95 by individuals aged 31-38 in 1995**

	Men	Women	White	Black	Hispanic
High school drop-out	75.2	48.8	68.8	48.2	62.2
High school graduate only	86.8	68.9	80.3	69.0	75.3
Some college	88.0	76.1	82.6	77.6	80.7
College graduate	95.4	81.1	88.2	90.9	88.7

Source: Bureau of Labor Statistics (1998a).

Table 5. **Employment-population rate,
16-19-year-olds**

	1978	1998
All	48.3	45.1
Male	52.2	44.7
Female	44.5	45.5
White	52.4	48.9
Black	25.2	30.1

Source: Bureau of Labor Statistics, calculated from the current population survey.

Table 6. **Youth unemployment rates,
January 1999** (Percentages)

	16-19 years of age	20-24 years of age
All	15.5	6.9
Males	16.9	7.1
Females	13.9	6.7
White males	14.1	
White females	11.9	
Black males	34.2	
Black females	25.0	

Source: Bureau of Labor Statistics, calculated from the current population survey.

Table 7. **Distribution of unemployment by duration,
annual average 1998** (Percentages)

Age	< 5 weeks	5-14 weeks	15-26 weeks	27 weeks+
Total, 16 years and over Average duration = 14.5 weeks Median duration = 6.7 weeks	42	31	12	14
16 to 19 years of age Average duration = 9.5 weeks Median duration = 4.4 weeks	51	33	8	7
20 to 24 years of age Average duration = 12.3 weeks Median duration = 5.6 weeks	46	32	11	11

Source: Bureau of Labor Statistics (1998*b*) annual averages. Note rows may not add up to 100% due to rounding.

Figure 1. **Unemployment rate, 16-24 year olds**

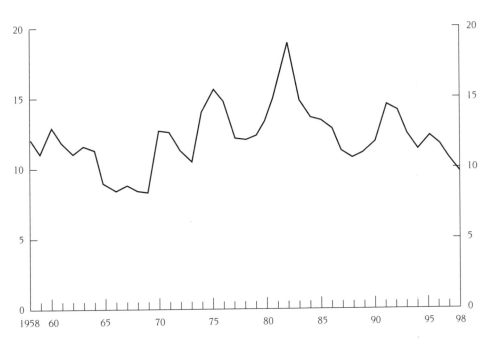

Source: US Bureau of Labor Statistics, "Employment and Earnings," various issues.

Figure 2a. **Percentage of high school drop-outs among 16-24 years old**

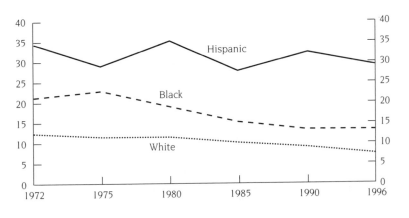

Source: US Bureau of Labor Statistics, "Employment and Earnings," various issues.

Figure 2b. **College enrollment rates of high school graduates**

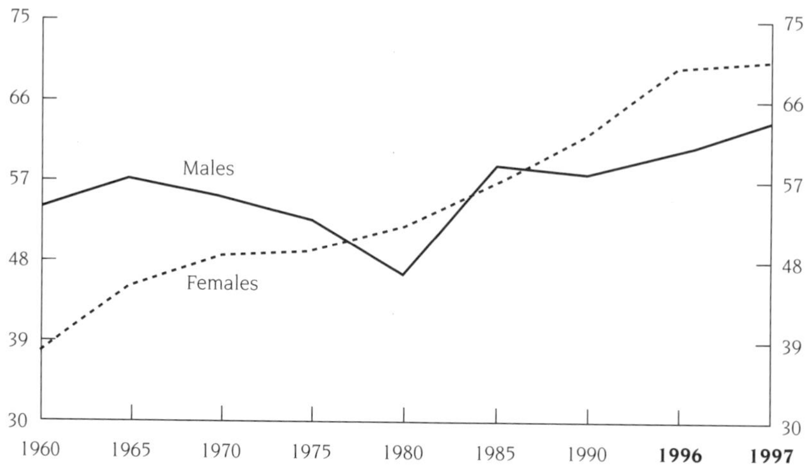

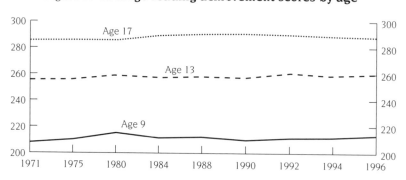

Source: US Dept. of Education, D*igest of Education Statistics* 1997 and Bureau of Labor Statistics Current Population Survey.

Figure 3. **Average reading achievement scores by age**

For Reading:
Level 150 – simple discrete reading tasks
Level 200 – partial skills and understanding
Level 250 – interrelates ideas and makes generalisations
Level 300 – understands complicated information
Level 350 – learns from specialised reading materials.

Source: US Department of Education, National Assessment of Educational Progress 1996 Trends in Educational Progress.

Figure 4. **Average reading achievement, age 17**

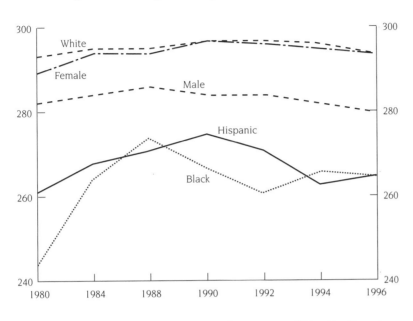

Source: US Department of Education, National Assessment of Education Progress 1996 Trends in Education.

Figure 5. **Percentage of employed 16-24 year olds with minimal mathematical skills**

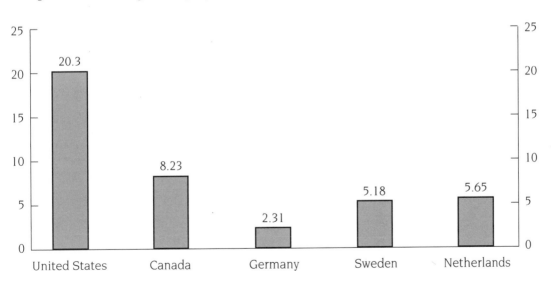

Source: OECD Adult Literacy Survey (1995), Employed Individuals, minimal quantitative score.

WORKSHOP 4

BEYOND THE INITIAL TRANSITION:
IMPROVING YOUTH'S ACCESS TO JOBS AND CAREERS –
THE ROLE OF LABOUR MARKET INSTITUTIONS AND REGULATION

THE JAPANESE EMPLOYMENT SYSTEM AND YOUTH LABOUR MARKET

by
Naoki Mitani
Faculty of Economics, Kobe University, Japan

Introduction

Under the current recession, conditions in the Japanese labour market have sharply deteriorated. The unemployment rate rose to an historical high of 4.4% in November 1998. Young workers are most affected together with older workers over 60 years old. Nonetheless, youth unemployment problems are not considered as a primary policy target. There may be two reasons. First, the rapid ageing of the population and the decreasing number of young people would imply the future improvement of the position of young workers in the labour market, and the increasing importance of older workers as the target of labour market policy. Second, the youth labour market has thus far performed relatively well compared with other OECD Member countries.

Much literature has discussed the special role played by high schools in the placement of their graduates and the Japanese employment system in which enterprises tend to hire and train young workers on OJT under long-term employment practices (Dore *et al.*, 1989; Hashimoto, 1994). If Japanese young workers enjoy relatively better employment opportunities, these factors must contribute to it.

This paper investigates the relationship between the performance of youth labour market and the Japanese school/employment system. We use some statistical data as well as a literature survey. We would like to pay more attention to economic factors rather than social or cultural ones. Namely, we would like to consider the efficiency of training within firms in the Japanese employment system, the contents of the skills on which Japanese firms put most emphasis and/or the structure of the firm.

The structure of this paper is as follows. In the next section, we will have a brief overview of the Japanese youth labour market. In Section 2, we discuss the Japanese education system and the placement activities by high schools. In Section 3, we will see the general features of the Japanese labour market. In Section 4, we will investigate the relationship between the firms employment practices and the youth labour market. In Section 5, we will discuss about the wage determination of youth with minimum wage system and collective bargaining practices. The final section summarises the implications.

1. Overview of the youth labour market

Recent developments

The labour force participation rates of youth have been fairly stable the past 20 years (Figure 1). The participation rates of teenagers for both sexes decreased sharply until the mid-1970s, and flattened to around 18% thereafter. The participation rate of young male adults has shown a similar pattern, although it flattened in the late 1970s. These tendencies reflect the trend of the increase in the proportion of youth going into higher education. The participation rate of young female adults shows somewhat different trends. It had been rising slowly until 1992. This may be attributable to the factors accounting for the rise in the participation rate of other female age groups such as the rise in the average marriage age and growing employment opportunities for women. For all young sex-age groups, the participation rates have decreased slightly, reflecting the current recession that began at the end of 1991.

The majority of young workers are full-time regular workers. The proportion of part-time workers is relatively high among young workers.[1] But most part-time employment is so-called *Arubaito*,[2] which is usually conducted by full-time students in high schools or universities.

The employment opportunities for youth have sharply deteriorated since the beginning of the current recession. For instance, the number of jobs offered to a new school leaver job applicant from senior high school declined from the peak of 3.3 in 1992 to 1.8 in 1997, according to the Statistics on Placement Activities of the Ministry of Labour.

The youth unemployment rate has risen to an historical high during the current long recession. It declined during the economic boom from the late 1980s to the early 1990s. But, from 1992 onwards, it began to rise rapidly. For male teenagers, it has risen to over 10% for the first time. The unemployment rate of young adults exceeds 6% (Figure 2). Recently, the ratio of youth unemployment to the overall unemployment rate stabilised at 2.6 and 1.8 for teenagers and young adults, respectively. However, the ratio for teenagers increased to over 3 during the last economic boom in the late 1980s.

The reasons for job search for the unemployed shed some light on the nature of the youth labour market. Young workers tend to be unemployed because of voluntary quits rather than involuntary separation. In fact, 75% of separations are voluntary (quit) for young workers aged 15-24 years old, while only 50% and 10% are for prime-age workers (25 to 54 years old) and older worker (55 years old and over), respectively (Table 1). This may account for the fact that the youth unemployment rate did not decrease as much as the overall unemployment rate during the boom beginning at the end of the last decade. Nonetheless, the recent increase in unemployment through quitting may imply that the deteriorated labour market situation made young workers take jobs with worse working conditions than before. In addition, the increase in unemployment among the new school leavers who have never had jobs also indicates the deterioration of youth labour markets. The number of young who remain unemployed after graduation (new school-leavers) increased from 50 000 in February 1991 to 70 000 in February 1998.[3]

Main features of the Japanese youth labour market

The youth labour market in Japan differs from that of other countries in a number of ways.

First, youth unemployment is relatively low. Although the recent recession has increased youth unemployment, its level is still lower, compared with other OECD Member countries. The unemployment rates for youth aged 15-24 years old was 6.1% in 1997. This figure was the second lowest following Switzerland among OECD Member countries. Under the worst recession since World War II, it rose sharply in 1998, but it still seems below 8%. The incidence of long-term unemployment among youth is also lower, compared with other OECD countries (OECD, 1996, Table 4.4).

Second, Japanese new school-leavers tend to be employed as full-time regular workers[4] from the start of their professional careers. According to the Ministry of Labour, *Jyakunensya Syugyo Jittai Chosa* (Survey on Young Employees), the proportion of young workers who were employed as full-time regular workers in their first employment after graduation was 83.8% in 1997 (Figure 3). This figure is much higher than other OECD Member countries (OECD, 1998, Table 3.5).

Third, the job change rate for a typical young worker is low in Japan among the OECD countries. The OECD (1996) reports the average number of jobs per year held by young persons after leaving school for some Member countries. It is 0.17 for men and for women in Japan. This is much less than the US. [0.86 (men), 0.76 (women), Norway (0.57, 0.63), Great Britain (0.26, 0.34) and Germany (0.26, 0.22)]. The turnover rate of young Japanese workers rose somewhat from the late 1980s to early 1990s but it has been stable thereafter. Nonetheless, it is noteworthy that the turnover rates of young workers are not negligible. Analysis of unemployment insurance data show that about one-half of the new school leavers from high schools and a little less than 30% of the new school leavers from universities quit full-time regular jobs in their first three years.[5]

The above features may be explained by various economic, social and/or historical factors. Here we would like to focus on the following institutional aspects of the Japanese employment system as well as those of the transition from school to work.

2. Education and the transition from school-to-work[6]

Overview of educational institutions

This section briefly describes the Japanese educational system. Compulsory education is composed of six years of elementary school and three years of junior high school education (Figure 4). Although a few classes of home economy and vocational technology are taught, the majority of classes taught at junior high schools are general education.

The careers of junior high school graduates are as follows. Three-year senior high schools admit about 96% of junior school graduates. In 1997, only 1.4% of junior high school graduates entered the labour force. Only 1% either had no job or did not go to senior high school. Another 1% went to vocational schools. Only 0.2% of all junior high school graduates entered public vocational training centres. In other words, after compulsory education only a few graduates go directly into work or other types of vocational training institutions such as Special Vocational Schools at the secondary educational level. Thus, vocational training institutions and apprenticeship programs play a very limited role in Japan.

Students pass the entrance examination to enter senior high schools, with the results serving to channel students into different types and ranks of high schools. There are different types of high schools. General high schools provide general and academic courses such as mathematics, languages, sciences, social sciences, physical education and arts. Besides general high schools, there are several types of vocational high schools: commercial high schools, industrial high schools, agricultural high schools, nurse training high schools and fisheries schools. Under these categories of vocational schools and courses, there are sub-categories of vocational education courses. For example, within industrial high schools, there are architecture, auto-mechanics, chemical industry, civil engineering courses, etc. Within commercial high schools, there are sales, accounting and information processing courses. There are about 300 kinds of vocational courses in vocational high schools.

The majority (about three-quarters) of Japanese students enter general high schools, while less than one-third go to vocational high schools. Among vocational high school courses, male students tend toward technical courses and female students are enrolled in commercial, home economy and nurse training high schools. As with general high schools, there is a ranking of vocational schools.

Less than 30% of high school graduates enter the labour force while over 50% are enrolled in higher education or vocational-training institutions at the post-secondary level. Higher educational institutions are composed of 4-year universities and colleges (*Daigaku*), 2-year colleges (*Tandai*) and technical colleges (*Koto Senmon Gakko*). Technical colleges are unique institutions, because they combine 3-year upper secondary education and 2-year post-secondary education.

Other than these official higher educational institutions, there are Special Vocational Schools (*Senmon Gakko*), Miscellaneous Schools (*Kakusyu Gakko*) and Vocational Training Institutions outside the educational system run by Ministries. Special Vocational Schools and Miscellaneous Schools provide a variety of training, such as computer programming and foreign languages. The years to complete these programs vary according to the diversity of training offered. The number of enrolled in these schools has grown rapidly since the last decade. In 1997, 29% of new senior high school graduates entered these schools.

Outside the formal education system, there are vocational training institutions mainly run by Ministries other than the Ministry of Education. Vocational Training Centres are training institutions run by the Ministry of Labour. There are 382 Vocational Training Centres. Ministries have certain professional schools such as the Police Academy, the College of Meteorology and Training Centre for Diplomats. Only 1% of senior high school graduates who receive any kind of post-secondary education or training enter these institutions. Therefore, they have negligible influence on the transition of youth from school to work.

Junior high schools and other types of vocational training institutions play a limited role in the transition to work. Most enter the world of work from senior high schools (especially vocational high schools) and other post-secondary educational institutions.

Transition from school-to-work

Placement by senior high schools

First, institutionally, some part of the job placement activities of students is delegated to high schools. The Japanese Employment Security Law stipulates that the Public Employment Security Office (PESO) can delegate some parts of their duties to junior or senior high schools for job placement of their students or graduates. Employers' recruitment, in general, should be implemented under the supervision of the PESO. This regulation thus allows employers to deal directly with schools or the PESO itself, rather than with individual students. Employers must specify the conditions of recruitment to the PESO, the number of job offers to the school, job contents, wages, work-time, etc. Then, based on the job offers, each school recommends students to employers. Employers rarely reject those recommended. Job placement activities begin more than a half-year before students graduate. Most senior students find their jobs before graduation. Thus high schools play a crucial role in the transition of students to work.

Second, there are semi-formal or implicit contracts (*Jisseki Kankei*) between specific employers and high schools, which ensure smooth transitions for high school graduates. Employers prefer to recruit from specific high schools year after year. Recruitment tends to be stabilised by highly trustworthy semiformal employment contracts. Contract employers represent a small proportion (about 10%) of those providing jobs. But about half of the graduates are employed by these contracts employers. They are dominant in this respect. In addition, they tend to offer desirable jobs in terms of job training, job security and perspectives for future careers. Contract firms dominate the labour market of the graduates of the school and the school relies heavily on them to place their graduates. Maintaining these relationships are important for schools wishing to successfully place their graduates and for firms wishing to recruit capable employees. Schools must select students who satisfy employers in order to keep on receiving their job allocations in the future and employers try to continue hiring the schools graduates so as to continue receiving a stable supply of capable employees.

Third, these recruitment practices are based on meritocratic criterions in terms of academic achievement. Firms give jobs offers to the schools in semi-formal contracts, according to the rank of each school in the area. As mentioned, students are admitted into schools of different ranks by the entrance examination. The rank in the hierarchy can be an indication by which firms screen the new school leavers. Within each school, the selection of the graduates to recommend is also based on academic achievement.

This is a strong incentive for students to study and is a device for schools to control their students. It should be noted that academic achievement is also important for vocational high schools. About two-third of the classes taught at vocational high schools are not vocational, but academic.

There is some evidence for the efficiency of this placement practice by school. For instance, a Ministry of Labour Survey on Young Employees investigates the labour market experiences after graduation as well as how the decision to take the first job was made. Apparently, the young workers who took the first jobs by the recommendation of the schools are the relatively stable jobs (Figure 5).

In sum, the placement practices of schools and informal relationships between schools and specific firms contribute to the efficiency of the transition from school to work and also motivate students to take difficult "academic" classes.

Drop-outs from school

Among the graduates from schools, there are those who refuse to take full-time jobs and work on temporary jobs or part-time jobs. The proportion of the students who quit schools or drop out before graduation has increased. Some graduates refuse to take full-time jobs and work on temporary jobs or part-time jobs. In 1995, the number of the drop-outs from senior high schools was 112 000 or 2.5% of all students.

The drop-outs rely on private job-search means, such as the information from their family, relatives or friends. According to a survey on drop-outs from senior high schools conducted by the Japan Institute of Labour, only 6.6% of drop-outs found their first regular jobs though schools, while 65.3% of graduates found them through schools. More than half of the drop-outs get their first regular jobs by the information from their family, relatives or friends, while only one-fifth of the graduates used this information. As a result, the proportion of regular jobs among their first jobs for drop-outs (36.7%) is much lower than for graduates (87.7%). In addition, the turnover rate is higher for drop-outs than for graduates. Seventy per cent of the drop-outs who had full-time jobs quit jobs within one year. This is far higher than the 36.9% among senior high school graduates and is almost the same as those of junior high school graduates.

Transition from school to work for university graduates

In the case of university graduates, the roles of schools are limited. Students begin to consider jobs after graduation around December of the third year. Around April in the final (the fourth) year, they begin job hunting. Almost all students terminate job hunting in late July, after having received Nainaitei (pre-informal promise of employment). They are usually employed the following April, after their graduation. The methods of job search are different between the students in sciences or engineering and those in social sciences. Students in social sciences tend to search by themselves, using guidebooks on job information, or pamphlets companies have sent to them. Students in sciences or engineering use the above methods as well, but they tend to use recommendations of professors. They also apply for job offerings sent to the placement office of the universities. To avoid the bad effects on education caused by too early recruitment activities, an agreement about the beginning date of companies' recruitment activities was made and it fixed the official beginning date of an informal promise of employment as October 1st. However, the agreement was abandoned in 1997.

In the recruitment of new graduates from university, the reputation of schools or their ranking is an important criterion. Certain large companies used to have a system under which only the students from the designated famous universities could apply for job offers. Officially, few companies have such a system. However, in practice, the name and reputation of the of the university are important factors used in determining which graduates to select. Some large companies have a quota to meet from certain famous universities. Here again, there is a hierarchy of universities, which large firms use in screening the students in their hiring process.[7]

3. General features of the Japanese labour market

Before investigating the relation between the employer's behaviour and the youth labour market, we would like to mention the general features of the Japanese labour market.

It is often pointed out that the following are the main features:

– Life-time employment.

– Seniority based wage or steep age-wage profile.

– Enterprise-based unions.

This section briefly overviews the first two points.

Long-term employment

As documented in OECD (1993, 1997), Japan is one of the countries with the longest average enterprise tenures among the OECD Member countries. In 1995, the average tenure was 11.3 years in Japan, which is much longer than Australia (6.4 years), the United States (7.4 years), Canada (7.9 years) and the United Kingdom (8.3 years). But Japan is not the only country with long average enterprise tenure. It is also long in Italy (11.6 years), France (10.4 years), Germany (9.7 years), the Netherlands (9.6 years), Finland (9.2 years) and Spain (9.1 years).

OECD (1997) estimated retention rates for nine Member countries. Between 1990 and 1995, the estimated retention rate was 64.2% in Japan. This was the highest rate, followed by Germany and Switzerland. The retention rate for young workers is especially high in Japan. The retention rate for young workers aged 15-24 years old was 50.8% for the same period, which is much higher than the unweighted average of 28.7% among other countries in the analysis.

In Japan, enterprise tenure has been getting longer, especially among male middle-aged and older workers. This may be accounted for by the fact that the current middle-aged and older workers entered the firms when the Japanese economy was growing rapidly (meaning that they could get good jobs in large firms) and it may also reflect the effect of the extension of the mandatory retirement age.[8]

However, it should be noted that the separation rate is not negligible, especially for young workers, as already mentioned. Moreover, it is not true that all regular workers are employed until their mandatory retirement age, which is now 60 years old for most firms. Some retire earlier than the mandatory retirement age, to receive advantageous early retirement lump-sum payments. Others are transferred to other companies or subsidiaries. Among those over 50 years old, one-third leave the company before the mandatory retirement age.

The labour turnover rate is increasing somewhat, reflecting the increase in the number of contingent workers such as part-time workers. The overall labour turnover rate had declined after the first oil shock as economic growth slowed. Then, after 1985 it has been increasing slowly, most notably for young workers and women. This is considered to be due to the increase in the number of contingent workers (Ministry of Labour, 1998). According to the Statistics Bureau's Employment Status Survey, the proportion of part-time workers among employees has increased from 14.1% in 1987 to 18.8% in 1997.

Age-wage profiles

Steep age-wage profiles are considered as another main feature of the Japanese labour market. Many have pointed to the steep age-wage profile and low labour turnover rate in Japan, compared with the United States (*e.g.* Hashimoto and Rasian, 1985; Mincer and Higuchi, 1988). However, the steep age-wage profile is not limited to Japan. Recent studies have revealed that age-wage profile is also steep in the other OECD Member countries such as Spain, Portugal, Italy and Ireland (OECD, 1998, Table 4.4).

After comparing the age-wage profiles in the manufacturing sector for several EU countries, the United States and Japan, Koike pointed out that while the steep age-wage profile is prevailing for white-collar workers in all countries, Japan is the only country where (in the large firms) it applies to blue-collar workers as well. He considered that the resemblance of the age-wage profiles between blue-collar workers and white-collar workers in large Japanese manufacturing companies reflects the high skills among production workers and the wage system, in which the wages of blue-collar workers are determined in a similar way to white-collar workers. He called this phenomenon the "White-collarization of blue-collar workers" (Koike, 1988). Recent data shows that it is still observable (Table 2).

Recently, age-wage profiles have flattened somewhat for all categories of workers. This is considered to reflect the ageing of the work force within enterprises, which is partly due to the extension of mandatory retirement age.

Historical developments

Historically, the main features of the Japanese labour market – such as long-term employment and the steep age-wage profile – were established in two periods. The first period was the 1920s when Japanese heavy industries such as steel, shipbuilding industries developed. During that period, the turnover rates that had been very high declined dramatically. The proportion of the short-term employees with enterprise tenures less than one year was about 44% in 1918. The proportion of the long-term employees with enterprise tenures over 10 years was only 4%. But it increased to 16% in 1924, and to 24% in 1933 (Chuma, 1989). In the meantime, steep age-wage profiles were found widely in large enterprises at latest until 1927. Although there remain only fragmental data, they suggest that the age-wage profile was flat at the end of the last century. Yearly increments in pay with merit rating appeared in large companies during 1920s. It is also during this period that "new" human resource management systems, such as bonus system and company unions were introduced from the United States. Although the separation rates declined, the level was still as high as in the United States.

The second is the period during World War II and immediately after it. During the war, under the state control of industries, the differentials in the pay level and pay method between blue-collar workers and white-collar workers were largely removed (Odaka, 1984). The wage differential between the two groups diminished substantially after the war. The wages for blue-collar workers had been based on hourly payments, but it has become monthly payment like white-collar workers. Meanwhile, the yearly separation rate has decreased gradually to less than 30% in the early 1960s. The training system with broad OJT discussed in the following section was established late in the 1950s and early 1960s in large companies (Koike, 1997).

Economic rationales and legal constraints

Historical developments suggest that the current Japanese employment system has been influenced by certain economic or technological environments as well as historical events like a war. The fact that long-term employment and steep age-wage profile can be found widely among OECD Member countries suggests also that there are economic rationales behind such phenomena.

The economic rationales for long-term employment or the existence of internal labour markets are summarised below.

First, the existence of firm-specific human capital is one of the reasons for long-term employment. Given the low separation rate, employers tend to invest more in human capital of young workers. Some part of the skills acquired by training is firm-specific. Thus, it increases separation costs, which in turn leads to low separation rates and long-term employment.

Second, to avoid the moral hazard of workers is another reason for long-term employment. If the skills or the performance of the worker is unverifiable by the third party, it is important for employers to give incentives for workers to work. For this purpose, certain wage system, like a deferred wage payment system is adopted under long-term employment contracts.

Further, long-term employment contracts are also economically rational, when it is difficult for firms to know the ability of the worker. Under the long-term employment contract, the firm gathers the information on the ability of the worker by observing performance over the long period. It is possible to increase the productivity by assigning suitable jobs to the worker on the basis of the accumulated personnel information of the worker.

These reasons are to some extent mutually complementary. And it is clear that these reasons also provide the economic rationales for steep age-wage profile for certain workers.

Some also argue that legal constraints contribute to the long-term employment. The Japanese Labour Standard Law stipulates that the employer must provide at least 30 days advance notice, if the employer wants to dismiss a worker. An employer who does not give 30 days advance notice is required to pay the average wage for a period of not less than 30 days. However, the right of dismissal is restricted by the doctrine of abusive dismissal established by the Supreme Court. It formalised the legal principles accumulated so far by declaring that "even when an employer exercises his right of dismissal, it will be void as an abuse of the right, if it is not based on objectively reasonable grounds so that it cannot receive general social approval as a proper act" (Sugeno, 1992). This legal constraint may be also mutually complementary with the economic rationales mentioned above.

4. Employment practices and the youth labour market

In this section, we examine employers' employment practices such as hiring, training, wages and promotions in Japan. These practices are closely related with the features of the Japanese youth labour market mentioned in Section 1.

Hiring policies

In 1997, 18 000 new school leavers from junior high schools, 353 000 from senior high schools, 150 000 from junior colleges and 349 000 from universities were employed. The proportions among total new school leavers employed are 2.1%, 40.6%, 17.2% and 40.1%, respectively. In addition to new school leavers, full-time regular workers are hired in mid-career and part-time workers are also hired. As mentioned above, almost all young part-time workers are students in full-time education. The hiring practices of new school leavers from senior high schools and those from universities are discussed in Section 2.

There is strong demand for new school leavers. Japanese companies, especially large ones, tend to hire new school-leavers regularly, mostly in April, when the fiscal/school year begins. This is usually "lump-sum" hire,[9] a term used to describe the practice of hiring individuals for the firm, but not for a particular job within the firm. These individuals are not assigned to specific jobs, but tend to move from one job to another within the firm.

As mentioned earlier, almost all new school graduates are hired as full-time regular workers. An establishment survey shows that there are more firms that will emphasise the hiring of new school leavers than firms that will give the same importance to the hiring of new school leavers and mid-career workers. This tendency is very clear for large firms (Ministry of Labour, Survey on Employment Management (1998). This suggests great willingness of the Japanese firm to hire new school-leavers rather than mid-career workers.

However, it should be noted that more mid-career workers are hired than new school leavers. The larger the firm, the greater the proportion of new school leavers among all those hired during a year. But even in large firms with 1 000 employees and over, it is only one fourth or one third (Figure 6).

Japanese firms tend to hire new school leavers on the basis of their trainability rather than their acquired qualifications. According to surveys on hiring management of firms, they attach more importance to "enthusiasm", and "general knowledge" in the hiring of new school leavers, while they attach more importance to "professional experiences", or "professional knowledge and skills" for mid-career workers (op. cit). Screening processes of new school leavers also suggests this. In the case of new high school leavers, they are screened by the reputation of the school and the academic achievement in general knowledge such as mathematics and foreign language. In the case of new university leavers in social sciences, they are screened by the reputation of the school and the results of interviews. In both cases, the criterion is trainability rather than specialised knowledge or skills.

Historically, the lump-sum hiring of new school leavers developed during the period of high economic growth of the 1960s. Before, new school leavers, mainly from junior high schools, were employed as temporary workers. Then after a certain period, some of them were selected as regular workers. But the labour shortage of young workers due to the rapid economic growth, as well as the rise in the proportion of the junior high school graduates going to senior high schools developed the lump sum hiring of new school leavers as full-time regular workers. Once these practices were established, they did not return to the earlier ones even during the period of low economic growth after the first oil shock. This is largely due to the presence of part time workers, who replaced young temporary workers.

The lump-sum hiring of new school leavers is considered to have several economic advantages. First, it reduces the costs of personnel management, such as promotion or wage management of individual workers, because those hired in the same year can be treated collectively. Second, it reduces training costs because firms can give them training (OffJT) at the same time. In addition, the fact that the newly hired are not attached to specific jobs facilitates the training by broad OJT, which is based on the broad move of workers among various related jobs. This will be discussed in detail below.

However, the firms with these hiring practices might not be able to hire various types of workers, whom they would need in order to cope with rapidly changing economic environments. Thus, some large firms began to introduce hiring throughout the year or the hiring by occupation.

Intellectual skills

Before investigating the training practices in Japanese firms, we would like to see what kinds of skills are formed in large Japanese enterprises. We will consider mainly the skills of production workers in large manufacturing enterprises, but in principle it applies similarly to white-collar workers in other industries in Japan (see, for instance, the Japan Institute of Labour, 1997).

In the production workshop there are two types of operations: usual operations and unusual operations. Most of the work in the workshops – such as mass production assembly – is usual, which is repetitive and apparently does not require high skills. However, changes and problems in the workshop often occur, and the skills to deal with such changes and problems are crucial to the efficiency of production. It would certainly be better if (unless it was a serious problem) production workers could do such operations on site themselves, without the help of the technicians or engineers.

The changes may occur in the following cases: diversification of the types of products; changes in the quantity of products; the changes in the methods of production due to technological progress; the changes in the composition of the workforce and so forth. To deal with such changes, workers need to be not only skilled enough to deal with changes in tools and jigs for themselves, or multi-skilled to perform most of the jobs in the workshop, but also be able to instruct other workers. For example, when the composition of the workers in the workshop changes due to mandatory retirement or the entrance of new school leavers in April, the workers must instruct the newly hired on the job.

Many problems do take place frequently in the workshop. To deal with such problems, it is necessary first of all to be aware of the problem as quickly as possible. The cause or causes must then be determined. And finally, the problem must be solved. In order to do these unusual operations, the workers must have certain level of knowledge on the structure of the machine and the procedure of production. These skills resemble those of technicians or engineers. Thus, Koike calls them intellectual skills (Koike and Inoki, 1990).

What would be the effects of technological developments such as computerisation of the production process on the importance of intellectual skills? Since computers or other machines can deal only with usual operations, the skills to conduct unusual operations will become more important as the computerisation of production process evolves. Thus intellectual skills become more important as technological progress occurs (op. cit.).

In sum, the skills formed in large Japanese enterprises are those used to deal quickly on site with the emergencies and the uncertainties that take place in the workshop. In the following subsections, we would like to see how intellectual skills are formed.

Training

There are two types training within the enterprise. One is OffJT (Off-the-job-training) which is conducted with an instructor and trainees who gather in some place other than the workshop. OffJT may be either theoretical or practical. On the other hand, the OJT (On-the-job-training) is conducted while the trainees are working. Their supervisors or more skilled colleagues instruct them. Normally, OJT takes longer than OffJT. A "career" is a series of jobs to which the worker is assigned. OJT is closely related with a career within the enterprise, because the skills acquired by OJT depend on the jobs to which the workers are assigned over their career. These two sorts of training within enterprise are complementary with each other. For example, a production worker learns the manipulation of a machine by OJT, and this training is complemented by OffJT on the theory of the technology or the mechanical structure of the machine.

Generally, the large Japanese enterprise tends to attach more importance to OJT. After entering the enterprise, employees receive initial training in the form of OffJT. Then the employee traces his/her career within the enterprise. A career begins by a relatively simple job.[10] The job is learned by OJT with the aid of colleagues and supervisors. Then, after a certain period, the worker is assigned to another job that is related to the previous one, but often more difficult. OJT is the key learning mechanism. This process continues. As experience in the enterprise accumulates, more difficult jobs, which need more competence and responsibilities, are taken on. The rotation of the workforce in the enterprise takes place regularly, although the manner of the rotation depends on the enterprise and the workshop. It should be noted, however, that the rotation is conducted among related jobs. Otherwise, training costs would be too large. In the case of production workers, the workers move between different jobs within one workshop or closely related workshops. The short-term OffJT is practised occasionally, for example on the occasion of entering into the enterprise or promotions. The OffJT inserted among OJT over the long career provides the worker with the opportunities to synthesise the experiences in the workshop.

Although the statistics on OJT are scanty, the data on OffJT shed quantitatively some light on the training practices in Japanese enterprises. According to the OECD, the proportion of the enterprises doing OffJT is higher in Japan than in France and the United States (OECD, 1993). According to the Ministry of Labour, *Minkan Kyoiku Kunren Jittai Chousa* (Survey on Training in the Private Sector), 73.3% of the establishments with 30 employees or more conducted OffJT or formal OJT[11] in 1996. Larger establishments tend to give more training opportunities. In 1991, three-quarters of all workers surveyed received OffJT during the previous year. The incidence of OffJT varies little across different age groups. Younger workers tend to receive OffJT at the time of starting their professional careers within firms, whereas older workers tend to receive it on the occasion of transfers or promotions. The incidence of OffJT is almost the same across different education attainment groups, except for university graduates or higher, for whom it is somewhat greater.

The system of training by OJT is not unique to Japanese large enterprises. It can be found in other western countries, where long-term employment relations are observed. However, evidences show that the Japanese OJT is less job-specific, compared with other countries.[12]

In sum, the training practices in Japanese large firms are characterised by broad OJT supplemented by inserted short-term OffJT.

Wage and promotion systems

Training within firms cannot be efficiently conducted, unless incentive mechanisms work. Wage increases and hierarchical promotions provide such incentives.

Under the Japanese wage system, wages are paid on a monthly basis for both blue-collar workers and white-collar workers. Wages consist of basic salary, overtime wages, various allowances and a bonus. The basic salary occupies about 70% of total wages and it is most important because the remaining wages are determined on the basis of the basic salary. A part of the basic salary is determined by age or seniority, but another part is determined by the degree of skill formation or the performance of the worker. Workers are classified into hierarchical ranks of skills called " job grades" (Table 3). The job grade is not the hierarchical ranking of jobs. Both are related, but not identical. A part of the basic salary is determined by the job grade with a certain range. The regular (once or twice a year) basic salary increases are called "yearly increments". The amount of yearly increments is larger for a worker in a higher job grade. However, the amount of yearly increments depends on the results of the assessment of the skills of the worker and the rank. The basic salary increases also as a result of a promotion to a higher job grade, which is determined on the basis of the assessment of skills. In other words, the Japanese wage system is like a pay-for-skill plan. The degree of skill formation is reflected in wages, and this provides strong incentives for the worker to acquire skills. The qualifications for higher grades in the job grade table suggest that the formation of intellectual skills such as multi-skills, or the skills to instruct others are appreciated in the assessment for the promotion (Table 3). Moreover, the fact that the Japanese wage system is a pay-for-skill plan is important for the Japanese system of skill formation. If it were pay-for-job plan, it could not motivate workers to move among different jobs within the workshop to enhance the range of their skills. If it were a pay-for-results plan, it would discourage workers from moving among different jobs. They would not want to take jobs to which they were not accustomed, because they would have poorer results at the beginning and their wages would decrease. The Japanese wage system is thus compatible with its training system, which is composed of broad OJT and short occasional OffJT inserted between OJT.

With regards to this pay-for-skill plan, the fair assessment of the skills of workers is crucially important. The Japanese labour unions, whose members are both blue-collar workers and white-collar workers, accept the assessment of skills because they consider that wages based on fair assessment - rather than equal wages regardless of the skills - is just. It is said that this is one of the unique features of the Japanese labour unions (Ishida, 1990). The supervisors make the assessment of the skills. In case of blue-collar workers, they are foremen or subforemen in the workshop. To avoid favouritism, job charts are put up on the walls of the workshop. They are the tables to show the width and the depth of the intellectual skills of individual workers.

Intellectual skills are formed by broad OJT with occasional OffJT and the incentive for the skill formation is provided by the merit-rating compensation/promotion system. This is clearly associated with long-term employment and steep age/seniority-wage profiles.

Employment adjustment

It is well known that in Japanese firms, employment adjustment is done first by the reduction of working hours and then by the reduction of the numbers of the entrants into the firm as well as the number of part-time/ temporary workers, and that both employers and labour unions try to avoid dismissal as much as possible.

However, dismissal is not uncommon in Japanese firms. During severe recessions, even large firms dismiss workers. According to the Ministry of Labour, *Koyo Hendo Sogo Chosa* (General Survey on Employment Changes), about 20% of total manufacturing establishments conducted dismissal during the period from January 1975 to June 1978 when the Japanese economy was in deep recession after the first oil crisis. Over 20% of large establishments with 1 000 employees or more conducted dismissals. According to the studies, which analysed the relationship between the profit and the dismissal for individual firms, firms dismiss their employees after two consecutive years of losses or large losses (Koike, 1996).

In Japan, the burden of dismissal is disproportionately distributed among older workers. Chart 7 shows the distribution of involuntary separation of regular employees by age. The incidence of dismissal or involuntary separation is much higher for older workers than for young workers, even if mandatory retirement is excluded. This is quite in contrast with the practices of employment adjustment in countries like the United States, where seniority-based lay-off/recall system is popular and young workers with less seniority suffer disproportionately the burden of employment adjustment.

Employment practices and firm structure

As discussed above, large Japanese firms tend to hire new school leavers and to provide them with intense training through broad OJT among different jobs within the firm, together with short inserted OffJT to nurture them with intellectual skills. The intense OJT is associated with long-term employment. Such employment practices are related with firm structure or the information structure within a firm.

Aoki (1988, 1990) presents a theoretical model of the large Japanese firm in the manufacturing industry. He called a typical American firm an A-firm and a typical Japanese firm a J-firm. The A-firm emphasises efficiency attained through fine specialisation and sharp job demarcation. The J-firm emphasises the capacity of the workers' group to cope with local emergencies autonomously, which is developed through OJT and sharing knowledge on the workshop. In the former, the operating task is separated from the task of identifying and finding necessary expedients to overcome and prevent emergencies, whereas in the latter, the two tend to be integrated.

In the hierarchical control system of the A-firm, management has *a priori* knowledge of the overall production technology. But their capacity to identify emerging events affecting production technology of sub-units and to enforce the implementation of appropriate operational decisions may be limited and costly, simply because management is removed from operational activities.

In the horizontal co-ordinating system of the J-firm, the tasks of monitoring and identification of emergent events and the implementation of corresponding operational decisions are delegated to sub-units. Since the centralised use of information about emergent events is absent, the problem-solving at the sub-units level may not satisfy the first best condition. But, through OJT, the sub-units can improve the ability to perceive emergent problems and to find corresponding solutions. Once a problem is recognised and a corresponding solution is found, the sub-units should be able to implement it quickly.

The relative efficiency of the J-firm depends largely on the "grass-root" information-processing capacities of the worker at the workshop level to cope with uncertain events, which are determined by initial educational level and experience. The relative efficiency of the hierarchical system depends largely on the professional capability of its managers and the quality of its communication technology.

Thus the Japanese firms are willing to invest in human capital of the employees though OffJT as well as broad OJT. Given the relative efficiency of the training of young workers, this would mean that Japanese firms have a relatively strong demand for young workers.

5. Minimum wages, collective bargainings and wages for new school-leavers

Given the steep age-wage profiles, the relative wages of young Japanese workers are lower compared with other OECD countries. This might provide the incentive to employ more young workers than older workers. However, if the labour market is sufficiently competitive, the strong demand for young workers would raise the relative wages of young workers to a certain equilibrium point, where the relative advantage of hiring youth disappears. Thus, the problem is rather how flexibly the youth wages are determined. If this flexibility is secured, then youth employment would not be disproportionately reduced.

We would now like to investigate the minimum wages system and collective bargaining system from this point of view.

Minimum wages

Minimum wages are considered to affect the wages and the employment of unskilled young workers. We shall see first the institutional aspects of the minimum wage system in Japan and then consider their levels as well as possible influences on the employment and wages of youth.

There are three sorts of minimum wages in Japan:

- *Regional minimum wages*: the major form of minimum wages is the regional minimum wage in a prefectural unit. There are uniform minimum wages for each prefecture, regardless of industry or occupation. There are thus 47 regional minimum wages corresponding to the number of prefectures.

- *(National) Industrial minimum wages*: they are determined for the workers in some specific industries or some crafts, where it is acknowledged by the Central Minimum Wages Council that the minimum wages should be higher than the regional minimum wages. In 1998, there were 253 industrial minimum wages.

- *Regional minimum wages based on collective agreements*: when the majority of workers of the same kind employed in establishments in the prefecture and the employers employing them are covered by a collective agreement containing a provision concerning the minimum wages, this can be extended to be applicable to all the workers of the same kind employed in the region under certain conditions. There were two regional minimum wages based on collective agreements in 1998.

The first two are determined by the deliberations of the Central Minimum Wages Council and the Local Minimum Wages Council. These councils are composed of an equal number of members representing workers, employers and the public interest.

The regional minimum wages are revised every year after the annual reports of the Local Minimum Wages Councils are received. Since 1978, the Central Minimum Wages Council divides all the prefectures into four categories and indicates the guideline amounts of minimum wage increases for each category. The guideline plays an important role in raising regional minimum wages and in the nation-wide adjustment of minimum wages. After the investigation of the historical developments of the minimum wage system in Japan, Sakasegawa (1996) concluded that minimum wages are revised so as to improve the wages of low-wage earners following the general wage increase.

As documented in OECD (1998), among the countries compared, the ratio of minimum wages to the average wage is lowest in Japan, Korea and the United States. The ratio is fairly stable with the minimum wage being about 40% of the average wage. Regional hourly minimum wages range from JPY 590 in nine prefectures to JPY 692 in Tokyo.

The ratio of minimum wages to the wages of new school-leavers from high school is about 60% across most prefectures. This is much lower than the ratio of minimum wages to the wages of female part-time workers which ranges from 66% to 86% with the unweighted average being 75%. The bulk of low-wage earners are concentrated among middle-aged female workers, while the proportion of low-wage earners is highest for young workers aged less than 17 years old (Table 4). These facts suggest that the direct effects of minimum wages on the wages and the employment of young workers are very limited. They affect the wages and the employment of middle-aged female workers and part-time workers.

Collective bargaining and the wages of youth

In Japan, collective wage determination in most firms is done in the spring, the so-called Shyunto (Spring Offensive). The collective wage determination system is essentially enterprise-based but co-ordinated within and across industries. Most Japanese labour unions are enterprise-based unions, which consist of both blue-collar workers and white-collar workers of individual enterprises. Thus the wage increase is negotiated and determined between the enterprise-based unions and the employer within each enterprise. However, most labour unions affiliate with industrial federations and industrial federations themselves affiliate with national centres. They set the scheduling of collective bargaining at the same period in the spring, and under their directions and co-ordination, the affiliated labour unions make wage demands and negotiate simultaneously to reinforce their bargaining positions to get higher wage increases. The wage increase in leading sectors tends to be regarded as a standard followed by other employers. The "Spring Offensive" serves to standardise the wage increase in individual enterprises, although under the current recession, its role is being questioned because the differentials of profits across enterprises have widened and the margin for wage increase is so small in depressed industries.

The wages of new school leavers tend to be more uniform across regions and firms than the wages of incumbent workers, because new school leavers are relatively more mobile and consequently their wages reflect to a greater degree the relation between supply and demand in the external labour market. The existence of firm-specific human capital and the incentive age-wage profile results in more wage differentials for older workers. However, they tend to be more sensitive to economic fluctuations. Figure 8 shows the larger fluctuations of wages of new male senior high school leavers, compared with those of older workers. Nonetheless, the adjustment by wages is not sufficient to absorb the external shocks. During recessions, the demand for new school leavers declines sharply.

6. Recession, future developments in the demographic structure and the youth labour market

Recession and the youth labour market

The internal labour market model predicts that the employment adjustment is mostly done at the port of entry. The employment of young workers, especially new school-leavers and older workers after the mandatory retirement age, is most sensitive to the economic fluctuations.

During recessions, good employment opportunities are reduced and new school leavers are obliged to take less attractive jobs with poorer training opportunities. In fact, the proportion of new high school leavers entering into large firms with 1 000 employees or over was 22.7% in 1996, while it was 35.7% in 1991, a boom year (Ministry of Labour, 1998). Given the limited chances to change jobs, this can have a negative effect on the professional careers of the generation that entered into the labour market during recessions. Some studies show the effect that this can have on the life-long earnings of workers (Inoki and Ohtake, 1997). The current long recession may have deprived many young workers of good training opportunities.

Demographic changes and the future of the youth labour market

There is a rapid ageing of the population in Japan, with the proportion of the elderly aged 65 years and over projected to increase rapidly from 14.6% in 1995 to 26.9% in 2020. On the other hand, the proportion of young people aged up to 15 years old is projected to decrease from 16.0% in 1995 to 13.7% in 2020.

Accordingly, it is projected that there will be: 1) a rapid ageing of the labour force; 2) a rapid decrease in the number of young workers; and 3) a decrease in the total labour force. The proportion of older workers aged 60 years old or over will rise from 13% to 20.6% between 1995 to 2015, while that of young workers aged less than 25 years old will decrease from 24% to 16.8% during the same period. The number in the labour force, which increased from 0.4% to 0.6% per annum during the 1980s and the early 1990s, will level off between 2000 and 2005 and it will decrease slowly thereafter (Figure 9).

Generally speaking, the relative scarcity of youth may improve, *ceteris paribus*, their relative situation in the labour market in the future. However, faced with the social demands for the prolongation of the employment period for older workers and the international competition as well as technological changes, firms might want to keep their work force longer and decrease the recruitment of new school leavers, with a more severe screening. The possible slow-down of economic growth might aggravate the situation for youth.

7. Concluding remarks

The Japanese youth labour market has so far shown a relatively good performance, compared with the other OECD Member countries, although it has deteriorated sharply during the current recession. The main factors behind this performance include:

- – The special role played by schools in placement of their graduates.

- – The large propensity for firms to train their employees under long-term employment system with merit-based compensation/promotion system.

- – The flexible wage determination of young workers.

The Japanese employment system is characterised by efficient human resource development or investment in human capital, especially in large companies. This is closely related to the decentralised informational structure of companies, in which the skills to deal with problems on site are relatively more appreciated. To ensure the relative advantage of this system, firms have developed efficient skill formation systems through broad OJT with incentives for workers to participate in training, such as merit-based compensation/promotion system and job charts. This system is complementary with long-term employment, as the return to investment in human capital is higher for young workers than for older workers. This means the relatively strong demand for, and flexible wage determination of, young workers. Job placements by senior high schools can be considered to serve as a screening device. It internalises the placement process to reduce the transaction costs between schools and firms.

However, this school/employment system is challenged by future structural changes. The changes in demographic structure, the ageing of the labour force and the decreasing number of youth, will have important effects. If the relative scarcity of young workers may improve their position in the labour market, the shift of the policy emphasis from youth to older workers may negatively affect the young low-qualified workers who are substitutes for older workers.

Second, the technological changes and the globalisation of the economy might affect the relative advantage of the Japanese employment system which might in turn affect the employment practices of Japanese firms. It should be noted, however, that in principle intellectual skills become more important as technological progress proceeds.

Third, the restructuring of the education system toward more diversification might change the role played by high schools in the placement of their graduates.

Fourth, the changes in the aspiration of young workers may change their behaviour in the labour market. It is often pointed out that young workers are increasingly less reluctant to quit their jobs. Although this is partly accounted for by the recent poor employment opportunities they receive at graduation, it may also reflect changes in their attitudes towards work.

Finally, the current recession has had a sharp negative impact on the youth labour market. Since the economic situation at the time of graduation affects largely the employment/training opportunities and consequently the life-long earnings for young workers, rapid economic recovery is vital.

NOTES

1. According to Statistics Bureau, Employment Status Survey, 69.6% of young workers aged 15-24 were full-time regular workers in 1997. The proportion of part-time workers was 27.4%.

2. A Japanese word derived from *Arbeit* in German.

3. Statistics Bureau, Special Survey of the Labour Force Survey.

4. This means full-time workers without any limit on the employment period. It should be noted that currently, the Japanese Labour Standard Law prohibits any employment contract which is longer than one year.

5. Ministry of Labour, *Shinki Gakusotusya No Syusyoku Risyoku Jyokyo Chosa* (Survey on the Employment and the Separation of New School Leavers).

6. This section owes much to Kariya (1994).

7. Takeuchi (1995) describes the details of the hiring practices of university graduates by large Japanese companies.

8. The proportion of the establishments with mandatory retirement age of 60 years old or over has increased sharply from 38.9% in 1985 to 81.8% in 1997 (Ministry of Labour, 1998).

9. According to the Ministry of Labour, Survey on Employment Management (1989), some 60% of the firms employ new school-leavers to firms rather than to specific jobs.

10. It is one of the salient features of the Japanese employment system that workers begin their careers at the bottom of the ranks regardless of educational attainment (Mitani, 1997).

11. This survey distinguishes between formal OJT and informal OJT. Formal OJT is the OJT conducted with a designated instructor and a check list of the training. In this paragraph, the figures for OffJT include formal OJT.

12. See, for example, Koike (1996) for production workers and the Japan Institute of Labour (1997) for professional workers.

BIBLIOGRAPHY

AOKI, M. (1988), *Information, Incentives, and Bargaining in the Japanese Economy*, Cambridge University Press.

AOKI, M. (1990), "Toward an Economic Model of the Japanese Firm", *Journal of Economic Literature*, Vol. 28, pp. 1-27.

CHUMA, H. (1989), "Nihonteki Koyokanko No Rekishiteki Bunseki (Historical Analysis of the Japanese Employment Practices)", The Labour Research Centre, mimeo.

DORE, R., BOUNINE-CABALÉ, J. and TAPIOLA, K. (1989), *Japan at Work: Markets, Management and Flexibility*, OECD, Paris.

HASHIMOTO, M. (1994), "Employment-Based Training in Japanese Firms in Japan and in the United States: Experiences of Automobile Manufacturers", in L.M. Lynch (ed.), *Training and the Private Sector: International Comparisons*, The University of Chicago Press.

HASHIMOTO, M. and RAISIAN, J. (1985), "Employment Tenure and Earnings Profiles in Japan and the United States", *American Economic Review*, 75, pp. 721-35.

INOKI, T. and OHTAKE (1997), "Roudousijyou Ni Okeru Sedaikouka Ni Tsuite (Cohort Effects in the Japanese Labour Market)", in K. Asako, S. Fukuda and N. Yoshino (eds.), *Gendai Makuro Keizai Bunseki Tenkanki No Nihon Keizai (The Japanese Economy in Transition: A Macroeconomic Analysis)*, Tokyo University Press, Tokyo.

ISHIDA, M. (1990), *Chingin No Syakai Kagaku-Nihon To Igirisu (Social Science of Wages: Japan and UK)*, Chuo Keizaisya, Tokyo.

THE JAPAN INSTITUTE OF LABOUR (1997), *Daisostu Howaito Kara no Jinzai Kaihatsu-Koyo Shisutemu Nichi, Ei, Bei, Doku no Dai Kigyo (1) Jirei Chaosa Hen (A Comparative Study of Human Resource Development of Professional Employees-Large Firms in Japan, UK, US and Germany (1) Case Studies)*, Japan Institute of Labour, Tokyo.

KARIYA, T. (1994), "Transition from School to Work and Career Formation of Japanese High School Students", OECD, mimeo.

KOIKE, K. (1988), *Understanding Industrial Relations in Modern Japan*, Macmillan Press.

KOIKE, K. (1995), "Learning and Incentive Systems in Japanese Industry", in M. Aoki and R. Dore (eds.), *The Japanese Firm: The Source of Competitive Strength*, Oxford University Press.

KOIKE, K. (1996), *The Economics of Work in Japan*, LTCB International Library Foundation, Tokyo.

KOIKE, K. (1997), *Human Resource Development*, The Japan Institute of Labour, Tokyo.

KOIKE, K. and INOKI, T. (1990), *Skill Formation in Japan and Southeast Asia*, University of Tokyo Press, Tokyo.

MINISTRY OF LABOUR (1998), *Rodo Hakusyo (White Paper on Labour)*, Tokyo.

MINCER, J. and HIGUCHI, Y. (1988), "Wage Structures and Labour Turnover in the United States and Japan", *Journal of the Japanese and International Economies*, 2, pp. 97-133.

MITANI, N. (1997), "France: Internal Labour Markets and Wage Structure", in T. Tachibanaki. (ed.), *Wage Differentials: An International Comparison*, Macmillan Press.

ODAKA, K. (1984), *Rodo Shijo Bunseki (An Analysis of Labour Markets)*, Iwanami, Tokyo.

OECD (1993), *Employment Outlook*, Paris.

OECD (1996), *Employment Outlook*, Paris.

OECD (1997), *Employment Outlook*, Paris.

OECD (1998), *Employment Outlook*, Paris.

SAKASEGAWA, K. (1996), *Chyushyo kigyo to rodo monda (Small Firms and Labour Problems)*, the Japan Institute of Labour, Tokyo.

SUGENO, K. (1992), *Japanese Labour Law*, University of Washington Press.

TAKEUCHI, Y. (1995), *Nihon No Meritokurasii Kouzou To Shinsyo (Japan's Meritocracy, Structure and Mentality)*, University of Tokyo Press, Tokyo.

Table 1. **Distribution of the unemployed by reason for job search, 1998**

Reasons for job-search	Males			Females		
	15~24	25~54	55~64	15~24	25~54	55~64
Those separated						
Dismissal	12.5	35.7	61.5	7.7	19.0	54.5
Quit	40.6	41.4	7.7	50.0	48.3	18.2
Those unemployed from not in the labour force						
New school-leavers	12.5	1.4	0.0	7.7	0.0	0.0
To earn money necessary for living	18.8	10.0	15.4	19.2	19.0	9.1
To use spare time	3.1	0.0	5.1	3.8	5.2	9.1
Other	12.5	11.4	10.3	11.5	8.6	9.1
Total	**100.0**	**100.0**	**100.0**	**100.0**	**100.0**	**100.0**

Source: Statistics Bureau, Special Survey of the Labour Force Survey.

Table 2. **Males age-wage profile in the manufacturing sector, 1995**
(20-24=100)

	-19 years old	20-24	25-29	30-44	45-54	55+
Japan	87	100	119	151	176	157
United Kingdom	79	100	115	126	125	113
Germany	86	100	107	110	107	105
France	92	100	116	135	155	173
Italy	87	100	109	118	125	116
Sweden	86	100	108	107	112	103
Non-manual workers						
Japan	83	100	121	177	241	228
United Kingdom	67	100	129	164	179	154
Germany	83	100	131	153	157	162
France	71	100	140	186	233	265
Italy	93	100	127	176	224	274
Sweden	-	100	122	152	164	146

Sources: Japan Ministry of Labour, Basic Survey on Wages, EU countries; Eurostat, Survey on Wage Structure 1995.

Table 3. **An example of job-grade system: a large car manufacturer, 1991**

Job grade	Qualifications
P1	
P2	Capable of performing about one-third of the positions in the sub-foreman's unit without help of others
P3	(1) Capable of performing nearly two-thirds of positions without help of others
	(2) Capable of being a leader of small group activities
P4	(1) Capable of performing all positions in the sub-foreman's unit
	(2) Capable of dealing with problems
P5 Group leader	(1) Capable of performing all positions in the unit at the level of being able to instruct others
	(2) Able, as leader, to promote quality and productivity in the unit
Highly skilled	(1) Capable of performing many positions in the foreman's unit
	(2) Capable of advising effectively when a new production starts
P6 Sub-foremen	Sub-foremen
P7 Foremen	Foremen
P8 Foremen	Foremen

Source: Koike (1997).

Table 4. **Distribution and proportion of low-wage earners defined as those earning less than JPY 120 000 per month, 1997**

	All ages	-17	18-19	20-24	25-29	30-34	35-39	40-44	45-49	50-54	55-59	60-64	65+
Distribution of low-wage workers													
Both sexes	100.0	0.7	3.0	8.4	6.2	6.3	7.1	10.0	13.5	12.4	12.9	12.6	7.1
Males	18.0	0.5	0.8	2.5	1.4	0.7	0.7	0.8	1.1	0.9	1.4	4.3	2.9
Females	82.0	0.3	2.2	5.9	4.8	5.6	6.4	9.2	12.4	11.5	11.5	8.2	4.2
Proportion of low-wage workers within the demographic group													
Both sexes	1.5	16.7	2.8	1.0	0.6	0.8	1.0	1.4	1.5	1.8	2.3	6.2	7.6
Males	0.4	15.8	1.4	0.6	0.2	0.1	0.1	0.2	0.2	0.2	0.3	3.0	4.2
Females	4.1	18.6	4.4	1.4	1.3	3.1	4.2	5.2	5.1	6.1	7.5	14.1	17.2

Source: Ministry of Labour, Basic Survey on Wages.

Figure 1. **Participation rates of youth**

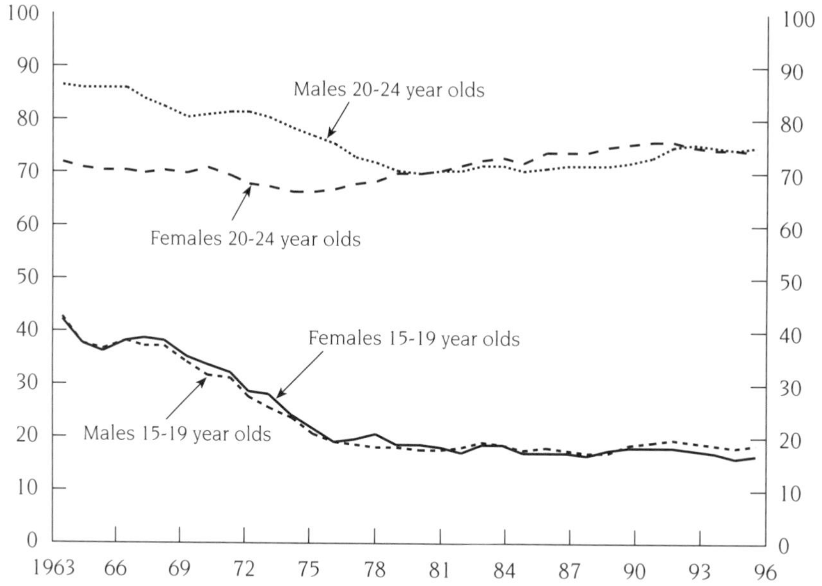

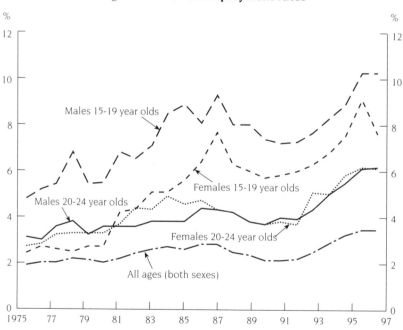

Source: Statistics Bureau, Labour Force Survey.

Figure 2. **Youth unemployment rates**

Source: Statistics Bureau, Labour Force Survey.

Figure 3. **Proportion of the new school leavers who were employed as full-time regular workers immediately after their graduation**
(15-29 year olds, both sexes)

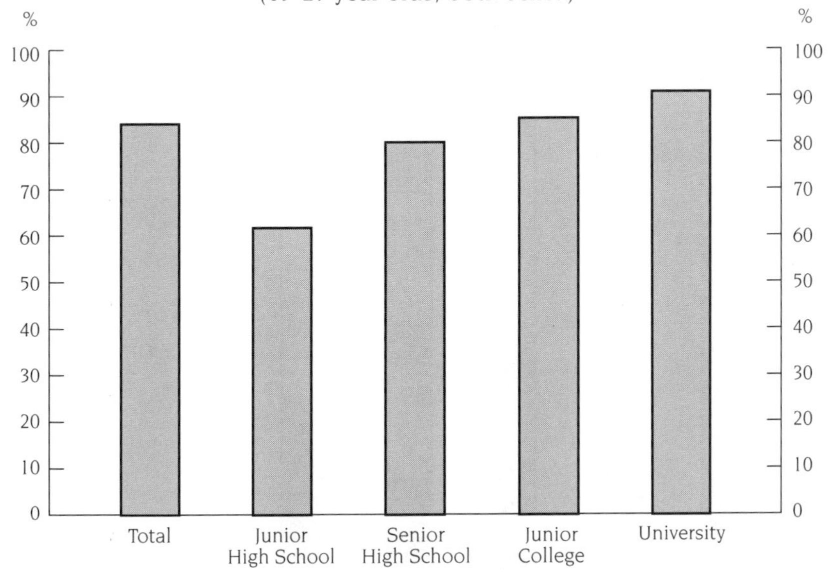

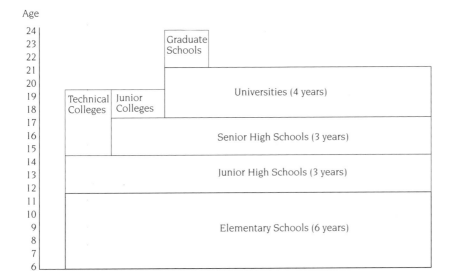

Source: Ministry of Labour, Survey on Young Employees (1997).

Figure 4. **Educational system in Japan**

Figure 5. **Number of job separations by how the first job was obtained**
(15-29 year olds, both sexes)

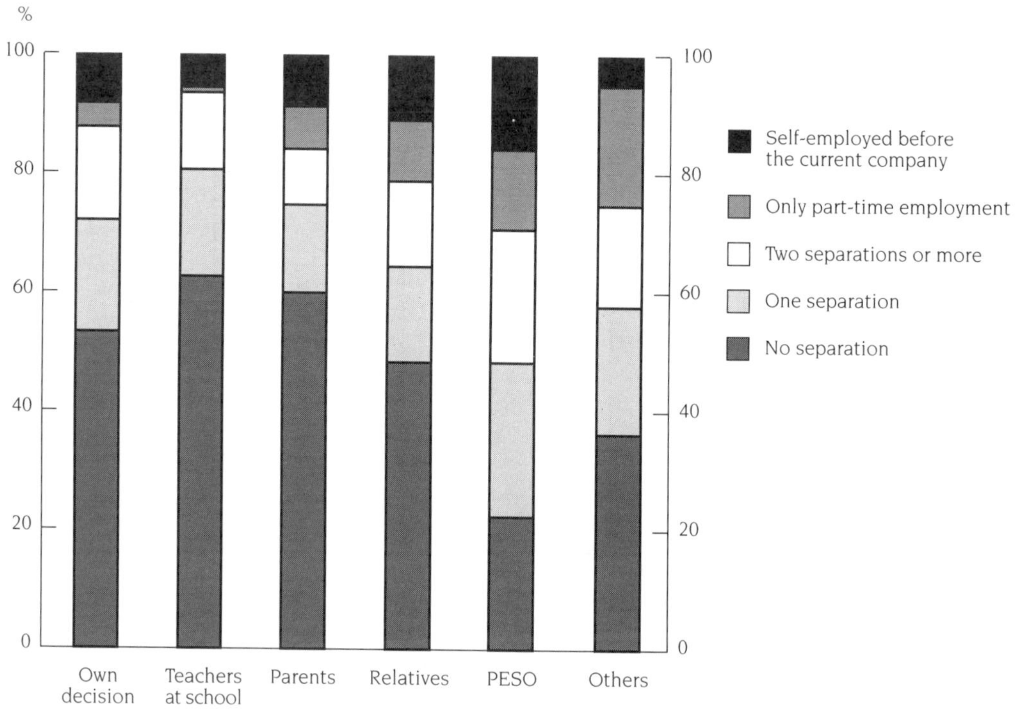

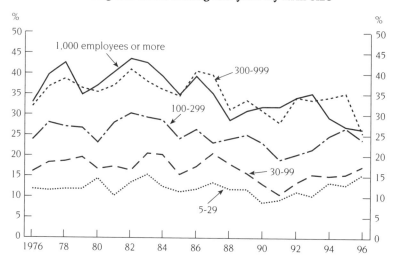

Source: Ministry of Labour, Survey on Young Employees (1985).

Figure 6. **Proportion of new school leavers
among the hired during the year by firm size**

Source: Ministry of Labour, Survey on Employment Trends.

Figure 7. **Distributions of involuntary separation[1] and employment by age, 1996**
(both sexes, all industries, establishments with 5 employees or more)

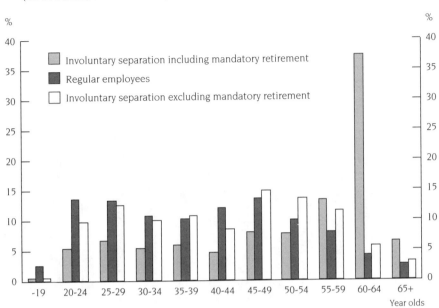

1. Separation for employers' reasons and mandatory retirement.
Source: Ministry of Labour, Survey on Employment Trends.

Figure 8. **Growth rates of wages of male new senior high school leavers and all workers**

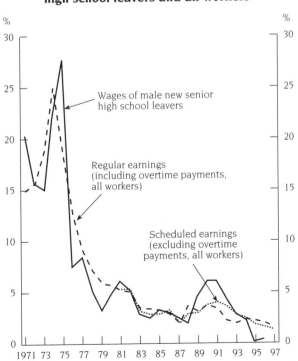

Source: Ministry of Labour, Monthly Labour Survey,
Basic Survey on Wages.

Figure 9. **Projection of the labour force population by age group**

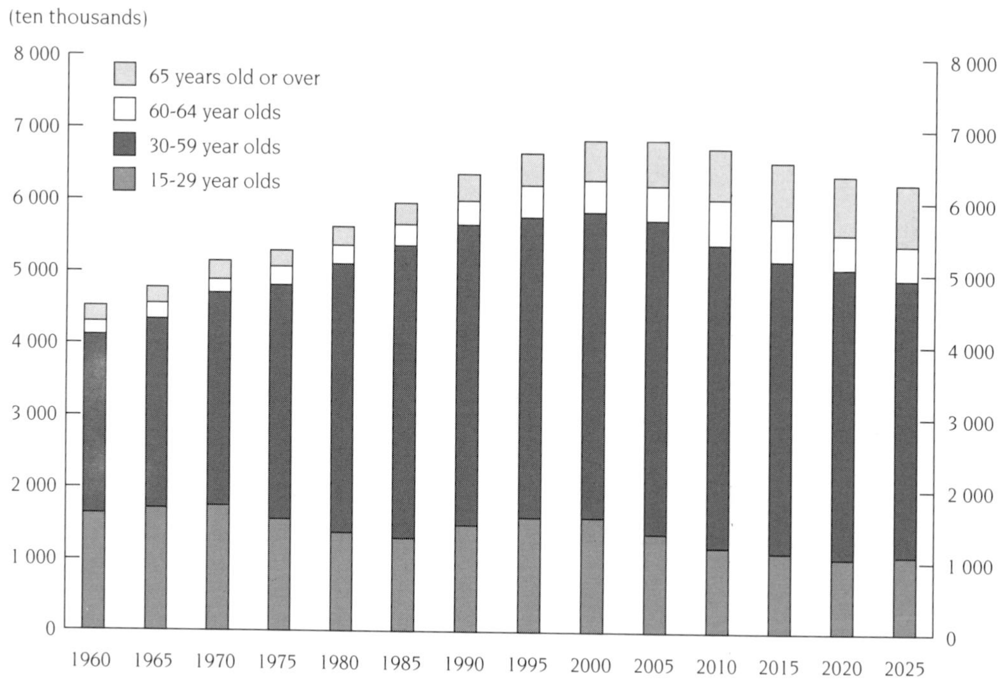

(ten thousands)

Source: Ministry of Labour (1998).

YOUTH UNEMPLOYMENT IN OECD COUNTRIES: HOW CAN THE DISPARITIES BE EXPLAINED?

by
Olivier Marchand
Direction de l'Animation, de la Recherche, des Études et des Statistiques (DARES),
Ministère de l'Emploi et de la Solidarité, France

This report will begin by surveying the labour market status of young people under 25 in the main OECD countries, and how their situation has evolved over the 1990s. It will then explore the factors frequently cited to explain cross-country differences, such as demographic factors, wage costs, training, and so on. Thirdly, it will probe the underlying dynamics of labour markets and employment systems, focusing in particular on the general issue of the productive sector's utilisation of youth labour.

1. A statistical finding: assessments differ, depending on the indicator used

From the youth unemployment rate...

The unemployment rate for 15-24 year-olds is the indicator most commonly used for comparing the job situation of young people from one country to another (Table 1). According to that indicator, the various countries ranked as follows in 1997, the most recent year available: the group scoring most favourably consisted of Japan and a number of continental European countries (Austria, Denmark, the Netherlands and Germany), with rates not exceeding 10%; at the other end of the spectrum were the southern European countries (Spain, Italy, Greece, France), with rates in excess of 28%; in between, with jobless rates ranging from 11 to 17%, were the English-speaking countries (United States, United Kingdom, Australia, Ireland, Canada), which were more favourably placed than a more diverse European group made up of Portugal, Belgium, Sweden and Finland, whose rates varied between 17 and 23%.

In 1987, this ranking was much the same, although the situation was more favourable in Finland, and especially Sweden, but more unfavourable in Ireland and the Netherlands. A further ten years earlier, in 1977, at the time of the first OECD conference on this same topic of young people, it was France and Spain that were relatively best placed, while Portugal, the United States and Canada had the weakest showings.

Moreover, it can be noted that in most European countries unemployment runs higher for young women than for young men, but that the opposite holds true in the English-speaking countries, as well as in Japan. Finally, it can be seen that in all cases, except for women in Germany, the rate of youth unemployment is higher – and frequently much higher – than overall joblessness. The ranking of countries on the basis of the absolute gap between the rate of youth unemployment and average joblessness is fairly close to the one obtained previously using youth unemployment rates, with Germany, Austria, Denmark, Japan and the Netherlands showing excellent figures and those of Greece, Italy, Spain and France being most unfavourable. The ranking changes, however, if it is based on relative differentials between young people and the total.

Even so, these results require substantial qualification, since the unemployment rate is increasingly inadequate as an indicator to describe the situation in countries like France, where the period of initial training has been extended considerably (see Box 1). Taking things to the extreme, if all young people pursued their studies until they were 25, their unemployment rate would become meaningless.

... to the proportion of young unemployed in a given generation

The countries in which the youth activity rate dropped most sharply – apart from France, where the average had fallen to 28% in 1997 – were Belgium (32%), Greece (35%) and Italy (37%). In respect of all these countries, it is increasingly justified to reason in terms of the ratio of young unemployed to the total number of young people, rather than the unemployment rate itself. In contrast, it is still meaningful to use both indicators with regard to countries in which young people show high activity patterns: Denmark (where the activity rate in 1997 was 74%), the United Kingdom (71%), the Netherlands (68%), Australia (67%), the United States (65%) and Canada (61%).

To analyse these wide disparities in activity, it is instructive to compare the situations of young people in the various countries by splitting the cohort of 15-24 year-olds into three groups: the unemployed (C), the employed (E) and the inactive (I) (students and non-students alike), which, when divided by the total population of young people (P), respectively yield the three indicators C/P, E/P (employment rate) and I/P (inactivity rate).

As a result, four broad categories of countries can be distinguished for 1997 (Figure 1):

– Japan, Austria and Germany, on the one hand, and Denmark and the Netherlands, on the other, all show a low percentage of youth unemployment, with employment (or activity) rates being average for the first group and high for the second.

– Belgium, Ireland, Portugal and France show relatively moderate youth unemployment with substantial inactivity rates (and thus modest employment rates).

– The United States and, especially, the United Kingdom, Canada and Australia combine slightly higher youth unemployment rates with high rates of activity or employment.

– Lastly, Finland and Sweden, on the one hand, and Greece, Italy and Spain, on the other, combine massive youth unemployment with inactivity rates that are fairly high for the first group and high for the second.

These findings, which also emerge, albeit with some minor discrepancies, if young men and young women are examined separately, are thus fairly different from the ones obtained earlier by examining unemployment rates. In particular, the relative positions of France, Belgium and Portugal seem more favourable, whereas those of the Scandinavian and English-speaking countries (except Ireland) become somewhat worse.

For 1990, the same analysis yields somewhat different conclusions, especially with regard to Denmark and Ireland, whose situations truly improved during the 1990s, and, conversely, Sweden and Finland, which experienced both a sharp drop in employment rates and a clear deterioration of their unemployment indicator over the same period (Figure 1).

Lastly, to reason on the basis of the differential (absolute or relative) between the proportion of youth unemployed in the total population of young people and the proportion of unemployed in the population at large yields the rankings shown in Figure 2. According to the absolute differentials (*i.e.* the differences between the two ratios), the relative standings of France and, to a lesser extent, Finland and

Box 1.

How should "young people" be defined, and which indicators of employment and unemployment should be used?

Analysis of the situation of young people vis-à-vis the labour market is generally based on one of two types of definitions of these "young people": either it focuses on a population having a certain age at the time the survey is conducted (most commonly 15-24, even if this is increasingly out of line with real-life situations, especially in countries like France where the average age of entry into work has risen to roughly 22), or it classifies young people on the basis of the length of time elapsed since they first entered the labour market (*e.g.* young people one or five years thereafter). Here the difficulty is exactly how to define this point of initial entry, as in the case of young people who study and work at the same time, or of those who return to training after an initial work experience.

The first method makes it possible to describe the situation of young people at a particular point in time, and it facilitates comparisons over time or space. It is this method that has been selected here, primarily on account of data availability. The second approach is better suited to describing the processes by which young people enter the labour market (see the third workshop). It enables clear analysis of the dynamics of the transition from initial education to the labour market, the whole problem being to determine how long this phase of integration or transition takes. In France, it is currently estimated to average about four years, although some take as long as six years, which for them would be an outer limit to the transition-to-work phase with its gradually diminishing particularities. Beyond these four and a half to six years begins what is known as the post-integration phase.

A second methodological issue is the choice of statistical indicators on which the analysis will be based. The one most commonly used is the unemployment rate – the ratio of the number of unemployed people to the work force as a whole – which theoretically reflects the difficulties young people have in entering the labour market. This is more or less borne out when young people are monitored after they leave the educational system, even if the unemployment rate needs to be supplemented by other indicators, and in particular by indicators of the quality and stability of the jobs they obtain.

However, if "young people" are defined in terms of their age, as is done here, the unemployment rate becomes less and less appropriate for describing their situation as the length of time they spend in school increases and the average age at which they start working increases. First, the number of young people in the labour force is increasingly low, making the unemployment rate less and less significant, but, above all, the population of young workers is increasingly less representative, since the least-skilled youngsters account for a larger and larger percentage. In countries like France, where the activity rate of people under 25 is now less than 30%, the unemployment rate of that population has an upward bias and is also subject to fluctuations that have little significance.

Studies on young people (defined as the population of persons between 15 and 24 years of age) should be based not on unemployment rates, but rather on the proportion of unemployed among all young people of the same age – an indicator to be compared with the employment rate and the inactivity rate (in or out of school), which share the same denominator. This is what has been done here, in order to depict the situations and recent trends in various countries.

Sweden are better than if based on the percentage of unemployed youth in their generation; using the relative differentials (*i.e.* the ratios of the two ratios), the same countries, as well as Spain, are situated most favourably, whereas the situations in Denmark, the Netherlands, the United Kingdom and, especially, the United States seem relatively worse.

It is clear then, that the appraisal hinges to a large extent on the choice of indicator, even if a number of "sure things" emerge from all this analysis: on the good side, Germany, Austria and Japan; on the bad side, Spain, Italy and Greece. For countries such as France, what emerges is not as clear-cut as is often claimed: ever-lower activity rates have gradually shifted the problem of youth unemployment to one of initial education and government-subsidised alternating classroom-workplace training. It is no longer business enterprises that steer young people's entry into work, but rather the public education system.

Issues arising from this finding

This statistical finding is obviously not enough to grasp the complexity of the situations in the various countries, or to rank them.

First, there are problems relating strictly to measurement: definitions of age (*e.g.* for France, age is considered the age attained during the year and not actual age), of the age bracket used to characterise "young people" (generally 15-24, but in some cases 16-24 or even 14-24), and of "activity" (national concepts may diverge significantly from ILO standards, especially in respect of situations that combine employment and training).

Beyond these problems, however, the respective roles of the educational system, the public training system and business enterprises in getting young people into work have an impact on the measure of activity and employment in these categories, at a time when alternating classroom-workplace experience is becoming the rule for them, when boundaries are becoming blurred, and when overall data are as much a reflection of the institutional forms of entry as of objective standings vis-à-vis employment and unemployment. The respective roles of apprenticeship and general schooling, theoretical internships and in-firm training in the various countries affect the measure of youth activity and employment just as much as they affect the actual conditions of young people's entry into the workplace.

Similarly, the very high unemployment rates for young people in certain countries (such as Spain and Italy) probably require qualification, given the scope of the informal economy: some temporary or occasional job situations can involve the underground economy and alternate with periods of unemployment or inactivity in a way that is difficult to detect.

More generally, the vulnerability of the various categories of young people, the frequency of recurrent unemployment and the duration of periods of joblessness are obviously crucial factors in explaining the problems involved in finding work for a population that frequently experiences repeated unemployment. Similarly, it is the concentration of joblessness in certain areas or certain segments of the population that poses the most difficult problems, in terms of social aspects as well as government action.

Lastly, integration processes depend on individual attitudes towards work, and on ways in which people build their family lives. In these respects as well, the frames of reference vary sharply from one country to another and cannot be disregarded.

2. The inadequacy of conventional explanations

A number of interpretations are generally advanced to explain young people's difficulties in the labour market. Here we shall not deal with aspects arising from differences between educational systems, which not only are shaped largely by national traditions, but have also been in great flux since the early 1980s. This is, in fact, a topic that falls under the scope of the work being done in the second and third workshops. Likewise, a comparative review of public programmes to facilitate the integration of young people, and especially the least skilled, into employment, and of the effectiveness of those programmes, will be addressed in the fifth and sixth workshops. Here we shall limit ourselves to factors of a more "institutional" nature specific to each country, incorporating the demographic context.

Demographics

The imbalance between the populous age groups entering the job market each year and the smaller groups, born before the Second World War, who leave it has at times been advanced as one explanation of young people's difficulties in the labour market. The OECD countries in which this demographic vitality has been sharpest over the past two decades are Australia, Canada, Ireland and the United States, judging from the indicator of average change in working-age population between 1976 and 1996. However, there is nothing to show that the unemployment situation of young people has deteriorated in these countries – on the contrary. Conversely, over the past twenty years, the population of 15-64-year-olds has grown far more slowly in Belgium, Italy and the United Kingdom, as well as in the Nordic countries (Denmark, Sweden and Finland). Here too, however, the correlation with an improvement in the labour market position of young people is not at all clear. Demographic pressure is therefore not a factor that can provide a compelling explanation of youth unemployment trends.

This somewhat empirical result is confirmed by a study by Béduwé and Giret (1998) on the ways in which young people are brought into European labour markets – an analysis that will be cited below. A certain competition effect can be noted here, however, between young people and women, and, although far less clearly, between young people and older workers.

Wage costs

The second factor that is frequently cited to explain the magnitude of unemployment, especially among the least skilled young people, is wage costs and the minimum wage. The influence of recruiting costs on youth joblessness has for years sparked recurring debate. This debate is losing its relevance in France, however, with the proliferation of mechanisms to lessen wage costs – mechanisms that target unskilled youths and are generally associated with integration and training policies.

The debate over entry-level salaries traditionally focuses on two aspects: the pay level of young people relative to that of adults, and the impact of the minimum wage on youth employment.

The problem of young people's relative pay level was posed by the OECD, among others, in the mid-1980s. The hypothesis put forward at that time was that, between the mid-1960s and the mid-1980s, the relative salaries of young people had substantially increased in countries like the United Kingdom, Japan, Sweden and France, whereas they had remained stable in Germany and declined in the United States. Youth employment is believed to be sensitive to such fluctuations in relative wages, and this may have affected young people's outlook for integration, at a time when new entrants to the labour market were especially numerous. However, the OECD did not present any direct estimation of these effects, due to uncertainty as to the "elasticities" thus highlighted. Moreover, it can be added that in France, but probably in other European countries as well, wage trends in the 1990s were highly unfavourable to the young, due in particular to the development of special forms of employment: in March 1997, their median monthly wage was FRF 5 750, or 74% of the FRF 7 800 average for all wage-earners – down four percentage points from six years earlier (Marchand and Minni, 1997). The aforementioned study by Béduwé and Giret (1998) also concludes that there is no significant linkage between the cost of unskilled labour and youth unemployment.

The impact of the minimum wage on youth employment has sparked special debate over the case of France, since in France young people account for a significant proportion of minimum wage earners, and the minimum wage (SMIC) has a wider scope than the industry minima found in a number of other countries. Moreover, the SMIC made significant gains in the 1980s, while in the United States the value of the minimum wage was eroded severely over the same period. A paper for OECD *Economic Studies* (Bazen and Martin, 1991) showed that, between 1970 and 1987, the ratio of the minimum wage to the average wage had dropped from 49.6 to 37.3% in the United States, whereas, at the same time, it rose in France from 39.3 to 49.9%. However, the ratio subsequently declined in France (it was 49.4% in 1996), while in the United States, the minimum wage, which had been constant for a number of years, was raised in 1991 and again in 1996 (the ratio was 42.1% in 1997). In this regard, it can be noted that over the years 1981 to 1989, which were characterised by a sharp relative drop in the US minimum wage, no more jobs were created than in 1989-1997, which saw a relative rise in the minimum wage.

Above all, the linkage between minimum wage trends and youth unemployment could not be clearly established by the OECD, and certainly not in the first study by John P. Martin in 1983. Published again in 1991 by Bazen and Martin, the estimates were somewhat more convincing, yet they show only that "at best" the elasticity of youth employment to the minimum wage is in the neighbourhood of -0.1 to -0.2. The resultant impact is therefore both modest and subject to substantial reservations. A similar study, carried out in California on increases in the minimum wage since 1988, reached the opposite conclusion by finding an increase in the employment of young people, who had previously been put off by excessively low wage levels. Other, more recent empirical studies focusing on the United States (Card and Krueger, 1995); France (Benhayoun, 1994; Cette *et al.*, 1996; Bruno and Cazes, 1997) or on a number of countries (Dolado *et al.*, 1996; OECD, 1998); also yielded highly mixed results. It would therefore appear very difficult to prove that the minimum wage has a significant effect on youth unemployment.

In any event, the relevance of a substantial portion of these discussions, which in fact centre on the total labour costs of employers who hire young people, would appear in France's case to be negated by the development of integration mechanisms. Indeed, youth employment assistance measures either adjust the minimum wage (for apprenticeships or special skills-acquisition contracts) or reduce its impact on the employer through subsidies or exemptions from social insurance charges (for "adaptation" contracts, "employment-solidarity" contracts and "youth employment" contracts). At year-end 1997, there were nearly 900 000 young people under such assisted work contracts, including 790 000 in the market sector. Of these, 160 000 qualified for part-time exemptions, 340 000 had apprenticeship contracts and 150 000 had alternating work-training contracts. As a result, at least 30% of young French workers were generating labour costs lower than the minimum wage for their employers. It is true, however, that this massive deployment of employment policy measures has successfully countered any negative effects of the minimum wage on the employment of the least skilled young people.

Training

The fact that those with low skills are over-represented among unemployed young people, or that young people whose education has included a large dose of workplace training do better at finding jobs, might suggest that youth training is either insufficient or not suitable. In France's case, this argument has become practically invalid, given the very significant improvement in the level of training that young people have received since the mid-1980s: today, fewer than 8% of the youths leaving school each year have either no diploma or only the lowest-level ones. Here, one could also point to instances of downgrading for first-time workers, which have grown more common in France in the 1990s, which also contradicts the idea that training is insufficient. Moreover, while a shortage of labour with suitable qualifications cannot be excluded, it would seem, on the basis of a 1989 survey by the Commission of the European Communities, that this shortage is no greater in France than in the other European countries (Gautié, 1997). In addition, if certain training specialities were in short supply in the late 1980s (in information technology in particular) this has become less common. It is therefore highly unlikely that, on the whole, joblessness among French youth could be attributed to any problem involving the suitability of their training.

3.   At the heart of the problem: how labour markets work

It is therefore necessary to go beyond single-cause approaches and look more comprehensively at how, in the various countries, the problem of youth unemployment is affected by the workings of labour markets, labour management policies and societal behaviours.

In a comparative analysis of youth unemployment in Sweden and France, Bourdet and Persson (1991) show first that in Sweden, joblessness among young people is more sensitive to demand, and that unemployed Swedish youth would therefore be more likely to benefit from economic upswings than their French counterparts.

Another type of analysis focuses on the interdependencies between labour market structures, training practices, patterns of labour management and industrial relations systems. In this regard, François Eyraud, David Marsden and Jean-Jacques Silvestre, in a 1990 article for the *International Labour Review*, noted the persistence in France of an "internal labour market", as opposed to the United Kingdom, in which the "occupational labour market" model was found to predominate. In the internal market model, which is based on the firm, young people must generally start in unskilled positions and may be promoted only after a period of internal probation. Experience is gathered within the firm, which updates the skills potential arising from the level of studies that is acquired elsewhere and used as a signal and a recruiting criterion. External mobility, which would entail downgrading, is therefore low. In contrast, the British apprenticeship system has built up an occupational model in which skills are transferable from one company to another, within the same industry, and young people have direct access to skilled jobs. This is also the system adopted by Germany, albeit in a different manner.

Florence Lefresne (1992) points out, however, in her comparison of the French and British integration systems, that the two came closer together in the early 1990s with the creation of the Youth Training Scheme, and of French programmes for alternating classroom-workplace training. In both instances, this led to an institutionalisation of occupational transition phases, based on particular provisions. In this framework, however, it can be seen that internal market mechanisms, involving a downgrading of new hires, continued to prevail more in France than in the United Kingdom. It was found that firms tended to stick to their old ways, using the prolonging of integration processes to filter access to skilled jobs.

Collective bargaining practices interfere with the relationship between training systems and systems of production

The two models of production systems – that of internal markets and that of occupational markets – yield different mechanisms for bringing young people into the labour market. In this respect, the 1989 analysis by Paolo Garonna and Paul Ryan warrants repetition. Focusing on the linkage between youth employment and industrial relations systems, they contrasted "regulated integration" (or negotiated entry) of young people, which is characteristic of occupational markets controlled by trade unions and industries (as in Germany or Austria), and the "selective exclusion" mechanisms at work in the United States and, especially, France, where the internal market system continues to prevail. The adult labour market is "protected", insofar as young people are trained in an external institutional educational framework and remain confined in unemployment or insecure or low-paid jobs until they are old enough to enter the primary market. Thus, in economic downturns, occupational markets maintain the flow of hiring and the place of young people, whereas internal markets pass the job shortage along to young people, as illustrated by the example of the iron and steel industry in France and Germany. In countries like France then, employment policy plays a structural role intended to counter this selective exclusion, even if it does not succeed in actually altering the underlying principle of having to wait one's turn ("queuing phenomena").

The scale and the role of temporary contracts and part-time jobs

To a much greater extent than adults, young people have jobs entailing fixed-term contracts: in 1995, this was the case for 23% of European Union youth, versus 7% of employed persons over the age of 30. The situation varies widely by country, however, depending in particular on each country's legislation governing work contracts. The percentage of young people on fixed-term contracts seems very high in Sweden, France, Finland and, especially Spain, in contrast to the situation in the United Kingdom, Belgium, Austria and Italy. The spread of this kind of employment involves cyclical aspects, but it is also structural when it reflects companies' efforts to achieve maximum flexibility.

Similarly, the rate of part-time work is generally high among young people and in countries like France, where it has risen sharply for them since the mid-1980s. In some countries (including Denmark and the Netherlands), this stems from the fact that part-timing makes it possible to reconcile further study with gainful employment. But for other countries, such as France, the explanation for this growth lies with the fact that part-time work has also become an essential component of flexibility policies. The correlation between the part-time rates for female and male youth, in contrast to the differential for adults, shows that for them this form of employment in fact constitutes a particular means of integration.

A principal components analysis in the aforementioned study by Béduwé and Giret (1998) on the 15 countries of the European Union tends to show that a high level of unemployment is often associated, for young people, with intensive recourse to fixed-term contracts, which lead to hiring but also put people frequently back on the job market (see the first part of the analysis, dealing with vulnerability to unemployment). This demonstrates the high risk of youth unemployment in countries like Spain, Finland and France. In contrast, Austria, Germany and Portugal exhibit relatively low youth unemployment and fairly long average tenure with the same employer.

The second finding contrasts fairly widespread long-term joblessness (in countries such as Greece and Italy) with intensive recourse to part-time work (in Finland, Sweden, Denmark and the Netherlands). In other words, this would suggest that part-time work enhances the employability of young people and promotes their occupational stability.

Fixed-term contracts are in fact a two-edged sword: when the frequency of fixed-term contracts is associated with unemployment rates, the emphasis is on the negative aspect of such jobs in terms of young people's vulnerability to unemployment; but when preferential use of fixed-term contracts for young people is associated with adults and low unemployment, the emphasis is on the positive integrative role of such contracts insofar as they enhance the employability of young people. On this subject, a very recent study addressed a question posed by the OECD Secretariat: do fixed-term contracts constitute a springboard to stable employment or an unemployment trap? The authors (Bloch and Estrade, 1998) took the same approach as Atkinson in a report to the French Government's Conseil d'Analyse Économique. Their response was of course mixed: at the beginning of a working life, fixed-term contracts can be considered part of a phase of integration (in a model of social mobility), except for people with the least education; at the end of a career, they are more characteristic of an exclusion phase (in a model of social separation).

Provisions to protect employment

Laws intended to protect employment in general (*e.g.* administrative authorisation for dismissal, severance pay, etc.) have frequently been cited as factors that impede hiring – which has in fact been borne out at certain times and in certain countries. However, such provisions are usually far less restrictive for young people, who are more frequently hired on fixed-term contracts, than for workers with high seniority in a company. In addition, a feature common to all of the countries studied is that they have gradually eased restrictions of this type. This is the case in France, for example, with the repeal in 1986 of administrative authorisation for dismissal and a loosening of the regulations governing temporary contracts. As we have seen, this has led to a sharp rise in the number of workers in these kinds of jobs, especially among young people.

Likewise, in the United Kingdom, deregulation of labour laws in the 1980s was conducive to the spread of part-time work and fixed-term contracts, and since that time it has not been seriously challenged. In contrast, the meagre results of this policy with regard to youth unemployment have prompted the new government to implement a five-year "Welfare to Work" plan to enable the 250 000 young people who have been unemployed for more than six months to find jobs.

4. The role of business enterprises

It is therefore necessary to take a closer look at the behaviour of business enterprises and their practices in mobilising young workers. For lack of detailed data that are comparable across countries, we shall deal essentially with the case of France, although in many cases the lessons to be learned will hold true across the board.

The first important point is that analysing young people's share of corporate employment (taking a stock perspective) yields fairly different results from those obtained by looking at their changing recruitment patterns (taking a flow perspective). In France, for example, the overall proportion of young people aged 15-26 in private sector salaried employment fell from more than 20% in 1990 to only 14% in early 1997, whereas, over the same period, the volume of hiring by the corresponding businesses remained very high: nearly four million hires, over half of which involved young people under 27 years of age. Much of the explanation for this seeming paradox stems from the increasing scope of recruitment on fixed-term contracts, and from the use of temps. By industry, the figures also differ, as will be shown by the analysis below, carried out using both types of approaches.

The declining proportion of young people in the various industries

In France, as stated above, the proportion of young workers aged 15 to 26 declined sharply in the 1990s. This trend stems in part from the fact that people are staying in school longer, of course, but also from the persistent difficulties of young first-time job-seekers and the fact that occupational integration now takes longer, with periods of unemployment, training and temporary work.

What is quite remarkable, however, is that the decline extends to virtually every one of the 36 industries studied, and that there is relatively little correlation with the employment trends of the respective sectors. Rather, there is a far greater association with an industry's labour management practices: 6% net job creation over seven years in transport and pharmaceuticals, for example, did not prevent youth employment from dropping by more than 20%.

The reduction in the proportion of young people has generally been accompanied by a rise in the percentage of workers over 50, although in some industries (agri-food, clothing-leather, retailing and agriculture) the proportion of older workers has declined as well, reflecting a concentration of the age pyramid at the intermediate levels.

While the overall industry rankings for youth employment changed little in seven years, in some cases the trends are extremely disturbing: between 1990 and 1997, the number of workers under 27 years of age dropped by over 50% in the textiles, clothing-leather, iron and steel, and electric and electronic industries – sectors in which overall employment was down sharply – but also by about 45% in chemicals and financial activities, in which job losses did not exceed 5%, and by over 40% in wholesaling, in which employment held steady overall.

Four groups of industries

Today, distinctions can be drawn between four groups of industries in which the conditions and problems are very different. The industries that employed the highest proportion of young people, both in 1997 and in 1990, have high turnover, stemming from the extensive use of fixed-term contracts, and in most cases offer low-skilled jobs. These industries primarily include i) hotels, cafés and restaurants; ii) retailing, automobile sales and repairs; iii) agri-food and; iv) personal and domestic services. Their problems stem mainly from the quality of the jobs on offer – in terms of security, skills level and attractiveness for young people, who take such positions without necessarily wishing to remain in them.

A second group is made up of fast-growing private service industries, which employ an average proportion of young people, but often in skilled positions. Examples include recreational and cultural activities, sport, health care and social welfare activities and non-profit functions. These sectors have strong potential for growth, and their problem is to attract more young people and offer them more secure jobs, because, like the first group, these industries resort massively to part-time work and fixed-term contracts (although their overall turnover is about average).

A third group of industries, which is said to be "out of phase", has more particular problems. Some industries (consumer goods, wood and paper) employ more young people than do others, whereas wholesaling, consulting and assistance activities and transport have a particularly low proportion of young people (as compared to services as a whole), with, in each case, different problems regarding skills.

The last group is made up of industries in which the labour force has lengthy average service and is ageing. With jobs that are generally open-ended and full-time, the proportion of young people is especially low (less than 9 or 10%), and even extremely low, as in energy and fuel, where the proportion is around 5%. These are primarily industrial sectors, belonging to the intermediate and capital goods industries, but they also include service activities such as real estate and finance. These industries have a very acute age-pyramid problem: they do little recruiting and tend to allow their workforce to age, not replacing everyone who retires. Some do make use of youth labour, but primarily as temporary workers: this is especially true in the automobile industry, in which youth employment accounts for 9% of the total if temporary workers are included, but also chemicals and metallurgy, in which there is also a problem of job consolidation.

The public policies that have been implemented over the past fifteen years by government, labour and management, and that have been centred on subsidies for hiring and training, have therefore not been able to prevent the relative employment situation of young people from deteriorating, nor have they addressed the labour management problems specific to the various industries.

Preserving the volume of youth recruitment

This important finding emerges less clearly if the analysis is limited to flows, because, as we have seen, the volume of young hires and youth's share of total recruiting always seem very high: in 1995, when the economy slowed down, young people accounted for 54% of the hiring in private sector companies that had at least ten employees, yet nearly four out of five of them were hired on fixed-term contracts, giving rise to substantial turnover. Since 1990, companies have offered more and more such contracts to new hires. The proportion rose from 59% of all hires (excluding temps) in 1990 to nearly 70% in 1995. The expansion of the service sector, which uses makes greater use of these contracts, unlike industry and construction, which favour temporary workers, provides a partial explanation for this trend. It would appear, however, that this type of hiring is spreading structurally, as employers seek to obtain the labour corresponding most closely to their needs.

By industry, recruitment rates are higher in services (averaging about 40% in 1995) than in industry (22%) or construction (23%). However, the proportion of young people aged 15 to 26 in total hires is greater in large establishments (56% in units with at least 50 employees) than in small ones (51% in establishments of between 10 and 19 employees). Similarly, the proportion is not always highest in service activities, which make extensive use of fixed-term contracts. While young people account for fewer than 50% of the hires of a number of service sectors (private education, transport, consulting and advisory services), this is less often the case in industrial sectors. The automobile industry, which did little recruiting in 1995, gave many of those jobs to young people (63%), as did certain intermediate-goods industries in which the average age of the workforce would appear to be getting relatively higher: chemicals (62%), wood and paper (61%) and electric and electronic components (58%).

Nevertheless, young people account for a substantial proportion of the hiring in retailing (72%), hotels, cafés and restaurants (64%), automobile sales and repairs (60%) and agri-food industries (59%).

The two viewpoints (stocks or flows) are therefore complementary, and they do not always lead to the same groupings or, on the contrary, the same distinctions, when the various sectors are characterised. Conditions in each industry call for specific reviews and solutions, covering the full range of their respective employment problems, age pyramids, forms of mobilisation of youth labour and changing skills profiles.

Other work carried out in France supports the idea that there are employment dynamics peculiar to each industry, and that these industries are fairly uniform in terms of the proportions they accord the various categories of labour and employment. This sectoral uniformity is not always present, however, in particular when an industry combines units of vastly divergent size. On top of industry-wide tendencies, there may be a dichotomy between large firms, which would favour medium-term manpower planning, a balancing of the age pyramid and renewal of skills, and small and medium-sized firms, which would favour short-term quantitative flexibility in the way they manage employment.

Forms of employment and pay that clearly reflect corporate policies

The characteristics of the jobs held by young people clearly reflect corporate policies on the recruitment and management of youth labour. They are heavily concentrated in a relatively limited number of occupations, many of which are low-skilled. Young people, who are nonetheless more highly trained, are much more likely than working adults to be employed temporarily (fixed-term contracts, reduced or occasional work, internships or subsidised contracts, and so on) or on a part-time basis. But this is especially true at the outset of a person's working life, which seems shaped by queuing phenomena: the risk of insecurity tends to diminish with age and labour market seniority. This trend towards rising insecurity for the youngest workers reflects special corporate strategies for adjusting more easily to fluctuating demand, and for enhancing the flexibility of their personnel management.

Going hand in hand with the relative insecurity of their employment, young people's pay is both low and uniformly so. Moreover, the situation has deteriorated further in the 1990s, in part because of the rise in part-time work among young people. In real terms, young people's starting salaries dropped by 7% between 1991 and 1995. Here too, the situation is one that occurs primarily at the beginning of someone's career. For a few years after young people enter the labour market, their salaries, initially concentrated at low levels, have a tendency to disperse. The fact that wages remain virtually fixed for many young people starting out, and fairly insensitive to general economic conditions, would suggest that their pay is not really determined by market forces. In any event, in a number of cases of subsidised employment, compensation is imposed in an institutional fashion.

Everything would therefore suggest that businesses play an essential role in structuring youth employment. To begin with, it is companies, in choosing whether or not to recruit, that determine the volume of employment that could satisfy the demand of young people. Additionally, it is companies that select the persons to be recruited and those whose jobs will be cut, and finally, it is companies that set the rules for employment and, apparently in a rather unilateral manner, for pay. Here, however, a decisive factor in corporate behaviour is the company's industry, and probably its size. Moreover, corporate intervention is external, but also in-house, through pay and training policies, mobility management and decisions on how work is organised.

Corporate behaviour and individual strategies

Given these transformations in corporate behaviour with respect to employment policy and personnel management, young people themselves adopt individual strategies, which can be to their collective detriment.

One example of this is the "diploma chase", in which everyone is motivated to try to protect themselves against the risks of unemployment or to await some improvement in job market conditions. But this prompts firms to require experience, along with degrees, as an additional criterion, and this favours older people at the expense of younger ones. In addition, it leads to a gradual devaluation of degrees and therefore to the downgrading of new hires aptly described by Gautié (1997), who also interprets this as a way in which businesses make labour costs more flexible. The scarcity of job offers makes young people less demanding, and although recruitment of the "overqualified" presents a certain risk, firms clearly prefer such people to those with lower levels of training. This induces a ripple-down effect: each category of graduate, from the highest to the lowest, suffers a reduction of pay and status, and, as a result, those with the least education have the most trouble breaking out of insecurity and unemployment.

Until now, however, a significant percentage of graduates have succeeded, later on in their careers, in attaining jobs more in line with their aspirations. Moreover, it is more common for the skills level of employment to go back up when the economy is strong, suggesting that a sustained recovery might lead to a reskilling of jobs (Minni and Poulet-Coulibando, 1998).

5. The French model: work for only one generation at a time?

In France, the recruiting policies that prevail not only in private enterprise, but in the public sector as well, are being called into question. The tendency of recruiters to require a higher level of formal education puts people under 25 at a disadvantage vis-à-vis those in the next-highest age bracket. One might wonder, however, whether – in firms and the civil service alike – policies intended to preserve the positions of adults are not partially responsible, in France, for the "externalisation" of young people, of whom public systems of education and integration are collectively taking charge. More specifically, the uniqueness of the French model may stem more from the difficulties inherent in the early years of working life, and in the various forms of acquiring work experience, than from any comprehensive discrimination that penalises all young people.

Youth unemployment can then be analysed as a queuing phenomenon arising from the overall scarcity of jobs, and from particular labour market mechanisms that shift a great deal of the flexibility to young people, and especially to the most inexperienced and least skilled among them, who are squeezed out.

From this standpoint, the problem of youth employment may be considered alongside that of the exclusion of older workers, for whom employment has also fallen off sharply since the early 1980s. Whereas the French social model has promoted access to activity and employment for adults, men and women, France is today feeling the effects of an "inter-generational" division of labour. Notwithstanding the efforts undertaken in connection with employment and training mechanisms, only by means of a thorough reassessment of how work is shared over the course of people's working lives can France provide better occupational integration for the young people who aspire to it.

BIBLIOGRAPHY

BAZEN, S. and MARTIN, J.P. (1991), "The Impact of the Minimum Wage on Earnings and Employment in France", *OECD Economic Studies*, No. 16, Spring.

BÉDUWÉ, C. and GIRET, J.F. (1998), "Analyse comparative des modes d'intégration des jeunes aux marchés du travail européens", Working Paper, No. 281 (98-20), LIRHE, October.

BENHAYOUN, G. (1994), "The Impact of Minimum Wages on Youth Employment in France Revisited", *International Journal of Manpower*, No. 15.

BLOCH, L. and ESTRADE, M.A. (1998), "Les formes particulières d'emploi en France: un marchepied vers les emplois stables?", *France, Portrait social*, INSEE, October.

BOURDET, Y. and PERSSON, I. (1991), "Chômage des jeunes et fonctionnement du marché du travail: les cas français et suédois", *Économie et Statistique*, No. 249, December.

BRUNO, C. and CAZES, S. (1997), "Le chômage des jeunes en France", *Revue de l'OFCE*, No. 62.

CARD, D. and KRUEGER, A. (1994), "Minimum Wages and Employment: A Case Study of the Fast Food Industry in New Jersey and Pennsylvania", *American Economic Review*, September.

CETTE, G., CUNÉO, P., EYSSARTIER, D. and GAUTIÉ, J. (1996), "Coût du travail et emploi des jeunes", *Revue de l'OFCE*, No. 56.

DARES (1998), "Emploi des jeunes et secteurs d'activité", Preparatory Document for the Conférence nationale sur l'emploi, les salaires et le temps de travail in October 1997, Paris, March.

DOLADO, J., KRAMARZ, F., MACHIN, S., MANNING, A., MARGOLIS, D. and TEULINGS, C. (1996), "The Economic Impact of Minimum Wages in Europe", *Economic Policy*, No. 23, October.

ELBAUM, M. and MARCHAND, O. (1993), "Emploi et chômage des jeunes dans les pays industrialisés: la spécificité française", *Premières Synthèses*, No. 34, DARES, October.

EYRAND, F., MARSDEN, D. and SILVESTRE, J.J. (1990), "Occupational and Internal Labour Markets in Britain and France", *International Labour Review*, Vol. 129, No. 4.

GARONNA, P. and RYAN, P. (1989), "Le travail des jeunes, les relations professionnelles et les politiques sociales dans les économies avancées", *Formation Emploi*, No. 25, CEREQ, January-March.

GAUTIÉ, J. (1997), "Insertion professionnelle et chômage des jeunes en France", *Regards sur l'actualité*, July-August.

INSEE (1995), "Les trajectoires des jeunes: transitions professionnelles et familiales", *Économie et Statistique*, Nos. 283-284, 1995-3/4.

INSEE (1997), "Les trajectoires des jeunes: distances et dépendances entre générations", *Économie et Statistique*, Nos. 304-305, 1997-4/5.

LEFRESNE, F. (1992), "Systèmes de formation professionnelle et insertion des jeunes: une comparaison France/Royaume-Uni", *Revue de l'IRES*, No. 9.

MARCHAND, O. and MINNI, C. (1997), "En mars 1997, un jeune sur neuf était au chômage", *Premières Synthèses*, 97.12-No. 52.1, DARES, December.

MINNI, C. and POULET-COULIBANDO, P. (1998), "L'évolution récente de la scolarité et de l'insertion professionnelle des jeunes (1996-1998)", *Premières Synthèses*, 98.12-No. 52.1, DARES, December.

OECD (1998), *Employment Outlook*, Paris.

OECD (forthcoming), *Labour Force Statistics 1978-1997*, Paris.

ROSE, J. (1998), *Les jeunes face à l'emploi*, Éditions Desclée de Brouwer, Paris.

Table 1. **Unemployment rates of youth aged 15-24 in selected OECD countries** (Percentages)

	Men			Women			All		
	1977	1987	1997	1977	1987	1997	1977	1987	1997
Australia	10.9	14.8	17.2	13.8	14.3	14.6	12.2	14.6	15.9
Austria	n.a.	n.a.	5.5	n.a.	n.a.	7.6	n.a.	n.a.	6.5
Belgium	n.a.	14.7	17.6	n.a.	28.6	25.7	n.a.	21.4	21.3
Canada	14.8	14.6	17.6	13.7	12.3	15.7	14.3	13.6	16.7
Denmark	n.a.	8.0	6.6	n.a.	10.0	9.9	n.a.	8.9	8.1
Finland	13.4	9.7	22.0	11.0	8.1	25.0	12.3	9.0	23.3
France	8.0	18.3	24.6	15.1	28.5	32.8	11.2	22.9	28.1
Germany[a]	4.6	8.0	10.3	6.6	9.0	9.6	5.5	8.5	10.0
Greece	n.a.	17.5	22.2	n.a.	33.8	40.6	n.a.	25.0	31.0
Ireland	15.3	27.2	18.9	10.4	21.4	15.2	13.2	24.5	16.1
Italy[b]	20.4	29.8	29.1	28.2	42.2	39.3	23.9	35.5	33.6
Japan	4.0	5.4	6.9	3.1	5.0	6.3	3.5	5.2	6.6
Netherlands	7.9	12.9	9.1	6.5	16.9	10.0	7.3	14.8	9.5
Portugal	13.7	12.7	14.5[c]	20.8	20.4	19.3	16.3	16.1	16.7
Spain[d]	10.2	33.7	30.3	12.7	49.3	46.1	11.2	40.2	37.1
Sweden[d]	3.8	4.6	23.0	5.1	4.6	21.9	4.4	4.6	22.5
United Kingdom[d]	n.a.	16.7	15.6	n.a.	14.7	11.0	n.a.	15.8	13.5
United States[d]	13.3	12.8	11.8	14.0	11.7	10.7	13.6	12.2	11.3

n.a. Data not available.

a. Western Germany in 1977 and 1987, the whole of Germany in 1997.

b. Refers to persons 14-24 years old.

c. Data for 1996.

d. Refers to persons 16-24 years old.

Source: OECD, *Labour Force Statistics*, non-standardised rates.

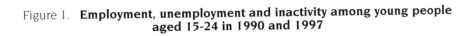

Figure 1. **Employment, unemployment and inactivity among young people aged 15-24 in 1990 and 1997**

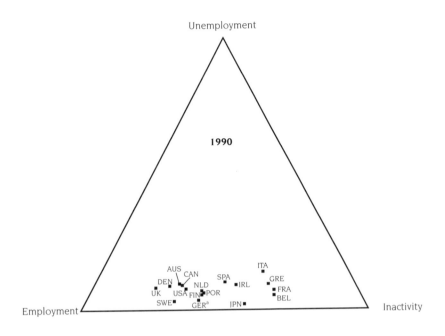

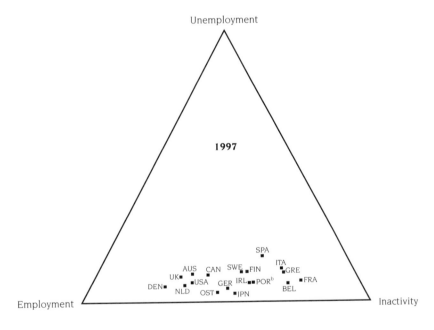

a. 1991.
b. 1996.

How to read the chart: The position of each country is given by its orthogonal distance to each of the three sides of the triangle. For instance, in 1997, France is at 0.079 from the side opposite the apex "unemployment", at 0.201 from the side opposite the apex "employment" and at 0.720 from the side opposite the apex "inactivity", these three values being respectively the unemployment/population ratio, the employment/population ratio and the inactivity rate for young French in 1997.

Source: OECD.

Figure 2. **Comparison between young people and the total (15 and more), 1997**

Difference or proportion between youth unemployment/population ratio and the unemployment/population ratio of the population aged 15 and more

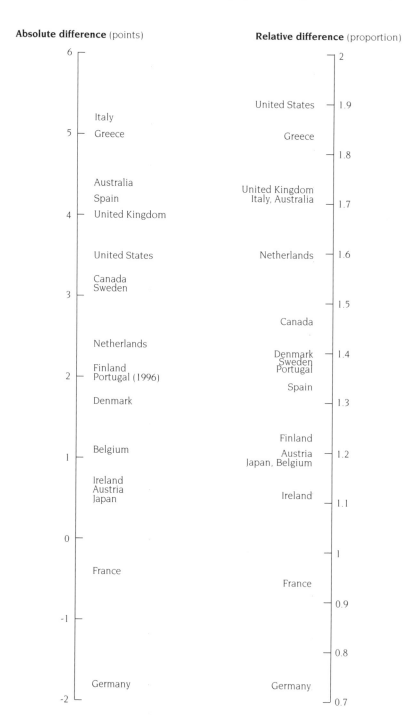

Source: OECD.

WORKSHOP 5

POLICIES TO IMPROVE THE EMPLOYABILITY OF DISADVANTAGED YOUTH: WHAT WORKS AND FOR WHOM?

LABOUR MARKET POLICIES FOR DISADVANTAGED YOUNG PEOPLE IN EUROPE*

by
Idès Nicaise
HIVE, Catholic University of Leuven, Belgium

Introduction

"In my municipality, social services place young people in integration projects for a period of 18 months. They have to work for up to 8 or 10 hours a day in voluntary organisations for USD 30 per day. It is cheap labour for the employers. The young people are forced to accept it because they have no alternative and they want to be independent. Once the "integration" is over, they are back on the street and are not entitled to anything because the law does not give them the same rights as other employees: they have no pay slip, no social security contributions, no sickness benefit fund, no minimum wage. When they leave they cannot go on the dole because their work is not recognised as real work, it is just an 'occupation'. What we are demanding for young people is that the work in these integration projects should give them genuine rights as employees, both during and after the project. During the integration period, they should be able to learn a real trade and obtain a recognised certificate. Afterwards, they must be entitled to unemployment benefits. If they are recognised as unemployed, it is easier for them to be recruited by employers, who are subsidised for re-employing unemployed re-employing people." This is how a mother from an underprivileged family summarises her son's situation and her vision of the integration policy (ATD Quart Monde, 1998).

1. Who is involved?

The image of "disadvantaged young people" is somewhat fuzzy. We are dealing not only with unemployed young people who have to be "integrated", but also with young people who started working when they were too young, for example, with no form of social protection. In some southern European countries, young people aged between 12 and 16 from needy families drop out of compulsory schooling in order to earn an additional income.[1] In other cases, young adults try to earn a living or simply make themselves useful doing "informal work" (which is not the same as illegal activities), *e.g.* by repairing televisions or mopeds, doing voluntary work in their neighbourhood, etc.

It is therefore best not to measure "disadvantage" one-dimensionally (by unemployment), but as an accumulation of deprivations, even if we confine ourselves to the labour dimension. Each of these elements in itself delineates a fairly broad group, while the intensity and duration of the deprivation, together with the accumulation of factors, leads to genuine disadvantage. Unfortunately, the statistics [mostly derived here from Eurostat's Labour Force Surveys (1996 and 1997)] are too general to give an accurate picture of our target group:

- *Level of education*: approximately 12.2% of the young people who have left school[2] (unemployed or not) in the EU have had no more than primary education. Even though more than half of them are employed, these youngsters are faced with extremely high risks of unemployment and poverty at later ages (see Figures 1 and 2).

* My special thanks to Nick Matheus for bibliographical assistance, and to Eurostat for providing unpublished data.

– *Social protection*: only 23.3% of unemployed people under the age of 25 in the EU were receiving unemployment insurance or assistance benefits in 1994 (CEC, 1995, p. 88; Eurostat, 1996).[3] It is not known whether these are better-placed or more underprivileged unemployed people: unemployment insurance favours those who have already worked long enough, while unemployment assistance is selectively targeted at families on the lowest incomes. Note, however, that in many countries young people also have no access to means-tested (public assistance) benefits (see Figure 3).

– *Duration of unemployment*: 37.8% of young unemployed people in 1996 had already been without work for longer than one year, 20.5% for longer than two years.

– *Regional disadvantage*: both youth unemployment in general and long-term youth unemployment are highly geographically concentrated in southern Europe.[4] While Finland may well have high youth unemployment, the proportion of long-term unemployment remains limited.

– *Gender seems not to be a highly discriminating factor among young people*. In some EU countries, the level of unemployment among young women is actually lower than among men, although this is compensated by a high level of inactivity. Young women are more likely to work part-time than young men, but the differences between the two sexes are much smaller among young people than among those aged over 25.

– *Qualitative aspects of employment*: part-time and temporary work are not typical youth concerns (European Commission, 1998a); they are actually more common among adults who go back to work after a period of unemployment. On the other hand, the labour market for young people is characterised primarily by low wages: the gap between them and higher age groups is increasing (OECD, 1996). Youth employment is also concentrated in sectors with higher flexibility requirements (hotel and catering, retail trade, building and personal services).

– Presumably, *young people with the lowest qualifications* are most likely to work in temporary, part-time and low-paid jobs, although no specific data are available to support this; and,

– *Other factors of disadvantage* include ethnic origin, health problems, handicaps, previous institutional history, a criminal record, etc.

2. Obstacles to participation in labour market programmes

Underprivileged groups in general (and to a less extent underprivileged young people) are paradoxically heavily under-represented in programmes for re-integration into the labour market: although they would benefit the most from them, they are the least likely to take part. Statistical material about this issue is widely available, although harmonised data can only be found for training measures (Figure 4). In this section, we look for possible explanations for this phenomenon.

The role of *cultural thresholds* (the attitudes of young people towards work) in the decision to take part in active labour market policies (ALMPs) must be put into perspective. In contrast to what is often expected, young people in general and unemployed young people in particular attach at least as much value to work as other age groups (OECD, 1996, pp. 113-117). So what are the genuine obstacles restricting access to ALMPs?

An initial group of stumbling blocks is *legal or administrative* in nature. Given that many young people cannot receive benefits, many of them do not register as job-seekers (although they are looking for work) or withdraw from the labour market. In addition to the 3.5 million young people in the EU who were registered as job-seekers in 1996, the Labour Force Survey counted another 1.3 million unemployed but not registered and 2.9 million young people (1/3 of whom are men) who are "inactive" for reasons other than receiving education.

Job-seekers who are not registered cannot of course be reached by the bodies implementing labour market programmes. However, even among those who are registered, attention is focused in the first instance on those entitled to benefit because the cost of their unemployment is higher for the government. This tendency is being reinforced by the new trend towards the activation of unemployment benefits. If no benefit is available, it cannot of course be activated.

Furthermore, within the group of those entitled to benefit, discrimination often takes place between those covered by "unemployment insurance" on the one hand and "unemployment assistance" or the minimum income on the other hand. For example, in Belgium in 1997 these categories were legally brought into line with one another in terms of access to ALMPs. However, subtle administrative rules still exist under which those receiving public assistance are removed from the registers of employment agencies after a certain spell of time.

Other legal or administrative reasons restricting access to ALMPs include: the inadequate definition of access conditions (*e.g.* a certain uninterrupted period of unemployment is required which means that those occasionally unemployed are excluded), the complexity of the legislation and the lack of publicity (towards both target group and employers).

A second cause of non-participation is the *mismatch between the programmes on offer and the needs and aspirations of the disadvantaged* young people (Nicaise *et al.*, 1995). Some (training) programmes impose excessively high requirements in terms of prior knowledge and skills, others follow too strict a pace; yet others are too schoolish and do not take into account young people's aversion to school as a result of a career full of failures. Those taking part in work experience programmes usually complain about their poor status or lack of prospects after the programme has ended. Most provisions suffer from a glaring lack of information and social guidance: they confine themselves to strictly work-related problems and lose sight of the link with other aspects of disadvantage.

We believe that *financial disincentives* do influence the participation of young people in labour market programmes, but not specifically where one would usually expect to find them in the literature. One view sometimes put forward is that the replacement ratios of social security benefits are too generous and have a demotivating effect. In other words, young people would turn up their noses at the low (minimum) wages in the segments to which they can gain access, compared to their unemployment benefits. We believe that this is too static an analysis. Generally speaking, the low wages paid to young people are still more attractive than the even lower or non-existent social security payments meted out to young people. The replacement ratios of the social security payments seem to work out very low, particularly for school-leavers (CEC, 1995, pp. 100-101). Moreover, we must not forget that participation in labour market programmes is itself a condition for receiving benefits in some countries (Nordic countries and the UK).

However, more complex financial thresholds may be at work, although little empirical research has been done in this respect. The considerations below are indeed based more on theoretical considerations and casual observation by field workers than on systematic econometric research.

In the first instance, interaction may possibly take place with the benefits received by other family members in means-tested systems of social protection. Indeed, in some cases, young people can be restrained from accepting a job offer if, as a result, the benefits paid to their parents or other family members would be cut.

The financial balance must also be examined dynamically, specifically with respect to low-income groups: sometimes acute short-term financial need takes precedence over the uncertain long-term benefit to be gained from investing in ALMPs. Even when the direct costs of participation (travel, child care etc.)

are refunded, they often have to be pre-financed by the participants. If the refunding procedure takes too long, this in itself may be sufficient reason for those most in need to drop out. However, in addition to direct costs, indirect costs must also be considered, *i.e.* the fact that no other work can be accepted for the duration of the integration programme – albeit low-paid or temporary work. For anyone weighed down by long-term deprivation or debts, the short-term prospect of occasional work is often more attractive. In contrast to the static analysis of financial (dis)incentives, this approach advocates an increase rather than a reduction in the replacement ratios for underprivileged job-seekers. The increase can best be allocated in the form of a bonus for participation.

Finally, we must mention the age-old tendency to *cream off* the target group in most labour market programmes. The cause may be found primarily in the desire of employment agencies to supply employers with the best possible candidates (Nicaise *et al.*, 1995). But this brings us to an apparent paradox, one we shall examine more closely in the next section. Employment agencies appear to be convinced that labour market programmes are more effective for the stronger job-seekers (higher skilled, men, natives, short-term unemployed, etc.), because ultimately these latter have better (gross) outflow opportunities. This is clearly a mistake: stronger groups may flow out faster, but the *added value of labour market measures* on their outflow rates is smaller.

3. The effectiveness of active labour market programmes

It is not our ambition to deliver a complete review of effect studies of ALMPs. Based on existing reviews (Fay *et al.*, 1996; Friedlander *et al.*, 1997; Meager and Evans, 1998; Nicaise *et al.*, 1995; Nicaise and Bollens, 1998; OECD, 1994), we draw lessons regarding disadvantaged target groups, young people, and the "intersection" of these two.

The big misconception: ALMPs are more effective for disadvantaged groups

Let us first consider the effects for the job-seekers in question at micro level. These effects are usually measured in terms of outflow rates from unemployment, or of wage rates or incomes. "Gross outflow rates" (as observed in bivariate analyses, *i.e.* without correction for the profile of the participants) argue against the disadvantaged groups: after participation, the long-term unemployed, the low-skilled, women and ethnic minorities still have lower outflow rates than stronger participants (the short-term unemployed, the better educated, etc.). However, the fact of participation means that the "net outflow effect", *i.e.* the *increase* of outflow rates is greater for the disadvantaged participant than for the average job-seeker (for European countries: Axelsson, 1989; Bollens and Hooge, 1996; de Koning, 1996; Gravesteijn-Ligthelm *et al.*, 1995; Hofbauer and Dadzio, 1987; Raaum and Torp, 1996; Van der Burgh and Bavinck, 1995). This general tendency has also been observed outside Europe in the general study by Friedlander *et al.* (1997).

Where a difference is made according to age groups, the findings are rather mixed: young people derive now more, now less profit from ALMPs. Few studies investigate the cross-effects of age and other group characteristics: they report quite a strong net effect among disadvantaged youth (Hofbauer and Dadzio, 1987; Korpi, 1992).

Insignificant macro-effects?

There is heated debate as to the effect of ALMPs at macro level. Attention has tended to focus on the unwanted side-effects, such as dead-weight, substitution and displacement effects (Fay, 1996). The increased outflow opportunities of one group are in fact partially offset by the lower employment opportunities of other groups. The net macro-effect for recruitment subsidies in particular is estimated at "only" 10 to 20% (or even less). Two important comments must be made in this connection.

– First, there are various reasons to assume that the dead-weight effects are smaller for programmes that selectively target the weakest groups. We are, after all, dealing with groups that would hardly stand a chance without government assistance (Bassi and Ashenfelter, 1986; OECD, 1993). As for substitution effects, the picture, in our opinion, is less clear: low and average qualified job-seekers are relatively more numerous and thus enter more readily into competition with each other (Nicaise and Bollens, 1998). Substitution can be avoided to the extent that ALMPs are focused on the bottlenecks in the labour market.

– Second, dead-weight and substitution may indeed be important parameters, but they also reflect no more than a part (that is, the negative side) of the macro-effects. Other, positive side-effects are generally "forgotten", *e.g.* the increased effectiveness of the job-seeking behaviour of the unemployed persons concerned can be expected to result in wage moderation effects [which have actually been measured by the OECD (1993)]. Furthermore, the recovery effects for the government (lower expenditure on social benefits and higher tax revenues after the intervention) should create more room for manoeuvre and thus also indirect employment. In the light of the strict European convergence policy (the Maastricht criteria), this is a not inconsiderable advantage.

In short, the macro-effects of ALMPs are broader and more complex than hitherto generally assumed. Such measures could be worth the trouble even with limited net employment effects at macro-level. The ultimate criterion of judgement is, in any case, not the total number of jobs created in a programme, nor even the cost per created job, but the social cost-benefit balance of the conducted policy per created job (Friedlander *et al.*, 1997).

This argument can be illustrated by the example of a Belgian programme for disadvantaged young people and adults. It is a (rather expensive) combination of work experience with training and counselling for welfare recipients ("Training and Employment for the Disadvantaged"). The gross transition ratio to further employment after the programme was "only" 40%, the net employment effect in comparison with the control group "hardly" 15%. However, it may reasonably be supposed that this programme sooner or later becomes profitable for the community because of the increased employability and productivity of the participants and the recovery effects for the government.[5] Instead of throwing the programme overboard for yielding too low employment effects, we do better to increase investment given its positive cost-benefit balance (Nicaise, 1996).

The above observations thus refute the prejudices held by many – including the policy makers and public employment services – that ALMP has dubious effects on the hard core of the unemployed. If ALMPs have one advantage compared with other types of employment policy (wage restraint, redistribution of employment, industrial policy, etc.), then it is in this area: they can drive back the structural unemployment, the so-called NAIRU – at least, if they are selectively targeted at the most disadvantaged target groups.

The theoretical foundation of this last condition is illustrated in Figures 5 and 6, showing the trade-off between unemployment and inflation by means of a Phillips curve. It is currently assumed that this trade-off is principally determined by the numbers of "effective" job-seekers. A reduction of the number of effective job-seekers implies an upward shift along the curve to the left; an increase is reflected in a shift along the curve, down to the right. Conversely, the number of hard-to-employ (or ineffective) job-seekers determines the lie of the entire curve: a fall in the numbers shifts the whole curve over to the left, an increase to the right. Point A is the point of departure for both figures.

If the active labour market policy is now brought to bear upon the average (effective) unemployed, the stock of the unemployed will decrease in the short term, but most likely at the cost of more inflation (shift of point A towards point B in Figure 5). On outflow, some of the participants find work in the regular employment market but, seeing the limited "added value" of the measures for the employability of the persons concerned, a substantial percentage flows back into unemployment (shift from B to C). Figure 6 shows the effect of selective measures for those caught in structural unemployment. In that this group has no influence on the wage formation, unemployment falls in the short term without exerting upwards pay pressure (from A to B) and nudges the Phillips curve to the left. When some of the participants end up in unemployment again after outflow, they are transformed into effective unemployed and exert a moderating influence on pay (shift from B to C along the new curve).

The above reasoning further explains why the empirical literature on the aggregate impact of ALMPs is not unambiguous (Layard *et al.*, 1991; Fay, 1996; Meager and Evans, 1998; Anxo *et al.*, 1998; Van der Linden and Dor, 1998). Our hypothesis is that the macro-effects regarding unemployment and pay pressure are more favourable as the policy is better focused on the structurally unemployed. An incorrect targeting brings wage-push inflation and a limited decrease in unemployment; selective measures for disadvantaged groups give a greater outflow from unemployment plus wage restraint. Thus far, macro-studies have tended to ignore the aspect of targeting.

What sort of measures, which modalities?

Can differences in effectiveness be observed between training, job search assistance, recruitment subsidies, relief work programmes, self-employment schemes or "intermediate employment (community business) initiatives"? Here again, the research findings are ambiguous: at present, it would seem rather premature to make firm statements regarding the superiority of this or that approach. For disadvantaged youth in particular, only certain tentative conclusions can be put forward:

– Recruitment subsidies appear more prone to dead-weight and substitution effects than direct employment schemes (relief work), and certainly more than job training (Meager and Evans, 1998). Temporary wage subsidies on the other hand allow employers to "screen" candidates from risk groups. Candidates can thus prove their employability and disabuse employers of their preconceptions. In other words, the main function of selective wage subsidies is that of redistribution of opportunities.

– Direct employment programmes have very mixed results (Meager and Evans, 1998). Some studies detect a substantial short-term effect on the outflow from unemployment, macro-level included (Anxo *et al.*, 1998). There is however a problem with the throughflow. Some cases display a "lock-in" effect, *i.e.* the beneficiaries reduce their job-seeking because of the fact of already having work. On the other hand, good throughflow results are booked in some countries (*e.g.* Flanders, the Netherlands, Germany, Austria), presumably because it is clear from the outset that these work experience programmes are of a temporary nature. Here, work experience acts as a springboard, especially for the long-term unemployed.

– Job training clearly has a greater impact on later employment chances when coupled with practical training periods with regular employers. More generally, however, combined measures (job search assistance, training, work experience, social guidance, etc.) appear to increase the chances of success. This, according to Meager and Evans (1998), argues the case for community businesses, which often adopt a more holistic approach than do other types of programmes. However, very little is yet known regarding the effectiveness of community businesses.

– There is strong evidence of the inefficiency of compulsory programmes such as workfare or learnfare programmes in which young people (sometimes also the long-term unemployed or welfare recipients) must participate in order to qualify for unemployment benefits. It is no accident that all these programmes have had negative effects on the outflow chances from unemployment and on the wages (Sweden: Andersson, 1993; UK: White and Mcrae., 1989; Dolton, 1993; Andrews *et al.*, 1996; Denmark: Jensen *et al.*, 1992; Rosholm. 1994, 1995; Finland: Hämäläinen, 1998). These disappointing results are ascribed to different factors (Aakrog *et al.*, 1991).

- "Mismatched" programmes, too homogeneous to accommodate the diversity of the needs and interests of the job-seekers. Compulsory participation relieves the providers of the programmes from any creativity in handling those needs.

- The demotivating effect of the obligation in itself (the training is seen more as a way of keeping the right side of the employment regulations than as a genuine springboard to employment).

- The stigma of the obligation, its aura of blameworthiness making the job-seekers even less attractive in the eyes of the employers.

– Denmark has drawn lessons from these evaluations and, since 1994, its labour market policy has become appreciably more flexible: the "obligation to co-operate in a re-integration plan" still remains, but more alternative options are now on offer, and initiatives are more made to measure and more preventive. In the same spirit, the UK abandoned the erstwhile Youth Training Scheme in favour of the national apprenticeship programme and the "Entry Level Provision" having better-fitting service packages for job-seekers.

– The pedagogic aspects of the measures have received scant critical attention. Brun *et al.* (1991) and Godinot *et al.* (1995) list the following quality criteria for the success of projects for the most deprived people: a holistic approach (see above), a sufficiently long training period (two or three years is not considered a luxury), alternating formulas combining training and work, preferably starting with work experience and with a gradually increasing training component, and sufficient remuneration in order to prevent dropout.

– Be this as it well may, we must not lose sight of the macroeconomic aspects of (youth) unemployment, nor of the problem of its regional concentration. Several studies (European Commission, 1998a; OECD, 1996) show that the aggregate volume of economic activity is the No. 1 determinant factor in youth unemployment. Active measures designed to increase the employability of youth may help, but are drops in the ocean in the context of areas such as southern Italy, where more than half the young are jobless. It goes without saying that an industrial and regional policy is also required there, directed towards the demand side of the labour market and towards the creation of new enterprise (Pugliese, 1995).

4. Recent trends and perspectives

It is impossible to give a quantitative summary of the different strategies currently in progress throughout the EU designed to combat youth unemployment. Many programmes are, in any case, not aimed at specific target groups. Low-skilled unemployed youth are targeted very actively in the countries of Northern Europe, more often than not by linking social allowances to work experience and job training programmes. Such a "watertight" approach is hardly feasible in Southern Europe. Here, we find greater reliance on the apprenticeship system and on the "intermediate labour market" (social co-operatives, workshop-schools, etc.). France and Germany make use of large-scale direct employment programmes.

The Structural Funds (the *European Social Fund* in particular) streamline policy at EU level. Here, the major accent rests on job training, though recent years have witnessed an interest in a diversification of measures. "Integrated pathways to employment" are the new fashion, with *a*) a provision of individualised services; *b*) partnership between diverse actors (government, the social partners, the third sector, etc.); *c*) a package of counselling, training, work experience, job clubs and labour cost subsidies; and *d*) a "trajectory" that must lead on to permanent integration. This concept is better suited to the needs of disadvantaged groups, though still limited to services in the field of employment integration and hard to implement.

Among the priority target groups of the ESF, a special place is accorded to (low-skilled) young persons as well as "persons threatened with exclusion from the labour market". Unfortunately, the category of "young persons" casts its net too wide for practical purposes, with the result that many countries complain of a "creaming-off" effect (European Commission, 1998b).

The European Social Fund is gradually being fitted into a broader *joint EU employment policy*.[6] This policy finds concrete form in the EU Employment Guidelines which are being applied in national action plans. Guideline number 1 merits particular comment here: "*Within five years (...) each Member State will ensure that every young person is offered a new start before reaching six months of unemployment, in the form of training*, retraining, *work practice, a job or other employability measure...*". A similar approach applies to persons over the age of 25 before they hit the limit of one year of unemployment.

These objectives go beyond the very ambitious. They also signal a *new approach in social protection* determined to go beyond the mere replacement of income from paid employment. We could, for want of a better name, call it *"activating social protection"*. This is anchored in a growing awareness that not only the right to a (minimum) income but, also, the right (and duty) to work is essential for social cohesion. What is more, it is common knowledge that both traditional Bismarckian and Beveridgian social protection systems cannot begin to cope with the present-day kind and scale of social exclusion. With Bismarckian systems, we note that more and more people are less and less able to consolidate their rights to social security through a track record of employment. Beveridgian systems are littered with the poverty trap. This being the case, a new sort of social contract is taking shape in which social protection is assured in exchange for a personal commitment to integration, via community service, training or participation in work experience programmes.

The new approach is very much inspired by the experience of the Nordic countries. All these countries have rubbed shoulders with one or another form of "learnfare" and "workfare", where young people receive benefits only if they attend a training scheme or sign up for a work experience programme.[7] The government then goes on to guarantee a sufficient supply of job training and work experience places, so as to strike a certain balance between the rights and obligations of individual and community. The New Deal in the UK and the *Jeugdwerkgarantieplan* in the Netherlands travel the same road. In many European countries, the access to public assistance is also linked to the conclusion of "integration contracts", where the receiving end and the municipal welfare agency join forces to put as swift as possible an end to the situation of dependence.

This trend can, in principle, be called positive. Whereas in the traditional Bismarckian systems millions of young people were unable to acquire rights to social security through earlier employment (*retro-active* insurance), they should now have meaningful chances to prove their readiness to work and to integrate if the new, *pro-active* formula is true to its promise.

The system also meets two of the three basic needs at a stroke: income, work and/or training – where previously there was naught but income replacement.

In the third place, the ALMP *creaming-off effects* are countered, meaning that the most underprivileged will also be invited to the table when the government seriously undertakes to make an offer to anyone who meets certain criteria.

Finally, these European guidelines are redolent of the will to prevent social exclusion by long-term unemployment rather than to cure it.

Denmark, Sweden and Finland are, at first sight, "runaway" success stories in this connection. In one twelve month period, Finland saw its youth unemployment drop by more than a third while the percentage of school attendance took the upward gradient (Aho and Vehviläinen, 1997, cited in MISEP, 1998); the number of low-skilled unemployed young persons in Denmark fell by a full 70% just one year after the introduction of the new compulsory training scheme (MISEP, 1997).

There are, however, certain fundamental *dangers*.

– To begin with, there is some fuzziness about the description of the target groups and their mutual relations. According the young such high priority – surely this is to eat off the plate of other, possibly even more disadvantaged target groups? By no means all young persons necessarily have integration problems. A sudden new tack on behalf of short-term unemployed youth may de facto, paradoxically, give way to even more stubborn exclusion of (younger and older) long-term unemployed ("reverse substitution effect").

– Will there be a priority for those who already draw benefits? The latest lever in the ALMPs is the activation of benefits and allowances. We have seen that only a small minority of young people draw any benefit at present. A watertight system of social protection, as described above, should provide cover for all school-leavers who appear unable to find employment past a certain cut-off point. Bearing in mind that many young people currently live at the margins of the labour market, there is the grim sensation that many a national action plan, unless re-thought, will miss those most in need of assistance.

– Targeting also has implications regarding the effectiveness of the measures put up. Measures aimed at the earliest possible intervention, irrespective of the job seekers' level of educational attainment, can by all means be expected to suffer considerable dead-weight and substitution effects. In our view, the urgent call for prevention has not altogether been founded in reason. A remedial approach can sometimes be more efficient than a "full frontal" preventive one. de Koning and van Nes (1998) have demonstrated that the a priori "expected duration of unemployment" (forecast based on econometric analyses of individual characteristics upon entry into unemployment) involves a high uncertainty margin. Allocation of services on this basis may to a large extent serve groups who do not need help.[8] Or, to put it another way, European Guideline number 1 might well turn out to be an expensive affair.

– In some countries, it has become clear that the government was not up to the job of matching supply quantity with quality within the set time-frame. In Denmark and the UK, the "iffy" quality of the early 1990s resulted in disappointing outflow rates. The Finnish authorities have recently been forced to loosen up as regards obligations on the part of youth: instead of actual participation in a training scheme, they now accept three 'applications' for job training sufficient to qualify for unemployment benefit.

– A further danger with "activating social security" is that of growing authoritarianism. There is already evidence of a systematic stiffening of unemployment regulations in Europe. The obligation to accept offers has always existed, but this was shaded by a set of criteria as to the nature of a "suitable offer": it must satisfy minimum or maximum requirements regarding mobility, working hours, match between the offer and the needs or capacities of the individual, pay, etc. These standards become increasingly unfavourable (Commission of the European Communities, 1997, pp. 102-105). So, we end up with the paradox that the public authorities themselves are developing a "secondary labour market", in which compulsion, uncertain statutes and, sometimes, near exploitation, rule. There is the added danger of increased exclusion from social protection: job-seekers who refuse the offer or drop out lose their benefits in greater numbers. It is puzzling, for instance, that the proportion of unemployed young people who are not registered at the public employment service is so high, not only in countries with a weak social protection system, but also in the Nordic countries where social protection is extremely well developed (see Figure 3). Does this signal non-compliance of youngsters with the coercive rules of the system, or sanctions, or is it a matter of definition? Could there be a trade-off between social protection and ALMPs? Different studies appear to point to a limited positive impact of sanctions on the outflow rates, but it should also be mentioned that the outflow often leads to inactivity instead of work (Abbring et al., 1995; Aho and Vehviläinen, 1997; Van den Berg et al., 1998; Van der Linden and Dor, 1998).[9]

There are practically no studies regarding the social side-effects of exclusion from unemployment (Wets, 1998; ATD Quart Monde, 1998). In the UK, the alarming increase in poverty and homelessness among young persons was brought into connection with the shortage of places in the Youth Training Scheme and the resultant exclusion of those young persons from social protection (Nicaise *et al.*, 1995, p. 59).

In short, the new model of social protection has opportunities and pitfalls. What is important is that the final objective (combating social exclusion) continues to have the upper hand over the pressure to score "good figures" as regards pushing back registered unemployment. These two objectives may not be mutually exclusive, but that does not make them synonymous. If we hope to prevent "activating social security" from degenerating into a bureaucratic mill or an exclusion machine, high standards will have to be imposed regarding quality, customised programmes and freedom of choice for job-seekers.

5. Conclusion

Disadvantaged youth in Europe will probably be the touchstone of the new social model. Given the combination of their vulnerable position in the labour market and their marginal position with regard to social protection, the national governments are obliged to search for new ways of integration. Guideline number 1 of the joint EU employment policy is, perhaps, the catalyst in this process of exploration. We are evolving – ideally – towards the linking of income transfers with packages of ALMPs.

In contrast to "common knowledge", research to date shows that ALMPs, both at individual and at macro-level, are more effective the more they are selectively targeted on the most disadvantaged groups.

It is then all a question of:

– Reaching out effectively to these groups (many disadvantaged young persons fall outside any system of social protection and have no more connection with the competent authorities)

– Putting together a suitable offer, *i.e.* a holistic approach in the form of "pathways to integration", sufficiently long and intensive, with a genuine prospect of paid employment at the outcome, a good balance between rights and obligations, positive support rather than a coercive approach, a solid status and sufficient freedom of choice.

The will in the Member States of Europe to arrive at a watertight offer within a period of five years must be viewed as ambitious. The most disadvantaged groups do not in fact really have a chance to benefit from policy measures until these take the form of guaranteed services. The undertaking, however, is not without risks, *e.g.* wrong definition of the target group, a pressure to 'statistical performance', and authoritarianism.

NOTES

1. In Portugal the government introduced minimum labour legislation in 1993 for young people of compulsory school age because they could not stop them dropping out. Occasionally, serious work accidents involving young people under the age of 15 crop up in the European media.

2. Young people between 15 and 24 who have left school (note that this definition implies an underestimation of graduation rates at upper secondary and tertiary level). The percentage is less than 5% in Austria, Denmark, Sweden and the UK and over 15% in Spain, France, Greece and Luxembourg. It exceeds 50% in Portugal.

3. CEC (1997) gives higher figures based on the EC Household Panel. However, these figures seem to us less reliable because of the limited size of the sample and possible selection biases in the calculations.

4. Both youth unemployment in general and long-term youth unemployment are expressed here as a percentage of the total population aged between 15 and 24 (therefore including those still studying. *Cf.* EC (1998*a*) for a justification of this definition: suppose only 10% of those in a certain age group are available on the labour market and half of them are unemployed, this is less of a problem than if 50% are available and 1 in 4 of them is unemployed. In the former case, we are dealing with 5% youth unemployment, in the latter with 12.5%.

5. The estimates are incomplete because displacement is left out of the equation but, conversely, so are the wage restraint effects. The time-horizon of the return period appears to be crucial: the balance is certainly positive if the profits on the investment last at least 2 to 3 years, which is plausible.

6. The four pillars of wisdom of this policy being: improving employability, developing entrepreneurship, encouraging adaptability in businesses and their employees, and strengthening the policies for equal opportunities.

7. The difference with hard-line workfare is that remuneration usually meets normal standards.

8. de Koning and van Nes advocate continual re-assessment of the outflow rates. Given that non-observed handicaps of individuals can only be "revealed" by the duration of unemployment, appropriate action should be taken as and when the outflow chance dips below a certain level.

9. It may further be assumed that outflow to work resulting from sanctions is also accompanied by deadweight and substitution. The aforementioned microstudies do not take this into account. Van der Linden & Dor (1998) report a macro effect near zero.

BIBLIOGRAPHY

AAKROG, V. et al. (1991), UTB, Uddannelsestilbud for langtidsledige, København: Danmarks Lærerhøjskole & Udviklingscenter for folkeoplysning og voksenundervisning, Denmark.

ABBRING, J., VAN DEN BERG, G.J. and VAN OURS, J. (1995), "The Effect of Unemployment Insurance Sanctions on the Transition rate from Unemployment to Employment", working paper, Department of Economics, University of Amsterdam.

AHO, S. and VEHVILÄINEN J. (1997), "Activating the Young Unemployed into Education? Studies on the Effect of a Recent Policy in Finland and on the Hidden Rationalities Among Uneducated Young People", University of Tampere, Research Institute for Social Sciences, No. 53.

ANDERSSON, H. (1993), "Choosing among Alternative Non Experimental Methods for Estimating the Impact of Training: New Swedish Evidence", mimeo, Swedish Institute for Social Research, Stockholm University.

ANDREWS, M.J., BRADLEY, S. and UPWARD, R. (1996), "Estimating the Costs and Benefits of Youth Training in the UK", paper presented at the 8th Annual EALE Conference, Chania, September.

ANXO, D., CARCILLO, S. and ERHEL, C. (1998), "Aggregate Impact Analysis of ALMPs in France and Sweden: A regional approach", paper presented at the 10th Annual EALE Conference, Blankenberge, September.

ATD QUART MONDE (1998), Sortir de l'inactivité forcée, Dossiers et Documents de la Revue Quart Monde, No. 8, France.

AXELSSON, R. (1989), "Svensk Arbetsmarknadsutbildning – en kvantitativ analys av dess effekter", Umea Economic Studies, Umea University.

BASSI, L.J. and ASHENFELTER, O. (1986), "The Effect of Direct Job Creation and Training Programs on Low-skilled Workers", in S. Danziger and D. Weinberg (eds.), Fighting Poverty: What Wworks and What Doesn't, Harvard University Press, pp. 133-151.

BOLLENS, J. and HOOGE, J. (1996), "Bereik, kwaliteit en effectiviteit van de VDAB-beroepsopleiding voor werkzoekenden", Luik 1, deelrapport 1, HIVA, Leuven.

BRUN, P., GUILLOT, F. and VIARD, T. (1991), "Le crédit-formation individualisé au regard des jeunes issus des milieux très défavorisés", Pierrelaye, IRFRH, ATD-Quart Monde, France.

COMMISSION OF THE EUROPEAN COMMUNITIES (1995), Social Protection in Europe, DG Employment, Industrial Relations and Social Affairs, Luxembourg, Office for Official Publications of the European Communities.

COMMISSION OF THE EUROPEAN COMMUNITIES (1997), Social Protection in Europe, DG Employment, Industrial Relations and Social Affairs, Luxembourg, Office for Official Publications of the European Communities.

DE KONING, J. (1996), "Strategies and Measures to Fight Long-term Unemployment: The Dutch case", NEI-paper, Nederlands Economisch Instituut, Rotterdam.

DE KONING, J. and VAN NES, P. (1998), "Prevention in Active Labour Market Policy: Is it possible and is it desirable?", paper presented at the 10th Annual EALE Conference, Blankenberge, September.

DOLTON, P.J. (1993), "The Economics of Youth Training in Britain", Economic Journal, 103(420), pp. 1261-1278.

EUROPEAN COMMISSION (1998a), Comparative Analysis of National Performance on Integrating Young People into the Labour Market, DG Employment, Industrial Relations and Social Affairs, Brussels, mimeo.

EUROPEAN COMMISSION (1998b), Conclusions of the ESF Mid-term Evaluations, DG Employment, Industrial Relations and Social Affairs Brussels.

EUROSTAT (1996), Labour Force Survey, Office for Official Publications of the European Communities, Luxembourg.

FAY, R. (1996), "Enhancing the Effectiveness of Active Labour Market Policies: Evidence From Programme Evaluations in OECD Countries", Labour Market and social Policy Occasional Papers, No. 18, OECD, Paris.

FRIEDLANDER, D., GREENBERG, D.H. and ROBINS, Ph.K. (1997), "Evaluating Government Training Programs for the Economically Disadvantaged", Journal of Economic Literature, XXXV, December, pp. 1809-1855.

GODINOT, X. *et al.* (1995), *On voudrait connaître le secret du travail*, Edition L'Atelier/Quart Monde, Paris.

GRAVESTEIJN-LIGTHELM J., DE KONING J., OLIEMAN R. and EN VAN DER WEIJDE, I. (1995), *Ex post evaluatie van de ESF hulpprogramma's voor doelstellingen 3 en 4 in Nederland*, NEI, Rotterdam.

HÄMÄLÄINEN, i. (1998), "The Impact of Active Programmes on Employment in the Eras of High and Low Unemployment", paper presented at the 10th annual EALE-Conference, Blankenberge, September.

HARTOG, J. (1997), "On Returns to Education: Wandering along the Hills of ORU Land", Keynote speech for the Conference of the Applied Econometrics Association, Maastricht, May.

HOFBAUER, H. and DADZIO, W. (1987), "Mittelfristige Wirkungen beruflicher Weiterbildung. Die berufliche Situation von Teilnehmern zwei Jahre nach Beendigung der Massnahme", *Mitteilungen AB*, 2/87, pp. 129-141.

JENSEN, P., PEDERSEN, P.J., SMITH, N. and WESTERGÅRD-NIELSEN, N. (1992), "Measuring the Effects of Labour Market Training Programmes", Fourth Annual Conference of the European Association of Labour Economists, Warwick.

KORPI, T. (1992), "Employment Stability Following Unemployment and Manpower Programs", Stockholm Research Reports in Demography, No. 72, Stockholm University.

LAYARD, R., NICKELL, S. and JACKMAN, R. (1991), *Unemployment: Macro-economic Performance and the Labour Market*, Oxford University Press.

MEAGER, N. and EVANS, C. (1998), "The Evaluation of Active Labour Market Measures for the Long-term Unemployed", ILO Employment and Training Papers No. 16, Geneva.

MISEP, *Policies* , quarterly journal of the EC's Employment Observatory, several issues.

NICAISE, I. (1996), "Donner du poisson ou apprendre à pêcher"? Analyse des coûts et bénéfices sociaux des projets d'insertion EFD des CPAS, *Revue Belge de Sécurité Sociale*, 38(4), December, pp. 909-923.

NICAISE, I. and BOLLENS, J. (1998), "Training and Employment Opportunities for Disadvantaged Groups", in M. Tessaring (ed.), *Vocational Education and Training – The European Research Field. Background Report*, Office for official publications of the European Communities, vol. II, Luxembourg, pp. 121-153.

NICAISE, I. (ed.), BOLLENS, J., DAWES, L., LAGHAEI, S., THAULOW, I., VERDIÉ, M. and WAGNER, A. (1995), *Labour Market Programmes for the Poor in Europe: Pitfalls, Dilemma's and how to avoid them*, Avebury.

OECD (1993), *Employment Outlook*, Paris.

OECD (1994), *OECD Jobs Study*, Paris.

OECD (1996), *Employment Outlook*, Paris.

OECD (1998), *Employment Outlook*, Paris.

PUGLIESE, E. (1995), "Special Measures to Improve Youth Unemployment in Italy", in McFate, K., Lawson, R. and Wilson, W.J. (eds.), *Poverty, Inequality and the Future of Social Policy*, Russell Sage Foundation, New York.

RAAUM, O. and TORP, H. (1996), "Impact of Training on Earnings. Testing Alternative Models", paper presented at the EALE Conference, Crete, September.

ROSHOLM, M. (1994), *Effektmaling af ATB m.v.*, Centre for Labour Market and Social Research, University of Aarhus.

ROSHOLM, M. (1995), "The Effect of Public Job Creation on the Exit Rate from Employment and Unemployment for Long-term Unemployed", paper presented at the 7th Annual EALE Conference, Lyon.

SPECKESSER, S. and HILBERT, C. (1998), "Active Labour Market Policy and Unemployment Outflows: an Aggregate Analysis for Germany", paper presented at the 10th Annual EALE Conference, Blankenberge.

VAN DEN BERG, G.J., VAN DER KLAAUW, B. and VAN OURS, J.C. (1998), "Sancties in de bijstand vergroten de kans op werk", *Economisch-Statistische Berichten*, 83 (4161).

VAN DER BURGH Y, and BAVINCK S. (1995), "Scholing en werkervaring voor de onderkant van de arbeidsmarkt", in Huygen et al. (eds.), *Naar volwaardige werkgelegenheid?*, SISWO.

VAN DER LINDEN, B. and DOR, E. (1998), "The Effect of Unemployment Benefits, Sanctions and Training on Unemployment Outflows", paper presented at the 10th Annual EALE Conference, Blankenberge.

WHITE, M. and MCRAE, S. (1989), *Young Adults and Long-term Unemployment*, Policy Studies Institute, London.

WETS, J. (1998), "Communicerende vaten? Een onderzoek naar de relatie tussen werkloosheid en sociale bijstand", Leuven, HIVA.

Figure 1. **Proportion of young people who have left school,
by level of education (EU14, 1997)**[1]

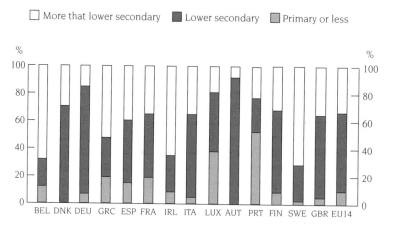

1. Figures for The Netherlands are not included because they are unreliable.

Figure 2. **Employment status of young people who have left school,
by level of education (EU15, 1997)**

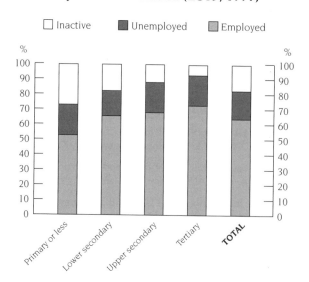

Figure 3. **Proportion of unemployed young people who are registered at the public employment service** (inactives not included)

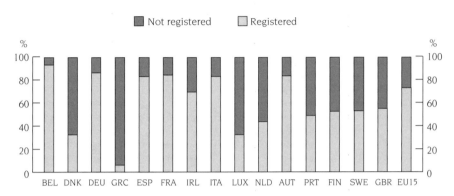

Figure 4. **Participation of 15-24 year old individuals who have left school in vocational training programmes (EU14, 1997)**[1]

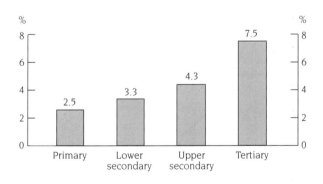

1. Figures for The Netherlands are not included because they are unreliable.

Figure 5. **Effects of non-targeted labour market policies on unemployment and wage inflation**

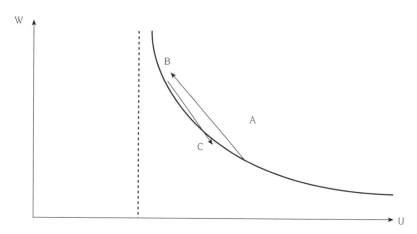

Figure 6. **Effects of targeted active labour market policies on unemployment and wage inflation**

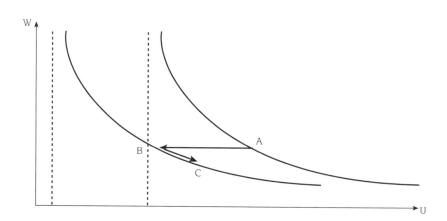

LESSONS FROM EDUCATION AND TRAINING FOR YOUTH: FIVE PRECEPTS

by
W. Norton Grubb
University of California, Berkeley, United States

Introduction

It's a confusing time on the world scene. In the realm of preparation for employment, at least four large ideas or policy narratives compete for attention.[1] One is the standard human capital vision that places its faith in education as a mechanism of both individual and social economic progress. In its more naive versions, this seems to hold that *any* type of education or training improves economic prospects, though more careful versions can be found.[2] The second, an amplified version of the human capital vision, waxes prophetic about the dramatic shifts in employment in most developed countries, with increasing use of new information, communication, and research-based technologies. These trends have caused many countries to redefine the competencies necessary at work to incorporate problem-solving, communications skills and teamwork, initiative and planning, judgement, and various other "higher-order" abilities, variously called key qualifications (*Schlüsselqualifikationen* in Germany and *cualificaciones claves* in Spain), "key" or "core" skills in Great Britain and Australia, and "SCANS" skills in the United States (SCANS, 1991). Like this conference itself, intent on "preparing youth for the 21st century", this school of thought tends to emphasise the "workforce of the 21st century" when such core or key or higher-order competencies will presumably be widespread.

A third vision, again a variant of the human capital model, expresses a concern for inequality, and emphasises programs for the disadvantaged, the working poor, the long-term unemployed, welfare populations, dislocated workers, and other groups having special trouble entering the mainstream of the population. And the final vision, embedded most obviously in the German dual system and in the recent efforts to provide work experience and work-based learning in many countries, is the idea that work itself a better form of preparation for employment that is formal education or training. The most extreme (or naive) version of this idea has emerged only in the United States, in the idea of "work first": in the reform of welfare in the United States, most programs are providing very little education and training and are instead providing incentives for welfare recipients to enter employment or, in a few cases, providing subsidised or unpaid employment in place of education and training.

These four visions are not necessarily consistent, of course. The extreme form of "work first" is directly antithetical to the human capital vision, in any of its varieties. The emphasis on the "skills for the 21st century" usually calls for relatively sophisticated or higher-order competencies, while programs for the disadvantaged often provide relatively low-level or basic levels of academic education and skill training, often remedial in their emphasis and pedagogy.[3] Different narratives apply to different programs within the education and job training systems that developed countries have created, and so we find quite inconsistent approaches within individual countries:

– Education is separated from job training.
– Concern with teaching methods and teacher training, as the foundation of developing various competencies, exists within some education programs while training efforts are largely indifferent to instructional issues.

– Programs for welfare recipients are segregated from those for individuals not on welfare.

– Generous public subsidies for students in public universities coexist with meagre subsidies for clients in job training programs or on welfare.

Furthermore, the research about different programs is carried on within different traditions so that information about education, about job training, about welfare-related programs, and about youth programs is often segregated in different literatures, unknown to other researchers.

In this paper I will try to draw on disparate traditions to develop some conclusions about what kinds of education, training, and work experience might be effective, focusing on youth rather than adult programs. I'll start in Section 1 with a review of the familiar job training programs, since these have often been the focus of attention when policy-makers become concerned with reducing youth unemployment. I will emphasise those in the United States partly because of the amount of evaluation in that country, and partly because of my own familiarity with such efforts (including direct observation), but I will also rely on a recent review including other countries (Grubb and Ryan, 1999). I will conclude this section with a tentative list of the reasons why these programs, some of which have been carefully designed and generously funded, have had such meagre results.

In Section 2 I will use a different tactic, exploring the nature of certain exemplary programs to see what lessons they hold for education and training more generally. But since programs for out-of school youth – that is, those who have dropped out of secondary school – have been so unpromising, prevention of dropping out may be a better strategy than creating second-chance programs, as many commentators have noted. I therefore shift in Section 3 to examining some of the evidence on dropout prevention programs and on promising reforms in secondary schools in the United States

In the final section, I draw together the various implications from a variety of education, job training, and work-based efforts into five precepts or recommendations. Many exemplary programs embody one or more of these precepts, and conversely the ineffective job training and work-based programs tend to violate all of them. But, while these recommendations can be inferred from some of the evidence about effective programs, they should be considered a series of hypotheses to govern the development of future programs, to be tested under different specific conditions, with different groups of students, under different economic conditions, in different countries. In effect, the development of such precepts is an effort to turn the attention of program designers, policy-makers, and administrators away from naive versions of human capital – and naive versions of "work first" as well, placing great faith in the transformative power of work – toward a greater concern with the more subtle dimensions of programs that enhance their quality and therefore their effectiveness.

1.   The effectiveness of youth job training: results and explanations

In countries where youth unemployment is high relative to adult unemployment, a standard practice has been to develop relatively short-term training programs aimed at youth, presumably to provide them the skills necessary for employment under a human capital rationale. These generally enrol youth who have dropped out of secondary school, though a few of them (like the STEP program reviewed below) are aimed at in-school youth and therefore overlap with the dropout prevention programs reviewed in Section 3.

The job training programs in the United States have been elaborated over about 35 years, since the early 1960s, and a clear consensus has developed about the effectiveness of these programs. A series of evaluations, including sophisticated random-assignment experiments, have shown that short-term job training and welfare-to-work programs increase earnings by trivial amounts (in the range of US 200 to 500 under most conditions), and fail to move individuals out of poverty or off of welfare.[4] Furthermore, even these paltry benefits tend to vanish after four or five years, so that the long-run effects are non-existent. To be sure, the benefits of these programs usually exceed the costs, so that they are "worth doing" in a benefit-cost sense; but in any substantive sense these programs are insufficient to move individuals out of poverty, or off welfare, or into the kinds of stable middle-income jobs where they can weather the ups and downs of labor markets and personal fortunes

Furthermore, these evaluations have consistently found that training programs have much smaller effects – and often negative effects – for youth compared to adults. For example, the largest job training program, the Job Training Partnership Act (JTPA), was evaluated using random-assignment methods. The results summarised in Table 1 describe the problem: while earnings increased by about USD 1 000 per year for adult men and women, they were unchanged for female youth and declined for male youth. Female youth did increase the rate at which they earned a General Equivalency Diploma (GED), which is supposed to be (but almost surely isn't) the equivalent of a secondary school diploma,[5] but male youth did not – and arrest rates for male youth actually increased. For youth, and particularly for the male youth that have the most trouble finding employment, the JTPA program violated the first principle of intervention: "do no harm".

Another large-scale job training program has been aimed at welfare recipients – the Jobs Opportunities and Basic Skills (JOBS) program, instituted in 1988 based on the presumably positive (but substantially trivial[6]) benefits of a series of experiments operated during the 1980s. The JOBS evaluations revealed that the effects of such programs were very small except for some unusual cases like Riverside County, California. Disentangling the effects for youth versus adults is difficult, because younger welfare recipients tend to have younger children and more difficult child care problems, though they may also have fewer children than older recipients. Perhaps for this reason, the patterns related to age and number of children are not clear.[7] Overall, however, these welfare-related programs had little influence on earnings or welfare rates, so they can't have been particularly effective for young welfare recipients.

In addition to widespread job training programs available to the working poor, or to welfare recipients, the United States has a rich tradition of experimenting with social programs by trying out promising practices on a small scale before potentially expanding them to larger programs. Several of these experimental efforts have focused on youth, and have been carefully evaluated:

- The Minority Female Single Parent (MFSP) Demonstration concentrated on young minority women with children but without husbands. The program emphasised remediation in basic academic skills and an extensive array of services like child care, counselling, guidance in managing daily problems, and help in finding jobs after the program. Three of the four sites had no influence whatsoever on employment and earnings; the fourth site, the Centre for Employment Training (CET), increased employment by 13%, wage rates by 11% and average earnings by 25% or USD 1 212 a year – huge effects compared with those of JTPA in Table 1, for example.[8] I review the special case of CET in Section 2 below, but aside from this exemplar, the pilot program did not suggest any way to improve the prospects of young women.

- Like MFSP, the New Chance program concentrated on young mothers, almost all of whom were high school dropouts. It assumed that they needed a range of supportive services in addition to remedial education and job training because they face a series of personal and psychological barriers to employment, and so New Chance provided career exploration, health education, family planning, various life skills, work experience, job placement, child care and some services to children, at a cost of about USD 9 000 per year. One particularly innovative element was a mentoring program, using community-based individuals to help women with various aspects of child rearing, pregnancy prevention, drug and alcohol abuse, and abusive family relationships. The women enrolled reported positive conceptions of mentoring (Quint, et al., 1994, especially Table 3.8). On the other hand, New Chance proved not to be as intensive a program as its designers planned, despite the high costs, since the average participant received only 300 hours of services – the equivalent of perhaps 10 weeks in a job training program, or six credits in a community college. Despite these various services, the program had few positive effects. The program did increase the rates of earning GEDs (though it reduced the receipt of high school diplomas, a more valuable credential), but it didn't significantly improve employment, wage rates, earnings, or receipt of welfare. Moreover, some indicators of well-being – the risk of homelessness, feelings of stress, and extent of depression, for example – were significantly worse (Quint and Bos, 1998).

Unlike many evaluations, the analysis of New Chance made an effort to go beyond simply crunching numbers, and collected information that provide some insight about why an carefully-devised program for young mothers had little effect. In a series of interviews with about 40 participants, Quint *et al.* (1994) found that many were entangled in family and personal relationships, including physical abuse, that made it difficult for them to attend the program regularly and to break out of a network of constraining obligations; abusive boyfriends seemed particularly responsible, though other family members were implicated as well. In addition, the evaluation included an assessment of mental health that revealed high levels of depressive and bipolar conditions. For women with relatively high scores on the scale of depressive disorders, the program actually had a negative effect because it increased their responsibilities and stresses without being able to do anything about the underlying problem (Quint and Bos, 1998). These results suggest that, as comprehensive as the support services offered by New Chance were, they were still not comprehensive enough.

– The JOBSTART program attempted to create programs for youth age 17 to 21 who had dropped out of school. It provided remedial education, vocational skill training, job placement assistance, and various support services like child care, transportation, counselling, instruction in work readiness and job skills; each program was required to offer at least 200 hours of basic education and 500 hours of job training, making the program more intensive than conventional JTPA programs. While the program did increase the rate at which individuals received GEDs, the effects over four years on employment and earnings were insignificant, rates of receiving welfare did not decrease, and rates of pregnancy and giving birth even increased. The only bright note is that rates of using drugs appeared to fall modestly. (Some of the result are summarised in Table 2.) As in the MFSP evaluation, the results for the Centre for Employment Training were much more positive. Otherwise, however, the results suggested that somewhat more intensive programs aimed at youth are not particularly effective.

– The Summer Training and Education Program (STEP) was an interesting effort to devise a program for youth still enrolled in school, rather than drop-outs. It was aimed at students considered likely to drop out (because of poor academic performance) or to become pregnant, and it was designed to combat the problem of "summer effects" – the fact that the academic achievement of many youth (especially low-income youth) regresses during the summer. Therefore the program provided two summers of activities; in each, students took remedial classes for half the day and worked for the remainder of the day, providing an opportunity to learn other work-related skills and to earn money. The inclusion of both school-based and work-based components in theory enabled students to see the connections between the two, since they could see how academic competencies are necessary on the job and could use the work component to explore the importance of initiative, persistence, and other work-oriented behaviour. In addition, because of the concern with pregnancy as a barrier to school completion, a half-day each week was devoted to issues about responsible sexual behaviour, contraception, and other aspects of personal responsibility. Some support services (counselling and guidance, and some tutoring) were also available during the intervening school year.

Despite this careful design, STEP youth experienced the same dropout rates, rates of postsecondary enrolment, employment rates, and rates of teenage pregnancy as did the control group, 3.5 years after enrolling in the program (Walker and Vilella-Velez, 1992; Grossman and Sipe, 1992). One widely-cited conclusion from the STEP experiment is that it may be possible to improve short-term academic performance through a short-term program; however, long-term results and effects on more fundamental behaviour like employment and pregnancy cannot be changed with a limited intervention that leaves the rest of schooling, the meagre opportunities in the youth labor market, and the general environment of poor youth unchanged.

My own observations suggest that the implementation of STEP may have badly undermined its intentions.[9] In practice the quality of work placements was poor, jobs required almost no school skills, job experiences were never incorporated into the schooling component, and teaching largely followed the conventional didactic, teacher-centred format with contrived materials that is so deadly to most students – and certainly to those considered "at risk" of school failure. The students we interviewed stayed in the program because they were being paid, but said nothing else good about it. What students may have learned from STEP is that school is irrelevant to work, that work is usually deadly, and that schooling never gets any better even in special programs – not the conclusions one would want any teenagers to draw. The effectiveness of well-designed programs may lie in the details of execution As Mies van der Rohe said, "God is in the details" – and here STEP was sorely lacking.

A number of programs have provided work experience alone, including various programs to provide summer jobs to disadvantaged youth (the Summer Youth Employment and Training Program and an earlier pilot program called the Youth Entitlement Pilot Project). The Supported Work demonstration was a more intensive effort, providing up to a year of subsidised work experience followed by job placement assistance. Most jobs were in the public and non-profit sectors, with few links to private-sector employers to place these youth in jobs after the program ended. None of the work only programs has been effective in increasing employment after the program has ended; the Supported Work evaluation also clarified that welfare rates and crime rates did not decline (US Department of Labor, 1995, pp. 10-12, 19-20). Of course, the educative content of the work provided may not have been very high, as was also true for STEP. Within short-term job training programs in the United States, Kogan *et al.* (1989) found that the training content of work experience was often weak or non-existent – partly because these programs were short, poorly-funded, and often devised to provide subsidised employees to firms rather than education and training.

Aside from the special case of CET, only one other youth program has been widely cited as effective. The Job Corps is predominantly an intensive residential program in which youth live in a centre away from home, and receive a variety of academic instruction, job training, ands other social services for an entire year. It has always been the most expensive job training program, costing about USD 15 300 in 1993 dollars (US GAO, 1995, p. 7), and has represented the most serious kind of intervention for those youth judged in the greatest need. A 1980 quasi-experimental evaluation using a matched comparison group revealed positive effects on employment rates and overall earnings, though not on wage rates, and it also reduced crime among those enrolled. These results provided some hope that intensive job training programs, even for youth with the greatest barriers to employment, would be worth doing. However, these positive assessments were based on quasi-experimental methods, with their tendency to be upwardly biased, and more recent evaluation has cast doubt on these results. In recent work (US GAO, 1995), only 36% of those enrolled completed vocational training, and only half found low-skilled jobs related to their training. Furthermore, students did not stay with their initial employers very long: one half worked two months or less, and two years after initial employment 88% were no longer working for the same employer: 45% had quit, 22%, were fired, and 13% were laid off. To be sure, given the focus of Job Corps on the most disadvantaged youth, it is possible that the results are better than they would have been if these individuals had not enrolled in the program – as the earlier quasi-experimental evaluation suggested. But on any absolute scale the employment outcomes seem pretty dismal – particularly for a program costing over USD 15 000 per student. Partly because of high costs and partly because of concerns about quality, the early support for Job Corps seems to have segued into ambivalence, though it remains a politically popular program based on the early results.

Even this brief review of the results indicates that there isn't much reason for optimism. About 35 years of experimentation have resulted in a series of programs – some of them widely available while others are pilot programs – that have been carefully evaluated and found to have essentially no effects for youth. The only consistently positive findings are that such programs sometimes increase rates of earning GEDs, but this credential isn't especially valuable in the labor market. This positive effect is counter-balanced by some negative effects – such as the increase in pregnancies in JOBSTART and the reduction of male earnings in JTPA – that are dispiriting, to say the least. And even the training programs for adults have effects on employment and earnings that are substantively trivial and temporary.

Finally, the results from European programs aren't much different, or any more encouraging (Grubb and Ryan, 1999, Ch. V). While the evaluation of remedial programs – those focusing on youth with special problems entering employment – generally rely on quasi-experimental rather than random-assignment evaluations, the results are quite similar to the United States While there is some evidence that French programs have improved employment rates, especially among the most disadvantaged youth, the results for the British Youth Training Scheme are generally negative or neutral. Furthermore, evidence from employers suggests that considerable displacement – hiring individuals from a program at the expense of other similar applicants – takes place, accounting for 80% (or more) of placements. "Insertion" contracts in which employers provide episodes of training and work experience, lasting from six months to two years, suggest positive employment (but not wage) effects, at least in programs with significant training content. However, in France, young people seem to lose more income while enrolled than they gain, and similar findings for Great Britain and Sweden also cast doubt on the overall effectiveness of such programs. In sum, the results indicate that some remedial and insertion programs can help participants find jobs, but do not enhance skills or overall earnings – and presumably not long-term earnings either. And the likelihood that benefits come at the expense of other disadvantaged youth suggest that aggregate effects are non-existent even when some participants appear to benefit.

This record demands some responses to the question of why the effects are so dismal. In most cases, there is no way to find much in the way of an answer to this question within the evaluations themselves – which is one of their liabilities to which I shall return. However, examining some clues within the evaluations, relying on my own observations of many job training and vocational education programs, and anticipating some results of the "exemplary" programs reviewed in the next section, reveals there are at least four major problems with these youth programs:[10]

- Intensity: The first and most obvious explanation is simply that most job training programs are short and small: they last a very limited period of time, rarely more than twenty weeks. However, the individuals in these programs often lack job-specific skills, general academic skills, and the kinds of values (including motivation, punctuality, persistence, the ability to work with others) necessary to find and keep employment, and by construction they have failed to learn them in perhaps ten to twelve years of formal schooling. The idea that a twenty week program, or two summers, can remedy these problems is somewhat astonishing. Indeed, Garth Mangum (1998), a long-time observer of job training, has concluded that this is the central explanation for the small effects of job training.

- Support services: Many job training programs, like the JTPA programs described in Table 1 and the GAIN programs mentioned above, provide some support services, though these services vary from program to program and it is difficult to learn anything about their quality and intensity. Most of the experimental programs reviewed in this section provide a wider variety of support services as part of their basic strategy. Some (like the community-based mentors in New Chance) seem quite innovative and well-regarded, but these are clearly exceptions. These support services include placement efforts, though there is at least a little evidence that training-related placement is low and may undermine economic benefits.[11] There's general agreement that youth in general – and certainly those having trouble finding employment – lack direction and need better guidance and counselling about job options and their requirements, though there is virtually no discussion within the job training world of what this should look like. The lack of motivation may be exacerbated by the special characteristics of youth culture in the United States: this culture, with its rejection of school and discipline and the premium placed on "cool", may work against youth programs in ways that do not affect adults with greater maturity and sense of responsibility. Finally, at least some of the youth participating in these programs have more serious problems like drug and alcohol abuse, physical handicaps, other health problems, depression and other mental health problems, and pressures from abusive family members or boyfriends. Some of these problems may not be treatable within the scope of public programs; for example, the depressive (or bipolar) manifestations and abusive conditions uncovered in the New Chance evaluations are extremely difficult to resolve, even in middle-class families with enormous resources.

– *Labor market conditions*: A possible explanation for mediocre employment effects is simply that there are not enough jobs for unskilled and semi-skilled workers.[12] In the past few years, with relatively low unemployment rates in the United States and even welfare recipients able to find jobs, this is not a plausible explanation for adults. However, many employers will not hire young people, so under the best of conditions they have a tendency to "mill around" until reaching their early or mid-twenties. In addition, for many of the moderately-skilled jobs in the sub-baccalaureate labor market, employers will not consider individuals without high school diplomas, effectively condemning high school drop-outs to completely unskilled positions.

– *Poor teaching*: Job training and youth programs are educational programs, whether they want to be or not: they try to provide individuals with academic (or basic) competencies like the three R's, with vocational skills, and with various other competencies including "soft" skills related to motivation, persistence, and punctuality. However, in the world of job training, there has never been any attention to the pedagogy of training, or to how instructors (or "trainers") can teach these complex competencies. The instruction I and my colleagues have observed – in the STEP program mentioned above, in CET described below, in various remedial efforts and adult education, and now in various welfare-to-work programs – has always been the most pedestrian "skills and drills" approach in which individuals labor through math and grammar drills, practice job-specific skills by rote, carry out fill-in-the-blank exercises with simplistic drill-oriented computer programs, and listen to untrained instructors lecture about the importance of getting to work on time.[13] The conventional didactic pedagogy of most job training may be especially abhorrent to youth because of their recent and almost entirely negative experiences with schools, where this kind of pedagogy is particularly pervasive with low-income students.

In contrast, within education there have been long debates about different pedagogies and the best ways to prepare instructors. The alternative ways of providing remedial (or basic or developmental) education have been the subject of extensive debate (Hull, undated; Grubb and Associates, 1999, Ch. 5), many different approaches to occupational education and training have been developed (Achtenhagen and Grubb, 1998), and the virtues of different settings – for example, the combination of classroom-based and work-based training found in the German dual setting – have been extensively debated. These discussions have not always proved conclusive, with the evidence about the effectiveness of different pedagogies not always being particularly clear. What evidence there is, however, supports constructivist or meaning-centred or systems-oriented teaching over behaviourist, didactic, and skills-oriented teaching.[14] But even in a world where there are no firm conclusions, the presence of debate is a critical signal of examining alternatives and weighing effectiveness. In contrast, where there is no discussion and no consideration of teacher preparation, as in job training and welfare-to-work programs, teaching is virtually certain to be of low quality and to follow the most conventional practices – the practices that have already failed to reach the youth and adults in these programs.

The existing evidence suggests two other conclusions. One is that the conventional evaluations of job training in the United States – based on random assignment methods, with outcomes compared for experimental and control groups – don't provide enough information. They say almost nothing about why such programs do or don't work, and therefore provide almost no guidance for administrators and program designers, or for policy-makers wanting to reform such programs. Only when there is supplementary information – for example, the interviews and information about depressive conditions available for New Chance, or the observational information available for CET – is there any possibility for learning why a program works or fails.

Finally, these programs often look worse the closer one gets to them – for example, as one observes what goes on in classrooms, where it's often clear that the content is simplistic and the teaching quite mediocre. But without such understanding, it's impossible to know how to identify the reasons for failure, and therefore to recommend the appropriate changes.

2. Lessons from exemplary programs

Although the general record of job training and youth programs is quite dismal, there are a few efforts that stand out for their effectiveness. Furthermore, in the current efforts to develop welfare-to-work programs in the new environment of "work first", a different set of programs is emerging with some promising characteristics.

In trying to learn from exemplary programs, it's necessary to remember that such programs can be selected in several different ways. Some are selected because their outcomes are known to be better than those of other programs. In other cases, programs are selected because of strong reputations, where observers who ought to know nominate them as especially effective. Unfortunately in our studies of workforce development programs, both state and local administrators and policy-makers are usually unable to name especially effective programs. They spend too little time visiting programs, and they often have few ideas of what characteristics effective programs might have.[15] Often they nominate programs with high profiles that result from working with large corporations. Community college programs are sometimes nominated as being effective when the colleges they are part of have high rates of transfer to four-year colleges – usually an indication of middle-class students that has nothing to do with the effectiveness of workforce programs. Thus the information provided by exemplary programs is highly varied and sometimes suspect.

One widely-cited program, on the basis of two random-assignment studies identifying it as unusually effective, is the Centre for Employment Training (CET). The early accounts credited its success to the practice of integrating remedial and vocational skills training (Burghardt and Gordon, 1990). In fact, however, the two kinds of training were not integrated in any way; CET provided both basic and vocational skills training, and the same instructors often provided both, but in different periods of time with little connection between them. Instead, the success of CET is probably due to a confluence of several factors:

– A long history in the San Jose area with close connections to local employers, which means that many employers turn first to CET as a source of employees.

– The presence of both basic education and vocational skills training, along with real work carried out in a series of small enterprises (a child care centre, a cafeteria, an auto body shop, a small print shop a janitorial service).

– A bilingual environment, where Spanish-speaking instructors stress the importance of English to the predominantly Latino population without breaking the connection to Spanish.

– Support services available on the site, including help with immigration status and child care.[16]

A second widely-cited program is the Riverside GAIN program; indeed, the increase in earnings of nearly 50% is one of the largest effects ever found for any job training program. The difference among sites could not be explained by local economic conditions – measured, for example, by unemployment rates and the growth rate of employment – and the effects of the Riverside program were remarkably consistent through varied economic conditions. Nor was there any obvious explanation of differences among counties based on the kinds of services offered. In the end, the evaluators concluded that the success of Riverside was due to a combination of practices: a strong message to participants about the importance of getting into jobs early; a strong commitment to job search and job placement efforts; a mix of job search, education, and training; and a commitment to enforcing mandatory participation of all eligible welfare recipients (Riccio *et al.*, 1994, Ch. 8). Another observer has concluded that the high expectations of the program staff were responsible (Bardach, 1993), and still others have attributed the success to the energy and charisma of the director.

In a different kind of study, King and his colleagues (King *et al.*, 1998) selected especially effective JTPA programs in Texas and Illinois based on earnings of 155% over the poverty level and on continuous employment. The outliers they visited had several characteristics in common:

– They were committed to a structured process for determining high demand and emerging occupations.

– They emphasised occupational skills training rather than short-term job search assistance and on-the-job training; they stressed intake, assessment, counselling, and case management continuing throughout the program and afterwards.

– And they constrained the choices of training activities, referring individuals only to approved providers and only in high-demand or emerging occupations.

Others have cited a variety of more recent pilot projects. For example, Project STRIVE combines long-term employment experiences with a variety of supportive services including counselling, "soft skills", and case management (but not academic or occupational education, apparently) and boasts a 75 to 80% retention rate in subsidised employment. The Youthbuild program sponsored by the Department of Housing and Urban Development engages youth in rebuilding housing in depressed urban neighbourhoods, providing them with various occupational skills in addition to a form of work experience. Similarly, various Youth Conservation Corps programs, modelled roughly on the Depression-era programs, provide youth with both work experience in various environmental and recreational projects, and some remedial education and supportive services.[17] These programs tend to combine work – particular work with a public service aspect – with various other supportive services and remedial education, rather than providing work experience alone.

In our own efforts to identify effective workforce development programs, my colleagues and I have relied on the nominations of state and local officials, with all their potential problems. An example of such a program is Project Quest in San Antonio, also profiled by Osterman and Lautsch (1996).[18] A community-based organisation serves to recruit clients and represent their interests, and also provides more intensive support services. The program targets high-growth jobs, particularly in health care and computer occupations, that are accessible to a population with relatively little education; the local community colleges provide remedial and occupational education in two-year programs, and participants earn credits so they can continue in other educational programs later. In this particular example the division of labor between the community-based organisation and the community college is instructive: the CBO provides a vision of the program, recruitment, various support services, and an advocacy role for its clients, while the college provides the educational components.

In the efforts to establish welfare-to-work programs under the new "work first" policies, two potentially effective models are emerging – unfortunately along with many more very short-term (3-4 week) programs with little skill development (Grubb *et al.*, 1998). Some high-profile programs train welfare recipients for a well-known large corporation (or perhaps a small consortium) – for example, Pacific Gas and Electric in the San Francisco area, Sprint in Kansas City, Disney World in central Florida, the Marriott Corporation in several locations. Typically, the corporation provides work experience placements; a local community college provides remedial/developmental education and job skills training; and sometimes a community-based organisation provides mentors, or "soft skills" or employability skills training, or other support services. These programs are relatively intensive, lasting perhaps 20 to 30 weeks, and they contain a number of related elements – academic (or remedial) preparation as well as occupational training, work experience as well as classroom instruction, support services as well as training. Usually the corporation involved hires many (but not all) of the completers of such programs, so there are clear incentives to do well. Unfortunately, there aren't many of these programs: they can provide visions of good practice, but they provide relatively few opportunities and they involve relatively few firms.[19]

In addition, a number of community colleges have responded to the challenge of welfare reform not by creating programs specifically for welfare recipients, but by creating programs for a range of the working poor. While the characteristics of these programs vary, in general they follow several of the precepts we outline in the concluding section. For example, one college in Washington follows an approach being developed in that state called "wage and skill progression", designed to allow low-income workers to get better jobs initially and then continue to obtain the skills necessary for advancement. This approach begins before employment with assessment and the development of a career passport specifying both a job ladder (with jobs of increasing earnings) and the skills necessary to move up that ladder. Training in technical and basic skills, and on-the-job experiences are used as necessary, and all short-term programs lead to associate degrees so that individuals can continue in the education system as they find the time. An example in one college is a 10-week manufacturing technician program with both classroom and on-the-job training, where the last three weeks is completed on the job with a mentoring component directed by on-line supervisors. The program includes technical skills as well as a 20-hour curriculum emphasising the rights and responsibilities of workers. Similarly, a Colorado community college has designed a series of four to seven month certificate programs in occupations including financial services, early childhood education, retailing, manufacturing, and surgical technician training. Individuals attend the college for 22 hours each week (for remediation, "soft skills" and work readiness, and vocational classes) and are employed 18 hours. Various support services (job coaching, a mental health group, child care information) are also included. These are all more intensive than conventional short-term job training, though they can all be completed within the limits of welfare legislation. They incorporate a variety of school and work activities as well as support services.

The exemplary programs I have profiled in this section have emerged under quite different conditions. Some of them are outliers among job training programs; some have been started by community-based organisations; some have been developed by especially aggressive community colleges, to respond to challenges of serving the working poor; and others have emerged in response to the challenges of devising effective programs within the serious constraints of "work first". There is, I think, some convergence in the characteristics of these exemplary efforts, though I have postponed describing these characteristics until the final section.

3. Reforming high schools: the strategy of prevention

Because youth programs serving high school dropouts have been so disappointing, a different tactic has been to prevent them from dropping out of high school. Indeed, this has been the dominant approach to improving the prospects of youth throughout this century, with periodic waves of interest in developing dropout prevention programs, followed by periods of relative indifference and then the "rediscovery" of dropping out as a social problem. For example, a decade-old review of drop-out prevention programs – with the subtitle "Enough is Known for Action" – concluded that "conventional education and remediation by itself isn't effective", and that "isolated work experience will not reclaim impoverished and troubled youth". Instead, it called for alternative schools (rather than conventional schooling that has alienated most youth) and an array of services including occupational skills training, support through counselling and mentorships, and case management to individualise services (Hahn et al., 1987). Another review similarly concluded that alternatives to conventional schooling for potential drop-outs needed to provide student support services, peer tutoring and co-operative learning (as well as more conventional academic materials), rather than conventional isolated instruction, and employability skills (Wircenski and Sarkees, 1990). While it's difficult to describe the vast array of drop-out prevention programs, most of them provide a wide array of services including support services to cope with personal and family problems; employment-oriented services including vocational training and job placements and remedial work in basic academic skills (Rumberger, 1990; US GAO, 1987). Many shift to alternative settings including special continuation schools, community-based schools, and schools located on college campuses, all intended to replace the constraining, authoritarian atmosphere and pedagogy of most secondary schools (e.g. Piemonte, 1995; Bradley, 1995; Heinemann, 1990).

There is currently a vast array of school reform efforts in the United States, intended to improve the learning of American youth – in response to complaints from employers and parents, and the perception that American education is lagging behind that of other advanced countries. There are too many of these to summarise adequately in a short space, and they vary substantially in their attention to the particular needs of disadvantaged youth. Some reforms rely on external standards and assessments, resolving not to let students receive a high school diploma or to progress through education without passing certain tests. In the absence of special efforts to help low-achieving students – efforts that are usually afterthoughts – they can only serve to sort students further and create even more high school dropouts. Some reforms are based on parental choice, under the assumption that parents will select more effective schools and that ineffective schools will be driven out of business. The variations among parents in the sophistication of their choices, however, as well as the problems in creating new schools, have not been thoroughly addressed. Some reforms foster new approaches to teaching and learning, particularly the Coalition of Essential Schools, whereas others, like Comer schools, try to provide a greater array of supports from the local community. The majority of them focus on improving academic achievement, since the high-status path in US education is a "pipeline" following a conventional academic curriculum to the baccalaureate degree.

A different approach, one that is closer to the efforts to develop better job training programs, has been various called "education through occupations" (Grubb, 1995a), or "college and careers" (Urquiola et al., 1997), or "school to work", or even the "new vocationalism" (Grubb, 1997). In this approach, both academic and occupational content is taught; the two are integrated by having academic courses develop more applications, and by incorporating more explicit teaching of academic underpinnings in occupational courses.[20] Typically, high schools are reorganised in some way. In the approach of career academies, students take four academic and occupational courses together, with the same teachers over two or three years (Stern et al., 1992). In other cases, students elect a "major" or pathway, focused on a broadly-defined cluster of occupations. Their occupational and academic coursework is modified in some way to be consistent with the demands of that cluster (Grubb, 1995b, Ch. 4). In a few cases an entire school follows a broad occupational area, like health occupations, agriculture, or business and commerce, with students educated for a variety of occupations within these areas. These reformed schools generally prepare students either for employment after high school, or for postsecondary education, or for the combination of further education with employment that has become so common in the United States – hence the slogan of "college and careers". A third component of these approaches, in addition to both academic and occupational content, is the use of work-based learning, ranging from job shadowing to short internships to lengthy co-operative education or apprenticeship programs. (The School-to-Work Opportunities Act of 1994 provided some additional support for work-based placements, among other services.) Ideally, these various forms of work-based learning are of high quality, and are closely linked with the school-based elements. Without much history of employer involvement in the United States, however, the extent and quality of work-based placement varies.[21]

There has still been relatively little evaluation of these broadly occupational programs, though what little there is suggests that they have reduced dropout rates, and increased completion rates and postsecondary enrolment.[22] In contrast to other reforms, which strengthen the conventional "pipeline" of academic programs, the vision of "education through occupations" provides a distinct alternative, a feature that is valuable for the large number of students who find the academic track insufferable. And the practices adopted by these school reforms provide some reinforcement about the characteristics of effective employment-oriented programs.

4. Five precepts for effective education and training

From this variety of education and training efforts, several common elements are starting to emerge. No doubt there are many ways to summarise the lessons from this history of experimentation,[23] but my version includes five precepts:

– Effective programs understand the local labor market, and target those jobs with relatively high earnings, strong employment growth, and opportunities for individual advancement. (Programs in high employment areas can get away with ignoring this recommendation, of course, but only at the expense of long-run effectiveness.) Some job programs do this by assessing the local job market carefully. CET and some community colleges (particularly those with extensive co-operative programs) accomplish this by maintaining stable links with local employers. The customised programs described in Section 3 achieve the same result by tying training to employment in large, stable firms – albeit, in some cases, in relatively low-level jobs. Career Academies and high schools with pathways or majors do something similar when they focus on broad clusters of occupations with strong levels and growth rates of employment in the local area – and they sometimes gain employer support as a way of overcoming local shortages of certain types of skilled labor. But those programs that fail to consider the quality of jobs for which they provide training are likely to place individuals in minimum-wage positions with few prospects for advancement and dismal prospects for the long run. Programs that fail to understand the hiring practices of local employers, or to actively change these practices (as some co-operative education programs do), are likely to be particularly ineffective for youth.

– Effective programs contain an appropriate mix of academic (or remedial, or basic) education, occupational skills, and work-based learning, in the best cases integrated with one another. These three components are complementary to one another since different components develop the range of competencies required in employment, including those necessary for long-run self-sufficiency and the "soft skills" necessary for job-keeping. Conversely, programs providing one component – basic skills only, or work experience only, for example – have generally been unsuccessful. The incorporation of all three was the foundation of the School-to-Work Opportunities Act of 1994. All three are present in the customised programs for high-profile corporations mentioned in Section 3, in the widely-cited Centre for Employment Training, in many exemplary community college programs, and in the secondary school programs following "education through occupations". Similarly, many of the programs incorporating basic skills profiled by the National Institute of Literacy provide other kinds of training and work experience in addition to basic skills (Murphy and Johnson, 1998).

Furthermore, while flexible and innovative scheduling may be necessary, the intensity of both academic and vocational education must be appropriate to the jobs being targeted. Short-term job training lasting 12 weeks on the average has been ineffective, and the very short 3 to 4-week programs now being offered cannot possibly be improvements. Even within the realm of job training, the exemplary programs like CET are longer than average; the welfare-to-work programs now being established with the help of leading corporations are also more intensive than the "work first" efforts; and Job Corps, which remains an attractive alternative despite chequered evidence of its success, remains the longest and highest-cost program of all.

Finally, effective programs pay attention to the pedagogy of everything they teach, whether classroom-based or work-based. Poorly-taught basic skills, or occupational education, or "soft skills", cannot possibly help individuals master the competencies they need for long-run independence. Unprepared instructors are inadequate to the teaching challenges in such programs, and the lack of attention to teacher training in many programs is a tip-off that the quality of instruction is likely to be poor. While it has been popular to cite the use of "technology" or computer-based instruction as an indicator of effectiveness, most programs are so drill-oriented, limited, and untested that scepticism about their effectiveness is appropriate. And it makes no sense to call for "key" or "core" or "higher-order" skills to prepare youth for the 21st century, and then use to remedial pedagogies that provide only the most conventional entry-level skills.[24]

– Effective programs provide a variety of supportive services as appropriate, given the needs of their clients or students. This precept has been incorporated in many programs providing such services as child care, counselling, and placement services, and caseworkers also act to provide (or find) a variety of services. Of course, there may be limits to the services a program can provide, and the experimental and pilot programs reviewed in Section 1 were ineffective despite providing a variety of support services; the New Chance evaluations in particular illustrate that it may not be possible to provide adequate services for some individuals.[25] However, a program that fails to consider the need for supportive services may have low completion rates and fail for that reason alone.

– Effective programs provide their clients or students with pathways or "ladders" of further education opportunities, so they can continue their education and training when they are able to. The widely-praised Centre for Employment Training has articulated its efforts with local community colleges, so that CET training can be applied toward Associate degrees (Strawn, 1998, p. 22). Many community college welfare-to-work programs are articulated with their certificate and Associate degree programs, and then through articulation agreements with four-year colleges providing baccalaureate degrees. Programs like QUEST in San Antonio deliberately provide their remedial and vocational skills training within the regular programs of the local community college, to provide them access to the educational system. Within current "work first" efforts, Wisconsin has articulated a conception of "stepping out and stepping back in", where welfare clients 'step out" of education to work but can then "step back in" to further education for more advanced employment. This plan is similar to the idea of creating ladders of opportunities, as is Illinois' Advancing Opportunities program. The creation of such ladders is the purpose of caseworkers in some states, and the caseworker model of post-employment services often stresses creating ladders with incremental advances, often with additional training.[26] But when short training programs are independent of further education, or when community colleges offer non-credit courses without facilitating transfer into regular credit-bearing courses, then the possibilities of such ladders are destroyed.

– Effective programs collect appropriate information about their results and use these to improve their quality. This precept has been embedded in job training programs, with performance measures required as a way to monitor and enhance effectiveness; performance measures are now required in the Workforce Investment Act of 1998 and the recent amendments to the Carl Perkins legislation for vocational education. The exemplary programs identified by King and his colleagues (1998) also used data to monitor their performance continuously. But while accountability requirements are expanding in the United States, they are still often viewed as requirements to be got around rather than mechanisms that might enhance performance.

Programs with different institutional sponsorship and funding vary in the extent to which they follow these precepts. Job training programs in the United States have probably been more faithful to the first precept (labor market targeting) and the fifth (data embedded in performance measures), but have completely ignored instructional and pedagogical issues and links with other programs. Education-based programs, including community colleges, have been better at instructional issues and linkages, but have generally not done much in targeting jobs or using data to improve outcomes, and their records on support services are spotty. A number of community-based programs have provided support services but not much else. And some low-quality programs in every setting, particularly adult education sponsored by school districts, have ignored every one of these precepts. There is therefore some systematic variation caused by the histories and institutional origins of various programs, though these precepts have been widely ignored in virtually every area.

These precepts are useful in various ways. Most obviously, they should be considered by those developing programs at the local level. Many of the exemplary efforts embrace several of these precepts. Conversely, many of the ineffective programs in job training and adult education violate one or more of these ideals, and many of the current welfare-to-work and "work first" programs also violate them.

Second, policy-makers should recognise the value of these precepts. In the United States with its three tiers of government, several states have recently articulated policies remarkably consistent with these precepts: Washington with its wage and skill progression; Wisconsin with Step Up and its affirmation of both education and employment, Iowa with its Family Independence Program, and Oregon with its provision for longer periods of education and training. At the national level, the conceptions of integrating both academic and occupational training, and incorporating work-based learning, have been included in the Amendments of 1990 and 1998 to the Carl Perkins Act supporting vocational education and in the School-to-Work Act of 1994. However, both state and federal policy are contradictory, sometimes relying on one policy narrative, sometimes on another conflicting one. In national welfare reform, in the recent

Workforce Investment Act of 1998, and in many states committed to the most barren version of "work first", the programs being supported pay virtually no attention to any of the five precepts I have presented. Particularly in welfare reform, I fear that the lack of appropriate education and training will doom a percentage of welfare recipients (and the working poor as well) to cycling on and off welfare, contrary to the image of self-sufficiency. In the competition between human capital and "work first" as visions of preparing the workforce of the 21st century, "work first" has often won out for the least well-prepared individuals.

Finally, I hope that these precepts, and more sustained attention to the requirements of effective programs in general, can raise the level of discussion. The human capital vision has provided support for a large variety of education and training efforts around the globe, and a large number of programs for the poor and working poor, but it has often been a naive version that supports any form of education and training. These precepts related to quality can in fact help us disentangle potentially effective programs from those that stand little chance of helping either individuals or employers. The emphasis on newly-defined "key" or "core" or SCANS skills, a development over the last decade that presumably responds (as the first precept requires) to changing employment needs, often ignores the instructional and pedagogical requirements of teaching these sophisticated competencies. This results in programs that claim to be "preparing the workforce of the 21st century" but in fact continue to provide the same low-level drills that conventional schools have emphasised. And replacing human capital visions with a naive version of "work first" – in which poorly-skilled individuals are sent off to work in low-skilled jobs, with no mechanisms of training either on or off the job – cannot possibly be successful over the longer run; they violate every one of the precepts I have presented in this section. There may be sophisticated versions of "work first", in which work-based placements are combined with learning both in work and school settings – as the German dual system, the American school-to-work vision, and some experimental efforts exemplify – but these are far different from the simple-minded efforts now being tried in the United States These five precepts can therefore help disentangle some of the discrepancies among the different visions behind education and training.

The large narratives that drive policy do not emerge overnight. They require sustained and consistent development. They develop only when a broad range of participants, policy-makers, citizens, and prospective students recognise their importance and understand them, and insist on policies that embody them. They need to become part of the culture surrounding policy and the stories related by educators and policy-makers and the research by academics must be relatively consistent and reinforcing. The five precepts I have presented (or others close to them) could serve as the basis for a narrative of quality and effectiveness, though doing so will require more consensus and support than now exists.

NOTES

1. I have been impressed with the extent to which policy in many countries is driven by narratives, or widely-accepted and simple "stories" about why certain programs are worthwhile. The creation of such narratives typically takes a considerable period of time and many different participants; once widely accepted, policy narratives are resistant to change, and empirical evidence – the kinds of results that academics can generate – is not usually enough to modify or complicate a policy narrative. See, for example, Roe (1994).

2. See, for example, the four-stage approach to the human capital model in Grubb and Ryan (1999), which distinguishes the implementation stage; the learning process, as the result of a program that has been successfully implemented; changed behaviour in the labor market and on the job, as the result of learning; and finally employment and non-employment outcomes, as the result of changed behaviour. The point is that education and training programs can fail to change outcomes through failures at any of these four stages.

3. By "remedial pedagogy", I mean one based on conceptions of teaching that emphasise mastering sub-skills before substantive uses of language and math, and that rely on conceptions of students as deficient. Some of the most dismal and ineffective teaching follows this approach.

4. There's a virtual industry summarising the effects of training; see Grubb (1996); LaLonde (1995); US Department of Labor (1995); Fischer and Cordray (1996); O'Neill and O'Neill (1997); Strawn (1998).

5. The evidence suggests that completion of a GED has at best a very small effect on subsequent earnings, compared to dropouts who have not earned a GED; see Cameron and Heckman (1993) and Murnane et al. (1995). Educators who have worked with the GED tend to report that this is the equivalent of an eighth or ninth grade education, not completion of a high school diploma – and this judgement is in effect confirmed by the evaluation results.

6. For example, see the summary of these experiments in Gueron (1987), Table 2, reproduced in Grubb (1996), Table 4.7. The most effective of five programs, in San Diego, increased earnings by 23%, which seems large – but this was only from USD 3 102 to USD 3 802 over fifteen months, or USD 640 per year, and did not significantly reduce the rate of receiving welfare.

7. For example, in the much-cited Riverside program, the effects on earnings are insignificant for recipients with one child, who are more likely to be younger; but the effects are similar for those with children under six and recipients in general.

8. On MFSP, see Gordon and Burghardt (1990), Rangarajan, et al. (1992). Some of the results are reproduced in Grubb (1996), Table 4.12.

9. These observations took place in the course of research for the Grubb and Kalman article in *The American Journal of Education* (1994). We observed a single program, and this might not have been representative of the many STEP sites around the country. However, we observed the program together with a representative of Public/Private Ventures, the developer of STEP, and she assured us that the program we saw was substantially similar to others.

10. See also Grubb (1996), Ch. 6. There are, of course, other explanations for the failure of youth programs and job training, including a certain amount of political manipulation and fraud, and simple incompetence in the implementation of programs.

11. The evidence about related placement in job training is sparse. However, in one data set – the Survey of Income and Program Participation (SIPP) – individuals were asked if they received different forms of job training, and whether this training was related to their current employment. Among those who were in JTPA programs, 49% of men and 46% of women reported that they used training on their current job; for those reporting having enrolled in CETA, 42% of men and 46% of women reported that their job training was related (Grubb, 1995b). And – consistent with the hypothesis that related training has a much higher economic return – the earnings of men with related JTPA training were on the average 55% higher than those with unrelated training, with the comparable figure for women 42%; for those with CETA training, men earned 21 more if their training was related to their current job, while women earned 6% more.

12. Equivalently, it may be that individuals completing job training programs find employment at the expense of others who do not – though this kind of displacement cannot be detected with conventional evaluation methods. In economic terms, a shift outward in the supply function for a particular kind of labor (e.g. for modestly-skilled employment) along a stationary

and inelastic demand function will result in very little additional employment and in a fall in the wage rate -- and so placement rates will be low, displacement high, and the increase in earnings modest. In effect, job training programs assume that the demand for relatively unskilled labor is elastic.

13. I have never seen any examination of pedagogy in job training programs within the job training literature. For observations from the perspectives of educators, see Grubb and Kalman (1994); Grubb et al. (1998); Hull (1993).

14. For vocational skills training see Achtenhagen and Grubb (1999); for basic writing see Hull (undated); for writing see Hillocks (1986) ; for the teaching of low-income students see Knapp and Turnbull (1990) and Knapp et al. (1995). Some specific practices in the meaning- and student-centred tradition have been found to be more effective, including co-operative learning and reciprocal teaching. In the community college realm, there is some evidence that interdisciplinary learning communities where instructors integrate material in several courses are effective in increasing retention, grades, and subsequent success in course. Some of this literature is reviewed in Grubb and Associates (1999), especially Ch. 1.

15. See especially Grubb and Associates (1999) and Grubb et al. (1998).

16. My comments about CET are based on visits in conjunction with the research for Grubb and Kalman (1994). See also Melendez (1996), particularly on the connections between CET and local employers. Unfortunately, these connections are difficult to achieve in a short period of time, and likely to indicate displacement -- that is, individuals hired from one source rather than another, without any overall increase in employment.

17. For some of these programs, see Sum et al. (1997), describing "programs of principles" following the principles of Walker (1997).

18. In addition, a spin-off program in the Rio Grande Valley named VIDA has many of the same characteristics of QUEST, though in a region with higher unemployment. Several smaller programs identified by state and local officials share many of the characteristics of these two.

19. See the Associated Press story, based on interviews of the 100 largest employers, that found only 34 have welfare-to-work programs, with another 13 planning them (San Francisco Chronicle, 1988).

20. These are the equivalent of the practices in Europe to reduce "parity of esteem"; see the review of eight countries in Lasonen and Young (1998).

21. In practice, the School-to-Work Opportunities Act has expanded work-based learning relatively little, and its greatest effect has been to expand relatively conventional school-based services like guidance and counselling (Hershey et al., 1998). It has proved easier to establish work-based placements when high schools have adopted academies or clusters, since then there is a school-based component congruent with work placements.

22. In addition to the review by Stasz et al. (1994), see especially Stern et al. (1992) on the effectiveness of career academies; McPartland et al. (1996) on the talent development high school model; Crain et al. (1992) on career-oriented magnet programs in New York City; and Roegge and Russell (1990) on an integrated approach to biology. Academies are now being evaluated by the Manpower Demonstration Research Corporation in a random-assignment study.

23. I have developed these five from a series of examinations of various education and training programs; see also Grubb et al. (1999), Grubb and Ryan (1999), and King et al. (1998). It's surprising to see how different such lists of principles can be; for a very different set of principles, focusing on how young people feel (e.g. "each young person needs to feel that at least one adult has a strong stake and interest in his or her labor market success"), see Walker (1997).

24. The need to shift pedagogies in order to teach higher-order skills has been argued more fully in Berryman and Bailey (1992); SCANS (1993), with its emphasis on applied instruction; Stasz et al. (1993); Hull (1993); Achtenhagen and Grubb (1999); Grubb and Associates (1999).

25. This kind of observation sometimes leads to triage strategies, where education and training efforts concentrate on a middle group on the assumption that the worst-off individuals cannot be helped except with extraordinary efforts, and that the best-off individuals will find employment on their own. For some evidence supporting a triage approach, see Grubb (1996), pp. 63-65. However, this conclusion has not been consistently supported by evaluations.

26. Many of the post-employment services profiled in Haimson and Hershey (1997) follow this caseworker approach.

BIBLIOGRAPHY

ACHTENHAGEN, F. and GRUBB, W.N. (forthcoming), "Vocational and Occupational Education: Pedagogical complexity, institutional diversity", in V. Richardson (ed.), *Handbook of Research on Teaching* (4th ed.), American Educational Research Association, Washington, DC.

BARDACH, E. (1993), *Improving the Productivity of JOBS Programs,* Manpower Demonstration Research Corporation, New York

BERRYMAN, S. and BAILEY, T. (1992), *The Double Helix of Education and the Economy,* Institute on Education and the Economy, Teachers College, Columbia University, New York.

BLOOM, H.S., ORR, L., CAVE, G., BELL, S.H., DOOLITTLE, F. and LIN, W. (1994), *The National JTPA Study: Overview: Impacts, benefits, and costs of Title II-A,* Abt Associates, Bethesda, MD.

BRADLEY, A. (1995), "Thinking Small", *Education Week,* 14 (256), pp. 37-41.

BURGHARDT, J. and GORDON, A. (1990), *More Jobs and Higher Pay: How an Integrated Program Compares with Traditional Programs,* Rockefeller Foundation, New York.

CAMERON, S. and HECKMAN, J. (1993). "The Non-equivalence of High School Equivalents", *Journal of Labor Economics,* 11(1).

CAVE, G., BOS, H., DOOLITTLE, F. and TOUSSAINT, C. (1993), *JOBSTART: Final Report on a Program for School Dropouts,* Manpower Demonstration Research Corporation, New York.

CRAIN, R.L., HEEBNER, A.L., SI, Y.P., JORDAN, W.J., and KIEFER, D.R. (1992), *The effectiveness of New York City's career magnet schools: An evaluation of ninth grade performance using an experimental design,* National Centre for Research in Vocational Education, University of California at Berkeley, Berkeley, CA.

FISCHER, R. and CORDRAY, D. (1996), *Job Training and Welfare Reform: A Policy-Driven Synthesis,* Russell Sage Foundation, New York.

GORDON, A. and BURGHARDT, J. (1990), *The Minority Female Single Parent Demonstration: Short-term economic impacts:* Mathematica Policy Research, Inc., Princeton, NJ.

GROSSMAN, J.B. and SIPE, C.L (1992), *Summer Training and Education Program (STEP): Report on long-term impacts,* Public/Private Ventures, Philadelphia, PA.

GRUBB, W.N. (1995a), *The Returns to Education and Training in the Sub-Baccalaureate Labor Market: Evidence from the Survey of Income and Program Participation, 1984-1990,* National Centre for Research in Vocational Education, University of California, Berkeley, CA.

GRUBB, W.N. (1995b), *Education through Occupations in American High Schools, Volume I: Approaches to Integrating Academic and Vocational Education,* Teachers College Press, New York.

GRUBB, W.N. (1996), *Learning to Work: The Case for Re-integrating Job Training and Education,* Russell Sage Foundation, New York.

GRUBB, W.N. (1997), "The New Vocationalism: What It Is, What It Could Be", *Phi Delta Kappan,* 77(8), pp. 535-546.

GRUBB, W.N. and Associates (1999), *Honoured But Invisible: An Inside Look at Teaching in Community Colleges,* Routledge, New York and London.

GRUBB, W.N., and KALMAN, J. (1994), "Relearning to Earn: The role of remediation in vocational education and job training", *American Journal of Education,* 103(1), pp. 54-93.

GRUBB, W.N. and RYAN, P. (forthcoming), *The Roles of Evaluation for Vocational Education and Training: Plain Talk on the Field of Dreams,* International Labour Office, Geneva.

GRUBB, W.N., BADWAY, N., BELL, D. and CASTELLANO, M. (1998), "Community College and Welfare Reform: Emerging Issues, Enduring Problems", Unpublished paper, School of Education, University of California, Berkeley, CA.

GRUBB, W.N., BADWAY, N., BELL, D., KING, C., HERR, J., PRINCE, H., KAZIS, R., HICKS, L. and TAYLOR, J. (forthcoming), *Order From Chaos: State Efforts to Reform Workforce Development "Systems"*, National Centre for Research in Vocational Education, Berkeley, CA.

GUERON, J.M. (1987), *Reforming Welfare with Work*, Ford Foundation Project on Social Welfare and American Future, Ford Foundation, Occasional Paper No. 2, New York.

HAHN, A., DANZBERGER, J. and LEFKOWITZ, B. (1987), *Dropouts in America: Enough is Known for Action*, Institute for Educational Leadership, Washington, DC.

HAIMSON, J. and HERSHEY, A. (1997), *Getting Help to Stay Employed: The Use of Post-employment Services*, Mathematica Policy Research, Princeton.

HEINEMANN, H. (1990), "Middle College High School: A comprehensive approach for at-risk students", in D. Inbar (ed.), *Second Chance in Education: An Interdisciplinary and International Perspective*, Falmer Press, London and New York.

HERSHEY, A., SILVERBERG, M., HAIMSON, J., HUDIS, P. and JACKSON, R. (1998), *Expanding Options for Students: Report to Congress on the National Evaluation of the School-to-Work Implementation*, Mathematical Policy Research, Princeton.

HILLOCKS, G. (1986), *Research on Written Composition: New directions for Teaching*, ERIC Clearinghouse on Reading and Communications Skills and National Conference on Research in English, Urbana, Illinois.

HULL, G. (1993), "Critical Literacy and Beyond: Lessons learned from students and workers in an vocational program and on the job", *Anthropology and Educational Quarterly*, No. 24, pp. 373-396.

HULL, G. (undated), "Alternatives to Remedial Writing: Lessons from Theory, from History, and a Case in Point", paper prepared for the Conference on Replacing Remediation in Higher Education, National Centre for Postsecondary Improvement, Stanford University, School of Education, University of California, Berkeley.

KING, C., LAWSON, L., OLSON, J., TROTT, C. and BAJ, J. (1998), "Training Success Stories for Adults and Out-of-School Youth: Past Effects and Lessons for the Future", in B. Barnow and C. King (eds.), *Improving the Odds: Increasing the Effectiveness of Publicly-Funded Training*, Urban Institute Press, Washington, DC.

KNAPP, M. and Associates (1995), *Teaching for Meaning in High-Poverty Classrooms*, Teachers College Press, New York.

KNAPP, M.S. and TURNBULL, B.J. (1990), *Better Schooling for the Children of Poverty: Alternatives to conventional wisdom, Volume I: Summary*, US Department of Education, Washington, DC.

KOGAN, D. et al. (1989), *Improving the Quality of Training Under JTP*, Berkeley Planning Associates and SRI International for the US Department of Labor.

LALONDE, R. (1995), "The Promise of Public Sector-sponsored Training Programs", *Journal of Economic Perspectives*, 2, pp. 149-168.

LASONEN, J. and YOUNG, M. (1998), *Strategies for Achieving Parity of Esteem in European Upper Secondary Education*, University of Jyväskylä, Institute of Economic Research, Jyväskylä, Finland.

MANGUM, G. (1998), "A Historical Perspective", in B. Barnow and C. King (eds.), *Improving the Odds: Increasing the Effectiveness of Publicly-Funded Training*, Urban Institute Press, Washington, DC.

MCPARTLAND, J., LEGTERS, N., JORDAN, W., and MCDILL, E. (1996), *The Talent Development High School: Early Evidence of Impact on School Climate, Attendance, and Student Promotion*, Centre for Research on the Education of Students Placed at Risk, Johns Hopkins University, Baltimore, MD.

MELENDEZ, E. (1996), *Working on Jobs: The Centre for Employment Training*, Mauricio Gaston Institute, University of Massachusetts, Boston, MA.

MURNANE, R., WILLETT, J. and BOUDETT, K.P. (1995), "Do High School Dropouts Benefit from Obtaining a GED?", *Educational Evaluation and Policy Analysis*, 17(2), pp. 133-148.

MURPHY, G. and JOHNSON, A. (1998), *What Works: Integrating Basic Skills Training into Welfare-to-Work*, National Institute for Literacy, Washington, DC.

O'NEILL, D. and O'NEILL, J. (1997), *Lessons for Welfare Reform: An Analysis of the AFDC Caseload and Past Welfare-to-Work Programs*, W.E. Upjohn Institute for Employment Research, Kalamazoo, MI.

OSTERMAN, P. and LAUTSCH, B. (1996), *Project QUEST: A Report to the Ford Foundation*, MIT Sloan School of Management, Cambridge.

PIEMONTE, C. (1995), "Alternative School Reform: Twenty years later", *Education Week*, 14(31), pp. 20-25.

QUINT, J. and BOS, J. (forthcoming), *The Challenge of Making A Difference: Lessons from a Program for Disadvantaged Mothers and Their Children*, Russell Sage Foundation, New York.

QUINT, J.C., MUSICK, J.S. and LADNER, J.A. (1994), *Lives of Promise, Lives of Pain*, Manpower Demonstration Research Corporation, New York and San Francisco.

RANGARAJAN, A., BURGHARDT, J. and GORDON, A. (1992), *Evaluation of the Minority Ffemale Single Parent Demonstration, Volume II: Technical supplement to the analysis of economic impacts*, Mathematica Policy Research Inc., Princeton.

RICCIO, J., FRIEDLANDER, D. and FREEDMAN, S. (1994), *GAIN: Benefits, costs, and three-year impacts of a welfare-to-work program*, MDRC, San Francisco.

ROE, E. (1994), *Narrative Policy Analysis: Theory and Practice*, Duke University Press, Durham, North Carolina and London.

ROEGGE, C. and RUSSELL, E. (1990), "Teaching Applied Biology in Secondary Agriculture: Effects on Student Achievement and Attitudes", *Journal of Agricultural Education*, 31, 27-31.

RUMBERGER, R. (1990), "Second Chance for High School Dropouts: The costs and benefits of dropout recovery programs in the United States", in D. Inbar (ed.), *Second Chance in Education: An Interdisciplinary and International Perspective*, Falmer Press, London and New York.

SAN FRANCISCO CHRONICLE (1988), "US Firms Slow to Hire Off Welfare", May 26, p. A3.

SECRETARY'S COMMISSION ON ACHIEVING NECESSARY SKILLS (1991), *What Work Requires of Schools: A SCANS report for America 2000*, US Department of Labor, Washington, DC.

SECRETARY'S COMMISSION ON ACHIEVING NECESSARY SKILLS (1993), *Teaching the SCANS Competencies*, US Department of Labor, Washington, DC.

STASZ, C., KAGANOFF, T. and EDEN, R. (1994), "Integrating Academic and Vocational Education: A review of the literature, 1987-1992", *Journal of Vocational Education Research*, 19 (2), pp. 25-72.

STASZ, C., RAMSEY, K., EDEN, R., DAVANZO, J., FARRIS, H. and LEWIS, M. (1993), *Classrooms that Work: Teaching generic skills in academic and vocational settings*, National Centre for Research in Vocational Education, Berkeley, CA.

STERN, D., RABY, M. and DAYTON, C. (1992), *Career Academies: Partnerships for reconstructing American high schools*, Jossey-Bass, San Francisco, CA.

STRAWN, J. (1998), *Beyond Job Search or Basic Education: Rethinking the Role of Skills in Welfare Reform*, Centre for Law and Social Policy, Washington DC.

SUM, A. et al. (1997), *A Generation of Challenge: Pathways to Success for Urban Youth*, Policy Issues Monograph, 97-03, Sar Levitan Centre for Social Policy Studies, Baltimore, MD.

US DEPARTMENT OF LABOR (1995), *What's Working (and What's Not): A summary of research on the economic impacts of employment and training programs*, Office of the Chief Economist, Washington, DC.

US GENERAL ACCOUNTING OFFICE (1987), *School Dropouts: Survey of Local Programs*, GAO/HRD-87-108., US Government Printing Office, Washington, DC.

US GENERAL ACCOUNTING OFFICE (1995), *Job Corps: High Costs and Mixed Results Raise Questions about Program's Effectiveness*, GAO/HEIS-95-180, Washington, DC.

URQUIOLA, M., STERN, D., HORN, I., DORNSIFE, C., CHI, B., WILLIAMS, L., MERRITT, D., HUGHES, K. and BAILEY, T. (1997), *School to Work, College and Career: A Review of Policy, Practice, and Results, 1993-1997*, MDS-1144, National Centre for Research in Vocational Education, Berkeley, CA.

WALKER G. (1997), "Out of School and Unemployed: Principles for More Effective Policies and Programs", in A. Sum et al. (eds.), *A Generation of Challenge: Pathways to Success for Urban Youth*, Policy Issues Monograph, 7-03, Sar Levitan Centre for Social Policy Studies, Baltimore, MD.

WALKER, G. and VILELLA-VELEZ, F. (1992), *Anatomy of a Demonstration: The Summer Training and Education Program (STEP) from pilot through replication and postprogram impacts*, Public/Private Ventures, Philadelphia.

WIRCENSKI, J.L. and SARKEES, M.D. (1990), "Instructional Alternatives: Rescue strategies for at-risk students", *NASSP Curriculum Report*, 19(4), pp. 1-6.

Table 1. **Impacts of JTPA on total 30-month earnings: assignees and enrolees, by target group**

	Mean earnings		Impact per assignee	
	Treatment group (1)	Control group (2)	In dollars	Percent (2)
Adult women	13 417	12 241	1 176***	9.6
Adult men	19 474	18 496	978*	5.3
Female youths	10 241	10 106	135	1.3
Male youth non arrestees	15 786	16 375	-589	-3.6
Male youth arrestees				
Using survey data	14 633	18 842	-4 209**	-22.3
Using scaled UI data	14 148	14 152	-4	0.0

Statistical significance: *** = 1%, ** = 5%, * = 10%.
Source: Bloom *et al.* (1994), Exhibit 5.

Table 2. **The effects of JOBSTART**

	Experimentals	Controls	Difference
Received GED or high school diploma by end of year 4			
Full sample	42.0	28.6	13.4***
Men	42.0	28.3	13.7***
Custodial mothers	42.0	26.7	15.3***
Other women	41.6	31.3	10.4**
Ever employed (%)			
Years 1-4	86.4	86.0	0.4
Year 1	56.5	60.8	-4.3**
Year 2	71.0	67.5	3.5*
Year 3	61.8	61.5	0.3
Year 4	65.7	64.5	1.3
Total hours worked			
Years 1-4	3 031	3 071	-40
Year 1	441	550	-109***
Year 2	760	775	-15
Year 3	899	855	44
Year 4	930	890	40
Total earnings (in USD)			
Years 1-4	17 010	16 796	214
Year 1	2 097	2 596	-499***
Year 2	3 991	4 112	-121
Year 3	5 329	4 906	423
Year 4	5 592	5 182	410
Custodial mothers			
Ever employed (%)			
Years 1-4	75.4	71.0	4.5
Total earnings (USD)			
Years 1-4	8 959	8 334	625
Other women			
Ever employed (%)			
Years 1-4	84.3	85.3	-1.0
Total earnings (USD)			
Years 1-4	13 923	13 310	613
Men			
Ever employed (%)			
Years 1-4	94.1	94.5	-0.4
Total earnings (USD)			
Years 1-4	23 364	23 637	-273

Custodial mothers

Ever received AFDC (%)			
Years 1-4	84.8	81.6	3.2
Total AFDC income (USD)			
Years 1-4	9 371	9 334	37
Ever pregnant (%)			
Years 1-4	76.1	67.5	8.6**
Ever gave birth (%)			
Years 1-4	67.8	57.9	9.9**

Other women

Ever received AFDC (%)			
Years 1-4	38.0	45.1	-7.1
Total AFDC income (USD)			
Years 1-4	3 204	3 979	-775
Ever pregnant (%)			
Years 1-4	64.4	65.6	-1.2
Ever gave birth (%)			
Years 1-4	52.7	56.5	-3.9

Men ever arrested

Year 1	35.1	35.1	-0.1
Years 1-4	68.9	74.8	-5.8

Ever used any drug in year 4	25.4	31.0	-5.5
Ever used any drug excluding marijuana in year 4	3.7	10.5	-6.9*
Ever used marijuana in year 4	25.3	30.2	-4.9

Statistical significance: *** = 1%; ** = 5%; * = 10%.
Source: Cave *et al.* (1993, Tables 2-7).

WORKSHOP 6

PROMOTING JOB CREATION FOR DISADVANTAGED YOUTH: WHAT WORKS AND FOR WHOM?

PROMOTING EMPLOYMENT FOR YOUTH: A EUROPEAN PERSPECTIVE*

by
Jérôme Gautié
École Normale Supérieure and Centre d'Études de l'Emploi, Paris

Introduction

In response to the magnitude of youth unemployment, since the second half of the 1970s many European countries have implemented active labour market policies (ALMPs). Some of these policies are more specifically aimed at promoting employment, and can be classified into three broad categories:

- Employment subsidies in the market sector (various forms of financial incentives, such as lump-sum payments, tax credits, reductions in social security contributions, etc.).

- Temporary subsidised employment in the non-market sector (the public and non-profit sectors).

- Various forms of aid to self-employment (financial aid, advice and training); this type of aid concerns young people only marginally, and those with the poorest skills, hardly at all. As Meager points out (1996), in most countries the beneficiaries of this type of aid are men over 30 with relatively high educational levels, who have experienced only a relatively short period of unemployment. In addition, there have been very few studies of the impact of this type of measure on young people.[1] Consequently, in this paper we shall focus only on the first two categories of measures, which we shall group together under the generic term of "subsidised jobs" in the broad sense.

Nearly 15 years ago, Wilenski (1985) drew attention to the paradox that it was the countries that relied most heavily on ALMPs that evaluated them least. Despite the substantial growth of the evaluation "industry" in Europe since the second half of the 1980s, this paradox still appears to hold true at the end of the 1990s, at least if Europe is compared with North America (Fay, 1996). And the more specific field of ALMPs for young people does not seem to be an exception to this rule.

But the specific situation of Europe should not be assessed solely in quantitative terms (*i.e.* more measures – in terms of diversity, percentage of GDP, number of beneficiaries among the youth population – and fewer evaluations). For many European countries, this quantitative difference also reflects, perhaps even more fundamentally, a qualitative difference with respect to the situation in North America. This difference resides in:

- The groups targeted (young beneficiaries are often defined in broader terms than the category of "disadvantaged youth", as defined in the United States, for example).

* I wish to thank D. Anxo, F. Lefresne, L. Schröder and L. Toharia for the information they sent me. I also would like to thank A. Gubian and B. Simonin very much for their comments. Obviously, I alone am responsible for any errors and for the opinions expressed in this paper.

– The nature of the measures implemented (some countries, such as France or Sweden and to a lesser extent the Netherlands, have and/or have had large programmes of temporary subsidised jobs in the non-market sector, which have no equivalent in the United States, for example).

– Evaluations: while in North America the focus is mainly on the impact of programmes on their beneficiaries (in terms of their wages and employment rates after the programme), in Europe many studies analyse the impact of AEP programmes on labour market outcomes and address concerns of a more macroeconomic nature, including for measures targeting specific groups such as young people.

It is this specifically European approach to promoting youth employment that we shall try to analyse in this paper, drawing upon the experience of the last two decades. How can we explain the use of these types of measures in European countries, in some cases on a mass scale? Who are the young people involved, and what are the different types of subsidised jobs? What do evaluation studies teach us and what lessons can be learned from them for the implementation of ALMPs for young people? This study will obviously make no attempt to be exhaustive, but will only try to provide some partial answers to these questions on the basis of the experience of a few European countries (chiefly France and Sweden, but also to a lesser extent the United Kingdom in the 1980s). Some aspects will be compared with what is known of the North American experience. The first part will present subsidised job programmes in the European context; the second will analyse the effects of these measures on their beneficiaries, and the third will study their impact on the labour market (in terms of net job creation, impact on youth unemployment and on overall employment and unemployment); lastly, the fourth part will try to draw some conclusions that will be useful for implementing ALMPs.

1. Subsidised jobs in Europe

Why do some countries rely more heavily on employment subsidies for young people?

Different labour market entry patterns of young people

The use of ALMPs for young people varies widely, not only between Europe and other OECD countries, but also within Europe itself. Some countries such as France,[2] and to a lesser extent Sweden[3] and Spain, operate employment subsidy programmes for young people on a mass scale, while others, such as Germany or the Netherlands, do so far less, if at all.[4] In order to understand better the specific national situations in this regard, it should be borne in mind that ALMPs are only one component of the youth transition system (Bourdet and Persson, 1994) specific to each country, the other components being the education and training system, labour market legislation and the wage formation and unemployment benefit systems. In Europe, there are two contrasting patterns of youth transition systems, the linkage between the education and training system and the productive system defining two modes of functioning of the labour market (Ryan *et al.*, 1991).

Occupational labour market

In an occupational labour market, skills are transferable from one firm to another, and qualify workers for specific jobs and a definite wage level. These skills are acquired through a training system that follows certain rules aimed specifically at making this transferability possible, thereby facilitating inter-firm mobility. The United Kingdom (until the 1980s) and especially Germany, albeit in different ways, are examples of these kinds of labour markets. France, and also to some extent Italy and Sweden, tend to be characterised by a labour market that functions along the lines of an *internal labour market*. The diplomas and credentials acquired outside firms act mainly as a criterion for recruitment, but it is the experience acquired inside the firm that transforms this "potential" skill into a skill recognised in classifications. The education and training system is primarily a "filter" that makes it possible to classify individuals according to their aptitudes, and firms consider a diploma more as a signal of individuals' potential than as a measurement of their immediately productive skills.

These two models differ in the ways that young people enter the labour market. In occupational markets of the German type, the apprenticeship system makes it possible to "disconnect" the wages young people are paid from the wages of adult workers, in exchange for which young people acquire skills recognised in classifications. This system is based on supervision by social partners, with trade unions ensuring the effectiveness and quality of training, in particular to prevent adult workers from being replaced by lower paid young people. In an internal labour market system, on the other hand, there is a danger of a "selective exclusion" of young people. For example, in France and Sweden wages are generally linked to jobs, and there is no institutional framework "disconnecting" young people's wages from those of adult workers. This results in young people being relegated to the lowest paid and most insecure jobs, especially in small firms, before they can enter jobs in the "primary" market of relatively closed labour markets.

The impact of the overall job shortage on the labour market entry of young people

The overall job shortage is the main cause of youth unemployment in most European countries. But it appears that it is in countries in which the internal labour market mode predominates that the overall shortage has the biggest impact on young people. Three factors have also contributed to this trend:

- The rise in the relative wages of the least skilled workers until the mid 1980s, and their level since then, has helped to penalise young people with the lowest education levels: this rise was due to the increase in the minimum wage (as in France), and/or the wage solidarity policy promoted by trade unions (as in Sweden[5]).

- In response to the crisis, wage-earners' unions have generally tended to defend the interests of the "adult" workers (aged over 30) who constitute their base; this was more especially the case in France where the initial diploma level of manual and non-manual workers was very low, and where, because of the internal labour market mode, the skills acquired subsequently were mainly specific and consequently less transferable.

- The destabilisation of internal labour markets, with the disappearance of the implicit subsidies from which young people sometimes benefited, also contributed to the deterioration of their situation on the labour market (Box 1).

The greater difficulties young people face on the labour market are reflected not only in higher unemployment, but also in greater occupational downgrading (see, for example, Blomskog and Schröder, 1995 for Sweden; and Forgeot and Gautié, 1997 for France). Employers can view this downgrading partly as a way of making the unit cost more flexible (W/MP, in which W and MP respectively stand for wages and marginal productivity) in a context of relative wage rigidity. Youth unemployment is thus partly due to "queuing", which, while it primarily affects the least skilled, can also affect young people with higher education levels.

The role of active employment policies

From a microeconomic standpoint, using Schröder's very simple formulation (1996), the policy of employment subsidies is based on the idea that the wage at which some young people could be hired (W) is higher than their marginal productivity (MP), minus their training cost (Tc), or:

$$W > MP - Tc \qquad [1]$$

Box 1.

Destabilisation of internal labour markets and youth employment

The accumulation of human capital in firms and the incentive value of tenure-based wages are the foundation of the standard wage career profile in the internal labour markets of large firms (Figure 1). In the initial phase (from t1 to t2), during which the specific human capital is accumulated, young employees are paid more than their productivity warrants. In the second phase (from t2 to t3), employees are paid below their productivity, both so that the employer can recover some of the costs of the investment in human capital of the preceding period and as an incentive [as presented in the theory of delayed payment contracts; cf. Lazear (1981)]. Lastly, the third stage (from t3 to T), in which older workers are paid above their productivity, is justified by these same reasons of incentive (seen in the second stage), since wages continue to rise in line with tenure until the end of the employee's career. Independently of considerations of specific human capital, the career profile during the first two periods (the young and the adult employee) can also be due to high wages at the time of hiring (because of a minimum or contractual wage), which requires the employer to pay newly hired employees above their productivity, a loss that the employer subsequently recoups by imposing a lower rate of tenure-based advancement. In the aggregate, the profile of wage and productivity trends is such that there is an equalisation of both variables (B = A + C) over time (longitudinally, over the entire career). On the other hand, cross-sectionally (at a given moment in time), this system entails a subsidy – that we shall call "implicit" since it is unintentional – by adult workers (of intermediate age) to younger and older workers (since these adult workers are paid below their productivity, while younger and older workers are paid above it).

Figure 1

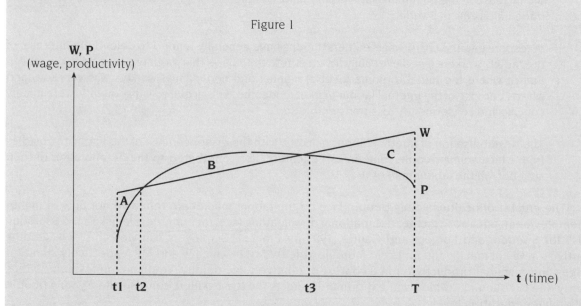

There are a number of signs that these implicit subsidy systems from which young people used to benefit in some firms are tending to be dismantled. This is due to the shorter time horizon of management – which itself is due to higher interest rates, the more rapid pace of technological progress and increased competition – as well as to new technologies, which perhaps make it more easy to individualise performance. The higher level of general and vocational training acquired in the education system has also contributed to weakening the on-the-job training model characteristic of traditional internal labour markets. The trend now is to pay all workers according to their productivity at a given time in their career, as is borne out by the increasing individualisation of wages: in new wage contracts, spot wages equal spot productivity. If, as we have suggested, younger and older workers tended to benefit from implicit subsidies in previous wage contracts, then it is understandable that in many countries they have been hardest hit by changes in the labour market, which have led to a drop in their relative wages and/or lower employment in countries in which wages are not flexible. This is the case, for example, in France, and more particularly in the sectors in which the internal labour market mode predominates.[6]

The German apprenticeship system is, as we pointed out earlier, an institution that makes it possible to disconnect young people's wages from those of adult workers (in exchange for effective training) and thus ensure equality [1] (W = MP - Tc). The other European countries, not having this kind of system, have sought to restore equality [1] in a variety of ways. Some countries have mainly sought to promote flexibility by lowering young people's wages (impact on W). This is the case in particular in the United Kingdom, where young people were removed from the jurisdiction of Wage Councils in the 1980s. The Netherlands have taken the same course of action in a more regulated way by introducing a minimum wage that varies with age until 23. But other countries have adopted ALMPs for young people, such as training measures (impact on MP), in-firm work contracts in which part of the training cost is paid (impact on Tc), employment subsidies to lower the labour cost of young people (impact on W) and temporary public jobs. France and Sweden are the two most characteristic countries of this second group.[7] More particularly, employment subsidies have a two-fold function:

- In firms in the secondary segment of the labour market, which as we have seen are more likely to hire young people, the subsidy, provided it is renewed, is aimed at offsetting structurally the gap between the statutory or contractual minimum wage and the productivity of young people in low-skill jobs: if S is the amount of the subsidy, then S = W-MP (with Tc = 0).

- In firms in with an internal labour market, in which the young people hired can acquire specific and general human capital, the subsidy can play the role of reducing the gap between W and MP - Tc, which is partly due to a starting wage that is too high waiting for MP to raise; the "explicit" subsidy thus replaces partly the "implicit" subsidy (Figure 1, Box 1).

All told, therefore, there are three standard models of labour market entry for young people in Europe: *"negotiated entry"*, via the German apprenticeship model, *"competitive entry"* through deregulation of the labour market of young people, and *"subsidised entry"*, in which ALMPs, and especially subsidised jobs play a key role, and are as it were the functional substitute for the German apprenticeship system, which is a form of bargained flexibility (Garonna and Ryan, 1991). These are more theoretical than actual models, however; the United Kingdom, for example, has also implemented programmes for young people in the 1980s and 1990s (in particular training programmes), which tends to show the limits of purely competitive entry.[8]

The groups targeted and the nature of programmes

Following the analysis in the preceding paragraph, we shall now turn to the groups that are targeted, as well as the nature of the programmes implemented.

Relatively broad targeting

Owing to the magnitude and nature of youth unemployment, which also concerns large numbers of diploma-holders,[9] in most countries employment promotion measures are not only intended for the most "disadvantaged" young people with no diploma whatsoever, who would be the equivalent of "high-school dropouts" in the United States. The very category of "young people" can also be extended, and is considerably broader than the group "teenagers" generally focused on in North America. In Sweden, for example, programmes initially targeted the 16-19 age group for some years, and were later extended to the 19-25 age group in the 1990s. In some countries such as Spain, France or Italy, where the youth unemployment rate is particularly high, eligibility for some programmes has been extended to "young people" as old as 29.

The large number of programmes and the difficulty of identifying them

The large number and diversity of programmes raises the problem of determining which ones are employment promotion schemes (and therefore demand-side programmes) and which are simply training schemes (*i.e.* supply-side programmes):

– The situation is unambiguous for straightforward job subsidy measures in the market sector (which we shall call "pure subsidies"). They may be based on different types of financial incentives. Tax credit schemes along the lines of the US Targeted Job Tax Credit are relatively rare in Europe. More often they are based on direct wage subsidies consisting of a lump-sum payment (in this case the size of the incentive is inversely proportional to the level of the wage the young person is paid) or a percentage of the wage, and/or a partial or full exemption from employer's social security contributions. It is important to point out that in many cases, the financial incentive is combined with certain clauses derogating from "regular" work contracts (this is the case in particular in France and Spain). In Sweden, however, the beneficiaries of subsidised jobs were traditionally covered by the same collective bargaining rules as other workers, particularly in terms of pay. But the introduction of Youth Practice in the beginning of the 1990s broke this rule for the first time, since young beneficiaries receive lower pay and do not have the same social insurance cover. But the status of this measure is ambiguous (are they subsidised jobs or a form of "training scheme"? see below). On the whole, in many countries, employment promotion measures combine financial incentives with the deregulation of work contracts, which raises a problem of evaluation, for, as Grubb (1994) points out, "in the countries concerned, the impact of subsidies is difficult to distinguish from the impact of the deregulation [...]" (p. 199).

– Temporary jobs in the non-market sector also seem easily identifiable, and clearly belong to the employment promotion measures that concern us here. It must be stressed that most jobs of this kind are not only, or even primarily, intended for young people (Erhel *et al.*, 1996). In Germany, for example, until the 1990s ABM programmes only marginally concerned young people (who also had relatively low unemployment rates, as we have seen). In France, although the programme of community work schemes (*Travaux d'Utilité Collective*, TUC) were exclusively intended for young people aged under 26, the programme that followed it (employment-solidarity contracts: *Contrats-Emploi-Solidarité*, CES) was extended to all groups experiencing the greatest difficulty (above all the long-term unemployed). In Sweden, "Relief Works" were not intended solely for young people, and were not limited to the non-market sector.

– The status of in-firm training programmes is far more ambiguous: some schemes that entail a work contract can be considered as subsidised jobs in the broad sense (or as a "mixed subsidy" – according to the terminology of Gautié, Gazier and Silvera (1994) – the financial incentive being given theoretically in exchange for training); in other words, if we refer to equation |1|, there is a simultaneous effect on W and Tc, in exchange for an investment by the firm to increase MP. Other measures have the status of training schemes, but are actually used by firms as subsidised jobs. In other words, the borderline between a "mixed" subsidy and a mere in-firm training programme cannot always be clearly drawn.

In France, for example, alternating classroom-workplace training programmes (*Formations en Alternance*) such as the skill formation contract (*Contrat de Qualification*, CQ), the adaptation contract (*Contrat d'Adaptation*, CA) and even the apprenticeship contract (*Contrat d'Apprentissage*), are classified in the Labour Ministry's official classifications as "subsidised jobs" (Emplois Aidés) together with "pure" employment subsidy measures such as the subsidy to give young people their first jobs (Aide au Premier Emploi des Jeunes, APEJ), the Exo-jeunes scheme or temporary public-sector jobs (TUC, CES). Similarly, the work experience programme (Stage d'Initiation à la Vie Professionnelle, SIVP) can be considered as a "subsidised job". The government tries to determine the impact in terms of *net job creation* (after deducting dead-weight loss and substitution effects in particular – see Section 3) of all these "subsidised employment" measures (Emplois Aidés), which strongly suggests that it considers them to be employment promotion measures. In Sweden, the Youth Practice programme, defined as an on-the-job training measure for young diploma-holders without job experience, is also *in fact* considered to be a job promotion programme because the evaluation studies also address its impact on employment. In the United Kingdom, the Youth Training Scheme and Youth Training were officially designed as training programmes, but trade unions tend to consider them as mere systems enabling employers to obtain cheap labour, in exchange for which there is often little or no training provided (Balchin and Ashton, 1994). But the evaluations of these schemes focus mainly on their effects on the employability of the beneficiaries, and virtually do not address their impact on job creation (Dolton, 1993). This would make it more logical to classify these measures as training schemes, although in practice (because of how they have been implemented rather than their initial design) it often seems difficult to distinguish them clearly from the French SIVP, for example.[10]

Table 1 lists the main employment promotion measures implemented for young people (or for other groups in difficulty, but which have particularly benefited young people) since the beginning of the 1980s in four European countries (France, Spain,[11] Sweden[12] and the United Kingdom[13]). We have classified these measures into the following four categories, although the status of the fourth category is ambiguous for the reasons we have mentioned above: 1) subsidised jobs in the market sector ("pure subsidies"); 2) temporary subsidised jobs in the non-market sector; 3) employment measures in firms with training aspects ("mixed subsidies"); and 4) "training schemes" that can to some extent be considered as forms of subsidised employment.

Evaluations in a European context

In the United States, evaluation procedures are relatively standardised[14] (US Department of Labor, 1995). They focus primarily on the impact of programmes on their beneficiaries, mainly in terms of their effects on wages (or earnings) and employability, although the evaluation is sometimes broadened so as to estimate the cost/benefits for society, but in a microeconomic perspective (see Bell and Orr, 1994) for an example of job subsidies not specifically intended for young people. Increasingly these evaluations are based on experimental methods. Although evaluation has developed significantly in Europe since the second half of the 1980s, the use of controlled experiments remains quite limited, and even non-existent (to the best of our knowledge) in the field of employment promotion programmes for young people (Björkland and Regner, 1996).

But the distinctive feature of evaluation in Europe is perhaps more specifically the emphasis many evaluations place on the labour market impact of programmes (in terms of employment and unemployment) both at the "micro" level (impact on employment in the firms receiving subsidies) and at force as a whole).[15] If we confine ourselves to employment policy for young people, its size and scope (in the more "macro" level (impact on the employment and unemployment of young people and of the labour terms of the percentage of young people affected and, in some countries, budgetary costs) warrant the evaluation of its macroeconomic impact.

2. Impact of programmes on beneficiaries

As Gélot and Simonin (1997) point out, to study the impact of employment policy on the groups concerned "means asking at least two types of questions: do the policy measures reach the persons for whom they were intended? And what are the consequences of having participated in the programme on its beneficiaries?" The first question is particularly relevant in the European context, where, as we have pointed out, youth unemployment is far from being limited to a core of economically and socially disadvantaged individuals. The second question implies that a clear distinction must be made, from a theoretical standpoint, between the various possible effects in order to interpret correctly the findings of empirical studies. But a third question must be added, *i.e.* to what extent has employability in the broad sense (measured in terms of the employment rate and wages) of non-beneficiaries itself been affected?

The selection of programme participants

The role of the various actors

The danger of targeting programmes too broadly is obviously that the more employable candidates will supplant the least employable young persons, all the more in that the number of places available is limited. The targeting of the programme in its design stage based on general socio-demographic criteria (age, education level) or on candidates' situations vis-à-vis the labour market (for example, length of unemployment) may prove to be inadequate, since these criteria may be arbitrary and insufficient to determine which young people are most in need of measures. Consequently, a certain leeway and freedom of action is usually left to the various actors (potential beneficiaries, local employment service staff, firms).

Studies on the attitude of young people towards the various schemes are relatively rare. According to a French survey (Maresca, 1994), based on interviews with young people aged between 20 and 26, it appears that overall they have a relatively negative view of the programmes in France, although the fear of being stigmatised (which was a factor for some subsidised programmes in the United States (*cf.* Dubin and Rivers, 1993) was not mentioned. The process by which they choose a programme seems to be a two step one, for instead of calculating the comparative advantages of various situations at the outset (in particular having to choose between taking advantage of unemployment to look for a job, and entering into a "subsidised employment" programme), they initially give priority to looking for a stable job, and only after a certain time (approximately one year) consider entering into a programme. They are somewhat reluctant to enter schemes that are so poorly paid that they will remain dependent on their parents, or they are afraid of being "stuck" in them for some time, and consider that they are highly unlikely to lead to a job. As a result, subsidised jobs in the non-market sector are sometimes preferred (CES: *cf.* Table 1), since they are better paid, to some alternating classroom-workplace training programmes (CQ, apprenticeship). Upon closer examination, young people's attitudes appear to differ depending on their education level. Living for the present and falling into a fatalistic attitude seem to be all the more prevalent when this level is low. What is more, the most disadvantaged young people may also be apprehensive about going to work in a firm, since they are afraid that they will not "make the grade" and prefer to "take refuge" in the more sheltered situation of temporary jobs in the non-market sector.

All things considered, there is a danger of self-selection that will cause the most disadvantaged young people (in terms of education and training) to shun the programmes most directly connected to private firms and/or that provide the most intensive training (in particular "mixed subsidy" measures). In order to prevent this from happening, the government must first seek to provide a coherent structure of incentives, ensuring, for example, that subsidised jobs in the non-market sector are not systematically better paid than ones in the market sector (or, for that matter, than training programmes). But more importantly, this danger of self-selection underscores the important role played by local employment service staff in providing guidance to young people.

The staff's approach will depend on their conception of their role. For example, Bessy *et al.* (1996) distinguish between several types of employment service employees: *"civic"* employees, who follow quite closely the rules of labour law, *"networking"* employees who try to establish lasting ties with other local actors, and lastly *"contract salesmen"*, who focus their activity on providing financial incentives to firms. While the first two types are more aware of the situation of the most disadvantaged individuals, the third group tends to maximise the placement rate by creaming off the best candidates in order to offer only the most employable young people to their "client" firms, or, conversely, to be less discriminating about the firms in which participants are placed.

To avoid this systematic creaming off of the most employable young people, maximising the placement rates of participants entering or leaving programmes should in no case be the only objective of local employment service staff. This is especially important given the fact that firms themselves obviously quite often tend to "filter" applicants (their goal being, for a given W, to maximise MP and minimise Tc: Equation [1]) in order to recruit the most productive individuals. Local employment service staff then face a dilemma, for if they make their criteria more stringent in order to try to force firms to take the most disadvantaged young people, they run the risk of discouraging firms, and especially the firms able to offer the jobs providing the best training (*i.e.* the most stable firms with better career prospects), which can then lead to a danger of adverse selection. When more stringent criteria are introduced, financial incentives must also be increased proportionally to firms' reluctance to take on the most disadvantaged young people.[16]

Selection and segmentation

In practice, it appears that the different types of measures benefit relatively different groups of young people: the most "employable" and highly motivated tend to enter subsidised programmes in the private sector (especially "mixed subsidies"), while the others are more frequently found in subsidised jobs in the non-market sector.

This is particularly true in France. There is a sharp distinction between subsidised market-sector jobs, especially those that provide the most valuable training, and non-market subsidised jobs. For example, at the beginning of the 1990s, some 60% of participants adaptation contract (CA) had a level equal or superior to the Baccalaureate (*i.e.* the equivalent of a high school diploma), as did nearly 50% of participants in skill formation contracts (CQ), as opposed to only some 15% of participants in employment-solidarity contracts (CES). According to the logistic study of Saucier and Sofer (1995), the likelihood of entering the various employment policy programmes (which they classify in three groups: subsidised market-sector jobs (CQ, CA, SIVP), CES and training schemes) is correlated with young people's various characteristics (age, mobility, sex, educational level and specialisation – industrial or tertiary). Nine months after leaving the education system, those who have participated in a subsidised market-sector job on the whole have characteristics similar to individuals who are already employed: other things being equal, they are older, more mobile, have a higher education level and are more often male. On the other hand, participants in CES have the opposite characteristics, more similar to those of the unemployed: they tend to be female, less mobile, with a low education level and tertiary-type training. It is also interesting to observe that, other things being equal, being female is a systematically unfavourable factor for finding a job, and that employed young people are older on average than young people in employment policy programmes. This appears to confirm that sex and age are the key criteria in the queuing process, which relegates the least "employable" persons – or those considered to be – to subsidised non-market sector jobs and unemployment.

The Swedish Youth Practice programme, which is theoretically intended to give young graduates initial work experience, has also proven to be relatively selective: according to one survey's findings, on average programme participants had 15 months of job experience before entering the programme, and in the 20-24 year-old group, over 40% had more than two years' job experience (Schröder, 1996).

Analysis of the impact of measures on their beneficiaries

Methodological problems

The problem with micro-econometric evaluations is isolating the *specific* effect of programmes. The idea is to compare the "outcomes" of beneficiaries (primarily in terms of employment rates, duration of employment and wages[17] after the programme) with those of non-beneficiaries, "other things being equal". To do so, it is necessary to control the differences between both groups of individuals so as not to attribute to the programme outcomes that are actually due to unobserved characteristics of individuals. Thus, there is a problem of a *selection bias*, which can be particularly important due to the fact that different programmes recruit groups with very different employability levels. Some of these are decisive, and can be identified at the local level by employment service staff or employers but do not show up in statistics. For want of experimental data, even if they do not entirely eliminate the problem (Heckman, 1992), European studies often come up against this type of problem.

Programmes treated as black boxes

Over and above the statistical problem of selection bias, there is the problem of the economic interpretation of the results obtained, for in most quantitative estimates of impact, the programme is reduced to a "black box". A number of factors can explain the impact observed in terms of wages and employment.

The first factor involves *human capital*. A drop in wages (in relative terms) after a programme is often interpreted as proof of a loss of human capital; but in fact, this loss in wages may simply mean that the programme channelled the young person towards the *secondary sector* of the labour market, where, other things being equal (and thus for a given human capital), wages are lower.

O'Higgins (1995), drawing on the example of the YTS in the United Kingdom, suggests that the lower wages of beneficiaries, observed following some programmes, may also be due, in some cases, to a drop in the reservation wages of beneficiaries. This would explain the fact that for some low-paid employment promotion programmes a negative effect on wages and a positive effect on the employment rate may be observed simultaneously. For it is possible that young people may systematically overestimate the wages they can expect on the labour market. Participating in a programme may then make them "more realistic" – or less demanding – and lead them to lower their wage expectations.[18]

Another factor can play a very important role: *stigmatisation*. It can not only account for lower employment rates, but also for lower wages.[19] It seems that this factor plays an important role in employment subsidies in the United States. Bishop (1989) has shown that, across a sample of firms, *other things being equal* – his data enable him to control some 20 variables – newly hired workers earned a lower wage when the employer knew that they were eligible for the Targeted Job Tax Credit than workers who were not eligible (the characteristics identifiable by the employer being equal. The negative effects of stigmatisation at hiring have been analysed by Burtless (1985), based on an experiment conducted in Ohio. The "clients" of a placement agency had been randomly divided into three groups; those in the first two groups were given a voucher entitling employers to an employment subsidy (in the form of a tax credit or an immediately payable lump-sum respectively); the last group was a control group, and its members were not informed of the experiment. After eight weeks of job search, only 13% of the beneficiaries of the subsidy had found a job, compared with 21% of non-beneficiaries. But a similar experiment reported by Dubin and Rivers (1993) makes it possible to qualify Burtless' findings. After 11 weeks, 37.9% of those in the "subsidised group" (who had received a voucher entitling prospective employers to a lump-sum of 500 dollars) had found a job, compared with only 35% of those in the control group. Either there had been no stigmatisation effect, or this time it had been offset by the subsidy. Nevertheless, the authors observed that the starting wages of subsidised workers were, other things being equal, *lower* than those of non-subsidised workers. In their view, this is due to a self-selection bias, since over 30% of the persons asked to join the subsidised group had refused to do so. According to Dubin and Rivers, the most likely explanation is that it was those who thought they had the best chance of being hired who refused, out of fear of being *stigmatised*. In other words, it was the least "employable" individuals, observed characteristics being equal, who had the greatest propensity to enter the subsidised group.

Some factors suggest that stigmatisation may play a less important role in the European context. It is true that in the United States: 1) employers find it very difficult to evaluate the quality of job applicants because of the extremely uneven quality of the education system, and because of legal restrictions on testing and enquiries prior to hiring (Bishop, 1993); 2) subsidies are reserved for particularly "disadvantaged" groups. In Europe, the few surveys that have been carried out suggest that neither young people nor employers consider stigmatisation to be an important factor.[20] But there is reason to believe that in the countries where, as we saw in the case of France, temporary public jobs attract the least employable and/or least motivated young people, this type of subsidised job may have a stigmatisation effect. But the same may also be true of "subsidised jobs" in the market sector. In France, where the practice of "job shopping" is far less widespread than in the United States,[21] surveys of firms show that the factor that most influences employers' perceptions at the time of hiring is not the socio-demographic profile (age, sex, diploma held, etc.), but the individual's employment record, for having held a number of short-term jobs is seen as a sign of instability. Thus a young person who held a subsidised job but did not remain in the firm when the subsidy expired may be judged negatively by prospective employers, although he or she was merely a victim of the attitude of some firms towards subsidy programmes, since they use them only to obtain cheap short-term labour, which they renew at the end of the subsidy period with another young person. Thus by increasing labour turnover in some firms, temporary short-term subsidies (such as the SIVP in France – *cf.* Table 1) may contribute to reducing the employability of some young people, since they fail to acquire human capital and run the risk of being stigmatised.

Lastly, in the more specific case of temporary jobs in the non-market sector, the "lock in" effect may also have negative repercussions on the subsequent employment rate, as young beneficiaries may stop looking for "regular" jobs. To avoid this unwanted effect, subsidised jobs of this kind are generally part-time.

Lessons from empirical studies

The interaction of the different factors mentioned in the preceding paragraph, in addition to the fact that not all the differences between beneficiaries and non beneficiaries are controlled, makes it particularly difficult to interpret many empirical studies. But we can nevertheless try to draw several lessons from European studies.

Relatively disappointing results for subsidised jobs in the non-market sector

As we have seen, France is the country that has most extensively developed subsidised jobs for young people in the non-market sector. However, the results of evaluations of this type of programme tend to be relatively negative, for the employability of participants does not seem to improve and sometimes even seems to deteriorate. According to Bonnal, Fougère and Sérandon (1994, 1995, 1997), young people with a diploma lower than the Baccalaureate (*i.e.* the equivalent of the high school level) who participate in a TUC (*cf.* Table 1) are less likely to find a job with an indefinite-term contract, have shorter tenure in this job and, particularly in the case of young women, are paid lower wages. According to Balsan, Hanchane and Werquin (1994*a* and *b*), young people who participate in a TUC or CES, compared with non-participants hired directly, undergo a loss in earnings greater than what they would have foregone by remaining unemployed or inactive before finding a job, whether they are men or women. Results in terms of employment rates are also negative, for in December 1991, the rate of "regular" employment

Table 1. **Main employment promotion measures for young people**

1. Subsidised jobs in the market sector ("pure subsidies")

France

Plan d'urgence pour les jeunes (1986-87)	Beneficiaries: young people under 25; reduction of employer's social security contributions (50% for a young person exiting another employment policy measure, 25% for others).
Exo-jeunes (1991-94)	Beneficiaries: young people under 25 without qualifications; reduction of employer's social security contributions (100% for one year, 50% for the next six months, up to 120% of the statutory minimum wage (SMIC).
Aide au premier emploi des jeunes, APEJ (1994-96)	Beneficiaries: all young people who have never held a job entitling them to unemployment compensation, whatever their level of qualifications; the employer is paid FRF 1 000 per month for the first nine months of the job.

United Kingdom

Young worker scheme, YWS (1982-86)	Beneficiaries: school leavers under 18; a subsidy of GBP 15 per week paid to the employer for a job paid less than GBP 40 per week (GBP 7.50 for a job paid between GBP 40 and GBP 45).
New workers scheme (1986-88)	Beneficiaries: young people under 20; a subsidy of GBP 15 per week paid to the employer for a job paid less than GBP 55.

Spain

Contratos temporales de fomento del empleo (1985-94)	Even though they are not reserved exclusively for young people, these contracts have been frequently used to hire young people; the advantage for the employer is their highly flexible nature (six months, renewable for up to three years).
Contratos permanentes de fomento del empleo (1985-88)	Beneficiaries: young people under 26 hired on an indefinite-term contract; the employer receives a lump sum equivalent to approximately half of the young person's average annual salary.

Sweden

Recruitment grant	Payment of 50% of the salary for the first six months for hiring an unemployed person (not limited to young people).

2. Temporary subsidised jobs in the non-market sector

France

Travaux d'utilité collective, TUC (1984-90)	Beneficiaries: young people aged 16 to 21, or up to 26 if they have been unemployed for over a year; "trainee" status: less social protection, low pay, 30% of salary paid by central government; maximum duration: one year, except in exceptional cases; TUCs are limited to the non-market sector.
Contrats emplois-solidarité, CES (1990-)	Replaced TUCs; extended to other groups in difficulty (in particular the long-term unemployed); half-time work contract, paid at an hourly rate based on the SMIC; maximum duration: one year, except in exceptional cases; CES are limited to the non-market sector.
Emplois-jeunes (1998-)	Beneficiaries: young people up to the age of 26 (or 30 for those not entitled to unemployment compensation); wages according to industry-wide collective bargaining agreements; duration = no more than five years; these jobs, in the non-market sector, must correspond to "new services" not existing on the "regular" market.

Sweden

Relief works (1933-)	Not limited exclusively to young people (and, until 1984, not limited only to the non-market sector); the central government pays between 50 and 80% of the salary for six months; as from 1992, young people under 25 are no longer eligible.
Youth jobs (1982-)	Beneficiaries: aged 16-17; jobs not limited to the non-market sector, fully subsidised; the employer receives a subsidy and the young person an allowance.
Youth teams (1984-89)	Beneficiaries: unemployed aged 18-19; "guarantee" of 100% subsidised work in the public sector four hours a day; measure replaced in 1989 by *Job Introduction Opportunities* (also in the market sector).

3. Subsidised contracts with training ("mixed subsidies")

France

Contrat d'apprentissage

Beneficiaries: young people aged 15 to 25; training both inside (mentoring) and outside firms (training centres); the employer receives a partial exemption from social security contributions, and, since 1993 tax credit and a lump-sum at recruitment (since abolished); young people are paid under the SMIC, according to their age; duration: up to three years.

Contrat de qualification, CQ (1984-)

Beneficiaries: young people aged 16 to 25; training both inside (mentoring) and outside firms (training centres); the employer receives a partial exemption from social security contributions, a training subsidy (FRF 60 per hour), and since 1993, a lump-sum at recruitment (since abolished); young people are paid under the SMIC, according to their age and tenure; maximum duration: two years.

Contrat d'adaptation, CA (1984-)

Beneficiaries: young people aged 15 to 25; in-firm training; the employer receives a partial exemption from social security contributions, a training subsidy, and since 1993, a lump-sum at recruitment (since abolished); young people are paid at least the SMIC, or at least 80% of the contractual wage corresponding to their qualifications; maximum duration: one year.

Spain

Contrato de aprendizaje-formacion

Its conditions have changed over time (recently: in 1994 and again in 1997); it is currently for young people under 21 with no diplomas; in exchange for providing effective training, employers receive a significant reduction in social insurance costs; young people are paid at least the statutory minimum wage.

Contrato de practicas (1981-)

For young people under 29; graduates who have been out of the education system for a maximum of two years; entitles employers to a significant reduction in social insurance costs for a maximum of two years.

4. "Training schemes" comparable to forms of subsidised employment

France

Stage d'initiation à la vie professionnelle, SIVP

Beneficiaries: young people aged 16-25, without job experience; very low pay (under the minimum wage), in exchange for "on-the-job" training; duration: between three and six months.

United Kingdom
Youth training scheme, YTS (1983-90), Youth training (1990-)

In-firm training schemes, supervised by employers, paid by the central government, in exchange for training "on-the-job" and outside the firm (13 weeks in some YTS); the trainee receives an allowance (approximately GBP 26 per week at the beginning of the 1980s).

Sweden
Youth practice (1992-95)

Beneficiaries: young unemployed people aged 18 to 25; are paid by the central government at less than the contractual rate; as from 1994, employers must pay a lump sum of SEK 1 000 to the central government (it is less than 10% of the cost of an unskilled employee); in 1995, this measure was replaced by the Work Place Introduction scheme, which is open to all unemployed persons over 20.

(*i.e.* not including "subsidised" employment) of young people who exited the education system in 1989 and participated in a CES in 1990, at a given education level, was lower, *whatever this level*, than that of the cohort as a whole (Aucouturier and Gélot, 1994); conversely, their unemployment rate was higher. What is more, the participants with the highest education levels had the highest negative employment rate differentials. All things considered, in the French case stigmatisation and lock-in effects and perhaps even loss of human capital seem to be at work (particularly for those with the highest education levels). However, it should be emphasised that these studies do not control the unobserved differences adequately, if at all, and that many important characteristics (such as the subject area of the diploma) are not taken into account in the data used. Consequently, it seems safe to assume that some of these results are explained by the fact that temporary jobs in the non-market sector are held, as we have seen, by the least "employable" young people, the observed characteristics being equal.

The findings are not as negative in the case of the Swedish Relief Works scheme. Thus, by following a sample group of 800 young people in the mid-1980s, Edin and Holmlund (1991) showed that participants had a lower short-term employment rate after exiting this programme than those who had remained unemployed, but that in the longer term their employment rate was higher. The authors argue that these results tend to show that although the Relief Works scheme has a lock-in effect in the short term (by reducing job-search intensity), it has helped to increase human capital, or at least to prevent it from deteriorating due to unemployment.

Mixed results for subsidised jobs in the market sector

We shall also discuss the findings of French studies, which deal with different types of measures. It seems that measures such as SIVPs (see Table 1) – which are short-term, very poorly paid, fail to provide training and are massively used by firms with a high proportion of low-skilled labour and a high turnover rate – do not have a positive impact on the employability of young people (some studies even show that, as in the case of subsidised non-market sector jobs, there is a loss of wage, compared with those who remained unemployed). On the other hand, "mixed subsidy" measures (in particular alternating classroom-workplace training, and CQ and CA in particular, see Table 1) seem to have a positive impact on the employment rate, as well as on the duration of employment (Bonnal, Fougère and Sérandon, 1994, 1995, 1997; Sollogoub, 1993). However, the results of these measures are more mixed with regard to young people's wages after they exit programmes, compared to the wages of young people recruited directly in a regular job, since some studies show a negative impact (Balsan *et al.*, 1994*a* and *b*; Sollogoub, *op. cit.*). Three explanations can be put forward for that which may seem paradoxical: that programmes simultaneously have a positive effect on employment and a negative effect on wages (Gautié, 1996):

– The segmentation of the labour market, for it is mainly small firms, paying lower salaries, that use these programmes and subsequently hire the participants; in this way, according to Werquin "participation in programmes reinforces the barriers to entry in the best jobs".

– There may be a downward adjustment of the reservation wage, but this has not been proven.

– Lastly, the unobserved differences (here again, poorly controlled) between participants and non-participants may play an important role.

Impact of programmes on the trajectories of non-beneficiaries

Little research has been done into the effects of programmes on the "employability" in the broad sense (as measured by employment and wage variables) of non-beneficiaries, *i.e.* of all the labour force, including those in the target group, who do not participate in the programmes.

Some negative effects are well known. The first is *substitution* between beneficiaries and non-beneficiaries – we shall come back to this point in the third part. But another adverse effect can result from the fact that, by targeting a measure according to a characteristic that is readily identifiable by employers (age, level of qualification, nationality, duration of unemployment, etc.), all the individuals who have that characteristic are *stigmatised* regardless of whether they are participating in the programme or not. The fact that they are targeted by special programmes implies that they are less employable.

The possible positive impact for non-beneficiaries is less often mentioned. Thus, if some young people get temporary public-sector jobs, the probability of other young people also finding jobs can increase – the mirror image, so to speak, of the crowding-out effect. A mirror image of the stigmatisation effect mentioned earlier is also possible: the fact that some employers hire individuals from a target group that they would not have hired otherwise, may prompt them to revise their opinion of the group, and product a lasting change in their hiring practices even after the scheme has ceased to exist. These schemes thus give employers an opportunity to "try out" workers and overcome any reservations they might have, stemming from lack of knowledge of the real productivity of the various labour categories (which can also stem from prejudice), or conversely, from a wrong assessment of the actual skills required for the jobs.

The French survey carried out by Gélot *et al.* (1993) of employers using subsidised youth employment schemes showed that while a third of the users of *contrats de qualification* (CQ – see Table 1) would have hired an older worker if the scheme had not existed, only 23% of them would envisage doing so for a future hiring (compared with respectively 19% and 14% for the Exo-Jeunes contracts – see Table 1). This apparent scaling-down of firms' requirements is also be found with the level of skills required, since the authors note, "these *programmes, which have prompted some firms to modify their hiring practices, in order to better adapt to the real characteristics of the jobs*".

3. Impact of programmes on the labour market

The previous section was devoted to the impact of programmes on youth employability. We shall now turn to the impact on the labour market. We shall try to determine the *net* effects of programmes on the employment and unemployment of young people, but also on the other categories in the labour market (adults). It is necessary to outline the theoretical framework for studying these effects before analysing the contribution of empirical studies on the subject.

Theoretical analysis of the various potential effects

An analytical framework

We can use the theoretical framework proposed by Calmfors (1994), which is itself based on a wage-setting/employment model (see Box 2) derived from Layard *et al.* (1991).

Calmfors *op. cit.* proposes to modify the initial theoretical framework by distinguishing normal or regular employment from employment policy schemes. It is thus necessary to think in terms of the normal employment rate (n'), the rate of participation in programmes[22] (r) merely shifting the vertical curve of the full employment rate to the left (Figure 3). This participation rate thus defines the *gross effect* of employment policy: if there were no other induced effects, open unemployment would fall by exactly the gross number of beneficiaries (from U0 to U1 where U1 = U0 - r). The net effects of employment policy will depend in particular on its repercussions on the two curves redefined accordingly, which we shall now examine.

Dead-weight loss and substitution effects

Total net job creation, corresponding to a certain number of subsidised jobs, is equal to the gross number of "non-regular" jobs less the possible loss of "regular" jobs resulting from subsidised programmes. At the level of the firms taking part in the programmes, the loss can result from a pure dead-weight loss effect (the firm would have created the job anyway and would have filled it with somebody with the same profile as the beneficiary) or a substitution effect (the firm would have created the job but because the programme existed filled it with somebody with a profile different from that of the person they would have otherwise hired, for example, a young person instead of an adult). In both cases, subsidised jobs

Box 2. **The wage-setting/employment curve**

The wage-setting/employment model is shown in Figure 2.

Figure 2.

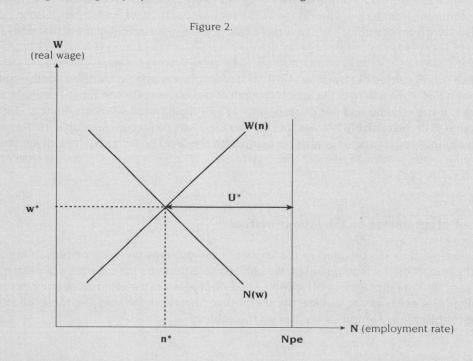

Let n be the *employment rate* (defined here as the share of employment in the labour force[23] – if Npe denotes the full employment rate, we get simply Npe = 100 %. Let w be the real wage. A given participation rate is assumed.

N(w), which denotes the employment curve, decreases with the wage. W(n) is the wage curve. The positive correlation between the wage and the employment rate can have several theoretical foundations. In terms of wage bargaining, the higher the employment rate, the more employees are in a stronger position to negotiate higher wages, if only because of the greater opportunities of finding another job in the event of redundancy. But efficiency wage considerations can also enter into the equation. When the unemployment rate is low, the loss of utility resulting from a redundancy is small, and enterprises thus have an incentive to pay higher wages to motivate their workers (Shapiro and Stiglitz, 1984). At the same time, high wages also reduce labour turnover – which is all the higher in that job opportunities are more plentiful outside (Salop, 1979) – and attract good workers (Weiss, 1980). Competition between firms increases when unemployment rate is low.

replace regular jobs. As result, the employment curve shifts to the left [from N(w) to N'(w), see Figure 4]. It may be noted that dead-weight effect can also arise with subsidised non-market jobs. In the case of local authorities (for example, communes), it is thus possible to talk of fiscal substitution in the sense that central government funds replace expenditure by the local authorities.

If r is the participation rate for subsidised jobs, and a and s the share of these jobs in the labour force corresponding respectively to the dead-weight loss and substitution effects, then the net job creation in percentage of the labour force is equal to $r - (a + s)$. It is also equal to the reduction in equilibrium unemployment (for an unchanged labour force) U0 - U1 (U0 denoting the initial unemployment rate and U1 the unemployment rate after the implementation of the programme).

Figure 3

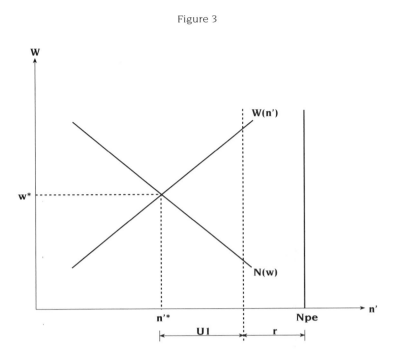

Crowding-out and displacement effects

A firm can take advantage of a subsidised job to lower its prices and win market share from its competitors, who will themselves be obliged to cut jobs (*crowding out*). The curve of regular employment N(w)[24] thus shifts to the left. Crowding-out can also take place in the labour market via a wage increase. Employment policy schemes can increase pressure on wages, more precisely, by shifting the wage curve W(n) to the left [for example from W(n) to W'(n), see Figure 5] – *i.e.* a *displacement effect*. However, it is certain that this displacement effect is of little importance for programmes targeted at young people (and especially the less qualified).[25]

Figure 4

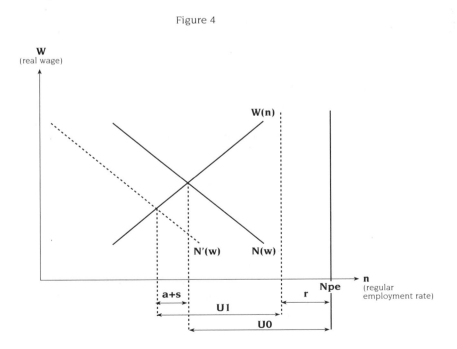

All told, if c denotes the share in the labour force of regular jobs that have been crowded out, and d that of displaced regular jobs, the net effect is equal to $r - (c + d)$, the reduction in unemployment falling to U0 - U1 (Figure 5).

Figure 5

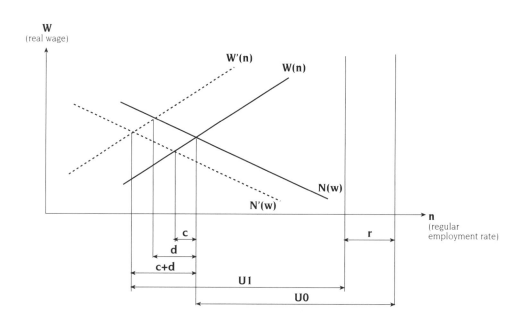

The effect on the labour force

A final effect that will reduce the impact of programmes on unemployment stems from the fact that any job creation causes a positive variation in the participation rate, other things being equal. This increase in the labour force can be represented graphically by a shift in the vertical axis from nr to nf (Figure 6), the gross "new worker" effect being equal to $r - f$, r being the share of beneficiaries in the initial labour force, and f the share of new workers "drawn" into the labour force as a proportion of the initial level of the latter. This increase in the labour supply increases competition on the labour market,[26] and should thus cause the wage curve W(n) to shift to the right, resulting in job creation of the amount g, as a proportion of the initial labour force. This effect is however probably smaller for programmes targeted at unskilled youth, whose wages exhibit downward rigidity (due, for example, to the existence of a minimum wage or collective wage agreement). All told, the loss of impact resulting from the increase in the labour force is equal to $f - g$, the unemployment rate moving from U0 to U1, without it being possible to determine *a priori* whether it is an increase or a decrease, even though the first hypothesis is more likely, while the rightward shift of W(n) ought to remain relatively moderate (one should thus have $f > g$).

The contribution of empirical studies

Evaluation of dead-weight loss and substitution effects

The dead-weight loss and substitution effects of subsidised jobs in the market sector have been studied the most. They are calculated at the microeconomic level of user firms, in percentage of the number of beneficiaries[27] – *i.e.* a' and s' (it means that the net employment creation corresponding to one hundred subsidised jobs is: 100-a'-s'). The first method is based on an econometric estimate.

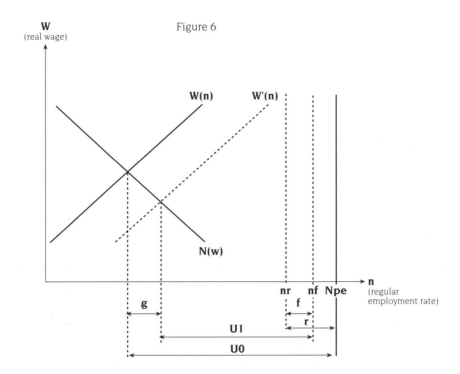

Figure 6

Bishop and Montgomery (1993), using firms panel data studied the effects of *Targeted Jobs Tax Credit* on youth and adult employment, using two equations. The first equation regresses the relative change in total employment in year t with respect to the number of subsidised hirings in t and t-1, and a large number of control variables (20 all told). Among the latter are cyclical variables (firms' demand in t, expected demand, etc.), labour turnover variables (hiring and exit rates in t-1), and a number of various characteristics (size, average wage, proportion of part-time workers, proportion of unionised workers, etc.). The second equation regresses the change in the share of young people in the total number of employees, with respect to the same variables, to which is added the share of young people in t-1 and t-2. According to their findings, the coefficient of net job creation (1-a'-s') lies between 0.13 and 0.3, the dead-weight loss is at least 70%, but the substitution effect between youths and adults is, in contrast, very small (on the most favourable estimates, adult employment would even increase slightly).

This type of estimate requires fairly detailed data; in addition, there is the difficulty of checking for simultaneity bias (*i.e.* perhaps it is when firms are taking on workers that they make the most use of subsidies). In Europe, estimates of dead-weight loss and substitution effects are usually based on the findings of surveys of firms using job subsidies. Although not all the findings point in the same direction, it seems possible to draw two lessons:

– On average, the losses (a' + s') are large (often 70% or over) regardless of the type of programme) (Gélot *et al.*, 1993) for the CQ and Exo-Jeune in France; Rajan (1985) for the YWS in the United Kingdom) (for which a' = 80% and s' = 4%); better results were obtained in Sweden for the Relief Work and Recruitment Grants since the figure for the same effects was only 40%, of which only 20% for the pure dead-weight loss effect (a') (Schröder, 1997); however, the losses seem smaller for "mixed subsidies" (Gélot *et al.*, *op. cit.*; Van der Linden, 1997 for Belgium).

– The losses rise with the size of the firm. According to Rajan, for example, in the case of the British YWS, in firms with fewer than 10 employees, a' = 32% and s' = 10%, while in those with over 500 employees, a' is over 85%, and s' = 2%. Gélot *et al.* (1993) confirms this increasing relationship. It may therefore be assumed that large firms draw up their hiring plans independently of the subsidies available, and it is only afterwards that they try to obtain subsidies, all the more in that it is easier for them to recoup the fixed cost of information and administrative formalities. On the latter point, in the case of the TJTC in the United States, see Bishop and Kang (1991).

These findings call for two remarks.

– There is a problem of reliability with the survey-based method. Often the questions asked are not sufficiently precise to allow the answers to be used for quantified estimates – for example, when firms are asked if they have hired somebody "older" or "more qualified – without specifying the age bracket or the level of diploma. But especially, firms' answers have to be treated with caution, due to the possibility of mistakes or manipulation of the data.

– It is generally considered that the losses are high, and this is thus an argument against subsidies. A priori, it is not surprising that the net effect of subsidised programmes in terms of job creation is modest: the effect of the modification of the cost of labour is only short-term and will thus affect (as noted above) only firms that need to offset temporarily the cost of training young workers or those that offer low-skilled jobs with low turnover costs (on this point, see Bishop and Kang, op. cit.). But to be rigorous, it is necessary to measure the number of net creations (1-a'-s') and substitutions (s') within the framework of the microeconomic analysis of the demand for labour, in terms of elasticities with respect to the reduction in the cost of labour corresponding to the subsidy. For example, if the losses (a'+s') on a subsidy reducing the cost of labour of a young person by 10% is around 90% (i.e. a net job creation of 10%), the corresponding elasticity is of the order of (-1), which is fairly large is for a short-term adjustment in employment compared with the long-term elasticities given in Hamermesh (1993).[28]

To conclude, it may be pointed out that the evaluation of the fiscal substitution resulting from job subsidies in the non-market sector is especially tricky. It may be assumed that, in most European countries, this type of substitution is not widespread given that the unions, which are particularly powerful in public administration, are quick to detect it.

Evaluation of crowding-out and displacement effects

While the framework outlined is used as a reference theoretical framework, it has hardly been used to estimate structural models that would allow the various potential effects to be differentiated. Thus, in most studies, it is the overall impact on regular employment and/or youth unemployment that has been estimated, without it being possible to distinguish clearly between the dead-weight loss (a'), the substitution effect (s'), the crowding-out effect (c') and the displacement effect (d') (and possibly the effect on the labour force) as defined above;[29] we shall thus use the term "overall loss". This kind of estimate has been done particularly in Sweden.

Skedinger (1995) estimated, using a VAR model on quarterly data, the effects on youth employment (18-24-year-olds) of the Swedish employment programmes implemented during the period 1970-1991. He found that the overall loss was over 100% for the first quarter. However, using the same data and a reformulated VAR model, Holmlund (1995) estimated the overall loss to be rather around 40% in the short term. Forslund (1996), on the basis of a panel of Swedish communes, estimated that the overall loss on youth employment programmes during the period 1990-1994 was around 95% in the short term and about 75% in the long term. Edin, Forslund and Holmlund (1998), using the same data, also highlighted the large losses: they estimated that about half of the steep fall in the youth regular employment rate between 1990 and 1994 (-28.7 percentage points of their sample of municipalities) was attributable to youth employment programmes. Calmfors and Skedinger (1995), exploiting pooled time series and cross section data from Swedish regions find that youth open unemployment would fall only by 0.1-0.4 percentage points when participation in job creations schemes increases by one percentage point.

All told, it would seem that one can agree with Calmfors and Skedinger, op. cit. that *"the evidence that targeting on young people has favourable employment effects is weak"*. However, while the findings of empirical studies seem to show fairly large overall losses, they do not make it possible to compare net job creations, even if they are small, and the cost of the measure, in order, for example, to give an idea of the cost of the reduction of unemployment obtained. Furthermore, in this type of study, the programmes are treated as black boxes: the links between the relative size of the losses and the nature of the programmes, the conditions in which they are implemented, etc. are not analysed, making it difficult to draw lessons for employment policy implementation.

For want of being able to calibrate a WS/PS general equilibrium model (see Box 2), some studies have used macroeconometric models to evaluate the impact of programmes on employment and unemployment, but also on GDP and the general government balance (Eyssartier and Gautié, 1996; Chouvel *et al.*, 1997). The usefulness of this type of study is to estimate the overall impact on employment, but the specific impact on youth situation depend on various assumptions made at each stage of the estimate.[30]

Evaluation of the new worker effect

The number of youths who enter the labour force as a result of the implementation of employment programmes (f, as a percentage of the initial young labour force, see "Theoretical analysis of the various potential effects", p. 401) can be estimated specifically. It may be assumed that f rises with the number of beneficiaries of programmes (r, as a percentage of the young labour force), and is also a function of the beneficiaries' remuneration. It is also necessary to relate f to other variables (characteristics of programmes other than remuneration, beneficiaries' level of education, etc.). Unfortunately, no studies have been done of these aspects. In France, the rare empirical work that has been done shows that, for 10 beneficiaries of employment promotion programmes, two to three youths enter the labour force (Chouvel *et al.*, 1997). We do not know of any similar studies in other countries.

4. What lessons can be drawn for youth employment policies?

Although the studies we have reviewed are not very numerous and leave a large number of points untouched, we can try to draw a few lessons, firstly regarding subsidies in the market sector, then subsidised jobs in the non-market sector, before concluding with a few more general remarks.

Promoting employment in the market sector

The relatively disappointing results of "pure" subsidies

The effectiveness of subsidies unaccompanied by training seems to have been relatively limited, especially when they are of short duration and broadly-targeted (see the experience of the SIVP in France). US and European studies tend to show that they do not have a lasting effect on the beneficiaries' "employability" in the broad sense (as measured by the wage and/or employment rate after the implementation of the programme). Furthermore, the risks of stigmatisation are high given that – especially in the European context – they accelerate the turnover in unskilled jobs, which can send out a negative signal to job markets in which job shopping is traditionally fairly limited. In terms of net job creation, the impact of this type of measure also seems to be relatively small, the overall loss effect probably being high. A massive dead-weight loss effect may be suspected in the case of large firms. The net job creation is perhaps larger in the case of small firms, but the fact that the financial incentive is limited in time may increase labour turnover,[31] subsidies may thus lock young people into insecure, poorly-paid jobs with no career prospects, and youths may eventually become discouraged and withdraw from the labour market.[32]

It should also be pointed out that a temporary subsidy cannot replace a lasting adjustment in labour costs when there is a structural problem of labour costs that are too high (due, for example, to a statutory minimum wage or a collectively-set wage).

Generally speaking, it seems very difficult to alter firms' selection procedures by a mere financial incentive. Perhaps it is mistaken to try and force the least employable young people into firms at any price: rather, they need a half-way house in the form of appropriate training and/or a subsidised job in the non-market sector. Perhaps a subsidy can have a positive, lasting effect for young people who are objectively employable but who have to overcome employers' prejudices. The role of the subsidy would thus be to give employers a chance to try them out and revise their preconceptions about them. But the financial incentive needs to be sufficiently large to overcome their preconceptions, which may even be reinforced by the stigmatising aspect of the programme. In other terms, large subsidies targeted at young persons who though unskilled have a certain degree of employability, may be effective.

Subsidies associated with training

The most effective programmes, both in terms of the impact on the employability of the beneficiaries and net job creation, seem to be "mixed subsidies" combining a financial advantage for the employer with training for the young person. In this case, a public subsidy can also be justified by the fact that the training does not only benefit the firm and the young person but society at large as well, due to the positive externalities that stem from the accumulation of human capital. Experience shows that it is very difficult to implement this type of measure, and that its success depends not only on the subsidy being well-designed by the authorities from the outset but also (and perhaps especially) on the involvement of employers and unions. There is a big risk that programmes will end up (as shown by the experience of the SIVP in France, the YTS in the UK, and Youth Practice in Sweden), being used by firms merely as a means of obtaining cheap labour, with all the attendant problems mentioned in the previous paragraph. It is the German apprenticeship system that can serve as model, even if it cannot be transferred intact to different national contexts. Trade union oversight of these schemes should ensure that; 1) the training is effective and leads to explicit recognition of the training received, both in and outside the workplace; 2) and that it is not used simply to replace adult workers by young workers. The German apprenticeship system was traditionally based on the family (the apprentice was dependent on his parents), which could also justify the low pay the apprentices received. But in the contemporary context (families that have split up, unemployed parents, the temptation to resort to illegal sources of income), there is also the problem of getting the young person to join a scheme (beyond the medium-term prospect of acquiring a qualification). The subsidy should thus also cover part of the cost of the remuneration so as to encourage youngsters to enrol on a scheme.

Temporary public sector jobs

Since the 1980s, temporary public sector jobs have been on the decline in OECD countries. However, the experience of the past 20 years shows that the track record of such jobs is less negative than one might think at first sight.

How to avoid the distorting effects?

Admittedly, these types of programmes potentially have a lot of negative effects. The studies done of them suggest that, in the case of France for example, they merely serve to occupy people (with the added advantage of reducing the unemployment figures in the short term), that they do not make the beneficiaries more employable and that they can even make them less so (as compared with if they had remained unemployed) because of the loss of human capital and the attached stigma, and by locking them into in low-grade jobs. It has been pointed out that these negative findings are probably partly due to the fact that the heterogeneity of the sample was not controlled. But similar evaluations in other pays (except for Sweden) tend to show that the lasting effects are small or non-existent (see, for example, the experience of Supported Work Demonstration in the United States, US Department of Labor, 1995).

To ensure that these "side tracks" do not become "dead ends" (to use the expression of Nicaise *et al.*, 1994), it seems necessary to provide more than a mere "occupation", all the more in that these kinds of programmes tend to attract those young people who are in the most difficulty and who cannot find a job directly in the market sector, even a subsidised one. It is necessary to provide both training and assistance with finding a job.[33] The experience of the *Youth Employment Strategies Demonstration* in the United States, for example, shows that combining work experience in the non-market sector with class-room training can have a positive effect on the beneficiaries (US Department of Labor, 1995). However, French experience shows that class-room training combined with a temporary public sector job may be unsuited to the needs of the beneficiaries.[34] Ideally, therefore, the work experience itself should provide training, though this requires that the job in question be clearly defined and that trainees have a mentor to look after them. In addition, the skills acquired during such work should be recognised by some form of official certificate.[35]

There is thus a potential conflict between the two objectives of this type of scheme, as Schmid noted a long time ago (1982): for a given cost, to achieve 1) the maximum impact on unemployment, and 2) a lasting improvement in the employability of the participants. The dilemma does not arise solely from the fact that the authorities may be more concerned with achieving a short-term reduction in unemployment, and with quantity rather than with quality. Often, in the non-profit sector rather than in the government sector in the strict sense, the jobs that provide the best training are those that are the most similar to jobs in the regular labour market, so the risks of crowding-out are all the greater. It is probably for this reason that commercial businesses that have been directly subsidised to operate with hard-to-place workers have not had much success.[36]

Following Nicaise *et al.* (1994, p. 13), several types of such enterprises can be distinguished: 1) "work experience initiatives" offering a temporary job often combined with on-the-job training, with a view to transferring the worker to the regular labour market in the medium run (for example, the *entreprises d'insertion* and *associations intermédiaires* in France); 2) the "social co-operatives" (Germany, Italy) functioning on a quasi-commercial basis, with the aim to create new and permanent jobs in a "niche" of the market; 3) "social workshops" (Netherlands, Belgium, Germany), that work on a non-profit basis, offering permanent subsidised jobs to the least "employable" job seekers.

Actually, subsidies should meet the condition of "additionality", *i.e.* subsidised jobs in the non-market sector should be added to existing jobs on the market, and not compete with them. In order not to lock people into completely unproductive jobs – which this condition may imply in some circumstances[37] – it is necessary to invent new activities which are not yet satisfied by the market but which meet a latent social demand (Schmid, *op. cit.*): this was the objective of the ABM in Germany, which were not aimed, at least initially, at young people, and it is the stated objective of the *Emplois Jeunes* recently introduced in France – see Table 1).

Which public?

From the foregoing remarks (see also subsection "Promoting employment in the market sector", p. 407), it would seem that temporary public sector jobs should be reserved to young people who are not sufficiently employable to find a job (even subsidised) in the "normal" or "regular" labour market. The purpose of such jobs should be to complement subsidised jobs in the market sector. However, two arguments have been put forward for extending this type of scheme to more employable young people: 1) if such jobs do actually correspond to innovative activities, they will require a minimum amount of general education and people skills, which rules out those young people who are the most desocialised; 2) in a context of job shortage in the regular job market, where even relatively skilled young people are hit by unemployment, this type of job creation can have beneficial effects, especially in the most disadvantaged districts; it is necessary to hold out the prospect of a job to the young people in these districts who have made the personal investment in training, thus attesting their resolve to become integrated members of society; to relegate them to unemployment would be to send a negative message to other young people, who would draw the conclusion that it was pointless to embark on training, and would be tempted to become delinquents;[38] these temporary public sector jobs should also be sufficiently well-paid to ensure that they are not devalued.[39] However, this strategy needs to steer between two dangers: first, in transforming itself into a sort of "employer of last resort", the state must not fail to give priority to implementing the necessary reforms and job creation policies in the regular market. Second, there is the danger that some young people will be locked into a "second" labour market (a danger that is all the greater when the jobs last a long time, like the *Emplois Jeunes* in France[40]).

Concluding remarks

From this overview of youth employment programmes, it would seem that the prerequisites for effective programmes are relatively few.

– A certain amount of complementarily is needed between the various programmes, according to the public they are aimed at; in this area too, there is no one-fits-all model. Likewise, the process of getting young people into jobs can be in several stages: some public sector jobs could be reserved to those are who the least employable in order to give them a first work experience (in an appropriate form: mentoring, additional training tailored to the individual's needs, etc.). Subsidies in the market sector could be reserved first and foremost to young victims of discrimination (*i.e.* of unwarranted prejudice as to their employability). Some temporary public sector jobs could be also be reserved to more qualified young people from disadvantaged areas in order to avoid the adverse spill-over effects on other youth that could result from their being unemployed. It is also important not to have too many programmes and not to be continually changing them,[41] because it confuses both young people and other actors (firms, associations and administrations, local employment officers). The ideal solution is thus to have a limited number of long-term initiatives.

– A lasting impact on the employability of the beneficiaries can be achieved only by providing more than a mere job, whether within the framework of subsidies to the market sector (obligation to provide effective training in return for subsidies) or in the non-market sector (need to provide training and help with job search). This entails a relatively costly outlay by the authorities. Small financial incentives provided without anything in return would merely constitute a massive windfall for firms but would not really change their hiring practices. Similarly, low-grade temporary jobs in the public sector created on a large-scale would have only a cosmetic effect on youth unemployment and could eventually turn young people against them.

The recommendations, – inevitably too general – which follow from this kind of survey, have to address two problems which to a large degree are still unresolved:

– It is crucial to target young people according to their degree of employability and the benefit that they can derive from the programme. This is not easy to do. It is unlikely that automatic *"profiling"* can completely replace the expertise of the local employment officer because – and perhaps increasingly – the individual's personal history can be as important as statistically identifiable characteristics.

– Often, it is not so much the way the programme is designed as the way it is implemented that explains its success or failure. The crucial factors are thus those that usually form the "black box" in quantified estimates; such estimates seek to determine the average impact of a programme, at best giving the variance according to the areas where it is implemented, whereas the most important thing is precisely to understand why a given result was obtained in a given context; as in other areas, in the area of youth employment programmes this question often remains unanswered.

Lastly, it should be reiterated that employment policy, no matter how active, cannot replace the reforms that are needed in the labour market, nor dynamic macroeconomics policies, since, as was pointed out in the first part of this paper, a large part of youth unemployment in Europe stems primarily from the overall shortage of employment. It is because this condition has not been respected that active employment policies for young people seem to have been given an impossible assignment in some European countries.

NOTES

1. However, some countries have developed measures of this kind specifically for young people, for example, the Departmental Funds for Youth Initiative (*Fonds Départementaux pour l'Initiative des Jeunes*), implemented in France between 1985 and 1993. Under this programme, between FRF 10 000 and 30 000 of aid was granted and entrepreneurs were entitled to receive low-cost advice (legal, financial, etc.). The impact of the programme was marginal, and it was later extended to other age groups and finally merged into a broader system of aid to entrepreneurship. More recently in Sweden (1995), the Youth Start Projects were introduced, which are pilot projects aimed at helping low-skilled young people under 20 find a job or start their own business. This project is based on close co-operation between the services of the central government and municipalities, and involves non-profit organisations. It is still too soon to evaluate this programme's effectiveness..

2. In France, in every year since 1986 at least 15 % of the jobs held by young people aged between 16-25 have been supported by some form of government subsidy ("subsidised jobs", cf. the description of programmes above). In 1996, the rate was nearly 35 %.

3. Since 1992, over 12 % of the Swedish labour force between the ages of 18-24 have participated in employment policy measures each year (17 % in 1993 and 18 % in 1994); most of these measures are employment promotion programmes (Schröder, 1997).

4. If the past 20 years are considered, Germany has only begun to use measures promoting youth employment quite recently, and primarily in the Länder of former East Germany.

5. This policy, which was initially aimed at equalising wages for a given level and type of job ("equal wages for equal work"), has subsequently, especially in the 1960s and 1970s, sought to reduce the relative wage gaps between the various skill levels.

6. For example, while the total number of employed rose by 2.9 % between 1983 and 1993, the number of employed aged between 16-24 and 50-59 fell by 30.1 % and 8.4 % respectively. The drop in the number of employed between the ages of 16-24 during this period was: -85.2 % in the energy sector, -66.5 % in capital goods, -62.5 % in consumer goods and -49.2 % in the banking sector (Gautié, 1997).

7. It is worth pointing out that in Sweden, ALMPs for young people were an important component of the youth transition system even before the emergence of mass unemployment in the early 1990s (Schober-Brinkmann and Wadensjö, 1991; Bourdet and Persson, 1994).

8. It can also be mentioned that in the 1990s the Netherlands introduced temporary public jobs in municipalities, associations and certain private firms for school-leavers aged under 23 as part of the *Jeugwerkgarantieplan*.

9. For example, in Sweden in the mid-1990s, 80 % of young unemployed people had an education level above the compulsory level; during the 1980s, *i.e.* even before the appearance of mass unemployment, as Schröder (1997) pointed out: "the relative insignificance of a "hard core" youth unemployment was also demonstrated in a study of the composition of youth unemployment [...]. At that time, only 10 % of unemployed youth registered with the Employment Services could be defined as being excluded from the labour market" (p. 9).

10. Lefresne (1994), for example, classifies YTS and YT as employment subsidy schemes in the broad sense. As Meager (1997) – following Dolton (1993) – points out: "There is a major question about the criteria against which the success or otherwise of YT and similar training schemes should be judged: 1) should they be judged on their impact on the subsequent employment chances and earnings capacity of participants? [...] 2) should they be judged in terms of their longer-term effects on human capital [...] ? 3) or should they be evaluated in terms of their wider social impact, and the extent to which they keep low skilled and disadvantaged young people out of unemployment [...] ?" (p. 79).

11. See Davia Rodriguez and Hernanz Martin (1998).

12. See Schröder (1997).

13. See Lefresne (1994); Balchin and Ashton (1994). We shall not take into account here the subsidised jobs under the New Deal for young people implemented since 1998. Nor shall we mention the Community Programmes from which many young people benefited at the beginning of the 1980s, since young people have been first and foremost been referred to YTS after they were created (1983).

14. The fact that since the 1980s evaluations are increasingly made by firms of professional evaluators is an aspect of this standardisation. This has not only had positive effects, since, as Manski and Garfinkel (1992) point out: "evaluation today is dominated by tightly focused applications with short horizons [...]. It discourages innovation in methods, efforts to understand the complex sets of processes that define a program, evaluation of long-term program impacts, and creative thinking about program design" (p. 20, cited by Perez, 1998, p. 120). In Europe, the standardisation process is less advanced, and a number of actors are involved in evaluation: government itself, academics, consultancy firms, each with different methods and viewpoints.

15. It is worth noting that US studies on employment subsidies also used to address macroeconomic aspects until the beginning of the 1980s (Palmer, 1978; Haveman and Palmer, 1982), but interest in these topics seems to have virtually disappeared in the 1980s. We can assume that in the United States, the level of employment and unemployment is considered to be primarily determined by labour market flexibility and macroeconomic policy (in particular, monetary policy). This being the case, unemployment is primarily frictional, or concerns a core of "hard-to-place" persons, on which employment policy will be focused as an integral part of anti-poverty policy. In Europe, however, ALMPs have played a major macroeconomic role because of their size (in percentage of GDP), and, in some countries, because of their very marked countercyclical character, which make them an integral part of macroeconomic policy regulation, as in Sweden for example.

16. The adjusting of financial incentives within the same programme according to the priority given to certain beneficiaries, as is done in certain programmes in France, is a policy along these lines.

17. The wage earned after the programme – and even earnings (which are a function of the wage and the duration of employment) – is often used as the main criterion for assessing measures in the United States (it has the advantage of making possible an evaluation in cost/benefits terms, since the beneficiaries' gains -- again in comparison with those for non-beneficiaries – can be compared with the cost of the programme.

18. But the fact that lower wages are earned after a programme compared with those for non-beneficiaries may also simply indicate that there is a self-selection bias: it may be that the young people who, other things being equal, initially have lower reservation wages are more willing to enter into a poorly paid programme.

19. As Bishop (1989) points out, firms have some leeway in setting wages, at least at the time of hiring and in the initial stages of the employment relation, when the employee's characteristics are still uncertain. Wages then reflect the employer's prejudices more than the real productivity of the newly hired young person.

20. For example, in Sweden, according to Schröder (1997): "Labour market programmes do not seem to have any 'stigmatisation effect' on programme participants. Very few employers (5 %) hesitate to employ someone because he or she has participated in a labour market programme" (p. 16).

21. This was above all true until the 1980s.

22. *i.e.* the number of beneficiaries/ the labour force.

23. Thus here the employment rate does not denote the share of the employed labour force in the total working-age population (the usual definition).

24. It may however be pointed out that, the better informed firms are of the existence and provisions of programmes, the more limited this effect should be. In response to the distortion of competition caused by subsidised jobs, the threatened firms may themselves have recourse to such jobs, giving rise to a *"domino effect"*, to use the expression of Deakin and Pratten (1982); they thus resort to a programme solely in order not to be penalised by competitors who are using it. Deadweight loss and substitution effects are probably increased in consequence.

25. It may even be considered that, by increasing competition for adult workers, job subsidies for young people may encourage the latter to show more wage moderation (*anti-insider effect*).

26. Unless all the new entrants are completely unemployable.

27. And not in percentage of the number of the labour force, as in Figure 3.

28. Using realistic long-term elasticities and short-term adjustment periods, one can systematically try to estimate *ex ante* the order of magnitude of net job creations corresponding to subsidies as a function of the reduction in labour costs stemming from them (see for example Chouvel, Confais, Cornilleau, Gubian and Roguet, 1997).

29. a', s', c', d' denote coefficients expressed in percentage of beneficiaries.

30. The medium-term results for employment and unemployment depend, for example, on the *assumed* degree of response of the average wage to the reduction in youth unemployment.

31. Generally speaking, as the report of the CGP (1997) notes in the French case, massive recourse to this type of short-term subsidy tends to encourage many employers to exploit subsidies opportunistically, while all that matters for local public services is to "place" as many young people as possible (p. 237).

32. According to Freeman (1995), the prospect of being able to find only a badly-paid insecure job has certainly been a factor in the rise in delinquency in the United States.

33. Thus, in Sweden, young people participating in *Youth Teams* met regularly to receive advice and encouragement with looking for a job.

34. Long training modules were offered to some TUC beneficiaries in the 1980s but the experience was dropped because it proved that they were not what the beneficiaries were looking for (Simonin et al., 1993).

35. For example, a certificate could be awarded for having learnt how to use a particular type of software.

36. The reservations about such programmes also stem from the fact that there is a big risk, especially for young people, that the beneficiaries will be locked into a "second market". This was also noted by Nicaise et al. (1994).

37. French experience shows, for example, that in order to comply with the condition that they must not compete with the market sector, some associations with TUC employees have used them for the least productive jobs, and by the same token, those that offer the least opportunity to acquire a skill (Simonin, Gomel and Schmidt, 1993).

38. As was noted in DOL (1995): "Improving the employment outcomes of some persons within a community can lead to 'spill over effects' as other people in the neighborhood are influenced by the positive actions of their peers" (p. 63).

39. The French example of the TUC shows how the image of a scheme in public opinion, and thus among young people, can change quickly. The TUC were initially well-received but then began to be denigrated following a series of articles in the press denouncing a few abuses ("fake" jobs). Despite the fact that it was not confirmed by the evaluation, studies were unable to shake off this image. Young people consequently turned against the scheme to some extent (see Simonin, Gomel and Schmidt, 1993).

40. The long-term effects of this type of scheme depend on the extent to which the authorities manage to promote the emergence of a "third sector", jointly funded with the private sector, and capable of transforming the activities created by the *Emplois-Jeunes* into lasting jobs.

41. As has been the case in France over the past 20 years, and also, though to a lesser extent, in Sweden since the beginning of the 1990s.

BIBLIOGRAPHY

AUCOUTURIER, A-L. and GÉLOT, D. (1994), "Les dispositifs pour l'emploi et les jeunes sortant de scolarité", *Économie et Statistique*, No. 277-278.

BALCHIN, A. and ASHTON, D. (1994), "Youth Integration Schemes in Europe: the Case of the UK", Centre for Labour Market Studies, University of Leicester and Institut de Recherche Économique et Sociale, Noisy-le-Grand.

BALSAN, D., HANCHANE, S. and WERQUIN, P. (1994*a*), "Salaire et évaluation des mesures jeunes", Working Paper GREQAM, No. 94B05, May.

BALSAN, D., HANCHANE, S. and WERQUIN, P. (1994*b*), "The French Youth Governmental Programmes for Transition from School to Work: Individual Choice or Selection Effect", European Association of Labour Economists Sixth Annual Conference, Warsaw, September.

BELL, S. and ORR, L. (1994), "Is Subsidized Employment Cost Effective for Welfare Recipients?", *Journal of Human Resources*, No. 1.

BESSY, C., EYMARD-DUVERNAY, F., GOMEL, B. and SIMONIN, B. (1996), "Les politiques publiques d'emploi: le rôle des agents locaux", *Les politiques publiques d'emploi et leurs acteurs*, Cahiers du CEE, No. 34, PUF, Paris.

BISHOP, J. (1989), "Toward more Valid Evaluations of Training Programs Serving the Disadvantaged", *Journal of Policy Analysis and Management*, No. 2.

BISHOP, J. (1993), "Improving Job Matches in the US Labor Market", *Brookings Papers on Economic Activity, I: Microeconomics*.

BISHOP, J. and KANG, S. (1991), "Applying for Entitlements: Employers and the Targeted Jobs Tax Credit", *Journal of Policy Analysis and Management*, No. 1.

BISHOP, J. and MONTGOMERY, M. (1993), "Does Targeted Jobs Tax Credit Create Jobs at Subsidized Firms?", *Industrial Relations*, No. 3, Autumn.

BJÖRKLUND, A. and REGNER, H. (1996), "Experimental Evaluation of European Labour Market Policy", in Schmid, O'Reilly and Schömann (eds.), *International Handbook of Labour Market Policy and Evaluation*, Edward Elgar, Cheltenham, UK.

BLOMSKOG, S. and SCHRÖDER, L. (1994) "Labour Market Entry and the Transition from Unqualified to Qualified Jobs in the Swedish Young Work Force 1950-1991", European Association of Labour Economists Sixth Annual Conference, Warsaw, September.

BONNAL, L., FOUGÈRE, D. and SÉRANDON, A. (1994), "L'impact des dispositifs d'emploi sur le devenir des jeunes chômeurs: une évaluation économétrique sur données longitudinales", *Économie et Prévision*, 4, No. 115.

BONNAL, L., FOUGÈRE, D. and SÉRANDON, A. (1995), "Une modélisation du processus de recherche d'emploi en présence de mesures publiques pour les jeunes", *Revue Économique*, No. 3, May.

BONNAL, L., FOUGÈRE, D. and SÉRANDON, A. (1997), "Evaluating the Impact of French Employment Policies on Individual Labour Market Histories", *Review of Economic Studies*, Vol. 64(4), No. 221, October.

BOURDET, Y. and PERSSON, I. (1994), "The Youth Transition Regime in Sweden", Lund University, and Institut de Recherche Économique et Sociale, Noisy-le-Grand.

BURTLESS, G. (1985), "Are Targeted Wage Subsidies Harmful? Evidence of a Wage Voucher Experiment", *Industrial and Labour Relations Review*, Vol. 39, pp. 105-114.

CACHON, L. (1994), "Dispositifs d'insertion professionnelle des jeunes en Espagne", Université Complutense, Madrid, and Institut de Recherche Économique et Sociale, Noisy-le-Grand.

CALMFORS, L. (1994), "Active Labour Market Policy and Unemployment: A Framework for the Analysis of Crucial Design Features", Labour Market and Social Policy Occasional Paper, No. 15, OECD, Paris.

CALMFORS, L. and SKEDINGER, P. (1995), "Does Active Labour Market Policy Increase Employment? Theoretical Considerations and some Empirical Evidence from Sweden", *Oxford Review of Economic Policy*, No. 1.

CASE, A. and KATZ, L. (1991), "The Company You Keep: The Influence of Family and Neighborhood on Disadvantaged Youth", National Bureau of Economic Research, Working Paper No. 3705.

CHOUVEL, F., CONFAIS, E., CORNILLEAU, G., GUBIAN, A. and ROGUET, B. (1997), "L'impact macroéconomique des politiques spécifiques d'emploi en France (1974-1994)", DARES: 40 ans de politique de l'emploi, La Documentation française, Paris.

COMMISSARIAT GÉNÉRAL DU PLAN (CGP), COMITÉ INTERMINISTÉRIEL DE L'ÉVALUATION DES POLITIQUES PUBLIQUES (1997), "La loi quinquennale relative au travail, à l'emploi et à la formation professionnelle", Evaluation Report, La Documentation française, Paris.

DAVIA RODRIGUEZ, M-A. and HERNANZ MARTIN, V. (1998), "Politicas de empleo para jovenes I", Universidad de Alcala.

DEAKIN, B. and PRATTEN, C. (1982), Effects of the Temporary Employment Subsidy, Cambridge University Press.

DOLTON, P. (1993), "The Econometric Assessment Of Training Schemes: a Critical Review", European Association of Labour Economists Fifth Annual Conference, Maastricht, September.

DUBIN, J. and RIVERS, D. (1993), "Experimental Estimates of the Impact of Wage Subsidies", Journal of Econometrics, No. 56, pp. 219-242.

EDIN, P.-A. and HOLMLUND, B. (1991), "Unemployment Vacancies and the Labour Market Programmes: Swedish Evidence", in F. Padoa-Schioppa (ed.), Mismatch and Labour Mobility, Cambridge University Press.

EDIN, P.-A., FORSLUND, A. and HOLMLUND, B. (1998), "The Swedish Youth Labour Market in Boom and Depression", Department of Economics, Uppsala University, mimeo, February.

ERHEL, C., GAUTIÉ, J., GAZIER, B. and MOREL, S. (1996), "Job Opportunities for the Hard-to-Place", in Schmid, O'Reilly and Schömann (eds.), International Handbook of Labour Market Policy and Evaluation, Edward Elgar, Cheltenham, UK.

EYSSARTIER, D. and GAUTIÉ, J. (1996), "Evaluating Employment Subsidies with a Macroeconomic Model: a Methodological Assessment and an Illustration", European Association of Labour Economists Eighth Annual Conference, Chania, September.

FAY, R. (1996), "Enhancing the Effectiveness of Active Labour Market Policies: Evidence from Programme Evaluations in OECD Countries", Labour Market and Social Policy Occasional Paper, No. 18, OECD, Paris.

FORGEOT, G. and GAUTIÉ, J. (1997), "Overeducation and the Youth Labour Market in France", European Association of Labour Economists Ninth Annual Conference, Aarhus, September.

FORSLUND, A. (1996) "Direct Displacement Effects of Labor Market Policy Measures" (in Swedish), Report to the Parliamentary Auditors.

FREEMAN, R. (1995), "The Limits of Wage Flexibility to Curing Unemployment", Oxford Review of Economic Policy, No. 1.

FRIEDLANDER, D., GREENBERG, D. and ROBINS, P. (1997), "Evaluating Government Training Programs for the Economically Disadvantaged", Journal of Economic Literature, December.

GARONNA, P. and RYAN, P. (1991), "The Regulation and Deregulation of Youth Economic Activity", in Ryan, Garonna and Edwards (eds.), The Problem of Youth, MacMillan.

GAUTIÉ, J. (1996), "L'évaluation de la politique de l'emploi en faveur des jeunes en France", Dossier du CEE, No. 8, La Documentation française, Paris.

GAUTIÉ, J. (1997), "Insertion professionnelle et chômage des jeunes en France", Regards sur l'actualité, No. 233, La Documentation française, Paris, July/August.

GAUTIÉ, J., GAZIER, B. and SILVERA, R. (in collaboration with D. Anxo, P. Auer, F. Lefresne) (1994), Les subventions à l'emploi: analyse et expériences européennes, La Documentation française, Paris.

GÉLOT, D. and SIMONIN, B. (1997), "Vingt ans d'évaluation de la politique de l'emploi", La Lettre du CEE, No. 48, June.

GÉLOT, D., TUCHSZIRER, C., ZILBERMAN, S. (1993), "Les effets des aides publiques à l'emploi des jeunes", Premières Synthèses, No. 26, DARES, Paris, June.

GRUBB, D. (1994), "Direct and Indirect Effects of Labour Market Policies in OECD Countries", in R. Barrell (ed.), The UK Labour Market, Cambridge University Press.

HAMERMESH, D. (1993), Labor Demand, Princeton University Press.

HAVEMAN, R. and PALMER, J. (1982), Jobs for Disadvantaged Workers: the Economics of Employment Subsidies, The Brookings Institution, Washington, DC.

HECKMAN, J. (1992), "Randomization and Social Policy Evaluation", in Manski and Garfinkel (eds.), *Evaluating Welfare and Training Programs*, Harvard University Press.

HOLMLUND, B. (1995), "Comments on Per Skedinger: Employment Policies and Displacement in the Youth Labour Market", *Swedish Economic Policy Review*, No. 2.

LAYARD, R., NICKELL, S. and JACKMAN, R. (1991), *Unemployment, Macroeconomic Performance and the Labour Market*, Oxford University Press.

LAZEAR, E. (1981), "Agency, Earning Profiles, Productivity and Hours Restrictions", *American Economic Review*, September.

LEFRESNE, F. (1994), "Le cas britannique: une intervention structurelle sur le marché du travail ", in Gautié, Gazier and Silvera (eds.), *Les subventions à l'emploi: analyse et expériences européennes*, La Documentation française, Paris.

MANSKI, C. and GARFINKEL, I. (eds.) (1992), *Evaluating Welfare and Training Programs*, Harvard University Press.

MARESCA, B. (1994), *Jeunes en attente d'intégration professionnelle*, CREDOC, Étude réalisée pour le Sénat, Paris, November.

MARTIN, J. (1998), "What Works Among Active Labour Market Policies: Evidence From OECD Countries' Experience", Labour Market and Social Policy Occasional Paper, No. 35, OECD, Paris.

MEAGER, N. (1996), "From Unemployment to Self-Employment: Labour Market Policies for Business Start-Up", in Schmid, O'Reilly and Schömann (eds.), *International Handbook of Labour Market Policy and Evaluation*, Edward Elgar, Cheltenham, UK.

MEAGER, N. (1997), "Developments in the Youth Labour Market in the UK", Report for the French Ministry of Labour, The Institute of Employment Studies, University of Sussex, UK.

NICAISE, I., BOLLENS, J., DAWES, L., LANGHAEI, S., THAULOW, I., VERDIÉ, M. and WAGNER, A. (1994), "Pitfalls and Dilemmas in Labour Market Policies for Disadvantaged Groups", European Association of Labour Economists, Sixth Annual Conference, Warsaw, September.

OECD (1993), "Active Labour Market Policies: Assessing Macroeconomic and Microeconomic Effects", *Employment Outlook*, Paris.

OECD (1996), "Growing into Work: Youth and the Labour Market over the 1980s and 1990s", *Employment Outlook*, Paris.

O'HIGGINS, N. (1995), "Less than Zero: YTS, Job Search, Human Capital Formation and Reservation Wages", European Association of Labour Economists Annual Conference.

PALMER, J. (ed.) (1978), *Creating Jobs: Public Employment Programs and Wage Subsidies*, The Brookings Institution, Washington DC.

PEREZ, C. (1998), "L'évaluation des programmes d'emploi et de formation aux États-Unis", *Conseil Scientifique de l'Évaluation: L'évaluation en développement en 1997*, La Documentation française, Paris.

RAJAN, A. (1985), *Job Subsidies: Do they Work?*, Special Report, Institute of Manpower Studies Series, Gower.

RYAN, P., GARONNA P. and EDWARDS, R.C. (eds.) (1991), *The Problem of Youth*, MacMillan.

SALOP, S. (1979), "A Model of the Natural Rate of Unemployment", *American Economic Review*, March.

SAUCIER, P. and SOFER, C. (1995), "L'accès des jeunes aux politiques d'insertion et à l'emploi", *Revue Économique*, No. 3.

SCHMID, G. (1982), "Public Finance Measures to Generate Employment for the Hard-to-Place People: Employer wage subsidies or public employment programs?", in R Haveman (ed.), *Public Finance and Public Employment*, Wayne State University Press, Detroit.

SCHOBER-BRINKMANN, K. and WADENSJÖ, E. (1991), "Contrasting Forms of Youth Training and Employment in Sweden and FR Germany", in Ryan, Garonna and Edwards (eds.), *The Problem of Youth*, MacMillan.

SCHRÖDER, L. (1996), "Patterns of Labour Market Entry and their Significance for Labour Market Policy", Nordic Council of Ministers, TemaNord, No. 592.

SCHRÖDER, L. (1997), "Programmes for Unemployed Youth in Sweden", Swedish Institute for Social Research, Stockholm University.

SHAPIRO, C. and STIGLITZ, J. (1984), "Equilibrium Unemployment as a Worker Discipline Device", *American Economic Review*, May.

SIMONIN, B., GOMEL, B. and SCHMIDT, N. (1993), "Un bilan d'évaluation des TUC", *Dossier de recherche du Centre d'Études de l'Emploi*, No. 49.

SKEDINGER, P. (1995), "Employment Policies and Displacement in the Youth Labour Market", *Swedish Economic Policy Review*, No. 2.

SOLLOGOUB, M. (ed.) (1993), "L'efficacité du système d'éducation et de formation: effets des structures sociales", Rapport pour le Ministère de l'Éducation Nationale, Paris, December.

US DEPARTMENT OF LABOR (DOL) (1995), What's Working (and what's not): a Summary of Research on the Economic Impacts of Employment and Training Programs, Washington, DC.

VAN DER LINDEN, B. (1997), "Effets des formations professionnelles et des aides à l'embauche: exploitation d'une enquête auprès d'employeurs belges", Économie et Prévision, No. 131-5.

WEISS, A. (1980), "Job Queues and Layoffs in Labor Markets with Flexible Wages", Journal of Political Economy, June.

WILENSKI, H. (1985), "Nothing Fails Like Success: the Evaluation Research Industry and Labor Market Policy", Industrial Relations, Vol. 24, No. 1.

IMPROVING JOB MARKET OUTCOMES FOR YOUTH: THE US EXPERIENCE WITH DEMAND SIDE APPROACHES

by
Robert I. Lerman
Urban Institute and American University, United States

Introduction

Since at least the 1950s, helping young people make a healthy transition to adulthood has remained high on the agenda of the American public and US policymakers. In the 1960s, a major focus of the US government's war on poverty was assisting poor youth to gain work experience and skills through such programmes as the Neighborhood Youth Corps and the Job Corps. When the 1970s brought a sharp rise in youth unemployment rates, especially among black youth, the federal government responded with new programmes, research and demonstration projects, and ultimately, a special Vice President's Task Force on Youth Employment. In the early 1980s, funding fell for youth employment programmes at the peak of the worst recession in post-war US history, when youth unemployment rates reached record levels.

The expansions of the 1980s and 1990s lowered youth unemployment rates to their lowest rate in thirty years. But even before these reductions, youth advocates and policymakers had begun shifting their emphasis away from the youth unemployment problem and toward the broader goals of improving educational outcomes and raising long-term wages (William T. Grant Foundation, 1988; US Commission on the Skills of the American Workforce, 1990). Last year, in a report that best illustrated the declining concern about the youth unemployment problem, a National Academy of Sciences panel (1998) expressed their worries about young people working too much and studying too little and recommended actions to limit the number of hours school-age youth can work per week.

Only part of the declining interest in employment of youth resulted from the reductions in US unemployment rates. Other contributing factors were reports about the low quality of education in US elementary and secondary schools, the slow growth of wages overall and declining wages for many workers, the widening earnings gap between high school educated and college educated workers, and the limited effectiveness of targeted youth employment and training programmes. As policymakers became disillusioned with existing targeted programmes and redefined the youth problem as a general concern with youth development and career success, they began emphasising approaches aimed at improving long-term schooling and career outcomes of non-college youth over short-term gains in the employment rates of disadvantaged youth. And, since few young people are the primary breadwinners in their households, the lost income associated with youth unemployment is less serious than losses linked to adult unemployment.

The shift in framing the nation's youth problem looks sensible today for young people as a whole. As in prior business cycles, youth unemployment rates have declined sharply in response to the expanding economy. By the last quarter of 1998, only about 6.5% of 20-24 year-old workers were unemployed, down from 10.6% in the last quarter of 1992. In addition, youth unemployment rates are trending downward on a long-term basis. Annual unemployment rates of 20-24 year-olds at business cycle peaks have fallen from 9.2% in 1979, to 8.6% in 1989, to 7.9% in 1998.

The tight labour markets have significantly improved the job outlook for disadvantaged youth as well. Black workers in their early 20s faced a 13% unemployment rate in late 1998, down by more than half from over 30% in the early 1980s and about 20% at the last business cycle peak. Still, large numbers of less educated and minority youth have trouble finding a job. Of the nearly 2 million black out-of-school youth with no college education, only about half were working and 20% of the labour force was unemployed. Education was a major factor. Only 54% of all high school dropouts were working, as compared to 86% of out-of-school youth who had at least some education beyond high school.

Notwithstanding the favourable US employment situation, it is worthwhile to examine the role of demand side programmes for young people. First, today's extraordinarily low unemployment rates may not last in the US and may be irrelevant to several countries with double digit unemployment rates. The US faces a demographic challenge in the coming years that may place a strain on the youth labour market. The 18-24 year-old population declined by 16% between 1981 and 1994, but will increase by at least 21% between 1995 and 2010 (Sum, Fogg and Fogg, 1997). Second, pockets of youth joblessness are important because of their association with poverty, race, educational deficiencies, criminal activity, and depressed geographic areas. As of September through November 1998, only 34% of 16-24 year-old black drop-outs and 59% of white drop-outs were employed.[1] Third, demand side policies targeted on young, disadvantaged workers may help restore wage growth for groups who have experienced sharp reductions in wages. Fourth, targeted job and wage subsidy initiatives may provide otherwise missing work experience that can translate into a stable future. Finally, advocates of national service argue a mandatory youth service programme could not only expand job opportunities for youth, but create social solidarity through the mixing of social classes and creating a spirit of civic equality (Kaus, 1992).

Even for the least advantaged young workers, the problem may be less one of finding a job than one of entering a promising career or obtaining a good job. In this case, demand strategies might still be useful so long as the work experience is real and not contrived. But other approaches may be more promising if the goal is to enhance the educational capacities, skills, and career prospects of the 65% of American youth whose highest degree is a high school diploma.

The main goal of the paper is to present the US experience with several demand side and supply side efforts to help young people. Unlike many of the youth programmes elsewhere in the OECD, most US programmes are highly targeted toward low income youth. I begin with an overview of the potential effects of the programmes. Next, I examine the evidence from a number of evaluation studies. After this review, I shall offer an overall assessment of the evidence and interpret the implications for the suitability of each type of policy. A key argument is that apprenticeship, internship and other intensive school-to-career initiatives have the potential to serve as effective supply and demand policies.

I. Demand side policies: a theoretical overview

Job creation programmes have a natural appeal. Who can object to giving the unemployed the chance to produce, to earn a basic income, to enhance their skills, and to avoid welfare? Even the sceptical economist concerned about inflationary effects of government spending should feel comfortable with jobs programmes that generate added production from otherwise idle resources.

One can also build a strong theoretical case against job creation programmes. If the primary objective is "creating" jobs *per se*, the jobs are likely to be artificial and produce little valued output. Workers will recognise the make-work, dead-end character of the programme and find little that is motivating or skill-enhancing. Some may even see their skills deteriorate. Since public jobs (PSE) programmes require overhead, materials, and skilled workers, they do cost the economy real resources. In fact, these resource costs may be so high as to make it cheaper to provide income support instead of artificially created jobs.

If workers in PSE are productive, they may displace other public workers, causing the funding for jobs programmes to end up going for other purposes, including tax reductions. Displacement is not necessarily a bad thing for the economy if the PSE workers are less skilled and/or more needy than the former public workers. To the extent that the government can produce its goods and services effectively with less skilled workers, it releases skilled workers to the private sector, thereby relieving shortages and/or inflationary pressures in skilled job markets.

Much depends on the goals, design, and context of the public employment programme. The primary goal of US programmes is to use work experience to develop the human capital of young workers, especially the disadvantaged. By having youth enter jobs where they gain valuable work experience, government programmes can raise their productivity, their value to employers, and thus their job and earnings opportunities. Avoiding unemployment and the consequent waste of human resources is a second goal. A third set of goals is to raise incomes of the disadvantaged by providing wages to the unemployed and by stimulating an increase in the wages of employed low wage workers. A final and important motivation for youth PSE programmes in the US is to prevent socially destructive behaviour, particularly criminal activity and drug abuse.

The design of PSE programmes may involve hiring low wage workers in general or a specific target group, the production of real services or the provision of simple work experience for large numbers of participants, paying market wages or below market wages, and emphasising current income or human capital formation. The programme may operate in a context of low or high unemployment, of structural or cyclical unemployment, and of a public sector paying market or above-market wages for regular public workers. Another possibility is that PSE is an element of an income support system that imposes tough work requirements on benefit recipients. Backing up work requirements with assured access to a public job may deter participation in welfare programmes and encourage many to accept low wage, private sector jobs.

In a recent paper, David Ellwood and Elizabeth Welty (1998) use a microeconomic perspective to show how the employment and earnings gains for low wage workers from public jobs programmes and wage subsidy programmes depend on the degree of public sector substitution, the crowding out of private jobs (as wages increase), and the responsiveness of labour supply to wage changes. Ignoring administrative costs, they find that public jobs programmes can be quite effective in expanding employment when unemployment is high and public sector displacement is moderate. Not surprisingly, for any rate of public sector substitution, the net jobs effect of PSE will be greatest in the case of unemployment involving wage rigidities, since the programme will not crowd out any private jobs. In the case of a counter-cyclical PSE programme with highly elastic labour supply (5.0), moderately elastic demand (0.4), and low substitution (25%), each 1 000 jobs financed under PSE translates into 692 added jobs (+750 public, -56 private) and earnings gains of USD 0.83 for each USD 1.00 spent on wages. In comparison, an employer wage subsidy in this setting raises wages only USD 0.44 per dollar spent.

When unemployment is low, an untargeted PSE programme may engender high substitution (67%) and perform poorly in terms of job creation (adding only 111 jobs for each 1 000 financed) and overall earnings growth. The impact of a targeted programme will vary with the elasticity of demand. At low elasticities, a targeted programme in low unemployment periods might still achieve more earnings growth per USD 1 than wage subsidies. However, the more targeted the group, the higher the elasticity of demand, the weaker will be the performance of PSE programmes in absolute terms and relative to wage subsidies. If disadvantaged youth are highly substitutable for other workers, then a slight rise in their wage induced by the PSE programme will generate a sharp decline in private sector employment. For example, given a demand elasticity of 1.5 (and supply elasticity of 0.4 and substitution rate of only 10%), an added 1 000 of PSE jobs will generate only 189 net new jobs. However, if the supply of labour is highly elastic (say 2.0), then the net job figures would rise to over 500. In the elastic supply case, the added workers generated by PSE demand could be attracted into the market even with a small increase in wages and thus lead to only a small decline in private sector employment.

Other perspectives on net job creation emphasise macroeconomic and worker heterogeneity factors. Suppose the macroeconomic constraint limiting policymakers from expansionary policies is the fear of induced wage inflation, partly linked to wage pressure in labour markets for skilled and semi-skilled workers. In this case, PSE can be an effective tool so long as the jobs are well targeted on workers in slack markets. The impact of substitution depends on whether the displaced workers are more capable than PSE workers. If so, then these relatively skilled workers add to the supply and lessen wage pressure in private markets for skilled workers. This type of substitution is likely if public agencies pay higher wages than necessary to attract capable workers. If the displacement is high and the displaced workers are other low skill workers, then PSE will be ineffective.

Employer wage subsidies are another way to stimulate demand for young workers. In a simple supply and demand model, lowering the labour cost paid by employers should expand employment, though the relative impact on wages and employment depends on the elasticities. However, effects vary markedly with the reason for unemployment or low wages and the design of the programme. Suppose unemployment occurs because of downwardly rigid wages for low wage workers but that the group targeted as eligible for employer wage subsidies are a small share of the relevant market. In this case, the induced demand stimulus will raise employment of the target group but leave total unemployment of low wage workers unchanged (Lerman, 1982). Measured unemployment may occur because wages are too low. Theoretically, those unwilling to work at available wages are outside the labour force or involuntarily unemployed. However, they may seek work and thus count as officially unemployed. In this case, employer wage subsidies will only increase employment if they raise wage offers. But employers may be unwilling to do so, perhaps because raising wages for some workers means having to raise wages for all workers. Employer wage subsidies may not work in these cases.[2]

Wage rate subsidies look more promising from macro and general equilibrium perspectives than from a partial equilibrium perspective. So long as producers are competitive, apparent gains to employers in the form of reductions in their wage costs are ultimately captured by consumers in the form of lower prices. In the short-run, the reduction in prices limits the inflationary impact of the reduction in unemployment.

Another issue relevant to demand-side policies is worker heterogeneity. Think of young workers along a continuum from those with the best to those with the worst chances of finding an unsubsidised job. Suppose managers in PSE programmes hire the most capable of the group into PSE jobs. Providing jobs to these relatively capable youth opens private sector positions for other workers, but the least capable youth may be able to fill them. The jobs may go to workers outside the target group or go unfilled.

As Ellwood and Welty point out, such considerations are only a starting point. One must also ask whether the PSE jobs are as productive as private sector jobs, whether the PSE jobs do as much as private jobs to raise the future earnings capacities of workers, whether the administrative costs are high in PSE jobs and whether long-run (general equilibrium) adjustments could mute the effects of PSE on wages.

Employer wage subsidies face other obstacles to success. The administrative costs of the programme may be high for the government and/or employers. Targeted programmes may generate a negative stigma, since eligible workers may have to declare themselves as members of a group not generally favoured in the market. To the extent that this declaration serves as a negative signal to the employer, the direct reduction in hiring costs associated with the subsidy may be offset by the subsidy's indirect increase in the costs of hiring a subpar worker.

2. US job creation and employer wage subsidy programs for youth

The modern history of US jobs programmes for youth begins with the Neighborhood Youth Corps (NYC), established under the War on Poverty in 1965. By its second year (1966), the NYC enrolled 422 000 youth, of which about 40% were out-of-school. Part of the Congressional response to the riots of the mid-1960s was an expansion of the NYC to over 1 million participants, with nearly all of the increase coming in the form of summer jobs. The Congress repeated this reaction in 1992 by expanding summer jobs programmes in response to the Los Angeles riot. During the Comprehensive Employment and Training Act (CETA) period, the Federal government provided monies for other youth work-related programmes, culminating in the Youth Employment and Demonstration Projects Act of 1977 (YEDPA), which sponsored a variety of work experience and job creation programmes. In the mid-1970s, the Department of Labor funded Supported Work, a major research and demonstration project testing whether a well-designed work experience programme could raise the long-term employment and earnings of hard-core unemployed workers and do so at an acceptable net cost. Sales of the programme's outputs would help pay the costs of salaries and training.

Since the early 1980s, the federal government has de-emphasised youth job creation but several programmes remain. The summer programme still finances over 500 000 positions for low income youth at a cost of nearly USD 900 million. The National and Community Service Act of 1990 funded the Conservation and Youth Service Corps programme as a way of expanding opportunities for 18-25 year-old out-of-school youth. About 100 corps programmes received funding in the 1993/94 programme year. In 1993, Congress created Americorps, another community service programme now providing about 18 000 jobs for young people. Americorps participants are hired by federal, state, and local agencies through grants from the Corporation for National and Community Service. Unlike other federal jobs programmes, Americorps has no income test and draws young people from a variety of education and income levels. In 1996-97, Americorps volunteers received a stipend of about USD 8 000 along with nearly USD 5 000 in an education award, health insurance, and childcare costs. Together with overhead, the overall programme costs amounted to over USD 20 000 per year per participant.

In 1993, the Department of Housing and Urban Development (HUD) began sponsoring job creation under a programme (Youthbuild) in which over 100 sponsors provide 2 000-3 000 disadvantaged youth with training and work experience primarily in the construction industry. In addition, the federal government helps support hundreds of thousands of work-study jobs for college and university students.

Wage subsidies targeted on disadvantaged youth began with the 1978 passage of the Targeted Jobs Tax Credit (TJTC) programme. When first enacted in 1978, the TJTC subsidised half of the first USD 6 000 (over USD 12 000 in 1998 prices) in first year wages and one-quarter of second year wages. The 1986 tax reform act limited the subsidy to 40% of first year wages only.

3. Evidence about the effects of direct job creation

The conventional view about direct job creation programmes for youth is sceptical. According to OECD's 1998 *Employment Outlook*, "(...) the effectiveness of many direct job creation programmes as a tool to improve the transition is in doubt. In practice, they are not only costly, but they also rarely lead to integration into the regular labour market. However, for some disadvantaged groups, they may be the only route into a job when all other possibilities have failed" (p. 89).

How warranted is this scepticism with respect to US programmes? Although few evaluations provide enough data to yield convincing estimates of the impacts of direct job creation, one can piece together some relevant findings. We begin with the simple objective of generating net employment gains for the disadvantaged.

4. Net employment impacts on disadvantaged young adults

When judging net employment impacts from the perspective of all workers or low wage workers, one naturally considers substitution of PSE workers for other public sector workers and crowding out of jobs in the private sector. Market and substitution effects are likely in large or untargeted programmes. In theory, such programmes should raise wages, increase public sector employment, and decrease private sector employment. If the programme's net effects are small, partly because of crowding out of private jobs, one would expect that those not employed in the programme have a lower rate of employment. However, for small and highly targeted programmes, where one can reasonably ignore market effects, one could draw the opposite conclusion when the employment is lower among the non-participants than among those eligible for PSE. As noted above, PSE may draw workers from the target group who would have been employed in the absence of the programme. When they leave their jobs, the odds are quite low that other target group members will be affected, since they represent a very small share of workers available for these positions. Assuming PSE does not affect the ability of other target group members to find a job, one can estimate net employment effects by comparing what eligibles do in the presence of the programme with what they would have been doing in the absence of the programme. This section examines evidence based on both perspectives.

One programme unlikely to have public substitution or market effects was the National Supported Work Demonstration. It placed hard-core unemployed workers in non-profit agencies in jobs that involved graduated stress, peer support, and close supervision. Young high-school dropouts were one of four target groups included in the demonstration (along with long-term unemployed welfare mothers, drug addicts, and former criminal offenders). The workers took jobs in a range of fields, including construction, manufacturing, business services and clerical work[3]. The programme began operations in 1975 at the trough of a deep recession, when unemployment rates reached over 10%; but most participants exited during the recovery of 1977-78.

Because applicants were randomly assigned to treatment and control groups, we can estimate the likely jobholding of participants in the absence of the programme from the experience of controls. On this basis, the Supported Work programme had a large impact on jobholding. In the first three months after enrolment, over 90% of the treatment group of high school dropouts had jobs while only 29% of controls were working. This implies that for each three jobs financed by Supported Work, two represented increases in jobholding among disadvantaged youth. In subsequent months, the gap narrowed so that by the third quarter after enrolment, each two Supported Work jobs meant a net increase of one new job.

Another, more recent youth job creation programme of modest scale is the Conservation and Youth Service Corps funded in 1990 as a way of expanding job opportunities for 18-25 year-old out-of-school youth (Jastrzab et al., 1996). This mixed array of service programmes has several goals: to produce goods and services beneficial to the public, to instil a strong work ethic and a sense of public service, and to enhance work-related skills. About 100 corps programmes received funding in the 1993/94 programme year.

Corps members participated in projects ranging from tutoring children, to assisting in child care and escorting patients to examinations, to planting trees along a highway, to renovating buildings for housing future participants, to improving parks and to helping clean up debris after a hurricane. About 70% of the work took place under the auspices of non-profit institutions and the remaining 30% involved government agencies. More than half the corps members were economically disadvantaged, and most did not have a high school degree or GED. To determine the effectiveness of service corps programmes, researchers conducted an intensive evaluation of eight sites and in four sites randomly assigned applicants either to a treatment group that entered the programme or to a control group excluded from the programme.

The analysis covers a period 15 months after entering the corps, a period during which most corps members were still working on projects. One, albeit imperfect, measure of net employment gains is the amount worked by the treatment group less the amount worked by controls. On this basis, net job creation appears to be only 30% of gross employment. While the corps stimulated additional employment, controls worked about 70% of the hours worked by the treatment group (1 465 to 2 030) and earned about USD 80 less per month. More than half of the earnings of corps members (USD 114 of the USD 197 per month) simply offset what they would have earned in the absence of the service corps. The net job and earnings gains were much higher for Black and Hispanic male participants. In contrast, white male participants apparently sacrificed to become corps members, as the control group earned substantially more than their counterparts in the treatment group.

Other evidence on net job creation can be gleaned from the Youth Incentive Entitlement Pilot Projects (YIEPP). The primary objective of YIEPP was to provide subsidised jobs to youth from poor families as a way of keeping them in school until they graduated from high school or to attract them back to school after they dropped out. YIEPP guaranteed jobs to any eligible 16-19 year-old living in the designated pilot area. To test the impact of YIEPP, the evaluators compared the impact of YIEPP in four sites with the experience of youth in comparison sites (Farkas *et al.*, 1984).

Since YIEPP attempted to saturate the market for poor youth, one would expect to observe market effects. If the comparison sites capture what would have taken place in the market in the absence of YIEPP, then one can calculate the net job creation effect of YIEPP by estimating the difference in employment rates between treatment and comparison sites in relationship to the jobs financed through YIEPP. With no displacement, the employment rate in YIEPP sites should equal the proportion of youth placed in YIEPP jobs plus the employment rate in comparison sites. Suppose, for example, YIEPP employed 40% of all eligible youth and the employment rate in control sites were 25%. If all the YIEPP jobs represented added employment, then the YIEPP employment rate would have been 65%. If the YIEPP employment rate were less than 65% (say, 45%), then some (half) of the YIEPP jobs must have replaced other employment for eligible youth.

Using this approach, one can estimate the net employment effects of YIEPP during the school year (when most YIEPP jobs took place) and during the summer. Virtually all the school year jobs appear to have represented net increases in employment. For example, in 1979-80, YIEPP employed about 22% of the eligible group and the employment rate in YIEPP sites was 22% points higher than in control sites. In the summers of 1979 and 1980, displacement of 30-48% apparently took place, since the gains in employment (12 and 6 percentage points) were lower than the proportion of eligibles (25 and 20%) working in YIEPP jobs. By implication, some of the YIEPP workers would have found jobs without YIEPP.

These indicators show displacement of low income youth. Studies of the broader impacts suggest displacements from the private sector close to 50%, though no displacement of part-time jobs.[4] The part-time finding is consistent with the low displacement effects observed during the summer.

Surprisingly, no one has produced other credible estimates of displacement and net job creation for job creation programmes involving out-of-school youth. Some studies are available for the Summer Youth Employment Program (SYEP) and these suggest either very little displacement (Clark and Summers, 1982) or displacement rates of about one-third of a job (Crane and Ellwood, 1984). However, a National Academy of Sciences review of the Crane-Ellwood study pointed out that their estimates were unreliable and lacked statistical significance (Betsey *et al.*, 1985, p. 151).

Other evidence on displacement comes from work by David Ellwood and David Wise (1987) on the impact of military recruitment on civilian employment of young adults. They found that jobs in the military led to no displacement among black young men but almost 30% displacement among white young men (though the estimate for Whites was not statistically significant). By implication, the downsizing of the military in the 1990s probably weakened the job market for young men, especially young black men.

5. Private sector subsidies for hiring disadvantaged youth

Evidence from the on-the-job (OJT) training component of the Job Training Partnership Act (JTPA) programme for youth illustrates how alternative perspectives can yield different conclusions. Under the OJT component of JTPA's youth programme, firms hired eligible participants (low income, unemployed youth) to work and to learn on-the-job in return for government subsidies. These were subsidised jobs in the private sector.

To determine overall job creation induced by the programme, one would want to know whether firms increased their total employment or simply substituted subsidised workers for unsubsidised workers. Observing no impact on employment rates of unsubsidised workers would be evidence of no substitution. However, if the focus is on net job creation for a target group that makes up a small segment of even the low skill work force, then substitution of subsidised for unsubsidised workers will have little effect on the employment rates of target group workers. In this case, using the worker heterogeneity perspective, net job gains to the target group depend on the extent to which the programme raised the employment rate of those with access to the programme over other target group members.

The National JTPA Study (Orr *et al.*, 1995) allows one to make this comparison because in several sites programme operators randomly assigned eligible applicants to a treatment group with access to JTPA services and a control group with no such access. Of the JTPA applicants assigned to the OJT/Job Search treatment, 30% actually obtained a subsidised job through an OJT contract. Assuming any private sector substitution has at most a marginal effect on jobs available to other disadvantaged youth, access to subsidised jobs for treatment group youth should raise their earnings over those of the control group during the first quarter of enrolment in the programme. In fact, the earnings levels of treatment and control groups within the OJT/Job Search component were virtually identical even during the in-programme or job subsidy phase. The absence of any in-programme gains indicates very high displacement in the sense that the added availability of government subsidised jobs did not add significantly to employment levels of young adults.

The Targeted Jobs Tax Credit (TJTC) is the one US employer subsidy with possible effects on the market for youth. In 1978, when unemployment was changing from a cyclical and to a structural problem, the Carter Administration proposed replacing the New Jobs Tax Credit, which paid employers subsidies for any increase in employment, with the TJTC, which subsidises only hires of economically disadvantaged youth, public assistance recipients, Vietnam-era veterans, some ex-offenders, and disabled individuals in vocational rehabilitation. According to Katz (1998), about 9% of employed, eligible youth were hired under the TJTC by the mid-1980s. The subsidy declined over time in generosity and in coverage, partly because of the concern that employers were using the credits to pay for workers they would have hired anyway. Another concern is one of stigma. The targeted nature of the subsidy requires workers to show that they are disadvantaged enough to qualify for a government subsidy. Two small studies (Burtless, 1985; Hollenbeck and Willke, 1991), indicate that employers interpret the designation of workers as eligible as a signal of lower quality; as a result, the value of the credit may only offset or be less than the added perceived cost of hiring eligible disadvantaged workers.

To analyse the impact of the TJTC on the employment of disadvantaged youth, Katz examined trends in employment before and after a change in the law taking hold at the beginning of 1989 that removed 23-24 year-old disadvantaged workers from eligibility. The test involved comparing employment-population ratios of economically disadvantaged 23-24 year-olds with those of other 23-24 year-olds before and after the change in the law. To account for differential trends between disadvantaged and other young workers unrelated to TJTC, Katz also compared group employment rates of 18-22 year-olds before and after 1989. While economically disadvantaged 23-24 year-olds saw their employment rates decline relative to non-disadvantaged 23-24 year-olds after the law changed, the 18-22 year-old economically disadvantaged youth gained over their non-disadvantaged counterparts. Results based on these "differences-in-differences" as well as based on regression-adjusted differences suggest that a large share of TJTC subsidised employment of 23-24 year-old disadvantaged workers represented net gains for the group. Katz estimates that TJTC accounted for about 3 percentage points of the 44% employment rate of 23-24 year-old disadvantaged workers. Put another way, Katz concludes that "(...) 40 to 52% of the jobs receiving TJTC subsidies reflected net employment additions for economically disadvantaged twenty-three to twenty-four year-olds at a cost of approximately USD 1 500 (1991 dollars) per net job created". With earnings of disadvantaged workers amounting to at least USD 9 000 per year, the cost per job would be less than 20% of a worker's salary. If these estimates are accurate, then the wage subsidy approach would be a far less expensive way to increase jobs for target group workers than PSE.

Other less optimistic evidence about employer wage subsidies comes from two demonstrations sponsored by the Department of Labor in the late 1970s. In the Wage Variation Experiment under YIEPP, firms were either randomly assigned or geographically assigned to qualify for a partial subsidy (50% in Baltimore, 75% in Detroit) or a 100% subsidy for hiring poor youth (Farkas *et al.*, 1984). Only a small proportion of the eligible firms were willing to hire poor youth, even when provided with a sizeable subsidy. However, the number of hires was sensitive to the subsidy rate, implying that at least some of the jobs represented new jobs for the target group. Going from a 50% to a 100% subsidy increased the number of jobs from 7.5 (per 100 firms contacted) to 20.1. If none of the jobs at the 50% subsidy rate represented new jobs, then the net increase in jobs for the 100% group was about 13 at a cost of about 20 salaries, or 1.55 times the average salary. This figure may sound high, but is no higher than the net cost of most jobs created through PSE.

In a second experiment, employers were randomly assigned to one of three groups - one provided with direct cash subsidies and TJTC, a second to whom employment counsellors marketed the TJTC, and a third exposed to neither treatment (Casale *et al.*, (1982). The results were entirely negative. Virtually none of the treatment group firms hired any low-income youth.

Overall, the evidence on highly targeted employer wage subsidies is mixed, though moderately positive. The value of output of subsidised workers must be considerable, at least large enough to offset the employer's contribution to the cost of cost of hiring them. And, the largest US wage subsidy programme appears to have generated a substantial number of jobs for economically disadvantaged youth at a modest budgetary cost. At the same time, even this positive evidence is not conclusive and other evidence points to negative signalling from highly targeted wage subsidies.

6. Value of PSE output

The resource costs - as opposed to the budgetary costs - of job creation programmes depend on the value of output generated in the programme compared to the real resources consumed by the programme (including labour time of participants and supervisors as well as materials and rent). Yet, few studies have provided direct estimates of output values. In part, this is because the subsidised jobs typically do not provide marketable output. Still, just a listing of accomplishments suggests that job creation programmes generate real output.

The usual approaches to valuation are: 1) estimating the costs of producing the output (supply estimates); and/or 2) estimating the value of the output based on market values or on the public's willingness to pay for public goods or services. Output estimates from Supported Work are most persuasive since this demonstration often produced and sometimes sold normal goods and services. However, since young adults worked alongside other target groups, one cannot isolate the youth contribution to the output. For all participants, the value of output approximated 45% of total costs and 96% of participant earnings. Behind these averages were substantial site differences, with some sites able to generate enough output to justify most of the programme's direct costs.

Remarkably similar estimates of output values come from two other studies of youth programmes. The Ventures in Community Improvements (VICI) demonstration provided work experience and skills training in the construction trades, with projects ranging from home rehabilitation to home weatherization. The costs of the programme were high, but so were the goals for increasing penetration in the construction trades and producing outputs in low income communities. Researchers (PPV, 1992) estimated output values based on what it would have cost to produce the VICI output. Such costs may be an upper bound, since neither governments nor individuals were purchasing the output for its own sake. Still, the supply-based figures indicated a value of output averaging 42% of total costs and 114% of youth wages. Again, the variability across sites was extreme.[5]

David Zimmerman (1978) tried to determine the value of output in ongoing CETA youth programmes, rather than special demonstrations. The results again indicated values averaging about 50% of programme costs and 90% of youth earnings, with wide ranges as well.

The evaluation of Youth Service Corps included an analysis of the value of output (Jastrzab et al., 1996). Evaluators obtained information about what projects accomplished, interviewed beneficiaries of the projects, and determined what it would cost a private, unsubsidised supplier to produce the output generated by the corps. The reports were largely positive. Over half the beneficiaries rated the quality of work by Corps members as excellent or very good; only about 30% stated the work had some problems or was poor. Using data from a representative sample of projects, the evaluators estimated value of programme output per service hour as averaging USD 13.24, with individual project values ranging from USD 8.64 to USD 15.18 per hour.

Combining the value of output estimates with the displacement estimates, we can derive the social costs of raising the employment of disadvantaged out-of-school youth. Suppose that for each newly employed young adult, the government must finance two jobs. Since in well-managed programmes the two workers probably produce about 40-45% of the costs of employing them, the net cost per newly employed worker is the outlays expended on about 1.2 or 1.1 jobs. If the displacement is higher and three jobs must be financed for each new worker, then the costs net of output values would amount to about 1.8 to 1.65 salaries.

7. Effects on human capital as measured by post-program earnings gains

The value of work experience is well-documented in the labour economics literature. Improving the long-term job market outcomes of young people, especially the economically disadvantaged is the primary motivation beyond most PSE programmes. (A major exception is the summer youth employment programme, whose main purpose is simply giving low income, young people a wage and something constructive to do when school is out.) In theory, job creation or work experience programmes could generate as much added human capital as training programmes since many people learn better in the context of their specific jobs, rather than in the abstract.

The Supported Work demonstration provided young drop-outs with jobs involving peer support, graduated stress and close supervision. In spite of the enhanced nature of the work experience, the programme exerted no significant effects on the earnings, hours of work, or wage rates of the treatment group. Another disappointing finding was the absence of any impacts on criminal behaviour. Even during the in-programme period, when jobholding was much higher for the treatment group, the arrest rates were similar for treatment and control groups. As Rebecca Maynard (1980) points out, the results show no evidence of a connection between employment and criminal behaviour. The reasons for the failure of Supported Work to improve the job market situation for out-of-school youth remain unclear. Another group involved in the experiment, AFDC mothers, did achieve gains. Perhaps, the problems were that the dropouts were an especially hard-core group (30% had been incarcerated) and that they had to work and learn alongside ex-addicts and ex-offenders.

One study (Couch, 1992) examined the earnings of AFDC and youth participants in the Supported Work treatment and control groups data for eight years following their participation. While modest, statistically significant gains continued among welfare recipients, youth in the Supported Work treatment group fared no better than youth in the control group.

The concept underlying YIEPP was to link the attraction of a job to staying in school or returning to school. Enhanced human capital development could thus occur both through work experience achieved in YIEPP and through increased educational attainment. Unfortunately, YIEPP's ability to achieve these human capital improvements was limited. It failed to achieve its primary goal of stimulating more poor youth to graduate high school. For eligible black youth who were 19 or 20 in the Fall of 1981, high school graduation rates in YIEPP sites were only 47%, a lower rate than the 50% level in comparison sites. By offering jobs to drop-outs if they returned to school, YIEPP did draw some young high school drop-outs back to school. The return to school rate rose by 55% in 1978 and by 10% in 1979. However, the programme was unable to stimulate these drop-outs to stay in school long enough to graduate from high school.

Despite the programme's weak performance in raising graduate rates, the work experience component may have raised employment levels. Evaluators estimated that YIEPP induced a post-programme gain in earnings of about USD 10 per week, a 39% differential between YIEPP and comparison sites. Most of the gains were due to higher employment levels rather than higher wages. Although these positive, statistically significant results are promising, they are based on comparisons of sites that are less reliable that comparisons of randomly assigned treatment and control groups. Moreover, well after YIEPP, the unemployment rates of YIEPP eligibles (most of whom participated) remained extremely high, reaching an incredible 60% among black young adults.

The Summer Training and Education Program (STEP) tried to enhance a temporary summer jobs programme with innovative instruction in math, reading, and life skills for 14-15 year-olds from poor families (Walker and Vilella-Velez, 1992). The major aims were to raise educational attainment and reduce the proportion of young people dropping out of school. The effects were also disappointing. Although STEP was able to raise grade equivalencies of treatment group members over a 15-month period, the programme was unable to produce positive effects on the education, employment, and parenting outcomes of treatment group members.

Few other job creation programmes for out-of-school youth have been able to provide robust findings about post-programme effects. The National Academy of Sciences study cites only the Supported Work programme as providing reliable evidence. Overall, the authors concluded that the long-term social and economic effects of temporary jobs programmes are not encouraging (Betsey *et al.*, p. 160).

Perhaps job-creation programmes for out-of-school youth have not generated earnings gains because they are trying to fulfil a variety of functions, from providing employment to producing output as well as raising skills. If so, perhaps jobs programmes geared more directly to training would achieve more for out-of-school youth.

8.   Overall assessment of demand-side programs

The US experience with demand-side programmes for young people offers some lessons but leaves many important questions unanswered. Job-creation programmes for youth and employer wage subsidy programmes are feasible to mount and probably are able to increase the employment of disadvantaged youth at modest resource costs (net of output values). These demand-side policies exert direct effects on joblessness, often providing disadvantaged young adults a way of earning income through work and producing worthwhile outputs. In a context of high unemployment for selected groups of young adults, these policies can help reduce structural unemployment.

Unfortunately, demand-side policies appear to have little impact on the subsequent employment and earnings of young people. Perhaps, this is too much to ask. After all, if the programmes are able to produce valued outputs and keep costs low or if the subsidies generate jobs at a low net cost, post-programme gains are desirable, though not necessary to justify the programme. To reinforce the point, note that many training programmes aimed entirely at human capital development do no better than PSE programmes in raising youth earnings on a long-term basis.

Several forces limit the expansion of existing demand-side programmes. Many policymakers are generally sceptical about whether employer subsidies create net new jobs or even redistribute jobs for the target group. Given the narrow target group of eligibles and their limited political clout, the only strong lobby for the continuation of these subsidies is public and private employers. But the more employers lobby for the benefits, the more policymakers see the subsidies as windfalls. Scepticism about PSE comes from the lack of strong credible evidence that the programmes are generating significant amounts of valued output and from their poor record in promoting human capital.

One chronic problem underlying virtually all employment and training programmes (including direct job-creation programmes) is their temporary, dispersed, on-off status. Few managers have the time to develop sound management and to learn from the experience of prior programmes. And, although the government supports multiple job creation and training programmes for at-risk youth, the incentives for programmes to compete in achieving the primary goals are limited (US General Accounting Office, 1998).

9. Future directions

Avoiding the proliferation of short-term programmes requires the development of a long-term strategy. But what should constitute a long-term demand-side strategy? Should the programme emphasise observable outputs or work experience, training, and education leading to enhanced human capital? Should eligibility be limited by family income and/or by educational level? Should the subsidies flow through government agencies, non-profit organisations, and/or private employers? How should the programmes be co-ordinated? How can such programmes attract and retain political support?

Sustaining the support of the public requires a broad and/or powerful group of beneficiaries or a clear record of cost-effectiveness in helping the disadvantaged. The problem is that budget analysts reasonably worry that the larger the group participating in the programme, the higher the cost, and the lower the cost-effectiveness for disadvantaged workers.

For this reason, most US demand-side programmes limit eligibility to low income youth. This income targeting is one way to channel scarce resources to those facing the most severe employment problems. However, such programmes generally rely on eligibility thresholds in which an additional dollar of family income can result in hundreds or thousands of dollars in lower benefits). One result is that families initially above the line end up with less income than families initially below the line. A second problem is that young people who set up separate households are treated more favourably than those who are equally disadvantaged in terms of employment but who live with their parents. Third, strict targeting creates groups made up entirely of youth with educational deficiencies and other significant barriers to employment. Separate programmes for the most disadvantaged can weaken educational components, keep low income youth in problematic peer groups, and lead graduates to experience the stigma of coming from a programme only for the weakest individuals. Though rarely noted, this kind of segregation draws harsh critiques when used in the educational sphere but escapes notice in the employment and training arena.

Devising policies that avoid these pitfalls is critical. One way out is to emphasise the service concept as a way of broadening the involvement of all types of young people. Such an approach could build on today's Youth Service Corps and Americorps in ways that keep costs per participant under control. Entry could be open to all, while the size of scholarship varies with income. At its best, this model can lead to increased ties between young people from the middle class and low income backgrounds. If the mix of social classes succeeds, indirect effects on job contacts might be especially valuable to disadvantaged young adults. As a service programme, it can operate without paying competitive wages and thus limit costs. Including people with a mix of skills and capabilities raises the chances of creating high value output.

Involving mainstream youth and promoting the service component raises the credibility of the programme in the eyes of the disadvantaged and of employers who might hire programme graduates. Even if a youth service programme were unable to improve post-programme outcomes any better than other programmes, participants should recognise that it is the services produced and their dignity as a volunteer that is of primary significance. Under this approach, young workers serve their communities for a low salary instead of receiving charity. Participants are then able to justify their work as a contribution to larger goals (say, helping guard or renovating parts of the neighbourhood), instead of having to admit that extremely low wages are the best they can do.

There is no presumption that the jobs will *necessarily* generate special new skills. The programme's key aim is to utilise idle capacity to produce something of value while providing income to the unemployed. Of course, where possible, the policy should encourage features that have a positive impact on the future job success of participants. One example is a monitoring component in which supervisors follow closely the progress of individual participants and are able to provide credible references to employers about their performance on the job. Participants should have access to basic education, but on a purely voluntary, unpaid basis. Ultimately, the programme should work toward the concepts of "functional context" education, as applied in the military (see Sticht, 1989). Under this approach, teaching would take place by relating the tasks that must be performed to the instruction in reading and math skills. The programme could even draw on materials developed by the military for functional context education, but also devise new materials that are linked to the tasks required on public jobs.

Sponsors should be responsible for documenting generic competencies learned by the participants and, where possible, for linking the work experience with skill standards required in various occupational fields. In these cases, participants should have the opportunity to obtain required academic instruction as well. Such an approach is likely to add to the rigor of the on-the-job training at the work site and to improve the incentives for participants to work hard as they see linkages between their work experience and their career opportunities.

Proceeding in this direction could allow a youth-oriented, PSE approach to set up models that could be replicated in the private sector. US employers often express scepticism about hiring young workers for even moderately responsible positions. And currently, the government employs a smaller proportion of young workers than does the private sector. If the government demonstrated ways of effectively hiring, training, and retaining young workers, the approaches could be diffused to the private sector as well. As an example, suppose the government helped develop occupational standards in the administrative assistant/clerical field and began to use them to hire youth in the context of a youth apprenticeship programme. The government might well find that employing and training young workers provides short-term labour for mundane tasks, but offers a source of well-trained workers for regular positions. Such a step would expand the demand for young workers and enhance the quality of the supply. If the programme succeeded in training these workers effectively, the infrastructure associated with these specific occupational models (especially the skill standards and methods of accountability) could be diffused to the private sector.

The US General Accounting Office and the Department of Labor identified other lessons from employment and training programmes for raising the earnings capacity of disadvantaged youth. While few programmes actually include these components, the most promising programmes build in all of the following:

– Make sure participants are committed to training and getting a job; one can do so by requiring a small payment by participants and strict discipline after initial counselling.

– Commit to removing geographic, attitudinal, family and other barriers to finding and keeping a job.

– Improve and document the skills employers require of all workers, such as dependability, working in teams, taking instruction, and resolving conflicts sensibly; some successful programmes require participants to use a time card to clock in when they arrive and leave and they sanction those who are late or miss days.

– Link occupational skills training with the job market to make sure that employers can absorb successful graduates.

– Integrate basic skills training with occupational training so that participants can learn by doing and can see the relevance of their skills.

– Use individual case management to mentor participants and to help them overcome temporary setbacks.

What about the role of employer wage subsidies? In a standard market framework, employer wage subsidies complement PSE programmes. Where the PSE stimulus to demand generally raises wages and labour costs, thereby crowding out private jobs, employer wage subsidies work to reduce labour cost, lower pre-subsidy wages and increase private employment. Thus, PSE offsets the wage reducing effect of wage subsidies and wage subsidies offset the labour cost increasing effect of PSE. Together, the two should lead to higher post-subsidy wages, higher public employment, and indeterminate effects on private employment.

Unlike PSE, employer wage subsidies avoid the costs of overhead, the need to monitor the quantity and quality of output, and the concern that work experience will be artificial. One can count on direct financial incentives to stimulate private employers to use subsidised workers effectively. Substitution arises in both PSE and employer wage subsidies; the evidence suggests no larger direct cost per job created under employer subsidies than under PSE.

The breadth of coverage and scope of the subsidy are critical design issues. A targeted programme limits the demand stimulus to a presumably needy group and thus permits a higher per-worker subsidy for the same total outlay. The targeted programmes are most appropriate when the untargeted groups have low unemployment rates. However, in situations with high unemployment due to wage rigidities, targeted wage subsidy programmes may only reallocate instead of reducing the unemployment. Moreover, inappropriately targeted programmes may generate high administrative costs and signal employers that the eligibles are not effective workers. Untargeted programmes are most appropriate in periods of high unemployment.

The mixed pattern of evidence from the US experience suggests that employer wage subsidies generate net gains in employment of target groups, but the size of the impacts vary. According to a recent estimate of the largest programme, the new jobs generated by TJTC represented about 40-50% of the TJTC subsidy awards. Yet, even with these significant windfalls to employers for workers they would have hired without the subsidy, the net cost per added job for workers in the target group amounted to about USD 1 500 (1991 dollars), or less than 20% of a typical worker's earnings. The limited evidence from other studies suggests a considerably high net cost per job for target group workers. Although no evidence is available about the effects of the private-subsidised jobs on the long-term earnings of disadvantaged youth, work experience in these jobs is unlikely to yield worse outcomes than the low or zero impacts observed in PSE.

In conclusion, raising youth employment through the use of demand side subsidies looks feasible and potentially desirable as a way of assisting selected groups. However, in the US context - here jobs are readily available for most young people and unemployment durations are short - the higher priority task is to help improve the long-term career prospects of the 65% of young people who leave school with at most a high school degree. In pursuit of this goal, US policymakers have focused on raising educational performance and increasing the number of years in school. A more promising approach would be to build on today's high demand for young workers by linking jobs with work experience and training toward a set of standards, work-based learning, school-based learning, and a system for verifying competencies. Creating job-training slots of this kind in the private and public sectors combines the best of demand and supply strategies. Employers increase their demand for young workers while young people gain the type of work experience and training that can lead to a rewarding career.

NOTES

1. These figures come from special tabulations prepared by the author from the Current Population Survey Microdata.

2. For a more extensive discussion of the cases in which employer wage subsidies are superior or inferior to worker wage subsidies, see Lerman (1982).

3. See Maynard (1980) for an analysis of the effects on young drop-outs and Kemper, Long and Thornton (1981) for the full benefit-cost analysis.

4. See the discussion in Ellwood and Welty (1998) of the studies of YIEPP displacement.

5. Unfortunately, no studies of the value of output are available for the Department of Housing and Urban Development (HUD) Program, Youthbuild.

BIBLIOGRAPHY

BETSEY, C., ROBINSON JR, H. and PAPAGEORGIOU M. (eds) (1985), Youth Employment and Training Programs: The YEDPA years, Committee on Youth Employment Programs, Commission on Behavioral and Social Sciences and Education, National Research Council, National Academy Press, Washington, DC.

CLARK, K and SUMMERS, L. (1982), "The Dynamics of Youth Unemployment", in R. Freeman and D. Wise (eds.), *The Youth Labor Market Problem: Its Nature, Causes, and Consequences,* National Bureau of Economic Research, The University of Chicago Press, Chicago.

COMMITTEE ON THE HEALTH AND SAFETY IMPLICATIONS OF CHILD LABOR, NATIONAL RESEARCH COUNCIL (1998), *Protecting Youth at Work,* National Academy Press, Washington DC.

COUCH, K. (1992), "New Evidence on the Long-term Effects of Employment Training Programs", *Journal of Labor Economics,* Vol. 10, No. 4, p. 380-388, October.

CRANE, J. and ELLWOOD, D. (1984), "The Summer Youth Employment Program: Private Job Supplement or Substitute?", Harvard University, Cambridge, MA.

ELLWOOD, D. and WELTY, E. (1998), "Public Service Employment and Mandatory Work: A Policy Whose Time Has Come and Gone and Come Again?", John F. Kennedy School of Government, Harvard University, Cambridge, MA.

ELLWOOD, D. and WISE, D. (1987), "Military Hiring and Youth Employment", in D. Wise (ed.), *Public Sector Payrolls,* The University of Chicago Press, Chicago.

FARKAS, G., ALTON SMITH, D., STROMSDORFER, E., TRASK, G. and JERRETT III, R. (1992), *Impacts from the Youth Incentive Entitlement Pilot Projects: Participation, Work, and Schooling Over the Full Program Period,* Manpower Demonstration Research Corporation, December.

FARKAS, G., OLSEN, R., STROMSDORFER, E., SHARPE, L., SKIDMORE, F., ALTON SMITH, D. and MERRILL, S. (1984), *Post-Program Impacts of the Youth Incentive Entitlement Pilot Projects,* Manpower Demonstration Research Corporation, June.

HOLLENBECK, K. and WILLKE, R. (1991), *The Employment and Earnings Impacts of the Targeted Jobs Tax Credit,* Upjohn Institute, Kalamazoo, MI.

JASTRZAB, J., MASKER, J., BLOOMQUIST, J. and ORR, L. (1996), *Impacts of Service: Final Report on the Evaluation of American Conservation and Youth Service Corps,* Abt Associates, Cambridge, MA, August.

KATZ, L. (1998), "Wage Subsidies for the Disadvantaged", in R. Freeman and P. Gottschalk (eds.), *Generating Jobs: How to Increase Demand for Less-Skilled Workers,* Russell Sage Foundation, New York.

KAUS, M. (1992), *The End of Inequality,* Basic Books, New York.

LERMAN, R. (1982), "A Comparison of Employer and Worker Wage Subsidies", in R. Haveman and J. Palmer (eds.), *Jobs for Disadvantaged Workers,* The Brookings Institution, Washington, DC.

MAYNARD, R. (1980), *The Impact of Supported Work on Young School Dropouts,* Manpower Demonstration Research Corporation, September, New York.

OECD (1998), *Employment Outlook,* Paris.

ORR, L., BLOOM, H., BELL, S., DOOLITTLE, F., LIN, W. and CAVE, G. (1995), *Does Training for the Disadvantaged Work? Evidence From the JTPA Study,* The Urban Institute Press, Washington, DC.

PUBLIC-PRIVATE VENTURES (PPV) (1992), *Ventures in Community Improvement: Final Report of the Demonstration,* March, Philadelphia, PA.

STICHT, T. (1989), "Functional Context Education: Policy and Training Methods from the Military Experience", *Investing in People,* Background Papers, Volume II, Commission on Workforce Quality and Labor Market Efficiency, US Department of Labor, Washington, DC.

SUM, A., FOOG, N. and FOGG, N. (1997), "Confronting the Demographic Challenge: Future Labor Market Prospects of Out-of-School Young Adults," *A Generation of Challenge: Pathways to Success for Urban Youth,* Sar Levitan Center for Social Policy Studies, Monograph 97-03, Johns Hopkins University, Baltimore, MD, June.

US COMMISSION ON THE SKILLS OF THE AMERICAN WORKFORCE (1990), *America's Choice: High Skills or Low Wages,* National Center for Education and the Economy, Rochester, NY

US GENERAL ACCOUNTING OFFICE (1996), *Employment Training: Successful Projects Share Common Strategy,* Washington, DC.

WALKER, G. and VILELLA-VELEZ, F. (1992), *Anatomy of a Demonstration,* Public/Private Ventures, Philadelphia, PA.

WILLIAM T. GRANT FOUNDATION COMMISSION ON WORK FAMILY AND CITIZENSHIP (1988), *The Forgotten Half: Non-College Youth in American,* Washington, DC.

ZIMMERMAN, D. (1978), *A Study of the Value of Output in Youth Employment Programs,* Report No. 21, Final Report, US Department of Labor, Washington, DC.

RAPPORTEUR'S REPORT

THE SCHOOL-TO-WORK TRANSITION TWENTY YEARS ON: ISSUES, EVIDENCE AND CONUNDRUMS*

by
Paul Ryan
University of Cambridge, United Kingdom

Introduction

The research effort of the last twenty years indicates both how much is known and how much remains unknown concerning the school-to-work transition in advanced economies. Much of what is known is reflected in the contributions to this volume. This paper attempts a selective overview of the issues and the evidence.

A key innovation of the past two decades has been the concept of the school-to-work transition itself. The concept draws together in a common arena a previously disparate set of issues in such areas as vocational education and training, youth unemployment, and wage structure. It does so by emphasising process attributes, as individuals flow from full-time schooling to full-time permanent employment, through various intermediate conditions, including vocational education and apprenticeship, fixed-term and part-time employment, and labour market programmes. The widespread adoption of a transition or flow perspective on these states has been encouraged by the increased availability of the longitudinal datasets within which individual trajectories can be traced over time. For a transition perspective to be more than simply descriptive, however, there must be path dependence along the way, with experiences at one stage affecting outcomes further on, if only temporarily.

It is difficult to assimilate the full range of issues and evidence in what is by now a vast international literature with variegated national components. The next section discusses the issues as they appear nowadays in various OECD economies, with their similarities and differences. The remainder of the paper draws primarily on the experiences of four economies: the United States, France, Japan and Germany. (Narrowing the focus to a small number of economies helps to highlight the issues; choosing these four ensures a wide range of evidence on those issues). Section 2 considers three detailed issues – path dependence, mobility in the youth labour market, and youth employment shares – in order to illustrate both the gains in our knowledge in the school-to-work area and the limits to those gains. Section 3 discusses the effectiveness of the main policies with which governments have responded to youth joblessness, which remains for most of us the key school-to-work problem. Section 4 considers the implications for public intervention of the two school-to-work institutions that have arguably been the most successful of all: the German dual system of mass apprenticeship and school-work networks in Japan.

* This paper is based on remarks made as rapporteur to the Washington conference. I would like to thank the OECD for encouragement and financial support; the Japan Institute of Labour for helpful discussions; Norton Grubb and Mitsuko Uenishi for advice and assistance; and John Martin for comments. All interpretations are my responsibility.

1. What are the problems?

Most commentators agree on the existence of significant problems in the school-to-work area in all advanced economies, but their nature and severity remain contentious. This section discusses the problems that cause concern, starting with widely accepted ones and moving on to more disputed ones.

Structure and conjuncture

The primary contemporary concern in the US and the UK is structural youth joblessness, associated with economic and social disadvantage.[1] The most vivid symbol is joblessness amongst teenage members of racial minorities in the US. Currently, even after prolonged economic expansion, as many as one third of black male teenager workers, and one quarter of females, are formally unemployed (see Lynch, p. 289 in this volume). When the other young people who are also out of work and out of school, but who have no contact with the formal labour market, are included, joblessness rates for teenage racial minority members rise towards one half, and exceed it when the aggregate labour market is slacker (Rees, 1986).

The presence of a large core of youth joblessness in countries that, as in the US and the UK at present, are at or near the top of the economic cycle, indicates a structural problem that cannot be removed by a general economic expansion. Public policy is consequently encouraged to concentrate on the problems of the least employable young people. Youth programmes have traditionally focused on urban minorities in the US. In the UK at present, the primary – initially, the exclusive – constituency of the leading labour market programme, the New Deal, is workers aged less than 25 years who have been unemployed for at least six months.

The labour market problems of disadvantaged youth are associated in part with educational failure. Internationally standardised tests of pupil attainment in mathematics and science generally indicate low cognitive achievements amongst students from disadvantaged backgrounds. Results for the UK and US point to lower means and higher variances in the distribution of pupil learning in compulsory education in mathematics than in Japan, Germany and Singapore in particular. A greater gap between the cognitive achievements of lower and higher achievers imposes cumulative labour market disability on the low achievers. It has led to acute policy concern to raise the attainments of the lower half of the achievement distribution in both the US and the UK (Prais, 1993; see Mortimore and Mortimore p. 103 in this volume).

Outside the US and the UK, concern over youth joblessness also embraces structural attributes (see Nicaise, p. 347 in this volume), but at present conjunctural ones dominate. In most advanced economies, youth unemployment is not just pro-cyclical but also "super-cyclical", i.e., more cyclically variable than is total unemployment (OECD, 1982; OECD, 1996, Table 4.18). The slack labour markets of the 1990s have wreaked havoc on youth access to employment. Countries previously immune to the problem, having broadly survived the shocks of the 1970s intact, notably Sweden, Japan and Finland, joined the club in the 1990s, their youth unemployment rates rising strongly, and, thus far at least, durably, in association with economic stagnation. In France, a potent mix of structural and cyclical factors has almost eliminated employment as an option for teenagers, and greatly depressed its availability for young adults.[2]

The balance between the structural and the conjunctural amongst the causes of youth employment problems varies considerably. The tight labour markets of the late 1990s in the US have left behind a problem that is exclusively structural. The slack labour markets of Europe and, increasingly, East Asia, have by contrast tended to conceal structural attributes. Nevertheless, major differences between countries and changes over time can be discerned in the importance of structural problems.

A structural change visible in many advanced economies is declining labour force attachment amongst young workers. The share of jobless young workers who are unemployed, rather than economically inactive, has fallen, in some countries to below one half (Table 1, columns 3 and 4). The tendency has been marked even in the Netherlands, where youth joblessness has remained low overall. Low labour force attachment amongst jobless youth makes economic expansion a less effective remedy for joblessness in the medium-term and in the longer-term may cause labour market difficulties for the young people involved (see Section 2 below).

The dangers are intensified by a tendency for the social concentration of youth joblessness to intensify, in terms of both locality and household. Youth economic activity has declined, even petrified, in many of the low-income housing estates located on the fringes of large cities in the UK and France. The share of unemployed teenagers living in households in which no one else is employed rose from one fifth to one quarter in the EU between 1985 and 1996, by which time it had reached 36% for young adults (see in this volume, Bowers, Sonnet and Bardone, Table 6a, p. 66 and Freeman, p. 89). Under such conditions, the difficulty of finding employment, and the will to do so, are both expected to deteriorate.

Problems associated with social disadvantage are visible in all countries: in Germany, as elsewhere, young members of racial minorities, primarily those of Turkish descent, do worse in terms of schooling, training and employment than do other young people.[3] But the extent and implications of social disadvantage are generally less outside than inside the US. In Germany and Japan, lower dispersions in the distributions of both household income and youth educational attainments are associated with less acute problems of economic and social marginalisation amongst young people than in the US (Franz and Pohlmeier, 1999; Dore and Sako, 1998).

Nor does depressed economic activity hurt youth disproportionately in all countries. Particularly in Germany, but also in Ireland and the Netherlands, youth unemployment has been no more sensitive to the economic cycle than has its adult counterpart (OECD, 1996, Table 4.18). The weakness of both the cyclical and structural sources of youth joblessness in Germany has provided an important cushion for school-to-work transitions as economic conditions have worsened. Recent data is not readily available. In the 1980s, when conditions were not as adverse, amongst young Germans who left school without completing upper secondary education, only 3% experienced at least two years cumulative unemployment during their first five years in the labour market, in contrast to the 33% of their French peers who had the same experience. Even so, this small minority of German youth represents a hard core of long-term joblessness, accounting for nearly one third of the total time spent in unemployment by their its education-age cohort (see Bowers, Sonnet and Bardone, Table 20, p. 80 in this volume).

Instability

A third area of concern is instability in early labour market experience. Movement between different labour market states, particularly to and from employment, is typically much higher amongst young than amongst adult workers. In all countries, young workers enter and leave jobs, and enter and leave joblessness, more frequently than do adults. Rates of job turnover amongst young people are particularly high in the US, and low in Japan and Germany (OECD, 1996, Table 4.7). In France, many young people cycle through various extended sequences of unemployment, fixed-term employment and public programmes before moving into more stable employment after five or more years in the labour market (Werquin, 1996).

Whether or not high turnover amongst youth is a problem remains controversial. In France, the mainstream interpretation views extensive *précarité* in early labour market experience as dysfunctional, a source of distress and damage to young people and of loss to the economy (*op. cit.*). This interpretation is mirrored in the US by institutionalist critics of high turnover in the youth labour market, who talk in terms of "churning", during an extended moratorium period that is spent between schooling and career employment in low-paid, unskilled, dead-end jobs (Osterman, 1980; Stern *et al.*, 1995).[4] Others accept the description but see in it not restlessness and waste but rather beneficial labour market search and job-worker matching that leads young workers and employers to better and more durable employment relationships than they would otherwise have found (Topel and Ward, 1992; Nicole-Drancourt, 1992; Bordigoni and Mansuy, 1997). The low youth turnover rates of Japan and Germany in particular are interpreted from this perspective as evidence, not of successful school-to-work institutions (Büchtemann *et al.*, 1993), but of undesirable restrictions on search and matching in the labour market (Heckman *et al.*, 1994). This highly polarised debate is considered further in the next section.

Vocational preparation

A second area of controversy is youth vocational preparation. In the US and the UK in particular, many young people acquire little vocational preparation, whether at school or in the labour market. Critics of such arrangements point to both the extensive vocational studies undertaken by young people in Germany, Austria and Denmark, where at least two fifths of each age cohort undertakes an apprenticeship that leads to a vocational qualification at craft or higher levels, and to the vocational curricula that occupy a large slice of secondary education in France, Sweden and the Netherlands. The high share of young workers that possesses a recognised vocational qualification in those countries, in an era of increasing returns to skill, has been depicted as a benefit to both individuals' career prospects and national economic performance (Prais, 1995; Stern, p. 155 in this volume).

Such arguments have in both the US and the UK prompted public intervention in support of vocational education in general, and apprenticeship in particular (Stern and Wagner, 1999). But the issue remains disputed. Others doubt the role postulated for vocational preparation in economic performance. Both Japan and the US have attained high levels of productivity without extensive vocational secondary education or apprenticeship. Some argue that early vocational preparation often goes to waste, and that it is better to restrict vocational preparation to post-secondary studies and labour market experience when young people are better placed to decide for themselves what they need to learn (Heckman *et al.*, 1994; Dougherty, 1996).

Youth incomes

Finally, there is the widespread decline in the youth share of personal income, associated not only with falling youth employment shares, but also with declining relative pay and access to social security benefits. The passivity of youth in the face of the decline is indeed noteworthy, and the family does cushion its effects on youth well-being, but the overall implications for youth well-being can only be adverse (Freeman, p. 89 in this volume).

Severity of problems

Agreement on the nature of the problem in the school-to-work area is therefore greatest for youth joblessness, particularly its long-term component, and least for vocational preparation and labour market mobility. Concentrating for the moment on joblessness, the key issues are: how severe is the problem and what are the alternatives?

Long-term joblessness can create problems on two counts: firstly, immediate loss of personal well-being associated with unemployment; secondly, subsequent damage to personal well-being arising from damage to skills, motivation and self-confidence. The latter represents a leading potential source of path dependence in school-to-work transitions.

The evidence suggests concern on both scores. Adverse effects of unemployment on youth personal well-being and mental health while unemployed have been reported by several European statistical studies that attempt to control for selection effects – i.e. in this context, a greater probability that intrinsically less happy and less healthy individuals will become unemployed than will happy and healthy ones (e.g., Korpi, 1997; Winkelmann and Winkelmann, 1998). Evidence of lasting scarring by youth unemployment, in Europe if not in the US, is considered in Section 2 below.

The tougher question is: given these adverse effects of joblessness on young people, what are the alternatives? The constraints on macroeconomic policy nowadays make increased employment hard to achieve. In the limit, the issue then becomes the distribution of a given level of joblessness. If attention is confined to youth, the alternative to long-term unemployment for a minority is to spread the pain more evenly, through exposing more young people to short spells, which means a less unequal distribution of the pain, and may mean less scarring overall. This has been a major effect of public interventions in France and the UK, for instance, which in effect encourage young workers to cycle through sequences of alternating activity and joblessness rather than to settle back into long-term inactivity.

Joblessness may also be redistributed from youth to adults. The question then is whether a given incidence of joblessness does less harm when borne by adults rather than by youth. The issue can be viewed either way: in favour of youths, by emphasising their less mature and fragile personalities; in favour of adults, by emphasising their greater household responsibilities and potentially lower resilience. Evidence on these matters is inadequate. Whether or not youths suffer greater losses of immediate well-being and more scarring as a result of joblessness than do adults has yet to be determined. Moreover, even were that the case, the relative priority of reducing youth relative to adult unemployment would require a value judgement as well.

The verdict on the issue that is implicit in public policy is often, but not always, that youth joblessness is a more grievous problem than its adult counterpart. In the UK in the early 1980s and again nowadays, in the US during the 1970s and 1980s, and in France nowadays, labour market programmes have by and large given the needs of youth priority over those of adults. By contrast, in Italy and Japan, public priorities are much less oriented to youth. Outlays on youth programmes in Italy do indeed account for a significant share of all public spending on labour market programmes, but not in proportion to youth's near-monopoly share of unemployment. In Japan, the steady rise in youth unemployment during the 1990s, taking it to nearly 10% by now, has yet to induce any significant share for youth in what is anyway a low level of public spending on labour market programmes (OECD, 1998, Table J)[5].

Some reasons for the low priority given to unemployed youth in Japan are considered in the following section. One general factor is particularly pronounced in Japan, Italy and other southern European countries: the possibility for many young people of relying on their parents for support, notably by continuing to live in the parental household. In advanced economies in 1997, around nine-tenths of teenage workers, and fully two-thirds of 20-24 year old males, lived with their parents. In Italy and Spain, so did as many as three in every four 25-29 year old males (see Bowers, Sonnet and Bardone, Table 3, p. 62 in this volume). Under such conditions, there is a case for giving lower priority to the young rather than to the prime-age unemployed, as long as attention is paid to the needs of young people who lack family support.

In sum, school-to-work problems are multi-dimensional, and the importance of some dimensions is disputed. The European perspective is dominated by a high incidence of long-term youth unemployment, associated with economic stagnation; the US one, by an irreducible core of structural joblessness. These two dimensions pose the major challenge to public policy. Outside them, there is little agreement. However, in my view, low vocational preparation and high labour market turnover constitute serious deficiencies in the school-to-work transitions of less highly educated young people in the US and the UK.

2. How extensive is our knowledge?

Our understanding of school-to-work issues has advanced during the past twenty years, but the gains have been uneven. This section considers three sets of issues across which the gain in knowledge has varied from high to low: path dependence, labour market turnover and youth employment shares.

Major gains in knowledge: path dependence

School-to-work transitions may show path (or state) dependence, in that outcomes may depend on events along the way. In particular, adverse events may blow the journey off course, temporarily or permanently. Potentially damaging events include educational failure, joblessness and instability; the outcomes potentially affected by them include pay and employment rates as adults.

During the past twenty years longitudinal datasets that cover early labour market experience have become widely available. Such data offer the prospect of isolating statistically the effects of early events on individuals' subsequent outcomes, while controlling for the effect of extraneous factors, both individual and contextual.

The resulting evidence is often far from robust, as it is potentially affected by various selection processes that allocate individuals between different states in ways that cannot readily be controlled statistically. For example, any apparently adverse association between the incidences of early and subsequent unemployment may reflect not scarring by unemployment, but rather joint selection into both states according to intrinsic individual attributes. Less able and motivated young people are more likely to experience both states even if no causal mechanism is present. Statistical analysis can cope readily when ability and motivation can be measured, but that is often not the case. Sophisticated statistical methods have been developed to deal with the resulting selection biases, but the limitations of those techniques are serious (Grubb and Ryan, 1999).

Nevertheless, the accumulated evidence undermines, for Europe at least, the early, US-based view that youth unemployment does not have major or lasting effects on the labour market prospects of those who undergo it. Studies of German, French, British and Swedish youth have found adverse effects on subsequent pay and employment rates. The uniformity with which state dependence is found in French studies, even after allowing for unseen selection processes, is particularly striking, given widespread concerns over *précarité* in early labour market experience in France (e.g., Allaire *et al.*, 1995; Balsan *et al.*, 1996).

Much remains to be determined. Firstly, it is hard to know how long adverse effects last when the data typically cover at most five years of labour market experience. The fact that, even in the slack labour markets of the 1990s, the great majority of French female workers who possessed low or no qualifications had achieved stable employment (*contrat à durée indéterminée*) within six years of leaving school provides some reassurance that the joblessness that affects most young French women may not have powerful long-term effects (Balsan *et al.*, 1996). Secondly, the relative importance of exposure to unemployment as opposed to time spent in unemployment in doing the damage remains unclear, as most of the evidence concerns the former only. Thirdly, adverse effects might be expected to be stronger for teenagers than for young adults, or in the first two years in the labour market rather than subsequently, but there is little evidence on either issue. Finally, it is not clear why state dependence should be stronger in Europe than in the US, if indeed the difference is really present in the first place.

It might be expected that Japan's labour market institutions, which have involved the direct hiring of large numbers of school-leavers into lifetime employment, would make the effects of unemployment on youth more durable than in other countries, by forcing the current generation of school-leavers permanently to "miss the bus" of access to career employment. Again, the evidence is limited. The outcome will depend on the extent to which small to medium sized employers, who nowadays compensate for the decline in school-leaver recruitment by large employers, prove to have offered career employment to their young recruits (Nitta, 1995; see also Mitani, p. 305 in this volume).

Notwithstanding such lacunae and the difficulty of truly controlling for selection effects, the evidence does point towards important scarring effects, arising from early failure in schooling and in the labour market, upon the subsequent fortunes of young people, thereby underlining the potential importance of school-to-work policies.

Unrecognised gains in knowledge: turnover in youth labour markets

Although the two, frequently opposed, views of instability in early labour market experience, *viz.* as unproductive churning or productive search and matching (see Section 1), remain largely unreconciled, comparative evidence can be used to narrow the issues, indicating that there is no need to chose between them.

To recap, one view interprets high turnover in early labour market experience as evidence of the institutional exclusion of young workers from good jobs in a segmented labour market, imposing a period of waiting and drifting until personal maturation permits entry to stable career employment. Evidence cited in support of this view includes: the low training content of most youth employment in the US; the sectoral and occupational segregation of youth employment, including inverse associations across sectors between adult pay and youth employment shares; and the effects of apprenticeship as a counter to such tendencies (Bishop, 1991; Marsden and Ryan, 1991).

In the alternative interpretation, young workers, lacking information on job location and attributes, and facing employers similarly ill-informed about them, move frequently between jobs as they reject prospects that turn out to be poor and as they locate better ones, settling down only when a match that is good for both parties has been attained. The process is seen as an efficient adaptation to imperfect labour market information. Evidence cited in favour of this view includes the marked growth of pay in association with turnover amongst US and French youth (Parsons, 1991; Topel and Ward, 1992; Mansuy, 1996).

Some perspective on the issue can be gained from comparative evidence, starting with Japan, whose youth labour market does not conform readily to either theory. Japanese school-leavers flow in large numbers directly from school to permanent employment. The institutional core is the *Jisseki-Kankei* ("contract") system of school-employer linkages at senior high school level, under which employers hire school-leavers from linked schools largely in accordance with the achievement rankings and recommendations that are provided by teachers. The term *Jisseki-Kankei* is used here as a shorthand for the wider institutional system of which the term forms only part, strictly speaking.[6]

Around one half of the secondary leavers who do not go into tertiary-level education and training make the short trip along this school-to-work superhighway direct to regular employment, and, amongst males at least, into career employment as well (Kariya, 1999). The system has, until recently at least, survived even the stresses of the 1990s: in 1997 four fifths of leavers at upper secondary level went straight to full-time regular employment (see Mitani, p. 305 in this volume).[7]

The sheer efficacy of *Jisseki-Kankei* in terms of the volume and speed of transitions from school to work contrasts with the weak to non-existent school-work linkages in the US, suggesting that US policy might gain from studying it and trying to develop similar institutions (Bishop, 1993; Rosenbaum, 1999). The apparent implication for this discussion is that *Jisseki-Kankei* dispenses with any need for young people to spend much time in early labour market experience, whether waiting or searching, in order to find a steady job.

The efficiency claims of the contract system are, however, less impressive in qualitative than in quantitative terms. It matches across two largely uni-dimensional rankings of jobs and workers. When job requirements and worker aspirations are highly standardised, that makes sense. When job requirements and worker aspirations are variegated, it becomes a matter of the mass hammering of square pegs into round holes. That can be done cheaply and quickly, but the quality of the match suffers, for both employers and young people. It can be argued that, as Japan's living standards have grown, the qualitative inefficiency of the contract system has become more important relative to its quantitative efficiency.

Such an interpretation is supported by official policies. Although some aspects predate World War Two, *Jisseki-Kankei* was formalised by government initiative in the 1960s, at a time of acute labour scarcity and national economic mobilisation. Nowadays, with labour no longer scarce, concerns to foster creativity to the fore, and attention to individual needs on the rise, the Japanese government seeks reform. The Ministries of both Education and Labour, who do not always see eye to eye, have both criticised national school-to-work institutions for paying little attention to individual needs and creativity. Evidence cited in favour of reform includes: dropping out in senior high school, which involved 7% of students in the mid-1980s before falling back; and the high quit rate amongst young workers, which accounted for almost one half of reasons for entering unemployment amongst 15-24 year olds in 1998 and which has been rising in small and medium sized companies since 1993, deteriorating labour market notwithstanding (see Mitani, p. 305 in this volume; Ministry of Labour, 1998). The government's intention is not to abolish *Jisseki-Kankei* but to increase the influence of personal aptitudes and interests on the choice of type of secondary school, subjects studied in school, and employment after school.[8]

If Japanese experience suggests that you can have too little turnover and matching in the youth labour market, its French counterpart suggests that you can have too much. In the slack labour markets of contemporary France, the matching potential of high turnover in the youth labour market is seriously reduced, at least as far as the needs of youth are concerned. Young people, seeking shelter from the storm, take whatever they can get: most young employees report not having had any choice of jobs, and having simply taken whatever was on offer. Employers have undoubtedly benefited from excess supply in youth labour markets, using fixed-term employment contracts and public training programmes to screen large numbers of young workers: the youth share of total recruitment has held up well while the share of total employment has plummeted (see Marchand, p. 329 in this volume). But there is little gain in this for young workers, most of whom must wait years to find career employment, and therefore correspondingly less for job-worker matching as a whole.[9]

The Japanese and French experiences suggest therefore: that the value of job-worker matching is indeed substantial, and the potential contribution of early labour market experience to it considerable; that the dichotomisation of churning and matching as interpretations of youth turnover is simplistic; that institutionalised school-employer linkages can reduce the need for matching in early labour market experience; and that, particularly in slack labour markets, the matching potential of youth turnover is partly wasted, at least for young people themselves.

More is therefore known, and less need be disputed, about the merits of turnover in youth labour markets than is usually recognised. Attention should be diverted to consider the other ways, including, for secondary education, the vocationalisation of curricula and the provision of careers advice, in which the matching burden may be prevented from falling as heavily upon early labour market experience as it does in the US (Bishop, 1993).

The conundrum: youth employment shares

Although we also know more than we used to about the determinants of youth employment, much remains to be understood. The tendency in many countries for youth employment to deteriorate, despite favourable movements in youth cohort sizes, youth relative pay and sectoral employment shares, is not easily explained (see Freeman, p. 89 in this volume). A comparison of the US, France and Japan helps point up the problem.

The past twenty years have seen in many economies declines in either youth employment rates or youth relative pay, or both. In the US, the main change has been in youth relative pay (Tables 2 and 3). The standard economic explanation looks to an increased demand for skills within competitive labour markets. From that standpoint, young workers might be expected to gain, insofar as "skill" is construed in terms of education: accelerating educational expansion has widened the gap between the schooling of young and adult workers. But if the skill dimension for which demand has expanded is experience, not education, then young workers must suffer, as they unavoidably possess less experience than adults. The fact that the decline in relative pay in the US was greatest for young workers in general, and less educated ones in particular, may therefore be explicable in terms of a particular "twist" in the trend in the demand for skill: *viz.*, a decline in the substitutability of schooling for experience in production technology, within a broader decline in the substitutability of less for more skilled labour. Young people may suffer from the Catch-22 problem of needing experience to get a good job, but finding it hard to get a job in order to get the experience, particularly if they did not acquire much education. In competitive markets, the price of youth labour then falls, avoiding any need, from the demand side at least, for youth employment rates to fall (Levy and Murnane, 1992).

So far, so orthodox – and, not surprisingly, consistent with the changes in the US experience that the theory was developed to explain in the first place: *viz.*, stable youth employment rates along with falling youth relative pay.[10] But does the explanation work for other countries? As the postulated causes of skill-oriented shifts in the demand for labour include technical change and international economic integration, similar trends in youth pay and employment should have occurred in all advanced economies, subject as all presumably are to similar trends in technology and trade.

In fact, the behaviour of youth pay and employment has differed greatly across the three countries considered here (Tables 2 and 3). Turning next to France, its experience is an anomaly for the mainstream economic interpretation: youth relative pay changed little over the same two decades, while youth employment rates plummeted. Such attributes can of course be reconciled with the postulated skill-intensive shift in labour demand as long as the assumption of competitive wage setting is abandoned, for France at least. Pay setting is indeed viewed as less responsive to labour market conditions in France than in the US, as a result of greater bargaining coverage, sector-level rather than plant-level bargaining, and a higher statutory wage floor in France. Moreover, in France internal labour markets (in which seniority-based job security – "last in, first out" – makes youth recruitment particularly sensitive to the economic cycle, while insulating internal pay structures from the same forces), are more extensive than in the US (Marsden 1990; Marsden and Ryan, 1990).

Under such conditions, one might hypothesise that similar economic forces have dissimilar implications for young workers. In the US, with more flexible pay structures, the impact is on relative pay; in France, with more rigid pay structures, on relative employment. The argument is familiar from studies of aggregate pay and unemployment in the US and EU (Krugman, 1994; OECD, 1994).[11] The evidence appears to be consistent with the hypothesis in the youth context, even if not in the aggregate (Tables 2 and 3).[12]

Japan again upsets the explanatory apple cart. The hypothesised changes in technology and trade are presumed to have affected Japan as well, and, if anything, to have done so earlier and more strongly than in the US and France. As in France, pay setting in Japan is often characterised in terms of extensive institutional co-ordination rather than of decentralisation and market forces; and internal labour markets are surely no less influential in Japan than in France. We might therefore expect developments for Japanese youth to resemble those in France: *viz.*, little change in relative pay combined with a marked decline in employment rates. Indeed, a particularly large fall in youth employment might be expected for Japan, in view of the protracted stagnation of the 1990s, the concentration of recruitment on school-leavers, and the difficulty for employers of laying off surplus employees, making recruitment cuts the easiest way of reducing employment (Nitta, 1995).

In practice, however, even though relative youth pay has declined only slightly, youth employment rates have remained high and stable in Japan during the 1990s (Tables 2 and 3), as had previously been the case after the oil price shocks of the 1970s (Nohara, 1988). There have indeed been changes under the more arduous conditions of the 1990s. The balance of youth recruitment has shifted in recent years from larger to smaller firms; higher proportions of school-leavers have not found regular employment by the time that they leave school; and the recruitment of college graduates, particularly females, has declined heavily (Ministry of Labour, 1996; see also Mitani, p. 305 in this volume).[13] Nevertheless, the contrast to the US and French experiences is sharp, and the challenge to the mainstream interpretation direct.

If technology and trade make young workers poorer substitutes for experienced adults, why has this not come through in a fall in either youth pay or employment patterns in Japan, as in the US and France? If institutionalised pay setting and internal labour markets mean that youth unemployment piles up during sustained recessions in France, why not in Japan during the stagnation of the 1990s?

Neither the competitive nor the institutional hypotheses, nor the combinations of the two in terms of which the US-France difference is often explained, can accommodate readily the attributes of Japanese youth employment (Sako, 1991).[14] Various lines of explanation can certainly be suggested, including: steep age-wage and seniority-wage profiles in Japan, strengthening the incentive to employ young rather than older workers; greater trainability amongst young than adult workers; higher levels of informal employer and worker organisation in Japan; socio-political pressures on employers to continue hiring from the schools to which they are contracted under *Jisseki-Kankei*; and an implicit social compact under which school-leaver recruitment is treated as a national priority. Whatever the merits of such explanations, it is clear that standard economic and institutional interpretations do not travel well, and that neither changes in technology and trade nor standardised institutional attributes provide the general explanations that are sometimes claimed for them. Indeed, the direct evidence for the postulated "twist" in trends in the demand for skill is hardly sufficient to induce confidence in the mainstream hypothesis in the first place.

Much remains therefore to be learned about the determinants of school-to-work transitions, particularly when it comes to international differences in their attributes. In such contexts, the only claim to wisdom is that, if the answers aren't clear, at least the questions are clearer than they were.

3.   What works?

An obvious question to pose after the last twenty years of policy experience and evaluation research is: what works, with respect to youth joblessness in particular? This section attempts a quick overview of the range of answers that has been given to the question.

One answer, commonly encountered nowadays in the US, is that "nothing works". Government should accordingly limit itself to improving the functioning of labour markets and general education and leave the rest to the self-interest of young people and employers (Heckman *et al.*, 1994). This stance has been encouraged by the generally unfavourable findings of evaluations of youth labour market programmes in the US (e.g., Bloom *et al.*, 1997). Nor are adverse assessments confined to the US. The main programme for unemployed British youth in the 1980s, the Youth Training Scheme, has proved similarly vulnerable to statistical evaluation (Ryan and Büchtemann, 1996). Similarly, macroeconomic evaluations of youth programmes in France and Sweden have found the displacement of non-participants by participants to be so extensive as to cast doubt on whether the programmes have had any net benefits for youth as a whole, or for the wider economy (see Gautié, p. 387 in this volume; Skedinger, 1995).

Nor has labour market deregulation helped youth much, judging by evidence on the employment effects of minimum wages. Controversy over the sign of the relationship between minimum wages and youth employment has obscured an implicit near-consensus that the youth employment effects of minimum wages, whether positive or negative, are economically small (Freeman, 1994). Moreover, *youth-specific* sub-minimum wages appear to have had little effect on youth employment, even when they cut as deeply across as wide an age band as is the case in the Netherlands (Dolado *et al.*, 1996).[15]

A second, slightly less pessimistic answer, is "not much works". An at least partial exemption from impotence must be granted to economic expansion, given the super-cyclicality of youth unemployment in most countries (see Freeman, p. 89 in this volume). The problem in the large continental European countries and in Japan at present is the difficulty of engineering a sustained economic expansion, even when the political will to do so is present.

Another encouraging exception involves programmes with serious learning content, as opposed to standard "training" and work experience ones. In France, where several labour market programmes function side by side, ranging from work-based, top-up programmes for the already qualified (*contrat d'adaptation*) to work experience for low achievers (*contrat emploi-solidarité*), participants appear to benefit significantly from programmes with substantial training content and private sector sponsorship, but not from the others (Bonnal *et al.*, 1994; Balsan *et al.*, 1996).

A third, still less pessimistic answer, is "some things definitely work, but we don't know why". This is the "San Jose" answer: outcomes for participants in public programmes as delivered by the CET site in San Jose, California, have proved favourable even when the programme as a whole has been evaluated as a failure. While CET's success may be attributable to some mix of employer links, broad training content, a bilingual environment, teaching, and support services, as those attributes are by no means as unique as CET's success, an aura of mystery surrounds the latter (see Grubb, p. 363 in this volume).

A fourth answer is "more works than is often recognised". Even in the US, some things do work, notably more ambitious and expensive programmes that aim higher than do the short-duration, low-quality interventions that have represented the mainstream. In the labour market, the leading potential example is the Job Corps, the long-running, intensive residential programme for disadvantaged minority youth – although the programme is only now being evaluated by the experimental methods that have demolished support for many other youth programmes, and its positive net benefits depend heavily on small changes in subsequent criminality (see Grubb, *op. cit.*). More promising results have been associated with more educationally oriented interventions, including: vocational Junior College courses in the US and apprenticeship in Europe (Grubb, 1997; Ryan, 1998); and the integrated vocational-academic curricula that have been developed in various US secondary schools, including career academies, magnet schools and Tech Prep programmes (see Stern, p. 155 in this volume).[16] The high cost per participant of such programmes may make their widespread adoption problematic, but that is a different obstacle from the ineffectiveness of the many "cheap and cheerful" alternatives on view.

A concern that is often expressed in connection with the more educationally oriented programmes, including mass upper secondary education and occupational training in Germany, Sweden and France is: what about the dwindling minority that is left behind? Such groups include the less than 10% of young Germans who do not enter upper secondary education, apprenticeship or equivalent vocational training (Franz and Pohlmeier, 1999). Won't their position deteriorate as a result? The shrinking size of such groups may intensify their members' consciousness of low status and social exclusion, but they will not necessarily lose out economically, whether relatively or absolutely. In Germany, unskilled young workers are so few that the market for their labour, which exists in all countries, slanted towards such sectors as catering and retailing, is less overstocked than in other countries, to the benefit of their pay and employment rates. The famous prediction by a British Chancellor of the Exchequer during the 1980s of an economic future stocked not so much with "low tech" as with "no tech" jobs may have been overstated, but it did point to the enduring importance of low-skilled service "McJobs" for young people, and the benefits to low skilled youth arising from any restriction, if only as a by-product of educational expansion, of supply relative to demand in such markets.

Moreover, viewed from a different standpoint, there is merit in even some of the US youth programmes that are commonly judged to have failed. The criterion conventionally used in evaluation research to assess programmes is an efficiency-related one: does the programme produce subsequent social and economic gains sufficient to justify the costs of providing the services? This criterion does consider benefits to participants: improvements in their subsequent labour market outcomes constitute in practice the main benefit category. But it does not consider the equity-related criterion, whether the programme makes participants better off while they are enrolled on it, whatever about afterwards. When the participants are predominantly the disadvantaged, as is common in the US, equity benefits may be present even when efficiency ones are negligible.

From an equity standpoint, even such frequently maligned programmes of temporary job creation for minority youth as the US' Supported Work have merit. Often criticised as no more than a means of keeping difficult teenagers off the street, while stigmatising participants in the eyes of employers, such programmes are nevertheless often accepted by the same teenagers because they offer a secure income during participation. The claim cannot, however, be made for all programmes, even those which cater to the disadvantaged. The US' Jobstart and New Chance programmes are both estimated to have reduced participant incomes during the programme: the allowances provided to participants were even lower than the expected value of labour market income in the absence of participation.[17]

More widespread acceptance of equity as a criterion in Europe than in the US is reflected in both the duration and entitlement basis of many European programmes. France's *contrats emplois consolidés* offer disadvantaged young workers who have been unable to find employment, despite having tried all the other options, up to five years' paid work in a public organisation (Stankiewicz, 1998). In the UK, the Youth Training Programme and its successors have since 1983 guaranteed a place to all unemployed 16 and 17 year olds. Efficiency goals remain important, not least in the apparent insistence on training content and increased employability in such programmes. In practice, however, YTS-type programmes have pushed many young people into what are in effect regular jobs, involving hard work, low pay and minimal learning, and done little for their skills and employability.

Better then in such cases to drop the rhetoric of work-based training and provide instead either a regular job or more user-friendly and socially useful activities for the young unemployed. The former option is now offered in France by the *contrats emploi consolidés* and in Britain through the private sector jobs subsidised by the New Deal programme. The latter option suggests building upon the concept of public service, as embodied in the US' Youth Service Corps, Americorps and Peace Corps programmes, and the environmental taskforces of the UK's New Deal. At the more user-friendly end of the spectrum, there are also the adventure-cum-challenge programmes for disadvantaged youth in the UK, offered by charities such as Outward Bound, that government had until recently become reluctant to support. While the goals of such activities include public service and personal development, that need not conflict with the standard efficiency criteria of enhanced skills and employability. The programmes can be designed to encourage the stable behaviour and work discipline that can subsequently help participants in the labour market (see Lerman, p. 419 in this volume).

From these wider perspectives, the view that "nothing works" is not only defeatist, it's wrong, in its preoccupation with subsequent labour market outcomes, its neglect of intensive and expensive programmes, and its indifference to in-programme benefits for disadvantaged participants. Those who remain pessimistic might at this point remember that the alternative for many disadvantaged youth, particularly in the US and the UK, is effectively imprisonment: a large minority of young black males in the US is incarcerated (Freeman, 1996). We know quite a lot about prison: it generally doesn't work, in terms of promoting personal reform and reducing recidivism, partly because it scars heavily at least some of those who go through it; and it's very expensive, for the economy, society and "participants" alike (Walker and Hough, 1998).

4. Programmes and institutions

Returning to economic efficiency, this section considers the possibility that more intensive and costly programmes, particularly educationally-oriented ones, may deliver lasting gains when standard labour market programmes do not. Another way of looking at it would be to contrast institutions and their development to programmes and their replacement.

The discussion is focused by considering the two leading examples of institutional success in the school-to-work area: Japan's *Jisseki-Kankei* system of school-employer linkages (Section 1 above), and Germany's mass apprenticeship system. Both sets of institutions are associated with high rates of youth transition from full-time schooling to potentially stable employment and training. They may be compared to the various packages of ephemeral labour market programmes, comprising short-cycle training and work experience, that have been adopted for unemployed young workers in the US, UK, France – and in this decade, even in Sweden – but that have hardly featured at all in Japan and Germany.

Before developing the contrast, we note that it is easily overdrawn, and the comparative merits of institutions over programmes easily overstated (see Teichler, p. 215 in this volume). Concerning the former, some programmes have been around for so long that it is no longer easy to distinguish them from institutions (Werquin, p. 265 in this volume). The difficulty is particularly marked in France, whose record of large-scale youth-related labour market interventions stretches back twenty years, and where the difference between the more training-oriented of those interventions, notably the *contrat de qualification*, and apprenticeship is often treated as trivial (Bonnal *et al.*, 1994). At the same time, the contrast between the ephemerality and low status of most youth programmes, on the one hand, and the longevity and improving, if not always high, status of apprenticeship suggests that the two categories should be separated, even in France (Lhotel and Monaco, 1993).[18]

Secondly, the comparative merits of institutions are often overstated relative to those of programmes. The qualitative drawbacks of *Jisseki-Kankei* were noted in Section 2. Similarly, the merits of apprenticeship are often exaggerated. From an individual standpoint, apprenticeship does improve labour market outcomes for participants, particularly in relation to alternatives in the youth labour market, but its benefits relative to those of full-time vocational education, and (in the US and the UK at least) for females as opposed to males, are more tenuous. From a youth labour market standpoint, apprenticeship promotes lower youth joblessness and greater youth access to skilled work. From the economy's standpoint, the high stocks of intermediate skills that Germany derives largely from mass apprenticeship are associated with superior productivity and trade performance in industry, particularly relative to that of the UK, but the advantages are less clear in services, and less clear relative to the US in general (Steedman and Wagner, 1989; Marsden and Ryan, 1990; Mason and Finegold, 1997; Ryan, 1998).

Even allowing for such reservations, the benefits of apprenticeship, particularly relative to those of labour market programmes, have induced many countries to increase public support for it (Ni Cheallaigh, 1995). Efforts to promote apprenticeship have been constrained, however, by a sense of onerous institutional preconditions that may render its growth infeasible in some contexts, particularly the more deregulated labour markets of the UK and the US. Examples of failed attempts to imitate the German dual system include Korea (Jeong, 1995).

The difficulty is real, but not necessarily insuperable, even in a country whose institutions have become as liberalised as in the UK. The key distinction is that between *institutional borrowing* from abroad, which typically fails, and *institutional development*, the scope for which is often neglected. An example is provided in the area of apprenticeship by recent Irish policies, which have tried, with at least moderate success so far, to revive a declining apprenticeship system by injecting a statutory basis, a stronger educational role, occupational skill standards and joint governance by employer and employee representatives at sectoral level.

The scope for institutional development is underlined by the origins of the two successful national institutions mentioned above: Japan's *Jisseki-Kankei* and German apprenticeship. These institutions did not spring ready made from some god's head. They were rather products of sustained development, subject to public steering at crucial junctures.

The point is particularly clear in the German case. In the first two decades after the war, apprenticeship in the Federal Republic of Germany was widely seen as a low quality, traditional institution, which many wished to scrap in favour of full-time schooling, as was indeed done in Sweden (Taylor, 1981). The path taken in West Germany, however, was major reform, as embodied in the 1969 Vocational Training Act, which, by stipulating improved training quality, laid the basis for the subsequent near-consensus on the merits of apprenticeship (Deißinger, 1996). Similar reforms were undertaken during the 1960s by the other European countries that took apprenticeship seriously, including Austria, Denmark, the Netherlands, Ireland and the UK. In all the relevant EU countries except the UK, governments have since continued to strengthen the institutional basis of apprenticeship, notably by increasing its educational content and functions, but without aiming at regulatory structures as elaborate as those in the German Federal Republic. The pragmatic, limited institutional development applied to industrial apprenticeship in Ireland during the past decade is particularly suggestive (Ryan, 1999).

In Japan, things moved swiftly on the equivalent front during the same decade. The *Jisseki-Kankei* system of recruitment linkages between schools and employers was set up in the 1960s when the Ministry of Labour handed to high schools the responsibility for placing school-leavers in jobs, previously the duty of the public employment service. The context was the rapid tightening of youth labour markets as the post-war boom took up the remaining labour market slack, along with a desire to restrain employer competition for young recruits (Kariya, 1999). The postwar Japanese youth labour market had until then resembled in many ways its western counterparts, particularly in the substantial share of school-leavers going into unemployment rather than a job.[19] Since the institutional change of the 1960s, however, the overwhelming majority of high school graduates (excluding those going on to higher education) has gone directly to employment.

Rising post-school employment rates were indeed fostered during the 1960s by tightening labour markets, not just by the introduction of *Jisseki-Kankei*. The latter's contribution has, however, been clarified during the 1990s, when, despite rising labour market slack, the great majority of secondary school-leavers bound for the labour market have continued to go direct into employment (see Mitani, p. 305 in this volume). The institutional innovation of the 1960s has proved not only durable but also highly resilient in the face of deteriorating labour market conditions.

These examples of successful institution building in German and Japan contrast to the national records of programme innovation in many other Western countries, notably the US and the UK, which have seen a succession of ephemeral and poorly funded youth programmes, with little continuity across programmes and limited learning from mistakes (see Grubb, p. 363 in this volume).[20] The weakness of the results of such programmes is, from this perspective, hardly surprising. The implication is that the UK and the US would be better served by a sustained effort geared to longer-term institutional development than by short-term policy innovation.

Institutional development is by no means unknown in the US, which has lately seen many and varied attempts to build linkages between schooling and early labour market experience through such initiatives as Tech Prep, "2+2" and youth apprenticeship programmes (see Stern, p. 155 this volume). But those efforts, valuable though they are, remain localised, limited in coverage and fragile.

The fundamental obstacle to institutional development in the US and the UK is the absence of widely-based and powerful employer and employee organisations. A further obstacle is short-termism, both economic and political. The UK and US economies, with their active takeover-based markets for corporate control, are renowned (or notorious) for the orientation of business investment decisions to short-term results, discouraging employers from training young people at work (Keep and Mayhew, 1996). Short-termism is also a political obstacle.[21] Modern democracy, notably in the UK and the US, rewards politicians who opt for well publicised programme innovation rather than the less spectacular long haul of institutional development (Keep, 1991).[22] What is remarkable from that perspective is the ability of German and Japanese democracy to support the latter when their counterparts elsewhere have proven so ill-adapted to the task.

5. Conclusions

The past twenty years show a mixed record in school-to-work terms. At one level an adverse verdict is inescapable. The problem of youth joblessness, reflecting variable mixtures of structural and cyclical factors, has endured since it first mushroomed after the 1973 oil price shock. Indeed, the problem now affects all advanced economies, including both those that remained largely immune to it through the 1980s and those that are enjoying or verging on boom conditions at the end of the 1990s. Youth joblessness often roots itself powerfully in particular localities and households. The damage that it does to those who experience it has become more clearly visible. Programmes to eradicate it have largely failed, and, though they have at least offered jobless youth something to do, in an era in which work experience is often treated as enough, "something to do" has left much to be desired in terms of interesting activity and personal development.

The extent to which vocational development and qualification are available to lower achievers in compulsory schooling is another area in which outcomes continue to be mixed. Large advances have been registered at secondary level in some countries, notably France, Sweden and the Netherlands, and at tertiary level in others, notably Japan and the US, but for the much discussed "lower half" or "bottom third" little change has been visible in the UK and US, where the need has been greatest (Halperin, 1998).

The brightest spot involves participation and progression in mainstream general, or "academic", education, which has been leveled upwards at upper secondary level across advanced economies as a whole; and where the previous situation in the UK, in which a majority of 16 year olds left school for jobs without formal training content, has at last been turned around. Increased participation, curriculum reform and improving schooling quality represent the leading gains of the contemporary period.

Finally, some reassurance can be drawn from the contemporary resilience, in the face of mounting labour market slack, of the two most successful school-to-work systems of the post-war period, Japan's *Jisseki-Kankei* network of recruitment linkages between schools and employers and Germany's dual system of mass apprenticeship. Each has bent under the strain; each has become the focus of reform initiatives; but each has continued broadly to function effectively, thereby allowing both countries – thus far, at least – to avoid recourse to the largely ineffective substitutes favoured by many other countries, i.e., labour market programmes of work experience and training for unemployed youth.

NOTES

1. Joblessness is defined here along conventional lines, including not just the unemployed but also the economically and educationally inactive, many of whom could under different circumstances form part of the labour force.

2. Increasing participation in full-time schooling has also reduced youth employment rates in France, but that is partly the effect of the paucity of employment opportunities, particularly for the less educated (Verdier, 1994; see also Marchand, p. 329 in this volume).

3. The share of 15-18 year old young people that undertook an apprenticeship in 1996 was only 39% amongst racial minorities, as opposed to 64% amongst non-minority youth (BMBW, 1998, p. 59).

4. Some deny that the process is all that protracted in the US in practice (Klerman and Karoly, 1995).

5. The Japanese government has since 1995 introduced various initiatives to subsidise both work-based and school-based training for unemployed school-leavers, particularly tertiary-level graduates, but entry to and outlays on these programmes appear to have remained low.

6. The two other attributes of the wider institutional structure, which has been termed "Job Selection Entrusted to Schools", are (i) the official prohibition of direct hiring of school-leavers by employers without making job offers to schools and (ii) the restriction of one job application per student. Even when a student is hired by an employer outside a *Jisseki-Kankei* relationship, the placement process remains under the control of the school (Kariya, 1993).

7. Other recent changes include a decline in the *Jisseki-Kankei* share of secondary leaver recruitment and increased scope for companies to choose as ratio of referrals to vacancies rises.

8. The Ministry of Education talks of the need to bring home to young people "the joy of work and the charm of skills"; the Ministry of Labour, of the merits of "job hopping [as] a means to find an ideal job", and the undesirability of trying to discourage quitting by young workers (Ministry of Education, 1994; Ministry of Labour, 1995). These considerations help explain the near-total absence of labour market programmes for unemployed youth in Japan (see Section 1, p. 438).

9. Similar conclusions have been reached for Sweden, where young people who work successively in many jobs achieve lower rates of upward occupational mobility than do those who occupy fewer – though selection bias may account for part or all of the difference (Blomskog and Schröder, 1997).

10. Employment rates may actually have increased for less advantaged US youth over the last two decades. The rate for black 16-19 year olds, for example, rose from 25 to 30% between 1978 and 1998, a period that saw the equivalent rate for whites fall from 52 to 49% (Lynch, in this volume, Table 5, p. 298).

11. The attempt to explain EU-US differences in aggregate labour market behaviour along such lines runs into the difficulty that the growth of unemployment in Europe has been as great amongst more skilled as amongst less skilled workers, when relative wage rigidity is expected to pass the burden of skill-oriented demand shifts primarily onto unskilled unemployment (Jackman et al., 1997).

12. The hypothesis is also consistent with trends in Sweden, where the skill content of youth employment has fallen while the skill content of both youth qualifications and overall employment has risen (Blomskog and Schröder, 1997). Card and Lemieux (1999), however, question the applicability of competitive models of wage setting to US youth labour markets in the first place.

13. Other data suggest declines in youth relative pay in both France and Japan since the late 1970s, albeit less marked than in the US (OECD, 1996, Chart 4.6).

14. Similarly, a recent explanation of divergent trends in aggregate unemployment in the US and the EU in terms of the effects of skill-biased technical change under different social insurance and employment protection institutions appears ill suited to explaining Japanese experience as well (Mortensen and Pissarides, 1999).

15. Many of the studies that report significantly adverse employment effects from either minimum wages or youth sub-minimum wages involve assumptions (e.g., on elasticities of factor substitution or on pay distributions in the absence of statutory minima) that by themselves make such results more likely.

16. Contemporary innovations in vocational secondary education in Denmark and Japan also look promising (see Moeller and Ljung, p. 141 in this volume).

17. Information on such programme attributes is summarised in Ryan and Büchtemann (1996), Table 10.2.

18. Stankiewicz (1998) counted 78 different labour market programmes (all ages) in operation at some time during 1973 and 1994, and 30 in force in 1997.

19. In the late 1950s, the share of junior high school graduates who entered the labour market – a category whose size dwindled rapidly after 1965 – whose first destination was unemployment rather than a job varied between 15 and 18% (Yoshimoto, 1996).

20. France represents an intermediate case, combining exceptional rates of programme proliferation and turnover with a sustained effort, since 1988 at any rate, to develop a small, low status, traditional artisanal apprenticeship system into a large, higher status, more educationally oriented and more industrially relevant one – a policy which has already been associated with changes in the desired direction in all these respects (Ministère de l'Éducation Nationale, 1998).

21. A Hollywood film producer replied during 1994-95 to Congressional allegations of short-termism and opportunism in the industry's production decisions with the assertion that short-termism was even more pronounced amongst its critics in national politics than it was in the film industry. The ability of political systems to sustain long-term institutional development is indeed often limited.

22. It is possible that the Modern Apprenticeship programme, introduced in the UK in 1995 to compensate for the weakness of the 1980s Youth Training Scheme and its successors may yet represent institutional development rather than simply programme innovation – though the institutional thinness of MA, as reflected in the absence of a statutory framework, of mandatory educational content and function, and of joint regulation in its administration, threatens to turn it into just another labour market programme, albeit one that aims higher than its predecessors (Ryan, 1999).

BIBLIOGRAPHY

ALLAIRE, G., CAHUZAC, E. and TAHAR, G. (1995), "Persistance du chômage et insertion", in A. Degenne, M. Mansuy and P. Werquin (eds), *Trajectoires et Insertions Professionnelles*, CEREQ, Marseilles.

BALSAN, D., HANCHINE, S. and WERQUIN, P. (1996), "Mobilité professionnelle initiale: éducation et expérience sur le marché du travail", *Economie et Statistique*, 299, pp. 91-106, September.

BISHOP, J.H. (1991), "Underinvestment in On-The-Job Training?", Working Paper 91-03, Centre for Advanced Human Resource Studies, Cornell University.

BISHOP, J.H. (1993), "Improving Job Matching in the US Labour Market", Brookings Papers on Economic Activity, Vol. 1, pp. 335-390.

BLANCHFLOWER, D. and FREEMAN, R.B. (eds) (1999), *Youth Unemployment and Joblessness in Advanced Countries*, University of Chicago Press/NBER, Chicago.

BLOMSKOG, S. and SCHRÖDER, L. (1997), "Labour Market Entry, Vocational Training and Mobility in the Young Workforce in Sweden, 1950-91", Chapter 4 of S. Blomskog, *Essays on the Functioning of the Swedish Labour Market*, Dissertation Series No. 27, Swedish Institute for Social Research, Stockholm.

BLOOM, H., ORR, L., CAVE, G., BELL, S., DOOLITTLE, F., LIN, W. and BOS, J. (1997), "The Benefits and Costs of JTPA Title II-A Programmes: Key Findings from the National Job Training Partnership Study Act", *Journal of Human Resources*, Vol. 32, No. 3, pp. 549-576, Summer.

BMBW (1998), *Berufsbildungsbericht 1998*, Bundesministerium für Bildung, Wissenschaft, Forschung und Technologie, Bonn.

BONNAL, L., FOUGÈRE, D. and SÉRANDON, A. (1994), "L'impact des dispositifs d'emploi sur le devenir des jeunes chômeurs: une évaluation économetrique sur données longitudinales", *Économie et Prévision*, No. 115, pp. 1-28.

BORDIGONI, M. and MANSUY, M. (1997), "Les parcours professionnels des lycéens et apprentis débutants", *Économie et Statistique*, No. 304-5, pp. 109-120.

BÜCHTEMANN, C.F., SCHUPP, J. and SOLOFF, D. (1993), "Roads to Work: School-To-Work Transition Patterns in Germany and the US", *Industrial Relations Journal*, Vol. 24, No. 2, pp. 97-111.

CARD, D. and LEMIEUX, T. (1999), "Adapting to Circumstances: the Evolution of Work, School and Living Arrangements among North American Youth", in D. Blanchflower and R.B. Freeman (eds), *Youth Unemployment and Joblessness in Advanced Countries*, University of Chicago Press/NBER, Chicago.

DEIßINGER, T. (1996), "Germany's Vocational Training Act: Its Function as an Instrument of Quality Control Within a Tradition-based Vocational Training System", *Oxford Review of Education*, Vol. 22, No. 3, pp. 317-336.

DOLADO, J., KRAMARZ, F., MACHIN, S., MANNING, A., MARGOLIS, D. and TEULINGS, C. (1996), "The Economic Impact of Minimum Wages in Europe", *Economic Policy*, Vol. 23, pp. 319-372, October.

DORE, R.P. and SAKO, M. (1998), *How the Japanese Learn to Work*, 2nd ed., Routledge, London.

DOUGHERTY, C.R.S. (1996), "Occupational Breaks, Their Incidence and Implications for Training Provision: Evidence from the NLSY", Working Paper 859, Centre for Economic Performance, London School of Economics.

FÁS (1998), *National Apprentice Statistics at 30th June 1998*, Foras Áiseanna Saothair, Dublin.

FRANZ, W. and POHLMEIER, W. (1999), "Young and Out in Germany: On Youths' Chances of Labour Market Entry in Germany", in D. Blanchflower and R.B. Freeman (eds), *Youth Unemployment and Joblessness in Advanced Countries*, University of Chicago Press/NBER, Chicago.

FREEMAN, R.B. (1994), "Minimum wages – again!", *International Journal of Manpower*, Vol. 15, No. 2, pp. 8-25.

FREEMAN, R.B. (1996), "Why do so Many Young American Men Commit Crimes and What Can be Done About it?', *Journal of Economic Perspectives*, Vol. 10, No. 1, pp. 25-42, Winter.

FREEMAN, R.B. and WISE, D.A. (eds) (1982), *The Youth Labour Market Problem*, National Bureau of Economic Research/University of Chicago Press, Chicago.

GRUBB, W.N. (1996), *Learning to Work: The Case for Re-Integrating Job Training and Education*, Russell Sage Foundation, New York.

GRUBB, W.N. (1997), "The Returns to Education and Training in the Sub-baccalaureate Labour Market 1984-1990", *Economics of Education Review*, Vol. 16, No. 3, pp. 231-246, June.

GRUBB, W.N. and RYAN, P. (1999), *Plain Talk on the Field of Dreams: the Roles of Evaluation for Education and Training*, ILO, Geneva.

HALPERIN, S. (ed.) (1998), *The Forgotten Half Revisited: American Youth and Young Families, 1988-2008*, American Youth Policy Forum, Washington, DC.

HECKMAN, J.J., ROSELIUS, R.L. and SMITH, J.A. (1994), "US Education and Training Policy: a Re-evaluation of the Underlying Assumptions Behind the 'New Consensus'", in L. C. Solmon and A. R. Levenson (eds), *Labour Markets, Employment Policy and Job Creation*, Westview Press, Boulder.

JACKMAN, R., LAYARD, R., MANACORDA, M. and PETRONGOLO, B. (1997), "European Versus US Unemployment: Different Responses to Increased Demand for Skill?", Discussion Paper 349, Centre for Economic Performance, London School of Economics.

JEONG, J. (1995), "The Failure of Recent State Vocational Training Policies in Korea from a Comparative Perspective", *British Journal of Industrial Relations*, Vol. 33, No. 2, pp. 237-252, June.

KARIYA, T. (1993), "Characteristics of Japan's New Graduate Labour Market for High School Graduates", *Monthly Journal of the Japan Institute of Labour*, October (in Japanese).

KARIYA, T. (1999), "Transition from School to Work and Career Formation of Japanese High School Students", forthcoming in D. Stern and D.A. Wagner (eds.), *International Perspectives on the School-to-Work Transition,* Hampton Press, Cresskill, NJ.

KEEP, E. (1991), "The Grass Looked Greener – Some Thoughts on the Influence of Comparative Vocational Training Research on the UK Policy Debate", in P. Ryan (ed.), *International Comparisons of Vocational Education and Training for Intermediate Skills*, Falmer Press, London.

KEEP, E. and MAYHEW, K. (1996), "Evaluating the Assumptions that Underlie Training Policy", in A. Booth and D. Snower (eds), *Acquiring Skills: Market Failures, Their Symptoms and Policy Responses*, Cambridge University Press, Cambridge.

KLERMAN, J.A. and KAROLY, L.A. (1995), "The Transition to Stable Employment: the Experience of US Youth in Their Early Labour Market Career", National Center for Research in Vocational Education, Berkeley.

KORPI, T. (1997), "Escaping Unemployment: Studies in the Individual Consequences of Unemployment and Labour Market Policy", Dissertation Series No. 24, Swedish Institute for Social Research, Stockholm.

KRUGMAN, P. (1994), "Past and Prospective Causes of High Unemployment", *Reducing Unemployment: Current Issues and Policy Options, Proceedings of Jackson Hole Conference*, Federal Reserve Bank of Kansas.

LEVY, F. and MURNAME, R.J. (1992), "US Earnings Levels and Earnings Inequality: a Review of Recent Trends and Proposed Explanations", *Journal of Economic Literature*, Vol. 30, pp. 1333-1381, September.

LHOTEL, H. and MONACO, A. (1993), "Regards croisés sur l'apprentissage et les contrats de qualification", *Formation Emploi*, 42, pp. 33-45, April.

MANSUY, M. (1996), "La gamme des emplois après un CAP ou un BEP", *Éducation et Formations*, Vol. 45, pp. 115-122, March.

MARSDEN, D.W. (1990), "Institutions and Labour Mobility: Occupational and Internal Labour Markets in Britain, France, Italy and West Germany", in R. Brunetta and C. Dell'Arringa (eds), *Labour Relations and Economic Performance*, Macmillan, London.

MARSDEN, D.W. and RYAN, P. (1990), "Institutional Aspects of Youth Employment and Training Policy in Britain", *British Journal of Industrial Relations*, Vol. 28, No. 3, pp. 351-370.

MARSDEN, D.W. and RYAN, P. (1991), "The Structuring of Youth Pay and Employment in Six European Economies", in P. Ryan, P. Garonna and R.C. Edwards (eds), *The Problem of Youth: the Regulation of Youth Employment and Training in Advanced Economies*, Macmillan, London, pp. 82-112.

MASON, G. and FINEGOLD, D. (1997), "Productivity, Machinery and Skills in the United States and Western Europe", *National Institute Economic Review*, Vol. 62, pp. 85-97, October.

MINISTÈRE DE L'ÉDUCATION NATIONALE (1998), "L'essor de l'apprentissage entre 1992 et 1996", Note d'Information 98.08, pp. 1-4, April.

MINISTRY OF EDUCATION (1994), *Japanese Government Policies in Education, Science and Culture*, Ministry of Education, Tokyo.

MINISTRY OF LABOUR (1995), *White Paper on Labour, 1995, Summary*, Japan Institute of Labour, Tokyo.

MINISTRY OF LABOUR (1996), *White Paper on Labour, 1996, Summary*, Japan Institute of Labour, Tokyo.

MINISTRY OF LABOUR (1998), *White Paper on Labour, 1998, Summary*, Japan Institute of Labour, Tokyo.

MORTENSEN, D.T. and PISSARIDES, C.A. (1999), "Unemployment Responses to 'Skill-Biased' Technology Shocks: The Role of Labour Market Policy", *Economic Journal*, Vol. 109, pp. 242-266.

NI CHEALLAIGH, M. (1995), *Apprenticeship in the EU Member States*, CEDEFOP, Berlin.

NICOLE-DRANCOURT, C. (1992), "L'idée de précarité revisitée", *Travail et Emploi*, Vol. 52, No. 2, pp. 57-70.

NITTA, M. (1995), "The Employment Practices and Employment of Young Workers in Japan: Past Experience and Present Situation", *Japan Labour Bulletin*, pp. 5-9, October.

NOHARA, H. (1988), "Formes d'insertion professionnelle des jeunes: le cas du Japon", in Ministère du Marché du Travail et Commisariat Général du Plan (eds), *Structures du Marché du Travail et Politiques d'Emploi*, Syros-Alternatives, Paris, pp. 341-354.

OECD (1982), *Youth Unemployment: the Causes and Consequences*, Paris.

OECD (1994), *The OECD Jobs Study: Facts, Analysis, Strategies*, Paris.

OECD (1996), "Growing into Work: Youth and the Labour Market over the 1980s and 1990s", *Employment Outlook*, Chapter 4, Paris, July.

OECD (1997), *Labour Force Statistics 1976-96*, Paris.

OECD (1998), "Getting Started, Settling In: The Transition from Education to the Labour Market", *Employment Outlook*, Chapter 3, Paris, June.

OSTERMAN, P. (1980), *Getting Started: the Youth Labour Market*, MIT Press, Cambridge.

PARSONS, D.O. (1991), "The Job Search Behaviour of Employed Youth", *Review of Economics and Statistics*, No. 73, pp. 597-604.

PRAIS, S.J. (1993), "Economic Performance and Education: the Nature of Britain's Deficiencies", Keynes Lecture, Discussion Paper 52, National Institute of Economic and Social Research, London.

PRAIS, S.J. (1995), *Productivity, Education and Training*, Cambridge University Press, Cambridge.

ROSENBAUM, J.E. (1999), "Preconditions for Effective School-work Linkages in the United States", in D. Stern and D.A. Wagner (eds.), *International Perspectives on the School-to-Work Transition*, Hampton Press, Cresskill, NJ.

REES, A. (1986), "An Essay on Youth Joblessness", *Journal of Economic Literature*, Vol. 24, No. 2, pp. 613-628.

RYAN, P. (1998), "Is Apprenticeship Better? A Review of the Economic Evidence", *Journal of Vocational Education and Training*, Vol. 50, No. 2, pp. 289-325, Summer.

RYAN, P. (1999), "The Institutional Attributes and Requirements of Apprenticeship: Evidence from Smaller EU Countries", Working paper, University of Cambridge.

RYAN, P. and BÜCHTEMANN, C. (1996), "The School to Work Transition", in G. Schmid, J. O'Reilly and K. Schöman (eds.), *International Handbook of Labour Market Policy and Evaluation*, Edward Elgar, Cheltenham.

RYAN, P., GARONNA, P. and EDWARDS, R.C. (eds) (1991), *The Problem of Youth: the Regulation of Youth Employment and Training in Advanced Economies*, Macmillan, London.

SAKO, M. (1991), "Institutional Aspects of Youth Employment and Training Policy: a Comment on Marsden and Ryan", *British Journal of Industrial Relations*, Vol. 29, No. 3, pp. 485-490, September.

SKEDINGER, P. (1995), "Employment Policies and Displacement in the Youth Labour Market", *Swedish Economic Policy Review*, Vol. 2, No. 1, pp. 135-171, Spring.

STANKIEWICZ, F. (1998), "Training and Employment – the French case", Background paper for World Employment Report, International Labour Office, Geneva.

STEEDMAN, H, and WAGNER, K. (1989), "Productivity, Machinery and Skills: Clothing Manufacture in Britain and Germany", *National Institute Economic Review*, No. 128, pp. 40-57, May.

STERN, D., FINKELSTEIN, N., STONE, J.R., LATTING, J. and DORNSIFE, C. (1995), *School to Work: Research on Programmes in the United States*, Falmer Press, London.

STERN, D. and WAGNER, D.A. (eds.) (1999), *International Perspectives on the School-to-Work Transition,* Hampton Press, Cresskill, NJ.

TAYLOR, M.E. (1981), *Education and Work in the Federal Republic of Germany,* Anglo-German Foundation, London.

TOPEL, R.H. and WARD, M.P. (1992), "Job Mobility and the Careers of Young Men", *Quarterly Journal of Economics,* Vol. 57, No. 2, pp. 439-480, May.

VERDIER, E.(1994), "Vocational Training of Young People in France: A Resource Difficult to Exploit", *European Journal of Vocational Training,* pp. 34-43, February.

WALKER, N. and HOUGH, M. (1998), "Schools for crime – dangerous drivers after imprisonment", *New Law Journal,* July 24, pp. 1119-20.

WERQUIN, P. (1996), "De l'école à l'emploi: les parcours précaires", in S. Paugam (ed.), *L'Exclusion: l'État des Savoirs,* Editions la Découverte, Paris, pp.120-134.

WINKELMANN, L. and WINKELMANN, R. (1998), "Why Are the Unemployed so Unhappy? Evidence From Panel Data", *Economica,* No. 65, pp. 1-15, February.

YOSHIMOTO, K. (1996), "Transition from School to Work in Japan", Paper prepared for planning meeting of Thematic Review of the Transition from Initial Education to Working Life, OECD, Paris.

Table 1. **Economically inactive as share of jobless young males, by age and country, 1987 and 1997**

	Out of school jobless (% population)		Unemployed (% out of school jobless)	
	1987	1997	1987	1997
16-19 year-olds				
France	10.2	6.8	78.1	66.0
Germany[a]	3.1	4.6	60.9	48.0
Italy	14.7	13.3	75.5	52.0
Netherlands	7.3	6.5	38.7	24.3
United Kingdom	13.1	19.4	87.4	44.5
United States	8.0	7.7	84.7	41.1
20-24 year-olds				
France	16.5	18.3	85.6	83.9
Germany[a]	8.6	12.5	72.3	67.8
Italy	21.7	24.9	81.7	62.4
Netherlands	9.0	7.8	74.3	37.5
United Kingdom	15.0	18.7	84.9	57.2
United States	10.5	10.9	85.9	50.1

a. 1996 instead of 1997.
Note: Out of school jobless = unemployed + economically inactive but not in school.
Source: See Bowers, Sonnet and Bardone, Figure 3, pp. 50-51 in this volume.

Table 2. **Youth relative pay in France. Japan and the United States, 1977 and 1996**
Mean earnings of 20-24 year olds as a percentage of those of 35-44 year old employees

	1977	1996	Change
United States	64.7	52.8	-11.8
France	64.6	64.9	0.3
Japan	56.7	53.6	-3.2

Source: See Bowers, Sonnet and Bardone, Figure 8, p. 59 in this volume.

Table 3. **Employment rates by age group and gender
in France, Japan and the United States, 1977 and 1996**
(Percentages of the population in each age group)

		16-19 years			20-24 years			25-54 years		
		1977	1996	change	1977	1996	change	1977	1996	change
United States	Males	50.4	43.6	-6.8	76.4	74.7	-1.7	90.1	87.9	-2.2
	Females	41.8	43.5	1.7	59.1	64.9	5.8	54.8	72.8	18.0
France	Males	24.1	7.6	-16.5	76.1	43.0	-33.1	94.2	86.3	-7.8
	Females	16.5	2.9	-13.6	60.7	32.0	-28.6	57.5	67.7	10.2
Japan	Males	17.3	16.5	-0.8	70.0	70.0	0.1	95.9	95.3	-0.7
	Females	19.3	14.8	-4.5	65.4	69.2	3.8	53.3	63.7	10.4

Source: OECD (1997), Part III (author's calculations).

OECD PUBLICATIONS, 2, rue André-Pascal, 75775 PARIS CEDEX 16
PRINTED IN FRANCE
(91 1999 03 1 P 1) ISBN 92-64-17076-6 – No. 50767 1999